INTERNATIONAL LAW

ANTONIO CASSESE

OXFORD
UNIVERSITY PRESS

OXFORD
UNIVERSITY PRESS

Great Clarendon Street, Oxford OX2 6DP

Oxford University Press is a department of the University of Oxford.
It furthers the University's objective of excellence in research, scholarship,
and education by publishing worldwide in

Oxford New York

Athens Auckland Bangkok Bogotá Buenos Aires Cape Town
Chennai Dar es Salaam Delhi Florence Hong Kong Istanbul Karachi
Kolkata Kuala Lumpur Madrid Melbourne Mexico City Mumbai Nairobi
Paris São Paulo Shanghai Singapore Taipei Tokyo Toronto Warsaw

with associated companies in Berlin Ibadan

Oxford is a registered trade mark of Oxford University Press
in the UK and in certain other countries

Published in the United States
by Oxford University Press Inc., New York

British Library Cataloguing in Publication Data

Data available

Library of Congress Cataloging in Publication Data

Data available

ISBN 0–19–829998–2

Typeset in Adobe Minion
by RefineCatch Limited, Bungay, Suffolk
Printed in Great Britain by
T.J. International Ltd., Padstow, Cornwall

INTERNATIONAL LAW

PREFACE

This book seeks to offer a general perspective for understanding the role of law in the international community. I have tried to expound the contents of those rules and legal institutions which to my mind deserve the attention of all persons alert to the current status of international affairs.

While most existing textbooks or treatises take a strictly legal approach, I have attempted not to look at international legal institutions as abstract entities 'petrified' in time and space. I believe that it is misleading to consider international law as a piece of reality cut off from its historical, political, and ideological context. To grasp international law in all its ramifications, one ought to look at it as a set of continuously changing elements of a whole. I have therefore tried to combine the strictly legal method with the historical and sociological approach, to expound the *dynamic* of international law: in particular, to illustrate the tension between traditional law, firmly grounded on the *rock* of State sovereignty, and the new or nascent law, often soft and hazy as a *cloud*, but inspired with new, community values.

Thus, my purpose has been to show *when* certain legal institutions have come into being in the world community. Indeed, it is important to know their origin, even when they have been supplanted or modified by new ones. Also, I have endeavoured to understand the rationale behind them. In addition to delineating their legal contents, I have asked myself *why* they have been created, what function they were intended to fulfil, and which one they in fact perform in the current reality of international relations.

As Bertrand Russell wisely wrote, 'without detail, a book becomes jejune and uninteresting; with detail, it is in danger of becoming intolerably lengthy'. As usually happens in life, I had to strike a compromise: I have endeavoured to be concise while sufficiently informative. One of the consequences of this attempt is that most references only intend to indicate the source of documents or cases cited, and notes have been put at the end of the book (where nothing is indicated to the contrary, translations from other languages into English are mine). In addition, no bibliography is given. The reader interested in consulting documents or looking up further writings may use the Oxford University Press web site: **www.oup.com/uk/best.textbooks/law/ cassese**, where he or she will find not only a select bibliography and the text of all the principal treaties and agreements cited in the book, but also links with the principal web sites containing further sources.

This book is therefore structured and organized to enable one to read it at four possible levels: (i) one can read only the text printed in bigger font, and ignore the passages in smaller font, the endnotes, and the references; (ii) or, one can also take a glance at the passages in smaller font, which are intended to illustrate by judicial or State practice the main propositions set out in the text; (iii) if one is interested in perusing citations, one may look up the references given in the endnotes; finally (iv), if one intends to go deeper into the matter and read the documents cited, one may go to the OUP web site, where it is possible to find all the most relevant documents, or reference to the most important links to relevant web sites.

I am deeply grateful to those colleagues and friends who have so kindly read and constructively commented on some chapters: Philip Alston, Roberto Barsotti, Paolo Benvenuti, Bardo Fassbender, Luigi Condorelli, James Crawford, Francesco Francioni, Thomas Franck, Giorgio Gaja, Marina Spinedi, Danilo Türk, Abdulqawi A. Yusuf. Paola Gaeta and Alain Pellet kindly read the whole book and offered perceptive criticisms.

I also am beholden to some junior colleagues and friends who, in addition to commenting on a few chapters, have greatly assisted me in finding documents, cases, and other materials and in checking references: Béatrice Bonafé, Micaela Frulli, and Salvatore Zappalà.

The usual caveat is however necessary: responsibility for any misapprehension that may remain, rests solely with me.

Finally, I wish to express my gratitude to the OUP staff, who once again have proved not only highly professional but also exceedingly understanding and patient.

CONTENTS

DETAILED CONTENTS

PART II CREATION AND ENFORCEMENT OF INTERNATIONAL
LEGAL STANDARDS

PRINCIPAL ABBREVIATIONS

AFDI	*Annuaire Français de Droit International*
AJIL	*American Journal of International Law*
AILC	B. D. Reams, Jr., ed., *American International Law Cases (1783–1968)* (New York: Oceana Publications, 1971)
Ann. Dig.	J. Fischer Williams and H. Lauterpacht, eds., *Annual Digest of Public International Law Cases* (London, New York, Toronto: Longmans, Green and Co., 1932–53)
Anzilotti, *Corso*	D. Anzilotti, *Corso di diritto internazionale* (1912, 1928), i, 4th edn. (Padua: Cedam, 1955)
Anzilotti, *Cours*	D. Anzilotti, *Cours de droit international*, I (trans. G. Gidel) (Paris, 1929)
ASDI	*Annuaire Suisse de Droit International*
BILC	*British International Law Cases* (London, 1965)
Bulletin crim.	*Bulletin des arrêts de la Cour de Cassation, Chambre criminelle*
BYIL	*British Yearbook of International Law*
CYIL	*Canadian Yearbook of International Law*
DSU	Understanding on Rules and Procedures Governing the Settlement of Disputes
ECHR	European Court of Human Rights
ECJ	European Court of Justice
ECOSOC	Economic and Social Council (of the UN)
EJIL	*European Journal of International Law*
El Derecho, Jurisprudencia	Consejo general del poder judicial (Madrid), Centro de Documentación Judicial, *El Derecho, Jurisprudencia penal, constitucional*, http://www.elderecho.com, also on CDRom
Encyclopedia	R. Bernhardt, ed., *Encyclopedia of Public International Law*, 4 vols. (North Holland: 1992, 1995, 1997, 2000)
Friedman	L. Friedman, ed., *The Law of War—A Documentary History*, 2 vols. (New York: Random House, 1972)
FRUS	*Foreign Relations of the United States* (Washington: Government Printing Office) many volumes; some of them are entitled: *Diplomatic Papers on the Foreign Relations of the United States*
GA	General Assembly (of the UN)

GAOR	UN General Assembly Official Records
GATT	General Agreement on Tariffs and Trade
GYIL	*German Yearbook of International Law*
Hackworth	G. H. Hackworth, *Digest of International Law* (Washington, DC: Government Printing Office, 1942)
HR	Recueil des Cours de l'Académie de La Haye
HRLJ	*Human Rights Law Journal*
ICAO	International Civil Aviation Organization
ICC	International Criminal Court
ICJ	International Court of Justice
ICJ Reports	Reports of the International Court of Justice
ICRC	International Committee of the Red Cross
ICTR	International Criminal Tribunal for Rwanda
ICTY	International Criminal Tribunal for the Former Yugoslavia
IJIL	*Indian Journal of International Law*
ILC	UN International Law Commission
ILC Draft (2000)	ILC Draft adopted in 2000 by the 2000 ILC Drafting Committee on second reading
ILM	International Legal Materials
ILO	International Labour Organisations
ILR	International Law Reports (since 1950; edited first by Sir H. Lauterpacht and at present by Sir E. Lauterpacht, C. J. Greenwood, and A. G. Oppenheimer).
IMT	International Military Tribunal
IYIL	*Italian Yearbook of International Law*
JAIL	*Japanese Annual of International Law*
JDI	*Journal du droit international*
JYIL	*Japanese Yearbook of International Law*
Kelsen, *Principles*	H. Kelsen, *Principles of International Law* (New York: Rinehart & Company, 1952)
La Fontaine, *Pasicrisie*	H. La Fontaine, *Pasicrisie internationale—Histoire documentaire des arbitrages internationaux* (Berne: Impr. Stämpfli and Co., 1902)
Lapradelle and Politis	A. de Lapradelle and N. Politis, *Recueil des Arbitrages internationaux*, 3 vols. (Paris: Pedone, 1905, 1923, 1954)
Moore, *Digest*	J. B. Moore, *A Digest of International Law*, 8 vols. (Washington, DC: Government Printing Office, 1906)

Moore, *History and Digest*	J. B. Moore, *History and Digest of the International Arbitrations to which the United States has been a Party*, 6 vols. (Washington, DC: Government Printing Office, 1898)
Moore, *International Adjudications*	J. B. Moore, *International Adjudications, Ancient and Modern, History and Documents*, 6 vols. (New York: Oxford University Press, 1929–31)
NIEO	New International Economic Order
NYIL	*Netherlands Yearbook of International Law*
OAS	Organization of American States
OAU	Organization of African Unity
PCA	Permanent Court of Arbitration
PCIJ	Permanent Court of International Justice
Parry	*The Consolidated Treaty Series*, edited and annotated by C. Parry, 155 vols plus Indexes (Dobbs Ferry, NY: Oceana Publications, 1969–86)
RBDI	*Revue Belge de Droit International*
RDI	*Rivista di Diritto Internazionale*
RGDIP	*Revue Générale de Droit International Public*
RIAA	Reports of International Arbitral Awards
RIDIPP	*Rivista italiana di diritto privato e processuale*
Right to Protect Citizens in Foreign Countries	*Right to Protect Citizens in Foreign Countries by Landing Forces*, Memorandum of the Solicitor for the Department of State, 5 October 1912, 2nd edn. (Washington, DC: Government Printing Office, 1929)
SC	Security Council (of the UN)
SCOR	UN Security Council Official Records
UN	United Nations
UNCIO	Documents of the United Nations Conference on International Organization, San Francisco, 1945, 16 vols. (London and New York: United Nations Information Organizations, 1945–6)
UNEP	United Nations Environment Programme
Whiteman	M. M. Whiteman, *Digest of International Law*, 15 vols (Washington DC: Government Printing Office, 1963–70)
WTO	World Trade Organization
YILC	Yearbook of the International Law Commission
ZaöRV	*Zeitschrift für ausländisches öffentliches Recht und Völkerrecht*

PART I

ORIGINS AND FOUNDATIONS OF THE INTERNATIONAL COMMUNITY

1

THE MAIN LEGAL FEATURES OF THE INTERNATIONAL COMMUNITY

1.1 INTRODUCTION

We all live within the framework of national legal orders. We therefore tend to assume that each legal system should be modelled on State law, or at least strongly resemble it. Accordingly, and almost unwittingly, we take the view that all legal systems should address themselves to individuals or groups of individuals, and in addition that they should include certain centralized institutions responsible for making law, adjudicating disputes, and enforcing legal norms.

However, the picture offered by the international community is completely different. This enquiry should therefore begin with a note of warning. The features of the world community are unique. Failure to grasp this crucial fact would inevitably entail a serious misinterpretation of the impact of law on this community.

1.2 THE NATURE OF INTERNATIONAL LEGAL SUBJECTS

The first salient feature of international law is that most of its rules aim at regulating the behaviour of States, not that of individuals. States are the principal actors on the international scene. They are legal entities, aggregates of human beings dominated by an apparatus that wields authority over them. Their general goals are quite distinct from the goals of each individual or group. Each State owns and controls a separate territory; and each is held together by political, economic, cultural (and frequently also ethnic or religious) links.

Within States individuals are the principal legal subjects, and such legal entities as public corporations, private associations, etc. are merely secondary subjects whose possible suppression would not result in the demise of the whole legal system. (However, the possible collapse of the governmental authorities may only be transitory; otherwise the whole State, as a distinct international entity, breaks down.) In the international community the reverse holds true: States are the primary subjects, and individuals play a limited role (see **4.2** and **4.5**). The latter are as puny Davids confronted by overpowering Goliaths holding all the instruments of power.

Although the protagonists of international life are States as legal entities or corporate structures, of course they can only operate through individuals, who do not act on their own account but as State officials, as the tools of the structures to which they belong. Thus, for instance, if a treaty of extradition is concluded by France with China, this deal should not blind us to what actually happens, namely that the international instrument is brought into being by individuals and is subsequently implemented by individuals. The agreement is negotiated by diplomats belonging to the two States; their Ministers of Foreign Affairs sign the treaty; the instrument of ratification is formally approved and signed by the Heads of State, if necessary after authorization by parliamentary assemblies. Once the treaty has entered into force, it is implemented by the courts of each country (indeed, it is generally for the courts to grant or refuse extradition in each particular case) and, if required, also by officials of the respective Ministries of Justice.

Similarly, a State may consider that another country has committed an international transgression, and therefore decides to react by resorting to peaceful reprisals such as the expulsion of all the nationals of the State in question. This response is decided upon and carried out by individuals acting as State agents: the decision is normally taken, at the suggestion of the Foreign Minister, by the Minister for Home Affairs, after possible deliberation by the Cabinet; the actual expulsion is carried out by police officers or officials of other enforcement agencies.

Indeed, in international law more than in any other field, the phenomenon of 'fictitious person', to which Hobbes drew attention,[1] manifests itself in a conspicuous form: individuals engage in transactions or perform acts not in their personal capacity, that is to protect or further their own interests, but on behalf of collectivities or a multitude of individuals.

Why is it that the world community consists of sovereign and independent States, while human beings as such play a lesser role? We shall see in **Chapter 2** how the international community evolved and how, after the first modern States (England, France, Spain) came into being in the fifteenth century, the various communities in Europe and elsewhere gradually consolidated and 'hardened' into States. It may suffice now to stress that this powerful drive has been a constant and salient feature of the world community, so much so that most individuals now belong to one State or another: the world population of about six billion human beings is currently divided up amongst nearly two hundred States. In the Middle Ages it was usual to say that outside the Church no salvation could be found (*extra Ecclesiam nulla salus*)—at least, this was what the Church encouraged people to believe. Today it could be maintained with greater truthfulness that without the protection of a State human beings are likely to endure more suffering and hardship than what is likely to be their lot in the normal course of events—witness the plight of stateless persons, which has only lately been taken up by international institutions.

1.3 THE LACK OF A CENTRAL AUTHORITY, AND DECENTRALIZATION OF LEGAL 'FUNCTIONS'

National legal systems are highly developed. In addition to substantive rules, which enjoin citizens to behave in a certain way, sophisticated organizational rules have evolved. Special machinery exists concerned with the 'life' of the legal order. These developments resulted from the emergence within the State community of a group of individuals who succeeded in wielding effective power: they considered it convenient to create a special structure aimed at institutionalizing that power and crystallizing the relationships between the ruling group and their fellow members. In devising the institutional apparatus, a common pattern evolved in all modern States. First, the use of force by members of the community was forbidden, except for emergency situations such as self-defence (the right to use force to impede unlawful violence which would otherwise be unavoidable); States monopolized lawful coercion. Second, the central organs acting on behalf of the whole community were responsible for the three main functions typical of any legal system (law making, law determination, and law enforcement). Accordingly, first the monarch and subsequently an assembly (generally called Parliament) held the power to create and modify law, courts ascertained breaches of law and special bodies of professionals (police officers) were the law enforcers. It should be added that these were functions proper and not simple powers. For all these bodies had to exercise their powers in the interest of the whole community and not in their own interest; they were vested with a power but also a legal duty to make the law, to establish whether legal rules had been breached and to enforce them, if necessary.

By contrast, in the international community no State or group of States has managed to hold the lasting power required to impose its will on the whole world community. Power is fragmented and dispersed. True, political and military alliances have occasionally been set up or a strong convergence of interests between two or more members of the community has evolved. However, these have not hardened into a permanent power structure. The relations between the States comprising the international community remain largely *horizontal*. No *vertical* structure has as yet crystallized, as is instead the rule within the domestic systems of States.

This situation is all the more striking and unsatisfactory today. At present, as everybody knows, most components of national structures and of the international community (individuals, groups, associations, State-like entities, multinational corporations, trans-national organizations, multinational financial structures, media networks, etc.) are so closely intertwined across national borders that they make up the phenomenon usually called 'globalization'. It has now become true that the fluttering of the wings of a butterfly in New York may trigger off a typhoon in Asia. However, global governance capable of settling all the problems that globalization may entail does not match this factual situation. Relative anarchy still prevails at the level of central management.

The major consequence of the *horizontal* structure of the international community is that organizational rules are at a very embryonic stage. There are no rules setting up special machinery for discharging the three functions referred to above, nor for entrusting them to any particular body or member of the international community. All three 'functions' are decentralized. (Clearly, in relation to the international community, one cannot speak of functions proper: when making law, settling disputes, or enforcing the law, States do not act in the interest and on behalf of the international community; they do not fulfil an obligation, but primarily pursue their own interests.) It is for each State, acting together with other States under the impulse of overriding economic, political, or other factors, to set new legal standards or to change them, either deliberately (as in the case of *treaties*, that is, contractual stipulations entered into by two or more States, and only binding upon the contracting parties; see *infra*, 6.3) or almost unwittingly (as in the case of *customary law*, that is, general rules evolved through a spontaneous process and binding upon all international legal subjects; see *infra*, 6.2). It is for each of them to decide how to settle disputes or to impel compliance with law, that is whether to iron out disagreements peacefully or enforce the law unilaterally or collectively. Of particular significance is the fact that each State has the power of 'auto-interpretation' of legal rules, a power that necessarily follows from the absence of courts endowed with general and compulsory jurisdiction.

In addition, in traditional international law, that is, the law which came into being and governed international relations between the Peace of Westphalia of 1648 and the First World War (see 2.3), resort to force was lawful both to enforce a right and to protect economic, political, or other interests. This state of affairs greatly favoured powerful States. As we shall see, some improvements, including the ban on the use of force by individual States, are to be found in the present international system (2.5).

1.4 COLLECTIVE RESPONSIBILITY

As in all primitive legal systems where groups play a much greater role than individuals, responsibility for violations of the rules governing the behaviour of States does not fall upon the transgressor but on the group to which he or she belongs (the State community). Here again we are confronted with a striking deviation from domestic legal systems.

Within the national legal orders which frame our daily lives, we are accustomed to the notion of individual responsibility: the one who commits a tort or any other breach of law shall suffer in consequence. One either must make good the damage or, in case of crime, is liable to a criminal penalty. Such is the rule. There are, however, exceptions. One is 'vicarious responsibility', which comes into play when the law provides that someone bears responsibility for actions performed by another person with whom the former has special ties (for example, a parent is legally responsible for damage caused by his or her children); sometimes a whole group is held responsible for the acts performed by one of its representatives on behalf of the group (as in the civil liability of corporations for torts).

In the international legal system the exception becomes the rule. A State official may break international law: for instance, a military commander orders his pilots to intrude upon the airspace of a neighbouring State, or a court disregards an international treaty granting certain rights to foreigners, or a police officer infringes diplomatic immunities by arresting a diplomat or maltreating him. In these and similar cases the wronged State is allowed to 'take revenge' against the whole community to which that State official belongs, even though the community has neither carried out nor ordered the infraction. For instance, the State which has become the victim of the international transgression can claim the payment of a sum of money (to be drawn from the State treasury), or will resort to counter-measures (traditionally called reprisals) damaging individuals other than the actual authors of the offence (for example, the expulsion of foreigners, the suspension of a commercial treaty, and so on).

Hence, collective responsibility means both that the whole State community is liable for any breach of international law committed by any State official and that the whole State community may suffer from the consequences of the wrongful act (on this matter see **Chapter 9**).

The incident of Corfu of 1923 is instructive in this regard. On 27 August 1923 the Italian members of the International Commission charged by the Conference of Ambassadors (a body consisting of diplomats from France, the UK, Italy, and Japan and responsible for the implementation of the peace treaties) to delimit the Graeco-Albanian frontier were killed at Zepi, near the town of Janina, on Greek territory, at the hands of unknown terrorists. Two days later Italy requested Greece to formally apologize, hold a solemn religious ceremony, pay honour to the Italian flag and military honours to the dead, conduct a most serious inquiry within five days, inflict the death penalty on all culprits, and pay an indemnity of 50 million Italian lire payable within five days. The next day the Greek Government responded that it regarded as unjust the Italian charges that Greece was responsible for the assassination of the Italians; it also dismissed the requests concerning a criminal inquiry, the imposition of death penalty, and the payment of compensation. At the same time Greece submitted the matter to the Council of the League of Nations, with a view to an amicable settlement of the matter. Nevertheless, the next day upon the orders of the Italian dictator, Mussolini, Italian ships bombarded Corfu, causing numerous casualties among civilians (16 people were killed and more than three times that number wounded); Italian troops occupied the island, to force Greece to comply with the Italian requests. In the event, following the initial report by an international commission of inquiry it had set up, the Conference of Ambassadors found that Greece had been negligent in pursuing the perpetrators of the crime; on 27 September Italian troops evacuated Corfu and Italy was awarded in compensation 50 million lire (which Greece had previously deposited as security in the Swiss National Bank, on the understanding that the PCIJ would determine the amount of the indemnity due; a determination that, however, never took place). Thus, even assuming that Greece was responsible (a matter that was never fully clarified), Greek civilians and the Greek Treasury bore the brunt of the consequences of the assassination perpetrated by some bandits at Zepi.[2]

For more recent and similarly instructive instances of collective responsibility, one may mention the reaction, in 1982, to the unlawful invasion by Argentina of the Falklands (Malvinas). The (then ten) members of the European Community adopted economic counter-measures (essentially the suspension of imports of textiles and meat from Argentina) and the USA followed suit, by among other things suspending 'new export-import credits and guarantees' (see *infra*, **11.4**); the parties adversely affected by such 'sanctions' were individuals and corporations, that is persons and entities other than the Argentine leadership that had decided the invasion. For another instance one may think of the economic sanctions adopted in 1992 by States against Libya, at the request of the UN SC (SC res. 748–1992) and as a reaction to the terrorist act at Lockerbie; these measures included the blocking of air communications with Libya (see *infra*, **11.4**); they clearly affected all Libyans as well as interests of Libyan corporations, in addition to Libyan State officials.

This form of responsibility is typical of primitive and rudimentary legal systems. Kelsen was one of the first authors to draw attention to this phenomenon. He pointed out that:

'[Co]llective responsibility exists in case of blood revenge which is directed not only against the murderer but also against all the members of his family. Criminal responsibility is established in the Ten Commandments when Yahweh threatens to punish the children and the childrens' children for the sins of their fathers'.[3]

Indeed, the law governing the international community is typical of primitive societies, with the aggravating circumstance—rightly emphasized by Hoffmann[4]— that unlike primitive communities (which are highly integrated, with all the ensuing benefits), the world community is largely based on the non-integration of its subjects, from the viewpoint of their social interrelations.

Later on we shall see that two new trends have significantly altered the traditional picture. First, next to traditional State accountability for 'ordinary' breaches of international rules, a new class of State responsibility has emerged for gross violations of fundamental rules enshrining essential values (so-called 'aggravated' *responsibility*: see *infra*, 9.5–6). Second, while previously the only category of individuals criminally liable under international law was that of pirates, since the end of the nineteenth century *individual responsibility* has gradually evolved. It was considered that serious offences committed by State officials in exceptional circumstances, for example war crimes, should entail the personal liability of their authors in addition to the possible international responsibility of the State to which they belonged. The category of war crimes gradually expanded after the Second World War and further categories were added: those of crimes against peace (chiefly aggression) and of crimes against humanity (chiefly genocide) (see *infra*, **Chapter 12**). However, despite these momentous advances, collective responsibility still remains the rule.

1.5 THE NEED FOR MOST INTERNATIONAL RULES TO BE TRANSLATED INTO NATIONAL LEGISLATION

As we shall see *infra* (**Chapter 8**), international rules to be applied by States within their own legal systems generally need to be incorporated into national law. This is because the international community is composed of sovereign States, each eager to control the individuals subject to its jurisdiction and consequently to decide on the extent to which they may hold rights and obligations. Hence, whenever international rules need to be applied within a State, or by a State official, in most cases they must be turned into municipal law.

Thus, for instance, for an international rule forbidding the use of certain categories of weapon (such as chemical or bacteriological weapons) to take effect, the Minister of Defence and the military commanders of a given State must be under a national obligation to comply with the rule, become cognizant of the scope of the rule, and take all the necessary measures to implement it. A provision such as Article 29 of the Vienna Convention of 1961 on diplomatic immunities ('The person of a diplomatic agent shall be inviolable. He shall not be liable to any form of arrest or detention. The receiving State shall treat him with due respect and shall take all appropriate steps to prevent any attack on his person, freedom or dignity') obliges the enforcement agencies of a State to refrain from arresting or detaining foreign diplomats, and to take all necessary measures to prevent undue attacks on them. Similarly, Article 34 of the same Convention ('A diplomatic agent shall be exempt from all dues, taxes, personal or real, national, regional or municipal' except for certain categories of taxes enumerated in the same provision) requires the tax authorities of the 'receiving State' (that is the State where he performs his diplomatic activity) to take the requisite regulatory or administrative steps to exempt foreign diplomats from all the dues and taxes to which they may not be subjected.

It is therefore apparent that most international rules cannot work without the constant help, co-operation, and support of national legal systems. Exaggerating somewhat (on account of his strictly dualistic approach), the German publicist H. Triepel observed in 1923 that international law is like a field marshal who can only give orders to generals. It is solely through the generals that his orders can reach the troops. If the generals do not transmit them to the soldiers in the field, he will lose the battle.[5]

1.6 THE RANGE OF STATES' FREEDOM OF ACTION

To illustrate yet another typical feature of the international community it is useful to refer once again, by way of comparison, to domestic legal systems.

In most national orders individuals—the primary legal subjects—enjoy great freedom in their private transactions. They can variously enter into agreements with other persons, or refrain from so doing, or they can set up companies, create associations, and so on. Their broad contractual freedom is not unfettered, however, in that central authorities usually place legal restraints upon them. Thus, for instance, one cannot make private transactions which are contrary to public order and morals (such as a contract whereby one party undertakes to hand over to another a next of kin, for purposes of prostitution); if such a transaction is made, it is null and void. It should be noted that national public order includes norms prohibiting physical persons from disposing of their body or their freedom. Thus, a contract whereby one party undertakes to mutilate his body or to deliver to another party one of his limbs is contrary to public order and consequently null and void. The same consideration applies to a contract whereby one party undertakes to commit suicide or to submit permanently to a position akin to slavery in relation to another party. Every domestic system contains a core of values that members of the community cannot disregard, not even when they engage in private transactions *inter se*. In the case of any such disregard, the response of the central authorities is to make the private undertaking devoid of legal effect. A fortiori individuals are not allowed to depart from certain basic values, which are held in such high esteem as to be embodied in rules governing criminal behaviour. If two or more persons enter into an agreement for the setting up of a criminal association, not only will their agreement be null and void, they will also incur penal responsibility and are punishable accordingly. A third set of restrictions on individual freedom derives from all the norms of public law concerning the functioning of State institutions: thus, for instance, in a State where political elections take place by law once every four years, citizens are not free to vote whenever they would like to do so. Limitations also derive from constitutional rules restraining the exercise of certain rights and liberties (as in the case of freedom of thought or association), and from labour laws (which often restrict freedom of contract in labour relations with regard to working time and working conditions, normally with a view to protecting the weaker party).

By contrast, subjects of the international community enjoy wide-ranging freedom of action. In traditional international law their freedom was in fact untrammelled; in modern international law some legal restrictions have been established.

Under traditional law States enjoyed great latitude as regards their internal set-up. The world community could not 'poke its nose' into how a State organized its political system. All States were free to establish an authoritarian power structure, or to uphold democratic principles; they could create a parliament or do without any representative assembly whatsoever; they could have a monarch or a democratically elected head of State. This was the private business of each country. In addition, international law was not interested in requesting States to give their internal legal order a specific content. With a few exceptions (for instance, international customary rules on the treatment of foreigners or on immunities to be granted to foreign diplomats), States were completely free to decide upon the tenor and scope of their national legislation. Again, general international law was not involved in the matter.

States also enjoyed complete freedom as regards the conduct of their foreign policy. It was up to them to decide whether or not to enter into international agreements; they also were free to choose their partners and the contents of agreements. They could shape their international relations as they pleased; they could recognize a new State or withhold recognition; they were free to enter into alliance with one or more States or refrain from doing so. The legal order even authorized States to use as much force as they wished and on any grounds they chose. States could engage in a war or resort to forcible measures short of war (see **11.1.1–11.1.4**) either on the grounds that one of their legal rights had been violated, or because they considered it politically and economically expedient forcibly to attack another State (for example, in order to occupy and annex part, or the whole, of its territory, or to set up a government subservient to their commands, etc.). Law was so 'generous' as also to allow States to intervene in the domestic and international affairs of other members of the world community, either by political pressure or by threatening the use of force, for the purpose of inducing the 'victim' of the intervention to change its policy (see **11.1.2**). Furthermore, even when they undertook to submit their legal disputes to arbitration, States usually excluded from the obligation to submit to arbitration, all the disputes affecting their 'vital interests', and each State retained the right to decide whether a specific case fell within that category. Freedom in the economic field was even greater.

Lack of legal restraints even allowed States to agree with other States that one of them must extinguish itself: they could conclude an agreement whereby one of them was incorporated into the other; or they could merge; or else one of them could agree to cede a portion of its territory to another State. No imperative rule prohibited self-mutilation or self-destruction.

I have, of course, been speaking of legal freedom. Power politics, the constant need for a balance of power, economic and social considerations, the geographical situation of States, prestige and traditions, as well as other factors—all these conspired to reduce that freedom. Nevertheless, the legal order adopted a laissez-faire attitude, thereby leaving an enormous field of action to States.

It is not difficult to understand why international law developed in this way. No State or group of States proved capable of wielding permanent control over the world community so as to impose a set of basic standards of behaviour calculated to govern the action of members. Hence, it was necessary to fall back on a negative regulation, leaving all members free to act as they liked, provided they did not grossly and consistently trespass on the freedom of other members. Clearly, this approach could not but favour the Great Powers. In practice, international law was modelled in such a way as to legitimize, 'codify', and protect their interests.

The unrestricted freedom of States has been subjected to increasing qualification since the First World War. Three factors account for new developments in this area.

First of all, there is the ever-expanding scope of the network of international treaties. Most States are now party to a very large number of treaties impinging upon their domestic legal systems. Consequently, at present most members of the world community are bound to obey a number of obligations that greatly restrict their latitude, as regards both their own internal system and their freedom in the international sphere. Many States have assumed obligations in the field of commercial, political, and judicial co-operation, in the realm of human rights, and so on. Similarly, as far as international action is concerned, many are parties to international organizations, to treaties of alliance, etc. True, all these undertakings derive from treaties; in theory, States can therefore get rid of them if they wish to do so. However, in practice, it is difficult for them to release themselves from all their various commitments: political, economic, diplomatic, military, and psychological factors stand in the way.

A second important reason is the increasing number of legal restrictions on the right to use force. The Covenant of the League of Nations in 1919 placed considerable restraints on a number of States. These restraints curtailed these States' power to wage war. The Paris Pact promoted by the USA and France, reinforced and extended them to a larger (and, in some respects, different) group of States in 1928. They became radical and sweeping in 1945, when the UN Charter required members to refrain from using or threatening the use of any sort of military force, with or without the label of 'war'. The ban on the use of force has now turned into a principle encompassing the whole international community, although the resulting limitation on State freedom is unfortunately beset with loopholes, which chiefly affect the enforcement mechanisms (see **5.4** and **Chapter 14**).

Thirdly, in the 1960s a customary rule evolved in the international community to the effect that certain general principles have greater legal force than other rules, in that States cannot derogate from them through international agreements. This set of peremptory norms was called *jus cogens* (see **6.5**). It follows that States are now duty-bound to refrain from entering into agreements providing for one of the activities prohibited by peremptory norms; if they nevertheless do so, their agreements may turn out to be null and void.

However, as we shall see (**Chapter 14**), despite these major advances, in reality and at least in some respects, the condition of the present international community is not far removed from that of classical international law.

1.7 THE OVERRIDING ROLE OF EFFECTIVENESS

International law is a realistic legal system. It takes account of existing power relationships and endeavours to translate them into legal rules. It is largely based on the principle of effectiveness, that is to say, it provides that only those claims and situations which are effective can produce legal consequences. A situation is effective if it is solidly implanted in real life. Thus, for instance, if a new State emerges from secession, it will be able to claim international status only after it is apparent that it undisputedly controls a specific territory and the human community living there. Control over the State community must be real and durable. The same consideration holds true for insurgents. If civil strife breaks out within a State, the rebels cannot claim international rights and duties unless they exercise effective authority over a part of the territory concerned. Similarly, in the case of the military occupation of a foreign territory, the occupying Power cannot claim all the rights and privileges deriving from the international law of warfare, until the territory is actually placed under that Power's authority and it is in a position to assert itself.

The principle of effectiveness permeates the whole body of rules making up international law. Under traditional law one of its corollaries has for long been that legal fictions had no place on the international scene. New situations were not recognized as legally valid unless they could be seen to rest on a firm and durable display of authority. No new situation could claim international legitimacy so long as the 'new men' failed to demonstrate that they had firmly supplanted the former authority. Force was the principal source of legitimation.

One may well wonder why force has played such an overriding role in the world community, giving the international legal system a 'conservative' slant. The answer probably lies in the fact that power has always been diffused and a superior authority capable of legitimizing new situations has not emerged, nor have States evolved a core of legally binding principles serving this purpose (because they are too divided to be able to do so). In consequence, legal rules must of necessity rely upon force as the sole standard by which new facts and events are to be legally appraised.

The foregoing observations essentially apply to the *traditional* setting of the international community. Since the First World War a number of States have attempted to make 'legality' prevail over sheer force or authority. The main impetus came from the Stimson doctrine of 1932 (see **14.3.2**). This suggested withholding legitimation from certain situations which, although effective, offended values that were increasingly regarded as fundamental.

1.8 TRADITIONAL INDIVIDUALISTIC TRENDS AND EMERGING COMMUNITY OBLIGATIONS AND RIGHTS

1.8.1 RECIPROCITY AS THE BASIS OF INTERNATIONAL RIGHTS AND OBLIGATIONS

The international community has long been characterized by a horizontal structure and the lack of strong political, ideological, and economic links between its members. (The Christian principles prevailing in the 'old' community were not allowed to override national interests.) These features have thus resulted in the tendency for every State to be self-seeking. Self-interest has held sway.

This phenomenon is also apparent in the way substantive rules govern the behaviour of States. International rules, even though they address themselves to all

States (in the case of customs) or group of States (in the case of multilateral treaties), confer rights or impose obligations on *pairs of States* only. As a result, each State has a right or an obligation in relation to one other State only. Such rules can also be termed 'synallagmatic' in that they impose reciprocal obligations. For instance, in the case of customary rules, they may confer on each member of the international community rights *erga omnes*, that is towards all other States. However, in their concrete application, they boil down to standards applying to pairs of States. Conspicuous instances are the rule on sovereignty (each State can claim from all other States full respect for its territorial integrity and political independence), and that on the free use of the high seas (each State is entitled to enjoy freedom of navigation, fishing, and overflight, as well as freedom to lay submarine cables and pipelines in all parts of the sea which are not under the jurisdiction of a coastal State). It should, however, be noted that as soon as one of these norms is violated, the ensuing legal relationship links only the aggrieved State and the offending party. In other words, the *erga omnes* character of the substantive rights is not accompanied by a procedural right of enforcement belonging to all the members of the international community. Once a State has infringed the sovereignty of another State, it is for the victim to claim reparation; no other State can intervene on the victim's behalf or on behalf of the whole international community to claim cessation of the wrong or reparation. The same holds true for the rules on diplomatic immunities; although they are general in character and address themselves to all States, in fact they split into a number of binary rules, each regulating a pair of States. Thus, for instance, the rule that 'A diplomatic agent shall enjoy immunity from the criminal jurisdiction of the receiving State' (codified in the 1961 Vienna Convention on Diplomatic Relations, Art. 31(1)) entails that in the relations between, say, the UK and Indonesia, either State has the right to claim from the other that its diplomatic agents be immune from the criminal jurisdiction of the other State. The same applies to all other pairs of States members of the international community.

The same holds true for international treaties, in particular multilateral treaties. For instance, a treaty on international trade providing for the establishment of a certain customs duty on a particular good confers on each contracting party the right to demand of all the other contracting parties fulfilment of that obligation; as soon as a contracting party breaches that obligation with regard to goods imported from another contracting party, the latter is entitled to claim reparation for that breach. In practice, this multilateral treaty can be broken down into a set of substantially similar bilateral treaties, each regulating the relationships between a particular pair of States. It is as if each contracting party were bound by as many bilateral treaties as there are other contracting parties.

Plainly, we are far from the system obtaining in all national legal systems. There, in cases of serious breaches (for example criminal offences), a representative of the entire community (the Public Prosecutor or a similar institution) can initiate legal proceedings irrespective of the attitude or action of the injured party. The system prevailing in international law has a number of serious drawbacks, among them the fact that the reaction to a wrong ultimately depends on whether the victim is stronger than or at least as strong as the culpable State. In the final analysis, respect for law is made dependent on power.

Probably one of the few exceptions to this network of legal rights and obligations was constituted by the general rule on piracy (on this notion, still applicable today, see *infra*, **4.5.1** and **12.1**). This rule authorized every State to seize and capture pirates on the high seas, whatever their nationality and whether or not they had attacked one of its ships or threatened to do so. Thus, this rule (which imposed on all individuals of the world the obligation to refrain from piracy) granted a right to all States unconnected to actual damage. However, when exercising this right, States did not act on behalf of the world community, for the protection of a community value; rather they acted merely to safeguard a *joint interest*. As a British court put it in 1817 in *Le Louis, Forest*, pirates are 'enemies of the human race, renouncing every country, and ravaging every country in its coasts and vessels indiscriminately, and thereby creating an [sic] universal terror and alarm'.[6] Hence, the right to capture piratical vessels 'has existed upon the ground of repelling injury, and as a measure of self-defence'.[7] This proposition clearly spells out that the right to capture pirates rested on the joint interest of all States to fight a common danger (and consequent damage), be it real or potential.

The same seems to hold true for the rights of riparian States with regard to navigable international rivers. Under customary law developed since 1815, every riparian State has a right to free navigation and to equality of treatment. Consequently, if one of those States performs an act preventing another State's free navigation, by the same token it infringes upon the right of any other riparian State, whether or not it actually causes damage to it. This is because, as the PCIJ put it in 1929 in *Territorial Jurisdiction of the International Commission of the River Oder*,

'the community of interest in a navigable river becomes the basis of a common legal right, the essential features of which are the perfect equality of all riparian States in the use of the whole course of the river and the exclusion of any preferential privilege of any one riparian State in relation to the others'.[8]

1.8.2 COMMUNITY OBLIGATIONS AND COMMUNITY RIGHTS

In the *present* international community traditional rules based on reciprocity still constitute the bulk of international law. Nevertheless, one can also find new rules with a different content and import. A number of treaties, many of which came into being after the First World War and more particularly in the aftermath of the Second World War, provide for obligations that are incumbent upon each State towards all other contracting parties and which are in no way reciprocal.

This category of rules has evolved from the emergence of *new values* that the international community has come to regard as being worthy of special protection. Thus, after the First World War, as a result of the ideological and political pressure of socialist doctrines, and also because, following the catastrophe of war, it came to be believed that the condition of workers was growing worse, the lot of workers was regarded as deserving greater international concern. Consequently, the International Labour Organization (ILO) was set up and international conventions for the protection of workers began being drafted and adopted, their implementation being under the scrutiny of the ILO (see, however, **4.5.2(c)**). Similarly, after the Second World War, as a reaction to the mass murder by the Nazis of ethnic and religious groups (chiefly Jews, as well as Gypsies) and the total disregard for the basic human rights of thousands of individuals both in Germany and elsewhere, the Allies decided to create better safeguards against genocide and other egregious violations of human rights. By the same token, the Nazi aggression against a number of European States and the attack by Japan on the USA prompted the UN to enact a sweeping ban on all forms of aggression. As stated above, all these new values resulted in numerous international treaties as well as a few international customary rules (see **Chapters 5** and **16**).

Community obligations possess the following unique features: (i) they are obligations protecting fundamental values (such as peace, human rights, self-determination of peoples, protection of the environment); (ii) they are obligations *erga omnes*, that is towards all the member States of the international community (or, in the case of multilateral treaties, all the other contracting States); (iii) they are attended by a correlative *right* that belongs to any State (or to every other *contracting* State, in the case of obligations provided for in multilateral treaties); (iv) this right may be exercised by any other (contracting) State, whether or not it has been materially or morally injured by the violation; (v) the right is exercised *on behalf of the whole international community* (or the community of the contracting States) to *safeguard fundamental values* of this community (for example, when a State makes a remonstrance to, or forcefully protests against, another State on account of atrocities committed by the latter against its own nationals, and demands the immediate cessation of those atrocities, it is not motivated by the desire to safeguard its own interests or to prevent any possible future damage; its sole (or primary) purpose is to vindicate humanitarian values on behalf of the whole international community). These rights can therefore be termed 'community rights'.

In a way, this body of values makes up what the Spanish international lawyer Francisco de Vitoria (1483–1546), a follower of modern natural law theory, termed *bonum commune totius orbis*, that is, the common good for the whole world—in other words, the assets and values that are shared by the whole of mankind and to which the particular interests and demands of individual States should yield. As we shall see, this is yet another confirmation that the emergence in modern times of the notions of community obligations and rights (and of the cognate concept of *jus cogens*, see *infra*, **6.5**) translates into the terms of the positive law ideas and constructs propounded by the advocates of natural law between the fifteenth and the eighteenth century.

How can the 'community rights' we are discussing be exercised? Customary rules do not provide for any particular mechanism. It follows that it is possible to resort to traditional means of redress (diplomatic steps, diplomatic pressure, peaceful countermeasures; see **11.3** and **11.4**). As for treaties, some simply proclaim a right, without specifying the means by which it can be put into effect. The means of redress just mentioned can also be used in such cases. By contrast, a number of other treaties set up special procedures or special machinery for facilitating the task of the claimant State. We shall return to this point later on (see **9.5** and **9.6** as well as **Chapter 10**).

In a Resolution adopted in 1989 the *Institut de Droit International*,[9] authoritatively restating and spelling out existing customary law, pointed out that the obligation to ensure observance of fundamental human rights as 'a direct expression of the dignity of the human person' is *erga omnes*; in case of breaches of human rights any other State is empowered to react by means of 'diplomatic representations as well as purely verbal expressions of concern or disapproval', whereas if the breaches are large scale or systematic, other States are entitled to take diplomatic, economic, and other peaceful measures towards the responsible State. In addition, Article 1, which is common to the four Geneva Conventions of 1949 and Article 1.1 of the 1978 First Additional Protocol provide that each contracting State undertakes to respect the Conventions and Protocol 'in all circumstances', and by the same token assumes the obligation 'to ensure respect' for these instruments 'in all circumstances'; in other words, it not only has the right but also is under the obligation to demand that any other contracting party comply with them.[10] Furthermore, as Judge E. Lauterpacht stated in his Separate Opinion in *Genocide (Bosnia and Herzegovina v. Yugoslavia (Serbia and Montenegro)*,[11] under Article 1 of the 1949 Genocide Convention each contracting party is authorized to react to any breach of the Convention by any other State engaging in genocide. Customary law restates and broadens these obligations and rights in the area of genocide.

Nevertheless, the significance of the recent emergence of 'community obligations', though considerable, should not be over-emphasized.[12] For one thing, the treaties or customary rules laying down these obligations are still relatively rare. For another, even those rules are seldom put into effect. A typical feature of the international community, namely the huge gap between the normative level and implementation, is more conspicuous in this area than anywhere else. Although States have the opportunity of acting in the interest of the whole international community, or of all the other contracting parties, they usually prefer to avoid meddling in other States' internal affairs. They end up by exercising their 'community rights' only when their own economic, military, or political interests are at stake. In the final analysis, most procedures based on State-to-State complaints have ended in failure, or, at least, have not been exploited fully (see **9.3.4–5** and **9.4**). This assessment ought, however, to be qualified to some extent. There are international procedures which can be set in motion not by States but either at the request of the aggrieved individuals or ex officio, that is by the international body responsible for supervising compliance with the treaty concerned (see **10.8.2**). Thus in such cases fulfilment of community obligations is sought by entities other than the various contracting States. Their action eventually compensates for the lack of consideration shown to ideals of a common good.

1.9 COEXISTENCE OF THE OLD AND NEW PATTERNS

Every legal system undergoes constant change, for law must steadily adjust itself to new realities. This sometimes results in old and new institutions living together: even in the case of revolutions, it is difficult to cast aside all the existing legal structures overnight. However, as a rule, fresh pieces of the legal fabric supplant outmoded ones so as to eliminate the most glaring inconsistencies.

In the international community two different patterns in law, one traditional, the other modern, live side by side. Taking up the distinction drawn by a distinguished British political scientist, M. Wight,[13] and developed by another outstanding British scholar, H. Bull,[14] we could call the traditional model '*Grotian*' and the new one '*Kantian*'. Under the former model the international community is based on a 'statist' vision of international relations; it is characterized by co-operation and regulated intercourse among sovereign States, each pursuing its own interests. In contrast, the more modern '*Kantian*' paradigm is based on a universalist or cosmopolitan outlook, 'which sees at work in international politics a potential community of mankind' and lays stress on the element of 'trans-national solidarity' (*jus cosmopoliticum*).

The new legal institutions, which have developed within the setting of the international community approximately since the First World War (and with greater intensity since 1945), have not uprooted or supplanted the old framework, the 'Grotian' strand. Rather, they appear to have been superimposed on it (even though their main purpose is to mitigate the most striking defects of the old system).

2

THE HISTORICAL EVOLUTION OF THE INTERNATIONAL COMMUNITY

2.1 INTRODUCTION

We should now ask how the international community acquired the unique features it currently shows. As a result of what historical events did it evolve in such a way as to appear so markedly different from all domestic legal systems?

In tracing the historical evolution of the world community, it is useful to divide it into various stages. Periodization is, of course, always arbitrary; nevertheless, it may prove helpful for a better understanding of some major turning points. The evolution of the international community can be roughly divided into four major stages: (1) from its gradual emergence (sixteenth–early seventeenth century) to the First World War; (2) from the establishment of the League of Nations to the end of the Second World War (1919–1945); (3) from the establishment of the United Nations to the end of the cold war (1945–1989); (4) the present period.

2.2 THE EMERGENCE OF THE PRESENT INTERNATIONAL COMMUNITY BEFORE THE PEACE OF WESTPHALIA

The origin of the international community in its present structure and configuration is usually traced back to the sixteenth century. It largely crystallized at the time of the Peace of Westphalia (1648), which concluded the ferocious and sanguinary Thirty Years War. Of course, international intercourse between groups and nations had existed previously. From time immemorial there had been consular and diplomatic relations between different communities, as well as treaties of alliance or of peace. Reprisals had been regulated for many years and during the Middle Ages a body of law on the conduct of belligerent hostilities had gradually evolved. And yet all these relations were radically different from current international dealings, for the fabric of the international community itself was different. Even in the late Middle Ages, when international relations of a kind resulted from the splitting of communities into various groups headed by feudal lords, the international community differed from the present one, and this for two reasons. First, fully fledged States—in the modern sense—did not yet exist. Centralized structures, which had gradually come into being in Europe between 1100 and 1300, did not assume the typical features of a modern State until after 1450.

Of the various historical enquiries into the origin of the modern State, it may suffice to quote here those of J. R. Strayer.[1] In his view, what characterizes the modern State and differentiates it from both 'the great, imperfectly integrated empires' of the past and the small, but highly cohesive units, such as the Greek 'city State', are the following characteristics: 'the appearance of political units persisting in time and fixed in space, the development of permanent, impersonal institutions, agreement on the need for an authority which can give final judgments, and acceptance of the idea that this authority should receive the basic loyalty of its subjects'. Underlying them are 'a shift in loyalty from family, local community, or religious organization to the State, and the acquisition by the State of a moral authority to back up its institutional structure and its theoretical legal supremacy'. In addition to these features, the modern State shows a very important distinguishing trait: the emergence of centralized bureaucracies, which gradually turn into ministerial departments. It was no doubt a slow evolution; nevertheless, in the seventeenth century, the permanent core of the State was the bureaucracy although, as Jellinek pointed out, one must wait until the adoption on 25 May 1791 of the French décret establishing the various ministries for the 'principle of division of labour to be completely carried through in public administration, and for ministers in the sense of administrative law to side by the monarch'.[2]

The period following the Peace of Westphalia inaugurated a new era in a second respect. Previously there had been the overpowering presence of two poles of authority: the Pope at the head of the Catholic Church, and the Emperor at the head of the Holy Roman Empire (which had been set up as early as AD 800 by Charlemagne and had encompassed most of Europe but dwindled in the seventeenth century to the German territory in central Europe).

Thus the necessary premise for the development of the present international community is the rise of modern national States between the fifteenth and seventeenth centuries. This momentous phenomenon, indisputably favoured by the discovery of America (1492) and the dissemination of Protestantism after the Reformation, led to the formation of a number of strong States, all of which sought to be independent of any superior authority. Western countries such as England, Spain, and France, followed by the Netherlands and Sweden, as well as the Ottoman Empire, China, and Japan in the East, increasingly regarded one another as separate and autonomous entities, and each struggled to overpower the other. New standards of behaviour became necessary. Consequently, either the old rules were given a new shape or new norms were developed.

In this respect an important contribution was made by a number of imaginative and forward-looking jurists, such as the Spaniards Francisco de Vitoria (1483–1546) and Francisco Suarez (1548–1617), the Italian Alberico Gentili (1552–1608), a Protestant who fled to England, where he taught at Oxford, and above all the Dutchman Hugo Grotius (1583–1645). They set out to lend a lucid legal justification to the interests of the emerging States in general, and of their own country in particular.

The Peace of Westphalia concluded a most appalling war, which had caused 'great effusion of Christian blood and the desolation of several provinces' (preamble to the Treaty of Münster). The major countries of Europe had been involved; the conflict had started in 1618 for religious reasons, namely the struggle between Catholic and Protestant countries, but it soon turned into an all-out struggle for military and political hegemony in Europe. The treaties of peace were signed in the Westphalian towns of Münster and Osnabrück.[3]

Questions of prestige accounted for the choice of two places for negotiating peace: France and Sweden, the former Catholic, the latter Protestant, quarrelled over the question of precedence; consequently France was given priority in Catholic Münster and Sweden in Protestant Osnabrück. However, from the legal point of view, the two treaties made up an integrated whole.

The treaties constitute a watershed in the evolution of the modern international community. First, they recognized Protestantism at an international level and consequently legitimized the existence of States based on Calvinist or Lutheran faith. Henceforth, even from the point of view of religion, it was recognized that the State was independent of the Church. Second, the treaties granted members of the Holy Roman Empire (some three hundred small States) the *jus foederationis*, that is the right to enter into alliances with foreign powers and to wage war, provided that those alliances or wars were neither against the Empire 'nor against the public peace' and the 'treaty' (Treaty of Münster, Art. 65). Thus, a number of small countries were upgraded to the status of members of the international community with quasi-sovereign rights. Third, the treaties crystallized a political distribution of power in Europe that lasted for more than a century. France, Sweden, and the Netherlands were recognized as the new emerging big powers; Switzerland (and the Netherlands) were given the status of neutral countries; Germany was split up into a number of relatively small States. In short, the Peace of Westphalia testified to the rapid decline of the Church (an institution which had already suffered many blows) and to the de facto disintegration of the Empire. By the same token it recorded the birth of an international system based on a plurality of independent States, recognizing no superior authority over them. The two treaties signed in 1648 also set up a scheme for collective security, which remained, however, a dead letter.[4]

2.3 STAGE 1: FROM THE PEACE OF WESTPHALIA TO THE END OF THE FIRST WORLD WAR

2.3.1 THE COMPOSITION OF THE INTERNATIONAL COMMUNITY

(a) The dominant States

Since its inception, the world community has encompassed States belonging to different geographic, cultural, and religious areas. While the most intense intercourse took place between European States, treaties were also concluded with other States with which Europe had come into contact, chiefly the Mogul Empire in India, the Ottoman Empire, Persia, China, Japan (since 1854), Burma, and Siam (which has been called Thailand since 1939), as well as with the States of Ethiopia and Liberia (the latter independent since 1847), and Haiti (independent since 1804). Only one year after the Peace of Westphalia, on 1 July 1649, the Holy Roman Empire concluded a treaty with Turkey for the continuation of the peace which had been agreed in 1642.

Nevertheless, for many centuries the most active and prominent members of the international community were the European States, joined by the USA in 1783 and by the Latin American countries between 1811 and 1821.

Paraphrasing Hegel's description of the role of Greece and Italy in the past, one might say that in this period Europe was the 'theatre of World History' and that there the 'World Spirit' (*Weltgeist*) found its home. All the States just mentioned had a common religious matrix: they were Christian. This common ideological background made for a better understanding. Despite political, economic, and military conflicts, culture and religion acted as cement uniting them. Another strong unifying factor was the pattern of internal economic and political development. All Western States were the outgrowth of capitalism and its equivalent phenomenon in the political field: absolutism (followed in subsequent years by parliamentary democracy).

In a number of respects non-Christian States lived for many years on the margin of the international community: they did not take a very active part, nor did they play any major role, in it. According to a number of scholars, for roughly three hundred years (from the beginning of the sixteenth to the eighteenth century) a few Asian powers (namely all State entities in the East Indies, as well as Persia, Burma, and Siam) had social intercourse with European countries on a footing of complete equality. However—so the argument goes—the industrial revolution that took place in Europe in the late eighteenth century created a gap between Europe and non-European States. In the nineteenth century the latter were left far behind and were gradually conquered by the former or at any event fell under their domination.

Be that as it may, three points are difficult to question: (1) since its inception the world community consisted not only of European States, but embraced other countries and nations as well, and there was some degree of intercourse between all sections of the community; however, many factors including geographical distance and the slowness of communication and transport rendered transactions between

European and other countries particularly difficult. (2) For various reasons, the European Powers set the tone from the outset and played a dominant role throughout. (3) Western jurists consistently theorized about and buttressed the idea of 'European' superiority.

(b) The capitulation system and colonialism

As pointed out above, non-European States bowed to Western 'superiority' and eventually submitted to the rules elaborated by European countries and the USA. Western States tended to develop two distinct classes of relations with the 'outside' world, depending on whether this 'world' consisted of States proper (the Ottoman Empire, China, Japan, etc.) or was instead made up of communities lacking any organized central authority (tribal communities or communities dominated by local rulers, in Africa and Asia). With the former, Europe and the USA to a large extent based their relations on the 'capitulation' system. They considered the latter mere objects of conquest and appropriation, and consequently turned them into colonial territories.

Let us consider first the capitulation system.

Capitulations were agreements (probably so called because they were divided into numbered *capitula* or brief chapters) concluded by Western States with Moslem rulers (later on with the Ottoman Empire), with some Arab countries (Egypt, Iraq, Syria, Morocco, Palestine), with Persia, Siam, China, and Japan ever since the sixteenth century. The capitulory regime was consolidated in the seventeenth and eighteenth centuries: the treaty of 1740 between France and the Ottoman Empire is usually mentioned as being of great significance for the delineation of the main traits of this regime. Capitulations served to impose conditions for the residence of Europeans (including US nationals) in the territory of non-European countries. They tended to include the following basic provisions: (1) Europeans who were nationals of a party to the agreement could not be expelled from the country without the consent of their consul; (2) they had the right to practise public worship of their Christian faith; to this end they could erect churches and have their own graveyards; (3) they enjoyed freedom of trade and commerce and were exempted from certain import and export duties; (4) reprisals against them were prohibited, especially in case of insolvency; (5) jurisdiction over disputes between Europeans belonged to the consul of the defendant or, in criminal cases, of the victim (hence not to the territorial court), while in the case of disputes between a European and a national of the territorial State the jurisdiction devolved upon the judges of the latter State.

Three features of this legal regime are striking. First, Europeans came to make up a legal community completely separate from the local one and actually subject to their own national authorities (which thereby extended their control beyond their own territorial area, and to a foreign country). Second, this regime was not based on reciprocity: it consisted of a number of privileges granted to Europeans on non-European territory, with no counterpart in favour of non-European nationals (the few instances adduced by Alexandrowicz of privileges granted in Europe to non-European partners are exceptional and of scant relevance).[5] The overwhelming inequality on which capitulations rested was clearly indicative of the existing relations. Third, at least in the eighteenth and early nineteenth centuries, certain non-Western States did not see capitulations as detrimental to their sovereignty. Thus, for instance, a Japanese author stated that 'The Japanese authorities in those days, which had little knowledge of the concept of extraterritoriality, regarded national laws of Japan as something sacred, for the benefit of which foreigners were not worthy of enjoyment'.[6] And Alexandrowicz has pointed out that capitulations rested on an ancient Asian tradition ('ancient custom in Asia allowed foreign merchants to govern themselves by their own personal law instead of submitting to the jurisdiction and the law of the host country and possibly to a different way of life').[7]

Nonetheless, Western rights of 'extraterritoriality' constituted serious restraints on the sovereignty of the 'territorial' State. Later on, towards the end of the nineteenth century, they were deeply felt as an undue encroachment even by the Japanese authorities and were gradually terminated (see *infra*, **2.4.4**).

Let us now turn to the relations of European States with another class of 'other' countries, namely those lacking any State-like structure, or governed by a great number of local authorities frequently feuding with one another. These countries were gradually subjected to the colonial domination of Western Powers.

Europeans first colonized the Americas in the fifteenth century. As soon as the first signs of rebellion were apparent in America, Asia became a desirable area. In the eighteenth century first France and then Britain appropriated large portions of India, until in 1773 most of India actually became a British colony. In the early nineteenth century, when the successful revolt of the USA was followed by the independence of South America, Europeans turned to Africa, while at the same time intensifying their interest in Asia. At the Berlin Conference of 1884–5, attended by such European countries as Austria-Hungary, Belgium, Denmark, France, Germany, Britain, Italy, the Netherlands, Portugal, Russia, Spain, Sweden-Norway, plus Turkey and the USA, and resulting in the General Act of 26 February 1884,[8] Africa was split up among Britain, France, Portugal, Belgium, Germany, and Italy. Furthermore, Britain, France, and the Netherlands either appropriated or consolidated their control over Asia. Even a State formerly under colonial domination, the USA, took part in the colonialist trend. It seized power over the Philippines in 1898 as a result of the war with Spain, concluded by the Peace Treaty of Paris in 1898.

We shall see *infra* (**18.1–3**) whether colonial domination proved beneficial at least in some respects. The question which should be raised here as particularly germane to the present enquiry is that of the role of international law in the process of colonial conquest. In short, it can be argued that this body of law greatly facilitated the task of European Powers, offering them, as it did, a large number of legal instruments designed to render conquest smooth and easy. International law authorized States to acquire sovereignty over those territories, both by downgrading the latter to *terrae nullius*, namely, territories belonging to no one, and by depriving the local communities or rulers of any international standing. Effective occupation and de facto control over the territory (coupled with the intent of appropriation) were sufficient for the acquisition of sovereign rights. Furthermore, if local rulers opposed the colonial conquest, international law offered two instruments: either war (without all the legal restraints applicable to wars between 'civilized' States), or the conclusion of treaties (indeed a great number of agreements with 'local rulers' or chieftains were entered into by European States, and they normally lacked any reciprocity).

The same legal instruments were available in case of conflict between colonial Powers and other Western countries wishing to appropriate the same territories: either the waging of a war or the conclusion of an agreement settled the matter.

2.3.2 THE ALLOCATION OF POWER

Throughout the whole period under consideration power was spread out: no single State became so strong as to subject all the other countries to its will. Legally, all members of the international community were on an equal footing. In practice, a group of great powers (France, Britain, Spain, Portugal, the USA, Russia, Austria, Prussia, Sweden, the Netherlands) dominated the international scene. However, this group never presented a united front because there were constant rivalries. A balance of power proved necessary and was in fact established.

It is against this general background that an experiment in collective systems for restraining power and enforcing the law should be considered. It was made in 1815 after the defeat of Napoleon. The French revolution and the genius of Napoleon had shattered deep-rooted principles and upset the existing order. The victors felt they had to protect the interests of European monarchies against the seeds of revolution. To this end they met to devise a system capable of putting a straitjacket on these new forces, which were urging the abolition of inequitable practices and the dismantling of aristocratic privileges. The new system, called the Concert of Europe, was set up in a number of treaties worked out in 1815 and supplemented by subsequent agreements. It rested on three principal elements:

(1) A *declaration of principles*, binding all States except for Britain, the Papal States, and the Ottoman Empire. It proclaimed that the contracting parties would adopt as standards of behaviour, both in their internal orders and in international relations, the precepts of the Christian religion.

(2) A *military alliance.* The 'Holy Alliance' was instituted by the Treaty of Paris of 20 November 1815, concluded by Austria, Prussia, Russia, and Great Britain, to which France acceded in 1818. It envisaged a system for collective security based on the agreement of the big Powers, designed to forestall or stifle any recurrence of Bonapartism, either in France or elsewhere. Under Articles 2 to 4 of the treaty, the contracting States undertook to agree upon the measures to be taken against those infringing upon the 'tranquillity' and the 'established order' in Europe; they also pledged themselves to agree upon the number of troops which each of them was bound to provide 'for the pursuit of the common cause'. While at the outset the main object was that of averting any threat to the stability of post-Napoleonic France, the system was subsequently extended so as to function against any revolutionary movement likely to overthrow European monarchies: see the treaty of 1818 and the protocol of 1820. The latter, ratified by Austria, Russia, and Prussia, provided for three measures in cases of revolution: (i) the State in which a revolution broke out would cease to be a member of the Concert of Europe; (ii) the new government resulting from a revolution would not be recognized; and (iii) the States directly concerned, or otherwise the Holy Alliance, would intervene to put an end to the revolution.

This system proved quite effective in practice. It was actually resorted to on two occasions: in 1821, when Austrian troops were sent to Naples and Turin to suppress liberal insurgents on behalf of the Holy Alliance; and in 1823, when French troops were dispatched to Spain, again to thwart a liberal attempt at independence. On both occasions one State only—the one directly concerned—made a military intervention. But the right to take action was considered as delegated by all the partners of the Holy Alliance, and was authorized by a general meeting (the Conference of Troppau and Laybach in the former case, the Conference of Verona in the latter).

(3) A *new procedure for the settlement of political questions*, consisting of meetings of all the sovereigns concerned where they might discuss 'great interests in common', consider measures conducive to the 'tranquillity and prosperity of peoples', and attempt to maintain peace in Europe. In short, a new diplomatic method was propounded: multilateral diplomacy, based on *periodical summit meetings*. It proved most useful and was indeed resorted to on a number of occasions in later years.

As soon as European monarchies came under strong attack from nationalist movements and were gradually overthrown or forced to turn into parliamentary democracies, the system set up in 1815 was replaced by the traditional policy of the *balance of power*: only the diplomatic method of summit meetings survived. Protected—at least in some respects—by this policy, the Great Powers revived their tendency to exercise hegemony, endeavouring not to trespass upon the respective spheres of influence.

Within this general framework, the emergence of the USA set a limit to European influence and power in the Americas. The new trend was formally proclaimed by the American president, Monroe, in the doctrine propounded in the famous message to Congress of 2 December 1823. This message stated, first, that 'the American continents . . . are henceforth not to be considered as subjects for future colonization by any European power'. Second, while the USA would not intervene in European matters, by the same token it could not allow European powers to intervene in America.[9] Thus a check was placed on European expansionism and at the same time the basic principle was enunciated that the American continent was under the control of the most powerful State of the area.

What is striking in this period is the spread of *forcible intervention* by major Powers in the internal or external affairs of other States.

As the German publicist Staudacher aptly emphasized in 1909,[10] this practice gained momentum after 1820 as a result of two developments. First, there was a growing tendency among major European countries to get together and police international relations by sending troops to troublespots; this tendency, evolved during the Napoleonic wars and dictated by the need of other European Powers to counteract Napoleon's hegemony, was consolidated after his downfall in the form of a strong feeling of solidarity linking reactionary monarchies, and led to the formation of the Holy Alliance. Second, the gruesome devastation entailed by the Napoleonic wars impelled States to avoid becoming involved in wars proper. The combination of the two trends led European States to intervene on a number of occasions both in Europe and elsewhere, without, however, engaging in fully fledged wars. For instance, after the downfall of Napoleon, as pointed out above the Holy Alliance provided for military intervention in European countries menaced by revolutions. Later, Great European Powers intervened against Turkey and

Egypt and in the colonial territories of other States, and the USA intervened in Latin American countries.

2.3.3 THE MAIN FEATURES OF THE LAW

The very expression 'international law' dates back to this period.[11] The legal regulation created in this period possesses two salient features:

(1) International rules and principles were the product of Western civilization and bore the imprint of Eurocentrism, Christian ideology, and of a 'free market' outlook (they rested on a laissez-faire philosophy, that is on the idea that all States should be legally equal and free to pursue their own interests, irrespective of any economic or social imbalance).[12]

(2) International norms and principles were mainly framed by the Great Powers or middle-sized States, particularly by those States which built up extensive colonial empires by dint of conquest and expansion. They elaborated the rules to serve their own interests. Among the norms of this category, particular emphasis should be laid on those concerning force: they placed no restraint on the threat or use of belligerent violence. Other important rules were those on the diplomatic and judicial protection of nationals abroad: whenever the citizen of a certain State claimed that a foreign Government had behaved unlawfully towards him, he could request his national Government to step in and claim reparation of the alleged international wrongful act. Clearly, these rules constituted important legal tools in the hands of those Great Powers whose nationals went abroad to initiate commercial undertakings.

A notable contribution to the elucidation and development of international customary rules, that often led to the elaboration of international treaties, was made by a group of eminent European and American scholars, who were instrumental in the establishment, in 1873, in Ghent (Belgium) of an association of distinguished academics, some of them involved in international affairs in different capacities: the *Institut de droit international*. Among them some stood out: the Dutch T. M. C. Asser, the Swiss (teaching in Germany) J. C. Bluntschli, the Argentinian C. Calvo, the British J. Lorimer, the Italian P. S. Mancini, the Swiss G. Moynier, the Belgian G. Rolin-Jaequemyns. The aims of the *Institut* were: promotion of the 'progress of international law' by stating its principles 'according to the judicial conscience of the civilized world'; promotion of 'progressive codification'; and the 'official acknowledgement' of the principles of international law. Over the years the *Institut* discussed important topics and passed resolutions that have been influential in the development of international law: in particular those on the liberty of navigation and neutrality within the Congo Basin, on rules concerning arbitration proceedings, on land and sea warfare, on international prize courts, on codification, etc.

Two qualifications should be made to the above remarks on the principal features of law in this period. First, in some cases big Powers were impelled to make concessions to smaller States (see, for example, the rules on the freedom of the high seas *infra*, **3.5.1** and **3.5.3**, and the rules on lawful combatants, see *infra*, **15.6.1**).

The second qualification is that while a number of treaties were dictated by humanitarian demands, others met the exigencies of all members of the international community, whether powerful or weak. The former include not only treaties on the slave trade, but also some international agreements placing restraints on the use of weapons causing inhuman suffering (see **15.6.2**).

At least one of the treaties banning weapons should be mentioned at this juncture, namely the declaration prohibiting the use of expanding bullets, adopted by the Hague Conference in 1899. Soft-nosed bullets which expanded on contact, thus causing gaping wounds and appalling suffering, had been developed by the British at the Dum-Dum arsenal in Calcutta in the nineteenth century. As E. M. Spiers recalled, the British authorities justified their production by saying that 'the demands of small colonial warfare warranted this deviation from the standards of European armaments. The enemies whom Britain encountered were not armies from the European countries who had signed the St Petersburg Declaration [of 1868, prohibiting the use in time of war of explosive projectiles under 400 grammes weight], but "fanatical natives", "savages", and "barbarians" '. The difference was deemed substantial: 'civilised man is much more susceptible to injury than savages . . . the savage, like the tiger, is not so impressionable, and will go on fighting even when desperately wounded'.[13] (It should be noted in passing that the distinction between civilized peoples and barbarians, as far as the use of weapons was concerned, was not new: back in 1625 Grotius had written that poisoning weapons and waters was 'contrary to the law of nations, not indeed of all nations but of European nations and of such others as attain to the higher standard of Europe'.)[14] Although Britain assured other Western Powers that it would not use those bullets in European wars, they managed to have the Hague Peace Conference pass the Declaration referred to above. Britain grudgingly adhered to it in 1907, and the prohibition gradually expanded so as to cover any international armed conflict.

The other category of rules intended to meet the demands of all States irrespective of their strength included treaties such as those on diplomatic and consular immunities, as well as the norms on neutrality and the neutralization of States. Although some of these norms were also motivated by particular interests, their intrinsic significance for the whole international community transformed them into lasting principles which continue to display their effects today.

2.3.4 EFFORTS TO RESTRAIN THE GREAT POWERS' DOMINANCE: THE CALVO AND DRAGO DOCTRINES

Timid attempts were made to restrain the domination of the Great Powers by international or national legislation. The first and probably the most important instance was the clause that, from the middle of the nineteenth century, many Latin American States began to insert into concession contracts with nationals of foreign countries, chiefly for the exploitation of national resources. It was the Argentine jurist C. Calvo (1824–1906) who had argued for this clause. It stipulated that in cases of dispute arising out of the contract, foreigners relinquished the right to request the diplomatic and judicial protection of their national State and agreed to have the dispute settled by local tribunals.

Plainly, the Calvo clause sought to limit the legal and political interventions of Western capital-exporting countries, which often constituted the pretext or the occasion for armed expeditions, strong political pressure, or other forms of interference. The attempt was ill-fated: numerous international courts and claims commissions ruled that the clause was legally ineffective, in that it could not deprive States of their rights of protection, since the latter derived from international law only. Consequently, the clause was either set aside or downgraded to a (superfluous) proviso requiring the exhaustion of local remedies before international diplomatic or judicial action could be initiated. No doubt the refusal to apply the clause was legally correct in the light of the international rules applicable at the time. The failure of the Calvo stipulation only proved that it was vain to seek to undermine existing conditions by means which fell short of a radical change in the legal regulation of the treatment of nationals abroad.

Another important attempt to place restraints on the Great Powers' hegemony was made, in the early twentieth century, by the Foreign Minister of Argentina, Luis María Drago (1859–1921). He argued that the Great Powers must not use military force to seek payment of debts from poor countries.

The unfettered right of States to resort to force included their right forcibly to recover payments due by foreign States to the nationals of the former. Three European countries, Britain, Germany, and Italy, used this right against Venezuela in 1902. They had requested Venezuela (i) to pay compensation for damage caused to their nationals during the civil strife which raged between 1898 and 1900, and for the seizure of fishing boats and other commercial ships by the Venezuelan authorities, and (ii) to repay loans made to Venezuela for the building of its railway. Venezuela demanded that the European claims be settled by a Venezuelan commission. This commission, however, partly rejected and partly reduced the European demands. The European Powers found the settlement unacceptable. After imparting an ultimatum, their men-of-war sank three Venezuelan ships, bombarded the locality of Puerto Cabello and, on 20 December 1902, instituted a naval blockade off the Venezuelan coast. Venezuela gave in. A few days later, on 29 December, Drago sent a diplomatic note to the US State Department, in which he claimed, first, that the European armed intervention was contrary to the Monroe doctrine (which he declared he was willing to uphold), and, second, that financial troubles and the consequent need to postpone payment of debts was no justification for foreign military intervention, since 'the collection of loans by military means requires territorial occupation to make them effective, and territorial occupation signifies the suppression or subordination of the governments of the countries on which it is imposed'.[15]

This note, which enunciated what was subsequently termed the 'Drago Doctrine', elicited a lukewarm response from the USA. In his note of 17 February 1903, the US Secretary of State, P. Hay, substantially dismissed Drago's claims and pointed out that, so long as Latin American countries fulfilled their international duties towards foreign States, they need not fear any foreign intervention. Hay quoted a message sent to Congress by President Theodore Roosevelt on 2 December 1902, which stated: 'It behooves each one to maintain order within its own borders and to discharge its just obligations to foreigners. When this is done, they [the independent nations of America] can rest assured that, strong or weak, they have nothing to dread from outside interference.'[16] In sum, the USA considered protection of foreign property to override the need to keep Europeans from intervening militarily on the American continent. It is hardly surprising that the so-called Drago doctrine was assailed by leading European jurists as being at variance with international law—a proposition which was indeed correct, in the light of the rules obtaining at the time.

No substantial headway was made in 1907, when Latin American countries endeavoured to pass, at the second Hague Peace Conference, a convention forbidding the use of force for the recovery of contract debts. The US delegate, General Horace Porter, took up, but also watered down, the ideas put forward by Drago in 1902. General Porter proposed to make resort to force conditional on the non-acceptance by the debtor State of international arbitration or its failure to carry out an arbitral award. The Conference largely accepted General Porter's proposals, and set up a Convention on the matter. Significantly, it was not ratified by any European country, thus showing again that even in an emasculated form, the efforts of Latin American countries to restrain international legitimation of force were to no avail.

2.4 STAGE 2: FROM THE FIRST TO THE SECOND WORLD WAR

Two major events mark the beginning of a new era: (1) the First World War which, although fought solely in Europe, involved the greater part of the international community and caused the members of the community to strive to rebuild it on better foundations; (2) the Soviet revolution and the consequent rise of the first State openly to oppose the economic and ideological roots of other States and of international relations.

2.4.1 THE TURNING POINT: THE FIRST WORLD WAR AND ITS CONSEQUENCES

The war had many important repercussions. It marked the passing of the 'European Age'.[17] When the war was over it became apparent that Europe no longer played a crucial part in the world community: the gradual erosion of its importance, initiated long before, culminated in Europe's demotion to the rank of merely one of the areas of power. Among the chief factors affecting its position were: (1) the rise of the USA; (2) the emergence in 1917 of the Soviet Union (as it was called after 1923); the substantial ideological and political unity of the 'old' community fell to pieces; (3) the end of colonial expansion—a striking phenomenon which marked the beginning of that long process that culminated in the collapse of colonial empires in the 1960s. The decline of Europe made itself felt in the field of economic, military, and political power, but also in that of culture and ideology. Europe's pivotal role in the previous centuries as the world's store room of values, institutions, political concepts, and standards of behaviour came to an end.

The war united the whole world—albeit in a forced and somewhat sinister way. For the first time a conflict assumed such magnitude as to involve all major members of the international community. The war proved that some major events were crucial to the world community at large. It became difficult for States to keep aloof from what was happening in other areas of the world.

2.4.2 THE SOVIET UNION'S PRESENCE SPLITS THE INTERNATIONAL COMMUNITY

It has already been pointed out that although some members of the international community (Turkey, China, Japan, Persia, Siam) had a different economic and ideological outlook to that of European States, they had actually yielded to the Christian majority geared to a market economy, which indeed set the tone throughout the development of the international community. In 1917 one Government came into being with an ideology and a political philosophy radically at odds with those upheld by all other States. In the international field, the USSR advocated the following principles:

(1) Self-determination of peoples, to be applied both to national groups in Europe (for example, the nationalities in Austria-Hungary) and to peoples under colonial domination (see **5.7.1**).

(2) The substantive equality of States (in contradistinction to their legal equality).

Point 6 of the proposals forming the basis for negotiations submitted by Adolf Joffe, the head of the Russian delegation to the Brest-Litovsk Peace Conference (which opened on 22 December 1917), proposed that the contracting parties should condemn the attempt of strong nations to restrict the freedom of the weaker nations by such indirect methods as economic boycotts, economic subjection by means of compulsory commercial agreements, separate customs agreements, restricting the freedom of trade with third countries, naval blockade without direct military purpose, etc. Thus, for the first time, there was outright condemnation of economic coercion, as a means of subduing weaker States, and unequal treaties.

(3) Socialist internationalism, whereby the USSR pledged itself to assist the working class and the political parties struggling for socialism in any State. Thus, again for the first time, a member State of the international community proclaimed a policy aimed at disrupting the fabric of other States and their colonial possessions (and the USSR officially pursued such a policy until at least 1927). This new state of affairs was soon fully appreciated by the American Secretary of State, Robert Lansing.

In a memorandum of 2 December 1917, speaking of Lenin and Trotsky, Lansing, among other things wrote the following: 'How can anyone deal with such people? They are wanting in international virtue. International obligations and comity mean nothing to them. The one thing they are striving to bring about is the "Social Revolution", which will sweep away national boundaries, racial distinctions and modern political, religious and social institutions, and make the ignorant and incapable mass of humanity dominant in the earth. They indeed plan to destroy civilization by mob violence . . . the Bolshevik program is to make way with the military and political authority in Russia and to incite similar destruction in other countries'.[18]

(4) The partial rejection of international law. The USSR proclaimed that since all the existing legal norms and institutions of the international community were the upshot of 'bourgeois' and 'capitalist' tendencies, they were by definition contrary to socialist interests, and would be endorsed by the new regime only to the extent that they proved useful to it. Consequently, many existing treaties were denounced.

In fact, the Soviet Government did not reject international law wholesale. Indeed, it could not have done so without becoming an outcast in the world community. One cannot be a member of a social group and at the same time dismiss all its rules. One must comply with at least some of them since otherwise international relations become impossible, with the group as a whole ostracizing the recalcitrant member by condemning it to complete isolation. The USSR rejected a number of bilateral and even multilateral treaties, but it tacitly or expressly bowed to a great many international standards. Thus, for example, in addition to emphasizing the importance of the customary rules protecting State sovereignty, it invoked a general norm (the rule *rebus sic stantibus*; see **6.3.1(e)**) to justify its repudiation of unacceptable treaties. Similarly, the USSR upheld many customary rules on treaty making (witness its entering into a great number of bilateral and multilateral treaties), and on diplomatic and consular immunities and privileges. In addition, it tacitly accepted the bulk of customary rules on the treatment of foreigners, as is proved by Articles 8 and 9 of the Soviet-German Treaty of 6 May 1921, which stated that Germany guaranteed Soviet citizens 'the prescriptions of international law and of the German common law'.

Nevertheless, the basic Soviet attitude towards the legal instruments of the international community inevitably undermined some of the community's basic doctrines. The USSR eroded—to a greater or lesser extent—many sacred principles (such as that on protection of investments abroad), while it resolutely opposed others, such as those on the rights of colonial powers.

2.4.3   AN EXPERIMENT IN COLLECTIVE CO-ORDINATION OF FORCE: THE LEAGUE OF NATIONS

Following the First World War the victors decided to set up an international institution designed to prevent the recurrence of worldwide armed conflict. The League of Nations was created, with a relatively small membership (42 States including five British dominions: India, New Zealand, Canada, Australia, and South Africa). For domestic reasons the USA held aloof. Its absence undisputedly weakened the institution from the outset.

The system set up in 1919 greatly resembles that devised in 1648 in the form of the Settlement of Westphalia.[19] Recourse to force was not generally prohibited, except for a limited number of cases. Articles 12, 13, and 15 of the Covenant subjected resort to war to a cooling-off period of three months. If a dispute was submitted to the League Council or to the Permanent Court of International Justice (PCIJ) or an arbitral tribunal, war could only be resorted to three months after the arbitral or judicial decision or the Council report. Consequently, there was a general prohibition on wars initiated before that delay or waged against a State which was complying with an arbitral award or a judgment of the PCIJ, or with a report adopted unanimously by the League Council.

The League system had major flaws. There was no ban on resort to force short of war. This qualification manifestly induced States to engage in war operations while claiming that they were merely using coercion short of war and were therefore not breaking any provision of the Covenant. An instance is the case of Manchuria, when Japan attacked China (1932). In addition, war was not banned altogether; it was only subjected to a cooling-off period, in the naïve hope that States would calm down and get less excited after a certain delay, and that the procedures for the settlement of disputes provided for in the Covenant would meanwhile induce them to refrain from using force. This proved illusory, as is shown by the case of the Italian aggression against Abyssinia, in 1935–6. Furthermore, no collective system was set up for enforcing law against a State that broke the procedural prohibitions of the Covenant. If a member State made war contravening the Covenant's stipulations, all the other member States were duty-bound to assist the victim against the aggressor—as long as they considered the use of force in the case at issue to be a breach of the Covenant. The League of Nations Assembly or Council had no power to send in troops against the aggressors; they could only recommend the use of force to member States. In short, the Covenant merely envisaged joint voluntary action on the part of States. There was no provision for an institutionalized enforcement procedure, there was no monopoly of force granted to the League organs, much less was an international army for the maintenance of peace and order set up. Plainly, the League system was a far cry from the enforcement machinery that existed within each State system. Indeed, in the only case when there was resort to sanctions (namely against Italy, 1935–6) they proved a failure, for political reasons. A further deficiency was that the Covenant's prescriptions remained treaty law; consequently they did not bind States outside the League (the USA, as well as a number of European and Asian countries, including at a certain stage Germany, the USSR, and Japan). As a result, the customary international rules authorizing war remained unaffected as far as third States were concerned.

Differences between member States, the lack of co-operation, the fact that the League gradually became a political instrument of Britain and France only, along with its inherent institutional deficiencies—all these account for its failure. A number of States resorted to force without being the subject of military sanctions or at any rate without the League bringing about a satisfactory settlement.

The USA and France endeavoured to obviate the most conspicuous deficiencies of the League by promoting the Paris Pact of 27 August 1928 on the Banning of War. The Pact, however, did not make much headway, for once again it was only war that was prohibited (although the ban was now more sweeping), and in addition there was no provision for an enforcement mechanism. Furthermore, the correspondence between the parties before the signing of the Pact made it clear that the right of self-defence was unaffected, and that a very liberal construction was placed on that right. Thus, Britain stated that it included its right to defend 'certain regions of the world, the welfare and integrity of which constitute a special and vital interest for our peace and security'. And the USA contended that self-defence embraced any action decided on by the US Government to prevent an infringement of the Monroe doctrine. The conspicuous merits of the Pact were that it laid down a more general prohibition of war, and that it was binding on States not parties to the Covenant such as the USA. However, the Pact itself was unable to supplant the customary rule authorizing war, in that it did not turn into a customary rule abrogating the previous one.

In short, even in the period between the two world wars, States gradually endeavoured to retrieve their traditionally unfettered right to use military force in international relations. The League served to slow down the process and reduce the instances of recourse to force. It was, however, unable to introduce a radical change in one particular structural element of the old international community.

2.4.4 LEGAL OUTPUT

During this period there was no conspicuous success in elaborating new rules. In its isolation the Soviet Union remained to a great extent on the defensive; on a number of occasions it attacked existing international institutions, but was unable to affect the new rules.

The principal area in which marked progress was made was that of the arbitral and judicial settlement of disputes. In the inter-war period international arbitration was in full bloom.

The PCIJ, set up in 1921, delivered 32 judgments, and 27 advisory opinions. The parties to the contentious proceedings were mostly European. Similarly, the members of the Court were mostly from European countries or from the USA (from 1922 to 1930, four of 16 judges were non-Western, while from 1931 to 1942 the proportion changed to seven out of 21). Numerous ad hoc arbitral tribunals were also set up.

Indeed, most European States strongly believed that arbitration was the best means of settling disputes and preventing the outbreak of wars. This, however, was an illusory view, both because on a number of occasions arbitral awards were not heeded, and because arbitration was inherently unable to restrain power politics.

However, frequent recourse to arbitration made it possible for international courts, particularly the PCIJ, to pronounce on many international issues. The case law which evolved was instrumental in filling many gaps in international legislation. Principles and rules were specified, elucidated, and elaborated upon. This, by itself, was a remarkable contribution to the improvement of the technicalities of international law.

In addition, a new wind began to blow through the international community, bringing with it a drive towards limiting inequalities between States, and greater concern for the demands of individuals.

The tendency to do away with the most glaring forms of inequality can be seen in the gradual abolition of capitulations. The only country where this regime had already been dismantled before the First World War was Japan (in 1899). Capitulations with other countries were gradually abrogated.

The emergence of a fresh concern with the exigencies of individuals manifested itself in two forms. First, while the slave trade had been prohibited long before, States now began to ban the institution of slavery as such. Second, groups of individuals were granted the right to lodge complaints with international bodies. Religious, ethnic, and linguistic minorities protected by post-war treaties were authorized to submit to the Council of the League of Nations 'petitions' designed to inform it of alleged violations of minority rights. Under Article 24 of the ILO Constitution trade union associations were entitled to file complaints with the ILO Governing Body. These normative innovations were indicative of the new tendency to pay greater attention to the interests of human beings, who until then had had no say whatsoever in the international community. As the Greek international lawyer Politis stated in 1927: 'Beforehand, the sovereign State was for its subjects an iron cage whence they could communicate legally with the outside world only through narrow bars. Under the pressure of the necessities of life, those bars have progressively loosened. The cage is starting to wobble. It will eventually fall to bits. Men will then be able to communicate beyond the frontiers of their respective countries freely and without any hindrance'.[20]

2.5 STAGE 3: FROM THE UN CHARTER TO THE END OF THE COLD WAR

2.5.1 THE MAIN CONSEQUENCES OF THE SECOND WORLD WAR

In 1945, over a period of less than two months, three momentous events occurred: on 26 June the Charter of the United Nations was signed in San Francisco (it came into force on 24 October 1945); on 6 August the atomic bomb was dropped on Hiroshima (two days later Albert Camus commented in France that 'the mechanical civilization has just reached its last degree of savagery';[21] on 9 August a second bomb was dropped on Nagasaki); and on 8 August the Agreement on the International Military Tribunal (IMT) for the Punishment of War Criminals was signed in London (the first session of the Tribunal was held in Berlin on 18 October). These three events were not formally linked to one another. Arguably they did, however, result from a unitary design: to put an end to the war, punish those responsible for it, and set the ground for a new international community.

In a way, these seemingly disparate events were destined to have a radical effect on the future of the international community. They increased the existing tension between the opposite poles of law and force. This tension was now dramatically enhanced: on the one hand, States came to possess potentially unrestricted physical power; on the other, new rules and principles were proclaimed and acted upon and a new international organization was established with a view to placing an ever-increasing number of legal restraints on State sovereignty.

Peace became the principal goal of the international community at large. In the past, wars had never been of worldwide magnitude; in addition, States had never possessed the means of destruction capable of annihilating mankind. The new appalling advances in man's ability to wreak havoc made it necessary to regard peace as the fundamental purpose of all States, a purpose to which all others—including respect for international law and promotion of justice—ought to be subordinated.

However, when the framers of the UN Charter upgraded peace to such high rank, they did not naïvely pursue the goal of permanent and universal peace. They were aware that international friction and inter-State armed conflict would not disappear by legislative fiat. They more realistically set about building up a system designed to make armed clashes exceptional events, to be controlled and terminated by means of international institutionalized co-operation. In short, States aimed at achieving a state of affairs where the absence of war was to be a fairly normal condition.

One means of pursuing this new purpose was to render the unleashing of wars more onerous than before. Waging war in breach of international law (that is, a war of aggression), was made an 'international crime' entailing the personal responsibility of its authors (in addition, of course, to that of the State for which they acted).

The Second World War had yet another remarkable consequence: it precipitated the downfall of colonial empires. It accelerated a process which had started earlier, and whose principal components were the gradual economic and political decline of European Powers, the disruptive presence of the Soviet Union on the world scene, the growing political and economic power of the USA which (despite its colonial domination of the Philippines, and the de facto direct or indirect exploitation of some Latin American countries) propounded an anti-colonialist ideology. These were the international factors that contributed to the demise of colonialism. There were, however, also domestic reasons, which various authors have rightly stressed. After the First World War, at least some Western European countries had witnessed both a gradual opening to democracy and also a drive towards the 'welfare State', largely motivated by greater sensitivity to and concern for the underprivileged. Thus, when the cost of maintaining colonial rule over distant territories increased (among other things because of rising unrest there), the metropolitan masses were able to transmit a clear message to their rulers: since the principal profits from colonial exploitation went to limited groups of people, whereas the military costs and also some welfare costs 'were rising rapidly and more and more becoming costs on the budget of the metropolitan country', it was no longer in the interest of the population to persist with colonial domination.

2.5.2 THE ESTABLISHMENT OF THE UNITED NATIONS

One of the major reactions to the devastations of the Second World War and the unfettered recourse to violence marking those dark years was the keen desire to set up a world organization that would be capable of preventing 'the scourge of war' and peacefully settling all major disputes between States. Thus the UN was created. As this organization is analysed in **Chapter 13**, it suffices here to outline briefly its main features.

The political premise to this major turning point was the rapprochement between two former political opponents, the USA and the USSR, which had gradually come about during the war and had led to some form of political co-operation. The major victorious Powers conceived of the UN as a sort of prolongation of their war-time alliance.

The Charter banned the use or threat of force (Article 2.4) and at the same time granted to the Security Council the power to take sanctions and measures involving the use of force against any State breaking that ban. It also regulated the gradual demise of the colonial empires, by providing for the trusteeship system with a view to ensuring a slow passage of colonial countries to self-government or independence. In addition, the Charter endeavoured to strengthen international co-operation in various fields.

No doubt the UN was a far better and more advanced experiment in world security than the previous ones (that of 1648, which to a large extent remained on paper; the Concert of Europe of 1815; and the League of Nations of 1919). Suffice it to mention just one element: for the first time the Charter prohibited not just war, but any threat of or resort to the use of military force. This, by itself, marked an enormous advance in international institutions. More specifically, the system for collective security created in 1945 bears a strong resemblance to the Concert of Europe of 1815 (see **2.3.2**). As in the post-Napoleonic era, in 1945 the big Powers considered it necessary to assume control of international affairs and to decide themselves on joint action to be taken in case of serious threats or breaches of peace. They therefore set up a 'directorate', consisting of the two superpowers (the USA and the USSR) plus a few other States which, although already on the wane, could still be regarded as indispensable to any effective direction of international affairs (Britain, France, and China, the latter being at that time formally represented by the 'nationalist' Government of Chiang Kai-shek). The superiority of a few powerful countries was formally acknowledged in law: Article 27.3 of the UN Charter lays down that the SC cannot adopt any deliberation on matters of substance unless all five permanent members agree (either by voting in favour or by abstaining, according to the practice evolved later). This is the so-called veto by any of the Big Five. By the same token, the Charter envisaged a system of collective security: if the SC, with the concurring vote of the Big Five, agreed that there was a threat to peace, a breach of the peace, or an act of aggression, it could either take sanctions or dispatch UN armed forces against the offending State.

However, two events undermined from the outset the whole edifice built at San Francisco. First, less than two months after the adoption of the Charter, the USA dropped atomic bombs on Hiroshima and Nagasaki: this immediately posed new and dramatic problems. Second, nearly a year after June 1945 the cold war set in, breaking up the political and military alliance born during the war and practically dividing the world into two conflicting camps. The disagreement between the Western Powers and the Soviet Union, which surfaced in 1946, with the cold war spreading everywhere, in most cases prevented the collective security system from working. As a consequence, the international community had to fall back on the traditional devices for preventing war or enforcing international law. Once again, an attempt at centralizing the use of force ended in failure, and the old institution of self-help acquired new importance, albeit with a number of qualifications.

2.5.3 THE COMPOSITION OF THE INTERNATIONAL COMMUNITY

Following the Second World War, the make-up of the world community changed radically. First, a handful of Eastern European countries became socialist 'democracies' (the German Democratic Republic, Poland, Bulgaria, Hungary, Romania, and Czechoslovakia, to which Yugoslavia should be added). As a consequence, the Soviet Union no longer felt isolated in its ideological and political fight against capitalist States. Second, a number of countries subjected to colonial domination gained political independence as a result of the erosion of the colonial empires of France, Britain, Belgium, the Netherlands, Portugal, and Italy.

Syria and Lebanon were granted independence in 1945 and 1946 respectively; India and Pakistan became formally independent in 1947; in 1948 the State of Israel was founded, and Burma became independent; independent status was granted to Libya in 1951, to Tunisia, Morocco, Sudan, and Ghana in 1956, to the Federation of Malaya in 1957, and to Guinea in 1958. Many other colonial countries gained independence in the 1960s.

After 1960 the bulk of the international community consisted of Third World countries. Together with socialist States they could easily muster a two-thirds majority in any international gathering.

The new make-up of the world community differs radically from that represented in its first phase. While in the seventeenth and eighteenth centuries a number of European countries dominated the world scene, and non-Western States were far less numerous and of marginal importance, now non-Western States constituted the overwhelming majority. However, one should refrain from jumping to the conclusion that the new position was the exact reverse of the former. In fact the Western minority still wielded enormous economic and military power, while the majority was chiefly endowed with political and rhetorical authority. Hence, the situation was now more complex and contradictory than its predecessor.

Along with newly independent States, a new category of international subjects became active in the international arena: intergovernmental organizations. They mushroomed in a short period of time, covering several fields (political, economic, social, technical, etc.) with a broad variety of activities, which had considerable impact on international affairs. Their existence had many consequences. It may suffice to emphasize one, which relates to the political field. Previously, some States, particularly middle-sized and small Powers, were to some extent able to refrain from becoming involved in international affairs which were not directly relevant to them. Once they started participating in the activities of international organizations where all major world events were discussed, often forming the subject of resolutions or leading to the taking of some sort of joint action, it became almost impossible for them to remain aloof. They were required to express their views on the matter, to take sides, to join in praising, condemning, or exhorting. In short, the creation of a wide network of intergovernmental organizations aroused or strengthened, if not a sense of solidarity, at least the sense of belonging to the same community and therefore of being concerned by any crucial event occurring in it. If the First World War made each State feel that it could no longer live in relative isolation, the emergence of organizations buttressed this trend and definitively established the notion that certain occurrences (aggression in one area of the world, one particular country's pursuit of a policy of destabilization of other States, widespread injustice in economic relations between two or more groups of States, etc.) were of concern to the whole international community.

2.5.4 THE LEGAL STRATEGY OF THE MAJOR GROUPINGS OF STATES

(a) Western countries

Many Western countries took widely different attitudes towards the international legal institutions: some were content with the status quo or 'law and order', such as the USA and the UK, whereas Scandinavian States tended to be quite responsive to Third World demands and support the need for sweeping social and legal change. In spite of these differences, it is possible to discern some general trends. Considering that for two and a half centuries the principal international lawmakers were the European States, and other States moulded in the European tradition, it comes as no surprise that in this third stage most of them were interested in maintaining the traditional legal framework intact as far as possible. Their primary concern was for stability. However, as the modern international set-up and the new realities called for profound alterations in that framework, they were disposed to accept legal change, provided it did not take the form of a radical break but was gradual, and so long as it was effected with their active participation.

The *concept of law*, strictly adhered to by Western countries in their domestic systems, could not but influence the attitude of Western States towards international law and impel them to take it relatively seriously. One should not, however, overemphasize the role of the Western legal stance. At least three qualifications are called for.

First, it was only natural for them to preach law abidance and to attempt to live up to legal imperatives which had been forged precisely to reflect and protect their interests.

Second, in many countries jurists, politicians, and diplomats tended to draw a distinction between municipal law—regarded as a distinct social value *per se*—and inter-State law—which was to be complied with so long as it did not turn out to be in conflict with national political goals.

Third, one should not forget that many of the most appalling violations of international morality and legal principles perpetrated in this third stage—in particular, the Nazi genocide during the Second World War, the dropping of atomic bombs on Hiroshima and Nagasaki, and the heinous system of apartheid enforced for so long in South Africa—were all perpetrated by white Western Powers. Fortunately, however, examples such as these of gross misconduct are the exception.

This description of the Occidental outlook allows us better to understand the legal strategy adopted by Western States in the international community. They were pre-pared to accede to the request for legal change put forward by other groups, on condition that this change be effected by the adoption of international treaties (writ-ten instruments being perceived as providing better guarantees than international custom because by definition they cannot impel States to accept something contrary to their own interests). In addition, they favoured the procedure of consensus (2.5.6) as a technique of negotiation and decision making in international bodies and diplo-matic conferences, for it ensured that they would not be left out of the negotiating process. Finally, when it came to drafting international legislation, they insisted on two major points, which in their view were crucial to the acceptance of new legal rules. Legal provisions ought to be clear and precise if they were to serve as reliable standards of behaviour. In other words, the margin of discretion which legal prescrip-tions leave their addressees should be as narrow as possible, so as to ward off the danger of easy evasion. Furthermore, substantive rules were always to be attended by implementation mechanisms, that is devices calculated to spot possible instances of disregard, and to impel transgressing States to abide by law. To Western States any form of international legislation lacking both, or even one, of these elements was of scant value and must be discouraged as much as possible

(b) Socialist States

Socialist States were motivated in international relations by their political interests, which largely pursued the following aims: (1) strengthening the 'socialist camp'; (2) averting any intrusion of Western States into their own domestic affairs; (3) maintain-ing relatively good relations with the West so as to ensure a satisfactory economic and commercial interchange and to keep open a channel of communication on matters of security and disarmament; and (4) attempting to convert developing countries as much as possible to socialist ideals. These objectives led Eastern European countries to insist on three main tenets in the field of international legal relations: sovereignty; peaceful coexistence with other groups of States; new principles allowing a shake-up of the international community along lines more acceptable to socialist political philosophy.

(c) Developing countries

It is common knowledge that these countries, which at present constitute the over-whelming majority of the international community (about 150 out of about 200 States), are in many respects very diverse.

They differ in their cultural and ideological backgrounds, in their degree of economic or social development, in political alignment, in their respective systems of public order, and so on. In spite of these huge differences, they do possess certain common traits, namely: (1) before reaching independence they were all subjected to some sort of Western domination, either direct or indirect; (2) they all suffer from economic underdevelopment (they do not have an advanced industrial economy comparable to that of the major Western Powers or Japan; exceptions are the newly industrializing countries such as Brazil, Malaysia, Thailand, Singapore, South Korea,

Taiwan, the Philippines); (3) they owe their independence not only to an armed or political struggle against domination but also to a whole arsenal of ideas borrowed from or moulded on Western or socialist philosophy, such as the concepts of the nation-State (developed by Bodin), of sovereignty (elaborated by Bodin and Locke), of equality (propounded by Rousseau and the French revolutionaries), of self-determination of peoples (advocated by Western political leaders such as Woodrow Wilson, and by Lenin). Furthermore, (4) as the British historian Fieldhouse emphasized, 'the concept of a permanent unitary State with fixed frontiers was largely a European importation into other parts of the world and "nations" based on such concepts and demarcations are the product of colonialism'.[22] In addition, (5) Third World countries have in common a concept of law which, while differing from one culture to another, has long been profoundly distinct from that predominating in the West. Finally, (6) many of these countries show a tendency towards authoritarian structures in their respective domestic legal systems.

For a number of historical, economic, and political reasons developing countries have 'inherited' from their colonial period 'highly centralized and basically autocratic' systems of government which tend to rely on power structures where law is easily disregarded whenever it suits the ruling group. This is often in consonance with their original culture. Thus, for instance, most of them are community-oriented countries, where the leader is not viewed as a sort of possible oppressor, and his being in a way *legibus solutus* (unbound by law) is not regarded, as it would be in the West, as an outrageous deviation from the sacred postulate of the rule of law. Furthermore, the State—which in the West is almost the incarnation of law—is often felt to be an extraneous entity. To quote a Nigerian publicist, B. O. Nwabueze, 'the State itself is an alien, if also a beneficial creation; its existence is characterized by a certain artificiality in the eyes of the people and it is remote from their lives and thought'.[23]

To developing countries international law was (and still is) relevant to the extent that it protected them from undue interference by powerful States and was instrumental in bringing about social change, with more equitable conditions stimulating economic development. Their legal strategy in international relations consequently hinged on two important principles: State sovereignty and radical legal change. A major feature of developing countries' strategy was their insistence on the need to elaborate general principles as opposed to detailed and precise legal rules.

A further characteristic of the Third World countries' strategy was its tendency to expand national jurisdictions. This tendency was apparent in claims over the high seas, which exhibited a marked insistence on the institution of the patrimonial sea or exclusive economic zone (3.5.1–2) under national jurisdiction. One of two possible objectives appeared to stand behind such claims: to appropriate areas that belonged to nobody, or to have such areas declared 'the common heritage of mankind' (see 3.5.4). The latter applies chiefly to areas that the countries in question were unable to exploit for want of technology (this consideration also applies to outer space and celestial bodies). Both objectives were reinforced by the need for these countries to develop their economies and by their hope of reaping benefits from new areas of the sea. The second objective was also motivated by the wish to prevent developed countries from increasing their economic advantage to the detriment of less developed nations.

Closely linked to the objectives just described were the Third World's attempts to restructure international economic relations with a view to acquiring a greater share of wealth. Developing countries pursued this goal by advocating new international standards on economic relations (**18.5**), international institutions more sensitive to development than the traditional economic and financial organizations, and the exploitation of important assets such as the ocean bed and its subsoil and outer space, in the interest of, and on behalf of, the whole of mankind.

2.5.5 LEGAL CHANGE

Once developing countries had, with the active support of socialist States, firmly established their command over the UN GA, they started devising and propounding a complex strategy. First, the powers of the UN were enhanced (at least at the rhetorical level), except in the area of collective security. Second, developing and socialist States kept insisting on self-determination and racial equality, and demanded that they be turned into legal principles. They achieved these demands, in 1965 when the UN Convention on Racial Discrimination was adopted, and again in 1966 when the two UN Covenants on Human Rights of that year included an article (Article I) laying down the principle of self-determination. These instruments were followed and amplified by a number of resolutions and other treaties laying down ancillary rules (see **5.7.1**). Third, the two groups of States proposed that all the basic principles governing international relations should be recast in such a way as to take account of their views. This was achieved in 1970, after many years of labour, when the UN GA adopted the Declaration on Friendly Relations (see **5.1**). Fourth, codification was expanded to cover a wide range of subjects (see **6.4**). Finally, developing countries tried to bring about radical changes in the economic set-up of the international community. After long and untiring efforts the so-called Group of 77 (in 1964, when they first united their efforts on an institutional basis, the African, Asian, and Latin American States numbered 77) succeeded in having the GA adopt a declaration and a plan of action on the 'New International Economic Order' (NIEO). Developing States opted for a resolution, for it would have been both unrealistic and premature to impose new economic principles with legally binding force on industrialized countries. The adoption of resolutions was seen as the stage preceding the gradual transformation of political guidelines into international legal rules.

In this period the contribution of the *Institut de Droit International* and, more generally, of individual writers, to the elaboration or codification of international law increasingly dwindled (at least, in contrast to what it was before: see **2.3.3**). This is mainly due to the UN's establishment of the ILC, which is charged with the task of contributing to the codification and progressive development of international law, as well as the increasing adoption, by the GA, of resolutions or declarations concerning important issues of international law.

2.5.6 CONSENSUS AS A TECHNIQUE OF REACHING AGREEMENT

In the early 1960s a new technique was introduced as a means of facilitating agreement within international organizations and diplomatic conferences: consensus. Developing States, siding with socialist countries, could easily muster a two-thirds majority. However, scoring easy victories would be self-defeating. It was evident that in consistently losing the support of a powerful segment of the international community (Western countries), they would alienate it for good and doom any international action to failure. Thus, consensus gradually evolved as a procedure for reducing differences and reaching solutions acceptable to everybody.

Consensus denotes a negotiating and decision-making technique, consisting of a collective effort to agree upon a text by reconciling different views and smoothing out difficulties. This process culminates in the adoption without vote of a text basically acceptable to everybody. Consensus is different from *unanimity*, for in the latter there exists full agreement on a given text and in addition the general consent is evinced by a vote. It is also different from *acclamation*, for although normally texts approved by acclamation are not voted on (as is true of consensus also), they are, however, the subject of unqualified agreement. In the case of consensus reservations and objections are often expressed either before or after it is declared that a decision has been taken. What distinguishes consensus from the usual adoption of decisions by a majority vote is that, in the case of consensus, possible 'reservations' do not affect major points of the decision (whereas, when there is a split between States favourable, those opposing, and those abstaining, the States casting a negative vote or abstaining usually entertain and express views that more or less radically differ from those of States supporting the text). Moreover, as a consequence of the lack of fundamental differences, and with a view to emphasizing the existence of a substantial convergence of views, no vote is taken.

The advantages of the new technique are self-evident: it implies that the active minority becomes involved in the process and can therefore act to safeguard its interests and concerns; it fosters negotiation and compromise; and it means that there is use neither of the overpowering (but only rhetorical) force of the many, nor of the veto of the few powerful States. This in turn increases the chance of resolutions being implemented and of conventions being ratified and observed by a large number of States. The drawbacks of consensus are no less evident, however: divergent views are often ironed out only on paper, by dint of vague compromise formulae which each of the draftsmen subsequently interprets in his own way; international instruments become tainted with ambiguity; and negotiations tend to get bogged down in interminable discussions and trade-offs, because each State or group feels that the more it holds out, the more likely it is that its counterpart will abandon its initial bargaining position and make substantial concessions.

2.6 STAGE 4: FROM THE END OF THE COLD WAR TO THE PRESENT

The collapse, in 1989, of the Soviet Union and the subsequent break-up of the group of socialist States led to the demise of the whole of this group. The newly born Russian Federation did not inherit the Soviet Union's position as a superpower.

At present there no longer exist in the world community three distinct groupings. Essentially, there is one superpower, the USA, politically and ideologically leading the Western States. This superpower tends to act as a world policeman, that is, it endeavours to settle political disputes or to promote settlements, as well as contributing to the maintenance of peace and enforcing international law. This role, however, is played selectively, that is, only to the extent that it proves consonant with, and favours, the superpower's strategic and geopolitical interests. Thus, in many cases where these interests were at stake, the superpower forcibly acted through the UN (Iraq, 1990–1, Somalia, 1992, Bosnia-Herzegovina, 1992–5); in other instances, where the UN support was not forthcoming, it acted through NATO, in clear disregard of the UN Charter (Kosovo, 1999). In yet other instances, it refrained from taking military action, for its interests were not involved (e.g. Rwanda, 1994, Sierra Leone, 2000, etc.). The USA also exercises its political role as a global mediator in many troublespots (for instance, in the Middle East, Northern Ireland, etc.).

The former socialist countries, no longer united, tend to lean on Western countries. Developing States are no longer divided into one group siding with socialist States and another siding with the West. They seem to be no longer ideologically oriented. They are instead united by their demands for more international economic and financial assistance and greater access to world markets. In the UN these countries form both the 'Group of 77' (see *supra*, 2.5.5), when discussing economic matters, and the Non-Aligned Movement (NAM), when they discuss political matters and endeavour to harmonize their international strategies.

What also seems to characterize the present period are: the relative decline of the UN as an international agency for the maintenance of peace and stability; the tendency of States to strengthen and broaden the role of military alliances such as NATO; the growing trend towards regionalization (a trend that appears more conspicuously in Europe, with the European Union).

Turning to groups of States, it would seem that at present the industrialized countries see as the main international problems free trade, nuclear disarmament, the fight against terrorism (including terrorism fomented or organized by the so-called rogue States), protection of the environment, and the need to prevent ethnic, racial, and religious conflicts—increasingly rife in so many parts of the world—from spreading across the borders of the countries where they break out. No fully fledged common legal strategy may be discerned in this group of countries.

As for developing States, they consider that the major problems are their poverty and backwardness, the lack of fair access of their products to world markets, and the dangerously widening gap with industrialized States. Their legal strategy in the world community reflects these concerns. As for the legal means of action they pursue, it would seem that they have drawn an important lesson from (a) the failure of both the NIEO and their doctrine of the so-called right to development, and (b) the fact that they now lack the ideological and political support they previously attracted from socialist States. They therefore no longer insist on passing GA resolutions proclaiming new rights or outlining new economic strategies. They have realized that it is more constructive to come to some sort of agreement or compromise with the industrialized countries. Consequently they tend to be less vociferous and more realistic in their claims and negotiations.

A characteristic feature of modern developments in international law deserves to be emphasized. In the previous developmental stages *special bodies of law* gradually emerged: for instance, human rights law, the humanitarian law of armed conflict, environmental law, international trade law, international criminal law, the law on international responsibility of States. They tended to make up separate and tight legal compartments. At present, they are gradually tending to influence one another, or States and international courts are coming to look upon them as parts of a whole. Thus, for instance, two bodies of law, namely international rules and guidelines on the protection of the environment and international trade law are increasingly linked to—and, to some extent, made contingent on the application of—the law of development as well as human rights law; international criminal law is more and more influenced by human rights law and linked to humanitarian law; the law of State responsibility is increasingly overlapping, or being influenced by, the law on individual criminal liability; in many respects the law of the sea has been connected to the law of development and is seen as a possible means of promoting the take-off of the economies of poor countries.

This gradual interpenetration and cross-fertilization of previously somewhat compartmentalized areas of international law is a significant development: it shows that at least at the normative level the international community is becoming more integrated and—what is even more important—that such values as human rights and the need to promote development are increasingly permeating various sectors of international law that previously seemed impervious to them.

3

STATES AS THE PRIMARY SUBJECTS OF INTERNATIONAL LAW

3.1 TRADITIONAL AND NEW SUBJECTS

National systems encompass very many legal subjects: citizens, foreigners residing in the territory of the State, corporate bodies, and State institutions (if endowed with legal personality). In contrast, only a limited number of legal persons, that is, holders of international rights, powers, and obligations, make up the international community. The fundamental or primary subjects are *States*. They are paramount because they are the international entities which, besides controlling territory in a stable and permanent way, exercise the principal lawmaking and executive 'functions' proper of any legal order. All other subjects either exercise effective authority over territory for a limited period of time only, or have no territorial basis whatsoever. States, therefore, are the backbone of the community. They possess full *legal capacity*, that is, the ability to be vested with rights, powers, and obligations. Were they to disappear, the present international community would either fall apart or change radically. For historical reasons, there are at present about two hundred States, including a few mini-States. In principle, all States are equal. However, one particular class—a handful of States with strong economic and military systems—holds authority in the international community.

There is another category of international subjects, namely *insurgents*, who come into being through their struggle against the State to which they formerly belonged. They are born from a wound in the body of a particular State, and are therefore not easily accepted by the international community unless they can prove that they exercise some of the sovereign rights typical of States. They assert themselves by force, and acquire international status proportionate to their power and authority. However, their existence is by definition provisional: they either win and turn into fully fledged States or are defeated and disappear.

States and insurgents are 'traditional' subjects of the international community, in the sense that they have been the *dramatis personae* (the characters of the play) on the international scene since its inception. In the twentieth century, and increasingly after the Second World War, other poles of interest and activity have gained international status. They are: *international organizations*, *individuals*, and *national liberation movements* (i.e. some categories of peoples possessed of a representative organization). The emergence of these relatively 'new' subjects is a distinct feature of modern international law.

Unlike States, all the other international subjects just mentioned, on account of their inherent characteristics (e.g. lack of territorial authority, etc.) possess a *limited legal capacity*. In particular, they have a limited capacity to be vested with international rights and powers or to be under international obligations, or a *limited capacity to act*, that is, to put into effect their rights and powers in judicial and other proceedings, or to enforce their rights.

3.2 COMMENCEMENT OF THE EXISTENCE OF STATES

As stated above, States are the primary subjects of the international community, just like the individuals in national legal systems. However, while individuals are normally very numerous, States are few and profoundly different. This does not simplify matters but rather complicates them in the world community. As the distinguished British political scientist, M.Wight, noted in the 1950s:

'The smaller the numerical membership of a society, and the more various its members, the more difficult it is to make rules not unjust to extreme cases: this is one reason for the weakness of international law. As a *reductio ad absurdum*, imagine a society of four members: an ogre twenty feet high, flesh-eating, preferably human; an Englishman six feet high, speaking no Japanese; a Japanese samurai, a military noble, speaking no English; and a Central African pygmy, early palaeolithic; and all on an island the size of Malta. This is a parable of what is called international society.'[1]

A further factor complicates matters. Generally municipal law lays down rules establishing when an individual or a body acquires legal status or legal capacity—that is, when they become holders of rights and duties. To this effect, most national legal systems provide that individuals become legal subjects at birth (or even on conception), although they may only exercise their rights and obligations when they come of age. As for entities (corporations, foundations, public agencies, etc.) domestic law usually specifies the requirements they must satisfy in order to be granted rights and duties. In short, municipal law normally includes special provisions on the 'birth' of juridical subjects. In a way, the application of such rules constitutes a kind of precondition to the operation of all other substantive and procedural norms.

By contrast, there is no international legislation laying down detailed rules concerning the creation of States. Yet, on careful analysis, it is possible to infer from the body of customary international rules granting basic rights and duties to States that these rules presuppose certain general characteristics in the entities to which they address themselves (reliance upon customary, that is, *general* rules is necessary, for the international legal personality must operate towards all the other members of the international community).

The rules under discussion usually require two elements. The first is a central structure capable of exercising effective control over a human community living in a given territory. The bodies endowed with supreme authority must in principle be quite distinct from, and independent of, any other State, that is to say, endowed with an original (not derivative) legal order. However, some forms of international interference by other subjects have in the past been considered compatible with statehood (for instance, protectorates, where the protecting State—say France in relation to Morocco and Tunisia—was authorized to control the defence and foreign policy of the protected State). The second element needed is a territory which does not belong, or no longer belongs, to any other sovereign State, with a community whose members do not owe allegiance to other outside authorities. It must be emphasized here that territory is an essential element to this class of subjects. Territory may be large or small, but it is indispensable if an organized structure is to qualify as a State and an international subject. International law requires *effective* possession of, and control over, a territory. Only in exceptional circumstances does it allow corporate entities that have lost effective control over territory to survive as international entities for some time (this was the case of the so-called 'Governments-in-exile' created during the Second World War: they were hosted in Britian and represented countries occupied by Germany, namely Poland, Norway, the Netherlands, Belgium, Luxemburg, Yugoslavia, Greece). Even in those cases the 'survival' of the international subjects rests on a legal fiction—politically motivated—and is warranted by the hope of recovering control over territory. Once this prospect vanishes, the other States discard this legal fiction.

If these requirements are met, then all the rules governing international dealings become applicable.

3.3 THE ROLE OF RECOGNITION

It is clear that the norms referred to above do not lay down very specific criteria. They merely provide a general yardstick. It is, therefore, difficult to ascertain in practice whether a State fulfils the requisite conditions. A major factor proves of great help here: the attitude of existing States, as reflected in their recognition, or non-recognition, of the new entity.

The act of recognition has no legal effect on the international personality of the entity: it does not confer rights, nor does it impose obligations on it. Many jurists, chiefly in the past, have advocated the view that recognition entails 'constitutive' effects, namely that it creates the legal personality of States. This view is, however, fallacious because it is in strident contradiction with the principle of effectiveness whereby 'effective' situations are fully legitimized by international law (according to the theory of constitutive recognition a State would not possess legal personality if not recognized, even where it possessed effectiveness). Furthermore it is inconsistent with the principle of the sovereign equality of States, for existing States would be authorized to decide when a new entity exhibiting all the hallmarks of a State may or may not be admitted to membership in the world community. The theory is also logically unsound, for it implies that a certain entity is an international subject in relation to those States which have recognized it, while it lacks legal personality as far as other States are concerned; thus the international personality would be split quite artificially, in defiance of reality. In fact, this theory is an outmoded survival from the nineteenth century, when, as I pointed out above (2.3.1), European States claimed the right to admit or exclude other States to the 'family of nations'. I have already emphasized that even at that time such a right was questionable and that the policy was devoid of formal legitimization.

At present, recognition of States has a threefold significance. First, it is politically important in that it testifies to the will of the recognizing States to initiate international interaction with the new State. Second, it is legally relevant for it proves that the recognizing States consider that in their view the new entity fulfils all the factual conditions considered necessary for becoming an international subject.

In a case dealing with recognition of a revolutionary government *(Tinoco Concessions (GB v. Costa Rica))*, in 1923 the sole arbitrator W. H. Taft made a pronouncement that might be extended to recognition of States. He stated that 'the non-recognition by other nations of a government claiming to be a national [sic] personality, is usually appropriate evidence that it has not attained the independence and control entitling it by international law to be classed as such'.[2]

Of course this assessment is not binding on other States. It is, however, indicative of the attitude of States and can therefore prove useful in deciding whether the new entity may be regarded as an international legal subject. In a community lacking any central authority responsible for formally passing judgment on legally relevant situations, the attitude of single States acquires considerable weight as evidence for, or against, the existence of new legal subjects. Third, recognition is legally relevant in that, once granted, it bars the recognizing State from altering its position and claiming that the new entity lacks statehood. In other words, the granting of recognition creates an *estoppel* precluding the recognizing State from contesting the legal personality of the new State. (It is widely recognized that international law upholds the common law concept of estoppel, whereby a party is barred from alleging or denying a fact or claiming a right, to the detriment of another party entitled to rely upon such conduct in consequence of previous allegation, denial, or conduct, or admission by the former party.)

In addition, recognition may have legal consequences when precipitately granted, particularly when the new entity results from secession from an existing State or from a civil war. *Premature* recognition, that is recognition accorded before the basic factual conditions for statehood are met, may amount to unlawful interference in the internal affairs of the State concerned.

According to some commentators,[3] the recognition of Croatia by the members of the European Communities, Austria, and Switzerland on 15 January 1992 was premature, because Croatia only controlled one-third of its territory. The Arbitration Commission on Yugoslavia, in its Opinion No. 5 of 11 January 1992, corroborated this view.[4]

State practice shows that over the years the *factual conditions many States require for recognition* have changed. In the past, it was sufficient for the new State to wield *effective control* over a human community and the territory where such community lived. In the 1930s some States began also to require that *the new State had not contravened some fundamental standards* of the international community (such as the ban on wars in breach of international treaties or effected to attack a foreign country). If these values had been disregarded, States withheld recognition, even if the new State was firmly in control of population and territory. More recently some States, chiefly of Western Europe, have begun also to require *respect for human rights and the rights of minorities* as well as *respect for existing international frontiers*, as further conditions for granting recognition.

Following the break-up of the Soviet Union and the radical changes that occurred in eastern European countries, on 16 December 1991 the foreign ministers of the member States of the European Community adopted a Declaration on the 'Guidelines on the Recognition of New States in eastern Europe and in the Soviet Union'.[5] In this Declaration they among other things required for the formal recognition of new States in eastern Europe: (1) respect for the UN Charter, the Helsinki Final Act, and the Charter of Paris, 'especially with regard to the rule of law, democracy and human rights'; (2) guarantees for the rights of ethnic and national groups and minorities; (3) respect for the inviolability of all frontiers 'which can only be changed by peaceful means and by common agreement'; (4) acceptance of all relevant commitments with regard to disarmament and nuclear non-proliferation as well as security and regional stability; (5) commitment to settle by agreement, including where appropriate by recourse to arbitration, all questions concerning State succession and regional disputes. In addition, the Declaration stipulated that 'the Community and its Member States will not recognize entities which are the result of aggression'.

On the same day a 'Declaration on Yugoslavia' was issued which applied the same 'Guidelines' to the States resulting from the collapse of the former Yugoslavia. It added that if those new States applied for recognition, the application would be submitted to the Arbitration Commission (chaired by the French leading jurist Robert Badinter) for advice. In its Opinions Nos. 4 and 5, of 11 January 1992,[6] the Arbitration Commission held that Bosnia-Herzegovina and Croatia had not yet met all the necessary requirements (subsequently, when these requirements were regarded as fulfilled, recognition was granted by States). In Opinions Nos. 6 and 7, also issued on 11 January 1992, the Arbitration Commission held instead that Macedonia and Slovenia met the requirements at issue.[7]

Furthermore, in its Opinion No. 10, of 4 July 1992, the Arbitration Commission stated the following: 'while recognition is not a prerequisite for the foundation of a State and is purely declaratory in its impact, it is nonetheless a discretionary act that other States may perform when they choose and in a manner of their own choosing, subject only to compliance with the imperatives of general international law, and particularly those prohibiting the use of force in dealings with other States or guaranteeing the rights of ethnic, religious or linguistic minorities'.[8]

New States are rarely successful in achieving recognition by all members of the international community within a short period of time (unless they are States that were granted independence by peaceful means). Usually, only a few States grant recognition and accordingly initiate dealings with the new entity, exchanging diplomatic envoys, entering into agreements, and so on. A segment of the international community may decide to hold aloof for some time: this attitude is usually motivated by political considerations (a lack of ideological or political affinity, or even open opposition, or else the existence of strong economic or geographic obstacles to the subsistence of the new entity). If this is the case, the new State will not be able to enter into active relations with those States: no treaties are concluded, diplomats are not exchanged, the nationals of the new State are not allowed to enter the non-recognizing countries and vice versa. This does not, however, necessarily mean that the new entity is devoid of legal personality in relation to non-recognizing nations. General international rules such as those concerning the high seas, or respect for territorial and political sovereignty, etc. do apply to the relationships between the new State and all other members of the community. It follows that non-recognizing States are duty-bound to refrain from invading or occupying the new State or from jeopardizing its political independence. Also, they are not allowed to subvert its domestic political system. Furthermore, they must respect its right to sail the high seas (in particular, no interference in the navigation of its warships is allowed).

It should be added that extreme situations may exist where a State, although it exhibits at least the traditional requirements based on effectiveness, is still not recognized by the overwhelming majority of the members of the world community. This anomalous situation results from the clash of two conflicting principles: the old principle of effectiveness and the new principle of withholding legitimacy to facts and situations inconsistent with the general values of the present world community. The coexistence of these two principles (because the latter has not been capable of displacing the former) may give rise to the disconcerting situation of a State meeting all the conditions and showing all the trappings of statehood but deprived of international intercourse.

This actually happened in the case of Southern Rhodesia, from its Unilateral Declaration of Independence (UDI, 1965) to when its internal political system accepted majority rule (1980). By resolutions 216 and 217 of 12 and 20 November 1965 the UN SC had called upon all States 'not to recognize this illegal act'. Until 1980 all States (except for South Africa) withheld recognition on account of Southern Rhodesia's racist policy. This general stand only meant that no other State (except for South Africa) was ready to enter into relations with Southern Rhodesia as long as it refused to change its domestic policies. Socially, Southern Rhodesia was regarded as an outcast, a pariah State. Legally speaking, other States looked upon Southern Rhodesia as a territory under British colonial administration. It did, nonetheless, possess autonomous rights and duties, although it was unable to make use of most of them.

Taiwan (Formosa) is another case in point. Although it has all the hallmarks of a State, China's claim that it is part of its territory and subject to its sovereignty prevents Taiwan from entertaining intercourse with all other States.

There have also been cases in which it was doubtful that a new State had actually been created, or else a new entity had been set up but in gross breach of international rules, and in addition other States did not consider it to be really independent of the State that had been instrumental in its establishment (with the consequence that they withheld recognition).

This last instance occurred with regard to the 'Turkish Republic of Northern Cyprus', pro-claimed on 15 November 1983 and recognized by Turkey only. The UN SC, the Commonwealth Heads of Government, and the Committee of Ministers of the Council of Europe considered the declaration of independence 'legally invalid', required its 'withdrawal', and called upon all States 'not to recognize any Cypriot State other than the Republic of Cyprus' (see in particular SC res. 541 of 18 November 1983).

3.4 CONTINUITY AND TERMINATION OF THE EXISTENCE OF STATES

How do changes in the life or existence of States affect their legal personality? A revolutionary change in the government does not have any major impact on this personality. The principal problem that may arise in the case of revolutionary change following a civil war is whether acts performed by a government are binding upon a State if that government is succeeded by another one. In *Tinoco Concessions* (*GB* v. *Costa Rica*) the arbitrator Taft satisfactorily clarified the matter in 1923.

In 1917, Tinoco, a political leader, overthrew the government of Costa Rica and proclaimed a new constitution. In 1919 the Tinoco government was toppled and the old authorities reinstated. In 1922 the government passed legislation quashing all the rights Tinoco had granted by con-tract to a number of British companies. The arbitrator held that, as Tinoco 'was in actual and peaceable administration without resistance or conflict or contest by anyone until a few months before the time when he retired and resigned'[9] those contracts were binding on Costa Rica.

In short, revolutionary or extra-constitutional changes in the government do not have any bearing on the identity of a State and consequently States are bound by international acts performed by previous governments.

In contrast, changes in the territory of a State may affect its legal personality. This happens when a State becomes extinct as a result of its break-up (*dismemberment*), or of its *merger* with one or more States (in which case all the merging States become extinct and at the same time give birth to a new legal subject), or when a State *incorporates* another one which, as a consequence, becomes extinct. In contrast, in case of *secession* of a part of the State's population and territory, the State continues to exist as a legal subject, but the seceding part may acquire international statehood.

Whenever on a territory a State replaces another one, the problem arises of whether there is a State succession, namely whether the rights and obligations of the former State are transferred to the other international subject (or subjects, in case of dismemberment) that has de facto replaced the old State, or part of it, in its control over the territory and the population living there.

The question is far from academic, as is shown by the merger of Egypt and Syria into the United Arab Republic in 1958 (which lasted until 1961), the merger of Tanganyika and Zanzibar to form Tanzania in 1964, the secession of Bangladesh from Pakistan in 1970, the merger of the two Yemens in 1990, the incorporation of the German Democratic Republic into the Federal Republic of Germany in 1990, the acquisition (or, rather, the re-acquisition) of independence from the Soviet Union of the three Baltic States (Estonia and Latvia in 1990 and Lithuania in 1991), the break-up of the Soviet Union in 1991, of Yugoslavia in 1991, and Czechoslovakia in 1992.

This matter is regulated by a number of customary rules, to some extent codified in two treaties: the 1978 Vienna Convention on Succession of States in respect of Treaties, and the 1983 Vienna Convention on Succession of States in respect of State property, Archives and Debts (the latter is not yet in force).

Let us first consider the question of succession to *treaties*. In short, under customary law a distinction must be made between various categories of treaties. The first are the so-called *localized treaties*, which impose obligations and confer rights with regard to specific territories (for instance, regulate frontier matters, lay down a right of transit over certain specific areas, demilitarize a territory, establish fishing rights in certain waters or rights of navigation in specific rivers, etc.). Since these treaties attach to a specific territory, for the sake of international stability these treaties are not affected by the mere fact of State succession; in other words, those treaties bind the new entity (see the 1978 Vienna Convention, Art. 12).

With regard to *non-localized treaties* customary law, as codified in the 1978 Vienna Convention, provides for a differentiated legal regime. For 'newly independent States' (namely successor States 'the territory of which immediately before the date of the succession of States was a dependent territory for the international relations of which the predecessor State was responsible', the 1978 Vienna Convention, Art. 2.1), the 'clean slate' principle applies, namely the principle whereby the new States are not bound by the treaties in force for the territory at the date of succession. This 'anti-colonialist' approach has been clearly dictated by the necessity to take into account the legal condition and the specific needs of States resulting from the decolonization process.

By contrast, with regard to other States, requirements for international stability have pushed to uphold the principle of continuity, whereby normally treaties binding on the predecessor State also apply to the successor State (see the 1978 Vienna Convention, Articles 34 and 35, which however do not correspond to customary law, that is instead based on the 'clean slate' rule, subject to the exception of localized treaties).

For a particular category of treaties, namely those on *human rights*, it would seem that a *general* rule has gradually evolved whereby the successor State (whether or not it belongs to the category of 'newly independent States') must respect them. The rationale for this rule is that human rights treaties are intended to protect and benefit individuals *vis-à-vis* the central authorities; hence, whatever the nature, character, and political allegiance of these authorities, what matters is that individuals should continue to be protected even after a change in sovereignty over a particular territory. In addition, human rights are now considered so essential that it would be inconsistent with the whole thrust of the present world community to discontinue protecting them only because one State has replaced another in operating as the governing entity responsible for the international relations of a particular territory.[10]

The question of succession also arises with regard to: (i) State assets and debts; (ii) State archives; (iii) membership of international organizations. It would seem that the content of the customary rules regulating these matters is still uncertain.

As for *State property*, the definition of what belongs to a State must be drawn from the relevant national law applicable at the moment of succession, as is laid down in Article 8 of the Vienna Convention of 1983 and was restated by the Arbitration Commission on Yugoslavia (in its Opinion No. 14).[11] Once it has been established whether the assets are public, it may normally be held that the State that wields control over the territory where the assets are located succeeds the previous territorial State with regard to ownership. The same holds true for *State archives*.

The question of succession with regard to *public debts* (that is, debts owed by the State) is more difficult, also because State practice is rather confusing. Under Article 40 of the 1983 Vienna Convention, when a State breaks up and new entities come into being, unless they otherwise agree, the State debt of the predecessor State passes to the successor States 'in an equitable proportion'.

With regard to *international organizations*, it is rational to believe that, if two member States merge thereby creating a new State, this State should apply for admission to the Organization. However, in UN practice, no admission has been required (this happened in 1958, when Egypt and Syria merged to form the United Arab Republic, and in 1990, when North Yemen and South Yemen merged). Furthermore, if a member State breaks up into two or more States, all of them must apply for membership (this happened in 1992–3, after the dissolution of Yugoslavia and the birth of six Yugoslav Republics; five were admitted immediately thereafter while the Federal Republic of Yugoslavia (Serbia and Montenegro) applied for, and gained, membership in 2000). An exception may be admitted for the one component that may successfully claim to be a continuation of the old State, as far as membership is concerned (this happened in 1990, when the Soviet Union broke up, and all newly born republics had to apply for admission, except for the Russian Federation which was considered a continuation of the Soviet Union, and Byelorussia and Ukraine which were already members of the UN in their own right). If a new State-like entity comes into being as a result of secession from a member State, it too must apply for membership.

3.5 THE SPATIAL DIMENSION OF STATE ACTIVITIES

3.5.1 GENERAL

Most activities performed by the primary subjects of the world community, States, take place within a geographic area. Territory is crucial not only to the very existence of a State (a State without a territorial basis, however tiny it may be, is inconceivable). Territory also constitutes the dimension within which States deploy their major activities.

In traditional international law the physical dimension of State activity was regulated in fairly simple terms. The earth, portions of the sea, and the air were divided up into areas subject to the sovereign authority of States. The general principles regulating the carving up of areas among sovereign States were relatively simple. First, whoever possessed a territory and exercised actual control over it acquired a legal title. Second, for areas subject to no one (*terrae nullius*) mere discovery on the principle 'first come, first served' rapidly became insufficient. Actual display of sovereignty, coupled with the intent to wield authority, has been needed since the Berlin Congress of 1885. On the strength of these elementary principles the land on the whole planet gradually became subject to the rule of one or other sovereign State. In addition to land, a small portion of sea around each area of land, the so-called territorial waters, was also subject to State sovereignty. The air above each territory was considered subject to the sovereignty of the territorial State up to the stars (*usque ad sidera*); of course, this stipulation was only theoretical in nature, for States did not possess any means of exercising de facto control over the airspace above their land.

Clearly, this distribution of space among the various members of the world community was inspired by aggressive individualism and a laissez-faire attitude: whoever had the physical means of acquiring, and effectively controlling, a portion of territory on land was legitimized to claim sovereign rights over it. As a consequence, the more powerful—militarily and economically—a State, the greater was its chance of acquiring a bigger territory.

The only exception to this partition among competing claims was the high seas, which—since the seventeenth century—were subject to the principle whereby it was a thing belonging to everybody (*res communis omnium*): every State could sail its ships or use the high seas' resources as it pleased, as long as it did not hamper the free use of the high seas by other States. However, the fact that the high seas were considered a 'common good' should not lead us to believe that this legal regime was the outcome of solidarity. Had a State, or group of States, proved strong enough to claim the exclusive right to use the high seas or large portions thereof, it would have had no hesitation in depriving the other members of the international community of access to them. Furthermore, the *res communis* concept means that every State is authorized to use a certain good for its own purposes and its own interest. It is not a community-oriented concept; it is geared to self-interest.

After the Second World War new technology and research made it possible to find out that the seabed off the coast of States and an area called the continental shelf contained important resources. In addition, advances in shipping rendered it possible to exploit fishing resources on the high seas. It was expected that mineral resources would be found on the ocean floor. The world community faced a choice: (i) to allow each and every State freely to appropriate or at least exclusively exploit the resources within its reach, on the individualistic principle of free competition; or (ii) to act on a community-oriented principle, whereby resources beyond the territorial waters of each State should be commonly exploited and shared, or at least should be used by the more industrialized and powerful States in such a manner as to take into account also the needs of the less advantaged States. States immediately opted for the first alternative. The whole development of the law of the sea was thus dictated by State sovereignty, nationalism, and a laissez-faire attitude. In the scramble for economic, scientific, or military control of the new resources, almost all new notions were inspired by self-interest and geared to competition. The only area where developing countries managed to get the adoption of new concepts was the seabed and ocean floor and the subsoil thereof, beyond the limits of national jurisdiction. With respect to this area they launched the notion of the 'common heritage of mankind'; they propounded the view that the mineral resources of this area should be exploited in such a way as to take into consideration the needs of poor countries. However, as we shall see (3.5.4), the concept proved unworkable, and, to a large extent, was watered down.

Thus, in the whole area of the law of the sea a nationalist, self-centred approach has displaced community interests and any idea of solidarity or joint utilization of resources. As we shall see (3.5.7), some progress was instead made in the legal regulation of outer space, a portion of air that is above the airspace normally used by aircraft, although it has never been delimited (it is conventionally and roughly considered to be higher than 90–100 miles; see 3.5.7). Probably this progress was due to the fact that modern technology did not yet allow the application to this area of State sovereignty-oriented notions.

3.5.2 TERRITORY

Territory is that portion of land that is subject to the sovereign authority of a State. At present no territory exists that is not subject to a sovereign Power. (Exceptionally, in the case of the Antarctic region, claims to territorial sovereignty by some adjacent and other States—Argentina, Australia, Chile, France, New Zealand, Norway, and the UK—based on discovery or symbolic annexation or the doctrine of contiguity called the 'sector principle', are suspended by treaty.) Today there therefore exists an absolute nexus between territory and sovereignty. In 1928, in his celebrated judgment in *Island of Palmas*, Judge Max Huber stated that 'sovereignty in relation to a portion of the surface of the globe is the legal condition necessary for the inclusion of such portion in the territory of any particular State'.[12]

States are entitled to exercise over their territories all those powers inherent in their sovereignty (see **5.2.2**). Such powers are of course subject to the limitations outlined below (**5.3**).

(a) Acquisition of territory

Traditionally the *principal* modes of acquiring territory were: (i) occupation of land belonging to no one (as stated above, occupation must be effective and accompanied by the intent to appropriate the territory); (ii) cession by treaty, followed by the effective peaceful transfer of territory; (iii) conquest (the occupation of a territory following resort to armed violence); and (iv) accretion (a physical process whereby new land is formed close to existing land, for example a new island in a river mouth or the formation of dry land as a result of the change of flow of a river; normally the new land becomes subject to the sovereignty of the State within whose territory it has come into being).

At present the first mode has lost importance, for the reason set out before, and the third is no longer admissible, as 'no territorial acquisition resulting from the threat or use of force shall be recognized as legal' (Declaration on Friendly Relations, of 1970, codifying a new principle of international law: GA resolution 2625-XXV).

(b) Delimitation of boundaries: the *uti possidetis* doctrine

Towards the beginning of the nineteenth century a practice developed in Spanish America whereby, on the accession of the various former colonies of Spain to independence, their boundaries followed the former colonial frontiers ('you will have sovereignty over those territories you possess as of law': *uti possidetis jure*). This sound practice, aimed at averting endless territorial claims and clashes, took shape in a host of bilateral treaties, as well as a number of national constitutions of newly independent Latin American countries. It is not clear whether the practice turned into a customary rule of international law endowed with a regional scope, or remained a simple practice devoid of any binding force, or rather crystallized into a general principle of law, as was held by two Latin American judges of the ICJ (Armand-Ugon and Moreno Quintana) in *Sovereignty over Certain Frontier Land*.[13]

The wave of decolonization in Africa, which started in the 1950s and continued until 1963, posed a crucial problem as to the borders of the new independent countries. Except for a few cases where the boundaries were agreed upon within the framework of the UN, the general trend was to accept the colonial boundaries that existed at the time of independence. This practice was sanctioned in various UN resolutions as well as an important resolution of 1964 of the OAU.[14] In *Case Concerning the Frontier Dispute*, a Chamber of the ICJ held in 1986 that *uti possidetis*

'is a general principle, which is logically connected with the phenomenon of obtaining independence, wherever it occurs. Its obvious purpose is to prevent the independence and stability of new States being endangered by fratricidal struggles provoked by the challenging of frontiers following the withdrawal of the administering power.'[15]

As a principle having a universal and not only a regional purport, the doctrine has also been applied by the Arbitration Committee established by the Conference on Yugoslavia in its Opinion No. 2, of 1992, with regard to Croatia and Bosnia-Herzegovina.

The Arbitration Committee, having been called upon to pronounce on whether 'the Serbian population in Croatia and Bosnia-Herzegovina, as one of the constituent peoples of Yugoslavia, have the right to self-determination', stated that 'whatever the circumstances, the right to self-determination must not involve changes to existing frontier[s] at the time of independence (*uti possidetis juris*) except where the States concerned agree otherwise'.[16]

3.5.3 SEA

In recent times the sea has gradually been *divided up* into sections or areas, each with a different legal status and consequently involving different rights and powers of States. This whole matter is regulated by the 1982 Convention on the Law of the Sea, which entered into force in 1994, largely replacing various codification conventions of 1958.

The *territorial sea* of States (that is, the waters surrounding a State's territory and including its bays, gulfs, and straits) had long been the subject of extensive dispute as to its width. In the past the principle was often advocated that the breadth of that belt was the same as the effective range of shore artillery, namely three nautical miles. However, probably on account of the development of more powerful guns, many States claimed a broader area. At present the question is settled by the 1982 Convention on the Law of the Sea, Article 3 of which provides that States have the right to establish the breadth of their territorial sea up to a limit not exceeding 12 nautical miles from the baselines.

The question of *from where to measure the width of the territorial sea*, that is, of how to define baselines, has been somewhat controversial in the past. It is now regulated by Article 5 of the Law of the Sea Convention, which reflects a customary rule. Under this provision 'the normal baseline for measuring the breadth of the territorial sea is the low-water line along the coast as marked on large-scale charts officially recognized by the coastal State'. This general principle of the 'low-water line' is however derogated from in the case of States whose coast is deeply indented and cut into, or if there is a fringe of islands along the coast in its immediate vicinity. For such States Article 7.1 of the same Convention provides, partly in keeping with, partly developing, customary international law, that 'the method of straight baselines joining appropriate points may be employed in drawing the baseline from which the breadth of the territorial sea is measured'. Some general criteria for the drawing of straight baselines are laid down in the same provision: (i) one 'must not depart to any appreciable extent from the general direction of the coast'; (ii) 'the sea areas lying within the lines must be sufficiently closely linked to the land domain to be subject to the regime of internal waters'; (iii) 'account must be taken . . . of economic interests peculiar to the region concerned'; (iv) the system in question 'may not be applied by a State in such a manner as to cut off the territorial sea of another State from the high seas or an exclusive economic zone'.

A particular problem may be posed by States having *bays*, defined in Article 10.2 of the 1982 Convention as:

'a well-marked indentation whose penetration is in such proportion to the width of its mouth as to contain land-locked waters and constitute more than a mere curvature of the coast. An indentation shall not however be regarded as a bay unless its area is as large as, or larger than, that of the semi-circle whose diameter is a line drawn across the mouth of that indentation'.

For these bays, under Article 10.4 and 10.5, if the distance between the low-water marks of the natural entrance points of the bay does not exceed 24 nautical miles, 'a closing line may be drawn between these two low-water marks, and the waters enclosed thereby shall be considered as internal waters'. If the bay's entrance exceeds 24 nautical miles, 'a straight baseline of 24 nautical miles shall be drawn within the bay in such a manner as to enclose the maximum area of water that is possible with a line of that length'.

Within the territorial sea (plus its airspace, seabed, and subsoil) the coastal State enjoys *full sovereignty*, subject to the *right of innocent passage* of foreign merchants' ships and warships. This right entails that foreign ships may, without prior notification or authorization, pass through the territorial waters if their passage is not prejudicial to the coastal State (for example, they do not engage in threat or use of force, spying, propaganda, breach of customs, fiscal, immigration, or sanitary regulations, interference with coastal communications, serious and wilful pollution, etc.) and as long as they comply with the laws and regulations enacted by the coastal State, notably in the area of transport and navigation. In addition, the coastal State may not exercise criminal jurisdiction over offences committed on board ships within territorial waters, except for the situations enumerated in Article 27.1 of the 1982 Convention.

Unlike the territorial sea, *internal waters* (comprising not only rivers and lakes but also sea waters within the baselines) are subject to the full and exclusive sovereignty of the State; hence, in internal waters along the coast of a State, no right of innocent passage accrues to other States.

The *contiguous zone* goes beyond the territorial sea and can extend to up to 24 nautical miles from the baselines. In this zone the coastal State may prevent and punish infringement of its customs, fiscal, immigration, or sanitary regulations within its territory or its territorial sea (the 1982 Convention, Art. 33).

The *exclusive economic zone* has been gradually established in recent years following the discovery of important fishing and mineral resources off the coast of many States. It is an area beyond and adjacent to the territorial sea, that extends to 200 miles. In this area the coastal State enjoys sovereign rights *in some specific matters*, namely only for the purpose of exploring, exploiting, conserving, and managing natural resources. In addition, it has 'jurisdiction' over artificial islands, installations and infrastructures, marine scientific research, and the protection and preservation of the marine environment.

While the areas discussed so far embrace sea waters and their resources, the *continental shelf* is part of underwater land. The shelf is the natural prolongation of a coastal

State's land territory into the sea, before it falls away into the ocean depths. Normally the shelf is covered with relatively shallow water (between 150 and 200 metres). Its length varies depending on the geology of the coast. For instance, off the US western coast it is not broader than five miles, while off the coast of other States it is very wide. Under Article 76.1 of the 1982 Convention the outer limit of the continental shelf is set out as follows:

'The continental shelf of a coastal State comprises the seabed and subsoil of the submarine areas that extend beyond its territorial sea throughout the natural prolongation of its land territory to the outer edge of the continental margin, or to a distance of 200 nautical miles from the baselines from which the breadth of the territorial sea is measured where the outer edge of [the] continental margin does not extend up to that distance'.

The coastal State has, again, sovereign rights *limited* to certain specific activities: exploration and exploitation of the natural resources of the shelf (essentially: oil and fishing resources). As the ICJ put it in *North Sea Continental Shelf*,

'the rights of the coastal State [in respect of the continental shelf] . . . exist *ipso facto* and *ab initio*, by virtue of its sovereignty over the land, and as an extension of it in an exercise of sovereign rights for the purpose of exploring the seabed and exploiting its natural resources. In short, there is here an inherent right'.[17]

In addition, under Article 80 of the 1982 Convention, the coastal State may construct and maintain installations for exploration of the shelf and establish safety zones around such installations up to a limit of 500 metres. These rights only relate to the shelf and its resources: under Article 78 of the 1982 Convention the status of the superjacent waters, if they are beyond the contiguous zone and are part of the high seas, remain unaffected, just as does the airspace above those waters.

The question of delimitation of the continental shelf between opposite or adjacent States has given rise to many disputes. Under Article 6 of the 1958 Convention on the Continental Shelf, in the absence of agreement between the States concerned, the boundary must be determined 'by application of the principle of equidistance from the nearest points of the baselines from which the breadth of the territorial sea of each State is measured'. The principle of equidistance could however lead to inequitable solutions, as became evident in the *North Sea Continental Shelf* cases (between the Federal Republic of Germany on the one side and the Netherlands and Denmark, on the other) brought before the ICJ. The Court held that the principle at issue was not enshrined in customary law; in its view the relevant general rule prescribed that the delimitation was to be effected 'by agreement in accordance with equitable principles'.[18] This view was repeated by the same Court in *Tunisia* v. *Libya Continental Shelf*,[19] in *Gulf of Maine*,[20] in *Libya* v. *Malta Continental Shelf*,[21] and in *Jan Mayen* (*Denmark* v. *Norway*).[22]

Beyond the contiguous zone, and subject to what has been said above with regard to the exclusive economic zone, the waters belong to the *high seas*. They are free for every State, being a good available to all of them (*res communis omnium*). Each State enjoys freedoms of navigation and overflight, laying submarine cables and pipelines, fishing, scientific research, construction of artificial islands and other installations (provided they are permitted by international rules). Each State has exclusive jurisdiction over its own ships. Exceptionally, a State, through its warships, may exercise jurisdiction over foreign ships, in the following cases: (i) It may approach and board foreign merchant ships to ascertain their nationality, or to establish whether they engage in piracy, slave trading, unauthorized broadcasting, etc. (ii) It may arrest and seize any ship engaging in piracy or slave trading, and bring to trial the persons practising such activities. (iii) It may pursue and seize a ship suspected of infringing its laws in its internal waters, territorial sea, or contiguous zone, or its laws relating to the exclusive economic zone or continental shelf. This right of 'hot pursuit' must be initiated in one of these areas and may be exercised on the high seas; it must be uninterrupted, but shall cease as soon as the pursued ship is in the territorial waters of its own State or of a third State.

3.5.4 THE INTERNATIONAL SEABED AND THE CONCEPT OF THE COMMON HERITAGE OF MANKIND

The *international seabed* is the soil and subsoil under the high seas. In the past it has been estimated to be rich in mineral nodules, notably manganese, nickel, copper, and cobalt. It would now seem that these riches have been overestimated and in any case it will be a number of years before exploitation will become feasible (and economically attractive, having regard to the decline in price of land-based minerals). Be that as it may, at the time developing countries considered that a new, community-oriented concept should govern the exploitation of undersea wealth. Thus, as early as 1967 the Maltese Ambassador Arvid Pardo launched the notion of the *common heritage of mankind* in the UN GA.[23] He noted that new technology as well as fresh developments in oceanography were making it possible for mankind to benefit from the 'immense wealth' existing on the seabed and the ocean floor beyond national jurisdictions. In his view there were two alternative courses of action. The first was to allow a 'competitive scramble for sovereign rights over the land underlying the world's seas and oceans, surpassing in magnitude and in its implications last century's colonial scramble for territory in Asia and Africa'; one of the consequences would be both a 'dramatic increase of the arms race and increasing world tension'; in addition, the 'strong would get stronger, the rich richer, and among the rich themselves there would arise an increasing and insuperable differentiation between two or three and the remainder'. The other alternative was to establish an international legal regime to ensure that the seabed and the ocean floor were exploited solely for peaceful purposes, and for the benefit of mankind as a whole. Thus the concept of the 'common heritage of mankind', as a general standard for the exploitation of new natural resources, was delineated. It incorporates five main elements: (i) the absence of a right of appropriation; (ii) the duty to exploit the resources in the interest of mankind in such a way as to benefit all, including developing countries; (iii) the obligation to explore and exploit for peaceful purposes only; (iv) the duty to pay due regard to scientific research; (v) the duty duly to protect the environment.

Pardo's ideas were to a large extent taken up in the 1982 Convention on the Law of the Sea. Article 136 provided that 'The Area [i.e. the seabed and ocean floor and subsoil therof, beyond the limits of national jurisdictions] and its resources are the common heritage of mankind'.

Other provisions specified that no portion of the Area and its resources could be appropriated or made subject to State sovereignty, that the Area should be used peacefully, marine scientific research must be promoted and the marine environment must be protected (see Articles 137 and 141–5). The crucial point was of course how the resources of the Area would be exploited. In short an organization, the International Sea-Bed Authority, was provided for. It was to consist of an Assembly, made up of all contracting parties, and a Council, consisting of 36 States selected in accordance with special criteria. The activities of exploration or exploitation were to be carried out either by the Enterprise (an organ of the Authority also charged with transporting, processing, and marketing the minerals recovered from the Area), or by States parties, State enterprises, or natural or juridical persons having the nationality of, or being controlled by, a State party. When entities other than the Enterprise carried out the various activities, they could do so only after receiving an authorization for production from the Author- ity. Each area for which an entity would apply was to be divided into two parts: one to be exploited by the applicant, the other by the Enterprise. As for the modalities for sharing the financial or other economic benefits, under Article 160 the question was left to the Assembly for future decision. It was only provided that the sharing should be 'equitable' and that one ought to take into account 'the interests and needs of developing States and peoples who have not attained full independence or other self-governing status'.

Industrialized countries firmly opposed the new concepts. Led by the USA, the UK, and Japan, they assailed this legal regime, on many grounds: (i) it did not ensure access to seabed minerals; (ii) majority voting did not enable industrialized States, which would have to bear the brunt of costly research and exploitation, to have a proportionate role in decision making; (iii) the legal regime of transfer of technology by industrialized countries to the Enterprise and developing States would be contrary to the free play of market forces and penalize the former category of States. This opposition prevented the Convention from entering into force.

A breakthrough occurred in 1994, when States reached agreement on a text designed to revise part XI of the Convention (on the Area). Thanks to this revision, an increasing number of States ratified the Convention, which entered into force in 1994. The agreement adopted in 1994 hinges on the following points: (i) The Author- ity shall be set up gradually, and its costs for member States will be kept at a min- imum. (ii) There is no longer an obligation for States to finance the Enterprise (previously it had been provided that States parties were to grant the Enterprise long- term, interest-free loans designed to cover 50 per cent of the cost of exploring and exploiting a site in the Area, of treating and marketing the minerals retrieved, besides covering the initial administration expenses). (iii) The Enterprise is now subject to market forces; both its funding and its operations are subordinate to cost- effectiveness criteria. (iv) In conformity with a new voting system, the Authority's Council can no longer impose its decisions on matters that States (in particular, industrialized States) deem contrary to their interests. (v) There is no longer an obligation to transfer technology to the Enterprise or to those developing countries which apply for a contract.

Thus, although the notion of the common heritage of mankind has not been scuttled, in practice all its major implications for developing countries, with regard to seabed resources, have been watered down to such an extent that one may well wonder when and how this bold concept will be translated into reality, even assuming the resources do exist.

3.5.6 AIR

Traditionally, States have claimed sovereignty over the whole of their airspace. This of course was theoretical, until balloons and then aircraft began to be used. At present each State enjoys exclusive sovereignty over the airspace above its territory and territorial sea. Consequently no foreign State may fly through its airspace without prior permission or authorization. Overflight by foreign aircraft is allowed under bilateral or multilateral agreements. In addition, the 1944 Chicago Convention on International Civil Aviation provides in Article 5.1 that aircraft of other contracting parties 'not engaged in scheduled international air services' may make 'flights into or in transit non-stop across' the territory of a contracting State and 'make stops for non-traffic purposes without the necessity of obtaining prior permission, and subject to the right of the State flown over to require landing'.

3.5.7 OUTER SPACE

As stated above, outer space is the space around the earth beyond an altitude that is still undefined. According to some commentators, it starts between 90 and 100 miles above the earth; according to others, it comprises the space beyond the height to which aircraft can ascend in the atmosphere while 'deriving support from the reactions of the air'.

Theoretically, until the first rockets and satellites were launched in 1957 into outer space, under the *usque ad sidera* principle (see **3.5.1**) each State had sovereign rights over its own portion of outer space. However, as soon as the USSR and the USA began launching rockets and orbiting satellites, a consensus instantly emerged to the effect that they were not required to ask for the authorization of the States above whose territory the satellites were orbiting. All States bowed to the technological superiority of the two Powers and gave up their theoretical rights of jurisdiction over their respective outer space. As a consequence, outer space was immediately considered open to everybody for exploration and use (*res communis omnium*). In the following years the UN GA approved a number of resolutions, in particular resolution 1721 (XVI) of 20 December 1961, the Declaration adopted by resolution 1962 (XVIII) of 13 December 1963, and the 1967 Treaty on Principles Governing the Activities of States in the Exploration and Use of Outer Space. Together with the 1979 Agreement Governing the Activities of States on the Moon and Other Celestial Bodies, they laid down a set of rules which, being unopposed and indeed universally accepted, may be deemed to have become part of customary law. The basic principles of the legal regime of outer space are as follows: (i) It is not subject to national appropriation by claim of sovereignty, by means of use or occupation, or by any other means. (ii) Its exploration and use must be carried out 'for the benefit and in the interests of all countries, irrespective of their degree of economic or scientific development', and shall be 'the province of all mankind' (Article 1 of the 1967 Treaty and Article 4 of the 1979 Treaty). (iii) It must not be used to put into orbit round the earth, or station in any other manner, objects carrying nuclear weapons or other weapons of mass destruction.

Clearly, States did not go beyond the concept of *res communis omnium*. Except for the ban on orbiting weapons of mass destruction and damaging the environment, outer space was subjected to a legal regime akin to that of the high seas. The notion that the exploration and use of outer space is 'the province of all mankind' is an emphatic proposition which should not lead one to believe that outer space is subject to the legal regime of the 'common heritage of mankind'. Indeed, States exploring and using the area in question are under no specific obligation to carry out these activities in the interest of all mankind. And it is well known that major Powers are using outer space primarily, if not exclusively, in their own interests (except, of course, for certain obligations of co-operation undertaken by treaty with a few other countries).

The 1979 Treaty on the Moon and Other Celestial Bodies, the provisions of which have to a large extent become customary law, provides that all substances originating in the moon and other celestial bodies are to be regarded as natural resources belonging to the common heritage of mankind (see Articles 4.1 and 11.1). In the event the treaty only commanded unanimous support, after initial strong opposition from some major Powers, because the crucial point concerning the concept of common heritage, namely the question of how to share the benefits deriving from the exploitation of resources in outer space, was left unresolved.

3.6 THE LEGAL REGULATION OF SPACE, BETWEEN SOVEREIGNTY AND COMMUNITY INTERESTS

In the international legal regulation of territory and other space more than in any other area the tension and conflict between a traditional, State sovereignty-oriented approach and a modern, community-oriented outlook have come to the fore. However, here more than in any other area self-interest and individualism have eventually gained the upper hand even at the *legal* level. As we shall see (for instance, **Chapters 16** and **17**), in other fields notable advances have been made at least on the legal plane; although they have not yet been fully matched by progress in practice, the fact remains that legal tools are available to States enabling them to take a new path, if they so wish. The legal regulation of space has instead remained under the aegis of the 'each for himself' principle. The launching of the common heritage of mankind paradigm should not lead one to believe that at least there some community interest was propounded. In fact, the real linchpin of the concept, the idea of equitable sharing of profits, was advanced in the exclusive, or primary, interest of developing countries and contrary to the interests of industrialized States. It is striking that at the very time developing countries appropriated the exclusive economic zone, they also declared that the ocean floor beyond that zone was part of the common heritage of mankind. One cannot avoid inferring that in the exclusive economic zone coastal States, including the poor ones, either were able to exploit their own resources directly or considered it advisable to allow other States to exploit those resources. In the area beyond that zone, being deprived of the high technology required for exploration and exploitation, developing countries urged that States able to do so should act in the interests of everyone. One could draw the conclusion that they acted out of national self-interest, more than on behalf of mankind.

Nevertheless, as the concept is still embodied in the 1982 Convention on the Law of the Sea as revised in 1994, as well as in the 1979 Treaty on the Moon, it remains possible that gradually, through patient and realistic compromise, it may be turned into a set of legal provisions and institutions designed to meet the needs of all countries, in particular those that are less advanced.

4

OTHER INTERNATIONAL
LEGAL SUBJECTS

As stated in the previous chapter, international legal subjects also include insurgents, national liberation movements, international organizations, and individuals. While insurgents, like States, constitute traditional subjects of international law, the other categories are new classes of subjects.

4.1 INSURGENTS

Often political and military dissidence within a sovereign State results in large-scale armed conflict, with rebels succeeding in controlling a modicum of territory and setting up an operational structure capable of effectively wielding authority over the individuals living there. When this happens the insurrectional party normally claims some measure of recognition as an international subject.

Insurgency has occurred frequently since the inception of the international community. Civil strife raged in North America between 1774 and 1783: the fight between American settlers and the British colonial power (which today would be styled a 'war of national liberation', although the rebels were white, like the colonial power) lasted a long time and wrought havoc; it ended with the victory of the rebels. Between 1810 and 1824 other rebellions broke out on the same continent, against Spanish and Portuguese rule in Latin America. Once again, the insurgents got the upper hand. In the nineteenth century a number of internal armed conflicts also erupted in Europe, yet the most important civil war of all took place in the USA between 1861 and 1865, and was attended by such appalling devastation and cruelty that the contestants regarded it as no different from a war proper, and consequently applied to it the bulk of the rules governing armed conflict between States. In the twentieth century internal conflicts were particularly serious, protracted, and destructive. The Spanish Civil War 1936–9 stands out for its magnitude and far-reaching repercussions. After the Second World War, conflicts broke out in some Western and socialist countries: in Greece (1946–9), in Hungary (1956), in Czechoslovakia (1968), in Turkey (1983 to the present), in the former Yugoslavia (1991–5 and 1998–9) and in Chechnya (1991–6 and 1999–2001). However, most major insurrections in modern times have tended to take place in developing countries.

What is the reaction of international law to civil strife? Later (15.7), it will be shown how international rules govern the conduct of hostilities. Here we shall establish the extent to which rebels acquire some standing in the world community.

States have traditionally been hostile to insurgents in their territory, on the obvious grounds that they do not like the status quo to be disrupted by people who seek to topple the 'lawful government' and possibly change the whole fabric of the State. Consequently they prefer to treat insurgency as a domestic occurrence and the rebels as common criminals. In their eyes, any 'interference' from the international community is bound to bolster insurgents and make them even more dangerous. Traditional reluctance to grant civil upheaval the status of international armed conflict has become even more marked in recent times, for two reasons. The first is the rapid spread of tribal feuds or other forms of conflict in many developing States, particularly in Africa, where the arbitrary borders decided upon by the colonial powers are likely to lead to secession. The second is the growing centrifugal influence of nationalist or religious groups, particularly in States resulting from the break-up of bigger entities (this holds true, among others, for the new States born out of the collapse of the Soviet Union and Yugoslavia). Consequently, feeling more and more insecure, the overwhelming majority of States show a growing tendency to withhold the granting of international legal standing to rebels and to treat them under the criminal law of the country concerned.

The inimical attitude of States towards insurgents has manifested itself in three principal forms.

First of all, the current regulation of the conditions for insurgents to acquire international legal personality is rather confused and rudimentary. International law only establishes certain loose minimum requirements for eligibility to become an international subject. In short, (1) rebels should prove that they have effective control over the territory, and (2) civil commotion should reach a certain degree of intensity and duration. It is for States (both the State against which civil strife breaks out and other parties) to appraise—by granting or withholding recognition of insurgency— whether these requirements have been fulfilled. If the State against which the insurgents are fighting grants them the recognition of belligerency, that is, admits that the conflict under way is an *international* armed conflict, or else third States so recognise it, then rebels are automatically upgraded to international subjects entitled to all the rights and obligations deriving from *ius in bello*. States are loath to grant such recognition, as is shown by the fact that it has very seldom been given.

Examples are rare. During the American Civil War, on 19 April 1861 President Lincoln issued a proclamation declaring the coasts of the seceded Confederate States to be under naval blockade; 'for this purpose a competent force' was posted 'so as to prevent entrance and exit of vessels' from the ports on those coasts. This Proclamation amounted to recognition of belligerency. On 14 May 1861 Britain issued a Proclamation of neutrality, thus recognizing in its turn the insurgents as belligerents.[1] In August–September 1918 Britain, France, Italy, and the USA recognized the state of belligerency between the Czecho-Slovaks (who had taken up arms against the central authorities and were led by a National Council), on the one side, and the German and Austro-Hungarian Empires, on the other).[2]

To some extent the existence of rebels as international legal persons may depend on the attitude of other subjects. Theoretically, if all members of the international community were to decide that a certain insurrectional party lacks the requisite conditions, that party would hardly be in a position to exercise the rights and fulfil the obligations inherent in its international status, however strong, effective, and protracted its authority over a portion of the territory belonging to a sovereign State.

In practice, things are different, for two main reasons. First, in the international community there are different political and ideological alignments; any insurrectional party is likely to enlist the support of one or more States with which it has political, religious, or ideological affinities, or because of military or strategic considerations. Consequently there will always be one or more States inclined to grant recognition to certain rebels. Second, even other States may at a particular point find it useful to concede that a group of insurgents has become a legally independent subject. This may occur when the rebellious party exercises effective authority over a territory where foreigners live. Since it would be unrealistic for third States to claim respect for their nationals from the incumbent government, they are forced to address their claim for protection of their citizens and their property to the rebels. They thus implicitly admit that rebels have a duty under international law to protect the lives and assets of foreigners.

Be that as it may, there is no gainsaying that recognition by existing States can play a more significant role in the case of rebels than in the 'birth' and legal personality of new States. The conspicuous reluctance of States to admit rebels to the 'charmed circle' of the family of nations, the inherently provisional character of insurgency, the embryonic nature of most international rules concerning civil strife, are all factors determining the practical and legal importance of recognition of insurgents.

There is a second way in which hostility to rebels comes to the fore. While third States are authorized to provide assistance of any kind (including the dispatch of armed forces for wiping out the rebels) to the 'lawful' government, they are duty-bound to refrain from supplying assistance (other than humanitarian) to rebels (whereas, as we shall see, *infra*, **4.4**, they are authorized to assist national liberation movements).

A third consequence of this hostility is the paucity of general international rules that address themselves equally to rebels and to States.

An example is the norms on treaty making: rebels are empowered to enter into agreements with those States that are willing to establish rapport with them. Another is the rules on the treatment of foreigners: rebels are to grant foreigners the treatment provided for under international law. In 1972, in his Report on the ILC Draft Articles on State Responsibility, R. Ago drew attention to three 'examples' of State practice where third States requested insurgents to make compensation for damage caused by the insurrectional authorities to the nationals of the States concerned.[3] These cases relate to the American Civil War (1861), to an insurrection which broke out in Mexico in 1914, and to the Spanish Civil War. (In relation to the latter, on three occasions in 1937 the British Government addressed a formal request for reparation to the Nationalist authorities, as a consequence of the destruction of a British destroyer, a merchant vessel, and two seaplanes at the hand of the insurgents.)

At the same time, rebels do not have a full correlative right to claim respect for their lives and property from all third States where their 'nationals' (that is, people owing them allegiance) may find themselves. Such respect can be exacted only by way of reciprocity. If a 'national' from an insurgent territory lives in a State unwilling to recognize rebels, that State's duty to protect that 'national' only exists in relation to the 'lawful' government, of which the individual has citizenship. With regard to the rules on the immunity of foreign representatives, insurgents must treat as State organs all officials of third States in the territory under their control; that is, they owe them a special duty of protection, and must grant them immunity from jurisdiction for official acts, etc. As to the persons acting for the rebellious party, they can claim international protection only from those States that have granted them recognition. Other States are entitled to regard them simply as nationals of the country where civil strife is in progress.

A few rules on the enforcement of international law (in relation to non-belligerent reprisals and other peaceful counter-measures) can also be applied. Insurgents can resort to all lawful sanctions to enforce international agreements entered into with third States or the general international rules on foreigners and respect for officials, when applicable. Finally, there are rules concerning the conduct of hostilities with the 'lawful' government (see **15.7**).

As I pointed out above, insurrectional parties are provisional in character (since insurgents are quelled by the government, and disappear; or they seize power, and install themselves in the place of the government; or they secede and join another State, or become a new international subject). It follows that they cannot claim rights contingent upon the permanent character of international subjects. Thus, *inter alia*, insurgents do not possess any right of sovereignty proper over the territory they control. That is, they may not lawfully cede the territory or part of it to another international subject; they merely exercise de facto authority.

To conclude, insurgents are State-like subjects, for they exhibit all the major features of States. However, they are *transient* and, in addition, they have a *limited international capacity* in two respects. First, they have only a few international rights and duties. Second, they are only 'associated' with a limited number of existing States (those which adopt the view that they fulfil all the conditions for international personality, and consequently engage in dealings with them).

4.2 THE REASONS BEHIND THE EMERGENCE OF NEW INTERNATIONAL SUBJECTS

The rationale behind the setting up of, and attributing international status to, inter-governmental organizations is different from that motivating the granting of international standing to national liberation movements and individuals.

As far as the former category is concerned, States have been motivated by reasons of *expediency* and *practicality*. In modern times many questions have acquired an international or trans-national dimension; they can therefore only be settled by inter-State co-operation. It is therefore only natural that States have refrained from looking after certain areas of mutual interest individually. They have preferred to set up joint bodies charged with the carrying out of international action, in matters of trans-national interest, on behalf of all the participating States. The setting up of such bodies began in the late nineteenth century. What is remarkable is that, particularly after the Second World War, a further step was taken and intergovernmental agencies were increasingly endowed with autonomous powers, with rights and duties distinct from those belonging to each member State. An ideological factor helped in strengthening the role of intergovernmental organizations and allotting international standing to them. This was the idea that to ward off the scourge of a third world war, a strong network of international instrumentalities should be created so as to impose heavier and more far-reaching restraints on States. However illusory and naïve this 'internationalist' outlook may have been, there is no denying that it led to the proliferation of organizations and contributed to their increasing importance.

In the case of individuals and national liberation movements the *ideological factor* was decisive. A different ideology accounts for the emergence of each of the two classes of international subject. A Western, liberal-democratic theory lay at the root of the granting of legal entitlements to individuals on the international scene: the human rights doctrine, championed by Western countries such as the USA and a few Latin American countries as early as 1944–5 and subsequently taken up by a number of other Western or Western-oriented States. This doctrine did not result only in the drafting of a number of international treaties protecting human rights. Its logical corollary was that individuals were granted the opportunity to call States to account before international bodies whenever they felt that their rights had been disregarded. In addition, new doctrines emerged (or took on new vigour) in the world community. They advocated full respect for some basic values (in addition to human rights, peace, the need to spare civilians as much as possible in armed conflict and, more generally, to uphold principles of humanity). Furthermore, States increasingly envisaged the direct imposition of international obligations upon individuals, regardless of what the national legal order within which they live may enjoin them to do. These obligations are designed to induce individuals to heed those values, with the consequence that, when they disregard them, they may be prosecuted and punished.

The doctrine of self-determination of peoples is behind the emergence of colonial peoples and peoples under racist regimes or foreign domination on the international scene. What gave impulse to the appearance of this category of subjects was the anti-colonialist version propounded by Lenin as early as 1917, rather than the moderate one put forward by Woodrow Wilson in 1918 (see **5.7.1**).

4.3 INTERNATIONAL ORGANIZATIONS

States increasingly find it convenient to establish international machinery for the purpose of carrying out tasks of mutual interest. They therefore institute distinct centres of action for the furtherance of common goals and designed to perform only those activities that States delegate to them. As the ICJ put it in its Advisory Opinion on *Legality of the Use by a State of Nuclear Weapons in Armed Conflict*, the object of the constituent instruments of international organizations 'is to create new subjects of law endowed with a certain autonomy, to which the parties entrust the task of realizing common goals'.[4] On this score organizations, when they are endowed with international legal personality, can be styled *ancillary* subjects of international law. This means that they are but instruments in the hands of States. They cease to exist internationally the very day the groups of States that created them decide to jettison them.

In the same Advisory Opinion, the ICJ also stressed another major feature of international organizations: unlike States, they have a limited competence and field of action. As the Court put it:

'[I]nternational organizations are subjects of international law which do not, unlike States, possess a general competence. International organizations are governed by the "principle of speciality", that is to say, they are invested by the States which create them with powers, the limits of which are a function of the common interests whose promotion those States entrust to them.'[5]

International organizations were first created in the late nineteenth and the early twentieth centuries; they were, however, very rudimentary, and primarily concerned with technical matters.

Think, for example, of the Universal Postal Union, set up in 1875; the Union for the Protection of Industrial Property, established in 1883; the International Institute for Agriculture, created in 1905; and the various 'River Commissions', for the Rhine, the Danube, etc. They were merely collective instrumentalities for the joint performance of actions that each member State would otherwise have had to undertake by itself.[6]

The League of Nations and the ILO—political institutions established after the First World War—were of greater importance. Yet they, too, were to a large extent conceived by member States as 'collective organs', that is, as structures under the control of those States, hence possessing hardly any really independent role or existence of their own. However, the question of their being endowed with international legal personality did crop up, and, although many scholars including D. Anzilotti rejected the idea,[7] some courts answered that question in the affirmative.

In particular, in 1931 the Italian Court of Cassation delivered a seminal decision in *Istituto internazionale di Agricoltura* v. *Profili*. Mr Profili, an employee of the International Institute for Agriculture (IIA), the international organization that was the predecessor of FAO and similarly headquartered in Rome, had been dismissed by the Organization. He sued the IIA before a court in Rome, asking among other things for severance pay. The IIA having challenged the jurisdiction of Italian courts, the case was brought before the Court of Cassation. The Court held that the Organization had international legal personality, as the States establishing the Organization had intended it to be 'absolutely autonomous *vis-à-vis* each and every member State'; consequently it was empowered to organize its own structure and legal order autonomously and without any interference from sovereign States. It followed that Italian courts lacked jurisdiction over employment relations with the Organization.[8]

The problem of the proper role and weight of intergovernmental organizations in international affairs chiefly arose after the Second World War, when many organizations were created and granted sweeping powers.

International institutions were set up in various fields. These include: (a) political relations — for example, the United Nations, which has universal scope; the Organization of American States, the Council of Europe, the Organization of African Unity, and the League of Arab States, all of which are regional in character; (b) military relations — for example, NATO and the former Warsaw Pact Organization; (c) economic co-operation — for example, the IMF, the World Bank, and the WTO (at the universal level); the EU (which also has a political dimension), at the regional level; (d) cultural relations — for example, UNESCO; (e) social co-operation — for example, ILO, FAO. At present there are more than 400 intergovernmental organizations.

Usually, these organizations consist of a permanent secretariat, an assembly in which all member States take part when it meets periodically, and a governing body made up of a limited number of member States, and entrusted with managerial tasks.

Of course, not all international organizations possess international legal personality. What is the test for determining whether or not they are international subjects? In its Advisory Opinion of 1949 on *Reparation for Injuries Suffered in the Service of the United Nations* the ICJ outlined two criteria.

First, it must be shown that the member States, in setting up the organization and entrusting certain functions to it, with the attendant duties and responsibilities, intended to clothe it 'with the competence required to enable these functions to be effectively discharged'.[9] In other words, it must be proved that the founding fathers intended to put into being an autonomous body, capable of occupying 'a position in certain respects in detachment from its Members'.[10] This *intention* can be inferred from various elements. For instance, it may be deduced from, among other things, the fact that decisions of the principal organs of the organization must not be taken (or must not always be taken) unanimously but can be adopted by a majority vote. That intention may also be spelled out by the draftsmen in the text of the charter or statute of the organization. In this respect, it may suffice to mention Article 4.1 of the 1998 Statute of the International Criminal Court (ICC), which states: 'The Court shall have international legal personality. It shall also have such legal capacity as may be necessary for the exercise of its functions and the fulfillment of its purposes.'

Second, it is necessary for the organization *in actual fact to enjoy the autonomy* from member States and the effective capacity necessary for it to act as an international subject. In the ICJ's words, it is necessary to show that the organization 'is in fact exercising and enjoying functions and rights which can only be explained on the basis of the possession of a large measure of international personality and the capacity to operate upon an international plane'.[11]

In 1985 the Italian Court of Cassation insisted upon this requirement in *Cristiani* v. *Istituto italo-latino-americano*.[12] The Court held that international legal personality is based on the effective position of an entity in the international community: the organization needs to constitute a 'collective unity detached from the member States'; it must consist of 'social organs' that are distinct from the organs of each member State and that in addition do not act as joint organs of those States; rather, they must act as organs proper to the organization.

Once this twofold test is met, it may be considered that international organizations possess international rights and obligations deriving from international customary rules.

As for organizations that do not satisfy the above tests, it may be said that they act on behalf of all the member States. They are organs common to all those States, with the consequence that acts they perform may be legally attributed to all such States. By the same token, any wrongful act perpetrated by one of the organs or officials of the organization is the responsibility of all the member States.

What are the international rights and duties conferred or, respectively, imposed on such organizations by international customary, that is *general*, rules? It is impossible to give a definite answer, for it is to a large extent left to the instituting States to decide in each case how to structure the international entity, and to what extent to grant to it powers and obligations that are then effectively exercised and discharged in practice. As the ICJ put it in *Reparation for Injuries*, 'the subjects of law in any legal system are not necessarily identical in their nature or in the extent of their rights'.[13] Bearing this caveat in mind, it may be noted that the international practice which evolved after the Second World War shows that at least a handful of international rules do confer rights on organizations in relation to non-member States on condition that the former are sufficiently autonomous from the member States and have a structure enabling them to act in the international field. Among the rights that we may safely regard as belonging to international bodies, the following should be mentioned.

(1) *The right to enter into international agreements with non-member States on matters within the organization's province.* Treaties concluded by the organization have all the legally binding effects of international treaties proper—provided, of course, that this was the intention of the parties to the agreement.

In fact, organizations have concluded numerous treaties covering a host of matters: headquarters agreements, conventions on privileges and immunities of international civil servants and members of international organs, treaties relating to activities performed by the organization concerned (for instance, those on technical assistance entered into by the UN), agreements with other organizations for the co-ordination of their fields of action, etc.

(2) *The right to immunity from jurisdiction of State courts for acts and activities performed by the organization.* Domestic courts of many States have held that disputes relating to employment with international organizations cannot be submitted to States' jurisdiction, for they concern activities falling within the purview of the organization concerned.

More generally, international organizations have the right to claim immunity from the jurisdiction as well as execution of national courts, with regard to activities performed to attain the goals laid down in the organization's statutes or constitution. The rationale for this immunity is that otherwise States could interfere with or affect the functioning of the organization; for instance the State where the organization is headquartered could seize or impound its assets.

(3) *The right to protection for all the organization's agents acting in the territory of a third State in their official capacity as international civil servants.* The ICJ in its Advisory Opinion on *Reparation for Injuries* (1949) authoritatively upheld this right.

On 17 September 1948, the UN Mediator, a Swede, Count Folke Bernadotte, and the UN Observer, a Frenchman, Colonel André Sérot, were assassinated by a Jewish terrorist organization while on an official mission for the UN. The murder took place in the eastern part of Jerusalem (then under Israeli control) after Israel had proclaimed its independence, and before it was admitted to UN membership. The Israeli authorities tried to discover and bring to justice the perpetrators and instigators of the crime but, as the Israeli representative stated to the UN GA on 5 May 1948, 'the results of the investigations had been disappointingly negative'.[14] The Government of Israel admitted that 'failure had been reported in the functioning of its security system in the past' but 'could not admit that any conclusions could be drawn from that event with respect to its present capacity to fulfil its international obligations'. Whatever the reasons behind its stance (it has been contended that it made a point of honouring its international obligations because it was keen to enter the UN), the fact remains that Israel declared itself to be ready to make reparation for its failure to protect the two UN agents and to punish their killers.

(4) *The right to bring an international claim* with a view to obtaining reparation for any damage caused by member States or by third States to the assets of the organization or to its officials acting on behalf of the organization. The ICJ upheld this right too in the same case. The Court held unanimously that the organization could bring an international claim for damage caused to its assets, and held by a large majority (eleven to four) that the organization could also bring a claim for reparation due in respect of the damage caused to an agent of the organization (so-called *functional* protection). Accordingly, the organization may bring claims on behalf of its agents, even where the offending State is the national State of the victim. The Court correctly implied that this right was *procedural* in character and presupposed the violation of a *substantive* right of the Organization, that is, the right to respect for and protection of its agents by any State in whose territory the agents performed their official functions.

The Court's majority adopted a very progressive stand on another issue. Instead of endorsing the traditional view whereby States alone can put forward claims on behalf of their nationals injured abroad (the so-called *diplomatic* protection), the Court held that when an individual acts on behalf of an organization, the organization may also exercise protection of its agents qua individuals. This view, needless to say, greatly privileged the *functional* bond as opposed to *national* allegiance. Some felt that this view actually undermined the authority of States over their citizens and constituted a dangerous precedent. Socialist countries, in particular, strongly resented and criticized the Court.

Despite the existence of these various rights, organizations do not always have the capacity to enforce them when member or non-member States breach them. True, organizations have the right to seek remedies before international bodies (provided of course that the defendant State has accepted the competence of such organs). However, in cases of non-compliance by States either with their own obligations or with international decisions concerning their wrongful acts, international organizations are often unable to enforce the law. They only have the power to suspend the delinquent member State from participation or voting, or to expel it from the organization. With regard to non-member States, organizations may perhaps invoke the general rules on State responsibility (see **Chapter 9**).

4.4 NATIONAL LIBERATION MOVEMENTS

The emergence of organized groups fighting on behalf of a whole 'people' against colonial powers is a characteristic feature of the aftermath of the Second World War. Liberation movements arose first in Africa, then in Asia; they then mushroomed in Latin America and—to a lesser extent—in Europe. Africa, however, has been the principal home of liberation movements. Along with the gradual expansion of the liberation phenomenon from Africa to other continents, the movements also broadened their objectives, invoking new goals, in addition to anti-colonialism, namely struggles against racist regimes and alien domination. Struggles of this type were prevalent from the 1960s until the 1980s. At present they seem to be on the wane. Consequently, this class of international subjects is dwindling.

Algeria was the first country to witness the emergence of a liberation movement (the FLN, in 1954). Other African movements were: PAIGC (African Party for the Independence of Guinea and Cape Verde), FRELIMO (Liberation Front of Mozambique), the three movements in Angola (MPLA, UNITA, and FLNA), the two movements which fought in Zimbabwe (ZAPU and ZANU); those fighting against South Africa (ANC: African National Congress, and PAC: Pan African Congress); SWAPO (South West Africa People's Organization), in Namibia; POLISARIO, struggling against Morocco in Western Sahara (annexed by Morocco in 1975), and others.

In the Middle East the PLO was founded in 1969. In Asia the FNLV actively participated in the struggle against South Vietnam from 1960 to 1974; FRETILIN sprang up in Timor in 1975 to fight against Indonesian rule. In Latin America similar movements emerged.

Many of these movements and the peoples of which they constituted the organized structure eventually acquired statehood (for instance, in Algeria, Zimbabwe, Comores, Seychelles, Angola, Mozambique, Vietnam, Eritrea). The ANC became an integral part of the new government in South Africa. In East Timor a new State is in the process of emerging. The PLO has been gradually given control over the Gaza Strip and parts of the West Bank, as the 'Palestinian Authority'. On the other hand, POLISARIO is still seeking independence in Western Sahara; a ceasefire signed in 1991 under UN auspices put an end to the guerrilla war that had started in 1976; however, UN-sponsored diplomatic efforts to hold a referendum on self-determination have led nowhere, for there still are many bones of contention involved in the question of how to hold the referendum.

A characteristic of a few of these movements has been the acquisition of control over some part of the territory in which they were (or are) fighting (for example, the FLN in Algeria, the two movements in Zimbabwe, the two liberation movements in Eritrea, POLISARIO in Western Sahara. However, most of them were hosted in a friendly country, from where they conducted military operations against their adversaries (for example, the PLO, SWAPO, ANC). *Control of territory*, therefore, is not their distinguishing trait, in contrast to insurgents. Their chief characteristic is their *international legitimation based on the principle of self-determination.* They are given international status on account of their political goals: their struggle to free themselves from colonial domination, a racist regime, or alien occupation (it is as a consequence of this legitimation that no ban is imposed on States to refrain from providing national liberation movements with humanitarian, economic, and military assistance short of sending armed troops; conversely, States are duty-bound to refrain from assisting a State denying self-determination to a people or a group entitled to it). However, this does not mean that the territorial factor is ruled out altogether: it is present, albeit in a very singular way. Liberation movements are elevated to the rank of international subjects because they tend (or at least strive) to acquire control over territory. In this context territory amounts to a 'prospective' factor. Liberation movements could not be recognized as members of the world community if they did not aspire to possess (once their struggle is over) the basic feature proper to primary subjects of the community, that, is, effective control over a population living in a given territory.

In order to be owners of rights and subjects of obligations, it is necessary for them to have an apparatus, a representative organization that can come into contact, as it were, with other international legal persons. Once a people falls into one of these three categories and is endowed with a representative organization or apparatus, it can claim to possess international status. This was clearly spelled out in Article 96.3 of the First Geneva Protocol of 1977 (see **15.6.1**). In indicating the categories of peoples entitled to make a declaration for the purpose of being bound by the Protocol, it specified that such a declaration could be made by '*the authority representing a people* engaged against a High Contracting Party in an armed conflict of the type referred to in Art. 1.4', that is, a conflict against a colonial, racist, or alien Power. In its judgment of 28 June 1985 in *Arafat and Salah*, the Italian Court of Cassation held that national liberation movements such as the PLO

'enjoy a limited international personality. They are granted *locus standi* in the international community for the limited purpose of discussing, on a perfectly equal footing with territorial States, the means and terms for the self-determination of the peoples they politically control, pursuant to the principle of self-determination of peoples, to be considered a customary rule of a peremptory character . . . Reference to the recognition, whether *de jure* or *de facto*, of the PLO granted by some Governments is irrelevant. Indeed, recognition does not constitute the international legal personality, for it belongs to the political domain and consequently is devoid of effects from the legal viewpoint.'[15]

What are the rights and duties of the organized peoples referred to above? In short:

(1) The right to self-determination. This right is general in character and applies to all member States of the international community: it is a community right (see **1.8.2**, **5.8.3**, and **5.8.9**).

(2) The rights and obligations deriving from general principles on the conduct of hostilities (*ius in bello*) (see **15.6**).

(3) The rights and obligations deriving from rules on treaty making. The existence of the power is evidenced by the numerous agreements various liberation movements have entered into on such matters as: the stationing of armed forces belonging to the movements on the territory of States, cessation of hostilities, and the granting of independence, as well as questions relating to borders.

(4) The right to claim respect for, and protection of, the persons acting in their official capacity as organs of the people's representative structure, as well as their immunity from the jurisdiction of States' courts for acts performed in that capacity. Arguably this right is inherent in the fact that the liberation movement acts as a distinct international entity. However, some national courts have denied this right, for instance the Italian Court of Cassation in its judgment of 1985 in *Arafat and Salah*, on the questionable grounds that customary rules only confer that right on entities endowed with 'complete international personality', such as States.[16]

By contrast, the organized peoples do not possess the right to dispose of the territory or its natural resources. However, as long as conflict between the organized people and the colonial or dominant State is under way, the colonial or dominant Power is barred from entering into international treaties concerning the territory of the people concerned. An arbitral tribunal in *Delimitation of the Maritime Boundary between Guinea-Bissau and Senegal* (award of 31 July 1989) laid down this principle.[17] It should be noted that in their submissions to the tribunal both Senegal and Guinea-Bissau agreed on the principle.

4.5 INDIVIDUALS

Many commentators contend that individuals may not be regarded as having the legal status of international subjects. In their view, individuals are still under the exclusive control of States. If treaties provide for rights and duties of individuals, this would only mean that each State undertakes by agreement *vis-à-vis* the other contracting States to confer such rights and impose duties on individuals solely within its own legal system. Those commentators regard the right of individuals to petition international judicial or quasi-judicial bodies as exceptional, viewing it as no more than a procedural right which lacks any attendant substantive right, or the power to enforce a possible decision of the international body that might be favourable to the individual.

We will see below that the international condition of individuals is much more complex and multifaceted. In any case, here too international law has undergone dramatic changes in recent times.

After briefly sketching out the condition of individuals under traditional international law, I will examine the relevant rules of modern international law, to establish to what extent it may be said that they grant rights to, or impose obligations on, individuals, and it is therefore warranted to regard human beings as international legal subjects.

4.5.1 TRADITIONAL LAW

Over a long period of time—in fact during the whole of the first stage of development of the international community, from the seventeenth to the early twentieth century—human beings were under the exclusive control of States. If, in time, individuals acquired some relevance in international affairs, it was mostly as 'beneficiaries' of treaties of commerce and navigation, or of conventions on the treatment to be accorded to foreigners, etc. Or else they constituted the 'reference point' of States' powers (think, for example of the customary rule granting States the right to exercise diplomatic and, if legally possible, judicial protection of their nationals wronged by a foreign country). The general position of international law with regard to individuals was aptly set out in 1928 by the PCIJ in its Advisory Opinion in *Danzig Railway Officials*, as follows:

'It may be readily admitted that, according to a well-established principle of international law, the *Beamtenabkommen* [a treaty between Poland and Germany] being an international agreement, cannot, as such, create direct rights and obligations for private individuals. But it cannot be disputed that the very object of an international agreement, according to the intention of the Contracting Parties, may be the adoption by the Parties of some definite rules creating individual rights and obligations and enforceable by the national courts.'[18]

Traditional international law did not include general rules conferring rights on individuals, regardless of their nationality. The question of a possible international legal status for individuals mainly arose with regard to *piracy* (any attack on a ship committed for private ends, on the high seas, by the crew or the passengers of a private ship; see **1.8.1** and **12.1**), a phenomenon that, while it was widespread in the seventeenth and eighteenth centuries, gradually disappeared, although more recently it has been somewhat revived in certain areas of the world. It thus remained a matter of controversy whether international rules reached individuals directly or through the intermediary of national legal systems.

Some leading scholars (such as Westlake and, in more recent times, Kelsen)[19] argued that international rules imposed direct obligations concerning piracy on individuals while at the same time exceptionally authorizing any State to seize pirates on the high seas and to punish them irrespective of their nationality. Others (e.g. Anzilotti)[20] contended that instead international rules merely obliged States to pass legislation prohibiting piracy and at the same time authorized all States to allow their national authorities to arrest, prosecute, and punish pirates.

The question remained controversial, on two main grounds. First, when piracy was in its heyday individuals were under the full control of States. As stated above, they were beneficiaries of diplomatic or judicial protection only when their national State decided to exercise such protection *vis-à-vis* another State. Second, it seemed rather odd to speak of individuals as subjects of international law, when allegedly they had obligations deriving from international rules, but were not at the same time granted rights and powers.

4.5.2 MODERN LAW

The situation appears to be different today. At present, as a result of historical events and the spread of new ideologies, States have lost their exclusive monopoly over individuals, in addition to gradually yielding some of their powers to other entities such as international organizations. Individuals have gradually come to be regarded as holders of internationally material interests but also as capable of infringing fundamental values of the world community. Their demands and concerns as well as their possibly reprehensible conduct have been taken into account. Thus, individuals have been granted legal rights that are operational at the international level. By the same token, States have deemed it fit to extend obligations to them, by enjoining them to comply with some new fundamental values and calling them to account for any breach of such values.

(a) Customary rules imposing obligations on individuals

It seems unquestionable that in recent times a number of international rules have come into being that directly impose *obligations* upon individuals. First, these general rules crystallized in the area of armed conflict. They provided that, should individuals engaging in an international war break the rules of warfare, they would be criminally liable for such breaches, regardless of their official position as State agents. Subsequently other general rules on the punishment of other international crimes evolved (on crimes against humanity, in particular genocide, on aggression and terrorism, as well as torture). In addition the scope of the rules on war crimes has expanded (see *infra*, 12.2.1).

Thus individuals are at present under many international obligations, some solely relating to armed conflict, others (those on crimes against humanity, genocide, aggression, terrorism, torture) also concerning peacetime. These obligations are incumbent upon *all individuals of the world*: they are all obliged to refrain from breaching the aforementioned rules; if they do not do so, they are accountable for their transgression. This is so regardless of whether the national legal system within which individuals live contains a similar or the same obligation (translated into national legislation). In other words, this is an area where the international legal system enters into direct contact, as it were, with individuals, without the medium of national legal systems. As the International Military Tribunal (IMT) at Nuremberg stated, 'the very essence of the Charter [of the IMT] is that individuals have international duties which transcend the national obligations of obedience imposed by the individual State. He who violates the laws of war cannot obtain immunity while acting in pursuance of the authority of the State if the State in authorizing action moves outside its competence under international law.'[21]

Furthermore, those obligations are incumbent on individuals both when they act as State officials (this is by far the most normal occurrence) as well as, under certain conditions, when they engage in the prohibited conduct *qua* individuals, that is, in a private capacity. Individuals who are in breach of one of the obligations under discussion are criminally liable and can be brought to trial before the courts of any country of the world: see **12.4.1** (or before an international criminal tribunal, if such a tribunal has been established and has jurisdiction over the crimes).

(b) The holders of the corresponding rights

Who is legally entitled to enforce the above-mentioned obligations? Two views are admissible. First, it could be maintained that at the present stage in the development of the world community it is not yet possible to consider that individuals are entitled to seek enforcement of those obligations. Only States would be in a position to advance such a claim, with the concomitant power to pursue enforcement by bringing to trial, before national courts or international criminal tribunals (such as the International Criminal Court: ICC), those allegedly responsible for breaches of the obligations. A different view could also be entertained. It could be contended that the 'foray' of international values, hence of international rights and obligations, into areas previously subjected to national legal systems has been so extensive as to give individuals a role that was previously unthinkable. As has just been pointed out, all individuals in the world, whatever their nationality and whether or not they are so enjoined by the national legal system of the country where they live, are now under the strict international obligation fully to respect some important values (maintenance of peace, protection of human dignity, etc.). It would be not only consistent from the viewpoint of legal logic but also in keeping with new trends emerging in the world community to argue that the international right in respect of those obligations accrues to all individuals: they are entitled to respect for their life and limbs, and for their dignity; hence they have a right not to become a victim of war crimes, crimes against humanity, aggression, torture, terrorism. At least for the time being, this international right, deriving from general international rules, is not, however, attended by a *specific* means, or power, of enforcement that belongs to individuals. At present individuals can only institute criminal proceedings against the alleged culprits of such crimes before national courts possessing territorial, or personal, or universal jurisdiction (see **12.4.1**). Or they can bring the alleged breaches to the attention of the Prosecutor of the ICC. That a substantive right is not attended by a specific legal entitlement to enforce that right is by no means novel or surprising, in legal terms. It may be noted that the power, granted by the ICC Statute to victims of international crimes, to put forward their legal views and concerns in proceedings set in motion before the Court by the Prosecutor, by States, or by the SC, may bear out, at least to some extent, the legal construction just delineated. It should be added that, strictly speaking, there is nothing to prevent States from providing in international rules for international obligations incumbent upon individuals and corresponding rights accruing to them, in the international field. What matters is the intention of the lawmakers. In terms of the view under discussion, it could be contended that the States that deliberately or unwittingly contributed to the formation of customary rules on international crimes intended to grant corresponding rights to individuals.

To grasp what this view implies, it may prove useful to emphasize the difference between the general rules under discussion and treaty provisions on human rights (e.g., those of the UN Covenant on Civil and Political Rights). The latter provisions seem to confer *substantive* (as opposed to *procedural* or *adjective*) rights and obligations on individuals; in fact all they do is to oblige States to grant rights and impose obligations on individuals *in their respective national systems*. As a consequence, should a contracting party fail to implement one of those provisions by legislative action in its domestic legal system, individuals would not possess the substantive rights and obligations laid down in that provision. By contrast, the obligations and rights we are discussing are *directly* conferred on individuals by international rules. They therefore accrue to, or are incumbent upon, persons even if a national legal system *has not implemented* those international rules domestically or has passed legislation contrary to them. Clearly, in this case the international legal order reaches out to individuals and gets to them without relying upon and going through national legal systems. This unique legal regulation is significant evidence of the *growing direct impact* of the international legal system on the action of individuals living in sovereign States.

Whichever of the two views expounded so far is considered sounder, there is no gainsaying that the emergence of the international obligations under discussion marks a significant advance in the international community.

(c) Treaty provisions conferring rights on individuals

In modern times, States have increasingly concluded agreements granting human rights to individuals subject to their jurisdiction. In some instances, they also have provided for the right of individuals to petition international bodies alleging that a contracting State has breached one of their human rights. The question arises of whether the *substantive* rights at issue have only a national dimension, that is, may only be exercised within the municipal sphere of each contracting party, or have instead international scope, that is, may be exercised at the international level. The same problem also arises with regard to the *procedural* right to petition international bodies.

As pointed out above, it is apparent from international treaties on human rights that the substantive rights they lay down may only be exercised by individuals within the domestic legal system of each contracting party. The position is different as regards the right to lodge a complaint with an international body.

This trend began in Latin America. The treaty concluded by five Central American republics (Costa Rica, El Salvador, Guatemala, Honduras, and Nicaragua) for the establishment of the Central American Court of Justice (1908–18) granted to individuals, as well as to States and domestic institutions, the right to appear as parties before the Court. Individuals could bring complaints against one of those States (other than their own), for violations of international law. Indeed, individuals brought five of the ten cases heard by the Court; however, none of these cases was successful.

After the First World War, the framers of the ILO decided to confer on industrial associations of workers and employers the right to demand compliance with ILO Conventions by member States. At the time this was a great improvement indeed. It went hand in hand with another similar development in the field of the international protection of minorities (racial, religious, or linguistic): representatives of such minorities gained the right to lodge 'petitions' with the League of Nations, if in their view the States concerned failed to honour their international undertakings. In both cases the rationale behind this significant change can easily be accounted for: as ILO Conventions and international treaties on minorities were calculated to protect workers (or employers) and minorities respectively, it was quite logical to grant their beneficiaries the right to protest in the case of alleged violations. This appeared all the more sensible since the treaties in question did not lay down any synallagmatic (reciprocal) rules (see **1.8.1**), but merely imposed obligations *erga omnes* (*contractantes*) relating to acts to be performed by each contracting State within its own municipal territory, regardless of any direct interest or benefit that might accrue to other contracting States. Consequently, had the groups of individuals directly concerned not been authorized to denounce possible violations, no State would have been likely to protest.

However, the practical benefits of this important new right failed to reach their potential. Associations of workers and employers lodged very few complaints with the ILO, and minorities made scant use of their right of petition. Historical conditions were manifestly not yet propitious to a legal development that was in many respects far in advance of its time.

After the Second World War the ILO principles were reaffirmed and the machinery for implementing them was gradually strengthened. Treaties on minorities, which had collapsed long before the outbreak of the war, were replaced by a number of Conventions on human rights, which no longer protected groups of individuals as such, but rather single human beings. Some of them granted their beneficiaries the right to make States accountable for possible contraventions. Individuals consequently came to possess a certain measure of international status.

On close scrutiny, it appears that, as stressed above, the right to petition international bodies is conferred on individuals regardless of whether or not they are accordingly authorized by the national implementing legislation of those treaties. In other words, this right is granted to individuals *directly by international rules*, and exists whatever the content of national legislation. The right therefore is an *international right* proper.

However, this right is also subject to the following limitations.

(1) Individuals are given only a *procedural* right, namely, the right to initiate international proceedings before an international body, for the purpose of ascertaining whether the State complained of has violated the treaty to the detriment of the individuals. In addition, this right is usually limited to forwarding a complaint, for the complainant is not allowed to participate in international proceedings.

A notable exception is the European Convention on Human Rights of 1950, as revised in 1998 by virtue of Protocol 11 of 1994: in addition to instituting proceedings, individuals may submit memorials, take part in, and make representations at the hearings; after delivery of a judgment by a Chamber, they may request that the case be referred to the Grand Chamber if they consider that it raises a serious question of interpretation or application or a serious issue of general importance.

Normally the individual has no right to enforce or promote the enforcement of any international decision favourable to him (again, a limited deviation from this rule can be found in the practice relating to the European Convention). Once the international body has pronounced upon the alleged violation, the applicant is left in the hands of the accused State: cessation of, or reparation for, the wrongful act will substantially depend on its good will (however, under the European Convention on Human Rights the State is under the obligation to comply and in addition the Council of Europe Committee of Ministers has the power to monitor compliance with the Court's judgment).

(2) The right in question is only granted by *treaties* (or, in a few instances, by *international resolutions*). Consequently, it exists only with respect to certain well-defined matters (e.g. labour relations, human rights).

As to the ILO, Article 24 of its Constitution grants associations of workers or employers the right to submit complaints with respect to any ILO Convention ratified by the State complained of; in addition, a few resolutions adopted in 1950 provide for the right of associations of workers to petition an ILO body (the Committee on Trade Union Freedom of Association) for alleged violations of the ILO Conventions on the matter, regardless of whether the accused State has ratified them.

In the field of human rights, mention should be made of the Optional Protocol to the UN Covenant on Civil and Political Rights of 1966, the Convention on the Elimination of Racial Discrimination of 1965 (Article 14), as well as of two procedures set up by ECOSOC in 1967 and 1970 respectively, whereby individuals or groups of individuals can submit 'communications' to certain human rights bodies (see **16.4.5(a)**). On the regional level, the most noteworthy treaty is the European Convention on Human Rights, referred to above. An Inter-American Convention on Human Rights was adopted in 1969, one of its provisions (Article 44) granting 'any person or group of persons or any non-governmental entity legally recognized in one or more member States' of the Organization of American States (OAS) the right to lodge with the Inter-American Commission on Human Rights petitions containing denunciations or complaints of violation of the Convention by a State party to it.

(3) Another limitation lies in the fact that not all States that are parties to the above treaties accept being made accountable to individuals (the European Convention on human rights being a notable exception).

To enable States opposed to the presence of individuals in the international community to ratify the treaties concerned without submitting to supervisory procedures set in motion by individuals, a special device has been resorted to: the authority of international bodies to consider individuals' petitions has been laid down in particular clauses of the treaties. Consequently, only those contracting States which *also* accept the clauses explicitly, submit to the control mechanisms.

(4) A further weakness is that the procedures individuals are authorized to initiate are quite different from those existing in domestic law. Three things in particular stand out. First, international bodies responsible for considering petitions are generally not judicial in character, although they often tend to behave in conformity with judicial rules. Second, often international proceedings are themselves quite rudimentary; in particular, there are notable limitations concerning the taking of evidence. Third, and even more important, the outcome of the procedure is not a judgment proper, but a fairly mild act, such as a report setting out the views of the international body, a recommendation, and the like: no legally binding decision is envisaged (again, the European and the Inter-American Conventions on human rights are important exceptions).

It is thus apparent that the role of individuals' international procedural rights is limited on many scores. In addition it is precarious, for it rests on the will of States. As soon as they decide to terminate the treaty or to repeal the international resolution granting procedural rights to individuals, these rights cease to exist in the international arena. Similarly, as soon as a State that has ratified one of the treaties in question withdraws its acceptance of the international bodies' authority to deal with complaints of individuals, the latter can no longer sue that State on the international plane.

Despite these deficiencies, the importance of individuals in relation to the right to petition international bodies directly should not be underestimated. It is not easy for States to deprive themselves of some of their sovereign prerogatives, such as their traditional right to exercise full control over individuals subject to their jurisdiction. Given the present structure of the world community and the fact that States are still the overlords, the limited status of individuals can be regarded as remarkable progress. In addition, individuals are granted the right to petition international organs irrespective of their nationality, whether they be citizens of the State complained of, or nationals of other States (be they parties to the treaty or not), or even stateless persons. The right is therefore granted to physical persons *qua* human beings. No bond of nationality nor any other form of allegiance is taken into account. This in itself represents a momentous advance.

Furthermore, in a great many cases where States have accepted the authority of international bodies to consider complaints of individuals, they have eventually come to respect the decisions by which those bodies have determined violations. In other words, international techniques of supervision set in motion by physical persons or non-governmental groups have indeed proved effective. This is hardly surprising. Once a State has taken the serious and momentous step of accepting the jurisdiction of international bodies acting at the request of individuals, it does not find it too difficult to attend to the decisions of those bodies and, if found guilty of violations, to take all the necessary measures for terminating a breach, or paying compensation to the victims.

All things considered, the existing international systems for protecting human rights that depend on the initiative of the very beneficiaries of the rights in question are no less effective than other international devices for ensuring compliance with international law. One should therefore not be discouraged by the paucity of international mechanisms based on individuals' petitions. Like all international instruments denoting a bold advance, treaties granting procedural rights to human beings are destined to be fruitful in the long run.

4.5.3 THE LEGAL STATUS OF INDIVIDUALS IN INTERNATIONAL LAW

In sum, in contemporary international law individuals possess international legal status. They have a few *obligations*, deriving from customary international law. In addition, *procedural rights* enure to the benefit of individuals, not *vis-à-vis* all States, but only towards the group of States that have concluded treaties, or the international organizations that have adopted resolutions, envisaging such rights. Clearly, the international legal status of individuals is unique: they have a *lopsided position* in the international community. As far as their obligations are concerned, they are associated with all the other members of the international community; in contrast, they do not possess rights in relation to all members of that community. Plainly, all States are willing to demand of individuals respect for some fundamental values, while they are less prepared to associate them to their international dealings, let alone to grant them the power to sue States before international bodies. To differentiate the position of individulas from that of States, it can be maintained that while States have international legal personality proper, individuals possess a *limited* locus standi *in international law*. Furthermore, unlike States, individuals possess a limited array of rights and obligations; on this score, one can speak of a *limited legal capacity* (in this respect, they can be put on the same footing as other non-State international subjects: insurgents, international organizations, and national liberation movements).

5

THE FUNDAMENTAL PRINCIPLES GOVERNING INTERNATIONAL RELATIONS

5.1 INTRODUCTION

Most States have written constitutions that lay down the fundamental principles regulating social intercourse. Principles are the pinnacle of the legal system and are intended to serve as basic guidelines for the life of the whole community. Besides imposing general obligations, they also set out the policy lines and the basic goals of State agencies. Furthermore, they can be drawn upon for the construction of legal provisions, in case rules on interpretation prove insufficient.

The position is different in the world community. When this community came into existence, no State or other authority set forth any fundamental principles for regulating international dealings: no member State had enough power to impose standards of behaviour on all other members. A body of law gradually evolved under the impulse of convergent interests and exigencies of States, but no general, overarching principle was agreed upon. However, the increase in the corpus of rules by the gradual accretion of new norms made it clear that States spontaneously and almost unwittingly based their lawmaking on a few fundamental postulates from which they drew inspiration. Close scrutiny of the legal standards emerging in the first stages of development of the international community shows that States substantially acted upon at least three *postulates*: freedom, equality, and effectiveness. They differ from the general principles of national legal systems, which are legally binding. The three postulates are merely legal constructs reached through an inductive process based on generalization of some of the distinguishing traits of international rules. Through such a theoretical process, the conclusion can be reached that most international rules grant a wide sphere of action to States; proclaim, or start from the assumption of, the legal equality of States; and tend to legitimize situations which have acquired de facto force.[1]

The three postulates are clearly the synthesis of what could be concisely defined as the 'laissez-faire approach' of classical international law. Under this approach, all States are equally free to do what they like provided they abide by certain 'rules of the game'. Moreover, if in the exercise of this almost unfettered freedom, they bring about new situations by force, the law gives its blessing to these situations.

The adoption of the UN Charter in 1945 heralded a very significant change: the draftsmen laid down in Article 2 a set of fundamental principles by which all the members of the UN were to abide. They were: sovereign equality of all UN Members; peaceful settlement of disputes; prohibition of the threat or use of force. Thus, an international treaty of overriding importance set forth the fundamental standards governing State action and established the main goals of international institutions. This new state of affairs was the direct consequence of the shake-up in the world community brought about by the Second World War, in particular of the keen desire of all States to lay the foundations of an international system more conducive to peace and justice. However, in spite of the great impact of the Charter principles on the evolution of the international community, it gradually emerged in the 1960s that they were too loose and did not meet the demands of new States. Indeed, far-reaching changes had taken place in the international community in the aftermath of the Second World War as a result of the demise of colonialism and the spread of the socialist State model. More particularly, numerous new members had joined the world community whose political outlook differed substantially from that of older States.

Socialist and developing countries thus initiated a process of revision that involved the expansion and updating of the Charter principles, with a view to turning them into standards of universal value. Both groups of countries were motivated by two basic factors. On the one hand, they were keen to inject their own basic demands into international law so as to make it more consonant with current international realities. On the other hand, they felt that, in order to satisfy the need for predictability and security underlying social relations, they had to discuss, negotiate, and agree upon the basic standards of conduct with the traditional members of the world community. The principles agreed upon in the 1960s and proclaimed in the UN 1970 Declaration on Friendly Relations (resolution 2625-XXV, adopted by consensus; not legally binding *per se*) were seven: in addition to those already laid down in the UN Charter (sovereign equality of member States of the UN, the ban on the threat or use of force, peaceful settlement of disputes, which were extended to all members of the international community), the ban on intervention in internal or external affairs of other States, the duty of co-operation, good faith, and the principle of equal rights and self-determination of peoples.

It should not be thought, however, that the mere fact of being included in the list proclaimed in the Declaration upgrades a standard of behaviour to the rank and status of a universal and fundamental principle. It also is necessary for the standard to be laid down in a set of norms of general import. Standards such as those on co-operation, or on good faith, as long as they are not enshrined in instruments elevating them to the rank of sweeping guidelines for the conduct of international subjects, may remain expressions of policy guidelines. By the same token, it is not true that only those principles laid down in the Declaration may make up the body of fundamental principles of international law. What is determinative of the matter is careful consideration of international practice: a wide range of factors (treaties; GA resolutions; declarations of States; statements by government representatives in the UN;

diplomatic practice, if any) must be taken into account when trying to determine whether certain international pronouncements have engendered a principle of universal scope and legally binding force.

In the present world community, even after the collapse of the Soviet Union and most other socialist countries, States are divided economically and politically and often their relations are beset with tensions. The principles therefore represent the fundamental set of standards on which States are not divided and which allow a modicum of relatively smooth international relations. They make up the apex of the whole body of international legislation. They constitute *overriding legal standards* that may be regarded as the *constitutional principles* of the international community.

5.2 THE SOVEREIGN EQUALITY OF STATES

5.2.1 GENERAL

Traditional international law was based on a set of rules protecting the sovereignty of States and establishing their formal equality in law. In 1945, while drafting the UN Charter, the 'founding fathers' proclaimed 'sovereign equality of all its Members' (Article 2.1) as one of the organization's principles. This formula was not adopted without opposition. The Belgian delegate to one of the Committees in the San Francisco Conference that drafted the Charter pointed out that 'the smaller States would regard it as somewhat ironical, in view of the striking inequalities evident in the Organization, to find at the head of the statement of principles a bold reference to the "sovereign equality" of all Members'.[2] By contrast, and for obvious reasons, neither the labours of the Special Committee on Friendly Relations (1962–70) nor the debates in the GA reveal any radical differences on this principle, so much so that it was reaffirmed in the 1970 Declaration along the lines of Article 2.1 of the Charter. However, in the Declaration, it was extended to *all* States, irrespective of their membership in the UN.

Of the various fundamental principles regulating international relations, this is unquestionably the only one on which there is unqualified agreement and which has the support of all groups of States, irrespective of ideologies, political leanings, and circumstances. It is safe to conclude that sovereign equality constitutes the linchpin of the whole body of international legal standards, the fundamental premise on which all international relations rest.

This being so, what is its present purport? The principle is an umbrella concept, covering various general rules, of which it provides a synthesis. Consequently, it can only be fully appreciated if these general rules are spelled out. As the principle embraces two logically distinct notions (sovereignty and legal equality), it makes sense to consider them separately.

5.2.2 SOVEREIGNTY

Sovereignty includes the following sweeping powers and rights.

(1) The power to wield authority over all the individuals living in the territory. This power might even be regarded as the quintessence of sovereignty. As a leading politician and publicist stated in 1923, the famous Cartesian dictum, if applied to States, should be set out as follows: '*iubeo, ergo sum*' (I command, hence I exist).[3]

(2) The power to freely use and dispose of the territory under the State's jurisdiction and perform all activities deemed necessary or beneficial to the population living there.

In 1921 the US Secretary of State Robert Lansing aptly synthesized, in *political* terms, the primary goal pursued by States in the exercise of this power, as follows: '[T]he chief object in the determination of the sovereignty to be exercised within a certain territory is national safety. National safety is as dominant in the life of a nation as self-preservation is in the life of an individual. It is even more so, as nations do not respond to the impulse of self-sacrifice'.[4]

(3) The right that no other State intrude in the State's territory (so-called *jus excludendi alios*, or the right to exclude others).

States have always vigorously protested and claimed compensation when foreign Sates have exercised on their territory public activities that had not been previously authorized. They have also reacted in this way when the public action on their territory had been performed secretly or by State agents allegedly acting as private individuals. This happened, for instance, in the following cases: in the *Salomon Jacob* case (in 1935 a German national was kidnapped in Switzerland by other Germans acting on behalf of Germany, and taken to Germany; Switzerland protested; in the end Mr Jacob was returned to Switzerland and a German civil servant was punished by the German authorities);[5] in the *Eichmann* case (in 1960 Eichmann was kidnapped by Israeli agents in Argentina posing as private individuals, and taken to Israel; Argentina, not content with the apology offered by Israel, took the case to the UN SC, which called upon Israel to pay adequate compensation);[6] in the *Argoud* case (in 1963 the French colonel Argoud was kidnapped in Germany by French agents and taken to France to stand trial; Germany protested and demanded the return of Argoud, adding that it was ready subsequently to extradite him to France; the French authorities claimed however that they were not accountable for the alleged kidnapping of Argoud adding that in any case it was not even certain that he had been kidnapped, for perhaps he had in fact returned to France voluntarily; Germany subsequently renounced its claim to the restitution of the French colonel).[7]

In other cases the doctrine of the inviolability of a State's territory was proclaimed with regard to actions performed publicly by foreign authorities. Thus, in 1921 a company of US soldiers, authorized by the US War Department to go into the territory of Mexico in pursuit of bandits, arrested a Mexican who had perpetrated a crime in Texas. The Mexican was brought to trial before a Texas court. On appeal, a US court held in *Dominguez* v. *State* that the US soldiers' 'entry of Mexico for the purpose of apprehending offenders would have been a violation of the law of nations in the absence of consent of the Mexican Government'. Since, however, that Government had given its consent, the apprehension of Dominguez had not been illegal and he could be tried in the USA.[8] However, in 1992 in *Alvarez-Machain* the US Supreme Court took a different stand. In 1990 a Mexican national had been kidnapped on Mexican territory and taken to the USA. A US District Court—before which Alvarez-Machain had been brought to trial for the alleged torture and murder of a US national in Mexico—found that US officials were responsible for the abduction, although they were not personally involved in it. The Court dismissed the indictment on the ground that it lacked jurisdiction since the abduction contravened the 1978 Extradition Treaty between the USA and Mexico, and ordered the respondent's repatriation. The Court of Appeals affirmed, holding that US jurisdiction was improper. The US Supreme Court held instead that US jurisdiction could be exercised, as the abduction was not contrary to the Extradition Treaty. It admitted that the respondent's abduction might be 'in violation of general international law principles' and that Mexico had 'protested the abduction through diplomatic notes'. It added however that 'the decision of whether the respondent should be returned to Mexico, as a matter outside of the Treaty, is a matter for the Executive Branch'. Hence a US court could lawfully try Alvarez-Machain.[9]

(4) The right to immunity for State representatives acting in their official capacity (so-called *functional immunity*). Acts performed by State officials in international relations must be imputed not to the individuals acting on behalf of the State, but to the State itself. Consequently individuals cannot be brought to trial and punished by foreign States for any official act, if such act happens to be contrary to international law (this rule emerged clearly in the well-known *McLeod* case).[10] They are exempt from the foreign substantive law for acts and transactions performed in their official capacity and may only be prosecuted and punished by their own national courts. However, as we shall see, this immunity may not cover international crimes (see *infra*, **12.2**), with the consequence that the relevant State official may be prosecuted and tried by the court of any State possessing jurisdiction over the crime, or by a competent international court. In addition there seems to have been emerging a trend towards subjecting foreign State officials to punitive measures that are hardly compatible with the right of each State to claim that any State official acting of its behalf be immune from both foreign jurisdiction and arrest: see the *Rainbow Warrior* case. [11]

(5) The right to immunity from the jurisdiction of foreign courts for acts or actions performed by the State in its sovereign capacity, and for execution measures taken against the use or planned use of public property or assets for the discharge of public functions. (The question, however, of defining these classes of acts or actions, or the public nature of assets, remains controversial.)

(6) The right to respect for life and property of the State's nationals and State officials abroad.

5.2.3 LEGAL EQUALITY

Legal equality implies that, formally speaking, no member of the international community can be placed at a disadvantage: all must be treated on the same footing. As de Vattel stated as early as 1758, 'a dwarf is as much a man as a giant; a small republic is no less a sovereign State than the most powerful kingdom'.[12] Consequently, possible legal hindrances or disabilities may be the result simply of factual circumstances (such as landlocked States; States without any natural and mineral resources and therefore heavily dependent on foreign aid). Alternatively, legal constraints, if any, are only valid if accepted, in full freedom, by the State concerned (an example is the status of a neutralized State, which entails a series of limitations on freedom of action in international relations; or the legal condition of member States of the UN other than the permanent members of the Security Council).

5.3 IMMUNITIES AND OTHER LIMITATIONS ON SOVEREIGNTY

State sovereignty is not unfettered. Many international rules restrict it. In addition to treaty rules, which of course vary from State to State, limitations are imposed upon State sovereignty by customary rules. They are the *natural legal consequence of the obligation to respect the sovereignty of other States*. We shall briefly consider the most important ones.

5.3.1 RIGHTS AND IMMUNITIES OF FOREIGN STATES

A State may not exercise its sovereign powers over, or otherwise interfere with, actions legally performed by foreign States on its territory. This legal inability stems from the general principle imposing respect for the independence and dignity of foreign States (*par in parem non habet imperium*, that is, equals have no jurisdiction over one another). More generally, a State may not carry out any of the following acts.

(1) Call to account on its own territory a foreign State official for acts performed in the exercise of his functions, except in the case of international crimes (as was recently restated by the ICTY Appeals Chamber in *Blaškić*).[13]

However, recently in the *Border Guards Prosecution* case the German Federal Supreme Court (*Bundesgerichtshof*) pronounced differently with regard to former members of the border guard of the German Democratic Republic (GDR), accused of 'unlawful homicide' (they had shot and injured persons attempting to escape to the West). The defendants had argued that they were acting as office holders by order, and in the interest, of a State (the GDR) and could accordingly not be called to account. In its decision of 2 November 1992 the Court held that the 'act of State doctrine' was not 'a general rule of international law' and that in the Federal Republic of Germany there was 'no binding rule that the effectiveness of foreign acts of State may not be reviewed by the courts'. It added that the defendants did not enjoy immunity from jurisdiction because they could not be treated as 'representatives of a foreign State for the simple reason that the GDR no longer exists'.[14]

(2) Interfere with foreign armed forces lawfully stationed on its territory (unless authorized by treaty rules or ad hoc consent).

(3) Perform coercive acts on board a foreign military or public ship or aircraft (for instance, it may not enforce the law there).

(4) Submit to the jurisdiction of their courts foreign States for acts performed in their sovereign capacity (the doctrine of the 'sovereign immunity of States'). These doctrines are grounded on a twofold rationale: first, States should not interfere with public acts of foreign sovereign States out of respect for their independence; second, generally speaking and with regard to both domestic decisions and decisions made by foreign countries, the judiciary should not interfere with the conduct of foreign policy, by either national or foreign governmental authorities, on the principle of separation of powers. It follows that it is not for courts, but for the organs responsible for foreign affairs, to take matters relating to foreign acts into their hands and use diplomatic channels to discuss, or argue over, them with the foreign State concerned.

These doctrines have been set out in many cases. For instance, in the celebrated *Underhill* v. *Hernandez* case, in 1897 a US court stated that 'Every sovereign State is bound to respect the independence of every other sovereign State, and the courts of one country cannot sit in judgment on the acts of the government of another done within its own territory'.[15] In *Buttes Gas and Oil Co.* v. *Hammer* the British House of Lords held that the transactions of foreign sovereign States 'are not issues upon which a municipal court can pass'.[16]

An important exception is made for acts performed *jure gestionis* or *jure privatorum*, that is, performed by a foreign State in a private capacity as a legal person subject to private law (a phenomenon that has acquired increasing importance since the First World War; particularly after the growing participation of Soviet authorities in commercial transactions, a practice that has also spread to all modern States).

That a foreign State can claim no immunity from suit in respect of ordinary commercial transactions, as distinct from acts of a governmental nature, was held by, among others, British courts in *Il Congreso del Partido*[17] and *Alcom Ltd* v. *Republic of Colombia*.[18] It should be noted that pursuant to Article 10 of the 1991 ILC Draft on Jurisdictional Immunities of States and their Property, States do not enjoy immunity from jurisdiction when they engage in a 'commercial transaction' with a foreign natural or legal person. Under Article 2(1)(c) of the Draft, 'commercial transaction' means: (a) any commercial contract or transaction for the sale of goods or supply of services; (b) any contract for a loan or other transaction of a financial nature, including any obligation of guarantee or of indemnity in respect of any such loan or transaction; (c) any other contract or transaction, of a commercial, industrial, trading or professional nature, but not including a contract of employment of persons.[19]

(5) Seize foreign State property or take any other measure of execution or preventive measure against the property of a foreign State intended for use for the discharge of public functions. In contrast, measures of constraint may be taken against property or assets destined for a private function, that is, intended for use for commercial purposes.

Thus, for instance, in 1992 the Italian Court of Cassation held that a possessory action could not be brought concerning property located in the US military base of Sigonella, Italy (an Italian national had rented some space for a beauty parlour within a building located in the military base; upon eviction by the US military authorities, he brought a suit against the USA before an Italian lower court; according to the Court of Cassation the organization of a military base and the protection of its security through strict regulation of access implies that the foreign State holding the base exercises sovereign powers there; in the case at issue Italian courts therefore lacked jurisdiction on the strength of the principle *par in parem non habet jurisdictionem*).[20] The same basic principle was upheld by the Italian Constitutional Court in 1992 in *Condor and Filvem* v. *Minister of Justice*, with regard to a writ of attachment concerning a Nigerian ship sought by Italian corporations.[21] The Swiss Federal Tribunal has taken the same approach.[22]

Normally courts have held that execution measures may be taken against bank accounts belonging to foreign States; however, in the case of accounts opened by foreign diplomatic missions, the courts of some States tend to hold that they are destined to accomplish public functions of the foreign State.

The German Constitutional Court took this stand in 1977 in *Philippine Embassy*[23], as did the House of Lords in 1984 in *Alcom Ltd* v. *Republic of Colombia*[24] and the Swiss Foreign Department (in a note of 28 February 1991, where mention is made of a 'presumption' that foreign embassies' bank accounts are used for public purposes and consequently enjoy immunity from execution).[25]

The Swiss Federal Tribunal held in 1960 that whenever accounts owned by a foreign State are not earmarked for a specific purpose, they may be the subject of enforcement measures such as attachment.[26]

5.3.2 IMMUNITIES OF DIPLOMATIC AGENTS

International customary law grants a host of privileges and immunities to diplomatic agents. They are laid down in the Vienna Convention on Diplomatic Relations, of 1961; most provisions of this Convention are to a large extent declaratory of customary law or have turned into general law. All these rules envisage two classes of privileges and immunities, which supplement the *functional* immunities diplomats enjoy as State officials for acts and transactions performed in their official capacity (see above, 5.2.2(4)). One class encompasses immunities that attach to the premises and assets used by the foreign State official for accomplishing his or her mission (these are immunities *relating to property*); the other class embraces immunities covering the personal activities of that official (*personal* immunities). These immunities are intended to shelter foreign officials from any interference with their private life that might jeopardize the accomplishment of their official function (traditionally the underlying rationale of these immunities was expressed with the dictum *ne impediatur legatio*, that is, they are granted in order to save the official mission from being hampered in its work).

In 1979, as a result of a claim against the Canadian military attaché in Rome for not paying the rent on his private dwelling in Rome, in *Russel* v. *S.r.l. Immobiliare Soblim* the Italian Constitutional Court was asked to establish whether the immunity from civil jurisdiction enjoyed by foreign diplomats was contrary to the constitutional principle of equality. The Court held that it was not, on the ground of the principle of speciality, and noted that the customary rule granting immunity to foreign diplomats for their private transactions 'sprang up not in order to bestow a personal privilege but for the purpose of assuring in all cases that the diplomat may fulfil his duties. Indeed, immunity from civil jurisdiction, although with some exceptions, became necessary precisely to guarantee complete independence in accomplishing the mission: *ne impediatur legatio*'.[27]

Personal immunities *differ* from functional immunities in various respects: (1) In contradistinction to the latter, they cover private acts and transactions. (2) They do not consist of exemptions from the substantive law of the receiving or host State, but only of exemption from the jurisdiction of their courts and enforcement of their enforcement agencies.[28] (3) They only apply in the relations between the sending and the receiving State (as well as towards the State through which a diplomatic agent is passing on his or her way to or from the receiving State). In contrast, the immunity enjoyed by the foreign State official for acts performed in his official capacity, besides being absolute (with the only exception relating to international crimes, see *infra*, 12.2), may be invoked towards *any other State*, that is, is *erga omnes*. (4) They cease with the cessation of the function (whereas functional immunities are permanent).

Among the privileges and immunities belonging to the first category the following stand out: (a) the premises of the foreign diplomatic mission are inviolable; consequently State officials of the local country may not enter them without the consent of the head of the mission. The area where the foreign mission is located is not subject to foreign sovereignty, that is, it is not foreign territory; rather, it is part of the territory of the local State, but the enforcement agencies of this State are not allowed to exercise their powers in that area, unless expressly authorized by the head of the foreign mission; (b) the property of the foreign diplomatic mission is immune from search, requisition, attachment, or execution; (c) the diplomatic bag as well as the use of a diplomatic courier and messages in code and cipher may not be violated.

Personal immunities include the following:

(1) Immunity from arrest and detention. If the diplomatic agent engages in criminal activity, the host State may notify the sending State that he or she is *persona non grata* (that is, a person unacceptable to the receiving State). In any such case, according to Article 9 of the Vienna Convention, 'the sending State shall as appropriate, either recall the person concerned or terminate his functions with the mission'; if that State refuses to do so or fails so to act 'within a reasonable period' the host State 'may refuse to recognize the person concerned as a member of the [diplomatic] mission'.

(2) Immunity from criminal jurisdiction.

(3) Immunity from the civil and administrative jurisdiction of the receiving State (except—under customary law as codified in Article 31 of the Vienna Convention— with regard to actions relating to: (a) private immoveable property located in the receiving State, 'unless he holds it on behalf of the sending State for the purposes of the mission'; (b) succession, 'in which the diplomatic agent is involved as an executor,

administrator, heir or legatee as private person and not on behalf of the sending State'; (c) 'any professional or commercial activity exercised by the diplomatic agent in the receiving State outside his official functions'; clearly in these three classes of actions, States have felt that it would have been unfair to exempt diplomats from the local jurisdiction, given that they deliberately engage in private activities or transactions not linked to their diplomatic functions. In addition, diplomatic agents are not exempt from administrative or civil proceedings whenever they voluntarily submit to jurisdiction; for instance, after initiating proceedings before a local court, thus waiving their right to immunity from jurisdiction, they may not invoke immunity in respect of a counterclaim directly connected with the principal claim, or in respect of an appeal).

(4) Inviolability of the diplomatic agent's private residence, papers, correspondence, and property.

(5) Exemption from all dues and taxes, personal or real, national, regional, or municipal (except for indirect taxes and other dues or taxes enumerated in Article 34(a)–(f) of the Vienna Convention).

However, the above immunities do not cover a diplomatic agent who has the *nationality* of the receiving State or '*permanent residence*' there (pursuant to Article 38.1 of the Vienna Convention, 'Except insofar as additional privileges and immunities may be granted by the receiving State, a diplomatic agent who is a national of or permanently resident in that State shall enjoy only immunity from jurisdiction, and inviolability, in respect of official acts performed in the exercise of his functions'). The rationale behind this exception is that otherwise he might be exempt from any jurisdiction and thus enjoy total unaccountability. This applies among other things to payment of taxes and dues. It also and *a fortiori* holds true for immunity from criminal jurisdiction.

The personal immunities and privileges normally applicable to diplomatic agents are also due to members of his or her family forming part of his or her household, if they are not nationals of the receiving State.

5.3.3 IMMUNITIES OF CONSULAR AGENTS

Consular agents are not diplomatic envoys: they are not in charge of transactions between two States. Rather, they perform activities designed to protect the commercial and other interests of the appointing State and in particular render assistance to nationals of that State (for instance, by giving them help and advice should they be arrested or detained in the host State, by communicating with nationals imprisoned by the local authorities, etc.). They also perform important notarial functions (for instance, by attesting and legalizing signatures, administering oaths for the purpose of evidence in trial proceedings, by concluding or registering marriages, by taking charge of wills of their own nationals, legalizing adoptions, registering births and deaths, etc.).

Customary rules on the legal status of consular agents were codified in the Vienna Convention of 1963. On account of the characteristics of their functions, consular agents do not enjoy *personal* immunities. They are only immune from criminal and civil jurisdiction for acts done in the official exercise of their consular functions (*functional* immunities). In addition, under Article 41.1 of the Vienna Convention, they are not 'liable to arrest or detention pending trial, except in the case of a grave crime and pursuant to a decision by the competent judicial authority'. Except in such a case, they may not be committed to prison and are not 'liable to any other form of restriction on their personal freedom save in execution of a judicial decision of final effect' (Article 41.2). Similarly, consular premises (the buildings where their activity is performed), as well as consular archives and documents are inviolable from search and seizure. Consular agents are exempt from taxation (Article 49 of the Vienna Convention) and from customs duties and inspection (Article 50).

5.3.4 IMMUNITIES OF HEADS OF STATES AND MEMBERS OF CABINET

Head of States, foreign ministers, and other members of cabinet on official mission abroad, in addition to immunity for official acts (functional immunity), enjoy privileges and immunities with regard to the premises where they perform their official transactions or live, and also their personal acts. There are differences in the legal literature about whether the aforementioned privileges and immunities conferred on diplomatic agents may be extended in their totality to this class of persons. The better view is that this extension is admitted by international law; case law bears out this proposition.[29] This conclusion has been based by national courts on a principle parallel to that applying to diplomats, namely *ne impediatur officium* (the need to protect the foreign senior official from possible interference in his or her official functions).[30]

It should be stressed again that, unlike acts performed by these persons in their official capacity, which are covered by functional immunity, the privileges and immunities we are discussing here either relate to property or are personal, and are intended to shelter the foreign State official from any undue interference by the host State in his or her private life, thereby jeopardizing his or her action as a foreign dignitary. However, they are only granted to senior State officials on an *official* visit. When they are on a private visit and are not travelling *incognito*, the host State is bound to afford them special protection; it may also grant them privileges and immunities out of comity, that is, politeness and good will; however, it is under no obligation to do so.

5.3.5 DURATION OF PRIVILEGES AND IMMUNITIES

As stated above, *functional* immunity does not cease with the cessation of the functions vested in the State official, as is confirmed by case law and State pronouncements, primarily concerning diplomatic agents.[31] In contrast, *personal* privileges and immunities terminate with the cessation of the mission. The rationale behind this international regulation was spelled out by the Paris Court in 1925 in *Laperdrix and Penquer* v. *Kouzouboff and Belin*, as follows: 'the principle of diplomatic immunity is set up in the interests of governments, not in that of diplomats; it cannot apply beyond the [diplomatic] mission . . . a contrary view would lead to creating to the benefit of diplomatic agents a sort of statute of limitations and an indefinite unaccountability'.[32] Thus, for instance, if an ambassador commits such an ordinary crime as the murder of his wife in the receiving State, that is the State to which he is accredited, he is immune there from criminal jurisdiction; however, if he goes back to that country after relinquishing his diplomatic position, he may be arrested and brought to trial.

The above proposition is clearly confirmed by State practice and case law, concerning instances where the diplomat had breached customs regulations[33] or the laws on explosives,[34] or committed rape,[35] or illegally parked, or refused to give his identity, and injured police officers,[36] or cases where criminal misconduct by a former foreign minister was at stake.[37]

However, the cessation of immunity does not coincide with the termination of his or her diplomatic functions in the host State. As the acting US Secretary of State Adee stated in 1908 in a note to the Brazilian Ambassador in the USA, 'the diplomatic immunity inherent in the persons of diplomatic agents extends for a reasonable time after the cessation of diplomatic functions in order that they may complete their arrangements to leave the country'.[38] This proposition has been borne out by case law,[39] and is codified in Article 39.2 of the Vienna Convention on Diplomatic Relations, whereby personal privileges and immunities 'cease at the moment when he [the diplomat] leaves the country, or on expiry of a reasonable period in which to do so, but shall subsist until that time, even in case of armed conflict'. Furthermore, the diplomatic agent enjoys immunity in the territory of third States while returning to his or her own country (see Article 40.1 of the Vienna Convention).

5.3.6 LIMITATIONS UPON A STATE'S TREATMENT OF FOREIGNERS AND INDIVIDUALS

Customary international rules on respect for human rights impose upon any State the obligation to respect the fundamental human rights of its own nationals, of foreigners residing or passing through its territory, as well as stateless persons. These rules do not provide detailed regulation of how a State must treat individuals. Such regulation can only be found in conventions such as the UN Covenant of Civil and Political Rights or the European Convention on Human Rights. Instead, customary rules, in addition to imposing certain obligations with regard to foreigners (for instance, they must be protected from unlawful attacks, they may not be subjected to military conscription, etc.), enjoin any State not to grossly and systematically infringe human rights (see 16.5).

5.4 NON-INTERVENTION IN THE INTERNAL OR EXTERNAL AFFAIRS OF OTHER STATES

5.4.1 GENERAL

The principle of non-intervention in the affairs of other States also belongs to the old pattern of the world community. Indeed, it constitutes one of the most significant tenets of the 'Grotian' model. Together with the principle of sovereign equality it is designed to ensure that each State respects the fundamental prerogatives of the other members of the community.

Since the period of classical international law the principle has been concretely enshrined in a few specific customary rules.

The first one is the rule prohibiting a State from interfering in the internal organization of a foreign State. For instance, one State may not decide which organ of a foreign State is competent to perform a certain act, nor may it enjoin a foreign State agent to discharge certain activities or accomplish a certain act. Another rule prohibits States from encroaching upon the internal affairs of other States. Thus, for instance, a State is not allowed to bring pressure to bear on *specific national bodies* of other countries (the legislature, enforcement agencies, or the judiciary), nor may it interfere in the relations between foreign government authorities and their own nationals. Yet another rule enjoins States to refrain from instigating, organizing, or officially supporting the organization on their territory of activities prejudicial to foreign countries. It should, however, be pointed out that this rule is not as sweeping as it may appear. For instance, it does not go so far as to prohibit any kind of subversive activity; in particular, it does not prohibit subversive activity against foreign States carried out by private persons without State involvement.

Measures to enforce compliance with the obligation imposed by this rule include: expulsion of foreigners who take advantage of the asylum granted to them to conspire against foreign countries; imposition of restrictions on the traffic of arms and ammunitions; prohibition against the creation of armed bands and the supply of the means of disturbing the domestic order of foreign countries.

Another customary rule has a more specific purport, in that it deals only with civil strife: it stipulates that whenever a civil war breaks out in a foreign country, States are duty-bound to refrain from assisting insurgents, unless they qualify for the status of national liberation movements (see **4.1** and **4**).

These rules are still in force. However, in the period before 1945, States did not have to comply with these rules if they considered that their interests overrode the rules. If a State did consider its interests to be paramount, it was legally authorized to disregard the rules in question and intervene by force, or by the threat of force, in the domestic or external affairs of another State, and impose a certain course of action. Consequently, the protection afforded by the aforementioned rules was precarious.

In the period after the First World War, and particularly in the years following the Second World War, instead of losing its significance and impact, the principle acquired new vigour. At present, a number of States, notably such States as Cuba and China, insist strongly on upholding it. Three major developments brought new life and authority to the principle. The first was the introduction of far-reaching legal restraints on the use or threat of force (which conferred on the principle of non-intervention a less precarious existence and a more clear-cut delimitation). The second was the drive towards international co-operation, which entailed the expansion of intergovernmental organizations and increasing opportunities both for these organizations and for States to meddle with the interests of other States. This development brought about the correlative need for States to define more clearly the areas where they were entitled to remain immune from outside interference. The third development was the spread of human rights doctrines, with the ensuing possibility for States and individuals to pressure other States to comply with human rights standards.

The principle of non-intervention thus acquired the fundamental value of a solid and indispensable 'bridge' between the traditional, sovereignty-orientated structure of the international community and the 'new' attitude of States, based on more intense social intercourse and closer co-operation. The principle currently plays the role of a necessary shield behind which States can shelter in the knowledge that more intense international relations will not affect their most vital and delicate domestic interests.

5.4.2 NEW FORMS OF INTERVENTION

The question arises of whether the ban on interference in the internal affairs of other States also embraces those interventions that do not take the form of sending, or threatening to send, military aircraft and warships, but include: economic pressure or even economic coercion; bringing about political destabilization; instigating, fomenting, and financing unrest in a foreign country. In addition, one may wonder whether international law bans the resort by powerful States to more subtle forms of undue interference, such as radio propaganda, economic boycott, withholding economic assistance, or influencing international monetary and financial institutions with a view to stifling weak States economically. Arguably, *economic force* is proscribed when used as a means of compelling a State to adopt a course of action contrary to its will and advantageous to the coercive State.

Not every form of economic pressure, be it direct or effected through international economic institutions, can be regarded as forbidden. Thus, for instance, the decision simply to withhold economic assistance to developing countries or the financing of international institutions promoting development, does not amount to an infringement of the principle, if this decision is warranted by serious difficulties on the part of the granting State or by a change in its policy that is motivated exclusively by domestic considerations. Only those economic measures designed 'to coerce another State in order to obtain from it the subordination of the exercise of its sovereign rights and to secure from it advantages of any kind' (paragraph 2 of Principle III of the UN Declaration of 1970) may be regarded as running counter to the principle on non-interference in internal affairs.

It is not easy to ascertain whether the conditions outlined above are fulfilled in specific cases: often the nexus between economic measures and the intended subjugation of the will of another State is impalpable. Frequently States are not explicit about making economic action conditional on the behaviour of the recipient. The conditioning is not stated in so many words, but can only be inferred from a host of clues. In these instances it is difficult to demonstrate that undue economic coercion has been effected. However, the difficulty of verifying compliance with the principle does not detract from its importance.

Traditional international law did not afford any protection against these forms of intervention. International practice was very confused, if only because—as pointed out above—until the gradual emergence of prohibitions on the use or threat of force, States could easily disregard the duty of non-intervention. In the 1960s and 1970s the aforementioned classes of encroachment on the freedom of States and peoples aroused the strong opposition of developing and socialist countries. Western countries, however, flatly rebuffed the claims put forward by other States. They repeatedly asserted that present international law only prohibits intervention by force or by the threat of force ('dictatorial intervention'). They also maintained that States are and should continue to be free to influence the policies and actions of other countries. Furthermore, they rejected the idea of extending any ban on intervention so as to benefit peoples. Other States consistently opposed these views. The conclusion is warranted that no general rule crystallized banning these instances of intervention.

However, there was at least one point on which there emerged full agreement among States: the need to extend the traditional prohibition of 'indirect armed aggression' (14.4.1(d)) to cover any 'toleration' by States of subversive activities against other States organized in the territories of the former.

5.5 PROHIBITION OF THE THREAT OR USE OF FORCE

The prohibition of the threat or use of force was first laid down in the UN Charter (Article 2.4). That this principle was proclaimed and strongly emphasized in 1945 is hardly surprising. As I pointed out above (2.5.1–2), after 1945 peace became the supreme goal of the world community and States decided to agree upon sweeping self-limitations of their sovereign prerogatives in the form of a mutual obligation to refrain from using or threatening force. The need to avert armed conflict likely to endanger the very survival of mankind prompted the international community to take a step that would have been unthinkable a few years before.

Let us briefly consider Article 2.4. Both the textual and logical interpretation of this Article and its drafting history warrant the following propositions:

First, the ban on force is an 'absolute all-inclusive prohibition', as was stated by the US delegate at San Francisco.[40] The threat or use of force was banned in all circumstances except for those provided for in: Chapter VII (collective enforcement measures); Article 51 (self-defence); Article 53 (enforcement action by regional agencies); and in other provisions (Articles 106 and 107, which have since become obsolete).

Second, only military force was proscribed. A Brazilian amendment calculated to prohibit also 'the threat or use of economic measures in any manner inconsistent with the purposes of the UN' was rejected,[41] for reasons which unfortunately were not reported.

Third, only the threat or use of force in inter-State relations was banned. Consequently, member States were by implication allowed to resort to forcible measures to suppress insurgents on their own territory, or to fight against liberation movements struggling for independence in territories subject to colonial domination—territories considered by colonial powers as an integral part of their own territory inasmuch as they were under their exclusive authority.

After 1945 the ban in Article 2.4 was gradually transformed into a general rule of international law, binding on non-member States as well.

A number of developments subsequently attracted the attention of socialist and Afro-Asian countries.

(1) The spread of wars of national liberation in colonial territories as well as in territories under foreign occupation (for instance, the Arab territories occupied by Israel following the war of 1967), or under racist regimes (for example, in Namibia and South Africa as well as in Rhodesia during the period 1965–80). Under existing international law the Powers against which liberation wars were being waged were authorized to use force to quell liberation movements, and this seemed to socialist and developing countries a negative feature of the Charter.

(2) Powerful States increasingly used economic coercion to subjugate developing countries, which easily fell prey to economic pressure. The lack of any rule prohibiting such behaviour was profoundly resented by the Third World, which managed to gain the support of socialist States in order to change the existing legal regulation.

(3) In some instances States resorted to war and managed to conquer foreign territory without there being any effective sanction on the part of the international community capable of bringing about the evacuation of the occupied territory (for example, the Arab territories occupied by Israel in 1967 and later on in 1973). Thus, the need arose at least to specify that conquest could not legalize the annexation of territory.

The clash between the demands of the West, sometimes backed up by a few of the Latin American States, and those of socialist and developing countries, resulted in lengthy and tiresome discussions within the UN. The ensuing compromise was set forth in the 1970 Declaration on Friendly Relations and in the Declaration on the Definition of Aggression of 1974. None of the competing groups gained the upper

hand. Rather, an agreement was reached which, to some extent, reconciled the opposing interests or gave pride of place to the demands of one or more groups of States in
a specific area while giving priority to the exigencies of the other group or groups in
another area.

The resulting situation can be summed up as follows:

(1) The threat or use of armed force must not be resorted to against (a) *States* or
(b) *peoples* having a representative organization (that is, national liberation movements) and falling within one of the categories entitled to self-determination (colonial peoples, peoples under foreign occupation or under racist regimes).

(2) As the ICJ held in 1986 in *Nicaragua*, it is necessary to distinguish 'the most
grave forms of the use of force (those constituting an armed attack) from other less
grave forms'. For instance, according to the Court, 'assistance to rebels in the form of
the provision of weapons or logistical or other support' may be regarded as a threat or
use of force (or amount to prohibited intervention in the internal or external affairs of
other States). However, it does not amount to 'armed attack'.[42] It follows that a State
that is the victim of the threat or use of force not amounting to an 'armed attack' is
not entitled to the right of individual or collective self-defence (see *infra* **14.4.1**).

(3) Force must not be used for the purpose of forestalling an imminent attack by
another State (that is, an attack which is presumed to be imminent). This is the
concept of *anticipatory self-defence* (see **14.4.1(c)**).

(4) Force in self-defence must not be used to repel an indirect armed aggression
(**14.4.1(d)**), although it might be admitted as an immediate armed reaction to a
minor use of force (see **14.4.4**).

(5) Territory belonging to a particular State cannot be 'the object of *acquisition* by
another State resulting from the threat or the use of force' (1970 Declaration, principle I, paragraph 10). This means that conquest does not transfer a legal title of
sovereignty, even if it is followed by de facto occupation, and assertion of authority,
over the territory. Furthermore, all other States are enjoined to withhold recognition
of the territorial expansion resulting from the threat or use of force.

(6) Extreme forms of *economic coercion* amounting to a threat to the peace are
prohibited (see **5.4.2**).

The principle in question should, of course, be considered in the light of the general
rules which exceptionally allow the use of force (see **14.4**). It is precisely the need for
the general principle prohibiting force to be supplemented by these exceptional rules
that constitutes its 'Achilles' heel'. Indeed, it is by dint of a broad interpretation or
even by bypassing those rules that various States—particularly the Great Powers or
the countries certain of their support—have endeavoured to dodge the principle,
thereby also abusing the exceptions laid down in the rules (see **Chapter 14**).

5.6 PEACEFUL SETTLEMENT OF DISPUTES

The UN Charter obliges member States to settle their international disputes peacefully (Article 2.3) so as generally to prevent peace and security, as well as justice, being imperilled. Chapter VI strengthens this obligation with regard to disputes likely to endanger the maintenance of peace and security. The SC may call upon parties to such disputes to settle them by peaceful means (or may 'investigate' the dispute or even make recommendations to the parties with regard to both the choice of the procedure and the settlement of the dispute).

This obligation has gradually been extended to all States as a logical corollary of the formation of a customary ban on the use of force. A customary rule has evolved on the matter, as evinced by the UN Declaration on Friendly Relations of 1970 (GA res. 2625-XXV) and the Manila Declaration on the Peaceful Settlement of Disputes of 1982 (GA res. 37/10). The ICJ authoritatively confirmed the principle in *Nicaragua.* The Court insisted that this principle is 'complementary' to the principles of a prohibitive nature such as that banning the use of force, and that 'respect for [the principle] is essential in the world today'. The Court went on to specify that the principle 'has also the status of customary law'.[43]

What exactly are the scope and the purport of the principle? First, States are mandated to *bona fide* endeavour to resolve their disputes peacefully. To this end, they must try the various means and procedures available (negotiation, mediation, conciliation, resort to arbitral or judicial mechanisms, etc.; see **10.2**, **10.3** and **10.6**). However, they are not bound to choose a particular means of settlement (unless this is envisaged in a treaty): as the PCIJ held in its Advisory Opinion in *Status of Eastern Carelia,*[44] States may not be obliged to submit a dispute to a particular mechanism without their consent. Second, in the event of failure to reach a solution by one of the means of dispute settlement just mentioned, States are legally bound 'to continue to seek a settlement of the dispute by other peaceful means agreed upon by them' (paragraph 3 of Principle II of the 1970 UN Declaration; paragraph 7 of the Manila Declaration). Third, while trying to settle the dispute peacefully, States must 'refrain from any action which may aggravate the situation so as to endanger the maintenance of international peace and security' (paragraph 4 of Principle II of the 1970 Declaration; paragraph 8 of the Manila Declaration).

Consequently, the principle is breached whenever a State wilfully and *mala fide* refuses to resort to negotiations or other peaceful means or procedures proposed by the counter-party; or, after the failure of a particular means or procedure agreed upon by the contending parties (for example, mediation), refuses to continue to seek a settlement; or takes action that is likely to aggravate the dispute or jeopardize peace. More generally, the principle is breached when a party manifestly engages in delaying tactics or in any other way shows that in actual fact it is not prepared to settle the matter peacefully.

If a party to the dispute considers that the counter-party has contravened the principle and that the dispute has important political overtones or implications, it may resort to an appropriate international body (at either the regional or universal level). Should such resort prove of no avail or unsatisfactory, the State can take counter-measures, subject to the stringent conditions provided for on the matter (see *infra* **11.3.1(a)**). One should bear in mind that one of the purposes of peaceful counter-measures may be to impel the counter-party to reach an amicable settlement of the dispute.

5.7 RESPECT FOR HUMAN RIGHTS

Unlike the principles on sovereignty and non-intervention—a typical expression of the Grotian model, to which dissensions in the world today have given a new lease of life—the principle imposing respect for human rights, like the ban on the threat or use of force, is typical of a new stage of development in the international community following the Second World War. It is one of the most significant aspects of the post-war phase: in a sense it is, in fact, competing—if not at loggerheads—with the traditional principles of respect for the sovereign equality of States and of non-interference in the domestic affairs of other States. As we shall see (**5.9**), it is for this very reason that the principle imposing respect for human rights is so difficult to co-ordinate with the other two.

The adoption of the UN Charter and the subsequent enactment of such fundamental international instruments as the Universal Declaration of 1948 and the two Covenants on Human Rights of 1966 had such an impact on the international community that no State currently challenges the concept that human rights must be respected everywhere in the world. As a result of, on the one hand, those general texts and a host of specific conventions and international resolutions, and, on the other hand, the consistent practice of international bodies, a general principle has gradually emerged prohibiting gross and large-scale violations of basic human rights and fundamental freedoms. States have gradually come to accept the idea that massive infringements of basic human rights are reprehensible; they make the delinquent State accountable to the whole international community. In contrast, isolated and sporadic instances of violation are not necessarily of *general* international concern.

The principle at issue does not impose on States the obligation to abide by specific regulations on human rights. Rather it requires States to refrain from seriously and repeatedly infringing a basic right (for example, the right not to be subjected to torture; or the right to a fair trial; or freedom from arbitrary arrest), and from trampling upon a whole series of rights (for instance, the fundamental civil and political rights, or social, economic, and cultural rights).

As in the case of other general principles, respect for human rights derives its most solid guarantee from the UN system. Legally, any State whatsoever is entitled to insist that the offending party discontinue its violations (and make reparations, as the case may require). However, for a number of historical, political, and diplomatic reasons States eschew bilateral action and prefer to bring the issue of gross disregard for human rights before international organizations, chiefly the UN. This practice is, to some extent, a healthy phenomenon, for in the UN a less partial examination of allegations can be made, and 'collective sanctions' (11.4.1–2) may be resorted to, which tend to be more effective than individual (peaceful) counter-measures.

5.8 SELF-DETERMINATION OF PEOPLES

5.8.1 HOW THE PRINCIPLE EVOLVED IN THE WORLD COMMUNITY

It may be fitting to trace the gradual emergence of self-determination as a general principle.

Propounded by the French Revolution and then strongly supported, albeit in differing versions, by such statesmen as Lenin and Wilson, self-determination was intended—at the international level—to brush aside the old, State-oriented approach prevailing in international dealings. Under this old approach, the world community consisted of potentates: the sovereign States, each of them primarily concerned with the interests of its own political élite. Relations between international subjects in actual fact amounted to relations between ruling groups that took into account the interests of their nationals only when these were threatened by foreign Powers, and only so long as the protection of those interests was of some relevance to the ruling élite concerned. By contrast, self-determination meant that peoples and nations were to have a say in international dealings: sovereign Powers could no longer freely dispose of them, for example by ceding or annexing territories without paying any regard to the wishes of the populations concerned, through plebiscites or referendums. Peoples were also to have a say in the conduct of domestic and foreign business; self-determination was advocated as a democratic principle calling for the consent of the governed in any sovereign State: the people should always have the right freely to choose their own rulers. Furthermore, peoples and nations were entitled to be free from any external oppression, chiefly in the form of colonial rule.

Clearly, this set of principles was directed toward undermining the very core of the traditional principles on which international society had rested since its inception: dynastic legitimation of power, despotism (albeit in increasingly attenuated forms), and agreements between rulers only. Self-determination suddenly introduced a new standard for judging the legitimacy of power in the international setting: respect for the wishes and aspirations of peoples and nations. This struck at the very heart of the traditional arrangements. Self-determination also eroded one of the basic postulates of the traditional international community: territorial sovereignty. Territorial sovereignty meant that every international subject was to pay full respect to any other Power wielding authority over a territory and the population living there, regardless of both how it had acquired its territorial title (whether by conquest, hereditary succession, or barter with another sovereign ruler), and in particular the aspirations of the populations concerned.

By promoting the formation of international entities based on the free wishes of the populations concerned, self-determination delivered a lethal blow to multinational empires. By the same token, it sounded the death knell for colonial rule. In short, the redistribution of power in the international community, advocated by self-determination, introduced a highly dynamic factor of change that deeply undermined the status quo. The US Secretary of State, R. Lansing, was therefore right when in 1919 he wrote that the 'phrase so deeply cherished and so warmly advocated by President Wilson was simply loaded with dynamite' and went on to point out that the 'fixity of national boundaries and of national allegiance, and political stability would disappear if this principle was uniformly applied'.[45] Further, he rightly raised some crucial questions:

'What effect will it have on the Irish, the Indians, the Egyptians, and the nationalists among the Boers? Will it not breed discontent, disorder and rebellion? Will not the Mohammedans of Syria and Palestine and possibly of Morocco and Tripoli rely on it? How can it be harmonized with Zionism, to which the President is practically committed?'[46]

5.8.2 LEGAL SCOPE OF THE PRINCIPLE

Like that on sovereign equality, this principle relates to international subjects. In particular, it touches upon both the inner structure and the legal legitimation of subjects on the international plane. However, unlike sovereign equality, the principle of self-determination strikingly reflects the new trends emerging in the world community. In addition, it has a markedly ideological matrix (this is why its transformation into a legal standard of behaviour has been a gradual process and has elicited strong opposition from many Western countries).

Self-determination appears firmly entrenched in the corpus of international law in only three areas: as an *anti-colonialist standard*, as a *ban on foreign military occupation*, and as a requirement that all *racial groups be given full access to government*. Peoples under colonial domination have the right to *external* self-determination, that is, to opt for the establishment of a sovereign State, or the free association or integration with an independent State, or 'the emergence into any other political status freely determined by the people' (1970 UN Declaration on Friendly Relations). The same right accrues to peoples subjected to foreign military occupation, after their obtaining or recovering independence. Any racial group denied full access to government in a sovereign State is entitled to either *external* self-determination (independence, integration into an existing State, etc.) or even *internal* self-determination (that is, in the words of the Supreme Court of Canada in *Reference re Secession of Quebec*, the 'pursuit of its political, economic, social and cultural development within the framework of an existing State').[47]

More specifically, there now exists in the body of international law both a *general principle*, serving as an overarching guideline, and a set of specific *customary rules* dealing with individual issues (the rule on the external self-determination of colonial peoples and peoples under foreign occupation; the rule on the internal self-determination of racial groups that have been subject to discrimination in being denied equal access to government). These rules specify, with regard to certain areas, the general principle. The role of the principle is to cast light on borderline situations and to serve as a general standard for the interpretation of both customary and treaty law. The principle therefore transcends, and gives unity to, the customary rules. It sets out the *essence* of self-determination. As the ICJ put it in the *Western Sahara* case, self-determination 'requires a free and genuine expression of the will of the peoples concerned'.[48] In other words, the principle lays down the *method* by which States must reach decisions concerning peoples: by heeding their freely expressed will. In contrast, the principle points neither to the various specific areas in which self-determination should apply, nor to the final goal of self-determination (internal self-government, independent statehood, association with or integration into another State, or the free choice of any other political status). Alongside this body of customary norms, there exists an important piece of international legislation: Article 1, common to the two 1966 UN Covenants on Human Rights. It essentially confers on the peoples of all the contracting parties the right to internal self-determination.

5.8.3 RIGHTS AND OBLIGATIONS

What are the rights and obligations deriving from the principle? In a nutshell, it can be said that, first, States which oppress peoples falling within one of the three categories are duty-bound to allow the free exercise of self-determination. In particular they are enjoined not to deny this right forcibly. Second, the peoples entitled to self-determination have a legal right in relation to the oppressor State, as well as a host of rights and claims in regard to other States (chiefly, the claim that third States must refrain from sending troops to assist the State denying self-determination; see also 4.3). Lastly, third States are legally authorized to support peoples entitled to self-determination, by granting them any assistance short of dispatching armed troops. Conversely, they must refrain from aiding and abetting oppressor States. Furthermore, they are entitled to claim respect for the principle from States denying self-determination. If self-determination is forcibly denied they can bring the question before the competent UN bodies and even resort to peaceful counter-measures, particularly if there has been a previous finding by the UN to the effect that the right at issue is illegally infringed.

Thus, in the area of the use of force, self-determination has had a twofold impact. On the one hand, it has *extended* the general ban on force: it has brought about the prohibition of resort to force by States against racial groups in their territory who are denied equal access to government. On the other hand, self-determination has resulted in granting to liberation movements a legal licence to use force for the purpose of reacting to the forcible denial of self-determination by a colonial State, an occupying Power, or a State refusing a racial group equal access to government (this licence amounts to a *derogation* from the customary ban on the use of force, referred to above: **5.4**). Self-determination—in addition to bringing about important changes in the area of humanitarian law of armed conflict (see **15.5–6**)—has also had a significant impact on the most traditional segment of international law, namely the acquisition, transfer, and loss of title over territory. It has cast doubt on traditional legal titles such as colonial conquest and acquisition by cession of sovereignty over overseas territories. In addition, as a result of the principle of self-determination, it is no longer possible for valid legal title to be acquired where territories are annexed in breach of self-determination. Self-determination also prevents States from regarding as *terra nullius* territories inhabited by organized aggregates lacking the hallmarks of State authority, in cases where, for example, the sovereign State previously wielding authority over a territory has abandoned that territory. Finally, self-determination renders null and void treaties providing for the transfer of territories where such treaties do not include provision for any prior and genuine consultation of the population involved (on the peremptory nature of the principle, see *infra*, **5.8**).

5.8.4 LIMITS OF THE PRINCIPLE

The acceptance of the principle into the realm of law has been *selective* and *limited* in many respects. In particular, current international law on self-determination is *blind to the demands of ethnic groups and national, religious, cultural, or linguistic minorities.* Not only does international law refrain from granting any right of internal or external self-determination to these groups, but it also fails to provide any alternative remedy *of a general character* to the present plight of so many of them. Clearly, political stability and the territorial integrity of States are important values that States do not accept being disregarded. To them, indiscriminately granting the right to self-determination to all ethnic groups would pose a serious threat to peace and bring about the fragmentation of States into a myriad of entities unable to survive. It should not come as a surprise that it is precisely those States that benefited from the principle of self-determination when they liberated themselves from colonial rule, which are now among the staunchest supporters of a strict interpretation of self-determination. It would seem that most member States of the world community have heeded the warning issued as early as 1952 by a leading champion of human rights, Eleanor Roosevelt, who, speaking as a US delegate, stated that: 'Just as the concept of individual human liberty carried to its logical extreme would mean anarchy, so the principle of self-determination given unrestricted application could result in chaos'.[49]

5.9 DISTINGUISHING TRAITS OF THE FUNDAMENTAL PRINCIPLES

Now that the various principles have been discussed separately we can sum up their common features.

First, the principles reflecting the 'classical' pattern of the world community, that is the traditional structure based on equality of States and marked by strong individualism, were not only standards that underpinned most rules of the international community and expressed the thrust of that body of law. They were also enshrined in general rules that attracted unanimous support and spelled out, in a fairly clear manner, the conduct of States in their international dealings. In contrast, the new principles are the expression and the result of conflicting views of States on matters of crucial importance. At present States, when they cannot agree upon definite and specific standards of behaviour because of their principled, opposing attitudes, but they need nevertheless some sort of basic guidelines for their conduct, tend to fall back on principles. These principles, being general, loose, and multifaceted, lend themselves to various and even contradictory applications, and in addition are susceptible to being manipulated and used for conflicting purposes. In this respect modern principles are a typical expression of the present world community, whereas in the old community—relatively homogeneous and less conflictual—fairly well-defined and unanimously supported principles tended to prevail, in addition of course to treaty and customary rules.

Second, these principles, with the exception of that on the sovereign equality of States, do not address themselves to States solely, but are binding on other international legal subjects as well: insurgents, peoples represented by liberation movements, and international organizations. All the legal entities operating in the international community must abide by them.

Third, the rights and claims deriving from the principles accrue to all members of the international community, all of which are entitled to exact observance by other international subjects (that is, they possess rights *erga omnes* in addition to obligations *erga omnes*). In addition, all new principles (hence not those on sovereign equality and non-intervention) confer *community rights*. In other words, the new principles legally entitle any relevant international subject (States and peoples endowed with a representative organization) to claim respect for the principles from any other international subject, whether or not the alleged non-compliance has materially damaged the former subject.

Thus, for instance, any State can claim respect for the principle on the use of force by any other State and, in case of violation, it is entitled to insist on its cessation or, if need be, reparation of the international offence. Similarly, the principle on respect for human rights grants to all members of the community the right to demand full compliance and, in the case of gross and large-scale infringements, to request their cessation (and the punishment of the responsible authorities, if allowed by the circumstances).

Fourth, the principles characteristic of the Kantian model belong to the category of peremptory rules or *jus cogens*, that is to say, to those principles and rules accepted and recognized by the international community as a whole, as standards from which no derogation is permitted. As will be specified later on (**6.5**), the special force of such peremptory principles lies in rendering null and void any international treaty contrary to them.

Clearly, the principle of *sovereign equality* does not produce all the effects of peremptory norms. For instance, it can be derogated from by treaty, and this is demonstrated by the numerous conventions providing for restrictions on State sovereignty, or on the equality of States. Derogations are permissible to the extent that the State on which the limitations are placed freely accepts the derogation. On the other hand, if two or more States enter into an agreement providing for impairment or restriction of the territorial integrity or political independence or legal equality of a third State, such an agreement is not null and void before it is implemented. As soon as it is implemented, the States concerned incur international responsibility for breach of a fundamental rule of international law. This also holds true for the principle of *non-intervention*. In this connection a pronouncement of the General Assembly must be mentioned. Operative paragraph II(*h*) of Resolution 36/103 of 9 December 1981 provides that one of the consequences of the principle is the duty of States 'to refrain from entering into agreements with other States with a view to intervening or interfering in internal or external affairs of other States'. This provision only entails that if an agreement is made and carried out, it will amount to a serious breach of international law.

That the *ban on the threat or use of force* has become part of international peremptory law was affirmed by various States at the Vienna Conference on the Law of Treaties and has been repeatedly asserted in subsequent years in the UN. The ICJ, although it did not formally endorse this view, in *Nicaragua* referred to the opinion of the ILC, favourable to the *jus cogens* character of the principle, as well as similar views submitted to the Court by Nicaragua in its Memorial in that case and by the USA in its Counter-Memorial.[50] Furthermore, in a memorandum of 29 December 1979 to the Acting Secretary of State Warren Christopher, the Legal Adviser of the US Department of State, pointed out that 'while agreement on precisely what are the peremptory norms of international law is not broad, there is universal agreement that the exemplary illustration of a peremptory norm is Article 2.4 [of the UN Charter]'. It follows that any treaty providing for the use of force contrary to the principle is null and void. The memorandum stressed that if the Treaty of Friendship, Good Neighborliness and Co-operation between the USSR and Afghanistan, of 1978, lent itself 'to support of [sic] Soviet intervention of the type in question in Afghanistan, it would be void under contemporary principles of international law, since it would conflict with what the Vienna Convention on the Law of Treaties describes as a "peremptory norm of general international law" (Article 53), namely, that contained in Article 2.4 of the Charter'.[51]

That the principle imposing *peaceful settlement of disputes* has peremptory nature follows from the fact that this principle is the natural and obvious corollary of the ban on the use of force; like that ban, it may not be derogated from.

The principle on *respect for fundamental human rights* also belongs to the category of *jus cogens*. For one thing, this character derives logically from the fact that certain general rules protecting specific human rights (those on racial discrimination, apartheid, slavery, genocide, self-determination of peoples) have had the nature of peremptory norms ascribed to them in official statements by government representatives (6.5.2). Logically, if a treaty that makes provision for genocide, slavery, racial discrimination, etc. is null and void on account of its inconsistency with *jus cogens*, there is no reason for denying the same character to a treaty that provides for large-scale infringements of similar gravity of human rights (for instance, massive denial of civil and political freedoms, of trade union rights, of basic economic, social, and cultural rights). Such a treaty too should be branded as 'illegitimate', on account of its incompatibility with the basic values of the international community. Even more important, however, than this logical argument is the fact that there is ample evidence in pronouncements by various States that the principle at hand is regarded as having a peremptory character.

Countries belonging to various groups made a number of statements to this effect at the Diplomatic Conference on the Law of Treaties in Vienna.[52] In addition, one should mention the authoritative dissenting opinion of the Japanese Judge Tanaka in the *South West Africa* case (1966), where he expressed a view that is all the more interesting for having been pronounced by an Asian jurist. (Although of course the view of a judge is no full substitute for the opinions of a group of States, it may nevertheless be regarded as indicative of the feelings and tendencies of that group.) Judge Tanaka stated that 'surely the law concerning the protection of human rights may be considered to belong to the *jus cogens*'.[53] Furthermore, in its Opinion no. 1 the Arbitration Commission on Yugoslavia held that 'the peremptory norms of general international law and, in particular, respect for the fundamental rights of the individual and the rights of peoples and minorities, [were] binding on all the parties to the succession',[54] and in its Opinion no. 2 restated this holding, as follows: 'The . . . now peremptory . . . norms of international law require States to ensure respect for the rights of minorities'.[55]

That the principle of *self-determination of peoples* cannot be derogated from by treaty has been repeatedly asserted in international practice. Many Third World and socialist countries (as well as such Western States as Greece and Spain) made statements to this effect in the UN GA on the occasion of the discussion on the Draft Articles on the Law of Treaties in 1963, at the Vienna Conference on the Law of Treaties in 1968–9, as well as in the UN GA in 1970, on the occasion of the discussion on the Declaration on Friendly Relations.

Spain, Algeria, and (to some extent) Morocco adopted the same attitude in their submissions in 1975 before the ICJ in the *Western Sahara* case.[56] It would seem that Italy also supported the view at issue in 1975, in the UN Human Rights Commission, as did the USA in the aforementioned 1979 Memorandum on the Soviet invasion of Afghanistan. The Italian Court of Cassation in 1985, in the *Arafat and Salah* case, also stated that self-determination is part of *jus cogens*,[57] as did the Arbitration Commission of the International Conference on Yugoslavia, in its Opinions no. 1, of 20 November 1991[58] and no. 2, of 11 January 1992.[59]

Finally, a common feature of the principles ought to be stressed. Although valid for and applicable to every State, they rely heavily for their implementation and enforcement on the UN. Plainly, the momentous advance represented by the emergence of a network of normative standards has not gone hand in hand with commensurate progress in the international instruments of law enforcement. In other words, no *specific* machinery has as yet been set up in the international community to give strength to the basic prescriptions destined to act as the backbone of the community. In this vacuum, the UN has been called upon to play the role of an implementation mechanism, by scrutinizing and enforcing the observance of the principles. In doing so, the UN ultimately acts in the interest and on behalf of the whole world community.

5.10 THE CLOSE LINK BETWEEN THE PRINCIPLES AND THE NEED FOR THEIR CO-ORDINATION

The principles discussed above are closely intertwined. They supplement and support one another and also condition each other's application. International subjects must comply with all of them. Also, in the application of any one of the principles, all the others must simultaneously be borne in mind. By way of illustration one may mention that the principles on respect for human rights and on non-intervention in the internal affairs of States are tightly connected. For example, the question of whether States can intervene to prompt a third State to discontinue alleged violations of human rights can only be settled in the light, and on the combined strength, of the two principles, which—taken together—can provide a correct solution to the question in specific cases. S. Hoffmann suggested a useful criterion:

'We must make a distinction between what one can normally call interference or meddling, which is practiced by every sovereign State, and which essentially consists of trying to change a sovereign regime so as to make it more favourable to one's own political or economic interests, and the kinds of measures I am advocating here [that is, peaceful steps to be taken on the bilateral and multilateral level, and within international organizations] and which are essentially aimed at getting governments to observe rules of behavior to which they have committed themselves.'[60]

It follows that any peaceful initiative aimed at requiring a State to discontinue large-scale and gross violations of human rights overrides the principle on non-intervention. Such initiative can also take the form of a proposal, within an international organization, that non-coercive sanctions should be taken against a State systematically engaging in violations of basic human rights. The situation is different in the case of sporadic infringements or single occurrences of serious disregard for human rights. In this case a balance between the two principles may consist in allowing foreign countries to take steps solely via diplomatic channels. Consequently, the State where the alleged violations have occurred must not regard as an unfriendly act a *démarche* by another State aimed at expressing concern and calling upon the former State to do its utmost to end the violations. By contrast the State where the violations have occurred can reject as undue interference any attempt by other States to exercise direct pressure on its State officials or on individuals or groups and associations acting on its territory.

Serious problems also arise as regards the question of how to co-ordinate the right of peoples to self-determination with that of the sovereign equality of States (inasmuch as the latter safeguards the territorial integrity of States).

A case in point is the conflict over the Falkland/Malvinas Islands (1982–83). In 1982, in the GA, Western countries, spearheaded by Britain, consistently argued that the crucial issue was whether or not the inhabitants of the Islands ought to exercise their right to self-determination. In contrast, Third World and socialist countries, following in the wake of Argentina, contended that the right to self-determination was not applicable owing to the historical circumstances of the occupation of the Islands by Britain, and that, therefore, the principle of territorial integrity should be overriding. This was to the advantage of Argentina, which maintained that the Islands should be legally subject to its territorial jurisdiction because the Argentines had been unlawfully evicted by the British in 1831.

A similar clash of views has opposed Britain and Spain over the question of Gibraltar, Britain insisting on the right of the inhabitants of the Rock to self-determination, Spain contending instead that the whole issue relates to sovereignty.

International law tends strongly to protect the territorial integrity of sovereign States. As a consequence, the international community does not recognize the right of secession. (A different case is that of peoples under a colonial power or military occupation, whose right to self-determination does not lead, if implemented, to the disruption of the territorial integrity of the colonial or occupying State.) As for peoples or groups entitled to internal self-determination, it does not follow from this legal entitlement that they have a right to secession. In 1998 the Supreme Court of Canada in *Reference re Secession of Quebec* rightly held that

'A State whose government represents the whole of the people or the peoples resident within its territory, on a basis of equality and without discrimination, and respects the principles [sic] of self-determination in its own internal arrangements, is entitled to the protection under international law of its territorial integrity'.[61]

A right to secession does not arise either when a racial group is refused equal access to government. True, in this case the group may resort to force. It has a legal licence to use force (with the consequence that third States are, among other things, legally authorized to grant assistance to the liberation movement that leads the racial group, while they are forbidden to assist the central government). However, the group in question does not have either a right or a legal licence to secession. Secession may only be brought about as a factual consequence of the war of national liberation. In sum, the international community still looks negatively upon secession, as was clearly shown by the 1970 UN Declaration on Friendly Relations and the attitude States take in their international practice.

PART II

CREATION AND ENFORCEMENT OF INTERNATIONAL LEGAL STANDARDS

6

INTERNATIONAL LAWMAKING: CUSTOM AND TREATIES

6.1 INTRODUCTORY REMARKS

6.1.1 TRADITIONAL LAW

From the beginning of the international community States have evolved two principal methods for creating legally binding rules: *treaties* and *custom*. Both were admirably suited to the exigencies of their creators. Both responded to the basic need of not imposing obligations on States that did not wish to be bound by them. No outside 'legislator' was tolerated: law was brought into being by the very States that were to be bound by it. Consequently there was complete coincidence of lawmakers and those to whom law was addressed. Treaties in particular, being applicable to the contracting parties only, perfectly reflected the individualism prevailing in the international community. Custom, although it gave rise to rules binding on all members of the community, also ultimately rested on consent. Accordingly in the past some leading authors contended that custom boiled down to 'tacit agreement' (*tacitum pactum*), that is, customary rules resulted from the convergence of will of all States.[1] Various national courts took substantially the same stand, for instance, British courts[2] and in 1927 the PCIJ, in *Lotus*.[3] It was consequently felt that any member could object to the applicability of a customary rule, at least at the moment of its formation, thereby avoiding being restrained by rules that were not to its liking. (For instance, in 1893 the British counsel so stated before the British-American Arbitral Tribunal in the *Fur Seal* arbitration,[4] as did in 1825 the US Supreme Court[5] and in 1903 the German-Venezuelan Mixed Claims Commission[6]).

The unfettered freedom of States was reflected in another feature of international lawmaking: the absence of any hierarchy between custom and treaties as sources of law. In other words, rules created by means of bilateral or multilateral treaties were not stronger than, or superior to, customary or 'general' rules, and vice versa. Both sets of rules possessed equal rank and status. It follows that the relations between rules generated by the two sources were governed by the three general principles which in all legal orders regulate the relations between norms deriving from the *same* source (a later law repeals an earlier one; a later law, general in character, does not derogate from an earlier one, which is special in character; a special law prevails over a general law).[7]

Furthermore, both categories of norms could regulate any subject matter, and in any manner to be decided upon by the parties concerned. Thus two or more States could elect to derogate *inter se* from customary international law; by the same token, a new customary rule could supplant a treaty concluded by two or more States. The complete interchangeability of the two sources plainly sanctioned the wish of sovereign States not to tie their hands for good; they were able to dispose of their obligations by mutual agreement as soon as fulfilling them proved contrary to the parties' interests.

In addition to not regulating the norm-creating process of customary rules (which is quite normal, given the inherent characteristics of custom), characteristically international rules did not define in detail the processes by which a treaty came into being (as we all know, in domestic legal orders the position is quite different: there, constitutional and similar legal precepts normally regulate the complex procedures for legislating; they define the subjects and bodies called upon to make law, the various stages of the law-making process, and so on). This is not accidental. States wished to be as free as possible in their dealings. Indeed, freedom of States was the fundamental feature of the international community (see above, **1.6**).

To a large extent this legal regime is still valid today, although some of its most glaring failings have been considerably attenuated.

6.1.2 NEW TRENDS

It should be noted, first, that the emergence in the twentieth century of a great number of States, many of them with different ideological, political, and cultural backgrounds (first the socialist countries and later developing States) meant that the international regulation of treaties had to become more certain, detailed, and consonant with the demands of these new States. As a result of the consequent need to codify, reshape, and develop traditional rules, States agreed to devote a whole treaty to the 'birth', 'life', and 'death' of international agreements. This was the 1969 Vienna Convention on the Law of Treaties, which regulated all the main features of international treaties (it was followed in 1986 by the Vienna Convention on the Law of Treaties between States and International Organizations).

Second, in recent years a set of fundamental values has emerged. States agree both on their content and on their crucial importance. By the same token, a new category of general international rules has come into being designed to enshrine those values: peremptory rules or *jus cogens* (see **6.5**). They place restraints on the otherwise unfettered freedom of States. They also establish some sort of *hierarchy* within the body of international law: States may not derogate from peremptory norms through treaties or customary rules that do not have the special legal force of such norms. It follows that *jus cogens* is hierarchically superior to all the other rules of international law; hence, the three general principles governing the relationship between international rules do not apply to them.

Third, as we shall see *infra* (**6.5.2**), it is now, at the least, questionable whether States may object to the formation of a customary rule thereby remaining outside it. The international community is less anarchic and individualistic, and far more integrated than in the past. Consequently community pressure on individual States, including Great Powers, is such that it proves difficult for a State to avoid being bound by a new general rule.

6.2 CUSTOM

6.2.1 GENERAL

Article 38.1(b) of the Statute of the ICJ[8] lists, among the sources of law upon which the Court can draw, 'international custom, as evidence of a general practice accepted as law'. This is the most authoritative definition, although a number of scholars have questioned it. It also reflects the widely held view that custom is made up of two elements: general practice, or *usus* or *diuturnitas*, and the conviction that such practice reflects, or amounts to, law (*opinio juris*) or is required by social, economic, or political exigencies (*opinio necessitatis*).

The main feature of custom is that normally it is not a deliberate lawmaking process. As we shall see, in the case of treaties, States come together willingly to agree upon legal standards of behaviour acceptable to all those participating in the lawmaking process. Their main and conscious intent is to bring about those standards. In the case of custom, States, when participating in the norm-setting process, do not act for the primary purpose of laying down international rules. Their primary concern is to safeguard some economic, social, or political interests. The gradual birth of a new international rule is the side effect of States' conduct in international relations. That is why Kelsen defined custom as 'unconscious and unintentional lawmaking'[9] and some Italian international lawyers (Giuliano, Ago, Barile) defined it as a 'spontaneous process'.[10]

As pointed out above, a second feature differentiating custom from treaties is that customary rules are normally binding upon all members of the world community (or of a regional group of States, in the case of regional customs), whereas treaties only bind those States that ratify or adhere to them.

6.2.2 ELEMENTS OF CUSTOM

Let us now go back to the fundamental elements constituting custom: State practice (*usus* or *diuturnitas*) and the corresponding views of States (*opinio juris* or *opinio necessitatis*).

As for practice, its scope is epitomized in a celebrated holding of the ICJ in the *North Sea Continental Shelf* cases. There the Court stated that 'State practice, including that of States whose interests are specially affected, should . . . [be] both extensive and virtually uniform'.[11] As the same Court stated in *Nicaragua*, possible instances of non-compliance with a rule do not necessarily mean that the rule has not come into being. State practice need not be absolutely uniform; hence, individual deviations may not lead to the conclusion that no rule has crystallized. In addition, often such instances can confirm the existence of a rule, in that either they are regarded as breaches of international law or the State concerned claims that its conduct was justified by exceptional circumstances.[12]

Should this practice always 'show a general recognition that a rule of law or legal obligation is involved', as the ICJ put it in the *North Sea Continental Shelf* cases?[13] It would seem that the two elements need not be both present from the outset. Usually, a practice evolves among certain States under the impulse of economic, political, or military demands. At this stage the practice may thus be regarded as being imposed by social or economic or political needs (*opinio necessitatis*). If it does not encounter strong and consistent opposition from other States but is increasingly accepted, or acquiesced in, a customary rule gradually crystallizes. At this later stage it may be held that the practice is dictated by international law (*opinio juris*). In other words, now States begin to believe that they must conform to the practice not so much, or not only, out of economic, political, or military considerations, but because an international rule enjoins them to do so. At that moment—difficult to pinpoint exactly, since it is the result of a continuous process—a customary rule may be said to have evolved. It would seem that it is only with regard to this stage in the gradual formation of a customary rule that one may require 'a belief that . . . [a given] practice is rendered obligatory by the existence of a rule of law requiring it', with the consequence that the 'States concerned must . . . feel that they are conforming to what amounts to a legal obligation', as the ICJ put in the *North Sea Continental Shelf* cases.[14]

Telling examples of nascent customary rules based on *opinio necessitatis*, that by now has turned into *opinio juris*, are the rules on the continental shelf (whereby each coastal State has exclusive jurisdiction over the natural resources of the subsoil and the seabed of the continental shelf beneath the high seas but contiguous to its coast: see above, (3.5.3) and on outer space (3.5.7).

It should be added that whenever there exist at the outset conflicting (economic or political) interests, the *usus* element may acquire greater importance for the formation of a customary rule. This, for instance, applies to the creation of the rule on the continental shelf. In other instances *usus* is less important: for instance, in the case of use of outer space, it is a fact that only two Great Powers (the Soviet Union and the USA) had the technological resources for using that portion of air; hence, once their substantial convergence had come about, it was easy for a customary rule to evolve in very little time (so much so that a distinguished commentator spoke of 'instant custom').[15] In other instances *opinio* acquires a prominent role, among other things because it is based on evident and inherently rational grounds; this, for example, holds true for the customary rules prohibiting genocide, slavery, and racial discrimination.

There are various examples of how international or national courts have established the existence of a customary rule. One of them, little known, is a case brought in 1939 before the Italian Court of Cassation (*De Meeüs* v. *Forzano*: decision delivered by the Court in plenary session on 16 November 1939).[16] In 1922 the same Court had held that diplomatic agents were not immune from civil jurisdiction for acts and transactions performed in their private capacity in the receiving State. That decision had triggered a firm note of protest lodged by the dean of the diplomatic corps in Rome with the Italian Foreign Ministry.[17] When a similar case arose a few years later concerning a Belgian diplomat, and the matter was brought before the Supreme Court, this found that a customary rule had envolved in the international community granting foreign diplomats immunity from civil jurisdiction for private acts (as for the few exceptions, see *supra*, 5.3.2(3)). As evidence of the existence of such a rule the Court mentioned the *protest*, just referred to. The Court noted that it emanated not from the diplomat concerned but from the whole diplomatic corps; it therefore had 'the value of an indication of the awareness, in the international circles concerned, of the legally binding nature of the customary rule and of its recognition by civilised States'.[18] The Court then referred to various *treaties*, some of them ratified by Italy, others to which Italy was not a party. It pointed out that, although Italian legislation did not regulate the matter by specific provisions, nevertheless it was of significance that in 1929 Italy had ratified and implemented a treaty with the Holy See that, in mentioning in Article 12 the immunity in question, did not provide for any restriction. The Court added that Italy had taken the same stand in the Hague Agreement of 22 May 1928 between the President of the PCIJ and the Netherlands concerning the immunities and privileges of members and staff of the Court; this Agreement laid down 'the rules that at the time were held applicable to diplomatic immunities and privileges'; Italy 'had not been extraneous to it'.[19] The Court then cited the Havana Convention of 28 February 1928 on diplomatic officers, which provided in Article 19 along the same lines.[20] It concluded that 'the combination of all these specific elements . . . proves the existence of the [customary] rule relied upon by the appellant. Hence, as there are no contrary legislative provisions in the national legal system [of Italy] and conversely there are elements showing that Italy has adhered' to the customary rule in question, this was applicable in Italy.

6.2.3 THE ROLE OF *USUS* AND *OPINIO* IN INTERNATIONAL HUMANITARIAN LAW

Usus and *opinio*, as elements of customary law, play a different role in a particular branch of international law, the humanitarian law of armed conflict. This is because of the celebrated Martens Clause, adopted in 1899 at the Hague Peace Conference and couched as follows: 'Until a more complete code of the laws of war has been issued, the High Contracting parties deem it expedient to declare that, in cases not included in the Regulations adopted by them, the inhabitants and the belligerents remain under the protection and the rule (*sous la sauvegarde et sous l'empire*) of the principles of the law of nations, as they result from the usages established among civilised peoples, from the laws of humanity, and the dictates of the public conscience.'[21]

The clause was first inserted at the suggestion of the Russian publicist Fyodor Fyodorovich Martens (1845–1909), in the preamble of the 1899 Hague Convention II containing the

Regulations on the Laws and Customs of War on Land, and was then restated in the 1907 Hague Convention IV on the same matter.

The Martens Clause was essentially adopted as a diplomatic ploy designed to avert a clash between small and Great Powers.[22] Nevertheless, it was subsequently taken up in a number of treaties, including the 1949 Geneva Conventions and the First Additional Protocol of 1977,[23] besides being referred to in numerous judgments delivered by both national courts and international tribunals (including the ICJ, in its Advisory Opinion of 1996 on *Legality of the Threat or Use of Nuclear Weapons*).[24] It thus acquired a weight in international legal relations that its proponent had not anticipated.

The clause puts the 'laws of humanity' and the 'dictates of public conscience' on the same footing as the 'usages of States' (that is, State practice) as historical sources of 'principles of international law'. In consequence it is logically admissible to infer (and is borne out by practice) that the requirement of State *practice* may not need to apply to the formation of a principle or a rule based on the laws of humanity or the dictates of public conscience. Or, at least, this requirement may not be so high as in the case of principles and rules having a different underpinning or rationale. In other words, when it comes to proof of the emergence of a principle or general rule reflecting the laws of humanity (or the dictates of public conscience), as a result of the impact of the Martens Clause on international law the requirement of *usus* may be less stringent than in other cases where the principle or rule may have emerged as a result of economic, political, or military demands. By the same token, the requirement of *opinio juris* or *opinio necessitatis* may take on special prominence. As a result, the expression of legal views by a number of States and other international subjects about the binding value of a principle or a rule, or the social and moral need for its observance by States, may be held to be conducive to the formation of a principle or a customary rule, even when there is no widespread and consistent State practice, or even no practice at all, to back up those legal views. Thus, arguably the Martens Clause (in its present legal dimension) loosens, in the limited area of humanitarian law, the requirements prescribed for *usus*, while at the same time elevating *opinio* (*juris* or *necessitatis*) to a rank higher than that normally admitted.

What would justify this conclusion? Essentially, the need—in the area of the law of warfare—for humanitarian demands to keep a balance between essential military activities and their devastating impact on human beings, even before such humanitarian demands have been translated into practice. What would be the purpose of requiring prior State practice for the formation of a general legal ban, when what is at stake is, say, the use of deadly means or methods of warfare that seriously imperil civilians? To wait for the development of practice would mean, in effect, legally to step in only after thousands of civilians have been killed. The original 'restructuring' of the norm-creating process in the area of humanitarian law, as suggested here, would thus serve as a sort of *antidote* to the destructiveness of war: combatants must comply with restraints on the most pernicious forms of belligerence whenever they are authoritatively required to do so by States and other international subjects, even if such restraints have not been previously put into practice.

Traditional State and judicial practice concerning the Martens Clause does not run counter to the above interpretation; recent judicial pronouncements would seem to uphold it, at least in part.[25]

6.2.4 DO CUSTOMARY RULES NEED, AT THEIR BIRTH, THE SUPPORT OF ALL STATES?

Mention has already been made of the previously prevalent view of custom as tacit agreement. Under this view the express or tacit consent of all States was required for a rule to emerge in the world community. This approach, assuming that it was formerly sound, is no longer tenable today. At present, when they gradually crystallize in the world community, customary rules do not need to be supported or consented to by all States. For a rule to take root in international dealings it is sufficient for a majority of States to engage in a consistent practice corresponding with the rule and to be aware of its imperative need. States shall be bound by the rule even if some of them have been indifferent, or relatively indifferent, to it (one may think of the position of landlocked States, in the process of formation of the law of the sea), or at any rate have refrained from expressing either assent or opposition. That universal (express or implicit) participation in the formation of a customary rule is not required is evidenced by the fact that no national or international court dealing with the question of whether a customary rule had taken shape on a certain matter has ever examined the views of all States of the world.

6.2.5 OBJECTION BY STATES TO THE FORMATION OF A CUSTOMARY RULE

Another important question arises: can a State that objects to the formation of a customary rule disassociate itself from such a rule and thus remain free from the obligations it imposes once it has been consolidated as an international legal standard of general value?

One of the consequences of the theory of custom as 'tacit agreement' was that any time a State could prove that it had tacitly or expressly opposed a customary rule, such rule could not be regarded as binding on it. This view did not go unchallenged. Possibly, it reflected the real state of affairs existing before the Second World War, when there were few States (mostly European) and their consent was necessary for a general rule to emerge. Whether or not that view rightly reflected the reality of the time, it can no longer be regarded as tenable today. True, a few distinguished commentators have maintained that at present a State that dissociates itself from a nascent rule cannot be considered bound by it (this is the so-called theory of the 'persistent objector').[26] The same stand was authoritatively taken in the US *Restatement of the Law Third* (1986), for which this view is 'an accepted application of the traditional principle that international law essentially depends on the consent of States'.[27]

However, arguably custom at present no longer maintains its original 'consensual' features. This proposition can be advanced on two grounds. First, no one could deny the current community-oriented configuration of international relations (which are much less individualistic, more integrated, and more social values oriented). At present it is extremely difficult for an individual State to eschew the strong pressure of the vast majority of members of the community. Second, there is no firm support in State practice and international case law for a rule on the 'persistent objector'. The only explicit contention in favour of this doctrine is set out in two *obiter dicta* of the ICJ (in *Asylum* and *Fisheries*) and in the pleadings of the UK and Norway in *Fisheries*.[28]

Hence, the contention is warranted that a State is not entitled to claim that it is not bound by a new customary rule because it consistently opposed it before it ripened into a customary rule. Admittedly, the strong opposition of major Powers to a new rule may either prevent or slow down its formation. But plainly this is a factual opposition, not amounting to a legal entitlement once the rule may be held to have crystallized.

Thus, although the world community still lacks a superior authority, and in particular a lawmaking body capable of enacting 'heteronomous' legal precepts (that is, subject to an external law), some sort of law also imposing obligations on those who were not willing or prepared to be bound, is gradually emerging.

Similarly, whenever a new State emerges in the international community, it is bound by all the pre-existing general rules of international law and may not challenge them legally (although of course it may contest their scope and purport politically, in the relevant international fora).

6.2.6 THE PRESENT ROLE OF CUSTOM

After the Second World War custom increasingly lost ground in two respects: existing customary rules were eroded more and more by fresh practice, and resort to custom to regulate new matters became relatively rare. These developments were largely due to the growing assertiveness of socialist countries and the massive presence of Third World States in the international arena. Both groups insisted on the need radically to revise old customary rules, which appeared to them to be the distillation of traditional Western values. Indeed, custom came to represent the quintessence of the outlook they opposed. They demanded legal change. Custom is not the most suitable instrument for achieving legal change. The insecurity inherent in its unwritten character and its protracted process of development rendered it disadvantageous to the Third World. As we shall see (**6.3**), treaty making, by contrast, had a number of merits. The majority of States accordingly turned to the codification and progressive development of international law through treaties.

Another general reason for the demotion of custom is that the membership of the world community is far larger than in the heyday of international customary law (in the space of one hundred years the number of States has risen from about 40 to nearly 200). Even more important, members of the world community are deeply divided economically and politically. It has, therefore, become extremely difficult for general rules to receive the support of the bulk of such a large number of very diverse States. By the same token, it is nowadays exceedingly difficult to ascertain whether a new rule has emerged, for it is not always possible to get hold of the huge body of evidence required.

Nevertheless, the existence today of so many international organizations to a great extent facilitates and speeds up the custom-creating process, at least in those areas where States are prepared to bring general rules into being. In particular, the UN makes a major contribution as it offers a forum, where States are able to exchange and, where possible, harmonize their views to arrive at some form of compromise with other groups. Within UN representative bodies, chiefly the GA, as well as in other international fora, general consent on the least common denominator often evolves: the majority of States eventually succeed in overcoming opposition by individual States, and in achieving general standards of behaviour. The latter come to constitute the normative core of subsequent practice and the basis for the drafting of treaties (or the evolution of customary rules). In other words, those general standards of behaviour represent a sort of bridge between the previous normative vacuum and the future detailed regulation afforded by treaty making or customary law. They provide basic guidelines; the treaty provisions (or customary rules) which usually follow in time provide the nuts and bolts, as it were—the technicalities calculated to bind international standards together and make them more detailed—besides, in the case of treaties, setting up the necessary techniques of supervision.[29]

It follows that custom is by no means on the wane everywhere. There are at least three areas where it plays a significant role, and is indeed acquiring growing importance.

The first is in *emerging economic interests* such as, for example, those relating to the law of the sea. The rapid growth of new economic demands often cannot be as rapidly co-ordinated and regulated by treaties in this area as in others. This is because numerous conflicts between groups of States and the complexity of all the closely interrelated matters need to be taken into account. By contrast, solutions to specific issues, propounded by one or more States, may come eventually to satisfy the interests and needs of others and thus bring about the gradual emergence of customary rules.

Typical illustrations of such newly emerged norms are those on the continental shelf (see above, 3.5.3), and on the exclusive economic zone (whereby States have the exclusive power to exploit fishing and natural resources in a zone reaching out as far as 200 miles from their coasts: see above, 3.5.3).

Second, there is the area of *major political and institutional conflicts*, where new needs in the international community give rise to strong disagreements between States, and it may therefore prove extremely difficult to achieve regulation via treaty rules.

An example of a customary rule that has evolved in this area is the customary modification of Article 27.3 of the UN Charter (requiring an 'affirmative vote of nine members including the concurring votes of the permanent Members' of the SC for a decision on a substantive matter to be adopted); through a customary process, a decision may now be made even if one or more permanent members abstain.

A third area where custom is relatively vigorous is the *updating and elaboration* of those parts of the body of customary law which newly independent States have considered to be more or less acceptable, although in need of some revision and clarification. Illustrations of this broad area are several rules on warfare and on the law of treaties (see *infra*, **15.6** and **6.3.2**). Here, the updating has been carried out by means of codification and 'progressive development'. However, the treaties of codification have often embodied provisions possessing a legal value going beyond that of conventional undertakings. In other words certain parts of traditional law have been supplemented and elaborated upon by conventional rules carrying the imprint of general rules in spite of their being consecrated in treaties.

6.3 TREATIES

6.3.1 GENERAL

The most frequent means of creating international rules is the conclusion of agreements. These are also called treaties, conventions, protocols, covenants, 'acts', and so on. The terminology varies but the substance is the same: they all denote a merger of the wills of two or more international subjects for the purpose of regulating their interests by international rules.

A major feature of treaties is that they only bind the parties to them, that is the States that have agreed to be bound by their provisions. As the PCIJ in 1926 put it in *Certain German Interests in Polish Upper Silesia (Merits)*, 'a treaty only creates law as between the States which are parties to it'.[30] Hence, for third States treaties are something devoid of any legal consequence: they are a thing made by others (*res inter alios acta*). To put it differently, treaties may neither impose obligations on, nor create legal entitlements for, third States (*pacta tertiis nec nocent nec prosunt*). Both in the old law and in the law that has gradually emerged in modern times and was codified in Articles 35–6 of the 1969 Vienna Convention of the Law of Treaties, it is provided that third States may derive rights and obligations from a treaty only if they consent to assuming the obligations or exercising the rights laid down in the treaty. (In the case of rights, the third State's assent may be presumed 'as long as the contrary is not indicated, unless the treaty otherwise provides'; in contrast, in the case of obligations, their acceptance by a third State must be in writing.) That means that only after entering with the contracting parties into a tacit (or, in the case of obligations) written, agreement designed to extend the rights or obligations of the treaty, may a third State derive a legal entitlement or an obligation from the treaty. In short, nothing can be done without or against the will of a sovereign State.

6.3.2 THE 'OLD' AND THE 'NEW' LAW

Traditional law upheld the principle of States' freedom in the field of treaty making. Under strong pressure from socialist and Third World countries momentous changes were introduced, and to a large extent 'codified', in the 1969 Vienna Convention on the Law of Treaties, entered into force in 1980.

Two observations are apposite here, one concerning the formal aspects of the law enacted through the Convention, the other regarding the political and ideological concepts underlying it.

As for the status of the Convention, most of its provisions either codify customary law or have given rise to rules belonging to the corpus of general law. Consequently, those which do not will retain their status of treaty stipulations as long as they do not turn into customary rules. It follows that, for the time being, the Convention as a whole does not yet constitute general international law. Nevertheless, it seems most likely that, as the 'old' law withers away, the 'new' one, destined gradually to replace it, will evolve along the lines set forth in the Convention. This instrument is therefore endowed with great significance, even in those areas where it only appears to be potential customary law.

Let us now consider the 'political' or ideological philosophy underlying the main innovations of the Convention.

Three principles inspire the bulk of the text. First, it introduces restrictions on the previously unfettered freedom of States. States are no longer free to do whatever they wish but must respect a central core of international values from which no country, however great its economic and military strength, may deviate (Articles 53 and 64, on *jus cogens*; see **6.5**). Second, there is a democratization of international legal relations. While the previous oligarchic structure allowed Great Powers formally to impose treaties upon lesser States, this is no longer permitted: coercion on a State to induce it to enter into an agreement is no longer allowed (see Article 52 and the Declaration on the Prohibition of Military, Political or Economic Coercion in the Conclusion of Treaties, annexed to the Convention). Moreover all States can now participate in treaties without being hampered by the fact that a few contracting parties can exercise a 'right of veto' (see Articles 19–23 on reservations). Third, the Convention enhances international values as opposed to national claims. Thus the interpretation of treaties must now emphasize their potential rather than give pride of place to States' sovereignty (see Article 31 on interpretation).

It should be emphasized, however, that the 'new' law has not completely superseded the 'old'. First of all, the Convention itself lays down in Article 4 that 'it applies only to treaties which are concluded by States after the entry into force of the present Convention with regard to such States'. It follows that treaties made before that date are still governed by the 'old' law. Second, not all members of the world community have become parties to the Convention. Consequently treaties made by countries that are not parties (or treaties made before the Convention's entry into force) are only governed by the Convention to the extent that it is declaratory of, or has turned into, customary law.

(a) Making of treaties

States enjoy full freedom as regards the modalities and form of agreement, for there are no rules *prescribing* any definite procedure or formality. However, over the years two main classes of (bilateral and multilateral) treaties have evolved in *State practice*. The first are treaties concluded 'in a solemn form'.

Plenipotentiaries (that is, diplomats endowed with 'full powers' to engage in negotiations) of the contracting States negotiate treaties. Once a written text is agreed upon and adopted, it is signed (or initialled and subsequently signed) by the diplomats and then submitted to the respective national authorities for ratification. Usually modern constitutions require the intervention of the legislature before the Head of State—or some other prominent State agency—signs the instrument of ratification. 'Ratification' does not mean *ex post* endorsement or confirmation of the manifestation of the State's will to be bound by the treaty. In fact, it is by ratification that a State expresses its intent to be legally bound by a treaty. Until the instrument of ratification is drawn up, signed, and exchanged with the other parties, or deposited with one of them or with an international organization, the State is not bound by the treaty, although it must refrain from acting in such a way as to stultify the object and purpose of the treaty. States that have signed a treaty are not obligated to ratify it.

Second, there are treaties concluded 'in simplified form' (also called 'executive agreements').

These are normally negotiated by diplomats, senior civil servants, or government experts, and become legally binding as soon as either the negotiators themselves or the Foreign Ministers of the contracting parties sign them. Sometimes they take the form of an exchange of notes between the Foreign Minister of a given State and the ambassador of another State accredited to the former. This class of agreement does not call for ratification by the Head of State, and consequently does not involve parliaments in their elaboration. The reasons behind their appearance are self-evident. There is a need to regulate urgent matters by procedures that have the merit of being expeditious and 'economically functional' (think, for example of agreements between postal administrations of two States). And there is the advantage of bypassing national legislatures in areas where the Executive deems it advisable to preserve a certain flexibility and latitude of power.

Generally speaking, it is however for States to decide how to bring into being legally binding undertakings. It all depends on their will. Hence, there have been cases in international practice where it was not clear whether a State had entered into an international binding agreement proper, or had instead undertaken only a political commitment.

The problem arose before the ICJ in *Aegean Sea Continental Shelf*, in 1978. The Court had to satisfy itself that its jurisdiction was based on a communiqué jointly issued in Brussels by the Prime Ministers of Greece and Turkey. The document was not signed or even initialled; it had been directly issued to the press during a press conference held at the conclusion of the Prime Ministers' meeting. The Court first pointed out that it knew 'of no rule of international law which might preclude a joint communiqué from constituting an international agreement to submit a dispute to arbitration or judicial settlement'.[31] It then noted that whether or not the communiqué constituted an agreement 'essentially depends on the nature of the act or transaction to which the Communiqué gives expression; and it does not settle the matter simply to refer to the form—a communiqué—in which that act or transaction is embodied. On the contrary, in determining what was indeed the nature of the act or transaction embodied in the Brussels Communiqué, the Court must have regard above all to its actual terms and to the particular circumstances in which it was drawn up'.[32] The Court then carefully considered the positions taken by the two States prior to the issuing of the Communiqué.[33] It concluded as follows: 'Having regard to the terms [of the Communiqué] and to the context in which it was agreed and issued, the Court can only conclude that it was not intended to, and did not, constitute an immediate commitment by the Greek and Turkish Prime Ministers, on behalf of their respective Governments, to accept unconditionally the unilateral submission of the present dispute to the Court.'[34]

By contrast, in *Maritime Delimitation and Territorial Questions between Qatar and Bahrain, Boundary*, the Court held in 1994 that the minutes of a meeting of 25 December 1990 of the Foreign Ministers of Bahrain and Qatar, in the presence of the Foreign Minister of Saudi Arabia, constituted an international agreement serving as the basis for the Court's jurisdiction. After examining the contents of the minutes, the Court noted that the minutes 'include a reaffirmation of obligations previously entered into; they entrust King Fahd [of Saudi Arabia] with the task of attempting to find a solution to the dispute during a period of six months; and lastly, they address the circumstances under which the Court could be seised after May 1991. Accordingly, and contrary to the contentions of Bahrain, the Minutes are not a simple record of a meeting . . . ; they do not merely give account of discussions and summarize points of agreement and disagreement. They enumerate the commitments to which the Parties have consented. They thus create rights and obligations in international law for the Parties. They constitute an international agreement.'[35]

(b) Reservations

Traditionally, when a State participating in the negotiations for a *multilateral* treaty found that some of its clauses were too onerous but nonetheless wished to enter into the treaty, it made reservations, that is, unilateral statements intended to either (a) exclude the application of one or more provisions, or (b) place a certain interpretation on them. However, reservations (attached to the signature or to ratification of the treaty) had to be accepted by *all* other contracting parties for the reserving State to become bound by the treaty. The principle of unanimity favoured the 'integrity of treaties'. However, in practice it gave a sort of right of veto to all other parties. (The situation is, however, different for bilateral treaties; 'reservations' to such a treaty in fact amount to a proposal for a new text and consequently they may only produce legal effects if accepted by the other party.)

This old regulation of reservations proved totally inadequate when membership in the international community increased, the more so because the newcomers belonged to political, economic, and cultural areas different from those of Western Christian countries. The very liberal doctrine of 'universality of treaties' came therefore to be upheld. Thus, a regime was envisaged, first in the important Advisory Opinion delivered in 1951 by the ICJ on *Reservations to the Convention on Genocide*[36] and then in the 1969 Vienna Convention.

Under the regime established in the Vienna Convention, States can append reservations at the time of ratification or accession, unless such reservations (a) are expressly prohibited by the treaty (either because the treaty prohibits any reservation or only allows reservations to provisions other than the one that is the object of a reservation), or (b) prove incompatible with the object and purpose of the treaty. The treaty comes into force between the reserving State and the other parties (as modified, between the State and the other parties, by the reservation). One of the latter States may object to the reservation within 12 months after its notification (among other things, because it considers the reservation to be contrary to the object and purpose of the treaty). Normally the objection does not have major legal consequences: just as in the case of non-objecting States, the objection merely entails that the provisions covered by the reservation do not apply as between the two States to the extent of the reservation. Therefore, when the reservation is aimed at excluding the applicability of a particular provision, there is no difference between acceptance of a reservation and objection to it: in both cases the treaty applies, except for the excluded provision, as between the reserving and the objecting State (or all not-objecting States). However, when the reservation places a certain interpretation on a treaty provision, if a State objects to the reservation, the treaty applies as between the reserving and the objecting State with the exception of the provision covered by the interpretative reservation. Instead, as between the reserving State and the States which have not objected to the reservation, the treaty applies in full, but the provision covered by the reservation will have the scope suggested in the reservation.

In addition, the objection may have a considerable legal effect if the objecting State so wishes: this State may oppose the entry into force of the treaty between itself and the reserving State.

This legal regime has the great merit of allowing as many States as possible to take part in treaties that include provisions unacceptable to some of them. However, it may impair the integrity of multilateral treaties (since they may end up being split into a series of bilateral agreements). Furthermore, in practice it leaves the question of whether or not a reservation is contrary to the object and purpose of a treaty to be decided by each contracting party. To be workable, this regime should always rely on the possibility that there is an international body to monitor and assess the admissibility of reservations, and rule on the matter. However, most multilateral treaties to date lack such a body. Hence the extreme subjectivity of any appraisal of reservations.

Important innovations have been recently introduced in the area of treaties on human rights by two monitoring bodies. First the European Court of Human Rights (notably in a number of cases: *Belilos, Weber,* and *Loizidou*),[37] and then the UN Human Rights Committee (in a General Comment of 1994)[38] and in a decision of 1999 on the *Rawle Kennedy* case,[39] have propounded the following view: if a State enters a reservation to a human rights treaty that is inadmissible either because it is not allowed by the treaty itself or because it is contrary to its object and purpose, it does not follow that the provision reserved does not operate with regard to the reserving State, or that this State may not join the treaty. It only follows that the reservation must be regarded as null and void, at least in those parts that prove to be incompatible with the object and purpose of the treaty. Clearly, under this view standards on human rights must prevail over the concerns of sovereign States. If there is conflict between the two requirements (the international community's need for contracting parties to remain bound as far as possible by international standards on human rights, and the intent of one of these parties to eschew the legal impact of such a standard), the former must prevail.

This view, although some major Powers have attacked it, is in keeping with the object and purpose of human rights law. It therefore commends itself as appropriate. It could also be extended to other treaties, whenever they set up supervisory bodies charged with monitoring compliance. These bodies, if endowed with judicial or quasi-judicial powers, could be in a position to appraise impartially whether a reservation is consonant with the purpose and object of the treaty, or even forbidden by the treaty, and decide accordingly.

(c) Grounds of invalidity

In the past the law also turned a blind eye to possible coercion of weaker States by stronger ones. Thus duress—economic, political, or military coercion exerted by one State over another to compel it to enter into a given agreement—was not considered to invalidate a treaty. Similarly, corruption of the State officials negotiating or, more generally, concluding a treaty did not render it null and void. Furthermore, there were no rules placing restrictions on the freedom of States as to the object of treaties. States were therefore allowed to regulate their own interests as they thought best, and even to agree on offences or attacks on other States or on the partition of their territory. The only grounds of invalidity were minor ones: (i) using force or intimidation against the State official making the treaty; (ii) inducing the other party through misrepresentation to enter into an agreement (for example, the conclusion of a boundary treaty based on a map fraudulently altered by one of the parties); (iii) the insertion of errors as to facts (for example, an incorrect map, in the case of a boundary treaty). In addition, (a) all of these grounds of invalidity were on the same legal footing: they could all make a treaty voidable if the party against which the grounds of invalidity had been invoked was willing to consider the treaty null and void, or a dispute resolution mechanism made it possible for the parties to reach agreement; (b) only the party to a treaty allegedly damaged by the treaty's invalidity was legally entitled to claim that the treaty was not valid; the other parties (in the case of a multilateral treaty) had no say in the matter.

The fact that it is not possible to glean many instances of grounds of invalidity from the international practice of the past is ample proof of their relative irrelevance. The paucity of international rules on this matter clearly played into the hands of the Great Powers.

Under the Vienna Convention a major cause of injustice in the making of treaties—

coercion exercised by a powerful State against another State—has been regarded as making the treaty null and void. Article 52 of the Convention covers coercion by the threat or use of military force contrary to the UN Charter, while a Declaration adopted by the Vienna Diplomatic Conference calls upon States to refrain from economic and political coercion as well. Thus the foundations have been laid for the gradual emergence of a customary rule on the matter. Article 53 constitutes another novelty, for it provides that Treaties may be null and void if contrary to peremptory norms (see *infra*, **6.5**). In addition, Article 50 stipulates that corruption of a State official of one of the negotiating parties is a cause of invalidity. Furthermore, the Convention provides significant clarification as regards error (Article 48), fraud (Article 49), and use of coercion against the State representatives negotiating the treaty (Article 51). Besides, Article 47 regulated a matter that was previously the subject of dispute: whether a State could claim that a treaty it had concluded was invalid because its consent had been expressed in violation of a provision of its internal law (it is now necessary for that violation to be 'manifest' and to concern a national rule 'of fundamental importance').

What is very novel, and marks a momentous advance in the field of the law of treaties, is the distinction drawn in the Convention between *'absolute'* and *'relative'* *grounds of invalidity*. The former (coercion against a State representative; coercion against the State as a whole; incompatibility with *jus cogens*; on this notion see *infra*, **6.5**) implies that: (1) any State party to the treaty (that is, not merely the State which has suffered from possible coercion or which might be prejudiced by actions contrary to a peremptory rule) can invoke the invalidity of the treaty; (2) a treaty cannot be divided into valid and invalid clauses, but stands or falls as a whole (Article 44.5); and (3) possible acquiescence does not render the treaty valid (Article 45). If one of these grounds is established, the treaty is null and void *ex tunc*, that is since the moment it was concluded.

In contrast, grounds of relative invalidity are: error, fraud, corruption, manifest violation of internal law or of the restrictions of the powers of the State representative who has concluded the treaty. These grounds may only be invoked by the State that has been *victim* of error, fraud, corruption or whose representative has acted in manifest breach of internal law or of the restrictions on his powers. Furthermore, these grounds of invalidity may be *cured* by acquiescence or subsequent express consent by the aggrieved party. Finally, these grounds of nullity may vitiate only *some provisions* of the treaty. Also these grounds of invalidity operate *ex tunc*, that is, they render the treaty or some of its provisions null and void as from the conclusion of the treaty. However, acts performed bona fide by the aggrieved party before the treaty is declared null and void may be regarded as valid and legally effective, depending upon the specific circumstances of each case.

The important question arises of whether, when a treaty is tainted with absolute nullity, this nullity may be invoked by a *State not party to the treaty*. Under Article 65 of the Vienna Convention only a party to the defective treaty may invoke its inconsistency with *jus cogens*, and the same seems to apply to other grounds of absolute invalidity (see Articles 52 and 54). However, it would seem that the *customary* rules corresponding to the Vienna Convention's provisions on invalidity of treaties should be interpreted to the effect that *any State concerned*, whether or not party to the treaty, may invoke *jus cogens* or coercion of a State representative or of a State. This construction is in keeping with the spirit, object, and purpose of the distinction between the two classes of invalidity or nullity. The distinction is of great importance, for it points to an area of values which the international community has upgraded by establishing a specific regulation: use of force or other behaviour inconsistent with a peremptory rule have been stigmatized to such an extent as to render treaties concluded by resorting to either of them particularly vulnerable. If this is so, one fails to see why one should deny the right to invoke the nullity of the treaty to a third State that may be *directly affected* by a treaty. Think, for example, of a treaty concluded by two or more States and providing for unlawful use of force in the area where the third State also is located, or genocide of ethnic groups, or the forcible suppression of the right of self-determination of peoples having ramifications in the third State. By the same token a third State is arguably entitled to invoke the nullity of a treaty between two other States resulting from the threat or use of force by one of them against the other, if the conclusion of such a treaty may have serious repercussions for the State in question (for instance, the treaty stipulates that force may be used to invade the third State).

Before which international institutions is the third State authorized to invoke the absolute invalidity? Arguably, before an international court or tribunal having jurisdiction under the relevant jurisdictional clauses; if such jurisdiction is lacking, the third State is entitled to call upon the relevant contracting States or State to either undertake negotiations with a view to legally settling the matter, or bring the issue before an arbitral or judicial body.

(d) Interpretation

As Anzilotti emphasized back in 1912,[40] in the past there were no binding rules on interpretation. The criteria for construing treaty law were merely 'rules of logic', borrowed from national law or developed by arbitral courts, or 'those very general criteria which could be inferred from the nature and character of the [international] legal order'. States and courts tended to agree that the main purpose of treaty interpretation was to identify and spell out the intention of the draftsmen. However, views differed when it came to specifying how this intention could be found. Some States, under the influence of their own legal systems, favoured resort to the negotiating history (so-called preparatory work or *travaux préparatoires*). This held true for such countries as France, Italy, the USA. Some commentators termed this approach 'subjective interpretation'. Other countries, such as Britain, preferred instead a construction based on the text of the treaty and the wording of its provisions (termed by some commentators 'objective interpretation'). Courts tended to take different views depending on the cultural background of the judges.

The adverse consequences of the lack of legally binding rules in such a delicate area are self-evident. Furthermore, the absence proved ultimately to be to the advantage of bigger States. It is hardly surprising that one of the few maxims on interpretation that evolved in this period stemmed directly from the structure of the world community and the overriding principle of States' freedom: the criterion whereby international obligations should be so construed as to place fewer curtailments on States, and no treaty could be taken to restrict by implication the exercise of sovereignty or self-preservation (*in dubio mitius*: if in doubt, the interpretation least unfavourable to the subject of an obligation must be chosen; in other words, limitations of sovereignty must be strictly construed).

This tricky area received balanced and satisfactory regulation in Articles 31–3 of the Vienna Convention. Although some important questions, such as inter-temporal interpretation, were left out, the rules on construction upheld the most advanced views. Basically the Convention gave pride of place to literal, systematic, and teleo-logical interpretation (Article 31.1: 'A treaty shall be interpreted in good faith in accordance with the ordinary meaning to be given to the terms of the treaty in their context and in the light of its object and purpose'). Thus, great weight was attributed to the purpose pursued by contracting parties, as laid down in the text of the treaty. Also, pride of place was implicitly given to the principle of 'effectiveness' (*ut res magis valeat quam pereat*), whereby a treaty must be given an interpretation that enables its provisions to be 'effective and useful', that is, to have the appropriate effect. This principle is plainly intended to expand the normative scope of treaties, to the detri-ment of the old principle whereby in case of doubt limitations of sovereignty were to be strictly interpreted.

Under the Vienna Convention recourse to preparatory work may only be regarded as 'a supplementary means of interpretation'. Pursuant to Article 32 the records of the negotiating history of a treaty may only be relied upon 'in order to confirm the meaning' resulting from literal, systematic, and teleological interpretation, or to determine the meaning when the interpretation based on those criteria either leaves the text 'ambiguous or obscure' or 'leads to a result which is manifestly absurd or unreasonable'.

Under Article 33, when a treaty has been authenticated in two or more languages, the text is equally authoritative in each language, and the terms of the treaty are presumed to have the same meaning in each authentic text. When however there appears to be a difference of meaning, the meaning must prevail which best reconciles the texts, having regard to the object and purpose of the treaty.

In modern times, international courts have increasingly applied the 'implied powers doctrine' when interpreting a particular category of treaties, that is, the constitutive instruments of international organizations. This doctrine was first suggested by the US Supreme Court when interpreting the US Constitution with a view to broadening the powers of the federal authorities with respect to those of member States: it was propounded in 1819 by Chief Justice Marshall in *McCulloch* v. *The State of Maryland*,[41] and reaffirmed, among others, in 1920 in *Missouri* v. *Holland*.[42] It was taken up at the international level by the PCIJ[43] and then the ICJ[44] to broaden the powers of the ILO and UN respectively *vis-à-vis* member States. Under this doctrine, organs of international organizations may be deemed to possess all the powers necessary for the discharge of their express powers or the fulfilment of the organization's goals. This doctrine, based on the so-called federal analogy (namely, the equation of relations between member States of a federal State and the federal authorities, to the relations between member States of international organizations and organs of these organizations) is controversial. In particular, opponents argue that this doctrine ends up granting excessively broad powers to organs of international organizations, especially when it is relied upon to derive implied powers from general and loosely worded goals of the organizations (as in the case of the UN).

(e) Termination

In the past, to an even greater extent than the 'birth' and life of treaties, their 'death' was regulated by a handful of rules containing numerous loopholes. Major Powers made treaties to their advantage and released themselves from treaty obligations when they deemed it fit. If the other contracting party was also a Great Power, resort to war could prove necessary. This explains the scepticism expressed as early as the eighteenth century by Frederick the Second of Prussia on the relative weights of treaties and State interests (in his view the latter must always prevail in the final analysis).[45] It also explains some acerbic comments made by Bismarck, in 1879[46]—which in recent times, it is reported, were (not suprisingly) taken up somewhat by de Gaulle.[47]

More specifically, it was not clear under what circumstances the material breach of treaty provisions authorized the other contracting party to consider itself released from treaty obligations. Similarly, it was unclear whether the outbreak of war between two contracting States terminated all treaties between them or whether it left some of them unaffected. The import of the principle *rebus sic stantibus* (whereby a change in the basic conditions underlying the making of a treaty could terminate it) was also confused, for international practice on the matter was not conclusive. The most widely accepted mode of terminating treaties was denunciation by one of the contracting parties. However, even in this field it was questionable if and under what circumstances a State could denounce a treaty when the right of denunciation was not provided for in the treaty itself.

One of the major advances made in this area in the Vienna Convention was clarification of the concept of 'material breach', which one of the parties could invoke as a ground for terminating the treaty or suspending its operation. Thus, under Article 60.3 such a breach consists in '(a) a repudiation of the treaty not sanctioned by the present Convention; or (b) the violation of a provision essential to the accomplishment of the object or purpose of the treaty'. Furthermore, the principle *rebus sic stantibus* was restated, clarified, and elaborated upon. In particular: (1) it was clarified that, to warrant recourse to the clause, the change of circumstances must meet two requirements: (a) 'the existence of those circumstances constituted an essential basis of the consent of the parties to be bound by the treaty'; (b) 'the effect of the change is radically to transform the extent of obligations still to be performed under the treaty' (Article 62 (a) and (b)). In addition (2), two exceptions to its operation were enunciated. Under Article 62.2 the clause cannot be invoked '(a) if the treaty establishes a boundary; (b) if the fundamental change is the result of a breach, by the party invoking it, either of an obligation under the treaty or of any other international obligation owed to any other party to the treaty'. *Jus cogens* (see **6.5**) was called into play for the termination of treaties as well. Under Article 64 'if a new peremptory norm of general international law emerges, any existing treaty which is in conflict with that norm becomes void and terminates'.

Provisions were also laid down to clarify the role and legal effects of withdrawal from a multilateral treaty, or termination of a bilateral treaty, upon *denunciation*, when the treaty does not contain any clause regarding its termination or denunciation. Article 56 provided that the treaty is not subject to termination or withdrawal unless: (a) it may be established that the parties had the intention of allowing for this possibility, or (b) 'a right of denunciation or withdrawal may be implied by the nature of the treaty'.

In light of these provisions the UN Human Rights Committee recently, in its General Comment 26(61) of 1997, held that the UN Covenant on Civil and Political Rights is not subject to denunciation or withdrawal because (i) 'the drafters of the Covenant deliberately intended to exclude the possibility of denunciation',[48] and (ii) 'the Covenant is not the type of treaty which, by its nature, implied a right of denunciation . . . [it] codifies in treaty form the universal human rights enshrined in the Universal Declaration of Human Rights . . . As such, the Covenant does not have a temporary character typical of treaties where a right of denunciation is deemed to be admitted, notwithstanding the absence of a specific provision to that effect'.[49]

The Convention also spelled out a cardinal principle, namely that, except for what is stipulated by Article 64, the various causes of termination do not make treaties come to an end automatically but can only be invoked by one of the parties as a ground for discontinuing the treaty. It was also provided that, in addition to authorizing a party to claim that a treaty should cease, the above clauses could also have a more limited effect: that is to say, they could authorize a party to claim the mere suspension of the treaty.

In addition to the aforementioned grounds of termination of treaties, the Vienna Convention also regulates other grounds, namely those which are explicitly or implicitly provided for by the parties in a treaty (final term, final condition (Article 54)); abrogation by subsequent treaty (Articles 54 and 59), and subsequent impossibility of fulfilment (Article 61). Furthermore, the Vienna Convention provides that some grounds of termination of treaties may also be invoked as grounds of *suspension* of the legal effects of the treaty. In contrast, the Vienna Convention did not regulate the effect of war on treaties.

6.4 CODIFICATION

As pointed out above, most members of the international community tend to prefer *treaties* to custom, for the former are more certain and result from the willing participation of contracting parties in the negotiating process. Between the 1960s and the 1980s this natural preference for treaties became more pronounced, because new

States began actively to participate in international relations and insisted that the old law be changed so as to take account of their needs and concerns. The 'old' States considered it advisable to update the law by a treaty-making process, so as to be in a position actively to discuss and negotiate the adaptation of the law to new realities. This process is called 'codification'.

Two major channels have been used to this end. In the more traditional and classical areas of codification (in particular: law of the sea; diplomatic and consular immunities; law of treaties; State succession; State responsibility) draft treaties were elaborated by the UN ILC (made up of 34 experts, many with diplomatic experience and, therefore, sensitive to States' demands) and subsequently discussed by the Sixth Committee of the GA. They were subsequently the subject of negotiation in diplomatic conferences.

Thus, important codification treaties were adopted such as four Conventions on the Law of the Sea of 1958 (superseded by the 1982 Convention of the Law of Sea), the 1961 Vienna Convention on Diplomatic Relations, that on Consular Relations of 1963; the Vienna Convention on the Law of Treaties of 1969, followed by the Convention on the Law of Treaties with International Organizations, of 1986; two Conventions on State Succession, of 1978 and 1983, etc.

In other areas, or in the same areas when existing law was in need of radical change or major differences persisted, the technical co-operation of the ILC was shunned: States preferred to keep the discussion and negotiation under their direct control. Accordingly, a Special Committee consisting of their representatives was set up to report to the GA. In some instances where the matter was too controversial for a detailed agreement to be reached, the upshot was the adoption of a Declaration (such as the 1970 Declaration on Friendly Relations). In other cases the GA, after taking account of the discussions in the Special Committee, referred the matter to a diplomatic Conference.

An important illustration of this process is the laborious work carried out from 1973 to 1982 on the new law of the sea, which led to the adoption of the 1982 Convention. In 1958, when four Conventions on the matter were adopted, the main purpose was to restate, codify, and update existing law, and consequently the co-operation of the ILC proved indispensable. By contrast, in the 1970s the main object was to change the law radically; to this end direct negotiation among States was regarded as a more suitable method.

The ICJ has lucidly stressed the relations between codification treaties and customary international law in a string of important judgments, and the legal literature has produced forceful theoretical treatment of the subject.[50] Codification treaties may have the following effects.

(1) A *declaratory effect*, that is they simply codify or restate an existing customary rule (as the ICJ noted in *Legal Consequences for States of the Continued Presence of South Africa in Namibia*[51] and *ICAO Council*,[52] where the Court noted that Article 60 of the Vienna Convention on the Law of Treaties concerning termination of a treaty relationship on account of breach was merely declaratory of existing law; the Court

stated the same with regard to Article 62 of the same Convention, on termination of treaties on the ground of change of circumstances, in *Fisheries Jurisdiction*;[53] see also the *Case Concerning the Gabcíkov-Ngymaros Project*;[54] in this same case the Court held that Article 12 of the 1978 Vienna Convention on Succession of States in Respect of Treaties reflected a rule of customary law).[55]

(2) A *crystallizing effect*, in that they bring to maturity an emerging customary rule, that is a rule that was still in the formative stage (as the ICJ stressed in the *North Continental Shelf* cases,[56] with regard to Articles 1 and 3 of the Convention on the Continental Shelf defining the continental shelf and the rights of States relating thereto, and in *Icelandic Fisheries*,[57] with regard to Article 52 of the Vienna Convention on the Law of Treaties, on coercion as a ground for the invalidity of treaties).

(3) A *generating effect*, which materializes whenever a treaty provision creating new law sets in motion a process whereby it gradually brings about, or contributes to, the formation of a corresponding customary rule (in the *North Sea Continental Shelf* cases the ICJ considered as legally admissible a process whereby a treaty provision, while only conventional or contractual in its origin, subsequently passes into the general *corpus* of international law and is 'accepted as such by the *opinio juris*' so as to have binding effects even for countries other than the parties to the treaty;[58] subsequently, in the *Icelandic Fisheries* cases it returned to the matter, although it did not find that the effect at issue had come about *in casu*).[59]

The aforementioned relations may also come about with regard to texts other than treaties, for example resolutions or Declarations adopted by the UN GA. Thus, for instance, the consent that evolved among States in the late 1950s on the use of outer space as soon as the first rockets and satellites were launched, was reflected and crystallized in a Declaration (1962-XVIII) adopted in 1963 by the GA (Article 2). It was subsequently restated and spelled out in the 1967 Treaty on Principles Governing the Activities of States in the Exploration and Use of Outer Space. This Treaty clearly elaborated upon a set of principles that were already part of general law. By the same token arguably some provisions of the Treaty led to the formation of corresponding rules of customary international law.

6.5 THE INTRODUCTION OF *JUS COGENS* IN THE 1960s

6.5.1 THE EMERGENCE OF *JUS COGENS*

In the late 1960s there occurred an upgrading of certain fundamental rules produced by traditional sources of law, with the introduction of *jus cogens*, as a result of the endeavours of the socialist and developing countries. These countries claimed that certain norms governing relations between States should be given a higher status and rank than ordinary rules deriving from treaties and custom. Consequently, treaties must not deviate from those supreme norms and, if they did, were to be regarded as null and void. According to the proponents of this view, the norms in question covered self-determination of peoples, the prohibition of aggression, genocide, slavery, racial discrimination, and, in particular, racial segregation or apartheid.

What were the political and ideological motivations behind this move? It seems that the two groups of countries were impelled by slightly different, though somewhat overlapping, motives.

To developing countries, the proclamation of *jus cogens* represented a further means of fighting against colonial (or former colonial) countries—as was made clear in 1968 at the Vienna Conference by the representative of Sierra Leone, who pointed out that the upholding of *jus cogens* 'provided a golden opportunity to condemn imperialism, slavery, forced labour, and all practices that violated the principle of the equality of all human beings and of the sovereign equality of States'.[60] To the socialist countries, on the other hand, the peremptory rules represented the hard core of those international principles which, by proclaiming the peaceful coexistence of States, permitted and safeguarded smooth relations between States having different economic and social structures. The upgrading of such principles to *jus cogens* further reinforced them, as it offered them protection against the risk of being nullified by any future treaty. In short, to socialist States *jus cogens* was a political means of crystallizing once and for all the 'rules of the game' concerning peaceful coexistence between East and West. This concept was set forth most clearly in the statements made at Vienna by Romania[61] and Ukraine[62] (which, curiously, were echoed by Mali[63]).

From the outset Western countries were on the defensive: some of them (in particular, France[64] and, less strongly, Switzerland[65]) immediately expressed serious doubts, while others (such as the Scandinavian countries and a number of others, including Greece,[66] Cyprus,[67] Israel,[68] Italy,[69] Spain,[70] and Canada[71]) became aware of the need to bow to the will of the majority, either because of their strong humanitarian or legal tradition, or under the influence of national jurists who had supported the concept of *jus cogens*. In the event, Western countries, with the support of some Latin American and Afro-Asian States, accepted the socialist and developing countries' initiative on condition that some mechanism for judicial determination of peremptory norms be set up. This mechanism was embedded in the ICJ.

Before moving to analyse various facets of peremptory norms, it is worth stressing that the introduction of this notion into international law in a sense translated into terms of positive law concepts and constructs that had been propounded in the seventeenth and eighteenth centuries by some lawyers, in particular, the German jurists Samuel Rachel (1628–91), Christian Wolff (1679–1754), and Georg Friedrich de Martens (1756–1821), and the Swiss publicist and diplomat Emer de Vattel (1714–67).

They had divided the legal order into *three spheres*: (i) internal law (*jus civile*) pertaining to the internal life of the State; (ii) the law applicable to relations among civilized States, that is the law pertaining to the international society, and primarily composed of treaties (*jus gentium*, also called *jus voluntarium*, on account of its consisting of the merger of the wills of the various States); and (iii) natural law (*jus naturae*), regulating the life of mankind, the *societas humani generis*; this law made up *jus necessarium*, or a necessary body of law, in that it derived from reason and humanity; as such it perforce prevailed over *jus voluntarium* or treaties.

6.5.2 ESTABLISHMENT AND CONTENT OF PEREMPTORY NORMS

In Vienna, a sort of package deal was made: *jus cogens* was accepted but on condition that any State invoking it be prepared to submit its determination to the ICJ. The Vienna Conventions on the Law of Treaties of 1969 and 1986 provided, in Article 53, as follows:

'A treaty is void if, at the time of its conclusion, it conflicts with a peremptory norm of general international law. For the purposes of the present Convention, a peremptory norm of general international law is a norm accepted and recognized by the international community of States as a whole as a norm from which no derogation is permitted and which can be modified only by a subsequent norm of general international law having the same character.' (See also Article 64, whereby 'If a new peremptory norm of general international law emerges, any existing treaty which is in conflict with that norm becomes void and terminates'.)

As a great authority, Jimenez de Aréchaga, rightly emphasized, the definition of peremptory rules contained in these provisions is very defective. As he put it,

'this description of *jus cogens* fails to apprehend its real essence, since the definition is based on the legal effects of a rule and not on its intrinsic nature; it is not that certain rules are rules of *jus cogens* because no derogation from them is permitted; rather, no derogation is allowed because they possess the nature of rules of *jus cogens*'.[72]

Article 66(a) (and Article 66.2 of the 1986 Convention) provide for resort to the Court in the event of disputes on the actual content of *jus cogens* in specific instances: pursuant to this provision, if, in the case of dispute on the applicability of *jus cogens*, no solution has been reached through means of conciliation, within a period of 12 months following the date on which the objection to the applicability of *jus cogens* was raised, 'any one of the parties to a dispute concerning the application or the interpretation of Articles 53 or 64 may, by a written application, submit it to the International Court of Justice for a decision unless the parties by common consent agree to submit the dispute to arbitration'.

Clearly, a peremptory norm can only take shape if the most important and representative States from the various areas of the world consent to it.

It is in this sense that R. Ago, the President of the Vienna Diplomatic Conference, authoritatively interpreted the formula of Article 53 of the 1969 Vienna Convention.[73] The president of the Drafting Committee in Vienna, Ambassador Yasseen, had to some extent specified this interpretation when he had noted that: '[B]y inserting the words "as a whole" in Article 50 the Drafting Committee had wished to stress that there was no question of requiring a rule to be accepted and recognized as peremptory by all States. It would be enough if a very large majority did so; that would mean that, if one State in isolation refused to accept the peremptory character of the rule, or if that State was supported by a very small number of States, the acceptance and recognition of the peremptory character of the rule by the international community as a whole would not be affected.'[74]

It could be contended that peremptory norms ultimately rest on the consent or acquiescence of the major members of the world community. However, it is difficult for a State, whether or not it is a Great Power, to oppose the formation of a peremptory norm: numerous political, diplomatic, or psychological factors dissuade States from assuming a hostile attitude towards emerging values which most other States consider to be fundamental.

For all its innovative impact, the concept of peremptory rules should not be over-estimated. Jimenez de Aréchaga, speaking as the delegate of Uruguay, rightly stressed this at Vienna.[75] He noted that at the time of their proclamation the provisions of the Vienna Convention on *jus cogens* aroused greater hopes, in some, and fiercer opposition and fear, in others, than was warranted by a realistic prospect of their application.

Nonetheless, much headway was made, in that a body of supreme or 'constitutional' principles was created.

Considerable agreement has evolved among States to the effect that certain rules indisputably belong to *jus cogens*. An important clue to the identification of peremptory norms can be found in the former Article 19 of the ILC Draft Articles on State Responsibility (now deleted for reasons other than the enumeration of fundamental norms; see *infra*, **9.5**). In that provision, proposed by the Special Rapporteur R. Ago and initially accepted by the ILC, mention was made of norms laying down international obligations 'so *essential for the protection of fundamental interests of the international community* that [their] breach [was] recognized as a crime by that *community as a whole*' (emphasis added). By way of illustration, reference was made there to the norms prohibiting aggression, 'the establishment or maintenance by force of colonial domination', slavery, genocide or apartheid, as well as 'massive pollution of the atmosphere of the seas'. One could add the norms prohibiting the use or threat of force (see **5.9**), those protecting fundamental human rights (see **5.8**), in particular the customary rules banning racial discrimination[76] or torture[77] as well as the general rules on self-determination (see **5.8**). In addition, at the Vienna Diplomatic Conference on the Law of Treaties, various delegates stated that the fundamental principles of humanitarian law belong to *jus cogens*,[78] a statement echoed by the International Criminal Tribunal for the former Yugoslavia (ICTY) in *Kupreškić et al.*, where the Tribunal referred to 'most norms of international humanitarian law, in particular those prohibiting war crimes [and] crimes against humanity'.[79] In a decision of 1993 the Hungarian Constitutional Court held that

The rules relative to the punishment of war crimes and crimes against humanity are *jus cogens* norms of international law, because these crimes threaten mankind and international co-existence in their foundations. A State refusing to undertake this obligation may not participate in the international community.[80]

Recently a Belgian judge and the Swiss Government have taken the same stand, with reference to crimes against humanity.[81]

It is apparent from the examples mentioned above that all the peremptory norms so far evolved in the international community impose community obligations and by the same token confer community rights (on these notions see **1.8.2**).

6.5.3 LIMITATIONS OF *JUS COGENS* AS ENVISAGED IN THE VIENNA CONVENTION

The provisions of the Vienna Convention on peremptory norms, however important, suffer from a major limitation: they may only be invoked by a State that is both party to the Vienna Convention and party to the bilateral or multilateral treaty it intends to have declared contrary to *jus cogens*. An outsider, that is, a State which is a party to a multilateral treaty but which has not ratified the Vienna Convention, or a party to the Convention that is not party to the multilateral treaty, is barred from invoking Articles 53 and 64. This situation presents a remarkable oddity, which however is indicative of the still rudimentary development of international law: on the one hand, there exist fundamental principles which comprise the international public order, principles from which consequently States cannot derogate in their dealings; on the other hand it is only possible to rely upon these principles in relatively exceptional circumstances. They remain essentially in a state of *potentiality*, rather than producing their legal effects on an everyday basis and in any direction (see, however, *infra*, **6.5.5**).

6.5.4 PARTIAL REMEDIES TO THOSE LIMITATIONS, PROVIDED BY CUSTOMARY INTERNATIONAL LAW

This flaw of the Vienna Convention is somewhat mitigated by (i) the customary rules on invalidity of treaties, whose content has gradually evolved following the adoption of the Vienna Convention; reference has already been made above (**6.3.2(c)**) to these rules; (ii) the gradual emergence of a customary rule on peremptory law.

As a result of the working of customary rules on invalidity, any State directly affected by a treaty contrary to a peremptory rule of international law, whether or not party to the treaty, may invoke the invalidity of the treaty. Examples have already been given above (**6.3.2.(c)**). Also, recall that in 1979 the USA pointed out that a 1978 Agreement between the Soviet Union and Afghanistan, if construed in such a manner as to support the Soviet intervention in Afghanistan, was null and void as contrary to the *jus cogens* prohibition against the use or threat of force[82] (however, it would seem that the USA did not follow up this statement with any action).

The customary rule on *jus cogens* operates instead with regard to States that are not party to the Vienna Convention (but party to a treaty assertedly contrary to a peremptory rule). Arguably, in late 1969 a very broad measure of consent was achieved on *jus cogens* (only France voted against, but it would appear that it is gradually coming to accept the doctrine of peremptory norms). The agreement resulted not only from the adoption of Articles 53, 64, and 66 in 1969 (and in 1986), but also from the statements made in the Conference, and was borne out in later years by the declarations concerning specific peremptory norms made by a number of States both within and outside the UN (see the numerous instances mentioned above, at **6.5.2**). In addition, various national courts have adverted to peremptory norms, albeit in *obiter dicta*. Furthermore, in at least two cases (*Aminol* v. *Kuwait* and *Guinea/Guinea Bissau Maritime*

Delimitation) international arbitral courts *implicitly* upheld the notion of *jus cogens* (they found that the specific rules invoked by a party were not peremptory in nature and hence did not make a contrary treaty provision null and void).[83]

The view is therefore warranted that in that short space of time a *customary* norm evolved to the effect that certain rules of international law (created either by custom or by multilateral treaties) possess special legal force, that is, the capacity to prohibit any contrary norms and to quash those made in spite of this prohibition.

Of course this general rule on *jus cogens* does not embody any reference to the ICJ's compulsory jurisdiction laid down in the Vienna Conventions. However, it would seem that the whole spirit of this doctrine is based on the notion that whoever invokes *jus cogens* must be prepared to submit to arbitral or judicial determination. In other words, the linkage of *jus cogens* with independent, third-party establishment of whether the claim grounded on the existence of a peremptory norm is well founded, is integral to the very concept of *jus cogens*.

Nevertheless, the effectiveness of this legal regulation remains limited. True, as noted above, a party to a multilateral or bilateral treaty that is not party to the Vienna Convention may invoke *jus cogens*. However, if the State against which *jus cogens* is relied upon objects to its application and also refuses to submit to negotiation, conciliation, or adjudication, there will again be no *judicial or, more generally, third-party* determination of *jus cogens*. The contestant States will have to fall back on the general mechanisms for settling international disputes, if applicable. If they are not applicable, the State invoking a peremptory norm is left without legal means of redress, except for the traditional remedies available in the case of State responsibility (see **9.5.2**), on the assumption of course that the application by the contested party of the treaty allegedly contrary to a peremptory rule has resulted in an international wrongful act giving rise to State responsibility.

6.5.5 THE EFFECTS OF *JUS COGENS*

As stated above, the typical effect of peremptory norms is that, as States cannot derogate from them through treaties or customary rules (which are not endowed with the same legal force), the treaty or customary rules contrary to them are null and void *ab initio* (that is, since the moment the rules came into being).

However, other less far-reaching consequences than *invalidity* may be envisaged. Thus, for instance, it is warranted to contend that a consequence of a peremptory norm may be that a court will simply *disregard* or declare *null and void* a single treaty provision that is contrary to *jus cogens*, if the remaining provisions of the treaty are not tainted with the same legal invalidity. Admittedly, the 1969 Vienna Convention does not explicitly allow for this possibility and can probably be taken to even exclude it (see Article 44.5). However, one fails to see why a whole treaty should be invalidated if only one of its provisions is contrary to a peremptory norm and the other provisions are not closely intertwined with, or dependent on, the invalid one. If Article 44.5 is literally construed and the possibility in question is excluded for States parties to the

Vienna Convention, one could nevertheless admit it under the customary rule on *jus cogens*, whenever the States at issue are not at the same time bound by that Convention.

In addition, a court may be led to *construe* a treaty provision possessing a dubious scope in a sense consistent with a peremptory norm on the matter, rather than in any other sense.

Peremptory norms can also produce other effects. A first effect is essentially meta-legal. As the ICTY emphasized in *Furundžija* (with specific reference to the norm prohibiting torture), peremptory norms produce a 'deterrent effect' in that they signal to all States and individuals that the prohibitions they envisage are absolute values 'from which nobody must deviate'.[84]

Furthermore, *jus cogens* may have a bearing on *recognition of States*. The Arbitration Commission on Yugoslavia rightly stated in its Opinion no. 10, of 4 July 1992, that

[W]hile recognition is not a prerequisite for the foundation of a state and is purely declaratory in its impact, it is nonetheless a discretionary act that other states may perform when they choose and in a manner of their own choosing, subject only to compliance with the imperatives [*normes impératives du droit international général*, in the French authoritative text] of general international law, and particularly those prohibiting the use of force in dealings with other states or guaranteeing the rights of ethnic, religious or linguistic minorities.[85]

It would follow among other things that whenever an entity with all the hallmarks of statehood emerges as a result of aggression, or is grounded on systematic denial of the rights of minorities or of human rights, other States are legally bound to withhold recognition.

Another effect of peremptory norms relates to the *entering of reservations* to multi-lateral treaties. Some members of the ICJ (Padilla Nervo, Tanaka, and Sørensen) had already noted in 1969, in their separate or dissenting opinions in the *North Sea Continental Shelf* cases, that inconsistency with a peremptory norm makes a reserva-tion inadmissible.[86] In 1994 the UN Human Rights Committee took up this issue and cogently stated in its General Comment no. 24 of 1994, that

Reservations that offend peremptory norms would not be compatible with the object and pur-pose of the [UN] Covenant [on Civil and Political Rights]. Although treaties that are mere exchanges of obligations between States allow them to reserve *inter se* application of rules of general international law, it is otherwise in human rights treaties, which are for the benefit of persons within their jurisdiction. Accordingly, provisions in the Covenant that represent custom-ary international law (and *a fortiori* when they have the character of peremptory norms) may not be the subject of reservations.[87]

Jus cogens may also have a bearing on *treaties of extradition*. As the *Institut de droit international* implied in a resolution adopted in 1983,[88] the possible violation of a peremptory norm, for instance those against torture or persecution on racial, religious, or ethnic grounds, would authorize a State not to comply with an extradi-tion treaty under which it would otherwise be obliged to extradite an individual. The Swiss Supreme Court has taken a similar and much clearer position in a string of recent decisions (see **6.5.6**).

Furthermore, peremptory norms may impact on *State immunity from the jurisdiction of foreign States*, in that they may remove such immunity. Judge Wald convincingly argued in her dissenting opinion in *Princz* v. *Federal Republic of Germany*, that 'a State is never entitled to immunity from any act that contravenes a *jus cogens* norm, regardless of where or against whom that act was perpetrated'.[89]

The plaintiff, a Jewish US national, when still a minor had been arrested with his family in 1942 in Germany and held in a series of concentration camps where they suffered barbaric treatment, which the plaintiff alone survived. After attempting for many years to obtain compensation or a pension, he brought an action for damages against Germany in a US District Court. Germany applied to have the action dismissed on the ground of State immunity under the US Foreign Sovereign Immunities Act of 1976. While the District Court upheld the plaintiff's claim, the Court of Appeal dismissed it on the ground that Germany was entitled to sovereign immunity. In her dissenting opinion one of the members of the Court of Appeals, Judge Wald, argued that (i) 'Germany [had] clearly violated *jus cogens* norms by forcibly extracting labor from Princz at the I. G. Farben and Messerschmidt factories and by subjecting him to unconscionable physical and mental abuse at the Auschwitz and Dachau concentration camps'; (ii) '*jus cogens* norms are by definition nonderogable, and thus when a State thumbs its nose at such a norm, in effect overriding the collective will of the entire international community, the State cannot be performing a sovereign act entitled to immunity'; (iii) 'under international law, a State waives its right to sovereign immunity when it transgresses a *jus cogens* norm'. Judge Wald concluded that the US Foreign Sovereign Immunities Act was to be construed as 'encompassing the principle that a foreign State implicitly waives its right to sovereign immunity in United States courts by violating *jus cogens* norms'.[90]

Also, as the ICTY held in *Furundžija*, peremptory norms may produce legal effects *at the municipal law level*: they de-legitimize any legislative or administrative act authorizing the prohibited conduct. Consequently, national measures (including national laws granting amnesty to the authors of the prohibited conduct) *may not be accorded international legal recognition* or at any rate are *not opposable* to other States[91] (Spanish courts have also taken this position recently).[92] In addition, according to the ICTY

Proceedings could be initiated by potential victims [of conduct contrary to *jus cogens*] if they had *locus standi* before a competent international or national judicial body with a view to asking it to hold the national measure to be internationally unlawful; or the victim could bring a civil suit for damage in a foreign court, which would therefore be asked *inter alia* to disregard the legal value of the national authorizing act.[93]

It is interesting to note that recently the Swiss Government has taken the same stand, with regard to genocide.[94]

Finally, according to the ICTY,[95] a Belgian court,[96] Judge Wald's aforementioned dissenting opinion,[97] as well as at least one judge of the House of Lords in *Pinochet*,[98] one of the consequences of the peremptory character bestowed upon the prohibition of certain acts may be the granting to State courts of *universal criminal jurisdiction* over the alleged authors of those acts.

6.5.6 DEFICIENCIES AND MERITS OF *JUS COGENS*

Strikingly, although the concept of *jus cogens* has been in existence for more than forty years in the world community, so far it has only been invoked in States' pronouncements, in *obiter dicta* of international arbitral or judicial bodies, and in declarations of international bodies such as the UN GA or the Commission on Human Rights as well as in legal arguments of some of the litigants before the ICJ.[99] In contrast, *jus cogens* has not been relied upon in legal disagreements between States, as one of the major issues in dispute, or by international courts for the purpose of settling international disputes. In other words, it has not yet been used to invalidate a treaty provision (as stated above, at **6.5.4**, courts have instead relied upon the notion of *jus cogens* to rule out the invalidation of a specific treaty). In addition, the ICJ has carefully avoided pronouncing on the matter or has used a rather elusive language.[100]

All this can be easily explained. As emphasized above, peremptory rules primarily pursue a *deterrent effect*. Jimenez de Aréchaga perceptively underlined this unique feature. After noting that a set of values of vital importance have emerged in the international community (peace, respect for human rights, etc.), he pointed out that it was not considered sufficient to attach special consequences to their violation (see *infra*, on aggravated responsibility, **9.5**). It also was felt

'necessary to lay down in anticipation the preventive sanction of absolute nullity in respect of one of the preparatory acts, namely the conclusion of a treaty by which two or more States contemplate the execution of acts constituting a violation of those basic principles. The function of *jus cogens* is thus to protect States from contractual arrangements concluded in defiance of some general interests and values of the international community as a whole.'[101]

Nonetheless, cases have been brought before national courts where *jus cogens* was in fact the *ratio decidendi* (that is, the proposition of law determining the outcome of the case), not however for declaring a treaty null and void, but rather for the limited purpose of not applying *in casu* one of its otherwise binding provisions. In this respect *Bufano et al.*, decided in 1982 by the Swiss Supreme Court (*Tribunal Fédéral*)[102] is indicative.

Two Argentinians, Bufano and Martinez, had kidnapped a Uruguayan banker and subsequently an Argentinian financier in Buenos Aires. They were arrested, with three accomplices, in Geneva, while they were trying to collect the ransom. Argentina requested Switzerland to extradite them, pursuant to a bilateral extradition Convention of 1906. Before a Swiss court the defendants argued, among other things, that, if extradited, they would not be given a fair trial in Argentina, because the two kidnappers (one a former policeman and the other a member of the army) had criticized the Argentinian authorities and had subsequently provided information against their violations of human rights to a French non-governmental organization; they would therefore risk facing a biased judiciary, if extradited. The Swiss Supreme Court, to which the case was brought, held that the crime at issue did not fall under the category of 'political crimes', for which the Convention excluded extradition although it did not contain a definition of such crimes. The Court held that for the interpretation of this notion it could rely upon Article 3.2 of the 1957 European Convention on Extradition (whereby a State may refuse to grant the extradition requested for a common crime when the extradition request is in fact aimed at prosecuting or punishing the person on grounds of race, religion, nationality, or political opinion, or the condition of the person is likely to be aggravated on one of those grounds), as well as on Article 3 of the European Convention on Human Rights (prohibiting torture or inhuman or degrading treatment or punishment). The Court held that, although only Switzerland and not Argentina was a party to both treaties, the provisions just mentioned were applicable *qua* 'general principles of international law'. It went on to specify that the former principle could help define the notion of 'political crime' as also embracing the common crimes envisaged in Article 3.2. In this respect the extradition could therefore be refused in the case at issue.[103] The Court then referred to Article 3 of the European Convention on Human Rights. It adverted to one of its previous judgments (in *Lynas*),[104] where it had raised the question of whether extradition must be refused by virtue of 'a peremptory rule of international law', without however settling this issue. The Court held that the prohibition of torture must be taken into account when pronouncing upon requests for extradition and went on to say that 'the question left open in *Lynas* could therefore be answered in the affirmative'.[105] The Court therefore refused the extradition on this ground as well.

Clearly, while the Court in one respect framed the issue as one of interpretation of the bilateral Convention on Extradition of 1906, in another respect it applied *jus cogens*, for it looked upon the application of the norm against torture as a question of non-fulfilment of a binding treaty obligation, imposed by a peremptory rule of international law.

Arguably it is on account of the novelty of the problem that the Court used a roundabout way of pronouncing upon *jus cogens* besides employing cautious language. In essence, however, it rightly applied the peremptory norm on torture, with the consequence that—on this score—it felt warranted in disregarding an international obligation imposed by a bilateral treaty.

The same Court, in a string of subsequent judgments, where it explicitly adverted to norms of *jus cogens* (although it never applied these norms as *ratio decidendi*), cited its judgment in *Bufano et al.* as setting out and relying upon a peremptory norm of international law, from which no derogation was admissible either at the international or at the national level.[106] Thus, in a way the Court rectified its previous cautious attitude by explicitly stating that Article 3 of the European Convention on Human Rights, as well as other norms, belonged to *jus cogens* or to what it also termed '*ordre public international*'.

The fact remains that, at the level of State to State relations, hitherto peremptory norms have largely remained a potentiality. How can we explain this state of affairs? Probably States still hesitate to raise crucial issues of alleged deviance from the basic values accepted in the world community, the more so because often to do so presupposes a general interest in invoking a peremptory norm. In other words, States still incline to act out of self-interest, within a 'bilateralist' or 'private' paradigm; they are therefore prepared to contest the inconsistency of a treaty with *jus cogens* only to the extent that this serves to promote their own interests. In short, the furtherance of 'public' interests still remains in the background, in the present international community.

On the other hand, one should not underrate the role peremptory norms may play in guiding and channelling the conduct of States. The existence of a core of fundamental values enshrined in peremptory norms may serve and indeed is serving to bar States from behaving in a certain manner and at the same time to induce them to fashion their conduct consistently with those values. In other words, *jus cogens* is already working as a host of 'world public order' standards, sometimes dissuading States from performing certain acts, and other times impelling them to behave in a certain manner. This preventive role may—to some extent—account for the lack of invocation of *jus cogens* in disputes between States.

7

INTERNATIONAL LAWMAKING: OTHER LAW-CREATING PROCESSES

7.1 GENERAL

Custom and treaties constitute the two most important sources of international law. They are envisaged by two basic 'constitutional' rules of the international community, which lie at the very apex of the legal order (they are often designated by the Latin expressions: *consuetudo est servanda*, that is, all international subjects must comply with customary rules, and *pacta sunt servanda*, that is, the parties to international agreements must abide by them).

Article 38 of the ICJ Statute refers to these two sources. In this respect this Article codifies existing general rules. However, other sources of international law exist. Article 38 mentions two of them (general principles of law recognized by civilized nations and judicial decisions taken *ex aequo et bono*, namely on the strength of equitable principles). There are other sources to which that provision makes no reference, but which are nonetheless envisaged by international law and applied by the ICJ itself: unilateral acts of States creating rules, general principles of international law, and binding decisions of international organizations.

Some of the above sources may be termed '*primary*', in that they are contemplated by general international law: custom, treaties, unilateral acts of States creating rules of conduct, general principles of international law. Binding decisions of international organizations, as well as judicial decisions made *ex aequo et bono*, are '*secondary*' sources, because they are provided for by rules produced by primary sources (treaties). Resort to these sources must be made in order of speciality; that is, one should first look for the most specific provision applicable to a particular case and, if it is lacking, fall back on the more general rule. Thus, one should first look for a treaty or a source deriving from a treaty; failing an applicable rule, one should look for a customary rule or a general principle of international law. Only at that stage, if no relevant rule can be found, may one apply general principles of law recognized by the domestic legal orders of States. This particular category of general principles makes up what one may term a '*subsidiary source*'.

7.2 UNILATERAL ACTS AS SOURCES OF OBLIGATIONS

This process for making law, although not provided for in Article 38 of the Statute of the ICJ, is envisaged by a general rule which has the same rank as those providing for custom and treaty-making.

Not all unilateral acts give rise to new binding rules providing for specific conduct, not predetermined in its content. Indeed, most unilateral acts produce other legal effects, that are always predetermined by customary law.

For instance, *protest* is a unilateral declaration designed to object to an act or action performed by another State; its purpose and legal effects is to show that the protesting State does not recognize, accept, or acquiesce in the act or action, or preserves the right to challenge that act or action. Similarly, *recognition* of a situation or conduct is a unilateral transaction (or, in the case of tacit or implicit recognition, conduct) aimed at considering as legitimate that situation or conduct; its legal effect is to bar the recognizing State from subsequently challenging what had been previously recognized; in other words, it produces estoppel (see above, 3.3). *Renunciation* is the willing unilateral abandonment of a right; this abandonment, although it may be explicit or tacit, must however be deliberate and clear; as Anzilotti rightly pointed out, it may not be inferred from simple inertia, or non-exercise of a right, or mere passage of time.[1] *Notification* is the act by which a State makes other States cognizant of a certain action it has performed (for instance, in the case of naval blockade in time of war, customary law requires that the blockading State should notify neutral States of the blockade). Its legal effect is to preclude the other States from subsequently claiming that, not knowing the action notified, they were entitled to behave differently.

Recently, in a decision of 22 December 1999 in *United States—Sections 301–310 of the Trade Act of 1974*, a Panel established by the World Trade Organization pronounced upon yet another legal effect of unilateral undertakings. The Panel had to pass judgment on the question of whether unilateral declarations may formally preclude a State from applying an internal law in such a manner as to breach an international obligation. The USA had passed in 1974 a Trade Act containing provisions that, if applied in a certain manner, could bring about an infringement of international obligations assumed by the USA towards the other participants in the Uruguay Round of 1986–94; in particular, Articles 3, 21, 22, and 23 of the Understanding on Rules and Procedures Governing the Settlement of Disputes (DSU) and Article XVI.4 of the WTO Agreement ('Each member shall ensure the conformity of its laws, regulations and administrative procedures with its obligations as provided in the Annexed Agreements'). The Panel held that the USA had formally, solemnly, and unambiguously undertaken before it to apply the Act in such a manner as not to contravene the international obligation.[2] Thus, as the Panel pointed out, the unilateral declaration by the USA did not create a new international obligation for that State, because after all the USA had already assumed such an obligation. According to the Panel the effect of the declaration was to preclude US authorities from using the discretionary power granted by the US Trade Act, in a manner that would be inconsistent with the international obligation of the USA.[3] Thus the practical effect of the unilateral declaration was to *forestall* a possible wrongful act by the USA giving rise to its international responsibility.

Promise is the only unilateral transaction giving rise to international obligations proper, that is, establishing a new rule binding the promising State towards one or more other States. Promise is a unilateral declaration by which a State undertakes to behave in a certain manner. This obligation is assumed independently of any reciprocal undertaking by other States (otherwise the declaration would amount to one element of a contractual legal transaction).

In the *North Sea Continental Shelf* cases the ICJ stressed that the unilateral assumption 'by conduct, by public statements and proclamations, and in other ways', by a State not party to a convention, of the obligations laid down in the convention was 'not lightly to be presumed', because 'a very definite, very consistent course of conduct' was required.[4] In *Nuclear Tests* the same Court held that France's declaration, that it would cease the conduct of atmospheric nuclear tests, entailed that it had assumed an obligation to do so. The Court required, for a unilateral declaration to produce this effect, that the State making the declaration should have the clear intention to be legally bound by it, and that the undertaking be given publicly.[5]

Promise was also considered as a legal transaction giving rise to obligations in *Nicaragua*,[6] and in the *Case Concerning the Frontier Dispute (Burkina Faso* v. *Mali)*.[7]

7.3 GENERAL PRINCIPLES OF INTERNATIONAL LAW

7.3.1 GENERAL

No legal order can regulate with specific rules any possible conduct of legal subjects. Gaps are bound to exist in the normative network of any community. Hence the need to resort to general principles, that is, sweeping and rather loose standards of conduct that can be deduced from the various rules by extracting and generalizing some of their most significant common points. This need, which a US-British Claims Tribunal aptly emphasized in 1923 in *Eastern Extension, Australasia and China Telegraph Co.*,[8] is all the more conspicuous in the international community, where there is no central lawmaking body, treaty law tends to regulate only the specific matters of concern to the relevant contracting parties, and customary rules normally come into being slowly and by definition cannot address all the interests and concerns of States. In this community, general principles constitute both the backbone of the body of law governing international dealings and the potent cement that binds together the various and often disparate cogs and wheels of the normative framework of the community. States tend to be rather wary of general principles for fear that they might unduly restrain their freedom of action; in consequence, they seldom invoke such principles, except when they consider it advantageous to use them against another State, and they claim that a certain principle exists limiting the sovereignty of that State. Normally principles are spelled out by courts, when adjudicating cases that are not entirely regulated by treaty or customary rules. In this respect courts have played and are increasingly playing an essential role: they identify and set out principles 'hidden' in the interstices of the normative network, thus considerably contributing to the enrichment and development of the whole body of international law. It cannot be denied that by so acting courts fulfil a meritorious function very close to, and almost verging on, the creation of law.

At present, in the world community, two distinct classes of general principles may be relied upon. First, there are general principles of international law, namely those principles which can be inferred or extracted by way of induction and generalization from conventional and customary rules of international law. Some of these principles have been restated by States in international instruments designed to set out the fundamental standards of behaviour that should govern the relations among members of the international community (see 5.1). Second, there are principles that are peculiar to a particular branch of international law (the law of the sea, humanitarian law, the law of State responsibility, etc.). These principles are general legal standards overarching the whole body of law governing a specific area.

See for instance Article 21 of the Statute of the ICC, providing that the Court shall also apply general principles of international humanitarian law.

Both categories of principles serve two major functions. The first is to fill possible gaps in the body of treaty and customary rules. It is often contended that the purpose of resort to principles is that of avoiding as much as possible a *non liquet* (this is an expression meaning 'it is not clear', used by Roman judges when they found that the law did not settle the dispute), that is, a ruling by courts that the dispute cannot be adjudicated for lack of legal rules governing the matter. In reality in contentious proceedings a *non liquet* cannot be envisaged, for, if the court cannot find any rule or principle material to the claim made by a party, it must simply dismiss the claim, on the strength of the principle that whatever is not prohibited is allowed by law. A *non liquet* can however arise in non-contentious proceedings, as happened in the *Threat or Use of Nuclear Weapons* case. The ICJ had been requested to issue an Advisory Opinion on the legality of resort to nuclear weapons. It held among other things that 'in view of the current state of international law, and the elements of fact at its disposal, the Court [could not] conclude definitively whether the threat or use of nuclear weapons would be lawful or unlawful in an extreme circumstance of self-defence, in which the very survival of a State would be at stake'.[9]

The second function is to choose between two or more conflicting interpretations of a treaty or customary rule.

7.3.2 RELIANCE ON PRINCIPLES BY INTERNATIONAL COURTS

International courts have often had recourse to the two categories of principles outlined above.

As instances of general principles of international law, one may mention that the ICJ held that there are 'certain general and well-recognized principles, namely:

elementary considerations of humanity, even more exacting in peace than in war; the principle of the freedom of maritime communication; and every State's obligation not to allow knowingly its territory to be used for acts contrary to the rights of other States' (*Corfu Channel*, 1949).[10] Other general principles are mentioned above (see **Chapter 5**).

As instances of general principles peculiar to a particular branch of international law, one may mention that in 1986 in *Nicaragua* the ICJ spoke of and applied 'the general principles of humanitarian law to which the [1949 Geneva] Conventions merely give specific expression'.[11] In the same year, in the *Case Concerning the Frontier Dispute* the ICJ held that the principle of *uti possidetis* is 'a principle of a general kind which is logically connected with this form of decolonisation wherever it occurs'.[12]

Some principles may first belong to a particular branch of international law and then gradually come to impregnate the whole body of this law. Thus, in 1998 in *Furundžija* an ICTY Trial Chamber held that

'the general principle of respect for human dignity is the basic underpinning and indeed the very *raison d'être* of international humanitarian law and human rights law; indeed, in modern times it has become of such paramount importance as to permeate the whole body of international law. This principle is intended to shield human beings from outrages upon their personal dignity, whether such outrages are carried out by unlawfully attacking the body or by humiliating and debasing the honour, the self-respect or the mental well-being of a person'.[13]

7.4 SOURCES ENVISAGED IN INTERNATIONAL TREATIES

7.4.1 BINDING DECISIONS OF INTERNATIONAL ORGANIZATIONS

Rules created by means of treaties sometimes provide for norm-setting processes (to date, no customary rule has ever envisaged such a process: this is quite natural, for States are still reluctant to be bound by legal standards enacted by virtue of a general rule over which they cannot exercise the control that is implied in the fact of accepting or not ratifying a treaty.) Normally, when treaty rules establish norm-creating processes, they do so within the framework of an intergovernmental organization. A body of the organization is empowered to adopt binding legal standards, normally by majority vote. The rules enacted by the body entrusted with this function by the treaty bind only the member States of the organization.

That secondary sources of law are hedged around with these limitations is quite understandable. States only accept being bound by written rules other than those based on consent, if they have previously accepted the norm-creating process through a treaty, that is, have previously manifested in writing their willingness to be bound in future by rules set by an international body. Furthermore, just as the treaty rules that make up the statute of an organization bind only the member States of that organization, similarly the rules enacted by a constituent body of an organization cannot bind third States.

It is apparent that the existence of this category of sources of law is a characteristic feature of modern international law. The needs it was intended to meet are clear: in some specific and well-defined areas it would be difficult and time consuming for States to get together and unanimously agree upon a set of rules as soon as the necessity for such rules arises. It is easier and more expeditious for an international body to enact such rules.

The power to pass binding resolutions is provided for in the UN Charter. The Security Council is empowered to issue binding legal standards, when acting under Chapter VII of the UN Charter (concerning action with respect to threats to peace, breaches of the peace, and acts of aggression). Article 41 of the UN Charter provides that 'The Security Council may decide what measures not involving the use of armed force are to be employed to give effect to its decisions'. When the Security Council decides not to resort to recommendations but to issue decisions, these are binding on the strength of Article 25 of the UN Charter ('The Members of the United Nations agree to accept and carry out the decisions of the Security Council in accordance with the present Charter'). The UN may impel compliance with these decisions by third States, namely those few States that are still not members of the UN (Switzerland, etc.), through sanctions or other measures taken on the strength of Article 2.6 of the UN Charter ('The Organization shall ensure that States which are not members of the United Nations act in accordance with these Principles [laid down in Article 2] so far as may be necessary for the maintenance of international peace and security').

Particularly since the end of the cold war, the UN Security Council has passed many decisions on sanctions, such as bans on exports and imports and other economic relations with particular States (for example, Iraq, the Federal Republic of Yugoslavia (Serbia-Montenegro), Somalia, Liberia, Libya, Haiti, etc.). It has also adopted the Statutes of the ICTY and the ICTR.

Another intergovernmental organization endowed with norm-setting powers is the International Civil Aviation Organization (ICAO), whose Council is authorized to pass by a two-thirds majority international standards concerning air traffic. These standards become binding on member States three months after their adoption unless the majority of member States has meanwhile notified their disapproval.

The Statutes of the three European Communities, which form one of the pillars of the European Union, grant even greater powers to the European Council of Ministers. The Council may issue regulations (which normally bind States and individuals 20 days after their publication in the *Official Journal* of the Communities), directives (which normally become binding on all member States upon their publication in the *Official Journal* of the Communities), and decisions (acts of a specific nature, that are normally binding upon their notification to the State, individual, or enterprise concerned). For some matters, absolute majority is sufficient for the adoption of regulations or directives; for other matters a 'qualified majority', as defined in Article 205(2) of the Treaty on the EC is required. Unanimity is necessary for some matters.

It would seem that the same principles of construction as apply to treaties are relevant to the interpretation of the rules under discussion, as is shown, among other things, by the case law of the ICTY and the ICTR relating to the interpretation of the Statute of each of these two tribunals.

7.4.2 JUDICIAL DECISIONS BASED ON EQUITABLE PRINCIPLES

Some treaties grant international courts and tribunals the power to make decisions based not on existing law, but rather on principles of equity. This power is also laid down in Article 38.2 of the ICJ Statute, although States have never granted the Court specific jurisdiction to make decisions *ex aequo et bono*.

Whenever an international court or tribunal applies equity, it creates law between the parties to the dispute.

For example, under Article V.3 of Annex II to the Dayton-Paris Accord of 1995 the Arbitral Tribunal charged with pronouncing on the establishment of an Inter-Entity Boundary Line between the Federation of Bosnia and Herzegovina and the Republika Srpska in the Brcko area, was authorized to apply 'the relevant legal and equitable principles'. In its first judgment, of 14 February 1997, the Arbitral Tribunal drew upon 'the demands of impartiality, justice and reason'.[14] In its second, 'supplemental award', of 15 March 1998, the Arbitral Tribunal put off a final decision on the matter, deciding that the interim international supervisory system set up by the first award should continue. It justified this decision as being equitable and not based on 'purely political considerations'.[15] In its third and final award, of 5 March 1999, the Arbitral Tribunal went so far as to legislate on the matter: it established a permanent self-governing Brcko District, independent of the two Entities, to be held in condominium by them, and subject to the sovereignty of Bosnia and Herzegovina.[16]

7.5 GENERAL PRINCIPLES OF LAW RECOGNIZED BY THE COMMUNITY OF NATIONS, AS A SUBSIDIARY SOURCE

In addition to primary and secondary sources of law, international law also encompasses subsidiary sources. These are norm-setting processes that bring about rules to which recourse may only be had if and when no rule produced by a primary or secondary source (treaties, customs, unilateral acts giving birth to obligations proper, general principles of international law, and so on) regulates a certain matter.

7.5.1 RESORT TO SUCH PRINCIPLES IN THE PAST

In the nineteenth century and at the beginning of the twentieth century courts adjudicating disputes between States, faced with cases where no treaty or customary rule regulated the matter submitted to arbitration, felt it necessary to have recourse to some general principles common to the domestic legal systems of most countries (in that period that of course meant European countries plus some advanced States of other continents such as the USA). This was an adroit manner of filling legal gaps, thereby developing the then rather rudimentary and incomplete body of international law. It should be noted that the courts set out these principles without engaging in a comparative survey of national law. They simply enunciated principles that had very general purport and which indisputably were common to all major Western legal systems. No State protested, which is not surprising since the courts applied general principles familiar to the States concerned.

The principles at issue embraced necessity,[17] *force majeure*,[18] *res judicata*,[19] denial of justice,[20] and, turning to more specific areas, the principle whereby in the case of wrongful acts, the delinquent State must pay compensation including both *damnum emergens* and *lucrum cessans*.[21]

7.5.2 THE ATTEMPT TO CODIFY RESORT TO PRINCIPLES IN 1921

After the First World War reference to these principles was codified in Article 38.3 of the Statute of the PCIJ, drafted in 1921 by an 'Advisory Committee of Jurists' appointed by the Council of the League of Nations and made up of ten members (eight from the West, a Brazilian, and a Japanese).[22] The Chairman, the Belgian E. E. F. Descamps, proposed that, in addition to treaties and custom, the Court should also apply 'the rules of international law as recognized by the legal conscience of civilized nations'.[23] Interestingly, in moving to adopt such an approach, he cited in support the Martens Clause[24] (referred to above: see **6.2.3**) and explicitly insisted that the new Court should 'conform to the dictates of the legal conscience of civilised nations'.[25]

In commenting upon and reacting to the proposal, the Committee split into two groups. The majority proved to be in favour. They had two aims in mind. First they wished to expand the sources of international law, by making applicable 'the fundamental law of justice and injustice, deeply engraved on the heart of every human being and which is given its highest and most authoritative expression in the legal conscience of civilized nations' (Descamps).[26] Plainly, the advocates of this doctrine endeavoured to introduce 'principles of objective justice', that is, natural law principles in international relations. Second, where a dispute was not governed either by a treaty or by custom, they wished to avoid the possibility that the Court might declare itself incompetent through lack of applicable rules. Three members (the American Root, the Englishman Lord Phillimore, and the Italian Ricci-Busatti) strongly opposed this approach, adopting one that was markedly positivist.[27] In an earlier meeting the leader of this group, Root, had emphatically stated that 'Nations will submit to positive law, but will not submit to such principles as have not been developed into positive rules supported by an accord between all States'.[28] And he asked, 'Was it possible to compel nations to submit their disputes to a Court which would administer not merely law, but also what it deems to be the conscience of civilised peoples?'[29] In short, the minority clung to the traditional concept that the Court should solely apply rules and principles derived from the will of States and embodied in treaties or custom.

Given this radical difference of views, Root and Lord Phillimore eventually suggested a compromise: the Court should be empowered to apply 'the general principles of law recognised by civilised nations'.[30] The proposal was accepted and in the end became Article 38.3 of the

Court's Statute. Clearly, the formula agreed upon followed a middle course between the two opposing views. The Court was empowered to apply something more than treaties and custom, and was thus able to go beyond the law resting on the will of States. However, it could not apply general and vague 'principles of objective justice' (in which case it would ultimately have been endowed with the power to create law), but only those principles which were clearly laid down in the municipal law systems of (dominant) States.

In spite of the looseness of the formula adopted in 1921, the fact that international courts had previously already drawn upon general principles of law proclaimed in national legal systems, and had not been challenged by the States concerned, justifies the view that Article 38.3 eventually codified what had become over the years an unwritten rule on general principles.

It should again be emphasized that the Court was not empowered to *create* those principles. It could only spell them out, after ascertaining by a process of induction whether they were shared by the vast majority of national legal systems.

What use did the PCIJ make of the new source of law? Even a cursory glance at the Court's case law makes it clear that, first, the Court very seldom resorted to the principles and, what is more important, it actually relied on principles of legal logic or general jurisprudence.

Mention may be made of the principle *nemo judex in re sua*,[31] the duty of reparation for international wrongs,[32] the principle whereby one cannot take advantage of one's own misconduct,[33] the *inadimplenti non est adimplendum* principle.[34] In addition, there are some principles relating to the interpretation of treaties, such as that *contra proferentem*.[35]

Second, the principles themselves were not identified through a detailed investigation of the legal systems of the various members of the international community. This, in itself, corroborates the view that they were actually not applied *qua* general principles obtaining *in foro domestico*, but as general tenets capable of being induced from the rules of international law or deduced from legal logic. Third, the principles resorted to were not indispensable for the final decision in the case. They were only mentioned *ad adjuvandum*, that is, to bolster a proposition that could already be formulated on the basis of other rules or principles.

When the ICJ replaced the PCIJ the new Court, and other courts, resorted even less frequently to these principles.[36]

Mention may be made of the principle of good faith,[37] the rule of law,[38] the principle *expressio unius est exclusio alterius*[39], and the principle whereby a rule must be construed 'within the framework of the entire legal system prevailing at the time of the interpretation'.[40]

It would seem that the main reason for the decline of these principles is that in the meantime in the international community a whole network of treaty rules had been established and in addition numerous customary rules had emerged, translating general principles of international law into treaty or customary rules. As a consequence, it was felt that there was no need in traditional areas of international law to have recourse to these general principles.

7.5.3 THE PRESENT ROLE OF PRINCIPLES

Could it be held that the general rule on general principles recognized by the community of nations, since it was so rarely invoked, gradually withered away? In fact it has not fallen into desuetude. It has remained dormant, as it were, for a long time. However, as soon as it has appeared that new areas of international law contained conspicuous gaps, the rule in question and the source it envisages have been revitalized. This applies to various areas, for instance international administrative law (governing the relations between international organizations and their staff). It applies in particular to international criminal law, a body of law that is still rudimentary and replete with lacunae. In this area the newly established ad hoc international criminal tribunals have frequently resorted to general principles of criminal law recognized in the principal legal systems of the world—common law systems and civil law systems. Also Article 21 of the ICC Statute envisages the possibility that the Court might resort to such a subsidiary source.

Courts have proclaimed general principles of law relating to the judicial process, such as those whereby tribunals must be established by law,[41] that of the equality of parties,[42] as well as the criminal law principle of specificity (also referred to by the maxim *nullum crimen sine lege stricta*).

In *Erdemović* in 1996 an ICTY Trial Chamber held that 'there is a general principle of law common to all nations . . . whereby the most severe penalties may be imposed for crimes against humanity';[43] in *Furundžija* another Trial Chamber of the same Tribunal held that the definition of rape as a crime against humanity resulted from the convergence of the principles of the major legal systems of the world;[44] in *Kupreškić et al.* the same Trial Chamber found in principles common to the various legal systems the 'criteria for deciding whether there has been a violation of one or more provisions' when the same conduct can be regarded as breaching more than one provision of criminal law (question of cumulation of offences);[45] in *Blaškić* another ICTY Trial Chamber held that the proportionality of the penalty to the gravity of the crime is a general principle of criminal law common to the major legal systems of the world.[46]

It should be added that of course, as international courts have repeatedly emphasized, the general principles under discussion can only be applied at the international level if they are compatible with the essential features and legal institutions of the world community. It would be inappropriate mechanically to import into the international legal system legal constructs that are not consonant with the specificities of international relations and which consequently cannot fit into the body of international law.

It would seem that courts, after looking for treaty rules (as well as, if needed, unilateral acts of states or binding decisions of international organizations), and subsequently for customary rules, should, in cases where there are gaps or an unclear regulation, search first for general principles specific to a certain branch of international law and then for general principles of international law. Only at this stage may a court look for general principles of law common to all the major legal systems of the members of the community of nations. The reason for so proceeding is that logically one should first of all apply principles that are peculiar to international law, hence more specifically suited to regulate a matter arising within the international community. Only subsequently may one turn to more sweeping principles that underpin all systems of law. In other words, one should gradually move from a more specific to a more general legal regulation, in keeping with the overarching principle whereby special law should always prevail over general law.

7.6 THE IMPACT OF PROCESSES THAT TECHNICALLY ARE NOT LAW-CREATING

7.6.1 JUDICIAL DECISIONS NOT BASED ON EQUITY

According to Article 59 of the ICJ Statute, the Court's decisions have 'no binding force except between the parties and in respect of that particular case'. Under Article 38(1)(d) of the same Statute, the Court 'shall apply, subject to the provisions of Article 59, judicial decisions . . . as subsidiary means for the determination of the rules of law'. It may safely be contended that these provisions have either codified customary international law or turned into customary rules. Hence, they apply to all decisions of international courts. It follows that judgments of such courts do not make law, nor is the common law doctrine of *stare decisis*, or binding precedent, applicable.

However, given the rudimentary character of international law, and the lack of both a central lawmaking body and a central judicial institution endowed with compulsory jurisdiction, in practice many decisions of the most authoritative courts (in particular the ICJ) are bound to have crucial importance in establishing the existence of customary rules, or in defining their scope and content, or in promoting the evolution of new concepts. As Judge Cardozo of the US Supreme Court stated in 1934,

'International law, or the law that governs between States, has at times, like the common law within States, a twilight existence during which it is hardly distinguishable from morality or justice, till at length the imprimatur of a court attests its jural quality'.[47]

It may suffice here to mention a few landmark decisions: the award rendered in 1872 in *The Alabama* (United States v. Great Britain), which laid down the basic principles on neutrality;[48] the award made in 1928 by the Swiss arbitrator Max Huber in *Island of Palmas* (United States v. The Netherlands), where the notion of territorial sovereignty was set out;[49] the arbitral award in *Naulilaa*, spelling out the requirements of reprisals.[50] One should also mention various judgments handed down by the ICJ: that in *Barcelona Traction*, which propounded, in a celebrated *obiter dictum*, the notion of obligations *erga omnes*[51] and in effect reversed the judgment of 1966 in the *South West Africa* cases (where the Court, by the President's casting vote, had held that a member of the League of Nations did not have legal standing to vindicate a right belonging to any member of the League, because *actio popularis*, that is, the right to institute proceedings on behalf of the community, did not exist in international law; the Court had consequently denied legal standing to Ethiopia and Liberia in their action against South Africa);[52] the judgment in the *North Sea Continental Shelf* cases, where the relations between treaties and custom were delineated in a masterly manner;[53] the judgment in *Nuclear Tests*, where the Court enunciated the doctrine of legal effects of promise;[54] that in *Nicaragua*, where the Court set out in compelling terms (i) the principal aspects of the body of customary law on the imputability to a State of acts of individuals not having the status of, or not acting as, State officials or agents; (ii) the principles on the use of force, in particular under Article 51 of the UN Charter; (iii) the principle of non-intervention; and (iv) the fundamental principles of humanitarian law.[55] One may also mention the judgment of the ICTY in *Tadić* (*Interlocutory Appeal*), delineating the category of war crimes in internal armed conflicts,[56] and in *Kupreškić et al.*, setting out the principles of international criminal law and international procedural law on 'cumulation of charges' (*concursus delictorum*).[57]

In addition, in a few instances the ICJ has even gone so far as, *in fact*, to set *new* international rules, in spite of its aforementioned lack of a formal power to do so. As one distinguished commentator noted,[58] this happened when the ICJ set out the implied powers doctrine whereby international organizations may be deemed to possess all the powers necessary for the fulfilment of their functions or goals (*Reparations for Injuries*);[59] developed a new regime of reservations to treaties (*Reservations to the Genocide Convention*);[60] held that in the exercise of diplomatic protection, even in the case of a single nationality what matters is the effective link between an individual and a State (*Nottebohm*);[61] and set forth the doctrine of 'equitable principles' in matters of delimitation of the continental shelf (*North Sea Continental Shelf* cases).[62] It is notable that no State has ever objected to, or complained about, these pronouncements. Thus, States have implicitly accepted or at least acquiesced in the normative role sometimes played by the ICJ.

7.6.2 SOFT LAW

In recent years a new phenomenon has taken shape in the international community: the formation of what has come to be termed 'soft law' (as opposed to 'hard law', which makes up international law proper). This is a body of standards, commitments, joint statements, or declarations of policy or intention (think, for instance, of the Helsinki Final Act of 1975), resolutions adopted by the UN GA or other multilateral bodies, etc. Normally 'soft law' is created within international organizations or is at any rate promoted by them. It chiefly relates to human rights, international economic relations, and protection of the environment.

These instruments or documents have three major features in common. First, they are indicative of the modern trends emerging in the world community, where *international organizations* or other collective bodies have the task of promoting action on matters of general concern. Second, they deal with matters that reflect *new concerns* of the international community, to which previously this community was not sensitive or not sufficiently alert. Third, for political, economic, or other reasons, it is, however, hard for States to reach full convergence of views and standards on these matters so as to agree upon legally binding commitments. As a consequence, the standards, statements, and other instruments at issue *do not impose legally binding obligations.* Nevertheless, these matters, although they remain legally unregulated, become the object of agreed guidelines, or statements of common positions or policies. They may thus lay the ground, or constitute the building blocks, for the gradual formation of customary rules or treaty provisions. In other words, gradually 'soft law' may turn into law proper.

How can one distinguish 'soft law' from a legally binding undertaking? It all depends on the *intention* of the authors of the specific document, as it may be inferred from the relevant elements: the drafters of the text may have intended to attach to it the legal value of a binding agreement, or they may have envisaged the document as a piece of 'soft law' (in this respect one could usefully make reference to two cases discussed in **6.3.2(a)**, namely *Aegean Sea Continental Shelf,* decided by the ICJ in 1978, and *Maritime Delimitation and Territorial Questions between Qatar and Bahrain, Boundary,* decided by the same Court in 1994).

Finally, the question may arise of the conditions on which a piece of 'soft law' may be regarded as declaratory, or indicative, of a customary rule, or instead as helping to crystallize such a rule. Clearly, these conditions are the general conditions to be fulfilled for establishing whether a customary rule exists or is in the process of formation: ascertaining whether *usus* and *opinio* have evolved on a certain subject (see above, **6.2.2**).

8

IMPLEMENTATION OF INTERNATIONAL RULES WITHIN NATIONAL SYSTEMS

8.1 RELATIONSHIP BETWEEN INTERNATIONAL AND NATIONAL LAW

8.1.1 THREE DIFFERENT CONCEPTIONS OF THE INTERPLAY BETWEEN THE INTERNATIONAL ORDER AND MUNICIPAL LEGAL SYSTEMS

The question whether international rules make up a body of law not only different but also radically autonomous and distinct from municipal (or national) legal orders has been the subject of much controversy. Three principal theoretical constructs have been advanced: first, the so-called monistic view advocating the supremacy of municipal law, then the dualistic doctrine, suggesting the existence of two distinct sets of legal orders (international law, on one side, and municipal legal systems on the other), and finally the monistic theory maintaining the unity of the various legal systems and the primacy of international law.

The first theory was essentially propounded in the eighteenth century by a German scholar, J. J. Moser (1701–85).[1] It was later elaborated, on the basis of Hegel's views (set forth, somewhat confusedly, in *Encyclopaedia*, 1817, and *Philosophy of Right*, 1821), into a fully fledged doctrine by some German international lawyers (C. Bergbohm, A. Zorn, and M. Wenzel)[2] in the late nineteenth century and the early twentieth century. In short, under this doctrine national law subsumed and prevailed over international legal rules, which were 'external State law'. It followed that international law proper did not exist, for it was made up of the 'external law' of the various members of the international community. International law was not a body of binding standards of behaviour. It was only a set of guidelines whose provisional value was removed as soon as a powerful State thought that they were contrary to its interests. Thus, this doctrine actually asserted the existence of a single set of legal systems, the domestic legal orders, and denied the existence of international law as a distinct and autonomous body of law. It clearly reflected the extreme nationalism and authoritarianism of a few great Powers, anxious to protect their respective interests.

The dualistic approach was based on the attitude towards international law taken in such countries as Britain and the United States. English case law and the US Constitution recognized the authority of international customary rules and duly ratified treaties approved by the competent constitutional authorities. Although international rules were only considered internally binding to the extent that they had been approved or accepted by the foreign policymakers, the fact remains that these States in principle intended to bow to international law. This attitude was in some respects developed into a theoretical construct in 1899 by the German publicist H. Triepel (1868–1946) and significantly elaborated upon by the Italian D. Anzilotti (1869–1950) between 1902 and 1928.[3] This doctrine started from the assumption that international law and municipal legal systems constitute two distinct and formally separate categories of legal orders. They differ as to (1) their subjects (individuals and groups of individuals in the case of domestic legal systems, States in the case of international law); (2) their sources (parliamentary statutes or judge-made law being the main sources of internal law, while treaties and custom are the two principal law-creating processes in international law); and (3) the contents of the rules (national law regulating the internal functioning of the State and the relations between the State and individuals, whereas international law chiefly governs relations between sovereign States). It follows, among other things, that international law cannot directly address itself to individuals. To become binding on domestic authorities and individuals, it must be 'transformed' into national law through the various mechanisms for the national implementation of international rules freely decided upon by each sovereign State. As Anzilotti stated in 1928, 'international rules are only possible to the extent that they can rely on national rules'.[4] In addition, international rules cannot alter or repeal national legislation and, by the same token, national laws cannot create, modify, or repeal international rules.

Clearly, this conception was inspired by a moderate nationalism: it advocated the need for national legal systems to comply with international rules by turning them into national norms binding at the domestic level. However, it envisaged at the same time a sort of 'emergency exit' for States in the case of serious conflict between international and national values: since international law is effective to the extent that it is actually applied within domestic legal systems, when national interests are regarded as prevalent, States may go so far as to thwart the legal import of international prescriptions by refraining from implementing them at the domestic level (although of course by so doing they may incur international responsibility).

The third theory, the monistic conception advocating the primacy of international law, was first outlined in 1899 by the German W. Kaufmann (1858–1926).[5]

Kaufmann argued that, as in Grotius' times, in modern times as well there was a clash between 'legal views representing common interests', to which he inclined, and 'views grounded on unilateral interests that lead to neglect [of] law'.[6] Starting from this basic assumption, he insisted in particular on the following points: (i) the notion that international rights and obligations accrue to, or are imposed on, not only States, but also individuals (for instance, when treaties regulate relations between individuals, or between individuals and States, or in the case of general rules prohibiting offences against the law of nations, such as piracy and the slave trade), as well as international bodies (for instance, international river commissions, international arbitral courts and tribunals), or State organs (for instance, prize courts, national courts provided for in treaties on the Rhine and other international rivers); (ii) the superiority of international rules over national legal systems; for Kaufmann international rules, and in particular treaties, lay down contractual obligations for the parties but, at the same time, make up an 'objective legal system' that derives its force from a legal source (the merger of the wills of the lawmaking States) over which each individual State has no authority, and which therefore begets rules superior to national law;[7] (iii) the immediate applicability of international rules within national legal systems of States, without any need for transformation of those rules into national norms, whenever international rules directly confer rights or impose obligations on individuals (whereas treaties granting rights or imposing obligations on States as such may need the enactment of national laws by each contracting State, in order for them to become applicable at the national level); (iv) the fact that international rules, taking precedence over national legislation, automatically repeal any national laws contrary to them; furthermore, if States subsequently pass laws contrary to international rules, they incur international responsibility;[8] in addition, at the international level, international rules, although violated by a national piece of legislation contrary to them, continue to be valid and applicable for all the relevant States; those international rules may not be set aside or deprived of their legal force by virtue of a national legislative act.[9]

These views, based more on scrutiny of State practice and case law than on theoretical postulates, were overshadowed by those, inspired by dualism, put forward that same year by Triepel. Probably this outcome was also due to Kaufmann's lacking the stringent logic and theoretical depth of Triepel. In addition his views were sometimes marred by inconsistencies; at times one is left with the impression that his propositions are based more on generous aspirations than on a dispassionate examination of the international reality prevailing at the time.[10]

'Internationalist' monism was propounded as a fully fledged doctrine after the First World War, between 1920 and 1934, by the Austrian H. Kelsen (1881–1973)[11] and was subsequently embraced by a number of distinguished scholars including A. Verdross (from Austria) and G. Scelle (from France). This theory is based on a number of postulates. First, there exists a unitary legal system, embracing all the various legal orders operating at various levels. Second, international law is at the top of the pyramid and validates or invalidates all the legal acts of any other legal system. Consequently, municipal law must always conform to international law. In cases of conflict, the latter declares all domestic rules or acts contrary to it to be illegal. A further corollary is that the 'transformation' of international norms into domestic law 'is not necessary from the point of view of international law'.[12] This is because international and national law are 'parts of one normative system'. Third, the subjects of international law are not radically different from those of national law: both in municipal law and in international law individuals are the principal subjects of law, although in international law individuals are often taken into account in their position as State officials. In addition, the sources of international law belong to a legal system that is hierarchically superior to municipal systems, not radically different from them. As a result, international rules can be applied *as such* by domestic courts, without any need for transformation. However, allowance is made for certain qualifications. National constitutions (be they written or unwritten) may require domestic courts to apply only statutes enacted by national legislatures. In this case courts will only apply international treaty rules after they have been transformed into national statutes. Nevertheless, this 'necessity of transformation is a question of national, not of international law'.[13] Furthermore, national courts may be required to apply statutes that are contrary to international rules. For Kelsen, although this occurrence shows the weakness of international law, nevertheless the fact remains that the State incurs international responsibility for this non-compliance with international rules.

According to this conception, the international legal system controls, however imperfectly, all national systems, which are subordinate to it. It follows that international values override national ones and State officials must always strive to achieve the objectives set by international rules.

It is clear that this theory rests on two basic ideological principles: internationalism and pacifism. Kelsen spelled out this underpinning with great clarity. He concluded, however, that the choice in favour of the primacy of international law cannot be based on scientific considerations, but is dictated by ethical or political preferences.[14] This somewhat non-committal attitude was probably motivated by Kelsen's adhesion to the philosophy of relativity. It is plausible that there was also another reason: Kelsen was aware that the international community was still far from the condition postulated by his theory: it still lacked the machinery for repealing those municipal provisions which are inconsistent with international rules.

8.1.2 MODERN CHANGES IN THE RELATION BETWEEN THE INTERNATIONAL AND MUNICIPAL LAW

How then should we explain the relation between the sphere of international law and that of municipal law? The first monistic theory is indisputably devoid of scientific value and was essentially intended to underpin ideological and political positions. In contrast, the dualistic approach did reflect the legal reality, particularly in the nineteenth and the first half of the twentieth century, although it was unable convincingly to explain some exceptional phenomena, such as the fact that a few international rules directly imposed obligations on individuals (think in particular of the rules prohibiting piracy; see 1.8.1, 4.5.1, and 12.1). Indeed, in that period the international world consisted of a community of sovereign States and their dealings belonged to a sphere of law substantially separate and distinct from that of each national legal order. The Kelsenian monistic theory, an admirable theoretical construction, was in advance of its time; in many respects it was utopian and did not reflect the reality of international relations. However, for all its inconsistencies and practical pitfalls, it had a significant ideological impact. It brought new emphasis to the role of international law as a controlling factor of State conduct. It was instrumental in consolidating the notion that State officials should abide by international legal standards and ought therefore to put international imperatives before national demands.

At present, as we shall see (below, 8.2), the dualistic conception is no longer valid in its entirety, whereas some of the postulates of the conception put forward by Kelsen are gradually taking a foothold in the international community. In short, international law no longer constitutes a sphere of law tightly separate and distinct (subject to one or two exceptions) from the sphere of the law of national legal systems. In many areas international law has made significant inroads into national legal systems, piercing their 'armour'. It no longer constitutes a different legal realm from the various municipal systems, but has a huge daily *direct* impact on these systems. It conditions their life in many areas and even contributes to shaping their internal functioning and operation. In addition, many international rules address themselves directly to individuals, without the intermediary of national legal systems: they impose obligations on them (this chiefly applies to rules on international crimes), or grant them rights (for instance the right to petition international bodies). Those obligations must be fulfilled, and the rights may be exercised, regardless of what national legal orders may provide. In short, in many respects individuals have become international legal subjects, associated to sovereign States. Thus, international law is no longer *jus inter potestates* (a law governing only relations among sovereign entities). It also embraces individuals, by directly legitimizing, or issuing commands to, them. Subject to the limitations set out above (**1.8.2** and **1.9**) and below (**9.7**), it is gradually heading towards a *civitas maxima* (a human commonwealth encompassing individuals, States, and other aggregates cutting across the boundaries of States). By the same token, it is increasingly tending to become, more than a *jus inter partes* (a body of law governing relations among subjects 'in a horizontal manner'), rather a *jus super partes* (a corpus of legal standards regulating international dealings 'from above': see, however, *infra*, **9.7** and **Chapter 14**).

8.2 INTERNATIONAL RULES ON IMPLEMENTING INTERNATIONAL LAW IN DOMESTIC LEGAL SYSTEMS

Whichever of the three theories outlined above is chosen, *most* international rules, to become operative, need to be applied by State officials or individuals within domestic legal systems. National implementation of international rules is thus of crucial importance. One would therefore expect there to be some form of international regulation of the matter or at least a certain uniformity in the ways in which domestic legal systems put international law into effect. The reality is quite different, however.

International law provides that States cannot invoke the legal procedures of their municipal system as a justification for not complying with international rules. This principle has been firmly stated by both the PCIJ (in *Polish Nationals in Danzig* and in *Free Zones*)[15] and other courts (for example, in *Georges Pinson* and in *Blaškić*),[16] and is now laid down, with regard to treaties, in the 1969 Vienna Convention on the Law of Treaties, Article 27 of which provides that 'A party [to a treaty] may not invoke the provisions of its internal law as justification for its failure to perform a treaty'.

The PCIJ held in *Exchange of Greek and Turkish Populations* (1925) and some commentators have contended[17] that, in addition, there exists a general duty for States to bring national law into conformity with obligations under international law. If such a duty existed, each time a State fails to comply with an international rule as a result of the failure of its domestic lawmaking body to pass the necessary implementing legislation, it would breach both that rule and the general principle imposing the duty in question. However, a perusal of State practice shows that no such general duty exists. When a State breaches an international obligation because the national legislation necessary for implementing the rule is lacking or inadequate, other States claim cessation of the wrongdoing or reparation only for that breach, without enquiring about the reasons for non-compliance or protesting at the lack or inadequacy of legislation. In other words, States are only interested in the final result: fulfilment or non-fulfilment of an obligation. They show no interest in the factors that brought about that result. Again, this state of affairs reflects the individualistic structure of the international community and the paramount importance of respect for other States' internal affairs.

What has just been pointed out primarily applies to *traditional* international law. The *current* regulation of the international community shows two important developments.

First, a number of treaties, in addition to laying down a set of obligations, also explicitly impose upon contracting States the duty to enact legislation for implementing the various provisions (or at least some provisions) of the treaties. One may mention some provisions of the four 1949 Geneva Conventions on the victims of war,[18] as well as a number of treaties on human rights,[19] or other international instruments such as the Statutes of the ICTY, the ICTR,[20] and the ICC.[21] Second, some general rules that have acquired the rank and status of peremptory norms or *jus cogens* (**6.5**) require that States adopt the necessary implementing legislation (thus for instance, the ICTY held in *Furundžija* that one of the consequences of the peremptory nature of international rules prohibiting and criminalizing torture is that States are bound to enact legislation prohibiting that heinous practice at the national level).[22] The motivation behind these two developments is clear: States regard certain treaties or general rules as so crucial that they take care to require that members of the international community change their national systems so as to ensure that international rules are implemented. The common goal is to cover even *potential* breaches of those international rules. International legislators seek to forestall breaches by seeing to it that States take all the national measures necessary to prevent or punish at the national level deviations from those international rules. In this way such deviations do not reach the level of international delinquencies, for they are remedied in the national sphere. It follows that a State may be called to account even if it simply fails to pass the necessary implementing legislation; it need not actually have engaged in any specific conduct inconsistent with the relevant international rule. In addition, if a State breaches one of those rules through lack of implementing legislation, it is answerable for a twofold delinquency.

Admittedly, even in the instances just mentioned, State practice does not contain many cases of complaints or requests by members of the international community that other States pass implementing legislation. The simple fact is that in their day-to-day dealings States still tend to cling to the old dogma of respect for the internal affairs of other international subjects. Fortunately, in some cases international monitoring mechanisms have been established, which among other things scrutinize whether parties to a specific international treaty have taken all the necessary legislative measures.

Apart from the general rule barring States from adducing domestic legal problems for not complying with international law, and the treaty or customary rules just mentioned that impose the obligation to enact implementing legislation, international law does not contain any regulation of implementation. It thus leaves each country *complete freedom* with regard to how it fulfils, nationally, its international obligations.

A survey of national systems shows a conspicuous lack of uniformity. This anarchic state of affairs can be easily accounted for: States consider that the translation of international commands into domestic legal standards is part and parcel of their sovereignty, and are unwilling to surrender it to international control. National self-interest stands in the way of a sensible regulation of this crucial area. As a consequence each State decides, on its own, how to make international law binding on State agencies and individuals and what status and rank to assign to it in the hierarchy of municipal sources of law.

As there is no international legal regulation of this matter, it falls to the commentator to undertake an analysis of comparative national law. In the following paragraphs I shall discuss the major tendencies that have taken shape among States. Furthermore, I shall try to pinpoint both the legal technicalities involved in each of the prevailing systems and the political and ideological motivations underlying each of such systems.

8.3 TRENDS EMERGING AMONG THE LEGAL SYSTEMS OF STATES

8.3.1 MODALITIES OF IMPLEMENTATION

Generally speaking, in the second half of the twentieth century domestic systems gradually opened the door to international values and States became increasingly willing to bow to international law. Although each State is free to choose its own mechanism for implementing international rules, even a cursory survey of national legal systems shows that two basic modalities, prevail.

The first is *automatic standing incorporation* of international rules. Such incorporation occurs whenever the national constitution, or a law (or, in the case of judge-made law, judicial decisions) enjoin that all State officials as well as all nationals and other individuals living on the territory of the State are bound to apply certain present or future rules of international law. In other words, an internal rule provides in a permanent way for the automatic incorporation into national law of any relevant rule of international (customary or treaty) law, without there being any need for the passing of an ad hoc national statute (subject to the exception of non-self-executing international rules; see **8.4.2(b)**). It follows that any time a treaty is duly approved and published in the State's Official Gazette or a customary rule of international law evolves in the world community, State officials and individuals must *ipso facto* and without further ado comply with it. This mechanism, among other things, enables the national legal system to adjust itself continuously and automatically to international rules. As soon as an international rule comes into existence, a corresponding rule evolves in the national legal system (subject to publication of the treaty, in the case of this category of international norms). By the same token, as soon as an international rule is terminated or changes in content, corresponding modifications in the national legal system take place (again, in the case of amendment of treaties, subject to publication of the amending provisions).

The second mechanism is *legislative ad hoc incorporation* of international rules. Under this system international rules become applicable within the State legal system only if and when the relevant parliamentary authorities pass *specific* implementing legislation. This legislation may take one of two principal forms. First, it may consist of an act of parliament translating the various treaty provisions into national legislation, setting out in detail the various obligations, powers, and rights stemming from those international provisions (*statutory ad hoc incorporation of international rules*).[23] Second, the act of parliament may confine itself to enjoining the automatic applicability of the international rule within the national legal system, without reformulating that rule ad hoc (*automatic ad hoc incorporation of international law*). Thus, *in substance*, this mechanism works in a similar way to the one that we have termed above automatic standing incorporation (the only difference being that now the incorporation is effected on a case by case basis). In this case as well, State officials, and all the individuals concerned, become duty bound to abide by the international provisions to which the act of parliament makes reference. The enabling legislation simply consists of one or two provisions stating that the treaty at issue must be complied with; the text of the treaty is annexed as a schedule. Courts, State officials, and individuals must infer the various provisions to be applied at the national level by way of interpretation. That is, these bodies or individuals must deduce from the text of the treaty, to which the piece of legislation refers, all the various rules to be applied at the national level.

For the purpose of ensuring a more complete and effective implementation of international law, preference should always be given to the legislative ad hoc incorporation of international rules whenever they turn out to be non self-executing (see *infra*, **8.4.2(b)**). Conversely, whenever international rules are self-executing, it would be preferable to resort to the automatic (whether permanent or ad hoc) incorporation of international rules. Indeed, this mechanism better safeguards the correct application of international rules because it does not ossify them: instead, it enables the national legal system to adjust itself fully to international rules as they are construed and applied in the international sphere.

8.3.2 THE RANK OF INTERNATIONAL RULES WITHIN DOMESTIC LEGAL ORDERS

A survey of national legislation and case law shows that some States tend to put the international rules incorporated into the national legal system (whether automatically or through ad hoc legislative enactment) on the same footing as national legislation of domestic origin. As a consequence, the general principles governing relationships between rules having the same rank apply: *lex posterior derogat priori* (a subsequent law repeals or modifies or at any rate supersedes a previous law), *lex specialis derogat generali* (a special law prevails over a general law), *lex posterior generalis non derogat priori speciali* (a subsequent general law does not derogate from a prior special law). It follows that the national legislature may at any time pass a law amending or repealing a rule of international origin. True, in this case the State, if it applies the national law in lieu of the international rule, incurs international responsibility for a breach of international law. The fact remains, however, that the international rule is set aside by a simple act of parliament.

In contrast, other States tend to accord international rules a status and rank higher than that of national legislation. Such an approach is normally linked to the nature of their national constitution. Where the constitution is flexible (that is, it can be amended by simple act of parliament, or in any case the principle of legislative supremacy obtains), the only way of giving international rules overriding importance would be to entrench them, so that it is not possible for legislation passed by simple majority to modify them. Such a course of action, however, does not seem to have occurred so far in those States which have a flexible constitution.

Things are different where the constitution is rigid, in particular where it is 'functionally rigid' (that is, the constitution lays down special requirements for constitutional amendments and in addition sets up a court authorized to undertake judicial review of legislation so as to establish whether the legislature exceeds its powers and infringes the constitution). In these constitutional systems, if the constitution provides for the incorporation of international rules, normally those rules enjoy constitutional or quasi-constitutional status and therefore rank higher than normal law. It follows that the legislature is precluded from passing a law contrary to an international rule, unless of course this law is enacted through the special procedure required for constitutional legislation. The logic behind this approach is that international legal standards should always be regarded as having overriding importance. Therefore, in addition to binding the executive branch and all citizens, they cannot be set aside by simple parliamentary majority. Only under special circumstances, when compelling national interests prevail and a special majority (say, a two-thirds majority) is mustered in parliament, may those rules be overridden.

8.3.3 EXIGENCIES MOTIVATING STATES IN THEIR CHOICE OF THE INCORPORATION SYSTEM

States tend to regulate national incorporation of international rules on the basis of two different requirements. First, they may have to choose between a statist (or nationalist) and an internationalist approach. Second, they may have to take into account the question of the relationship between the executive and legislative branch of government, and shape the mechanism for implementing international law accordingly.

States choosing a statist or nationalist approach incline (i) to adopt legislative ad hoc incorporation and (ii) to put international rules on the same footing as national legislation of domestic origin. In contrast, States taking an international outlook tend (i) to opt for the automatic incorporation (whether standing or ad hoc) of international rules and (ii) to accord international rules a status and rank higher than that of national legislation.

States often take into account a second requirement, which concerns the general question of reserving to the legislative branch a competence that belongs to it alone and not to the executive branch. In those States where the government (chiefly the foreign ministry) makes international treaties without any parliamentary participation, a special problem may arise in two sets of circumstances: (i) whenever the treaty covers areas that come within the purview of the legislature; (ii) whenever parliaments do not play any role, or play a limited role, in the decision to be bound by a treaty. In the first case, it is necessary to prevent the government from bypassing parliament by making a treaty and having it incorporated into national legislation without going through parliament. Hence, in these countries the intervention of parliament is always required for the treaty to be transformed into national legislation. Consequently, these countries do not opt for the automatic standing incorporation of treaties, but rather for the ad hoc incorporation (whether legislative or automatic). In other words, parliament may be required to enact a special law either setting out in detail the various rules contained in the treaty or simply enjoining all the relevant State agencies and the individuals concerned to abide by the treaty.

In the second case, where parliaments are excluded from the decision on whether or not to be bound by a treaty, to enable parliaments to exercise some control over foreign policy-making, it may be required that they formally give their consent to the incorporation of the treaty, for the treaty to take effect at the municipal level. In this case as well, the automatic standing incorporation mechanism proves to be inadequate and States resort to the legislative ad hoc incorporation system.

8.4 TECHNIQUES OF IMPLEMENTATION

8.4.1 CUSTOMARY INTERNATIONAL LAW

Although there is very great diversity in the ways of implementing customary rules, nevertheless a common feature stands out. All national systems adopt the same basic modality of implementation: automatic standing incorporation. National constitutions or statutes or judicial decisions of most States stipulate that customary international rules become domestically binding *ipso facto*, that is, by the mere fact of their evolving in the international community. As soon as they come into being in the world community international customary rules become binding within national legal systems; in addition they have, at the national level, the same content as that of the corresponding international rules.

The reason for the choice of this implementation system is self-evident: it is the only suitable one for rules that emerge gradually in the world community and whose content is not immediately definable. Were States to decide that a customary rule only becomes binding upon State officials and individuals after the enactment of a statute setting out the contents of such a rule, the parliamentary assembly would have to play a very difficult role, namely, to decide whether the customary rule has taken shape, and with what contents. Given the characteristics of customary law, it is far more fitting and practical to leave it to judges and other States officials to establish whether and to what extent a customary rule is binding within the legal system of a State.

It should however be noted that in some States (for example, Belgium) until recently a customary rule of international law could not be brought before, and applied by, the Court of Cassation: under Belgian legislation only alleged violations of a 'law' can be raised before the supreme Court, and international customary rules, as such, were not regarded as amounting to such law unless incorporated into Belgian legislation. This approach, supported by some Belgian cases going back to 1947–1950,[24] merits criticism: indeed, because of a domestic legal technicality the Court of Cassation might end up being barred from ensuring the full consonance of the national system with general rules of international law.

However, it would seem that in more recent times the Belgian Court has revised its approach. In two cases, one of 1966 (*Pittacos* v. *Etat belge*),[25] the other of 1979 (*Vafadar*),[26] it held the claim based on customary international law inadmissible, not however because it did not entail a violation of law, but because of 'lack of legal interest' (*défaut d'intérêt*).

Clearly, there may be customary rules that need to be supplemented by national legislation, in order for them to become operative at the domestic level. As an example of such non-self-executing customary rules, one may mention the rule providing that the maximum outer limit of the territorial sea should be 12 sea miles. Plainly, it is for each State to decide on the width of its territorial sea, by enacting national legislation or regulation on the matter. Having made this general point, let us now consider the *rank* of customary international law within major national systems.

In some States with rigid constitutions, constitutional provisions and judicial practice proclaim that international customary law overrides any inconsistent 'ordinary' national legislation. (This holds true for Italy, Germany, Japan, Greece; the same applies to Uzbekistan, Turkmenistan, and Belarus as well.)[27] In some of these States (for example, Italy, Germany, Japan) there is a constitutional court entrusted with judicial review of legislative acts and consequently responsible for ensuring that no law is passed which conflicts with the constitution. Hence, the enactment of any ordinary law contrary to international customary rules is safeguarded through judicial review by that court.

Other States (such as the USA, China, France, the UK) do not lay down provisions according customary international law a rank higher than that of ordinary legislation. (In the UK this is also due to the lack of a written constitution and the upholding of legislative supremacy.) Consequently, should parliament pass a law clearly conflicting with a customary rule of international law, the national law, being later in time, would prevail. This approach, also upheld in such countries as Belgium, has been laid down in terms in the 1996 South African Constitution (in spite of the fact that this is a rigid constitution and the country has a constitutional court endowed with the powers to undertake judicial review of legislation).[28]

8.4.2 TREATY LAW

(a) Modalities of implementation

While, as shown above, customary international law is normally incorporated by means of the *standing automatic* mechanism, with regard to treaties States tend to resort to all three aforementioned mechanisms of incorporation: *standing automatic; statutory ad hoc incorporation; automatic ad hoc incorporation.*

Some national systems provide that domestic authorities are to comply with treaties upon their publication in the *Official Bulletin* (see, for example, France and many African countries); in the case of the USA, treaties duly ratified by the President after the Senate's approval are 'the supreme Law of the Land' (Article VI of the Constitution). By contrast, other domestic systems (such as the UK and the Russian Federation) provide that treaties do not bind national authorities unless they are translated into detailed national legislation (in the UK, however, this principle does not apply to treaties concerning the conduct of war or to treaties of cession). In other countries, such as Italy and Germany, practice shows a frequent resort to *automatic ad hoc* incorporation.

(b) Non-self-executing treaties

A particular problem may arise with regard to treaties containing non-self-executing provisions, that is, provisions that cannot be directly applied within the national legal system because they need to be supplemented by additional national legislation for them to be implemented. Whenever treaties contain such provisions, even in those national legal systems where the mere publication of international treaties is sufficient for them to produce effects domestically, the passing of implementing legislation proves necessary for applying those international provisions.

The notion was formulated as early as 1829 by Chief Justice Marshall (of the US Supreme Court) in *Foster and Elam* v. *Neilson*. He wrote: 'Our Constitution declares a treaty to be the law of the land. It is, consequently, to be regarded in courts of justice as equivalent to an act of the legislature, whenever it operates of itself without the aid of any legislative provision. But when the terms of the stipulation import a contract, when either of the parties engages to perform a particular act, the treaty addresses itself to the political, not the judicial department; and the legislature must execute the contract, before it can become a rule for the court'.[29]

In *Fujii* v. *State of California* the Supreme Court of California held in 1952 that Articles 55 and 56 of the UN Charter, on human rights, were non self-executing and could not be applied unless the requisite state legislation was enacted.[30] Similarly, in 1979 the Italian Constitutional Court held in *Lockheed* that Article 14.5 of the UN Covenant on Civil and Political Rights (whereby 'Everyone convicted of a crime shall have the right to his conviction and sentence being reviewed by a higher tribunal according to law') was not applicable to the judicial proceedings that could be instituted against the Prime Minister and other members of cabinet under Article 96 of the Constitution, unless and until the legislature passed a law governing appellate proceedings in this matter.[31] In 1981 the Dutch Supreme Court delivered a similar decision.[32]

The distinction between self-executing and non-self-executing provisions of international treaties was taken up, in practice, in the Russian Federal Law on International Treaties of the Russian Federation, adopted by the Duma on 16 June 1995 and entered into force on 21 July 1995. Article 5 of the Law provides *inter alia* that: 'The provisions of the officially published international treaties of the Russian Federation which do not require the adoption of internal acts for their application are directly applicable. Corresponding legal acts *shall be adopted* for the application of other provisions of the international treaties of the Russian Federation' (emphasis added).

It should be emphasized that national courts often tend to broaden the notion of non-self-executing treaty provisions, with a view to wittingly or unwittingly shielding national legal systems from legal change. Thus, for instance, not until 1991 did the French Council of State (*Conseil d'Etat*), after many contrary decisions, come to the right conclusion, that Article 8 of the European Convention on Human Rights is self-executing (under this provision 'Everyone has the right to respect for his private and family life, his home and his correspondence'; see also paragraph 2).[33] Similarly, it was only in 1989 that the Italian Court of Cassation held that Article 5(1)(f) of the same Convention (on the condition of a person who has been arrested or detained with a view to preventing his unauthorized entry into the country, or pending his deportation or extradition) is self-executing.[34]

(c) Status of international treaties and possible conflict with later legislation

The legal standing of treaties within domestic legal orders and the possibility of conflict between international treaties and subsequent national legislation vary greatly, depending upon the rank and status of the national rule providing for the incorporation of international treaties within the legal system. In countries where a constitutional provision (of a rigid constitution) provides for the incorporation of treaties, duly ratified treaties override national legislation.

Thus, in France treaties acquire a status higher than national 'ordinary' legislation, with the obvious consequence that, in the case of conflict, the former prevails. Article 55 of the 1958 Constitution provides that 'Treaties and agreements duly ratified and approved shall, upon their publication, have an authority superior to that of laws, subject, for each agreement or treaty, to its application by the other party'. However, as the *Conseil d'Etat* stated recently in *Sarran, Levacher et al.*[35] and as did the plenary Court of Cassation in *Pauline Fraisse*, international treaties may not override constitutional provisions.[36] It is for this reason that recently, following a decision of the Constitutional Council (*Conseil constitutionnel*),[37] the French Parliament decided that, to implement the Statute of the ICC and those provisions of the Statute that were contrary to the French Constitution, it needed to pass a constitutional law. Such a law was indeed enacted: it added to Article 53 of the Constitution a new paragraph providing that the French legal order shall conform to the Rome Statute.[38] This Statute has thus been given constitutional rank in the French legal system.

Similar provisions on the incorporation of treaties are contained in the constitutions of such countries as Greece[39] and a number of French-speaking African countries, such as the Ivory Coast. The Spanish Constitution of 1978 also contains such a provision, but without the reciprocity clause.[40] Furthermore, Article 15(4) of the 1993 Constitution of the Russian Federation provides that 'the generally recognized principles and norms of international law and the international treaties of the Russian Federation shall constitute an integral part of its legal system' and goes on to state that 'if an international treaty of the Russian Federation establishes other rules than those stipulated by the law, the rules of the international treaty shall apply'.

The supremacy of international treaties is also laid down in the constitutions of such States as Bulgaria (Article 5(4)), Moldova (Article 8), Estonia (Article 123), Armenia (Article 6), Azerbaijan (Article 151), Kazakhstan (Article 4), Georgia (Article 6), and Tadzhikistan (Article 11). In the Netherlands treaties are granted a status that is even higher than the Constitution, at least in some cases.[41] It should be added that in many countries that have constitutional courts, these courts have acted upon the principle of primacy of international treaties over 'ordinary legislation'.[42]

In contrast, in other countries constitutions or national laws provide, either explicitly or implicitly, that treaties possess the same rank and status as laws enacted by parliament. Clearly, the rationale behind this trend is to grant parliament the power to change legislation implementing a treaty whenever national interests are regarded as paramount. Indeed, a later statute can override an earlier treaty. In the USA treaties have the status of federal law and prevail over State law, but can be superseded by a later federal law. (It follows, among other things, that interpretations of treaties made by the US Supreme Court are binding upon State courts.)

There are, however, many States (such as China, Italy, and a number of English-speaking African countries such as Ghana, Uganda, Nigeria, Tanzania, etc.) that have not made any provision in their constitutions or national legislation for the implementation of treaties. In these countries, treaties are incorporated by means of ad hoc mechanisms. The rank and status of treaties within the national legal order thus depend on the rank and status of the ad hoc implementing legislation.

In those States (such as the USA, Italy, etc.) where treaties, once incorporated, assume the rank of ordinary legislation, conflicts between treaties and subsequent legislation may frequently arise. To narrow the range of such possible conflicts, courts tend to uphold the principle of interpretation whereby in case of doubt a national statute must be so construed as not to conflict with an international treaty ratified by the State.

The Italian Court of Cassation clearly set out this principle in 1954. In upholding the prevalence of the Brussels Convention of 1924 on the unification of certain rules on the bill of lading, over the Italian maritime code of 1932, the Court stated that: 'The existence of an international undertaking . . . and, even more, its implementation by the national legislature cannot but amount to a means of interpretation of subsequent legislation. Consequently, failing a clear and manifest intention of the law-makers to repeal the law implementing a treaty, that is to say to cast off the international undertaking, one ought to think that the legislature intended to abide by the general and fundamental rule of international law commanding respect for the treaties.'[43]

US courts have taken the same approach. Thus, for instance in *US* v. *Palestine Liberation Organization* the Southern District Court of New York, in a decision of 29 June 1988, decided that the Anti Terrorism Act of 1988 did not supersede the Headquarters Agreement made by the USA with the UN in 1946, on account of the principle at issue, which the Court set out as follows: 'Only where a treaty is irreconcilable with a later enacted statute and Congress has clearly evinced an intent to supersede a treaty by enacting a statute does the later enacted statute take precedence.'[44]

Some legal scholars have criticized this approach, which the courts of other States have also taken. In their view, to claim that a national statute can derogate from an international treaty only when the lawmakers have clearly expressed the intent to make the law prevail over the previous treaty is to propound a hypothesis that is abstract and pointless. In fact, so they argue, parliaments very seldom deviate from treaties with the express intent to do so. When national legislation turns out to be contrary to international rules, this is often so merely as a result of lack of co-ordination or even owing to an oversight. It could, however, be objected that this principle of construction, however artificial, ultimately constitutes a sound device forged by courts to make good mistakes or oversights of the legislature, with a view to ensuring consistency of national legislation with international legal standards.

An approach akin to that just outlined was taken in the 1996 South African Constitution, section 233 of which provides that:

'When interpreting any legislation, every court must prefer any reasonable interpretation of the legislation that is consistent with international law over any alternative interpretation that is inconsistent with international law.'

It would seem that this wording is sufficiently flexible to grant much leeway to courts when confronted with cases of conflict between national legislation and international treaties.[45]

In any case, a number of Italian international lawyers, and a Russian scholar, have propounded a better view, designed to make treaties prevail over subsequent contrary domestic legislation.[46] Under this view, when interpreting and applying international treaties that might be inconsistent with national legislation, one ought to proceed on the notion that the legislation implementing the treaties makes up 'special' law. This special character does not lie in the fact that that legislation governs a class of facts or persons more limited than that envisaged by the general rule (the usual notion of speciality). Rather, it lies in the origin and the role of the rules implementing the treaty at the national level. These rules differ from ordinary municipal legislation in that they have the particular aim of adjusting the national legal order to an international treaty. They derive their origin and *raison d'être* from the existence of the treaty, and are designed to put it into practice in municipal law. This is the sort of 'speciality' that should make them prevail over subsequent legislation, on the strength of the traditional principle that a later and general rule does not supersede an earlier and special rule.

Ultimately the Court of Cassation in Belgium reached the same conclusion in *S.A. Fromagerie Franco-Suisse 'Le Ski' v. Etat Belge*.[47] The Court held that treaties must prevail over national legislation because 'the primacy of the treaty results from the very nature of international treaty law'. It would seem that the Italian Constitution Court also took the same attitude in a 1993 decision in *Kasim, Noureddin*.[48]

8.4.3 RIGHTS OF INDIVIDUALS *V.* DISCRETIONARY POWER OF STATES IN TREATY IMPLEMENTATION

When a State party to an international treaty fails to implement some of its provisions within its domestic legal order, it may follow that fundamental rights to which individuals would be entitled in the national system of another contracting party fail to accrue to them. This often happens when a foreign State violates international rules granting rights to nationals of a contracting party. In this and similar cases, if the injured State does not take any action to react to a breach of the treaty, and in particular fails to exercise diplomatic or judicial protection of its nationals, individuals' rights may end up being jeopardized. Normally States enjoy discretionary power in their international transactions; it thus often occurs that individuals' rights remain unfulfilled at the national level. A case recently brought before the Spanish High Court best illustrates this adverse upshot.

In *D. Juan*, Argentina, bound by the Treaty of extradition and judicial assistance in criminal matters with Spain, of 3 March 1987, had failed to execute the letters rogatory (that is, letters of request for judicial assistance, normally to gather evidence abroad) sent by the Spanish authorities in relation to crimes of genocide and terrorism allegedly perpetrated by D. Jorge and 95 other persons. The petitioner complained before the Spanish High Court (*Tribunal Supremo*) that the failure of the Spanish authorities to react to this Argentinian breach of the Treaty resulted in the violation of his fundamental right to effective judicial remedy. In a decision of 24 July 2000, the Court dismissed the petition. It held that Spain was under no international or national obligation to respond to the alleged breach of the Treaty by Argentina. The Spanish authorities only had the power (*facultad*) to take international action against this alleged breach; within the Spanish legal order individuals had no right to the exercise of such international power by the Spanish foreign policy-making authorities. The petitioner could only institute proceedings before Argentinian courts with a view to impelling the relevant authorities of Argentina to execute the letters rogatory.[49]

Of course, in the final analysis it is for each State, within its national legal system, to find the way to best settle conflicts and tensions that may arise between (i) respect for the fundamental rights of individuals at the national level, and (ii) political discretion of States in the conduct of international affairs.

8.4.4 IMPLEMENTATION OF BINDING DECISIONS OF INTERNATIONAL ORGANIZATIONS

One of the most striking features of modern international law is that some inter-governmental organizations are empowered to adopt binding decisions, some laying down rules producing outside effects, others consisting of 'administrative acts', that is, binding decisions concerning the internal life of the organization. To be put into operation, these decisions too need to be implemented at the national level. This in particular holds true for such acts as the economic and diplomatic sanctions adopted by the UN SC (for example, those against South Africa, Southern Rhodesia, Iraq, the Federal Republic of Yugoslavia (Serbia and Montenegro), etc.), as well as for the Statutes of the ICTY and the ICTR, enacted by the SC in 1993 and 1994 by a decision taken under Chapter VII of the UN Charter. Of great importance also is the implementation of regulations, directives, and other acts adopted by the organs of the European Community.

Normally national legal systems do not contain any special provision on the automatic or ad hoc incorporation of decisions of international organizations. Exceptions can be found in the constitutions of such States as the Netherlands, Greece, and Spain,[50] or in the judicial practice of such States as France.[51] These countries take a modern and internationally oriented attitude, by providing that internationally binding resolutions and decisions of intergovernmental organizations become binding within the internal legal system simply upon their publication in the State's Official Journal. (It is submitted that it would be excessive to claim that those decisions or resolutions should become binding *ipso facto*, without even being published in the Official Journal of the relevant State. Since normally there is no international judicial review of binding acts of international organizations, it would seem that States are entitled to exercise some sort of minimal scrutiny of the legality of those acts, that is, their consonance with the organization's rules, before applying them internally.)

Whenever this is not the case, or if the international normative acts, being non self-executing, require implementing legislation, specific legislative enactments prove necessary. There have been many such enactments. A number of States have passed legislation for the specific purpose of adjusting their national legal system to the

Statutes of the ICTY and the ICTR, in particular with a view to specifying the national judicial bodies entrusted with the task of ensuring co-operation with the Tribunals. Other States, including the Russian Federation, did not need such legislation to put the Statutes into practice.

The situation is different in relation to the national implementation of acts adopted by organs of the European Communities. The treaties establishing these Communities provide that regulations are 'directly applicable' in the national legal order of the various member States (see, for instance, Article 249 EC). As for directives, the case law of the European Court of Justice (ECJ) has clarified that in at least three categories of cases, they are directly applicable in national legal systems.[52] In other cases the passing of implementing legislation by each member State is needed.

This feature of EC acts, that is, their being directly applicable in the national legal systems of member States, is warranted (1) by the need for the EC immediately to produce the same legal effects within the legal systems of all these States; and (2) by the existence of a court (the ECJ) entrusted with the task of undertaking judicial review of any Community act allegedly contrary to the treaties.

8.5 STATIST VERSUS INTERNATIONAL OUTLOOK: EMERGING TRENDS

The choice of mechanisms for implementing international rules within national legal systems is the acid test for establishing to what extent States are open to international values. Those States which are sensitive to international demands opt for automatic standing incorporation mechanisms for customary law, treaty rules, and decisions of international organizations. In addition, they grant those international rules and decisions a higher rank than 'ordinary' law.

Very few countries adopt such an overall internationalist outlook. Three in particular stand out: Greece, the Netherlands, and Spain. They all adopt the automatic standing incorporation system. In addition, in Greece, both customary international rules and treaties override national legislation, a clear demonstration of Greece's consistent and courageous internationalist approach. In the Netherlands international treaties override the Constitution. In Spain provision is made not only for the primacy of international treaties over national legislation, but also for the obligation of national authorities to construe national legislation on human rights in the light of international instruments[53] (however, to safeguard the requirements of democratic governance, this internationalist attitude is counterbalanced by the firmly required intervention of Parliament: under the interpretation the Council of State (*Consejo de Estado*) has set forth in numerous 'opinions', Parliament's authorization or approval is required by Article 94 of the Constitution[54] not only for making treaties, including agreements 'in simplified form' (for instance through exchange of diplomatic notes),[55] but also for appending or withdrawing reservations,[56] making unilateral declarations (whether creating new obligations or simply interpreting existing obliga-tions),[57] amending multilateral treaties,[58] denouncing treaties or agreements,[59] as well as in cases of adhesion or accession of States to a multilateral treaty already binding upon Spain;[60] in contrast, parliamentary authorization is normally not required for the provisional application of treaties).[61]

Conversely, most States still take a rather nationalist approach to the implementa-tion of international law. They do not make international values, as sanctioned in international rules, prevail over domestic interests and concerns, as laid down in national legislation. By putting international rules on the same footing as ordinary national legislation, they retain the power to disregard international values at any time, by passing municipal legislation inconsistent with international rules. The most extreme of nationalist attitudes would seem to be that of States such as the UK which, out of respect for parliamentary prerogatives, require, for treaty rules to be binding at the national level, that the treaty be translated into national legislation by act of parliament.

Other States, such as France and the Russian Federation, which have adopted a partially internationalist approach, in that they make at least a part of international law prevail over national legislation, tend to take this attitude only with regard to treaties (whereas they take a traditional, statist approach with regard to customary law). This trend is probably accounted for by a widespread distrust of customary law, a body of law regarded as uncertain in its contents, and at any rate as not so reliable as written law. There may be another possible factor: in the case of treaties, normally parliament is associated with their birth, at least in that it authorizes their ratification or their implementation, and such association gives an imprint of popular legitimation to the rules contained in the treaty.

In sum, most States do not accord primacy to international rules in their national legal systems. Thus, it may be concluded that most members of the world community tend to play down the possible role of international legal standards in their domestic legal setting. This does not mean that they normally and systematically disregard international norms. The contrary is rather the rule. The failure of States to accord to international law pride of place in their legal systems only means that they do not intend to tie their hands formally, at the constitutional or legislative level. In other words, subject to the few exceptions already referred to, States ultimately prefer not to enshrine in their constitutions or in their laws a firm and irrevocable commitment to unqualified observance of all international rules.

To limit, at least in part, the markedly statist outlook taken by many States, courts may play a crucial role by stepping in to ensure compliance at the national level with international legal standards. Whenever their national legislation does not provide them with the legal means for making international values prevail, they have at least two interpretative principles available: that concerning the presumption in favour of international treaties, and the principle of speciality (see 8.4.2(c)). By judiciously resorting to either of these principles courts may make international law advance in a significant way.

Furthermore, one should consider that in modern international law we are faced with a phenomenon of increasing importance: there are more and more international rules that address themselves directly to individuals, either by imposing obligations (**4.5.2(a)**) or by granting rights (**4.5.2(c)**). These rules intend to, and do, reach individuals directly, that is, not through the medium of the municipal law of States. They are thus effective and operative as soon as they emerge, regardless of what is provided for in any particular national legal systems, and even contrary to possible national rules. Whereas in the old international community international law and national legal systems made up two distinct spheres of law, there has been an increasing tendency, since at least the First World War, for many international rules to operate everywhere in the world immediately, that is, to penetrate and directly affect individuals living under national systems of law. Clearly, for these rules, the possible passing of national implementing legislation only serves to strengthen their effectiveness. If they are matched by national rules, their impact on the conduct of individuals becomes even stronger.

9

STATE RESPONSIBILITY

9.1 GENERAL

As was pointed out in **Chapter 1**, the international community is so primitive that the archaic concept of collective responsibility still prevails. Where States breach an international rule, the whole collectivity to which the individual State official belongs, who materially infringed that rule, bears responsibility. The State official may have to suffer punishment or be blamed within the national legal system to which he belongs, if that system so provides. On the international plane, it is the whole State that incurs responsibility and which has to take all the required remedial measures.

Within this general framework one may however discern two different stages of development of law: the traditional legal regulation of this matter, and the new law evolved in recent years. As usual, the traditional has not been obliterated by the new, which has largely improved upon and developed some major features of the traditional system. It is therefore worth taking a quick glance at the old law before dwelling in some depth on the recent trends currently shaping up in the world community.

At the outset, a definition of State responsibility may prove useful. This notion designates the *legal consequences of the international wrongful act of a State*, namely the obligations of the wrongdoer, on the one hand, and the rights and powers of any State affected by the wrong, on the other. However, when discussing State responsibility, one must also enquire into the *preconditions* of this bundle of obligations, rights, and powers, and ask what is meant by 'international wrongful act'. We will therefore also discuss the subjective and objective elements that are necessary for an international wrongful act of a State to come about.

9.2 TRADITIONAL LAW

The old law on State responsibility primarily consisted of customary rules evolved out of the practice of States and a wealth of cases brought before international arbitral tribunals. Very few treaty rules existed, the most notable being Article 3 of the Fourth Hague Convention of 1907, on the Laws and Customs of War on Land, providing that 'A belligerent party which violates the provisions of the said Regulations [i.e. the

Regulations annexed to the Convention] shall, if the case demands, be liable to pay compensation. It shall be responsible for all acts committed by persons forming part of its armed forces'. In the period 1924–30, under the auspices of the League of Nations, an attempt was made to codify customary law governing various matters. A committee of jurists appointed by the League Council concluded that one of the seven topics ripe for codification was 'Responsibility of States for Damages done in their Territory to the Person or Property of Foreigners'. However, a Codification Conference held at The Hague in 1930 showed that there was disagreement on the matter of responsibility, among other things on the issue of responsibility for the treatment of aliens (some States proposing that they should be granted the 'national treatment', that is, equated with the nationals of the host State, others—principally Western countries—suggesting that they should instead be treated according to the 'minimum standard' principle, that is, they must be afforded the possibly higher protection deriving from the set of international rules making up the so-called 'minimum standards of civilization').

Customary rules provided that if a State violated an obligation imposed by an international rule, it bore international responsibility for such violation. Consequently, it had to make reparation for the breach; alternatively, the injured State was entitled to resort to self-help. Hence it could take forcible action (armed reprisals, war) or non-forcible measures (economic sanctions, suspension or termination of a treaty, etc.) designed either to impel the delinquent State to repair the wrong, or to 'penalize' it.

The traditional regulation of this matter exhibited a few major features.

First of all, *rules on State responsibility were rudimentary*. In particular, they did not specify some general elements of the notion of international delinquency, or the general conditions of the legal consequences of international wrongs. As to the content of the obligation to make reparation, it was not specified whether one form of reparation was to be preferred to another and, if so, subject to what conditions. It was generically provided that reparation could take the form of restitution in kind (re-establishment of the situation as it existed before the wrongful act), compensation (payment of a sum of money), or satisfaction (apology, expression of regret, etc.). As a rule of thumb it was held that satisfaction should be the consequence of a breach of an international rule protecting the honour or dignity of a State. However, all these classes of reparation were resorted to in State practice as possible instances of reparation, not as legal categories to which recourse should be made under certain circumstances and not under others. The choice of each class was left to the parties concerned. Furthermore, it was left to the injured State to decide whether and at what stage to resort to enforcement measures, as well as what measures to take.

In addition, it was not clear whether State responsibility could arise only if State officials of the allegedly delinquent State had acted either wilfully and maliciously, or negligently, or if instead the simple fact that one or more of a State's officials had broken a rule of international law was sufficient, without there being any *intent* or *fault (culpable negligence)*.[1]

Furthermore, State responsibility amounted to a *bilateral relation* between the delinquent State and the injured State. It was for them to agree (or, depending on the case, disagree) on the form of reparation; it was for the injured State alone to choose—subject to a few requirements including proportionality—the form of self-help, if it decided to enforce its rights. Only if the parties entered into negotiations and reached an agreement could they establish a dispute settlement mechanism.

Another feature of traditional law is that accountability for international wrongs hinged on the aforementioned concept of '*collective responsibility*', that is, the bulk of international rules provided that only States as such could be held accountable for any action contrary to international rules, performed by a State official. The only areas where individuals could be held liable for their actions were: (i) piracy (an international crime imputable to individuals acting *in their private capacity*, and widespread until the seventeenth century) and, (ii) since the nineteenth century, war crimes, namely offences committed in inter-State wars, normally by individuals acting *as State officials* (members of the armed forces of one of the belligerents). However, as for this last class of offences, liability applied only to soldiers and lower officers, and was not extended, at least in practice, to military leaders and commanders. By and large, the whole area of individual criminal liability was held to be rather inconsequential.

Lastly, the customary rules on the legal consequences of wrongful acts were normally *lumped together, both by States and by a number of Anglo-American publicists, with the substantive rules governing State behaviour*, chiefly with the customary rules concerning the treatment of foreigners. This was clearly due to the fact that the customary rules on State responsibility primarily crystallized as a result of disputes concerning the treatment, chiefly in non-industrialized countries (often, Latin American countries), of nationals of industrialized States. Hence a tendency evolved to associate rules on State responsibility to breaches of those international rules which imposed on States the obligation to respect the rights of foreign nationals and their property.

9.3 THE CURRENT REGULATION OF STATE RESPONSIBILITY: AN OVERVIEW

The present regulation of this difficult area of international law has gradually grown over the years. It has been greatly influenced by the works of the UN International Law Commission (ILC). The reports prepared by a number of successive outstanding Special Rapporteurs (F. V. García Amador, R. Ago, W. Riphagen, G. Arangio-Ruiz, J. Crawford), the debates in the Commission, and the reaction of States expressed both individually and in discussion in the UN General Assembly (GA), have gradually led to the laying down of general rules that to a large extent reflect existing law, while in some respects progressively developing that law. These rules are expected to become the subject of a sort of 'restatement of law', possibly to be enshrined in a General Assembly Declaration rather than becoming a codification convention to be adopted by a Diplomatic Conference.

The salient traits of the new law may be summarized as follows.

First, the law of State responsibility has been *unfastened from the set of substantive rules on the treatment of foreigners*, with which it had been previously bound up. Chiefly R. Ago must be credited for this major clarification of the matter. It is now generally acknowledged that a distinction can be made between '*primary rules*' of international law, that is, those customary or treaty rules laying down substantive obligations for States (on State immunities, treatment of foreigners, diplomatic and consular immunities, respect for the territorial sovereignty of other States, etc.), and '*secondary rules*', that is, rules establishing (i) the conditions on which a breach of a 'primary rule' may be held to have occurred and (ii) the legal consequences of this breach. The latter body of international rules encompasses a separate and relatively autonomous body of international law, the law of State responsibility.

Second, current rules on State responsibility have *clarified and given precision* to a number of previously controversial rules: for instance, the question of whether fault is necessary, the nature of the damage required for a State to be considered 'injured' by the wrongful act of another State, the circumstances precluding wrongfulness, etc.

Third, agreement has now crystallized on the need to distinguish between *two forms or categories of State accountability*: responsibility for 'ordinary' breaches of international law, and a class of 'aggravated responsibility' for violations of some fundamental general rules that enshrine essential values. The first class embraces responsibility for breaches of bilateral or multilateral treaties, or general rules, laying down 'synallagmatic' obligations, that is, rules protecting reciprocal interests of States (economic and commercial relations, the reciprocal treatment of nationals and of consuls or diplomats, etc.). The consequences of any breach of any such rule creates a 'bilateral relation' between the delinquent State and the wronged State. Hence the whole relation remains a '*private*' *matter* between the two States. 'Aggravated responsibility' has markedly distinct features from 'ordinary responsibility'. It arises when a State violates a general rule laying down a 'community obligation' (see **1.8.2**), that is a customary obligation *erga omnes* protecting fundamental values (chiefly: peace, human rights, self-determination of peoples) or an obligation *erga omnes contractantes* laid down in a multilateral treaty safeguarding those fundamental values, and entitling respectively any State, or any other party to the multilateral treaty, to demand cessation of any serious violation. In the case of this 'aggravated responsibility' the *material* or *moral* damage, if any, is not an indispensable element of State responsibility. What matters is that the breach results in the infringement of a State's right to compliance by any other State (or contracting State) with the obligation. Following such a breach of one of the aforementioned rules, a '*public relation*' comes into being between the delinquent State and all other States or, as the case may be, all the other contracting States. The 'public' nature of the relation lies in the fact that any other State, regardless of whether or not it has been materially or morally damaged by the breach, can invoke the responsibility of the wrongdoer (this invocation may also be made by a competent international body, either on its own initiative, or at the request of a State). In other words, the States that take action to invoke this class of responsibility *do not pursue a personal or individual interest*; they pursue *a community interest*, for they act on behalf of the whole world community or of the collectivity of States parties to the multilateral treaty. In addition, all the States entitled to demand compliance with the obligation that has been infringed may take a host of remedial actions designed to impel the delinquent State to cease its wrongdoing or to make reparation.

Third, as pointed out above, previously in cases of international wrongdoing the injured State could decide whether immediately to take forcible action, so as to 'punish' the delinquent State or instead to first request reparation. Furthermore, if no reparation was made, that State could again decide on its own whether to try to settle the dispute peacefully by resorting to the various procedures and mechanisms available, including arbitration, or rather enforce its right to reparation by using military or economic force. In contrast, this is no longer permitted now. A general obligation evolved following the expansion of the scope of Article 33 of the UN Charter. The requirement to endeavour to settle disputes by peaceful means before resorting to possible counter-measures (see **5.6** and **9.4.2(ii)**) currently obliges States to take a set of successive steps. They must first request reparation; then, if no reparation is made or reparation is considered unsatisfactory, they must *endeavour to settle the dispute peacefully*, by having recourse to negotiations, conciliation, arbitration, or other means of settling disputes (on this obligation, denied in *Air Service Agreement*, see *infra*, **9.4.2(ii)**). Only if such recourse proves to be of no avail, can the injured State (as well as, in the case of 'aggravated responsibility', the other States entitled to claim compliance with the obligation breached) take peaceful counter-measures (the only exception being individual or collective self-defence under Article 51 of the UN Charter; see **14.4.1**).

Fourth, *individual criminal liability*, as opposed to State responsibility, has enormously expanded. Individuals, be they State officials or private persons, are now accountable for serious breaches of international law (war crimes, crimes against humanity, genocide, terrorism, etc.; see **12.2**) both in time of peace (except of course for war crimes) and in time of war. In addition, not only simple soldiers and junior officers, as in the past, but also military leaders as well as senior politicians, members of cabinet, industrialists, etc. may be held accountable for any international crime. National and international prosecution and punishment of these crimes ensure that the international rules of human rights law and international humanitarian law are respected and enforced. This body of international criminal law has developed as a separate branch from the international law on State responsibility, although overlaps may come about (particularly in the case of genocide) between individual criminal liability and State responsibility.

Fifth, current needs have resulted in the possibility for States to be held *accountable for lawful actions.* This is provided for in rules that of course no longer pertain to State responsibility proper.

Thus, for instance, under Article 110 of the 1982 Law of the Sea Convention the warship of a State may stop and search a foreign merchant vessel on the high seas if 'there is reasonable doubt for suspecting' that the ship is engaged in piracy, or the slave trade, or in unauthorized broadcasting, or is without nationality, or if the ship, though flying a foreign flag or refusing to show its flag, is in reality of the same nationality as the warship. However, if it turns out that the suspicions are unfounded, the State to which the warship belongs must pay compensation 'for any loss or damage that may have been sustained' by the merchant vessel. Similarly, under some treaties on the use of outer space (for example, the 1972 Convention on International Liability for Damage Caused by Space Objects) or on the exploitation of nuclear energy (for example, the 1960 Convention on Third Party Liability in the Field of Nuclear Energy, or the 1962 Convention on Liability of Operators of Nuclear Ships) States are liable to pay compensation, either under international law or within a municipal law system (in the form of civil liability) to States or persons injured by their lawful but ultra-hazardous activities.

9.4 'ORDINARY' STATE RESPONSIBILITY

9.4.1 PRECONDITIONS OF STATE RESPONSIBILITY

As pointed out above, the basic precondition of State responsibility is the commission of a wrongful act by a State. For a wrongful act to occur, it is necessary that some subjective and objective elements come into being. The subjective elements are: (i) the imputability to a State of conduct of an individual (action or omission) contrary to an international obligation; (ii) in some instances, the fault (*culpa*) of the State official performing the wrongful act. The objective elements are: (i) the inconsistency of particular conduct with an international obligation; (ii) material or moral damage to another international subject; (iii) the absence of any of the various circumstances precluding wrongfulness.

We shall here discuss only the most important aspects of these elements.

(a) Subjective elements of international delinquency.

(1) *Imputability of an international wrong to a State.* States act on the international level through individuals. Hence, for a State to be responsible it is necessary first of all to establish whether the conduct of an individual may be imputed to it.

For the purpose of imputation of a wrongful act to a State, normally one must first establish whether the individual who materially committed the breach has the status of State official under the national legal system of a particular State, whether or not he is an official of the central government (including legislative and judicial authorities) or of a territorial unit, for example, the member State of a federal State such as the USA. As the ICJ held in *Immunity from Legal Process of a Special Rapporteur of the*

Commission on Human Rights, 'according to a well-established rule of international law [of a customary character] the conduct of any organ of a State must be regarded as an act of that State'.[2] Hence, if the individual has that status, the attribution of his acts and transactions to the State can be justifiably effected. Plainly, the State official must act in his official capacity, and not *qua* private individual.

For cases where the USA or Mexico were held responsible for acts of member States, see *Davy*,[3] brought before a UK-Venezuela Mixed Claims Commission, *Pellat*,[4] (where a France-Mexico Claims Commission held in 1929 that 'a federal State is considered responsible for acts of member States causing damage to citizens of other States, even when the Constitution denies to the central government the right to supervise the action of the member States or the right to demand that they conform their conduct to the prescriptions of international law'), and *Galvan*.[5]

A wrongful act is imputed to the State even if the State official performed that act *outside his instructions or even outside his remit*, as long as he acted by using the means and powers pertaining to his public function. Foreign nationals and foreign States are not expected or required to be cognizant in each case of the allotment of powers to the various State officials. Hence, the rule whereby the State incurs responsibility even when its organ acted outside his competence (this rule is restated in Article 9 of ILC Draft (2000)).

In *Caire* an officer and two soldiers of the forces in control of Mexico had asked Mr Caire, a French national, to give them $US 5,000 in gold, under threat of death; as he refused to comply, stating that he did not possess so much money, they detained him for some time and then had him shot. Verzjil, the President of the France-Mexico Claims Commission, held Mexico responsible for the act. He stated that States bear international responsibility for all acts committed by their officials or organs which are contrary to international law, regardless of whether the official or organ has acted within the limits of its competency or has exceeded those limits. However, in order to justify the admission of this 'objective responsibility' of the State for acts committed by its officials or organs outside their competence, it is necessary that 'they should have acted, at least apparently, as competent officials or organs, or that, in acting, they should have used powers or measures proper to their official character'.[6]

In *Youmans* some American nationals, following a labour dispute, were threatened by a mob of Mexican nationals. At the request of the mayor of the town, Mexican troops were sent to quell the riot and put an end to the attack on the Americans. However the troops, on arriving at the scene of the riot, instead of dispersing the mob, opened fire on the house where the Americans had withdrawn. As a result, two Americans were killed by the troops and members of the mob. No one appeared to have been punished for the crime, although some prosecutions were begun and some mobsters were sentenced in absentia, but then the sentences were modified. In 1926 the Mexico-US General Claims Commission found Mexico responsible, stating the following: '[W]e do not consider that the participation of the soldiers in the murder [of one of the Americans] can be regarded as acts of soldiers committed in their private capacity when it is clear that at the time of the commission of these acts the men were on duty under the immediate supervision and in the presence of a commanding officer. Soldiers inflicting personal injuries or committing wanton destruction or looting always act in disobedience of some rules laid down by superior authority. There could be no liability whatever for such misdeeds if the view were taken that any acts committed by soldiers in contravention of instructions must always be considered as personal acts.'[7]

In *Mallén*, a Mexican consul had been violently attacked and beaten twice by an American police officer, who had evidently a profound aversion for the consul. As for the first attack, with respect to which Mexico did not allege the 'direct responsibility' of the USA, but a denial of justice, the Mexican-US General Claim Commission found that the evidence indicated 'a malevolent and unlawful act of a private individual who happened to be an official'. On the second attack, the American policeman, 'showing his badge to assert his official capacity', struck Mallén among other things with his revolver, and then took him at gun point to the El Paso county jail. The policeman was brought to trial and contended in court that he had arrested Mallén because of his illegally carrying a gun, a contention that according to the Mexico-US General Claims Commission had no merit. The police officer was sentenced by a US court in Texas to pay a small fine, which he never paid. The Commission held that there was no doubt as to 'the liability on the part of American authorities for this second assault on Mallén by an American official' and stressed that he 'could not have taken Mallén to jail if he had not been acting as a police officer'.[8]

International rules also cover the case where individuals who do not fulfil State functions in fact play an important role in the exercise of governmental authority in that they may actually wield authority and control over senior State officials. It is only logical that acts performed by those persons should be attributed to the State as a whole; hence, if these acts are contrary to international law, the State shall bear international responsibility.

Another category of individuals whose activity may be attributed to a State is that of *de facto State organs*. These are individuals who, although they do not have the formal status and rank of State officials, in fact act on behalf of State. They can be so regarded when they (i) act under instructions from a State, or (ii) act under the overall control of a State, or (iii) in fact behave as State officials.

As instances of the State officials under discussion mention could be made of the secretary-general of a political party in a one-party State.

In addition, a recent case may be recalled. On 20 October 2000 the Paris Court of Appeals ruled that it was permissible to prosecute in France the Libyan leader Muammar Qaddafi for complicity in murder of French nationals in relation to a terrorist act, that is the bombing of a French airliner over Niger in 1989.[9] When it was objected that under the Libyan Constitution Qaddafi was not Head of State or Government, the French Foreign Ministry issued a press release stating among other things that 'the whole of the international community considers Qaddafi as the head of the Libyan State' and drawing attention to the fact that 'when international summits are convened it is Qaddafi who represents Libya. We consider, as a matter of fact, that when there are international gatherings and the international community must invite the head of State of Libya . . . its is Colonel Qaddafi who is invited; nobody has ever thought that there might be anybody other than he to be regarded as head of State'.[10]

The rule is to some extent codified in Article 5 of the ILC Draft (2000), which concerns public entities that are not State organs under national law. Under this Article 'The conduct of an entity which is not an organ of the State . . . but which is empowered by the law of that State to exercise elements of the governmental authority shall be considered an act of the State under international law, provided the entity was acting in that capacity in the case in question'.

The judgment of the ICJ in *Nicaragua* and that of the Appeals Chamber of the ICTY in *Tadić* (*Merits*) should be recalled.

In *Nicaragua*,[11] the Court had to establish whether in the civil war in Nicaragua of *contras* (rebels) against the central authorities, the breaches of international humanitarian law perpetrated by some individuals were to be attributed to the USA. The Court distinguished three classes of individuals. First, there were the members of the US Government administration (such as members of the CIA) and members of the US armed forces. Their acts were no doubt attributable to the USA. Second, there were some Latin American operatives (so-called UCLA, or Unilaterally Controlled Latino Assets). The Court held that their acts were to be attributed to the USA either because, in addition to being paid by that Government, they had been given specific instructions by US agents or officials and had acted under their supervision, or because 'agents of the US' had 'participated in the planning, direction, support and execution' of such specific operations by the UCLA as attacks on oil and storage facilities, or the blowing up of underwater oil pipelines in Nicaraguan ports. Third, there was the category of *contras*. The Court stated that for their violations of international humanitarian law to be legally attributed to the USA it was necessary to show that they had been under 'the effective control' of this State, namely that this State had issued specific instructions to the *contras* concerning the perpetration of the unlawful acts at issue. It would seem that the Court essentially propounded two alternative tests for the attribution of wrongful acts: first, whether or not individuals were State officials; second, if they were not, whether they were under the 'effective control' of a State, namely whether (i) they were paid or financed by a State, (ii) their action had been co-ordinated and supervised by that State, and (iii) the State had issued specific instructions concerning each of their unlawful actions.

It would seem that the ILC, in its latest Draft (2000), has substantially upheld the *Nicaragua* tests. In Article 6 the ILC has envisaged the following forms of authority by a State over individuals, for such individuals to be regarded as de facto State organs acting on behalf of the State: (i) acting under instructions from a State or (ii) acting under the direction or control of a State, '*in carrying out the unlawful conduct*' (emphasis added).

In *Tadić* (*Merits*) the ICTY Appeals Chamber had to tackle the question of de facto State organs from a different viewpoint: it had to establish whether some individuals (Bosnian Serbs) fighting within a prima facie civil war (between Bosnian Serbs and the central authorities in Bosnia and Herzegovina) had in fact acted on behalf of a foreign country (the Federal Republic of Yugoslavia (Serbia and Montenegro)), thus turning the civil conflict into an international armed conflict. Departing from *Nicaragua*, the ICTY held that international law provides for three alternative tests, to establish whether an individual acts as de facto State organ. First, whether single individuals or militarily unorganized groups act under specific instructions or subsequent public approval of a State. Second, in the case of armed groups or militarily organized groups, whether they are under the overall control of a State (without necessarily this State issuing instructions concerning each specific action). Third, whether individuals actually behave as State officials within the structure of a State.[12] The German Supreme Court (*Bundesgerichtshof*) has recently taken up this approach by the ICTY, in a judgement of 21 February 2001.[13]

In the case of unlawful acts committed by *individuals not acting as de facto State officials*, for instance against foreigners or foreign authorities, the State on whose territory the acts were committed incurs international responsibility only if it did not act with due diligence: if it omitted to take the necessary measures to prevent attacks on foreigners, or foreign assets, or, after the perpetration of the unlawful acts, failed to search for and duly punish the authors of any misconduct, besides paying compensation to the victims. In other words, in the case of violence and other unlawful acts against foreigners, the State is not responsible for the acts of the individuals; it is accountable only if its own 'conduct by omission' may be proved, that is, there is failure to act in conformity with international legal standards.

In this connection, the *US Diplomatic and Consular Staff in Tehran* case, decided in 1980 by the ICJ, is illuminating.

The Court divided the Iranian militants' attack on the US embassy and consular premises in Tehran into two phases. In the first stage the attack was carried out by militants who had no 'form of official status as recognized "agents" or organs of the Iranian State'.[14] Therefore, according to the Court, the militants' conduct in mounting the attack, storming the embassy, and seizing the inmates as hostages could not be 'imputable to the State on that basis'. Nevertheless, Iran was held responsible in that it failed to protect the US premises as required by international law.[15] The second phase started after completion of the occupation of the US embassy. At this stage the Iranian Government was legally bound to bring to an end the unlawful occupation and pay reparation. Instead, it approved and endorsed the occupation and even issued, on 17 November 1979, a decree stating that the US personnel 'did not enjoy international diplomatic respect'. As a result, in the view of the Court, the 'occupants' 'had now become agents of the Iranian State for whose acts the State itself was internationally responsible'.[16]

The Special Rapporteur J. Crawford pointed out in his First Report on State Responsibility (1998) that that acknowledgement and approval by a State of conduct 'as its own' may have retroactive effect. He rightly noted that in the *Diplomatic and Consular Staff* case this question did not have practical relevance, because Iran was held responsible in relation to an earlier period on a different legal basis. In other cases it could instead become material.[17]

(2) *The question of whether the fault of State officials is required for State responsibility to arise.* By 'fault' is meant a psychological attitude of the wrongdoer consisting of either 'intention' (the intent to bring about the event resulting from the conduct; for instance, the intent to expel all the nationals of a foreign country in breach of an international treaty), or 'recklessness' (awareness of the risk of the prohibited consequences occurring; for instance, a State puts in place provisional military installations on the high seas, knowing that it may thus jeopardize the freedom of other States to fish in that area or that those installations may imperil important natural resources).

Normally international courts do not inquire whether or not State officials who have allegedly performed an international wrong acted intentionally. In other words they do not look into the subjective attitude of the wrongdoer. They only consider the question of fault if the State complained of objects that it did not act willingly and invokes, for instance, *force majeure.*

The ILC Draft (2000) has endorsed this approach in that it does not envisage intention or fault as a distinct subjective element of State responsibility, but only takes fault into account when dealing with circumstances precluding wrongfulness (when lack of fault may exclude, in some instances, the arising of State responsibility; see *infra*, **9.4.1(b)(3)**), or for establishing the amount of compensation due (see Article 40 of the ILC Draft (2000)).

However, at least in two cases, fault—in the form of knowledge—amounts to an indispensable subjective element of State responsibility: (i) when a State 'directs and controls another State in the commission of an internationally wrongful act by the latter'. In this case it is internationally responsible for that act if, among other things, 'that State does so with knowledge of the circumstances of the internationally wrongful act' (Article 17); and (ii) when a State coerces another State to commit an act; in this case the State is internationally responsible for that act if (a) the act would, but for the coercion, be an internationally wrongful act of the coerced State; and (b) the coercing State does so with knowledge of the circumstances of the act (Article 18).

(b) Objective elements

(1) *Inconsistency of State conduct with an international obligation.* International law requires that for the conduct of a State to be inconsistent with an international obligation, it must be contrary to an obligation stemming for that State from an applicable rule or principle of international law, whatever the nature of the obligation breached (that is whether it is imposed by a customary rule, a treaty provision, a binding decision of an international organization, etc.). Plainly, for State responsibility to arise, it is necessary that the obligation was in force when it was breached (the principle of *tempus commissi delicti*). The wrongful conduct may consist either of an action or of the failure to take a prescribed action. Furthermore, wrongful acts may be *instantaneous* in nature, or *continuing* wrongs.

(2) *The question of damage.* As stated above, a State that has a right corresponding to the obligation breached is *legally entitled* to call to account the wrongdoer and in particular to bring an action against it (if the necessary procedural conditions are fulfilled). Some courts and many commentators have asserted that, in addition to this legal entitlement, a distinct specific element is also required, namely *material* or *moral damage*. Material damage is any prejudice caused to the economic or patrimonial interests of a State or its nationals; moral damage is any breach of a State's honour or dignity (for example, burning the flag of a State, or the violation by a military aircraft of the airspace of a foreign country, without causing any material damage, or, as in a recent case involving members of the Israeli intelligence, when sovereignty is violated by foreign agents planting listening devices in a private apartment abroad; see *infra*, (4)). According to one school of thought, an international wrongful act may only be committed when, in addition to the violation of an obligation and a corresponding right (*legal injury*), a State also causes material or moral damage, which it is then obliged to repair. In contrast, Ago, in the footsteps of Anzilotti,[18] suggested in the ILC a view that was accepted by the Commission,[19] namely that a legal injury is necessarily *inherent* in any breach of an international right of a State. If—so the argument goes— what matters is that a damage or prejudice be caused to a *legal right* of another State,

there is no point in insisting that damage, or prejudice, should be regarded as a *distinct* objective element of wrongfulness. And indeed it is not considered so in ILC Draft (2000). However, under this doctrine the material or moral damage may be taken into account when appraising the modalities and the *quantum* of the ensuing reparation.

This view is no doubt sound. However, one may object that it is no coincidence that most illustrations of responsibility arising out of a mere breach of an international obligation without involving any material or moral damage, advanced in the ILC Reports, belong to an area where State responsibility takes on different connotations, namely, the area of what is here called 'aggravated responsibility' (the ILC referred to breaches by a State of the human rights of its own nationals, as well as violations by a contracting State of ILO conventions, which, as is well known, are conventions laying down obligations *erga omnes* the violation of which does not bring about material or moral damage to other contracting parties).[20] This bears out the notion that whereas damage—at least under customary international law—is a necessary objective element of the wrongful act in the case of 'ordinary responsibility', as we shall see it *is not indispensable in the case of 'aggravated responsibility'*. In the former category, based on a one-to-one legal relation (between the responsible State and the victim State) normally the injured State is entitled to request reparation only because (a) one of its rights has been breached and (b) this breach has caused a material or moral damage. It is easy to explain why in international case law damage has not been *explicitly* required as one of the basic elements of international responsibility (except in those cases where courts have insisted that only direct damage, and not the so-called indirect damage, gives rise to responsibility):[21] when the States concerned in an alleged breach have brought cases to international courts, courts have not felt the need to satisfy themselves that the State other than the one allegedly breaching international obligation was a damaged party. This was simply taken for granted. Indeed, international substantive rules aim at protecting specific interests of States in their bilateral relations with any other member of the international community. In practice States undertake legal démarches with a view to invoking State responsibility *vis-à-vis* another State only when the action of that State directly affects them in their economic, commercial, diplomatic, or political sphere. State practice shows that, most of the time, if a State is not injured at the material or moral level by the action of another State, it does not invoke international rules on State responsibility against that State (unless the legal regime of 'aggravated responsibility' may be triggered, on the conditions we will set out below, and the State decides to exercise its right to invoke the international responsibility of the offending State).

What has just been pointed out applies to the legal regime of State responsibility envisaged in *customary* international law. Nothing of course precludes States from setting up *by treaty* a legal regime whereby a State incurs responsibility for the breach of an obligation towards another contracting party even if it has caused no material or moral damage, but only a legal injury (this legal injury resides in the violation of the right accruing to the other contracting State, in correspondence to the obligation

breached). It would seem that some Agreements concluded within the WTO envisage such a legal regime (see *infra*, **10.8.1**). In the WTO, a contracting party can
invoke the responsibility of another party on account of the mere contravention of an
obligation laid down in the Agreement, even in the absence of a material or moral
damage.

(3) *Circumstances precluding wrongfulness*. Another objective element to be taken
into account when establishing State responsibility is whether there are circumstances
precluding wrongfulness. State practice and case law, as codified in ILC Draft (2000),
provide for seven principal such circumstances: (i) consent of the State injured; (ii)
compliance with peremptory norms; (iii) self-defence; (iv) counter-measures in
respect of an international wrong; (v) *force majeure*; (vi) distress; (vii) state of
necessity.

Consent to carry out activities that would otherwise be prohibited by international
law renders those activities lawful (think of consent to station foreign troops on
national territory; to allow foreign military aircraft to cross the airspace; to authorize
a foreign State to fish, or drill for oil, in territorial waters, etc.). However, consent is
not valid if it is directed to permitting activities contrary to *jus cogens* (such as consent
for foreign armed forces to enter the territory to massacre civilians or a specific ethnic
group).

According to ILC Draft (2000), breach of an obligation imposed by *the need to
comply with a peremptory rule* does not give rise to a wrongful act. Arguably this might
happen, for instance, were a State to refuse to abide by a bilateral treaty imposing
mutual military assistance at the request of the other party, because the request is
directed to use that assistance for the purpose of carrying out crimes against humanity or forcible suppression of the right to self-determination.

Self-defence (see **14.4.1**) and *counter-measures* (see **11.3.1**) are discussed elsewhere.
Some clarification is needed here with regard to the last three circumstances precluding wrongfulness.

Force majeure is defined as follows in Article 24(1) of ILC Draft (2000): 'the occurrence of an irresistible force or of an unforeseen event, beyond the control of the State,
making it materially impossible in the circumstances to perform the obligation'.
Paragraph 2 adds that *force majeure* does not apply if '(a) the occurrence of *force
majeure* results, either alone or in combination with other factors, from the conduct
of the State invoking it; or (b) the State has assumed the risk of that occurrence.'

Gill is often mentioned as an illustration of *force majeure* but does not seem to be germane to
this matter.[22] In the *Serbian Loans* case the PCIJ did not admit the Serbian claim that the First
World War had made it impossible for Serbia to repay loans.[23]

In the *Rainbow Warrior* case France claimed that urgent medical reasons had imposed
repatriation to France, without the consent of New Zealand, of a French agent, Major Mafart,
from a French military facility on the island of Hao. For France those medical reasons
amounted to *force majeure*. The Arbitral Tribunal rejected the French claim. Quoting the works
of the ILC, it held that *force majeure* 'is generally invoked to justify involuntary, or at least
unintentional conduct' and relates to 'an irresistible force or an unforeseen event' against which

the State has no remedy and which makes it 'materially impossible' for the State to act in conformity with its obligation. The Tribunal went on to note that the test for applying the doctrine of *force majeure* was one of 'absolute and material impossibility', whereas a 'circumstance rendering performance [of the obligation] more difficult or burdensome' did not constitute such a circumstance precluding wrongfulness.[24]

Distress has been defined in Article 25(1) of ILC Draft (2000) as a situation where 'the author of the [otherwise wrongful] act . . . had no other reasonable way, in a situation of distress, of saving the author's life or the lives of other persons entrusted to the author's care'. Paragraph 2 goes on to provide that distress does not apply if '(a) the situation of distress results, either alone or in combination with other factors, from the conduct of the State invoking it; or (b) the act in question was likely to create a comparable or greater peril'.

According to the ILC,[25] illustrations of distress are the unauthorized entry of an aircraft into foreign territory to save the life of passengers, or the entry of a military ship into a foreign port without authorization due to a storm (this happened in the case of *The Creole*).[26] In 1946, following a diplomatic incident caused by some unauthorized flights of US military aircraft over Yugoslavia, the two countries agreed that only in cases of emergency rendered necessary by the need to save the life of the crew, could such flights be admissible in absence of consent.[27] In the *Rainbow Warrior* case the Tribunal held that France's violation of the obligation to obtain the prior consent of New Zealand to the removal to mainland France of Major Mafart was justified by distress, namely 'the existence of very exceptional circumstances of extreme urgency' involving medical considerations.[28] However, the Tribunal found that France incurred responsibility in not returning Major Mafart to the island of Hao once the medical reasons had terminated.[29]

State of necessity has been defined in Article 26(1) of ILC Draft (2000) as the condition where an otherwise unlawful act is performed and such act '(a) is the only means for the State to safeguard an essential interest against a grave and imminent peril; and (b) does not seriously impair an essential interest of the State or States towards which the obligation exists, or of the international community as a whole'. Paragraph 2 adds that 'In any case, necessity may not be invoked by a State as a ground for precluding wrongfulness if: (a) the international obligation in question arises from a peremptory norm of general international law; (b) the international obligation in question excludes the possibility of invoking necessity; or (c) the State has contributed to the situation of necessity'.

The *Neptune* case, decided in 1797 by a United States-Britain Mixed Commission, ought to be mentioned. In 1795, during the Anglo-French war, an American-owned vessel, 'laden with rice and other foodstuffs' on a voyage from the USA to France, was captured by a British ship of war, and the cargo was taken over for the British government, the owners being allowed the invoice price plus a mercantile profit of 10 per cent. The owner claimed before the United States-Britain Mixed Commission the difference between what had thus been paid to them and the price the goods would have fetched at Bordeaux, if they had not been seized. Britain claimed among other things that the seizure was justified by necessity, for Britain 'was threatened with a scarcity of those articles directed to be seized'. Judge Pinkney, writing as a member of the majority that issued the award, relied for the issue of necessity upon such authorities as the

Dutch Hugo Grotius (1583–1645), the British Thomas Rutherforth (writing in 1754–6), and the Swiss Jean Jacques Burlamaqui (1694–1748). He admitted that in case of 'scarcity which produces severe national distress or national despondency unless extraordinary measures [are] taken for preventing it' a State could be 'authorized to have recourse to the forcible seizure of provisions belonging to neutrals' 'for averting the calamity' it feared. However, in the case at issue the judge dismissed the British argument, essentially on two grounds: (i) the 'evil' was only 'seen in perspective', namely was 'imaginary', not 'real and pressing', and in addition (ii) no attempt had been made to find other means of supply 'which were consistent with the rights of others and which were not incompatible with the exigency'. The judge also tackled the issue of compensation. He held that, assuming a necessity existed in Britain for the seizure of the cargo, the British Government could have pre-empted the cargo only upon giving the neutral traders as much as they would have earned in the port of original destination.[30]

Similarly, one may think of the case where a State fails to honour an international agreement imposing the payment of money previously loaned by another State, because this payment would seriously jeopardize the whole national economy and trigger a grave economic crisis.

The case of *Torrey Canyon* can also be mentioned. In 1967, the Liberian oil tanker had run aground on the high seas off the British coast. To avoid further damage to the British and French coasts and the sea environment, and as salvage operations were hindered by rough seas, the UK bombed the vessel so as to open the cargo tanks and burn the oil therein. The British authorities invoked necessity and no concerned State protested. The ILC also relied upon the case as an instance of necessity.[31] In 1969 the International Convention Relating to Intervention on the High Seas in Cases of Oil Pollution Casualties[32] was made: it among other things authorizes States parties 'to take such measures on the high seas as may be necessary to prevent, mitigate or eliminate grave and imminent dangers to their coastline' from oil pollution.

In the *Case concerning the Gabcíkovo-Nagymaros Project* Hungary had contended that in 1989 it had suspended a treaty obligation imposing the joint construction with Czechoslovakia of a dam in the Danube on account of 'a state of ecological necessity'. The other party to the dispute, Slovakia, contested the claim. The Court dismissed the Hungarian submissions. It noted that 'the state of necessity is a ground recognized by customary international law for precluding the wrongfulness of an act not in conformity with an international obligation . . . Such ground . . . can only be accepted on an exceptional basis'. The Court then enumerated most of the conditions set forth in ILC Draft (2000), adding that they 'reflect customary international law'. After applying some of those conditions to the case at issue, the Court concluded that 'the perils invoked by Hungary, without prejudging their possible gravity, were not sufficiently established in 1989, nor were they "imminent"; and . . . Hungary had available to it at that time means of responding to these perceived perils other than the suspension and abandonment of works with which it had been entrusted. What is more, negotiations were under way which might have led to a review of the Project and the extension of some of its time-limits, without there being need to abandon it.'[33]

Clearly, while in the case of distress the wrongful act is justified by the urgent necessity to save the life of the *person* performing the act or of the lives *other individuals* entrusted to the State, necessity aims at warranting a breach of international law imposed by the need to avert a serious danger for the *whole* State or the *population* (or part of the population) of the State.

(4) *Circumstances excluding wrongfulness and duty to pay compensation for the*

damage caused. Although when one of the circumstances discussed above can be proved no responsibility is incurred by the State invoking that circumstance, the State may nevertheless have to pay compensation for any material harm or loss caused. Article 27(b) of ILC Draft (2000) provides that 'the invocation of a circumstance precluding wrongfulness . . . is without prejudice to . . . the question of compensation for any material harm or loss caused by the act in question'.

It would seem appropriate, and in keeping with the spirit of international principles on the law of State responsibility, to hold that compensation must not be always paid.

First of all, one should exclude the case of self-defence or counter-measures, where the action is only taken to react to the wrongful act of another State. As for self-defence, the right to compensation could accrue to the aggressor only if self-defence resulting in material harm or loss had been disproportionate. One fails to see why, instead, a State acting in self-defence to repel aggression should also be called upon to pay compensation for the material harm it may have caused (for example, for lawful collateral damage to civilians or civilian objects, destruction of such lawful military objectives as railways, bridges, or radio communication centres). The same holds true, *mutatis mutandis*, for counter-measures.

It seems that compensation should also be excluded with regard to some other circumstances precluding wrongfulness. For instance, if a State has consented to the commission of a specific activity that otherwise would have been unlawful, one might consider as implicit in the specific consent to the specific activity the waiver of any claim to compensation in the case of damage. This conclusion is grounded on the assumption that the consenting State knew or should have known that material harm or loss was most likely to occur.

9.4.2 CONSEQUENCES OF THE WRONGFUL ACT

(i) Obligations of the responsible State. The delinquent State is under several obligations, owed to the victim State and to it alone. First, it must cease the wrongdoing, if it is continuing. Second, it must 'offer appropriate assurances and guarantees of non-repetition, if circumstances so require' (Article 30 of ILC Draft (2000)). Third, it must 'make full reparation for the injury caused' (Article 31 of the same ILC Draft). Fourth, if it refuses to make reparation or to pay compensation to the extent required by the injured State, pursuant to Article 33 of the UN Charter the responsible State must accede *bona fide* to any attempt to peacefully settle the dispute made by the injured State.

As far as reparation is concerned, it is now clear that modern international law establishes a hierarchy between the various modes of making reparation. In case of *material damage*, the responsible State must provide *restitution in kind*, to the extent possible. Pursuant to Article 36 of ILC Draft (2000), restitution means 'to re-establish the situation which existed before the wrongful act was committed, provided and to the extent that restitution: (a) is not materially impossible; (b) would not involve a burden out of all proportion to the benefit deriving from restitution instead of compensation'.

Examples of restitution are: making the use of a house available (under a treaty with Britain, the Sultan of the Spanish zone of Morocco had built a house for the private residence of the British consul. Later the house was destroyed by Spanish troops; the arbiter Huber held that Spain—the protector State—was to give Britain 'the usufruct for a consular residence', that was to be 'as convenient' as the destroyed house);[34] deciding that, 'as a form of reparation', the respondent State must recognize the rescinding of the obligation or payment previously imposed;[35] ordering that Government taxes and import duties unlawfully paid must be returned.[36]

If restitution is not possible, or can allow only partial recovery of the material damage suffered, the delinquent State must make *compensation*. Under Article 37 of ILC Draft (2000) this obligation means that the responsible State must 'compensate for the damage caused thereby, insofar as such damage is not made good by restitution. The compensation shall cover any financially assessable damage including loss of profits insofar as it is established'.

A wrong causing *moral damage* may be redressed by *satisfaction*, which under Article 38(2) and (3) of ILC Draft (2000) 'may consist in an acknowledgement of the breach, an expression of regret, a formal apology or another appropriate modality' but shall not be 'out of proportion to the injury and may not take a form humiliating to the responsible State'.

For instance, on 19 February 1998 five Israeli secret agents tried to plant listening devices in an apartment building on the outskirts of Bern (one of the tenants was suspected of being connected to a Palestinian or Lebanese militant group); the Swiss police detained them, but then released four and held one. The Swiss authorities accused Israel of violating Swiss sovereignty and demanded an apology; on 27 February Israel formally apologized and the Israeli agent was released.[37] Similarly, on 11 April 2001 the US government apologized to China for a US military aircraft entering China's airspace and landing in Hainan airport without prior authorization.[38]

Other instances of satisfaction may be the symbolic payment of a very modest sum. In the *Cathage* and *Manouba* cases,[39] France had asked the PCA to hold that Italy having breached international law by capturing and temporarily detaining, on the high seas, during the Turco-Italian war in 1912, two French steamers allegedly carrying war contraband, Italy was to pay to France, in addition to compensation for moral and material damage, also one French franc for the offence on the French flag. In both cases the PCA held that finding that Italy had breached international law was by itself a 'serious sanction' and only obliged Italy to pay compensation for the moral and material damage. The decision by an arbitral or judicial body that the State had committed an international wrong was also held to constitute a fair satisfaction in *Corfu Channel* and in the *Rainbow Warrior* case.[40]

Another instance of satisfaction may be the punishment by the national authorities of the responsible State of the individuals who have caused the wrong; or formal assurance by the responsible State that it will not repeat the wrong.

Although restitution and compensation should normally be resorted to in the order outlined above, nothing prevents States from combining them, and if need be also providing satisfaction, to the extent that this is feasible or asked for.

(ii) Rights, powers, and obligations of the injured State: in particular, the right to resort to counter-measures. In correlation to the obligations incumbent upon the responsible State, rights and powers accrue to the injured State (in particular, the right to claim cessation of the wrongful act, assurances and guarantees of non-repetition, and full reparation for the material or moral damage caused), together with some obligations.

The injured State, if it decides to invoke the responsibility of another State, must take the following steps.

(1) It must 'give notice of its claim to that State' and specify in particular '(a) the conduct that the responsible State should take in order to cease the wrongful act, if it is continuing; (b) what form reparation should take' (Article 44 of ILC Draft (2000)).

(2) If the responsible State does not comply with its request, the injured State must endeavour to settle the dispute by peaceful means and in particular embark upon, or at least propose, negotiations, or mediation, conciliation, or arbitration (Article 53(2) of ILC Draft (2000) requires only resort to negotiations).

(3) Only if the responsible State refuses to make reparation or to enter into negotiations, conciliation, or arbitration, or manifestly does not act *bona fide* in responding to the offer for negotiations or dispute settlement, is the injured State entitled to resort to counter-measures (according to Article 53(2) and (4) of ILC Draft (2000), counter-measures may be taken after the failure of the parties concerned to negotiate so as to settle the matter). As stated above (**5.5** and **9.3**), the need to go through this process before initiating counter-measures follows from the general obligation to endeavour, in good faith, to settle disputes peacefully.

In 1978 a US-France arbitral tribunal took a contrary view in the *Case concerning the Air Service Agreement of 27 March 1946.* France had contended that counter-measures could be resorted to only in the absence of other legal channels to settle the dispute. The Tribunal dismissed this submission, stating that 'Under the rules of present-day international law, and unless the contrary results from special obligations arising under particular treaties, notably from mechanisms created within the framework of international organizations, each State establishes for itself its legal situation *vis-à-vis* other States. If a situation arises which, in one State's view, results in the violation of an international obligation by another State, the first State is entitled, within the limits set by the general rules of international law pertaining to the use of armed force, to affirm its rights through "countermeasures" '.[41] It is submitted, with respect, that the Tribunal did not take into sufficient account the recent evolution of general international law, and in particular its emphasis on the peaceful settlement of disputes, as can be inferred from the evolution of the obligation of Article 33 of the UN Charter into a general obligation laid down (or codified) in the aforementioned 1970 Declaration on Friendly Relations (see above, **5.6**).

As for the other conditions on which counter-measures are admissible, see above, **11.3.1(a)**.

9.5 'AGGRAVATED' STATE RESPONSIBILITY

This new form of responsibility has come into being as a result of a number of concomitant factors. The UN Charter provisions and mechanisms on aggression and the modalities for both centralized and non-centralized responses to aggression gradually brought about the idea that there existed rules envisaging reactions to international delinquencies different from and more serious than the usual response. The practice concerning reaction to gross and large-scale violations of human rights has also shown that in other areas as well responses to breaches are permissible which, although less institutionalized and conspicuous than those against aggression, may however take a collective dimension unusual in the consequences of 'ordinary' wrongs. More generally, the emergence in the world community of values (peace, human rights, self-determination of peoples) deemed of universal significance and not derogable by States in their private transactions has led many States to believe that gross infringements of such values must perforce require a stronger reaction than those normally taken in response to violations of bilateral legal relations. By the same token it has been felt that this reaction should also be 'public' and collective, as opposed to the 'private' and bilateral responses to ordinary responsibility.

The works of the ILC took these developments into account. The elaboration by R. Ago, and the adoption on first reading by the Commission, of Article 19 of the former Draft, on 'international crimes of States'[42] stimulated an extensive debate and triggered reactions, both positive and negative, from States. Eventually the ILC jettisoned this version of Article 19, chiefly because of the reluctance of States to accept the notion that they may be accused of 'crimes', as well as the difficulty for the ILC in pinpointing the consequences of these 'crimes'. However, the basic ideas behind that draft provision remain valid, as will be shown below.

9.5.1 SUBJECTIVE AND OBJECTIVE ELEMENTS OF THE WRONGFUL ACT

The essential features of aggravated responsibility have already been discussed above (see **9.3**). Let us now enlarge on the main traits of this form of responsibility, that differentiate it from 'ordinary responsibility'.

Both categories share the legal regulation of the subjective and objective elements of responsibility, except for the question of (i) the nature and gravity of the international obligation breached, (ii) fault, and (iii) damage.

The obligation whose breach may give rise to 'aggravated responsibility' must be a '*community obligation*' (see **1.8.2**), that is, an obligation (i) concerning a *fundamental value* (peace, human rights, self-determination of peoples, protection of the environment), (ii) *owed to all the other members* of the international community, or to the States bound by a multilateral treaty, (iii) having as its correlative position a '*community right*', that is, a right belonging to any other State (or to any other contracting party, in the case of a multilateral treaty); (iv) this right may be exercised by any other State (or contracting party), whether or not damaged by the breach; and (v) the right is exercised on behalf of the international community and not in the interest of the claimant State.

Furthermore, the breach of this obligation must be gross or systematic; in other words, it may not be a sporadic or isolated or minor contravention of a community obligation (for instance, the infringement upon the right of an individual to fair trial). It must be serious or large scale (for instance, aggression, genocide, or grave atrocities against one's own nationals or all persons belonging to an ethnic group).

The gravity of the breach and the fact that the obligation violated is of fundamental importance for the community as a whole entails that in cases of 'aggravated responsibility', intent, or fault, or *culpa gravis*, that is, serious negligence, is always inherent in this class of responsibility. This *psychological element* is thus always required and must consequently be proved by the claimant State.

Let us now move on to *damage*. As we saw above, material or moral damage is an indispensable element of the wrongful act that may trigger the 'ordinary responsibility'. Things are different in the case of 'aggravated responsibility'. Here a State is responsible towards all other States simply for breaching an international obligation, regardless of whether or not a particular State has been materially or morally damaged. If a State grossly violates human rights of its own nationals, no material or moral damage is caused to any other State, but only a *legal injury* is brought about to the right of *every other State*. Or it may happen that by the same wrongful act (for example, a massacre of a State's nationals together with the nationals of another State, belonging to the same ethnic or religious or racial group) a State may cause a material or moral damage to one particular State, and by the same token bring about a legal injury to all States.

Things are more complex for the so-called 'interdependent' or 'integral' obligations, such as those laid down in treaties on disarmament or some treaties on the environment. These are obligations that are necessarily dependent on a corresponding performance by all the other parties, since it is of the essence of treaties laying down such obligations that the undertaking of each party is given in return for a similar undertaking by the others.[43] Clearly, a breach of these treaties by a State party *vis-à-vis* one of the contracting parties automatically affects and injures the *interests* of all the other contracting States. However, only some of the treaties in question give rise, in case of violation, to aggravated responsibility. This is the case of disarmament treaties which do not entitle the other parties—in cases of violation—to suspend the treaty or withdraw from it, but solely to take collective or collectively authorized 'sanctions'. Only in these particular situations, may such treaties be considered as falling within the class of agreements imposing 'community obligations' and granting correlative 'community rights'.

In contrast, some treaties on disarmament are clearly based on the assumption of similar performance by the other contracting States, with the consequence that, if a State breaches the treaty, the other States may suspend its application or withdraw from the treaty, pursuant to Article 60 of the Vienna Convention on the Law of Treaties. Plainly, these obligations, although laid down in a multilateral treaty, are based on reciprocity.[44] Only 'ordinary responsibility' ensues from their violation.[45]

9.5.2 THE CONSEQUENCES OF THE WRONGFUL ACT IN CASES OF AGGRAVATED RESPONSIBILITY

(i) Legal regime. The most notable differences between the two classes of responsibility can be found in the consequences of the wrongful act. In particular, in the case of 'aggravated' responsibility, under customary law the offending State has obligations *towards all other States*; correspondingly, *all other States* have rights, powers, and obligations consequent upon the wrongful act, *vis-à-vis* the delinquent State.

We will now set out the legal regulation of the consequences of the international delinquency in the case of aggravated responsibility, as it has evolved in international law as a result of State practice (outlined *infra*, **9.5.3**), of the works of the ILC and the consequent debates in the UN General Assembly, and on the strength of the general principles of the international community.

Subsequently we will attempt to establish to what extent States have had resort, in practice, to all the legal tools available to them under the notion of aggravated responsibility.

(ii) Obligations incumbent upon the delinquent State. The wrongdoer is under all the obligations incumbent upon any author of an international delinquency, and discussed above (see **9.4.2**) with regard to 'ordinary responsibility'. However, now these obligations are owed not only to the damaged State, if any, but also to all the other members of the international community. In other words, the legal consequences of the wrongful act no longer consist merely of a 'bilateral relation' (between the responsible State and the State victim of the wrongful act), but of a 'community relation', namely a relation between the wrongdoer and all other States.

Restitution, compensation, or satisfaction in some instances may prove relevant when the wrongful act has caused a material or moral damage to a particular State (for instance, in cases of aggression, or in cases of serious violations of the human rights of nationals of that State). In such case the offending State is obliged to make reparation to the State damaged. In *most* cases of serious and massive breaches of 'community obligations', however, reparation in its various forms may turn out to be inconsequential. Take the example of crimes against humanity, genocide, or other large-scale or gross violations of human rights perpetrated by a State against its own nationals. Plainly, it is difficult to see how, under normal circumstances, it is possible to demand ordinary forms of reparation from the responsible State. Nevertheless, one may envisage the possibility that the responsible State may pay compensation to the victims, or to the relatives of the victims, of those gross breaches.

(iii) Rights, powers, and obligations of other States. It is more important to establish the

legal position of other States (namely, any member State of the international community, whether or not damaged by the wrong, provided it has the legal entitlement
or right corresponding to the obligation breached by the responsible State).

The ILC, while proposing a whole array of innovative ameliorations to existing law, or spelling
out some of its significant implications, has substantially taken a *minimalist approach*, by
pointing to a limited number of rather minor consequences of the form of responsibility at issue.
What is even more striking, the ILC has substantially envisaged a reaction to those grave
breaches hinging on the action of individual States, more than on a collective and in a
way 'public' action (see Article 54 of ILC Draft (2000)). As a result, while the perpetration of
those breaches amounts to conduct infringing upon universal and 'public' values, the response
contemplated is primarily of a 'bilateralist' and 'private' nature.

The first set of consequences of breaches of community obligations has been rightly
set out by the ILC in its Draft Articles and relates to *obligations* of all States other than
the delinquent one. These States are under the obligations: (a) not to recognize as
lawful the situation created by the breach; (b) not to render aid or assistance to the
responsible State in maintaining the situation so created; (c) to co-operate as far as
possible to bring the breach to an end (Article 42(2) of ILC Draft (2000)).

In addition all States other than the wrongdoer have the following *powers, rights, or
claims*.

(1) To invoke the aggravated responsibility of the delinquent State, by bringing
their claim to the notice of that State.

(2) To demand cessation of the wrong, if it is continuing, and to request assurances
and guarantees of non-repetition.

(3) To claim reparation in a form consistent with the nature of the wrong (if a
State has been materially or morally damaged, as in the case of aggression, the victim
State may claim reparation as may other States to the benefit of the victim State, or, as
in the case of gross violations of human rights, to the benefit of the individuals that
have suffered from the wrongful act).

(4) If the responsible State has not taken immediate action to discontinue the
wrongful act or has not complied with the form of reparation sought by the claiming
States, the right to bring the matter to the attention of the competent international
bodies. Thus, they can request the competent body of a universal organization (such
as the UN) or a regional organization (such as the OAS, the OAU, or the Council of
Europe), or of intra-regional organizations, publicly to discuss the wrong done by the
delinquent State with a view to attaining public exposure of that wrongdoing, or to
adopting collective sanctions (see *infra*, **14.3**), etc.

The need for States *first* to take steps within international organizations or other
appropriate collective bodies seems to be warranted and indeed dictated by the inherent nature of this class of responsibility. This responsibility arises out of a gross attack
on community or 'public' values. The response to the wrongdoing must therefore be
as much as possible *public and collective*. It would be incongruous and contradictory

to contemplate on the one hand a form of States' aggravated accountability for gross breaches of fundamental values of concern to all members of the world community, and then to envisage, on the other hand, a response left to the 'private' initiative and will of each individual member of such community.

(5) If those bodies take no action, or their action has not brought about cessation of the wrong or adequate reparation (if only in the form of strict assurances not to repeat the same or similar wrongs in the future), all States are empowered to take peaceful counter-measures on an individual basis.

When States opt for individual counter-measures, these must be subject to the conditions enumerated above with regard to 'ordinary responsibility' (see above, **9.4.2(ii)** and **11.3.1(a)**). In particular, before taking counter-measures, the claimant States must (a) offer to negotiate with the responsible State as well as propose other means of peacefully settling the dispute such as mediation and conciliation, if appropriate, or arbitral or judicial settlement; (b) duly notify the responsible State of their intention to resort to counter-measures. Plainly, in this case a problem of co-ordination among States resorting to counter-measures may arise (Article 54(3) of ILC Draft (2000) rightly provides that 'Where more than one State takes counter-measures, the States concerned shall cooperate in order to ensure that the conditions laid down . . . for the taking of countermeasures are fulfilled').

(6) In case of armed aggression, States are entitled to resort to collective self-defence (subject to the request or consent of the victim of aggression; see **14.4.1(e)**).

A caveat must however be entered. The above measures do not affect or prejudice the possible operation of the *UN security system*. If the UN Security Council considers that a gross violation of community obligations amounts to a threat to the peace, a breach of the peace, or an act of aggression, it may recommend or decide what measures not involving the use of force States are entitled or obliged to take under Article 41 of the UN Charter, or may authorize States to take forcible measures against the wrongdoer. In other words, faced with an international wrongful act that it deems covered by Article 39 of the UN Charter, *the Security Council takes over*, and individual States may only take action to the extent allowed by the UN Charter (individual or collective self-defence), or recommended, authorized, or decided upon by the Security Council.

A final point also proves necessary. As has been stressed above, violations of community obligations may well cause material or moral damage to a particular State. Thus, for example, in the aforementioned case of gross violations of human rights by a State, the victims of those violations may include both nationals of that State and citizens of, say, other States. In this case all States members of the international community may invoke the aggravated responsibility of the wrongdoer. In addition, the State whose nationals were victims of the wrongful act may complain that it has been damaged by the international delinquency, and claim reparation accordingly. For this purpose, it is necessary for the State to prove that some of the victims had its nationality. In contrast, for other States it is sufficient to prove that gross violations of human rights have been perpetrated, regardless of the victims' nationality.

9.5.3 TRENDS IN STATE PRACTICE

Let us now ask to what extent this legal regulation has been matched by State practice.

The most frequent cases of implementation of this form of responsibility can be discerned in instances of resort to collective self-defence (see **14.4.1(e)**). In some cases of aggression or at any rate of resort to force in breach of the UN Charter, other States have also resorted to counter-measures against the wrongdoer.

This for instance happened in 1980–1 after the Soviet intervention in Afghanistan: the USA applied in 1980 a host of embargo measures against the Soviet Union. In other cases of serious breaches of community obligations, States have always preferred to react through international bodies such as the UN Security Council or the General Assembly. This in itself is a healthy development, for central organs of the organized community may be in a better position to recommend individual or joint action against the delinquent State. Thus, for instance, the Security Council imposed or recommended economic measures against Southern Rhodesia in 1966. In 1980, in keeping with a Security Council resolution against the taking of hostages by Iran, the European Community adopted a decision whereby all contracts concluded with Iran after 4 November 1979 (the beginning of hostage taking) were to be suspended.[46] The Security Council recommended, or adopted, economic and other sanctions against South Africa in 1986 and, more recently, against Iraq (1990–1), the Federal Republic of Yugoslavia (Serbia and Montenegro) (1992), Libya (1992–9), Liberia (1993–4), Haiti (1993).

In a few instances States resorted to counter-measures even in the absence of a specific decision or recommendation of the Security Council. This happened, for example, in 1982, in connection with the crisis in Poland, when the European Community reduced the import of Soviet products (Regulation no. 596, adopted by the EC Council on 15 March 1982), and in relation to the Falklands/Malvinas conflict, when the EC suspended the import of goods from Argentina (Council Regulation no. 877, of 16 April 1982). In 1983 the downing by Soviet military aircraft, of a civilian Korean airliner, was termed by many States in the Security Council 'a flagrant violation of the current rules of civil aviation';[47] however, no resolution was adopted by the Council; thereafter a number of States, including Canada, the USA, Japan, adopted counter-measures against the Soviet Union.[48] Other instances of third party reaction to breaches of community obligations have been pinpointed in the legal literature.[49]

More recently, in 1999, faced with the massacres perpetrated by the Federal Republic of Yugoslavia (Serbia and Montenegro) on its own territory and against its own nationals, the member States of NATO reacted by using military force; this, however, was done in clear breach of the UN Charter, more specifically of the *jus cogens* principle banning the use of force unless such use is authorized by the Security Council.

Nonetheless, it can be pointed out that so far States and international organizations have not fully utilized the enormous legal potential provided by the rules on 'aggravated responsibility'. One cannot fail to note the reluctance of many States to 'interfere' in matters of no direct interest or concern for them; in other words, their proclivity not to pursue community interests. However, international practice shows that States have come to see the availability of such international organs as the UN Security Council and General Assembly, as well as organs of regional organizations or such organizations as NATO, as a useful means of channelling community interests. It has been rightly felt that collective action was preferable to the action of individual States, which may have political, ideological, or economic underpinnings, or may lend itself to distortions, or may acquire political overtones.

On some recent occasions international courts have emphasized the importance of 'aggravated responsibility'. Thus, in *Furundžija* Trial Chamber II of the ICTY, while discussing torture, made reference in an *obiter dictum* to the notion of 'aggravated responsibility'. After mentioning torture as a war crime and as a crime against humanity, it went on to say the following: 'Under current international humanitarian law, in addition to individual criminal liability, State responsibility may ensue as a result of a State official engaging in torture or failing to prevent torture or to punish torturers. If carried out as an extensive practice of State officials, torture amounts to a serious breach on a widespread scale of an international obligation of essential importance for safeguarding the human being, thus constituting a particularly grave wrongful act generating State responsibility.'[50]

9.6 THE SPECIAL REGIME OF RESPONSIBILITY IN CASE OF CONTRAVENTION OF COMMUNITY OBLIGATIONS PROVIDED FOR IN MULTILATERAL TREATIES

So far we have discussed the legal regime of 'aggravated responsibility' envisaged by customary international law, as well as the relevant State practice. We will now consider some multilateral treaties that protect the same fundamental values safeguarded by the rules on 'aggravated responsibility', in particular peace and human rights, by laying down community obligations and community rights. These treaties also set up complex mechanisms for ensuring compliance with the substantive provisions they contain, and in addition envisage *institutionalized reactions* to breaches of those provisions, which to some extent *replace* the modes of reaction to gross breaches of fundamental obligations provided for in customary international law. What also is unique with these treaties is that the 'collective' or institutional response to violations not only covers gross or large-scale or systematic breaches, but also extends to *any* contravention of the treaty. Except for the European Convention on Human Rights, as amended in 1994 and the Inter-American Convention on Human Rights (see *infra*, 16.4.5(b)), the sweeping nature and scope of this response is however compensated for by the weakness of the supervisory and 'sanctioning' mechanism.

9.6.1 TREATY REGULATION

With regard to serious violations of these categories of community obligations also, all the contracting States are under the general obligations arising in cases of aggravated responsibility and laid down in customary international law (see *supra*, 9.5.2(iii)).

As for the legal rights, powers, or claims of all the contracting States other than the wrongdoer, one must first turn to the provisions of each relevant multilateral treaty.

It is of course impossible to mention all the treaties that establish a legal regime of aggravated responsibility. Mention will be made, by way of illustration, of only some such regimes: that provided for in the four 1949 Geneva Conventions on the victims of war, the regime laid down in the 1966 UN Covenant on Civil and Political Rights and the legal regime that, according to the ICTY, is provided for in the Statute of the International Tribunal. (I will also omit consideration of the *regional* systems for the protection of human rights that exist in Europe and in America, on which see *infra*, 16.4.5(b)).

(i) The 1949 Geneva Conventions. It is widely accepted, and has been recently restated by the ICTY in *Kupreškić et al.*,[51] that the 1949 Geneva Conventions lay down community obligations. They also provide for two principal mechanisms designed to enforce State responsibility.

First, pursuant to Article 1 (common to all four Conventions) they oblige any contracting party 'to respect and to ensure respect' for the Conventions 'in all circumstances'. This provision (which the ICJ in *Nicaragua*[52] considered to have become part of 'the general principles of humanitarian law') empowers and even obligates any State party to demand of another State party that it comply with its obligations under the Conventions. It follows that the provision also entitles each State party to demand the cessation of a serious violation of the Conventions (as well as, as the case may be, the punishment of the culprits). Also the other entitlements and obligations following from a serious breach of international law apply. As the representative of Oman stated in 1980 in the UN General Assembly debate on Israeli practices in Occupied Territories, the obligations that the common Article 1 of the Geneva Conventions, in particular of the Fourth Convention, imposes on all contracting parties 'involve collective action to ensure adherence to the Convention, non-recognition of measures taken in contravention of its provisions and refraining from offering any aid to the occupying Power which might encourage it in its obstinacy'.[53]

Second, the Conventions institute a special regime for 'grave breaches' (illustratively enumerated in the relevant provisions of each Convention). If a belligerent commits any such breach, any other contracting State may react at two different levels: at the inter-State level and at the level of internal criminal punishment. At the former level, any State has the right to invoke the international responsibility of another contracting party for 'grave breaches' perpetrated by members of its armed forces or other individuals acting on its behalf (Articles 51, 52, 131, 148). At the national level, each State is under the obligation (i) to enact penal legislation to punish 'grave breaches'; (ii) to search for persons alleged to have committed such breaches; (iii) to bring them before its own courts, unless it decides to hand over those persons to another contracting State 'concerned' (Articles 49, 50, 129, 146). Thus, the *obligation* to search for, prosecute, and try or extradite State officials (or de facto organs) accused of 'grave breaches' might be viewed as a way of implementing the 'aggravated responsibility' of a State. It should be added that the Conventions do not include any provision ruling out the invocation of 'ordinary responsibility' in cases of breaches of the Conventions by a contracting State which damage the interests of another contracting party.

(ii) The 1966 UN Covenant on Civil and Political Rights. The UN Covenant, as do similar international instruments on human rights, extends the notion of 'aggravated responsibility' to any breach of the Covenant. Indeed, any State party is legally entitled to demand cessation of a violation of the Covenant *even if this violation is not gross and large scale.* In other words, any State is obliged towards all other contracting parties fully to respect the Covenant, and any other State is empowered to claim fulfilment of this obligation even if the violation is minor. However, this entitlement does not operate in a bilateral context. The Covenant, as did other similar international instruments, set up a body responsible for handling allegations by States or individuals of violations of the Covenant (provided of course that the necessary procedural conditions laid down in Article 41 of the Covenant and in the Optional Protocol are fulfilled). It is before this body—the UN Human Rights Committee—that a State may invoke the responsibility of the other contracting party, by asking the Committee to declare that the State complained of has indeed breached the Covenant. As the tasks of the Committee will be described below (**16.4.5(a)**), it is not necessary here to dwell on the matter. It may suffice to recall that, in addition to the right of individuals to submit 'communications' against a State for violations of the Covenant, each State party may be entitled, under Article 41 of the Covenant, to submit a case to the Committee.

What happens if the supervisory mechanism cannot work (if, for instance, the State that has breached the Covenant has neither made the declaration under Article 41 nor ratified the Protocol), or proves unable to put a stop to the violation, for instance because the offending State does not comply with the Committee's findings? It would be contrary to the spirit of the whole body of international law on human rights to suggest that the monitoring system envisaged in the Covenant and the Protocol should bar States parties from 'leaving' the self-contained regime contemplated in the Covenant and falling back on the customary law system of resort to peaceful counter-measures. This resort, it is submitted, is not however admissible if the offending State has not grossly and consistently breached human rights, but has only committed an individual or sporadic violation. In other words, States parties can fall back on the customary regime of 'aggravated responsibility', but are not authorized, on the strength of their Covenant's rights and obligations, to *extend* that regime to breaches of human rights that, as a rule, are not covered by it (see *infra,* **9.6.3**).

(iii) The Statute of the ICTY (1993). Let us move on to the regime established under the ICTY Statute. In *Blaskič,* the Appeals Chamber of the ICTY held that Article 29 of the ICTY Statute, imposing on all States the obligation to comply with orders and decisions of the Tribunal, laid down an obligation *erga omnes partes* and by the same token posited 'a community interest in its observance'.[54] 'In other words [so the Appeals Chamber went on to say] every member State of the UN has a legal interest in the fulfilment of the obligation laid down in Article 29.' As for the manner in which

this 'legal interest' could be exercised, the Chamber specified that, after a 'judicial finding' of the Tribunal that a State had violated Article 29,

'each Member State of the UN may act upon the legal interest referred to: consequently it may request the State to terminate its breach of Article 29. In addition to this possible unilateral action, a collective response through other intergovernmental organizations may be envisaged. The fundamental principles of the UN Charter and the spirit of the Statute of the International Tribunal aim to limit, as far as possible, the risks of arbitrariness and conflict. They therefore give pride of place to collective or joint action to be taken through an intergovernmental organization. . . . [T]his collective action . . . may take various forms, such as political and moral condemnation, or a collective request to cease the breach, or economic or diplomatic sanctions'.[55]

9.6.2 STATE PRACTICE

The regime provided for in the 1949 Geneva Conventions has not been consistently used.

In less recent years there were very few public individual démarches (only Switzerland and Austria made public appeals to Iran and Iraq during the war between these two countries in the years 1979–89).[56] In addition, some sort of collective action was taken: for instance Security Council members invited the parties to the same armed conflict to abide by the Geneva Conventions, and in February and March 1984 the then ten members of the European Community called upon Iran and Iraq to respect humanitarian law.[57] In addition, States members of the 'Contadora Group' made appeals to the conflicting parties in the case of the civil strife in El Salvador. In most cases resort to Article 1 has been made privately, in confidential démarches.

However, more recently there have been more cases where States have gone public, or at least have subsequently made public their action.

Thus, it would seem that on many occasions Jordan has protested against violations of international humanitarian law in the Arab territories occupied by Israel, requesting Israel to refrain from committing further breaches and also asking the ICRC to urge Israel to comply with international humanitarian law.[58] In 1995 the German Foreign Minister stated that the German Government had 'repeatedly reminded Russia of the latter's duty to abide by its obligations under Protocol II of 1977' in the conflict in Chechnya.[59] A few bodies of the organized community have also taken some kind of public action. Thus, for instance, on many occasions the UN Security Council, as well as the General Assembly and the Secretary-General, have called upon all the States parties to the Geneva Conventions to ensure compliance by Israel with these Conventions.[60] Similarly, in 1993 the Committee of Ministers of the Council of Europe, after discussing reports about massive rape of women and children being committed in the former Yugoslavia, appealed to 'member States and the international community at large to ensure that these atrocities cease and that their instigators and perpetrators are prosecuted by an appropriate national or international penal tribunal'.[61]

As to the provisions on national prosecution of grave breaches, it would seem that they were not applied until 1994, when national courts of some European States began to prosecute persons allegedly guilty of serious breaches in the former

Yugoslavia. This breakthrough probably occurred under the impulse of ICTY action. By and large international humanitarian law laid down in the Geneva Conventions still remains an area where the gap between the legal potential and its implementation in daily life is exceedingly broad.

As for the UN Covenant on Civil and Political Rights, the central supervisory mechanisms have been constantly utilized, and have become more and more effective (at least as far as 'communications' of individuals are concerned). This probably accounts for the absence of any 'sanctioning' action by individual States after the possible failure of the central monitoring bodies to impel compliance with the Covenant.

Regretfully, also, States have made scant use of the legal regime envisaged by the ICTY Appeals Chamber. In the many instances where the Tribunal's President forwarded to the Security Council findings about breaches of Article 29 by some States, Member States of the UN did not take any counter-measure against the delinquent State, leaving the matter with the Security Council (which, in its turn, confined itself to adopting exhortations, condemnations and other verbal censures).

Arguably, the Serbian authorities' arrest of Milosevic, on 1 April 2001, was a first step towards compliance by the Federal Republic of Yugoslavia (Serbia and Montenegro) with Article 29 of the ICTY Statute. Allegedly, this step was the consequence of the US Government's threat to withhold granting US\$ 50 million assistance. From this viewpoint the US threat could thus be regarded as a measure (technically speaking, retortion) designed to impel observance of Article 29. The US Government would have acted in lieu of the Security Council to attain at least partial enforcement of Article 29.

9.6.3 TREATY REGIMES AND RESORT TO INTERNATIONAL CUSTOMARY LAW MEASURES

The question may arise of the relationship between the remedial actions provided for in a multilateral treaty imposing community obligations, and the right to resort to measures envisaged in customary international law as a reaction to breaches of community obligations.

As pointed out above (**9.6.1(ii)**) this problem may only arise with regard to gross or systematic violations of a community obligation provided for in a treaty. As for minor or isolated or sporadic infringements of the treaty, no remedy is made available by customary rules on aggravated responsibility, for, as stated above, these rules only contemplate responsibility arising out of gross and serious breaches of community obligations.

Let us therefore concentrate on the category of gross contraventions. Take the case of a State party to a multilateral human rights convention engaging in a massacre against both its own nationals and the citizens of another contracting State. Clearly, the victim State may request reparation only through the institutional means available under the treaty and refrain from resorting to counter-measures. (The same holds true for other contracting States, which may act on behalf of all the victims of the massacre, be they nationals of the delinquent State or of the aggrieved contracting State.) It is only if the institutional remedies fail that the aggrieved or any other contracting State may activate the legal means available under customary law, including resort to unilateral counter-measures. The need to exhaust institutional or collective mechanisms first derives from the very spirit and object of the conventions in question (and any similar treaty): they protect community values and provide for a 'public interest' in their implementation; hence, collective remedial action should always trump any unilateral response to breaches.

The same holds true for other treaties, for example a treaty banning nuclear tests (and clearly not based on reciprocity). If a contracting State breaches the treaty by undertaking a nuclear test on the high seas but off the coast of another contracting party, it may cause damage to that particular State; in addition, it simultaneously injures the right of all the other contracting States. Again, at least the initial response must be collective, provided of course an institutional mechanism is envisaged in the treaty at issue.

An important point must here be duly stressed: whenever one is faced with a failure of institutional treaty-made mechanisms to react effectively to gross or systematic violations, the solutions available as a fall-back, under customary international law, to States parties to the multilateral treaty are also available to other States *not parties to that treaty*. In other words, in the event of failure of the multilateral treaty and its machinery, customary law takes over to the benefit not only of the contracting parties but also of the whole international membership of the international community: the treaty collectivity may be replaced by the whole international community.

9.7 THE CURRENT MINOR ROLE OF AGGRAVATED RESPONSIBILITY

There may be a basic reason for the *scant invocation of 'aggravated responsibility'*. States still cling to the idea that they should take action in international dealings primarily to protect their own interests. They are bent on shunning any meddling with matters that are not of direct concern to them. As a consequence, they are inclined to invoke State responsibility principally when they are materially or morally injured by another State. For them State responsibility is still primarily a private matter, arising within the framework of a bilateral legal relation. Thus there is seldom resort to 'aggravated responsibility' and its underpinning of 'public action on behalf of a community interest', whereas the old concept of 'ordinary responsibility' still holds sway.

Nevertheless, here, as in other areas of international law, it is important for *forward-looking legal means and instrumentalities* to be available to States. Sooner or later States will make use of them, thus implementing those fundamental values they tend to proclaim and even tout, but then often forget to put into practice.

10

MECHANISMS FOR PROMOTING COMPLIANCE WITH INTERNATIONAL RULES AND PURSUING THE PREVENTION OR PEACEFUL SETTLEMENT OF DISPUTES

10.1 INTRODUCTION

In every national legal system there are various rules establishing the authority of courts of law to adjudicate disputes arising between members of the community. By virtue of these rules a person can be brought to trial even if he is unwilling to submit to court. Normally, for the institution of proceedings a suit by another subject is sufficient. In addition, the system for establishing whether in specific instances substantive rules are violated is so elaborate and complex that a basic dichotomy exists between civil and criminal proceedings. In the latter, most offences can be submitted to court by any individual who happens to be cognizant of the offence, by a prosecutor or other enforcement officers. While this is the rule, there is also the exceptional procedure of arbitration whereby disputes on civil or commercial matters can be settled by a third party chosen by the litigants. The main feature of arbitration is that, if admitted by State legislation and within the limits set out by such legislation, it rests on the agreement of the contending parties: the arbitrator cannot pronounce on the dispute if he has not been granted the power to do so by both sides.

By comparison, the position of the international community appears totally rudimentary. Until the adoption of the UN Charter in 1945 States were authorized to resort to force to impose their terms of settlement, unless they had entered into treaties requiring self-restraint on the matter (the Covenant of the League of Nations, of 1919, and the Paris Pact of 1928 were among these treaties; see **2.4.3**). States were authorized to enforce, even militarily, their rights without previously endeavouring to seek a peaceful solution of their differences. Thus, while in municipal systems third-party ascertainment of possible breaches of law normally precedes resort to enforcement measures, in international law this intermediate stage was not necessary, and in fact was normally skipped.

However, one should not think that no means other than war were available to States for settling their disputes. Over the years States had gradually forged some institutions or mechanisms, available to those willing to resolve their disagreements peacefully.

Things changed considerably after the Second World War, chiefly as a result of the establishment of the UN and the introduction of a general ban on the use or threat of force. States revitalized and strengthened the traditional means for settling disputes and in addition established innovative and flexible mechanisms for preventing disputes or, more generally, inducing compliance with international law.

10.2 TRADITIONAL MECHANISMS FOR PROMOTING AGREEMENT

From the outset States have forged two classes of means of settling disputes: those which aim at inducing the contesting parties to reach agreement, and those which instead are designed to confer on a third party the power to settle the dispute by a legally binding decision.

The most elementary method of settling international disputes is resort to *negotiation* between the contending parties. Characteristic of this method is the total absence of a third party, be it another State or an international institution. The advantage is that the solution is left entirely to the parties concerned, without any undue pressure from outside. In addition, as the goal of negotiation is to achieve agreement over the conflicting claims, a further and more important element is that there will be no loser and no winner, for both parties should derive some benefit from the diplomatic exchange. However, it has two major shortcomings. First, negotiation seldom leads to an in-depth determination of the facts or, when legal disputes are at issue, to the identification of the rules applicable in the specific case. Second, the stronger party is more likely to apply pressure to its counterpart than the other way about. More important still, the stronger State may easily subdue the other litigant by resorting to a host of means available to it on account of its de facto superiority. Thus, of course, negotiation may turn out to be a way by which powerful States bend the will of lesser States, settling the issue to their own advantage.

Whenever the parties decide to depart from direct diplomatic exchanges and to involve a third entity in the dispute, they have various methods at their disposal: inquiry, good offices, mediation, or conciliation.

Inquiry is a method envisaged in the 1899 (revised and improved upon in 1907) Hague Convention for the Peaceful Settlement of Disputes (the Russian publicist Fyodor Fyodorovich de Martens must be credited with strongly and successfully advocating at the Hague Conferences this means of promoting the settlement of disputes). By inquiry is meant a scheme whereby the contending parties agree to set up an international body, consisting of independent and impartial individuals, for the limited purpose of 'elucidating the *facts* [in dispute] by means of an impartial and conscientious investigation' (Article 9 of the 1907 Convention; emphasis added), the presupposition being that they agree on the applicable law. It is for the contestants to decide whether the findings of the body conducting the inquiry shall, or shall not, be legally binding on them. Inquiry may also be, and more often is, a stage of a more complex settlement of disputes process: it aims at establishing facts with a view to facilitating the task of a conciliation commission or an arbitral or judicial body (see for instance Article 50 of the Statute of the ICJ, pursuant to which 'The Court may, at any time, entrust any individual, body, bureau, commission, or other organizations that it may select, with the task of carrying out an enquiry or giving an expert opinion').

The most famous case is that relating to the *Dogger Bank* incident (1904). During the Russo-Japanese war (1904–05) Russian warships fired on a British trawler fleet that was fishing on the Dogger Bank in the North Sea, believing that they were Japanese torpedo boats. The Commission of Inquiry was asked not only to clarify the facts but also to establish where the responsibility lay.[1] Other cases involved France and Italy. In particular, the *Tavignano* incident may be mentioned: during the Italo-Turkish war of 1911–12, in 1912 the Italian warship *Fulmine* seized off the coasts of Tunisia the French postal ship *Tavignano*, suspected of carrying war contraband and took it to Tripoli; the French ship, not having on board any goods likely to be considered as contraband of war, was released the day after. The same day and in the same area the Italian warship *Canopo* opened fire on two Tunisian vessels. France requested compensation for both cases, claiming that the ships seized or attacked were within the Tunisian territorial waters (at that time Tunisia was a French protectorate); Italy, on the other hand claimed that the acts at issue had occurred on the high seas. However, the commission of inquiry was unable to make any finding, the data provided by the parties being too inaccurate for the commission to reach any certain conclusion.[2] Also the *Tubantia* case, between Germany and the Netherlands, is notable. The sinking of the Dutch steamer *Tubantia* on 16 March 1916 had been caused by the explosion of a torpedo launched by a German submarine.[3]

Good offices, mediation, and conciliation denote three different gradations of third-party participation in the settlement of disputes. In the case of *good offices* a third State or an international body is asked, or offers, to induce the contending parties to negotiate an amicable settlement. In *mediation* the third party takes a more active role in the dispute settlement, by participating in the negotiations between the two disputants and informally promoting ways of settling the dispute. As a rule mediation is all the more effective when the mediator is a dignitary of a Great Power or a senior civil servant of an international organization. *Conciliation* designates an even more active role of the third party, which carefully considers the various factual and legal elements of the dispute and formally proposes the terms of settlement (that, however, are not legally binding on the disputants).

10.3 TRADITIONAL MECHANISMS FOR SETTLING DISPUTES BY A BINDING DECISION

In many respects, *arbitration* involves a qualitative leap. The dispute is no longer settled for the sole purpose of safeguarding peaceful relations and accommodating the interests of the conflicting parties in a mutually acceptable manner. An additional goal is pursued—that of patching up the differences on the basis of international legal standards previously accepted by States. Another salient trait is that the court makes a thorough examination of both the facts at issue and the law governing them. A further significant feature is that the court's findings concerning both the facts and the law are legally binding on the contending parties, in as much as they are set out in the disposition (*dispositif*).

Numerous treaty rules providing for resort to arbitral courts have been adopted since the late nineteenth century. What is more important still, permanent bodies were set up and a whole corpus of rules of procedure was developed. This process began in 1899, when the First Hague Convention on the Peaceful Settlement of International Disputes set up the Permanent Court of Arbitration (PCA, still in existence). It consisted of a standing panel of arbitrators from among whom States in conflict could select suitable persons to assist with settling their specific dispute, plus an administrative infrastructure (the Permanent Administrative Council and the International Bureau) created to act as a secretariat in the event of the Court being called into being. The essential features of the Court were described in 1907 by Fyodor Fyodorovich de Martens, who had played a central role in setting it up in 1899. He said that 'The Court of 1899 is only a shadow which, from time to time, materialises, only to fade away once again'.[4] In a similar vein, the Dutch jurist Asser, at the same 1907 Conference, stated that the PCA was 'only a phantom, an impalpable ghost, or, in plain words, it consisted of a Registry and a list'.[5] Actually, since 1900 the PCA has heard only 23 cases, 20 of which were dealt with between 1900 and 1932. The methods of conferring jurisdiction on the PCA were twofold: (a) the conclusion of an agreement submitting a certain dispute to the Court (so-called *compromis*); and (b) the making of a treaty containing a clause whereby each contracting party was empowered to submit to the Court any dispute with another contracting party relating to the interpretation or application of the treaty (the so-called *arbitral clause*).

It is hardly surprising that the heyday of arbitration was the period between the two World Wars, when Western States still made up a relatively homogeneous group and were still paramount in the world community. Tradition, domestic legal philosophy and attachment to the principle of the rule of law, all prompted Western States to submit to adjudication. Even more important, during that period States were under the influence of the Wilsonian concept of 'open diplomacy', according to which the 'reign of law', and voluntary submission to impartial judgment would save the world community from another conflagration by relaxing dangerous tensions.

The Permanent Court of International Justice (PCIJ) was created in 1921 (it was replaced in 1946 by the International Court of Justice, ICJ). The Court was really a permanent body. The framers of its Statute found four great merits in its institution: (1) Since it consisted of a group of sitting judges, 'the contesting parties no longer [had] the choice of the judges'. (2) As it was made up of judges 'permanently associated with each other in the same work, and, except in rare cases, retaining their seats from one case to another', the Court could 'develop a continuous tradition and assure the harmonious and logical development of international law'. (3) While in the PCA it could be feared that judges would be inclined to regard cases 'from a political standpoint', in the case of the PCIJ 'Law necessarily [became] more authoritative and also, possibly, more severe'. (4) While the PCA could include 'politicians in addition to Jurisconsults', the Court would comprise, 'besides Jurisconsults, great judges'.[6] In short, the Court was not a court of arbitration 'but a Court of justice'.[7]

Arbitral courts or tribunals vary in effectiveness and technical sophistication and, in addition, their jurisdiction is usually limited to a relatively small number of States. They all share, however, the characteristic of resting on the *consent* of States: they are set up by treaties and their jurisdiction is accepted by means of contractual obligations. In short, the system representing the exception in domestic legal systems, that is, arbitration, is the rule in the international community.

10.4 THE NEW LAW: AN OVERVIEW

The law that emerged after the Second World War and the adoption of the UN Charter exhibits a few unique features.

First, hand in hand with the general ban on the threat or use of force, a *general obligation* to settle legal or political disputes peacefully evolved under the impulse of Articles 2(3) and 33 of the UN Charter. In addition, precisely because of this ban, there have been two important developments. On the one hand, *States have increasingly resorted to traditional means of settling disputes* and even *strengthened* them by turning them into standing or at least compulsory institutions (in particular, States have more and more established permanent or semi-permanent judicial bodies). On the other hand, the principal political bodies of the UN, that is the *SC and the GA*, have handled disputes or situations likely to jeopardize peace.

Another distinguishing trait of modern law is that, in some areas (in particular, international trade relations) States have imaginatively crafted *new compulsory mechanisms* that share many features with adjudication without however properly falling into this class.

Finally, States have realized that in many areas dispute settlement should be replaced by the establishment of mechanisms designed to *monitor compliance* with international legal standards on a permanent basis, and thus *prevent* or *deter* as much as possible deviation from those standards. In other words, instead of setting up bodies calculated to act *after* a breach of international rules has allegedly occurred, mechanisms have been established aimed at forestalling possible infringements and inducing compliance with law.

10.5 THE GENERAL OBLIGATION TO SETTLE DISPUTES PEACEFULLY

Article 2(3) of the UN Charter is broad in scope, encompassing the peaceful settlement of all disputes, while Article 33 only imposes the obligation of peaceful settlement with regard to 'disputes, the continuance of which is likely to endanger the maintenance of international peace and security'. However, this loose terminology makes it clear that, since in practice any dispute may be likely to jeopardize peace and security, the obligation of peaceful settlement might concern all disputes. In any event, as stated above (5.5), the matter was clarified in 1970, when the UN Declaration on Friendly Relations, adopted by consensus by the GA, laid down the principle that States must seek a peaceful settlement for *any dispute* that may arise between them. Arguably the Declaration codified a customary rule that was fully consistent with, and spelled out the essence of, the new legal system inaugurated by the UN Charter.

States are thus enjoined to *endeavour* to resolve their disputes peacefully, before taking any enforcement action (although they are not duty bound to *settle* those disputes at any cost). The need to go through this intermediate stage means, among other things, that States may find it advisable to have the dispute settled by an arbitral court empowered to determine whether the law has been breached and, if it has, what remedial action may lawfully be taken. In spite of its momentous importance, this general obligation is marred by the absence of any provision establishing by what specific modalities disagreement should be solved. No general rules have evolved to the effect that States must submit to the authority of bodies empowered to dictate the terms of settlement; in particular, no adjudicating organ endowed with *general and compulsory* jurisdiction has ever been created. Hence, States are at liberty to choose any means of peaceful settlement they prefer. Thus, whereas States are mandated to try to settle their differences by means other than force, such stringent obligation is accompanied by complete freedom as to the choice of the means of settlement.

It is not difficult to grasp the reasons for this utterly unsatisfactory state of affairs. All members of the world community have come to realize that it is too dangerous to allow disagreements to be resolved forcibly: the threat or use of force between two States can easily involve other countries as well, since international subjects are interconnected by a variety of links. Hence, the establishment of the general obligation referred to above. However, a profound chasm exists among States as to the modalities for settlement. On the one hand, many countries claim that conciliation and judicial review are the best means of settlement and that they should therefore be compulsory for all States. In contrast, many other nations contend that negotiation is more appropriate; more generally, they argue that States should be left free to choose the best means in each specific case.

10.6 RESORT TO TRADITIONAL MEANS

As a result of the aforementioned ban on the use of force and the consequent obligation of States to settle their disputes peacefully, States have *increasingly* resorted to traditional mechanisms for settling disputes.

Whereas, as in the past, inquiry as a 'bilateral' method organized by the disputant States has been scantily used (with few notable exceptions),[10] inquiry or *fact-finding*, as it is now more often termed, has increasingly acquired importance as a means of establishing facts employed by international organizations or bodies. For instance, the ILO has frequently resorted to this method (under Article 26 of the Organization's Constitution), as have the UN SC (Article 34), the GA or the UN Secretary-General, as well as the Council of the International Civil Aviation Organization (ICAO).[11] Mention should also be made of the International Fact-Finding Commission, provided for in Article 90 of the First Geneva Additional Protocol of 1977. However, this Commission has not yet become operative due to the lack of will of any party to an international conflict to request its action.

Also *mediation* has been resorted to. For instance on 8 January 1979 Chile and Argentina asked Pope John Paul II to mediate the dispute between them over the Beagle Channel; following the Pope's 'proposals, suggestions and advice', of 12 December 1980, they made an agreement in 1984.[12]

Similarly, in 1979 the US President, Carter, mediated between Egypt and Israel and achieved the Camp David Agreement. In 1994–5 the so-called Group of Contact (consisting of a number of States including the USA, Britain, and Russia) mediated between the conflicting States in the former Yugoslavia, and promoted the conclusion of the Dayton/Paris agreement of November 1995. In 1999, at the request of the Foreign Ministers of the Group of Seven Industrialized Countries and the Russian Federation, the President of Finland, Mr Ahtisaari, and the Russian former Prime Minister, Mr Chernomyrdin, discharged the task of finding a political settlement of the Kosovo crisis; they eventually proposed a settlement that was accepted both by the Federal Republic of Yugoslavia (Serbia and Montenegro) and by NATO countries, and was later endorsed by the UN SC by resolution 1244 (1999).[13]

Furthermore, after the end of the cold war States have increasingly had recourse to international *arbitration* and *adjudication*, in the right belief that independent and impartial third-party binding settlement of disputes constitutes a helpful way of bridging international differences. In particular, an increasing number of States, chiefly developing countries as well as States belonging to the former Socialist bloc, submit disputes to the ICJ (conversely many Western States, contrary to the previous trend emphasized above, have tended to shun the Court, presumably out of distrust for the judicial settlement of disputes). The docket of this Court has greatly augmented, and the judgments delivered by the Court tend to cover a growing range of subjects, including politically sensitive issues such as self-defence, indirect armed aggression, self-determination of peoples, the legality of the threat or use of nuclear weapons, genocide, and so on.

Like its predecessor, the PCIJ, the Court has a fixed set of rules of procedure, and has developed an important case law over the years. In addition, means for facilitating a wider acceptance of the Court's jurisdiction are available to States, the most significant being the so-called *optional clause*. By virtue of this clause every State can declare that it accepts *ipso facto* and without special agreement the compulsory jurisdiction of the Court in relation to any other State accepting the same obligation (Article 36.2 of the Court's Statute). In addition, the Court has developed in its case law another method of accepting the Court's jurisdiction, based, as much as the other modes, on consent (which in this case may be tacit or implied): the so-called *forum prorogatum* (a State institutes proceedings before the Court against another State that has not previously accepted the Court's jurisdiction; if, by some acts—such as appearing before the Court and arguing the case on its merits—the respondent State shows that it accepts the Court's jurisdiction, the Court is empowered to pronounce on the merits of the case). This doctrine was first set out by the PCIJ in 1925, in the *Mavrommatis Palestine Concessions* (*Merits*) case (Greece v. Great Britain),[14] then taken up by the ICJ in 1951 in the *Haya de la Torre* case (Colombia v. Peru).[15]

Together with the increasing importance of the ICJ, another signal phenomenon of recent decades is the proliferation of permanent or semi-permanent international courts and tribunals.

In this connection, one can mention the courts and tribunals set up in the area of human rights (for instance, the European Court and the Inter-American Court of Human Rights), within the European Community and the European Free Trade Association (EFTA), the International Tribunal for the Law of the Sea, the two ad hoc UN criminal tribunals (ICTY and ICTR), the Special Court for Sierra Leone, and so on.

Another significant judicial mechanism is the Iran-US Claims Tribunal. It was established in 1981 under the Algiers Accord concluded following the 1979 hostage crisis and the consequent freezing by the US Government of Iranian assets in the USA or under US jurisdiction or control, and the taking of trade sanctions against Iran. The Tribunal was granted jurisdiction over: (a) claims of US nationals against Iranian authorities as well as claims of Iranian nationals against the USA; (b) claims of each State against the other, arising out of contractual arrangements for the purchase or sale of goods or services; (c) claims of one State against the other concerning the interpretation and performance of the obligations laid down in the General Declaration forming part of the Algiers Accord.

Some commentators have considered the multiplication of international arbitral or judicial bodies as likely to lead to discrepancies and conflicts in the interpretation or application of international law, hence to a fragmentation of this body of law. Also, it has been suggested that the ICJ, as the principal international judicial organ, should be given the role of the judicial body having the final word on international legal issues. It may be contended that, by itself, the proliferation at issue is not a negative phenomenon, as it may stimulate courts and tribunals to hand down better-reasoned and more convincing judgments. As a consequence, those judgments which stand out for the compelling nature of their legal reasoning will also enjoy greater authority and standing.

10.7 STRENGTHENING AND INSTITUTIONALIZATION OF TRADITIONAL MEANS

The aforementioned obligation, currently incumbent upon all States, to settle disputes peacefully, has entailed that States have also endeavoured to strengthen traditional mechanisms and, what is even more important, to establish them upon a permanent or quasi-permanent base. This in particular holds true for conciliation or adjudication mechanisms. Furthermore the UN has increasingly dealt with international disputes and, in a few cases, has even gone so far as to set up bodies entrusted with judicial functions.

As far as *negotiation* is concerned, still the most widespread means of settling disputes peacefully, some treaties make recourse to it compulsory, in the form of mandatory 'consultations' or 'exchange of views' (see for instance Article 283 of the UN Convention of the Law of the Sea, Article VIII (2) of the 1959 Antarctic Treaty). Other treaties, especially those on the protection of the environment, have institutionalized recourse to negotiation, by establishing permanent commissions.

10.7.1 RESORT TO COMPULSORY CONCILIATION OR ADJUDICATION

In recent times the traditional system of providing for the right to unilaterally resort to conciliation or arbitration (so-called compulsory conciliation or arbitration) has been revived and strengthened, as follows: (1) Compulsory conciliation or adjudication procedures are laid down in multilateral treaties of great importance. (2) They rest on the basic consent of the overwhelming majority of member States of the international community.

In the case of *conciliation*, the conclusions and proposals of the conciliatory organ are not binding on the parties. In spite of this major shortcoming, the mere facts of (a) providing for a right to initiate, or the obligation to submit to, conciliation; (b) establishing a procedure to be followed in the conciliation stage; and (c) setting up a body responsible for seeking to induce the contending parties to reach an amicable settlement, represent a major step forward, given the present state of the world community.

The establishment of compulsory conciliation is the upshot of two conflicting approaches. On the one hand, there is the position of those countries which argue that the drafting of new international substantive rules can only make sense if some compulsory means of settling disputes is established. On the other hand, there are the views of the vast majority of States. These States, while conceding the paramountcy of the general principle on peaceful settlement of disputes, do not wish to tie their hands by accepting *a priori* the obligation to have recourse to one or another of the specific methods of settlement; in particular, they strongly oppose any settlement procedure leading to a 'win or lose' conclusion. Faced with this rift, international lawmakers have eventually struck a balance by making resort to conciliation compulsory.

It should be noted that even this modest advance is not general, but has only been achieved in certain very definite areas.

Under the Vienna Convention on the Law of Treaties of 1969 disputes concerning any provision on the invalidity of treaties other than those on *jus cogens* can be submitted to conciliation within 12 months of their beginning (Article 66(b)). Any party to the dispute can set in motion the conciliation procedure by submitting a request to this effect to the UN Secretary-General. The Conciliation Commission, appointed from a list drawn up by the Secretary-General, 'shall hear the parties, examine the claims and objections, and make proposals to the parties with a view to reaching an amicable settlement of the dispute' (Article 5 of the Annex to the Convention). Clearly, the Commission has quasi-judicial powers, for it can look into both the facts and the law. However, its findings and proposals are not binding, for the report of the Commission 'shall have no other character than that of recommendations submitted for the consideration of the parties in order to facilitate an amicable settlement of the dispute' (Article 6 of the Annex). Nonetheless, the authority of the Commission's conclusions and recommendations cannot fail to have a great impact on the parties. It is likely, therefore, that in actual fact the weight of the Commission's report will be no less than that of a legally binding judgment. It should, however, be added that, in practice, the mechanism has never been utilized.

In some exceptional cases States have decided to make *adjudication* compulsory. A number of devices have, however, been introduced to render the system more acceptable to those States which oppose judicial review. Furthermore, the very specific character of the substantive law to which the system for compulsory adjudication relates, accounts for the exceptional acceptance, in principle, by all groups of States, of a method of settlement which so many States still look upon with suspicion. The system is *inter alia* provided for in two important treaties, the 1969 Vienna Convention on the Law of Treaties and the 1982 Convention on the Law of the Sea. The complexity and intricacy of the subject matter, as well as the need for developing countries to take account of the views of industrialized States in shaping a new law, explain why developing countries had to barter advanced modes of settling disputes with developed States, for the acceptance by those States of many of the Third World's demands.

Under the Vienna Convention disputes relating to *jus cogens* may be submitted to the ICJ at the request of one party only, after 12 months have elapsed since the start of the dispute without any settlement being reached (Article 66(a)).

In keeping with Article 33 of the UN Charter, Article 279 of the Convention on the Law of the Sea of 1982 reiterates the duty of States to settle their differences peacefully. It then imposes on them the duty to 'exchange their views' as to the mode of settlement to be adopted (Article 283). If no other method is agreed upon, each contending party has the right to propose resort to conciliation. If the offer is not accepted or the parties do not succeed in agreeing upon the conciliation procedure (under Article 284), any party to the dispute is entitled (under Article 287) to initiate judicial proceedings before one of four courts, namely: (1) the International Tribunal on the Law of the Sea (ITLOS), established under Annex VI to the Convention (the ITLOS has exclusive jurisdiction, through its Seabed Disputes Chamber, over disputes relating to activities in the international seabed area; in addition, it has special jurisdiction in matters calling for provisional measures). (2) The ICJ. (3) An arbitral tribunal set up in accordance with Annex VII to the Convention. (4) A special arbitral tribunal constituted in accordance with Annex VIII. These provisions are, however, subject to the limitations provided for in Article 297–9.

It should be apparent from this short survey that the system under consideration is much stronger than the one laid down in the 1969 Vienna Convention. Whilst conciliation is not compulsory, adjudication becomes obligatory if the parties fail to agree upon another method of settlement.

So far States (notably developing countries) have used the judicial mechanisms envisaged in the Law of the Sea Convention in a number of cases, submitting their disputes either to the ICJ or to the ITLOS; furthermore, in a recent case between Australia and New Zealand versus Japan (*Southern Bluefin Tuna*), an Arbitral Tribunal was instituted.[16]

The mechanisms discussed so far are designed to settle disputes relating to the interpretation or application of some specific multilateral treaties. They are provided for in so-called *compromissory clauses* or *clauses on compulsory conciliation*. Other mechanisms are established by general conventions and are charged with the settlement of disputes arising in general or in a particular area.

In this last respect the International Centre for Settlement of Investment Disputes (ICSID) stands out. In 1965 a Convention was concluded under the auspices of the World Bank. The purpose was to establish a mechanism that could take into account and protect the interests of both investors (normally nationals or corporations from industrialized countries) and States where investments were made (normally developing countries). Thus a legal framework was set up, available to States, individuals, and corporations. No permanent tribunal was established, only an Administrative Council, consisting of all member States, and a Secretariat. In addition, panels of conciliators and arbitrators (experts in the fields of law, industry, or finance) were set up. Parties to investment disputes may thus select conciliators or arbitrators from those panels. So far ICSID has proved very successful, primarily in the field of arbitration.

10.7.2 THE INCREASING DISPUTE-SETTLEMENT ROLE OF UN ORGANS

Another major feature of the new law is that a development started with the League of Nations has now acquired a crucial role: the *handling by the SC* (or, under the conditions set out in Article 12.1 of the UN Charter, by the GA) *of disputes or situations* likely to lead to a threat or a serious danger to peace and security (see **Chapter 13**). Thus, a central political body of the international organized community now monopolizes (or should monopolize) all those disputes or situations that pose a threat to friendly international relations. That body is empowered to call the parties concerned to explain their position and may try to narrow their differences, reconcile their opposing views, and, if need be, recommend an equitable solution. By the same token, any party to a dispute or even a third party may bring a situation or dispute likely to jeopardize peace and security to the attention of the SC (or the GA). Thus, these two bodies act as centralized organs of conciliation, while at the same time also possessing the authority to call upon the parties to adopt a certain settlement.

Interestingly, the SC has contributed to the settlement of disputes in another way as well, by establishing various bodies entrusted with judicial functions. In 1991, the SC set up the UN Compensation Commission charged with considering claims for 'any direct loss, damage, including environmental damage and the depletion of natural resources, or injury to foreign Governments, nationals and corporations, as a result of Iraq's unlawful invasion and occupation of Kuwait' (SC Res. 687 (1991)). The Commission, which plays a judicial role, verifies the validity of the claims, evaluating losses, assessing payments and resolving disputed claims.

In 1993 and 1994, the SC set up ad hoc international criminal tribunals charged with prosecuting and punishing persons responsible for serious violations of international humanitarian law respectively in the former Yugoslavia and Rwanda (the ICTY and ICTR). The SC conceived the establishment of these tribunals as a means of reacting by a judicial process to a threat to the peace and security and also of forestalling disputes between States likely to jeopardize peace and security.

10.8 THE ESTABLISHMENT OF MORE FLEXIBLE MECHANISMS FOR EITHER PREVENTING OR SETTLING DISPUTES

10.8.1 QUASI-JUDICIAL COMPULSORY SETTLEMENT OF TRADE DISPUTES

An extremely inventive method for settling disputes was worked out in the area of trade relations, first under the General Agreement on Tariff and Trade (GATT), established in 1947, and later, in 1994, within the system of the World Trade Organization (WTO). Here the latter system will be outlined.

The *substantive* provisions of the relevant agreements on trade are designed to liberalize world trade by providing for non-discrimination and most-favoured-nation treatment (see **Chapter 18**), by limiting subsidies and dumping and reducing tariff barriers to world trade (see **18.7.3**). To ensure that this complex network of international rules is complied with, an innovative procedure was devised in 1994, based on the Dispute Settlement Understanding (DSU) annexed to the WTO Agreement. It hinges on the following points.

(1) Each contracting State must *notify* the Organization and the other parties of its adoption of trade measures affecting the operation of the substantive provisions of an

agreement on trade. Notification is followed by *consultation*. The other contracting parties must respond to requests for consultation promptly and conduct these consultations with a view to reaching mutually satisfactory solutions. Should consultations fail to lead to an acceptable settlement, the parties may ask for the use of *good offices* or *conciliation* by WTO.

(2) If no settlement is attained, a contracting party may submit a *complaint* to a panel of independent experts. The complaint, it should be emphasized, does not necessarily concern a breach of a WTO provision. What a State may complain of is the *'nullification and impairment' of benefits accruing to it*, brought about by the measures adopted by the party complained of. What matters is not whether a State has violated a specific treaty provision, but rather whether or not it has caused that 'nullification or impairment of benefits' (indeed, a 'nullification or impairment of benefits' may come about even in the absence of a breach of the relevant agreement; conversely, a State can effect a breach of the agreement without such breach amounting to a 'nullification or impairment of benefits').

(3) The complaint may emanate from a single State or more States (multiple complaint). It is submitted to a panel of three (unless the parties agree on a panel of five) experts in international trade law or policy, serving in their individual capacity. Panels are established by the WTO Dispute Settlement Body (DSB), on which representatives of all contracting parties sit. The members of each specific panel are however nominated by the WTO Secretariat; if the parties do not agree to the composition of the panel, membership is determined by the Director-General of the WTO in consultation with the chairman of the DSB and the chairman of the Council or Committee established under the relevant WTO Agreement.

(4) The panel hears submissions from each complainant as well as the State complained of. Third States may also be heard. In making their findings on the facts and law, panels proceed in two stages. First they issue an *Interim Report* with their findings and conclusions. The parties may comment on it and request a further meeting of the panel to discuss their comments. The panel then adopts a *Final Report*, which is transmitted to the parties and the DSB.

(5) The panel's report is adopted by the DSB unless (a) it decides by consensus not to adopt it, or (b) a party to the dispute appeals against the report.

(6) If an appeal is made, it is heard by a standing seven-member *Appellate Body* established by the DSB. The Appellate Body has jurisdiction solely on questions of law. That body may of course also pronounce on questions of interpretation of the relevant provisions, but it is bound by the *interpretations* of the WTO Agreement and the various Multilateral Trade Agreements, adopted by the WTO Ministerial Conference and General Council (both consisting of representatives of all member States of WTO), interpretations taken by a three-quarters majority of States.

(7) Reports of the Appellate Body are *automatically adopted* by the DSB unless it decides by consensus not to adopt them.

(8) *Monitoring* of compliance with the panel's or Appellate Body's report is exercised by the DSB. In addition, if the State concerned does not comply with the report, the complainant State may request the DSB to authorize it to take counter-measures, namely to *suspend* the application, towards the State concerned, of concessions or other obligations laid down in the relevant agreement. This suspension may concern either the same trade sector or another sector or even obligations deriving from another WTO agreement.

(9) If the State against which the suspension is carried out objects to it, the matter must be referred to *arbitration* and the findings of the Arbitral Court are final.

As is apparent, the whole procedure is an inventive admixture of conciliation, negotiation, and adjudication, with an interesting follow-up of enforcement, and traditional arbitration as a final and *extrema ratio* mode of resolution. Clearly, this unique procedure is warranted by the subject matter: trade relations involve huge economic interests; in addition there is often the need to take account of the specific problems besetting certain countries or some sectors, a need that, however, must be reconciled or balanced with the requirement to ensure non-discrimination, that is equality of treatment and absence of unjustified distortions of world trade.

So far this procedure has proved exceedingly useful and successful. A great number of cases have been brought before the competent WTO organs or panels. When we consider that at present WTO membership runs to 140 States and that all are bound by this procedure, we may surely contend that it has proved to be one of the best means, by far, of settling international disputes in the world community.

10.8.2 INTERNATIONAL SUPERVISION

To obviate many deficiencies of the international order in the resolution of conflict, a new system of inducing compliance with international rules has gradually been introduced for the purpose of scrutinizing the behaviour of States parties to specific treaties. This system (which was established in some areas as early as 1919, but mushroomed particularly after the Second World War) differs from international adjudication in many respects.

First, the *composition of the organ* responsible for monitoring the implementation of international rules is normally different from that of judicial bodies, for the supervisory body may also be made up of representatives of States instead of individuals acting in their personal capacity.

In addition, overseeing functions are frequently entrusted to *more than one body*, and in this case the various organs often differ as to their composition, for one or more are composed of independent individuals, whereas others consist of State officials.

Furthermore, normally *the initiative of the supervisory procedure* is not left to the aggrieved State, but can be taken either by the beneficiaries of the international rules (for instance, individuals or groups of individuals), or even by the supervisory organ itself acting *proprio motu*, that is to say, on its own initiative. Sometimes there is no need for anybody to initiate the proceedings, for the simple reason that the procedure is a standing and automatic one, consisting of a periodic scrutiny of the behaviour of the States concerned. Thus, while in the case of adjudication the existence of a *dispute* (that is, a clash of opposing views and demands as to the facts and their legal appraisal) is necessary for the proceedings to be initiated, in the case of supervision the existence of a dispute is almost never a necessary prerequisite of international action.

Also, while—as has just been pointed out—adjudication is triggered *after* a dispute has arisen, supervision is normally carried out with a view to *deterring* States from infringing international legal standards. In other words, normally supervision is designed to have a *preventive purpose*.

In addition, while the hearings of judicial bodies are public, normally the debates between the contending parties before an overseeing body (or, where the procedure is not contentious in character, the investigatory activities of the body) are carried out *in camera*, so as to avoid attracting publicity to possible violations committed by the State under scrutiny while the investigation is under way.

Finally, as a rule the *outcome of the procedure* does not consist in a binding decision but takes various forms (report, recommendations, etc.) which, whatever their official label, have only moral and hortatory force.

Why did international law-makers resort to this ingenious system for impelling States to abide by international law? There are two closely interrelated reasons.

First, in the aftermath of the First World War, States started to resort to international treaties to regulate matters which until then had remained within their domestic jurisdiction.

These issues included the protection of minorities; the regulation of labour conditions and the rights of workers; the establishment of international mandates over territories which up to that time had been under the exclusive control of sovereign Powers; the regulation of narcotic drugs; and unique matters such as the relations between the Free City of Danzig (now Gdansk) and Poland and more generally the protection of the rights of the City laid down in the Treaty of Versailles. The new international legislation presented one remarkable feature: it did not impose reciprocal obligations, that is to say obligations entailing each contracting party being interested in complying with the rule for fear the other contracting State might feel free to disregard it. Rather, the new rules belonged to that unique class of norms which protect the interests of entities other than the subjects assuming the rights and obligations in question—such as individuals, groups, populations subject to the mandate system, associations of workers and employers, and so on.

The second reason is that in these new areas it was difficult to establish mechanisms for ensuring that the new international rules were faithfully observed. Resort to adjudication was not feasible on a number of grounds, including the fact that States, although they had accepted such new and bold obligations, were reluctant to submit to judicial bodies. Furthermore, the unique features of the subject matter meant that adjudication was scarcely appropriate. Indeed, the non-reciprocal character of the obligations laid down in those rules meant that infringement of one of them might be passed over in silence, if it was only the other contracting States that had the right to demand compliance. It was, therefore, only logical to bestow the right to exact respect for the rules upon the very entities for whose benefit they had been agreed upon. However, it would have been impossible for States to accept the granting of *locus standi* before international courts to individuals or groups. A compromise was reached. It lay in allowing individuals or groups to petition international bodies that were devoid of any judicial function and powers.

To satisfy all the requirements mentioned above, imaginative monitoring systems were contrived. To make them acceptable to States, it was deemed necessary to water down their possible impact on State sovereignty. To this effect, no binding force was attached to the final assessment of supervisory bodies. In addition, side by side with organs consisting of impartial individuals, bodies composed of State representatives were set up (plainly, they are more sensitive to States' exigencies and, therefore, more inclined to attenuate possibly harsh evaluations). It was also decided, as pointed out above, that the meetings or sessions of the monitoring bodies should normally be held *in camera*, for the manifest purpose of shielding States from public exposure.

Supervisory systems proved a balanced and relatively effective means of impelling States to live up to their international undertakings. It is, therefore, not surprising that certain of them survived the Second World War (for example, the ILO mechanisms for monitoring the application of international labour conventions, and the systems for scrutinizing conventions on narcotic drugs). In other areas new control machinery was instituted. The *fields in which supervision is at present most widespread* are (a) international labour conventions; (b) treaties and other international standards on human rights; (c) the peaceful use of atomic energy; (d) the environment; (e) the Antarctic and outer space; (f) international and internal armed conflict; (g) international economic law.

Plainly, the expansion of supervision to so many important areas testifies to its responsiveness to States' needs. In addition, it also proves that all groups of States are ready to submit to supervision, for even those countries which are more recalcitrant in respect of other international means of investigation do not oppose international monitoring. This, of course, is mainly due to its flexibility and to the fact that supervisory bodies do not put States in the dock, but tend to persuade them, even before any possible breach occurs, by dint of cautious diplomatic and moral pressure, to abide by those rules which they may be inclined to disregard.

There are four *principal modalities* through which supervision is effected.

(1) Examination of *periodic reports* submitted at predetermined intervals by the States concerned.

For example, reports by the member States of the ILO concerning the application of international labour conventions under Article 22 of the ILO Constitution; the reports provided for in various human rights conventions, such as the 1965 Convention on Racial Discrimination

(Article 9); the 1966 Covenants on Human Rights (Articles 16 and 40 respectively); the 1956 Slavery Convention (Article 8); the 1984 UN Convention against Torture (Article 19).

(2) *Inspection,* far more effective and penetrating than the examination of States' reports, where the inquiring body must confine itself to the data provided by the State concerned. On-the-spot investigations allow international organs (or, as in the case of the treaties on Antarctica and outer space, the other States parties to the treaty) to satisfy themselves as to whether a State respects or disregards the treaty.

This class of monitoring is, for example, provided for in the treaty on the International Agency for Atomic Energy (Article 12.6), the Antarctic Treaty (Article 7), the 1967 Treaty on the Peaceful Use of Outer Space (Article 12). Inspection is also provided for in many treaties on protection of the environment (see **17.3.4**).

(3) Supervision carried out through a *contentious procedure* where the parties to a dispute, or the State under control and the supervisory body, engage in a contentious examination of the case.

See, for example, the procedures provided for in Articles 22–3, 24–5, and 26–9 of the ILO Constitution; in Article 41 of the Covenant on Civil and Political Rights; and in the Optional Protocol to the Covenant (the Human Rights Committee is entrusted with looking into alleged violations of the Covenant, either at the request of a contracting State or of individuals subject to the jurisdiction of a party to the Protocol); in Article 21 of the Torture Convention.

(4) Adoption of measures designed to forestall the possible commission of international delinquency by a State. So far this unique form of '*preventive*' supervision has been chiefly established in the area of the peaceful use of atomic energy and protection of the environment (see **17.3.4**). The special nature of the subject matter in these areas accounts for the exceptional characteristics of this international scrutiny.

Take, for example, certain bilateral agreements such as those between Canada and the Federal Republic of Germany of 11 December 1957; between Canada and Australia of 4 August 1959; between the UK and Italy of 28 December 1957; or the treaty instituting EURATOM (Article 103). All of them make the delivery of nuclear material conditional on a preventive control of the facilities of the recipient party by the granting State. Only if those facilities are considered consistent with the general standards set out in the agreements can the material be delivered. In this case, the extreme importance of the matter, that is, the danger that nuclear material might be used for military purposes, warrants resort to a very advanced type of supervision which States would otherwise find unacceptable.

11

ENFORCEMENT IN THE CASE OF VIOLATIONS BY STATES

11.1 TRADITIONAL LAW

11.1.1 GENERAL

In domestic legal orders enforcement strictly denotes all those measures and procedures, mostly taken by *public authorities*, calculated to impel compliance, by forcible and other coercive means, with the law. Consequently there exists a clear-cut distinction between those measures and procedures, that is, *sanctions*, on the one hand, and, on the other hand, forcible acts which, since they do not amount to an authorized reaction to a wrong, are unlawful. By contrast, in the old international community this distinction could not be made. There existed no central authorities responsible for enforcing the law on behalf of the whole community: *self-help* prevailed, that is, only the aggrieved State was authorized to react to what it considered a breach of its rights by another State. What is even more striking, the law applicable before the First World War also allowed resort to force for the protection of one's own interests. Consequently, there was *no substantial difference* between legitimate forcible 'sanctions' and resort to military force for safeguarding or furthering one's own interests. States were only to respect certain modalities: if they decided to engage in war, they were to express their *animus belligerandi* (intent to wage war) in some way, with the consequence that all the rules on war and neutrality became applicable. If, instead, they preferred to resort to coercion short of war, they were to make it clear that they did not mean to render the laws on war and neutrality applicable, but preferred to remain within the province of the laws of peace. Other modalities concerned the proper use of force: in the case of war, various rules on warfare placed restraints on the conduct of hostilities; in the case of forcible measures short of war, a few general principles gradually evolved.

A further distinguishing trait of traditional law was that even when a State resorted to armed force in order to react to wrongful behaviour by another State, no prior exhaustion of peaceful remedies was requested; much less was the State required to wait for a third party to pronounce on whether international law had actually been broken. Thus, while in domestic legal systems enforcement is normally carried out after judicial ascertainment that a breach of law has indeed occurred, in traditional international law States were authorized to judge by themselves, that is to base their possible resort to force on their own unilateral assessment of wrongdoings by other countries.

In the following pages I shall summarize, albeit briefly, traditional law, on two main grounds: (i) this body of law has not been completely superseded, let alone obliterated, by the new law; (ii) it is impossible to fully grasp the purport of the current law without knowing the fundamentals of traditional law.

11.1.2 CLASSES OF ENFORCEMENT MEASURES

Both before and after the First World War State practice and legal literature tried to identify the various forms which the use of force could take. The classification which I shall set forth below is primarily intended to serve practical purposes and to unravel the maze of States' conduct. Except for the differentiation between the use of force short of war and war proper, which is based on legal differences between the two categories and is therefore of scientific value, all the other distinctions serve a classificatory purpose only. In particular, the distinction between armed intervention (whereby States act to protect their own interests) and armed reprisals (reactions against wrongful acts of another State), a distinction States often relied on, was rather blurred in actual practice, for two reasons. First, States were, in any case, authorized to use force to pursue their interests, and so it did not make much difference whether they engaged in military action to react to an instance of unlawful conduct on the part of another State, or to safeguard their own interests. Second, all too frequently States invoked legal considerations as a cloak to cover their action in cases where they acted out of mere political interest; conversely, in some instances, when they were the victims of breaches by other States, their reaction was not explicitly based on legal arguments.

11.1.3 FORCIBLE INTERVENTION

By forcible intervention in the internal or external affairs of another State is meant compelling the State, by the threat or use of force, to do something (for example, to change its government, to enter into a treaty with a third State, to cede territory, or to carry out certain actions in its territory) in the interest of the intervening State. Forcible intervention took the form of military occupation of the territory of another State, naval demonstrations, naval blockade (that is to say the blocking by men-of-war of a portion of the coast of another State), embargo (in the old sense, that is the seizure of ships belonging to the other State or its nationals), and so on. International practice is replete with cases of armed intervention.

In some instances armed intervention in the territory of other States was officially justified by the intervening State on the grounds of 'self-defence and self-preservation'.

As early as 1817 the USA occupied *Amelia Island* (off East Florida, at the mouth of St Mary's river, near the boundary of the State of Georgia) then under Spanish sovereignty, on the grounds that it had become a centre of illicit trafficking harmful to the USA and over which the Spanish authorities were unable to exercise control.[1] In 1817 the American troops invaded Western Florida, which was also still under Spanish sovereignty, to repel the Seminole Indians living in Florida.[2]

Another famous incident is that of the *Caroline*. On the occasion of the Canadian rebellion of 1837 against the British authorities (Canada being at the time under British sovereignty), rebels were assisted by American citizens who several times crossed the Niagara (the border between Canada and the USA) on the *Caroline* to provide the insurgents with men and ammunitions. A party of British troops headed by Captain McLeod was then sent to attack the ship. They boarded it in the US port of Fort Schlosser, killed a number of men, set the ship on fire, and set it adrift towards the Niagara Falls. The US Government protested against this violation of its territorial sovereignty. A characteristic feature of the *Caroline* incident is that Britain saw no need to justify its behaviour by invoking a breach of international law by the USA. Rather, it claimed that its violation of US sovereignty had been rendered necessary by the fundamental right of 'self-defence and self-preservation'. However, the ensuing diplomatic correspondence enabled the two States to agree upon a delimitation of the instances in which armed attack on the territory of another State was allowed. According to the definition by the US Secretary of State, Webster, the attacking State must show a 'necessity of self-defence, instant, overwhelming, leaving no choice of means and no moment for deliberation'. This formula, which became famous and was taken up in subsequent years, initiated an international practice which gradually led to the placing of some restrictions on the unfettered freedom of States to use force for the protection of their interests.[3]

In other instances States sent armed troops abroad for the purpose of protecting their own nationals. In such cases the justification normally invoked by the invading State was that the territorial State had failed to take all the precautionary and other measures necessary for safeguarding the life and property of foreigners. It, therefore, proved imperative to substitute for this omission. Plainly, this sort of justification lent itself to many abuses.

According to the American writer Offutt,[4] between 1813 and 1928 US troops were sent abroad at least seventy times in order to protect US nationals or 'US interests'. Not unexpectedly, most military expeditions were effected by the USA in Latin American countries, but US troops also landed in other countries, such as Japan (1853, 1854, 1863, 1864, 1868); China (1854, 1856, 1859, 1900); Egypt (1858 and 1882); in Kisembo (on the west coast of Africa) in 1860; Formosa (now Taiwan) (1867); and Korea (1871, 1888, 1894). During the same period British forces landed in Honduras in 1873 and in Nicaragua in 1895 and 1910, and German forces in Samoa in 1899.

In other instances, chiefly in the nineteenth century, States used force abroad allegedly for the purpose of protecting the life or assets of individuals (not necessarily their nationals) threatened by civil commotion (so-called *humanitarian intervention*). In fact there were military interventions by European countries in other States (for instance, the Ottoman Empire) designed to further political or diplomatic interests of the intervening Powers.

11.1.4 REPRISALS

Reprisals are acts or actions in response to an unlawful act by another State. They consist of violations, by the allegedly wronged State, of international rules *vis-à-vis* the wrongdoer. In other words, reprisals are unlawful acts that become lawful in that they constitute a reaction to a delinquency by another State. It obviously follows that, if the State against which reprisals are taken had not in fact breached international law, the State resorting to reprisals can be held responsible for a violation of international law. In traditional international law reprisals were aimed at either impelling the delinquent State to discontinue the wrongdoing, or at punishing it, or both.

They are usually divided into peaceful and military. The former term covers actions that may consist of the failure to apply towards the alleged author of a breach of international law, a treaty or a customary rule (for instance, on the treatment of foreigners), the mass expulsion of nationals of a State with which the State taking reprisals had concluded a treaty prohibiting such expulsion, and so on. The latter category includes any act implying the threat or use of military force against the State responsible for a wrongful act. This category, therefore, covers the actions indicated above under the heading of intervention (blockade, embargo, and so on).

The famous *Naulilaa* case may be mentioned. In 1914, while Portugal was still neutral, German forces from the German colony of South West Africa (at present Namibia) crossed the border with Angola, then under Portuguese domination, in order to meet Portuguese authorities and initiate negotiations concerning the importation of food and the setting up of postal relations with Germany through Angola. At the Portuguese post of Naulilaa, on the southern border of Angola, the head of the German team, the governor of a district in South West Africa, and two German officers were killed following a misunderstanding caused primarily by the linguistic incompetence of the German interpreter, who hardly spoke and read Portuguese. By way of reprisal German troops were sent to destroy Portuguese posts and kill Portuguese soldiers. The Special Arbitral Tribunal instituted by Germany and Portugal determined in 1928 the following concerning reprisals: first, they comprise acts which would normally be illegal but are rendered lawful by the fact that they constitute a reaction to an international delinquency; second, they must be 'limited by considerations of humanity (*les expériences de l'humanité*) and the rules of good faith applicable in the relations between States'; third, they must not be excessive, although they need not be strictly proportionate to the offence; fourth, they must be preceded by a request for peaceful settlement (they must 'have remained unredressed after a demand for amends'); fifth, they must 'seek to impose on the offending State reparation for the offence, the return to legality and the avoidance of new offences'. It is interesting to note that in this case, the Tribunal held that Germany had violated international law because: (1) the Portuguese had not acted contrary to international law, since the killing of the three Germans was not a wilful but a fortuitous, if deplorable, incident; (2) the Germans had not made a request for peaceful settlement before resorting to force; (3) the force used by Germany was 'excessive' and 'out of any proportion' to the conduct of Portuguese authorities.[5]

Clearly, the requirement whereby armed reprisals are lawful only to the extent that they constitute a reaction to a wrong committed by another State presupposes the emergence of a rule prohibiting forcible intervention, that is, any interference in another State by the threat or use of force (see **2.5.2** and **5.4.1**). So long as such intervention was admitted, armed reprisals hardly made up a separate category, for it did not matter very much whether forcible measures short of war were to be labelled 'intervention' or 'reprisals'.

International law did not impose the choice of one form of reprisal rather than another. Until the First World War international law did not exercise any restraints. Afterwards the restrictions on war laid down in the Covenant of the League of Nations and the concomitant limitations on forcible intervention led States to gradually restrict resort to armed reprisals as well.

11.1.5 WAR

As stated above, until 1919 States were free to resort to war whenever they considered it fitting. In 1899 a Convention adopted by the Hague Peace Conference prescribed a declaration of war or an ultimatum (namely a declaration making the beginning of hostilities contingent on the non-observance by the other party of the conditions set forth therein). The 1899 Hague Convention, which was restated in 1907 and arguably turned into customary international law (unless it is held that it in fact codified a pre-existing customary rule), can, however, be violated without this breach implying that war, in the full sense of the word, has not started: if a State initiates warlike action against another State without complying with the Convention, it only makes itself answerable for a breach of international law; nevertheless the so-called state of war (namely the entering into operation of the laws of war and neutrality) comes into force.

11.2 NEW TRENDS FOLLOWING THE FIRST WORLD WAR

Sweeping restrictions on resort to war proper were laid down in the Covenant of the League of Nations (1919) and later on in the Kellogg–Briand Pact of 1928 (see **2.4.3**). In addition, it was felt that armed force should not be used to settle international disputes, in particular to recover money and other assets loaned to foreign States (the Hague Convention II of 1907 respecting the Limitations on the Employment of Force for the Recovery of Contracts Debts, also called the Drago–Porter Convention; see above, **2.3.4**). This view resulted in three major developments between 1918 and 1938: (1) A customary prohibition of war as a means of protecting one's own interests slowly emerged. (2) Consequently a set of rules evolved permitting recourse to armed force under exceptional circumstances (reprisals; self-defence; protection of nationals abroad whose life and assets were in peril because the territorial State was unable or unwilling to protect them); in particular rules evolved setting out the conditions on which armed reprisals were lawful, and better distinguishing them from retortion, on which see *infra* **11.5** (these rules crystallized both as a result of the aforementioned *Naulilaa* case and under the impulse of a resolution adopted in 1934 by the *Institut de droit international*).[6] (3) A gradual process circumscribing the grounds for forcible intervention in the territory of another State led to the formation of a rule prohibiting 'dictatorial intervention', that is, the threat or use of force for the purpose of imposing on the will of another State.

11.3 ENFORCEMENT OF INTERNATIONAL RULES IN MODERN INTERNATIONAL LAW

At present, as stated above (see **5.5**), force and the threat of force 'against the territorial integrity or political independence of any State, or in any other manner inconsistent with the Purposes of the United Nations' are prohibited by the ban laid down in Article 2.4 of the UN Charter and a corresponding customary rule. In consequence, reprisals have become the most widespread means of enforcing international rules. Two trends have emerged.

First, on account of the ban on force, *armed* reprisals in time of peace are considered unlawful (in time of war belligerent reprisals against some limited targets are allowed; see **15.6.5(ii)(1)**). Hence to differentiate these prohibited reprisals from those permitted, it is now preferred to term the latter 'counter-measures' (an expression used for the first time in 1978 by the US-France Arbitral Tribunal in *Air Service Agreement*).[7] There is no point in objecting that, if armed reprisals are ruled out, the weakness and the frequent failures of the UN collective security system, as well as the ineffectiveness of many economic sanctions, would leave a victim State at the mercy of States bent on violating international law. In fact, the collective security system was not engineered in 1945 to *enforce international law*, but only to *maintain or restore international peace and order*. Any time a violation of international law does not amount to a threat to the peace or a breach of the peace, that collective security system may not be triggered. By the same token States remain bound by the prohibition laid down in Article 2.4. Consequently, they may only resort to peaceful counter-measures.

Second, there is a growing tendency towards the adoption of 'sanctions' by international organizations, particularly as a *reaction to serious and large-scale breaches of international law* (see *infra*, **14.3**). Clearly, while counter-measures are actions taken by *individual* States, sanctions are *collective* responses undertaken within an institutional framework.

11.3.1 COUNTER-MEASURES

In the event of a breach of international law, the injured State is legally entitled to *disregard* an international obligation owed to the delinquent State.

Counter-measures, whether taken to react to cases of 'ordinary responsibility' or to respond to instances of 'aggravated responsibility' (see *supra*, **9.4.2(ii)** and **9.5.2(iii)**), must, however, fulfil some basic conditions, and in addition are subject to a set of limitations.

The general conditions are that:

(1) States are not allowed to resort to them as soon as the wrong occurs; the injured State must first call upon the responsible State to discontinue the wrongful action (in cases of a continuing delinquency) or make reparation, in other cases.

(2) If the cessation of the wrong is not obtained or no reparation is made, the injured State must endeavour to obtain it through *negotiations*. The aim of negotiations is either to settle the dispute or to agree upon another means of settlement. This requirement follows from the general principle, already referred to (**5.6** and **10.5**), whereby States are under the general obligation to settle their disputes peacefully. Only when the author of the wrongdoing refuses to engage in negotiations, or wilfully or *mala fide* hampers the working of other means of adjustment available, can the injured State consider in good faith that no other choice is available, and resort to counter-measures.

In the particular case where States have already undertaken to submit their disputes to a compulsory settlement mechanism, counter-measures are not allowed until such time as the settlement mechanism has been activated.

This view is not unanimously shared. Whether or not one agrees to it, it seems nevertheless certain that some treaties implicitly or explicitly rule out resort to counter-measures, as a settlement of dispute mechanism is available and in addition it is backed up by an international organization. This applies, for instance, to disputes relating to the interpretation or application of the European Convention on Human Rights, the Inter-American Convention on Human Rights, the European Community Treaty and WTO Agreements. This principle was clearly stated by the US-France Arbitral Tribunal in *Air Service Agreement*: the Tribunal held that any State can establish for itself whether another State has violated its international rights and, if so, take counter-measures, 'unless the contrary results from special obligations arising under particular treaties, notably from mechanisms created within the framework of international organizations'.[8]

As for the different question of whether a State may resort to counter-measures in a case of *failure* of an institutional settlement of dispute mechanism, see (with specific reference to 'aggravated' responsibility arising out of gross violations of community obligations enshrining fundamental values) *supra*, **9.6.3**.

(a) Limitations on counter-measures

There are limitations on the counter-measures that may be taken within the framework of both 'ordinary' and 'aggravated' responsibility. Counter-measures (taken in time of peace) cannot consist of a violation of a host of international rules enshrining basic values protecting the interests of the international community as a whole.

(i) Obligations concerning the threat or use of force. Counter-measures may not

derogate from the obligations concerning the threat or use of force. The principle, evolved after the gradual turning of Article 2.4 of the UN Charter into a customary law endowed with the force a peremptory norm, was clearly laid down in Principle 1.6 of the 1970 UN Declaration on Friendly Relations, whereby 'States have a duty to refrain from acts of reprisal involving the use of force'. This provision may be deemed to reflect or codify customary international law (see also Article 51.1(a) of ILC Draft (2000)).

The ICJ, when it has pronounced on the matter, which admittedly has only been in passing, has never *explicitly* held armed reprisals to be contrary to law. This holds true both for *Nicaragua*[9] and *Legality of the Threat or Use of Nuclear Weapons* (when the Court stated that the reprisals at issue 'are considered to be unlawful').[10] When faced with cases of armed reprisals, the UN SC has often tended to condemn them, not because of their inconsistency with the Charter and general international law, but rather because they were 'disproportionate'.[11] Nevertheless, the principle at issue is firmly rooted in the present international legal system.[12]

(ii) Protection of human rights. Counter-measures may not disregard international rules for the protection of human rights or, more generally, the dignity and welfare of human beings. This serious limitation follows from the general principle on respect for human rights discussed above (**5.7** and see also **Chapter 16**), which has acquired such importance in the world community that it is no longer possible to sacrifice the interests and exigencies of human beings for the sake of responding to wrongs caused by States. Consequently, if a State breaks an international rule, the aggrieved party is not authorized to violate international rules protecting the rights or interests of nationals of the delinquent State. States cannot make the consequences of international misbehaviour fall upon innocent people.

The limitation under discussion, upheld in Article 51.1(b) of ILC Draft (2000), was partially codified in the 1969 Vienna Convention on the Law of Treaties (even though it is open to debate whether this belongs to the same branch of international law). Article 60.5 of this Convention lays down that a material breach of a bilateral or multilateral treaty cannot be invoked by a party as a ground for terminating the treaty or suspending its operation, in whole or in part, in the case of 'provisions relating to the protection of the human person contained in treaties of a humanitarian character, in particular to provisions prohibiting any form of reprisals against persons protected by such treaties'.

This provision codifies only in part the general limitation upon reprisals, for it rules out disregard of a treaty whenever the treaty itself is broken by another party. By contrast, the general limitation set forth above is intended to protect human beings even if the breach relates to a rule other than that which might be violated by way of reprisal. International rules designed to protect human beings must be observed under any circumstance, whether or not they themselves are the subject of a breach and regardless of whether they are contained in a treaty or are customary in nature.

The general qualification under discussion does not apply solely to treaties or general rules on human rights or to the humanitarian law of armed conflicts. It also extends its reach to rules protecting *fundamental interests or needs of human beings*. Thus, for instance, if a State acts contrary to international law (for example, by mistreating foreign diplomats, or unlawfully hampering innocent passage through its territorial sea), the injured State cannot reciprocate by terminating (or suspending the application of) a treaty which provides for economic aid to the defaulting State for the purpose of alleviating the plight of a segment of its population. This kind of retaliation would ultimately damage the needs and interests of human beings. Similarly, if a State unlawfully expropriates the assets of foreigners, the national State of the expropriated companies cannot react by terminating a commercial treaty intended to benefit poor segments of the population of that State. (In this instance, we are also dealing with the breach of an international rule protecting interests and rights—those relating to property—which the two 1966 UN Covenants consider as not worthy of the same international protection as other interests and needs of the human person. Consequently, we are faced with two conflicting interests, one of which outweighs the other in international consideration. This condition reinforces the obligation not to disregard, by way of counter-measure, the rule protecting human interests.) In a nutshell, the reciprocity principle does not apply when concerns and exigencies of human beings are at stake.

(iii) Obligations imposed by peremptory norms of general international law. Counter-measures may not disregard obligations imposed by peremptory norms of general international law (see also above). This prohibition, restated in Article 51.1(d) of ILC Draft (2000), aims at filling any gap left by the ban on counter-measures derogating from norms on the threat or use of force, or human rights and humanitarian law. It is therefore a 'residual' prohibition. It covers such areas as self-determination of peoples and protection of the environment.

It is doubtful whether counter-measures consisting of violations of diplomatic or consular immunities are prohibited. Article 51.1(c) of ILC Draft (2000) rules out counter-measures directed to derogate from 'obligations to respect the inviolability of diplomatic or consular agents, premises, archives and documents'. The ICJ judgment in *US Diplomatic and Consular Staff in Tehran*,[13] as well as State practice[14] seem to support this proposition, subject to a caveat: practice shows that States feel authorized to derogate from diplomatic or consular immunities by way of *specific* counter-measures against *violations of these immunities* by the counter-party.[15]

(iv) Counter-measures must not breach the rights of third States. Generally speaking, counter-measures may only target the State allegedly responsible for an international wrongful act. Hence, among other things, it is not permitted to violate, through a counter-measure, an international rule imposing community obligations (that is to say, obligations *erga omnes* giving rise to correlative rights *erga omnes*: see above, 1.8.2). For instance, it is not permitted, through a counter-measure, to disregard treaty obligations granting rights to other States. Indeed, the violation of such an obligation would result in the breach of the right of all the States other than the wrongdoing State; it would be inadmissible, for these States have nothing to do with the initial delinquency.

It is in the light of these principles that one should consider the application by the US authorities of the Helms–Burton Act of 12 March 1996 and the D'Amato–Kennedy Act of 5 August 1996. The first Act, intended both to help the Cuban people 'to restore its freedom' and to protect US nationals against Cuban acts of confiscation and illicit traffic of confiscated assets, allowed among other things unilateral measures against foreigners or foreign companies engaging in commercial activities involving assets 'confiscated' in Cuba in early 1960. The second Act aimed at depriving what the USA considered 'rogue' States of financial means for supporting international terrorism; it provided for 'sanctions' against any person or company investing in Iran or Libya $US 40m. in oil activities. The implementation of these laws entailed that, to 'punish' Cuba, Iran, or Libya, the US authorities were empowered to breach international agreements (bilateral treaties or the WTO rules) *vis-à-vis* third States whose nationals or companies engaged in forms of 'prohibited' trade with Cuba, Iran, or Libya. Plainly, the two Acts were in breach of international law. This is borne out by the harsh reaction of Latin American countries, Canada, the EU, as well as OECD and the Secretariat of the WTO.

(v) Proportionality. A further limitation upon counter-measures is that they *must not be out of proportion* to the breach by the delinquent State.

The application of the proportionality principle raises two problems: the exact scope of proportionality, and the standards by which proportionality should be gauged.

As the Arbitral Tribunal in the *Naulilaa* case stated, no strict proportionality was required at the time in the case of armed reprisals.[16] The same consideration holds true for counter-measures, if only because it is always difficult to ascertain whether they are strictly commensurate with the wrongdoing. What is exacted by international law is that counter-measures be not grossly disproportionate in gravity and magnitude: the importance of the rule disregarded by way of counter-measure, as well as the duration and global effects of its non-application, should roughly correspond to those of the unlawful act to which one retaliates.

The US-France Arbitral Tribunal rightly held in *Air Service Agreement* that 'it is essential, in a dispute between States, to take into account not only the injuries suffered by the companies concerned but also the importance of the questions of principle arising from the alleged breach'.[17] And in *The Gabcíkovo-Nagymaros Project* the ICJ held that 'the effects of a counter-measure must be commensurate with the injury suffered, taking account of the rights in question'.[18]

As for the standard of evaluation to be taken into account, it may be noted that in the aforementioned cases, that is, both in *Naulilaa* and in the judgments delivered by the US-France Arbitral Tribunal and the ICJ, courts have pronounced upon proportionality by balancing the *injury* caused by the wrongdoing State with that brought about by the counter-measure: the latter was proportionate if it did not seriously exceed the injury resulting from the previous international wrongful act. The rationale behind this approach lay in the idea that counter-measures aimed at 'punishing' the delinquent State for its misconduct. However, in current international law the purpose of counter-measures must be seen in impelling the offender to discontinue its wrongful conduct or to make reparation for it. If this is so, the proportionality must be appraised by establishing whether the counter-measure is such as to attain this *purpose*. For instance, in the case of violation by a developing State of an obligation owed to a major Power it may not prove necessary to retaliate by bringing about an injury of the same magnitude as that caused by the breach; to obtain cessation of the wrong or reparation, it may suffice to respond by causing a damage of lesser magnitude, in view of the impact that such a damage may in any case have on the weaker State.

(b) Counter-measures and aggravated State responsibility

As has been pointed out (see **9.5.2(iii)**) in the case of aggravated responsibility, counter-measures, in addition to having to meet the limitations set out above, are subject to a special legal regime.

Here it may suffice to mention that the current international practice of States includes cases where countries, individually or jointly, have decided to react against gross violations of basic international norms by other States by adopting economic measures against the delinquent State. Thus, for example, the USA put into effect economic counter-measures (suspension of deliveries of corn, withholding of industrial goods, etc.) against the USSR as a consequence of the Soviet 'invasion' of Afghanistan in 1979. Also, the USA decided to call the USSR to account for the Soviet attitude towards Poland in 1981.

The difficulty of making an impartial and balanced assessment of economic and other collective counter-measures taken so far by States outside any prior specific authorization of a representative international body helps to explain why counter-measures produce such widely varying reactions in the world community.

Thus, for example, the USSR consistently rejected as unlawful the counter-measures applied by the USA in response to the Soviet invasion of Afghanistan. As for Argentina, a few socialist countries (Albania, Bulgaria, Byelorussia, the then German Democratic Republic, the former Czechoslovakia), plus Laos, argued in November 1982 in the GA that the 'collective sanctions' imposed by some European countries against its invasion of the Falklands/Malvinas were unlawful. (However, they did not specify to which international norms they ran counter.) Poland, the Soviet Union, and Panama had contended in May 1982, in the SC, that the sanctions violated the UN Charter.

11.3.2 CAN NATIONAL COURTS ENFORCE INTERNATIONAL RULES?

The problem has arisen on many occasions of whether national courts of a State can contribute to enforcing international rules by either (a) denying legal domestic recognition to acts performed by foreign States contrary to international law, or even (b) deciding that, in the event of a foreign State taking an internationally unlawful decision or conducting a transaction injuring the interests of the court's nationals, the court could oblige the foreign State to pay compensation to the injured individuals.

The question has cropped up in the matter of nationalization by a foreign State (after the 1917

Soviet nationalizations, those of Iran in 1951, those in Indonesia in 1959, the Cuban nationalization of US-controlled banks, as well as tobacco and sugar plantations in 1959–60, the
Chilean nationalization of the copper industry in 1971).

The question also arose of (a) whether a court could pass judgment over the
domestic validity and enforceability of foreign legislation on nationality contrary to
international law; or (b) whether a court could pronounce on the internal validity of
measures taken by a foreign State as a result and on the strength of internationally
unlawful annexation of territory. Finally, the question arose of (c) whether individuals
could, before their own national courts, sue for damage a foreign State that had
caused them injuries as a result of an allegedly illegal bombing in the course of an
international armed conflict.

National courts have taken conflicting approaches. Thus, for instance Japanese and German
courts tend to exclude the power to adjudicate allegedly illegal foreign sovereign acts.[19] In
particular, in *Shimoda*, the Tokyo District Court upheld the doctrine of sovereign immunity of
foreign States[20] (see **5.3.1**) and therefore dismissed the claim for compensation lodged by the
victims or relatives of the atomic bombing of Hiroshima and Nagasaki. Other courts, for
instance, in France,[21] the Netherlands,[22] Aden,[23] Italy,[24] consider themselves authorized to find
whether the foreign act is contrary to international law, particularly with regard to foreign
nationalization. US courts, after admitting judicial review of foreign State acts only under strict
conditions (*Sabbatino* case, 1964),[25] have eventually broadened the scope of this judicial
review.

It would seem that there exist in this matter *two conflicting requirements*. On the
one hand, there is the need to respect the independence and sovereign equality of
foreign States. The rationale is that inter-State transactions are to be dealt with at the
diplomatic and political level, by organs that may take decisions on the strength of
broad political and diplomatic criteria. Judicial decisions simply based on the illegality
of a foreign act could easily beget frictions and unsettle international relations. There
also exists another, and conflicting, requirement: to ensure by all means the supremacy of international law and, in a way, supplement the failings of international
mechanisms for enforcing international rules by having recourse to national courts
whenever inter-State dealings prove unsatisfactory.

Probably a balanced solution may reside in considering national courts as entitled
to pronounce on the international legality of those foreign (legislative, administrative,
or judicial) acts which, depending on their conformity or inconsistency with international law, may or may not take effect in the *domestic legal system of these courts*. In
contrast, it is still doubtful whether, because of risks of abuse, it is in keeping with the
spirit of general international law to authorize national courts to pronounce judicially
on cases involving individuals allegedly injured by a public executive action of the
foreign State that does not take legal effect abroad (the penalty for which could be
payment of damages by the State to the individual). Such cases might take the form of
egregious violations of international law in the responsible State's territory. Nevertheless, any time there is a link between the gross violation of international law and a
foreign State, this State is warranted to pronounce judicially on the matter.

Thus, in the *Letelier* case,[26] a US court held that the Chilean authorities' order to assassinate a Chilean national in the USA was contrary to international law; thereafter, Chile paid compensation, although it claimed that this was made *ex gratia* and without admission of any responsibility.[27]

Of course, national courts contribute to the enforcement of many international rules on human rights or on the prohibition of international crimes, by instituting *criminal proceedings* against individuals allegedly guilty of violations of those rules (see **12.4**) or, as is the case in the USA, by authorizing aliens to sue for compensation, before US courts, foreign State officials (or persons acting in a private capacity) who have assertedly perpetrated abroad gross breaches of human rights or humanitarian rules (see **16.4.6**).

11.4 SANCTIONS

11.4.1 GENERAL

One of the most notable trends of the present international community is for international bodies, and principally international organizations, to react to gross breaches of international law by States. This is to be regarded as a healthy development: for all its defects (in particular, the possible slowness of the response to a wrong and the frequent need to resort to complex or even cumbersome procedures), collective responses (that may be termed 'sanctions') are to be preferred to counter-measures by individual States. Sanctions may be based on a more balanced appraisal of the illegal situation and take into account the general interest of respect for law combined with the need to safeguard peaceful international relations.

In practice one can distinguish between sanctions *decided* by international bodies, and those *authorized* or *recommended* by such bodies. In both cases it is States that take the sanctions; in the former case States are legally bound to do so, whereas in the latter case they are not.

The Security Council of the UN has on many occasions decided on or recommended economic sanctions such as the breaking off of economic relations, embargoes on imports and exports, the blocking of financial operations, as well as other sanctions (such as embargoes on weapons, the suspension of co-operation in the scientific and technical fields, etc): against South Africa, Southern Rhodesia, Iraq, Somalia, the former Yugoslavia, Libya, Liberia, Angola, Rwanda, Sudan, Sierra Leone, etc.[28] The UN General Assembly has recommended sanctions: for instance, against Spain (in 1951), North Korea and China, South Africa, Israel, etc.[29] In 1982 the ten EEC countries decided upon economic sanctions against Argentina for her invasion of the Falklands/Malvinas.

Such economic and other measures are often taken in consequence of a breach of international rules imposing community obligations. Sanctions such as these may consist of actions that undo previous legal commitments made by the sanctioning

States (for instance, suspension of trade agreements) or actions that are not *per se* illegal, but which amount to unfriendly conduct (for instance, the breaking off of diplomatic relations). Attention however must be drawn to the fact that the UN may decide upon or recommend sanctions even in instances of threats to the peace not amounting to violations of international law (see **14.1.1–3** and **14.3**).

In the case of Afghanistan, the resolution adopted by the UN GA by a very large majority, on 14 January 1980 (resolution ES-6/2), 'deploring' the 'armed intervention in Afghanistan as being contrary to the fundamental principle of respect for sovereignty, territorial integrity and political independence of States' (the USSR, however, was not named), can be regarded as warranting the economic sanctions taken by individual States or a group of States. In the case of the Falklands/Malvinas the resolution adopted by the UN SC on 3 April 1983, to the effect that Argentina had committed a 'breach of the peace' (resolution 502), can be considered sufficient international authority for imposing economic sanctions on that country. Of course, the decision of the EEC Council of Ministers gave added weight to the Security Council pronouncement.

There is a basic requirement that economic and other sanctions should meet: they must aim at inducing the delinquent State to discontinue its misbehaviour; they ought not to be used as an instrument for gaining political or diplomatic advantages. In short, they must not be abused.

Let us now ask ourselves what motivates economic and other peaceful sanctions, and whether these sanctions have proved effective. It seems that they may serve two purposes. First, they may act as the catalysing factor uniting a group of States opposed to the alleged misbehaviour of another State: by taking sanctions the collective bodies intend to rally States behind their censorious attitude. Second, they may be a symbol of public exposure and condemnation of the States allegedly misbehaving. They are not intended to damage the delinquent State in the economic field—the history of international relations speaks volumes for the ineffectiveness in practice of economic sanctions. They are primarily intended to dramatize and articulate the condemnation of a certain form of behaviour and, by the same token, to 'delegitimize' it, or, to put it differently, to prove to world public opinion that the responsible State was wrong, inasmuch as it had acted contrary to internationally accepted standards. Illustrations of these trends may be found in the sanctions decided upon by the SC against Iraq, Libya, and the Federal Republic of Yugoslavia (Serbia and Montenegro) (see **14.3**).

From this point of view the sanctions may be said to have been relatively effective. On other scores they have not achieved major results.

11.4.2 SANCTIONS AND RESPECT FOR HUMAN RIGHTS

It has become increasingly clear that international sanctions designed to impel ruling elites of States grossly violating international legal standards to discontinue such violations may have serious adverse impact on the most vulnerable groups in the targeted country. Some of these consequences were illustrated in 1997 by the UN Committee on Economic Social and Cultural Rights (CESCR, the body monitoring compliance with the UN Covenant on Economic, Social and Cultural Rights of 1966), in its important General Comment no. 8: collective sanctions

'often cause significant disruption in the distribution of food, pharmaceuticals and sanitation supplies, jeopardise the quality of food and the availability of clean drinking water, severely interfere with the functioning of basic health and education systems, and undermine the right to work'.[30]

It follows that economic sanctions, in particular, may seriously affect and jeopardize the basic human rights of children, the elderly, the sick, women, and other vulnerable members of the civilian population. Aware of these consequences, the SC has increasingly included in its resolutions on sanctions humanitarian exemptions with a view to permitting the flow of essential goods and services destined for humanitarian purposes. However, as noted by the CESCR in its aforementioned General Comment,[31] these exemptions have not produced the intended effects.

What does international law prescribe with regard to these situations? A few general standards may be drawn from the general spirits and tenor of both principles and rules on human rights.

First, as rightly pointed out by the CESCR, the *general assumption* from which all States and international organizations must start is that

'the inhabitants of a given country do not forfeit their basic economic, social and cultural rights by virtue of any determination that their leaders have violated norms relating to international peace and security'.[32]

Second, the general community obligation to refrain from engaging in, or bringing about, gross and large-scale violations of human rights is binding upon both States and international organizations. In particular, they are bound to refrain from causing, to the vulnerable members of the civilian population, suffering that is *manifestly disproportionate* to the aim of stopping the State's misconduct. It follows that international bodies such as the SC, when deciding on collective sanctions against a State, must consider whether such sanctions may cause egregious violations of the social, economic, or cultural rights of the vulnerable members of the civilian population. If this consequence looks likely to come about, they must opt for alternative courses of action, or differently shape their sanctions. By the same token, if after sanctions have been imposed it turns out that they cause very serious and disproportionate infringements of the human rights of the population concerned, collective bodies are under the obligation to take all the necessary measures to alleviate the plight of vulnerable groups, including, if need be, discontinuance of sanctions.

Third, the State targeted by the sanctions must take all the measures necessary to *spare as much as possible its civilian population*: that State

'remains under an obligation to ensure the absence of discrimination in relation to the enjoyment of such rights [that is, economic, social, and cultural rights], and to take all possible measures, including negotiations with other States and the international community, to reduce to a minimum the negative impact upon the rights of vulnerable groups within the society'.[33]

11.5 RETORTION

Retortion embraces any retaliatory act by which a State responds, by an unfriendly act not amounting to a violation of international law, to either (a) a breach of international law or (b) an unfriendly act, by another State. Illustrations of retortion include the breaking off of diplomatic relations; non-recognition of acts of a law-breaking State; withholding of economic assistance; discontinuance or reduction of trade and investment; denial of economic or financial benefits; curtailment of migration from the offending State; expulsion (on condition that such expulsion does not infringe upon treaty or customary rules) of nationals of the State that has taken the unfriendly act; imposition of heavy fiscal duties on goods from the offending State; requiring visas for entry into the country or enforcing other strict passport regulations, etc.

Retortion must meet two conditions. First, the noxious act by which a State retaliates against a breach or an unfriendly act should be *proportionate* in gravity to that conduct. Second, the act should be *discontinued* as soon as the unfair, unfriendly, or wrong behaviour to which it is intended to react ceases.

Typical instances of retortion can be seen in the measures adopted since 1989 by the USA against Burma/Myanmar on account of the gross violations of human rights perpetrated by that country, violations strongly condemned by various UN bodies including the GA. In 1989 the US President suspended Burma's eligibility for the trade preferences normally available to developing countries. In 1993 the USA suspended munitions export licences to Burma. In 1997 the US Congress prohibited bilateral aid to that State and the President prohibited new investment by US nationals.[34]

12

ENFORCEMENT IN THE CASE OF VIOLATIONS BY INDIVIDUALS

12.1 TRADITIONAL LAW

Traditionally, individuals have been subject to the exclusive jurisdiction of the State on the territory of which they live. Hence, any violations of international rules that they might commit, particularly rules on the treatment of foreigners and foreign State officials (for example, ill-treatment of foreigners, attacks on foreign diplomats, wrongful expulsion of foreigners, etc.), were prosecuted and punished by the competent authorities of the State where these acts had been performed. Clearly, prosecution and punishment only occurred if the State authorities were entitled to take such action under their national legislation, and provided they were willing so to proceed. If they did not, the State of which the victim was a national was authorized to claim internationally from the relevant State that it either punish the perpetrators or pay compensation (so-called diplomatic protection). As what was involved was the accountability of the State, the individuals who had materially breached international rules could not be called to account by the foreign State. In particular, where the international wrongful act had been performed by one or more State officials, they were entitled to immunity if they had acted in an official capacity. Hence, if they travelled to the territory of the aggrieved State, they could not be arrested and brought to trial (see **5.2.2(4)**).

A few exceptions existed. One of them was piracy (see **1.8.1** and **4.5.1**), a practice that was widespread in the seventeenth and eighteenth centuries, and has recently regained some importance. (An authoritative definition of piracy can now be found in Article 101 of the 1982 Convention on the Law of the Sea.)[1] All States of the world were empowered to search for and prosecute pirates, regardless of the nationality of the victims and of whether the proceeding State had been directly damaged by piracy. Also, the fact that the pirates happened to have the status of State officials when they had engaged in piratical acts while pursuing private ends did not impede their prosecution and punishment by other States (unless of course they could show that they had acted on behalf of a State, in which case State responsibility arose). The pirates were regarded as enemies of humanity (*hostes humani generis*) in that they hampered the freedom of the high seas and jeopardized private property.

12.2 INTERNATIONAL CRIMES

As we shall see, things gradually changed, and new classes of acts emerged that were considered in the international community punishable as crimes, namely, offences entailing the personal criminal liability of the individuals concerned (as opposed to the responsibility of the State).

Before considering some of the major categories of such crimes, it should be specified that international crimes can be held to embrace: (1) violations of international *customary rules* which are intended to protect values considered important by the whole international community and consequently bind all States and individuals. Furthermore, (2) since there exists a universal interest in repressing these crimes, under international law their alleged authors may be prosecuted and punished *by any State*, regardless of any territorial or nationality link with the perpetrator or his victim (see *infra*, **12.4.1**). Finally, (3) if the perpetrator has acted in an official capacity, that is, as *de jure* or de facto State official, the State on whose behalf he has performed the prohibited act is *barred* from claiming that he enjoys the immunity from the civil or criminal jurisdiction of foreign States, accruing under customary law to State officials acting in the exercise of their functions (see **5.2.2(4)**).

Under this definition international crimes include piracy, war crimes, crimes against humanity (in particular, genocide), torture (as distinct from one of the categories of war crimes or crimes against humanity), aggression, and terrorism. By contrast, it does not embrace apartheid, the illicit traffic in narcotic drugs and psychotropic substances, the unlawful arms trade, the smuggling of nuclear and other potentially deadly materials, and money laundering. This broad category of crimes is only provided for in international treaties or resolutions of international organizations, not in customary, that is, general law (as for apartheid, it would seem that under customary international law it is prohibited as a State delinquency; as a crime of individuals it falls within the broad category of crimes against humanity, as may also be inferred from Article 7(1) of the Statute of the International Criminal Court).

12.2.1 WAR CRIMES

(a) Definition

War crimes were defined very broadly as 'violations of the law of war'. This, for instance, is the definition given both in the 1956 US Military Manual[2] and in the 1958 British Manual.[3] A more accurate notion was given by the Appeals Chamber of the ICTY in *Tadić* (*Interlocutory Appeal*). Although strictly speaking the Tribunal was only referring to the scope of Article 3 of the Tribunal's Statute, it clearly intended to propound a more accurate definition. Under this definition, such a crime consists of (1) 'a serious infringement' of an international rule, that is to say, 'it must constitute a breach of a rule protecting important values, and the breach must involve grave consequences for the victim'; (2) the rule violated must either belong to the corpus of customary law or be part of an applicable treaty; (3) 'the violation must entail, under customary or conventional law, the individual criminal responsibility of the person breaching the rule'.[4] (This last requirement must probably be construed to mean that persons may be deemed criminally liable for a war crime if under existing case law there have been instances of criminal punishment of such breaches, or there is a treaty or another international instrument such as the Statute of the ICTY or the ICTR providing for such prosecution and punishment, or, as was held by the ICTY in *Blaškić*,[5] if the national legislation of the accused attaches criminal liability to the breach of the rules at issue.)

It should be added that while traditionally war crimes were held to embrace only breaches of international rules regulating war proper, that is, international armed conflicts and not civil wars, since the aforementioned ICTY decision in *Tadić*,[6] it is now widely accepted that serious infringements of customary or applicable treaty law on *internal* armed conflicts must also be regarded as amounting to war crimes proper. As evidence of this new trend, suffice it to mention Article 8 of the ICC Statute, which embraces as war crimes serious violations of both the law regulating international armed conflict and rules covering internal armed conflicts.

(b) The objective and subjective elements of the crime (*actus reus* and *mens rea*)

In the case of war crimes, in order to identify the main legal features of the prohibited conduct it is necessary to consider in each case the content of the rule that has been allegedly breached. This should not be surprising. In international criminal law the principle *nullum crimen sine lege* (traditionally cherished in national legal systems, particularly those of civil law countries) is upheld only in a limited way. No list of war crimes exists in customary law (such a list can only be found in the Statute of the ICC, under Article 8, which however is not intended to codify customary law on the matter). Hence in each case the objective element of the crime can only be inferred from the substantive rule of international humanitarian law assertedly violated. For a sub-category of war crimes, namely those acts that are defined by the 1949 Geneva Conventions and Additional Protocol I of 1977 as 'grave breaches', a further requirement is provided for: such acts must be committed within the context of an international armed conflict. (However, as the ICTY Appeals Chamber held in *Tadić*, (*Interlocutory Appeal*), a customary rule is *in statu nascendi*, that is, in the process of forming, whereby 'grave breaches' can also be perpetrated in internal armed conflicts.)[7]

As for the subjective element of the crime, it is sometimes specified by the international rule prohibiting a certain conduct.

Thus, for instance, Article 130 of the Third Geneva Convention of 1949 (on war prisoners) enumerates among the 'grave breaches' of the Convention the 'wilful killing [of prisoners of war], torture or inhuman treatment, including biological experiments' as well as 'wilfully causing great suffering or serious injury to body or health' of a prisoner of war, or 'wilfully depriving a prisoner of war of the rights of fair and regular trial prescribed in [the] Convention'.

The word 'wilful' clearly presupposes a criminal intent, namely the intention to bring about the consequences of the act prohibited by the international rule. (For instance, in the case of 'wilful killing' proof must be produced of the intention to cause the death of the victim; in the case of 'wilfully causing great suffering' it must be proved that the perpetrator had the intention to cause great suffering, etc.) The same holds true for other similar provisions, such as Article 147 of the Fourth Geneva Convention (on civilians) as well as provisions of other treaties, such as Article 15 of the 1999 Second Hague Protocol for the Protection of Cultural Property in the Event of Armed Conflict; this provision, in enumerating the serious violations of the Protocol entailing individual criminal liability, makes such liability contingent upon the fact that the author of the 'offence' has perpetrated it 'intentionally'.

When international rules do not provide, not even implicitly, for a subjective element, it would seem appropriate to hold that what is required is the intent or, depending upon the circumstances, knowledge or recklessness prescribed in most legal systems of the world for the underlying offence (murder, rape, torture, destruction of private property, firing on undefended localities, pillage, etc.). Generally speaking, it appears admissible to contend that, for war crimes, recklessness (*culpa gravis*) may be sufficient; that is, the author of the crime, although aware of the risk involved in his conduct, is nevertheless convinced that the prohibited consequence will not occur (whereas in the case of 'knowledge' or *dolus eventualis* the author knowingly takes the risk). Indeed, the consequent broadening of the range of acts amenable to international prosecution is in keeping with the general object and purpose of international humanitarian law.

12.2.2 CRIMES AGAINST HUMANITY

During the Second World War the Allies became aware that some of the most heinous acts of barbarity perpetrated by the Germans were not prohibited by traditional international law. The laws of warfare only proscribed violations involving the adversary or the enemy populations, whereas the Germans had also performed inhuman acts for political or racial reasons against their own citizens (Jews, trade union members, social democrats, communists, gypsies, members of the church) as well as other persons not protected by the laws of warfare. In addition, in 1945 such acts as mere persecution for political or racial purposes were not prohibited, even if perpetrated against civilians of occupied territories.[8]

In 1945, at the strong insistence of the USA, the Allies decided that a better course of action than simply to execute all the major war criminals (as initially suggested by Winston Churchill and other members of the British Cabinet),[9] would be to bring them to trial (it appears that Stalin also opposed summary execution).[10] The London Agreement embodying the Charter of the International Military Tribunal (IMT) included a provision under which the Tribunal was to try and punish persons guilty, among other things, of 'crimes against humanity'. These were defined as:

'murder, extermination, enslavement, deportation, and other inhuman acts committed against any civilian population, before or during the war, or persecutions on political, racial, or religious grounds in execution of or connexion with any crimes within the jurisdiction of the Tribunal [that is, either "crimes against peace" or "war crimes"], whether or not in violation of the domestic law of the country where perpetrated'.

One major shortcoming of this definition is that it closely links crimes against humanity to the other two categories of offences. As Schwelb rightly remarked, this association meant that only those criminal activities were punished which 'directly affected the interests of other States' (either because these activities were connected with a war of aggression or a conspiracy to wage such a war, or because they were bound up with war crimes, that is, crimes against enemy combatants or enemy civilians).[11] Plainly, in 1945 the Allies did not feel that they should legislate in such a way as to prohibit inhuman acts regardless of their consequences or implications for third States.

Despite this limitation, the creation of the new category marked a great advance. First, it indicated that the international community was widening the category of acts considered of 'meta-national' concern. This category came to include all acts running contrary to those basic values that are, or should be, considered inherent in any human being (in the notion, humanity did not mean 'mankind' or 'human race' but 'the quality' or concept of human being). Second, inasmuch as crimes against humanity were made punishable even if perpetrated in accordance with domestic laws, the 1945 Charter showed that in some special circumstances there were limits to the 'omnipotence of the State' (to quote the British Chief Prosecutor, Sir Hartley Shawcross) and that 'the individual human being, the ultimate unit of all law, is not disentitled to the protection of mankind when the State tramples upon his rights in a manner which outrages the conscience of mankind'.[12]

The IMT did act upon the Charter provision dealing with 'crimes against humanity'. In so doing, it indubitably applied *ex post facto law*; in other words, it applied international law retroactively, as was rightly stressed by the defence counsel at Nuremberg.[13] The Tribunal gave two justifications for its application of the Charter. First, it stated that it was 'the expression of international law existing at the time of its creation; and to that extent [it was] itself a contribution to international law'.[14] This, however, was not the case so far as crimes against humanity were concerned, and, indeed, it is striking that the Tribunal did not consider it fitting to argue its general view with regard to this class of offences (probably this was also due to the fact that in their joint Motion of 19 November 1945, all defence counsel insisted on crimes against peace being contrary to the *nullum crimen sine lege* principle, whereas they passed over in silence crimes against humanity).[15] The second proposition of the Tribunal—chiefly articulated with regard to 'crimes against peace' (see 12.2.5) but also applicable to the offence under consideration—was that 'the maxim *nullum crimen sine lege* is not a limitation of sovereignty, but is in general a principle of justice'.[16] This proposition is no doubt valid for grave atrocities and inhuman acts. In the case of newly established crimes, however, the courts would have been wise to refrain from meting out the harshest penalty, namely the death sentence, to defendants found guilty of these new crimes only (this view was forcefully defended by

Röling, the Dutch member of the Tokyo International Tribunal, in his dissenting opinion appended to the Tokyo judgment).[17]

In the wake of the major war trials momentous changes in international law took place. On 11 December 1946 the GA unanimously adopted a resolution (res. 95–1) 'affirming' the principles of the Charter of the Nuremberg International Tribunal and its judgment. A conspicuous number of international instruments, including the Statutes of the ICTY, the ICTR and the ICC, were then drawn up embodying the prohibition of crimes against humanity, certain of which improved and extended the London Agreement.[18]

The French Court of Cassation strikingly misapprehended the notion of crimes against humanity, as it had evolved in international law following the Nuremberg and Tokyo trials, in the famous *Sobanski Wladyslav* v. *George Boudarel* case (judgment of 1 April 1993).[19] The question at issue was whether the atrocities allegedly committed in 1952–4, in Vietnam, by the accused (a French serviceman who had deserted eventually siding with the Viet-minh) against French prisoners of war was covered by the French law of 26 December 1964, whereby crimes against humanity are not subject to the statute of limitation, or instead by the French law of 18 June 1966 granting amnesty for all crimes committed in Indochina before 1 October 1957. The Court noted that the 1964 law adverted to the provisions of the London Agreement of 8 August 1945 on crimes against humanity, as well as GA resolution 3(1) of 13 February 1946 (recommending the extradition and punishment of persons accused of the crimes provided for in the Nuremberg Charter). According to the Court, the London Agreement only related to 'offences perpetrated on behalf of the Axis European States', hence could not apply to atrocities committed elsewhere. Consequently, the 1964 French law was to be construed as only relating to crimes against humanity committed by the Axis European Powers during the Second World War and did not apply to the alleged crimes committed in Indochina. It followed that (i) the alleged offences of the accused could not be classified as crimes against humanity, (ii) the law of 1964 did not apply whereas (iii) that of 1966 did. Clearly, the Court wrongly derived the notion of crimes against humanity from a narrow construction of both the French law of 1964 and the London Agreement. It should have inferred that notion from *general rules* of international law, as they had evolved before 1964. Those rules *did cover* the atrocities assertedly committed by the accused. Furthermore, the French law on amnesty could not apply on account of the *peremptory nature* of the international rules on crimes against humanity (see above, **6.5.5**).

(a) *Actus reus* and *mens rea*

Under general international law the category of crimes encompassed by *actus reus* and *mens rea* is sweeping but sufficiently well defined. It covers actions that share a set of common features.

(1) These crimes are particularly odious offences in that they constitute a serious attack on human dignity or a grave humiliation or degradation of one or more human beings.

(2) They are not isolated or sporadic events, but are part either of a governmental policy (although the perpetrators need not identify themselves with this policy, as was stated in 1951 by the District Court of Tel Aviv in *Enigster*)[20] or of a widespread or

systematic practice of atrocities tolerated or condoned by a government or a de facto authority. Murder, extermination, torture, rape, political, racial, or religious persecution, and other inhumane acts reach the threshold of crimes against humanity only if they are part of a practice. Isolated inhumane acts of this nature may constitute grave infringements of human rights or, depending on the circumstances, war crimes, but may fall short of meriting the stigma attaching to crimes against humanity. On the other hand, an individual may be guilty of crimes against humanity even if he perpetrates one or two of the offences mentioned above, or engages in one such offence against only a few civilians, provided those offences are part of a consistent pattern of misbehaviour by a number of persons linked to that offender (for example, because they engage in armed action on the same side, or because they are parties to a common plan, or for any other similar reason).

Consequently, when one or more individuals are not accused of planning or carrying out a policy of inhumanity, but simply of perpetrating specific atrocities or vicious acts, in order to determine whether the necessary threshold is met one should use the following test: one ought to look at these atrocities or acts against their background and verify whether they may be regarded as part of an overall policy or a consistent pattern of inhumanity, or whether they instead constitute isolated or sporadic acts of cruelty and wickedness.

(3) Crimes against humanity may be punished regardless of whether they are perpetrated in time of war or peace. While in 1945 a link or nexus with an armed conflict was required, at present customary law no longer attaches any importance to such requirement.

The determination of the *mental element* of crimes against humanity has proved particularly difficult and controversial. A perusal of the relevant case law is helpful. In particular, courts have insisted on three points. First, in crimes against humanity criminal intent involves both the intent to bring about a certain result and the awareness of the factual circumstances that make up or are required for the *actus reus*. Second, the agent must be cognizant of the link between his misconduct and a policy or the systematic practice. Third, it is not necessary for an agent who does not directly and immediately cause the inhumane consequences to anticipate all the specific consequences of his misconduct; it is sufficient for him to be aware of the risk that his action might bring about serious consequences for the victims, on account of the violence and arbitrariness of the system to which he was delivering the victim (this point has been particularly stressed by the German Supreme Court in the British Occupied Zone, with particular reference to cases of denunciation of Jews or political opponents to the police or Gestapo).[21] Finally, it is worth mentioning that courts have not required, as part of *mens rea*, that the perpetrator should have a specifically racist or inhuman frame of mind.

To sum up, the requisite subjective element or *mens rea* in crimes against humanity is not simply limited to the criminal intent required for the underlying offence (murder, extermination, deportation, rape, torture, persecution, etc.). The viciousness of these crimes goes far beyond the underlying offence, however wicked or despicable it may be. This additional element—which helps to distinguish crimes against humanity from war crimes—consists of *awareness* of the broader context into which this crime fits, that is, knowledge that the offences are part of a systematic policy or of widespread and large-scale abuses. In addition, when these crimes take the form of persecution, another mental element is required: a persecutory or discriminatory animus. The intent must be to subject a person or group to discrimination, ill-treatment, or harassment, so as to bring about great suffering or injury to that person or group on religious, political, or other such grounds. This added element for persecution amounts to an aggravated criminal intent (*dolus specialis*).[22]

12.2.3 GENOCIDE

Genocide, that is, the intentional killing, destruction, or extermination of groups or members of a group as such, was first conceived of as a category of crimes against humanity. Neither Article 6(c) of the Charter of the IMT nor Article II(1)(c) of Control Council Law no. 10 explicitly envisaged genocide as a separate category of crimes against humanity. However, the wording of the relevant provisions clearly shows that these crimes encompassed genocide. The IMT and the Tokyo International Tribunal did not explicitly mention genocide; in dealing with the extermination of Jews and other ethnic or religious groups, they mostly referred to the crime of persecution.

However, genocide was discussed in a few other cases: in particular *Hoess,* decided by a Polish court in 1948[23] and *Greifelt et al.,* decided in 1948 by a United States Military Tribunal sitting at Nuremberg.[24]

Genocide acquired autonomous significance as a specific crime in 1948, when the UN GA adopted the Genocide Convention. The Convention has numerous merits. Among other things, (a) it sets out a careful definition of the crime, (b) it punishes other acts connected with genocide (conspiracy, complicity, etc.); (c) it prohibits genocide regardless of whether it is perpetrated in time of war or peace; (d) it considers genocide both a crime involving the criminal responsibility of the perpetrator (and other participants), and an international delinquency entailing the responsibility of the State whose authorities engage in, or otherwise participate in the commission of genocide (this international wrongful act may be the subject of an international dispute and in any case entails all the consequences of international wrongdoings).

However, one should not be unmindful of the flaws of the Convention. These are the most blatant ones: (1) The definition of genocide does not embrace the extermination of a group on political grounds, nor cultural genocide (that is, the destruction of the language and culture of a group). (2) The enforcement mechanism envisaged in the Convention is ineffective.

In Article IV the Convention contemplates trials before the courts of the State on the territory of which genocide has occurred, or before a future 'international penal tribunal'; Article VIII provides that any contracting party 'may call upon the competent organs of the United Nations to take such action' under the Charter 'as they consider appropriate' for the prevention or suppression of genocide, whereas Article IX confers on the ICJ jurisdiction over disputes between States concerning the interpretation, application, or fulfilment of the Convention.

Indeed, at the *enforcement* level the Convention has for long proved a failure. Only once did a United Nations body pronounce on a case of genocide: this occurred in the case of *Sabra and Shatila*, when the UN GA described the massacre as 'an act of genocide' in its resolution 37/ 123 D of 16 December 1982. Subsequently in 1993 for the first time a State brought a case of genocide before the International Court of Justice: *Bosnia and Herzegovina* v. *Federal Republic of Yugoslavia (Serbia and Montenegro)*. Similarly, only a few cases of genocide have been brought before national criminal courts (on the legal ground of universality): *Eichmann* (decided in 1961 by the District Court of Jerusalem and subsequently by the Israeli Supreme Court),[25] *Jorgić*, decided in 1997 by the Higher State Court (*Oberlandsgericht*) of Düsseldorf[26] and confirmed by the Federal High Court (*Bundesgerichtshof*) in 1999,[27] as well as *Sokolović* and *Kusljić*, both decided by the same High Court on 21 February 2001.[28]

By contrast, much headway has been made both at the level of prosecution and punishment of genocide by *international* criminal tribunals, and at the *normative* level. Genocide having been provided for in the Statutes of both the ICTY and the ICTR as well as the ICC, the first two courts have had the opportunity to try quite a few persons accused of this crime, and have delivered important judgments on the matter (the ICTR particularly in *Jean-Paul Akayesou*,[29] and *Clément Kayishema and Obed Ruzindana*[30] and the ICTY in *Jelisić*).[31] At the normative level, some major advances should be emphasized. The major substantive provisions of the Convention have gradually turned into customary international law, as has been admitted, although in somewhat erroneous terms, by the ICJ in its Advisory Opinion on *Reservations to the Convention on the Prevention and Punishment of Genocide*.[32] In addition, at the level of *State* responsibility it is now widely recognized that customary rules on genocide impose community obligations, that is, towards all other member States of the international community, and at the same time confer on any State the right to require that acts of genocide be discontinued. Finally, those rules now form part of *jus cogens* or peremptory norms, that is, they may not be derogated from by international agreement (nor *a fortiori* by national legislation).

(a) *Actus reus* and *mens rea*

Article IV of the Genocide Convention, and the corresponding rule of customary law, clearly define the conduct that may amount to genocide: (a) killing members (hence more than one member) of a national or ethnic, racial, or religious group; (b) causing serious bodily or mental harm to members of the group; (c) deliberately inflicting on the group conditions of life calculated to bring about its physical destruction in whole or in part; (d) imposing measures intended to prevent birth within the group; (e) forcibly transferring children of the group to another group.

Although, as stated before, genocide emerged as a sub-category of crimes against humanity, it soon acquired autonomous status and contents. This is among other things proved by the fact that in the case of genocide international rules do not require the existence of a widespread or systematic practice as a legal ingredient of the crime. This, of course, is material at the procedural level, for it implies that the prosecutor in a national or international trial need not lead evidence on that practice. In reality, genocidal acts are seldom isolated or sporadic events; normally they are part of a widespread policy, often approved or at least condoned by governmental authorities. These circumstances remain however factual events, not provided for as legal requirements of the crime.

Article IV does not cover the conduct currently termed in non-technical language 'ethnic cleansing', that is, the forcible expulsion of civilians belonging to a particular group from an area, a village, or a town. (In the course of the drafting of the Genocide Convention Syria proposed an amendment designed to add a sixth class of acts of genocide: 'Imposing measures intended to oblige members of a group to abandon their homes in order to escape the threat of subsequent ill-treatment.' However, the draftsmen rejected this proposal.)[33]

The *mental* requirement for genocide as a crime involving international criminal liability is provided for in Article II, paragraph 1 (and in the corresponding customary rule): the 'intent to destroy, in whole or in part, a national, ethnical, racial or religious group'. This intent amounts to *dolus specialis*, that is, to an aggravated criminal intention, required in addition to the criminal intent accompanying the underlying offence (spelled out above). It follows that other categories of mental element are excluded: negligence, recklessness (*dolus eventualis*).

12.2.4 TORTURE IN TIME OF PEACE

(a) General

Torture is not only prohibited as an international crime when it is part of a widespread or systematic practice thus amounting to a crime against humanity. Torture is also proscribed when it is perpetrated as a single act, outside any large-scale practice. In this case, if torture is perpetrated in time of war, against the 'enemy', it is a war crime. If instead it is resorted to in time of peace, or is practised in time of war for reasons not connected with war and against persons that are not 'enemies', it may be classified as an international crime under customary international law.

There is an important difference among these various categories. Torture in time of war may also be perpetrated by a private individual not acting in an official capacity; in this case, to qualify as a *war crime*, it must be committed against a protected person having the nationality of the enemy or (particularly in the case of internal armed conflict) under the control of the adversary.

Torture in time of internal or international armed conflict or in time of peace, to amount to a *crime against humanity*, needs among other things to be part of a widespread or systematic practice. It may be committed by private persons; again, there is no need for the participation of a State official in the specific act of torture brought to trial. However, it is implicit in the very definition of this class of crimes that, in addition to the specific case of torture prosecuted, numerous acts of torture are being or have been perpetrated without being punished by the authorities; in other words, there is, or has been, implicit approval or condonation by the authorities, or at least they have failed to take appropriate action to bring the culprits to book. To put it differently, there must be at least some sort of 'passive involvement' of the authorities.

Things are different as regards torture as a distinct crime, as the ICTY rightly held in 2001 in *Kunarać et al.*,[34] with a slight departure from the previous judgments of the ICTR in *Akayesu*[35] and the ICTY in *Furundžija*.[36] Under Article 1.1 of the UN Convention of 1984 on Torture, applying both in time of peace and of war, the 'pain or suffering' must be inflicted 'by or at the instigation of or with the consent or acquiescence of a public official or other person acting in an official capacity'. The need for this sort of participation of a *de jure* or de facto State official stems from: (a) the fact that in this case torture is punishable under international rules even when it constitutes a single or sporadic episode; and (b) the consequent necessity to distinguish between torture as a common or 'ordinary' crime (for example, torture of a woman by her husband, or of a boy by a group of hooligans) and torture as an international crime covered by international rules on human rights.

The ban on torture perpetrated under these circumstances has evolved over a long time, during which significant contributions at the norm-setting level were made by: (a) an important Declaration passed by the UN GA (resolution 3452(XXX) adopted on 9 December 1975); (b) the increasing importance of the 1984 UN Convention on Torture; (c) general treaties on human rights and the judicial practice of the bodies responsible for their enforcement; (d) national case law (in particular cases such as *Pinochet*);[37] and (e) the judgments of the ICTY in *Furundžija*[38] and the European Court of Human Rights in *Aksoy*[39] and *Selmouni*.[40] Suffice it to mention that in *Filartiga* a US court held that 'the torturer has become, like the pirate or the slave trader before him, *hostis humani generis*, an enemy of all mankind'.[41] And in 1998 in *Furundžija* the ICTY, after mentioning the human rights treaties and the resolutions of international organizations banning torture, stated that 'the existence of this corpus of general and treaty rules proscribing torture shows that the international community, aware of the importance of outlawing this heinous phenomenon, has decided to suppress any manifestation of torture by operating both at the interstate level and at the level of individuals. No legal loopholes have been left'.[42]

By now a general rule has evolved in the international community: (a) prohibiting individuals from perpetrating torture, regardless of whether it is committed on a large scale, and (b) authorizing all States to prosecute and punish the alleged author of such acts, regardless of where the acts were perpetrated, and whatever the nationality of the perpetrator or the victim.

(b) Objective and subjective elements of torture

As for the conduct prohibited, one can safely rely upon the definition of torture laid down in Article 1.1 of the 1984 UN Convention. As the ICTY held in *Delalić et al.*,[43] *Furundžija*,[44] and *Kunarać et al.*,[45] 'there is now general acceptance [in the world community] of the main elements contained' in that definition. The objective elements of torture may therefore be held to consist of: (a) 'any act by which severe pain or suffering, whether physical or mental, is . . . inflicted on a person'; (b) 'such pain or suffering is inflicted by or at the instigation of or with the consent or acquiescence of a public official or other person acting in an official capacity'; (c) such pain or suffering does not arise 'only from' or is 'inherent in or incidental to lawful sanctions'.

As for *mens rea*, the same definition, and the practice of international courts and other judicial or quasi-judicial bodies require that (a) the purpose of the infliction of pain or suffering be 'obtaining from him [the person tortured] or a third person information or a confession', or 'punishing him for an act he or a third person has committed or is suspected of having committed' or 'intimidating or coercing him or a third person', or else the infliction of pain or suffering be carried out 'for any reason based on discrimination of an kind'; (b) the infliction of pain or suffering be 'intentional'. It is warranted to hold that in the case of torture criminal intent (*dolus*) is always required. Other subjective criteria (knowledge, recklessness, fault by negligence, etc.) are not sufficient.

12.2.5 THE CRIME OF AGGRESSION

Aggression was first regarded as an international crime in the London Agreement of 8 August 1945 establishing the IMT. Article 6(a) of the IMT Charter, annexed to the Agreement, provided as follows:

'The following acts, or any of them, are crimes coming within the jurisdiction of the Tribunal for which there shall be individual responsibility: (a) CRIMES AGAINST PEACE: namely planning, preparation, initiation or waging of a war of aggression, or a war in violation of international treaties, agreements or assurances, or participation in a Common Plan or Conspiracy for the accomplishment of any of the foregoing'.

Thus, wars of aggression were only one of the sub-categories of the broad category of 'crimes against peace'. The IMT dwelt at some length on this category to prove that it had already been established before 1945 and consequently the punishment of such crimes did not fall foul of the *nullum crimen sine lege* principle. The IMT went so far as to define aggression as the 'supreme international crime'.[46] Some defendants were found guilty on this count and sentenced either to death or to long terms of imprisonment. Subsequently the Tokyo Tribunal found some defendants guilty of aggression. On 11 December 1946 the UN GA unanimously adopted resolution 95(I) by which it 'affirmed' the 'principles of international law recognized by the Charter of the Nuremberg Tribunal and the judgment of the Tribunal'. Thus, both the definition of crimes against peace and its application by the IMT were formally approved by all the States that at that stage were members of the UN. However, there was no follow-up to this specific matter in the subsequent years, whilst other crimes were spelled out in various conventions.

The problem with aggression was that the major Powers preferred to avoid defining this breach of the ban on force laid down in Article 2.4 of the UN Charter, so as to retain as much leeway as possible in the application of that provision both by each of them individually and by the SC collectively. The definition of aggression remained in abeyance, with regard to aggression both as a State delinquency entailing the international responsibility of the State and as an international crime involving criminal liability. Later the UN GA adopted a definition in resolution 3314 (XXIX) of 14 December 1974. However, it was deliberately incomplete, for Article 4 provided that the definition was not exhaustive and left to the SC a broad area of discretion, by stating that it was free to characterize other acts as aggression under the Charter. Furthermore, the resolution did not specify that aggression may entail both State responsibility and individual criminal liability: in Article 5.2 it simply provided that war of aggression is a crime against international law, adding that it 'gives rise to international responsibility'. In addition, the definition propounded in the Draft Code of Crimes against Peace and Security of Mankind, adopted by the ILC in 1996, is rather poor and disappointing[47] and the Statute of the ICC, while providing for the crime of aggression in Article 5, stipulates that the Court shall exercise jurisdiction over such crime once a provision defining it is adopted through an amendment of the Statute.

Not surprisingly, since 1948 there have been no national or international trials for alleged crimes of aggression, although undisputedly in quite a number of instances States have engaged in acts of aggression, and in a few cases the SC has determined that a State had committed such acts.[48]

It would however be fallacious to hold the view that, since no general agreement has been reached in the world community on an exhaustive definition of aggression, perpetrators of this crime may not be prosecuted and punished.

(a) Objective and subjective elements

Aggression is an area where States deliberately want to retain a broad margin of discretion. Nevertheless, at least some more *traditional* forms of aggression are prohibited by customary international law, which therefore can be held to provide the objective elements of the crime. These instances of aggression, constituting the core of the notion at issue, are basically those envisaged in terms in the 1974 Definition, and confirmed, at least in part, by the ICJ in *Nicaragua*.[49]

It would seem appropriate to consider as conduct prohibited by customary international law as an international crime the planning, or organizing or preparing or participating in the first use of armed force by a State against the territorial integrity of another State in contravention of the Charter, provided the acts of aggression concerned, or their consequences, are large scale and serious.

This category comprises the following instances: (1) The invasion or the attack by the armed forces of a State on the territory of another State, or any military occupation, however temporary, resulting from such invasion or attack, or any annexation by the use of force of the territory or part of the territory of another State. (2) Bombardment, or use of any weapon, by the armed forces of a State, against the territory of another State. (3) Blockade of the ports or coasts of a State by the armed forces of another State. (4) Attack by the armed forces of a State on the land, sea, or air forces, or marine and air fleets of another State. (5) The use of armed forces of one State which are within the territory of another State with the agreement of the receiving

State, in contravention of the conditions provided for in the agreement, or any extension of their presence in such territory beyond the termination of the agreement. (6) The action of a State in allowing its territory, which it has placed at the disposal of another State, to be used by that other State for perpetrating an act of aggression against a third State. (7) The sending by or on behalf of a State of armed bands, groups, irregulars, or mercenaries, which carry out acts of armed force against another State of such gravity as to amount to the acts listed above, or the State's substantial involvement therein.

This crime too requires criminal intent (*dolus*). It must be shown that the perpetrator intended to participate in aggression and was aware of the scope, significance, and consequences of his action.

(b) Judicial versus political appraisal of aggression

In the area of aggression, involving both State responsibility and individual criminal liability, courts trying persons accused of this crime may legitimately take a judicial approach different from the political stand international political bodies such as the UN SC or the GA may prefer. It follows that there may be cases where one of those bodies does not consider that it is faced with aggression, whereas a national or international court may find that the contrary is true and consequently that the individuals involved in aggression are criminally responsible. This consequence is quite understandable, in an area politically so charged. However, national or international courts should not be bound by any decision taken by a political body, and vice versa. Of course, it remains true that whenever the SC or the GA concludes that in a particular instance acts committed by a State amount to aggression, it will be easier for a national or international court to find that aggression was perpetrated and therefore to pronounce on the issue of whether the individuals involved are criminally liable.

12.2.6 TERRORISM

(a) General

For more than thirty years States have debated in the UN the question of punishing terrorism. However, they have been unable to agree upon a definition of this crime. Third World countries staunchly clung to their view that this notion could not cover acts of violence perpetrated by the so-called freedom fighters, that is, individuals and groups struggling for the realization of self-determination. In consequence, the majority of UN members preferred to take a different approach, namely to draw up conventions prohibiting individual sets of well-specified acts. In this way the thorny question of hammering out a broad and general definition was circumvented. The Conventions at issue are those of 1963, 1970, and 1971 on the hijacking of aircraft, the Convention of 1973 on crimes against internationally protected persons including diplomatic agents, the 1979 Convention on the taking of hostages. In addition, in 1971 the USA and various Latin or Central American countries plus Sri Lanka agreed upon a Convention for the prevention and punishment of acts of terrorism.[50] However, condemnation of terrorism increased. In addition, it is probable that many States became convinced that the First Additional Protocol of 1977 provided an acceptable solution to the problem of avoiding labelling 'freedom fighters' as terrorists (Article 44.3 of the Protocol granted, on certain conditions, legal status as combatants, and prisoner of war status in case of capture, to fighters who are not members of the armed forces of a State and who normally do not carry their arms openly). All this led to the formation of broad agreement on the general definition of terrorism. This agreement was laid down in a resolution passed by consensus by the UN GA (resolution 49/60, adopted on 9 December 1994). In the annexed Declaration it contains a provision (paragraph 3) stating that:

'Criminal acts intended or calculated to provoke a state of terror in the general public, a group of persons or particular persons for political purposes are in any circumstance unjustifiable, whatever the considerations of a political, philosophical, ideological, racial, ethnic, religious or any other nature that may be invoked to justify them'.

This provision sets out an acceptable definition of terrorism. Three main elements seem to be required: (1) The acts must constitute a criminal offence under most national legal systems (for example, murder, kidnapping, arson, etc.). (2) They must be aimed at spreading terror among the public or particular groups of persons. (3) They must be politically motivated. It would seem that terrorist acts, if they fulfil these conditions and in addition are very serious or large scale, may be regarded as international crimes.

The general revulsion against this crime, as evinced by statements and declarations of very many States, warrants the conclusion that any State is legally entitled to bring to trial the alleged authors of such acts of terrorism who happen to be on its territory.

(b) Objective and subjective elements of the crime

The objective elements of the crime of terrorism may substantially be inferred from the various treaties on the matter, referred to above.

As for *mens rea*, State practice, national legislation as well as the conventions mentioned above all point in the same direction, namely the requirement that there should be a criminal intent to perpetrate the acts, and kill or injure persons, or destroy property, as well as the intent to spread terror.

12.3 INTERNATIONAL CRIMES AND IMMUNITY FROM JURISDICTION

Often persons accused of international crimes claim that they are immune from criminal jurisdiction for they acted as State officials (heads of State, foreign ministers, etc.).

As we saw above (5.2.2(4)), all State officials are entitled to claim immunity from the civil and criminal jurisdiction of foreign States for acts or transactions performed in their official capacity (so-called *functional* immunities, which entail exemption from the *substantive* legislation of the receiving State and apply even after the State official has relinquished his position). However this privilege does not apply when they are accused of international crimes, and they may be brought to justice for such crimes. The removal of immunities was first applied in the case of war crimes to members of the army of belligerents and other lawful combatants; then, by virtue of the London Agreement of 8 August 1945, it was extended to senior State officials, and made applicable to war crimes, crimes against peace, and crimes against humanity. The cancellation of immunities was then reaffirmed in the Statutes of the ICTY, the ICTR, and the ICC. As these treaty rules or provisions of 'legislative' acts adopted by the SC have been borne out by State practice, it is safe to contend that they have turned into customary law.

However, in the *Qaddafi* case, contrary to what the *Chambre d'accusation* of the Paris Court of Appeal held on 20 October 2000,[51] on 13 March 2001 the Court of Cassation held that no customary rule has evolved on the matter, with specific reference to the international crime of terrorism.[52] This last decision has been rightly criticized in the legal literature.[53] In contrast, the removal of immunities for official acts performed by heads (or former heads) of State was affirmed by the Brussels *Juge d'instruction* on 6 November 1998 in his order in *Pinochet* and by the House of Lords in *Pinochet*.[54]

One should not however confuse the *functional* immunity discussed so far with the *personal* immunities and privileges that heads of State, foreign ministers, and other members of cabinet, as well as diplomatic agents, enjoy when on missions abroad. These immunities cover acts and transactions pertaining to the private life of State officials and terminate with the cessation of the official's functions. They include exemption from criminal jurisdiction and are due to foreign officials whenever they are on official missions (whereas they do not cover the private life of officials when they are abroad for private purposes). This distinction was rightly made by the Belgian *juge d'instruction*, Damien Vandermeersh, in his indictment against the former Foreign Minister of the Congo, which subsequently gave rise to an international dispute, brought before the ICJ as the *Congo* v. *Belgium* case.[55]

12.4 PROSECUTION AND PUNISHMENT BY STATE COURTS

12.4.1 LEGAL GROUNDS OF JURISDICTION

Traditionally States bring to trial before their courts alleged perpetrators of international crimes on the strength of one of three principles: *territoriality* (the offence has been perpetrated on the State territory), *passive nationality* (the victim is a national of the prosecuting State), or *active nationality* (the perpetrator is a national of the prosecuting State). Normally the territoriality principle is preferred, both for ideological reasons (need to affirm the territorial sovereignty) and because the territory where the alleged crime has been committed is the place where it is easier to collect evidence (it is therefore considered the *forum conveniens*, or the adequate place of trial, as was restated in *Eichmann*).[56] This principle was also considered as the most appropriate as long ago as 1764, by Cesare Beccaria.

In his *Crimes and Punishments* he wrote that 'There are those who think, that an act of cruelty committed, for example, at Constantinople, may be punished at Paris; for this abstracted reason, that he who offends humanity, should have enemies in all mankind, and be the object of universal execration; as if the judges were to be the knights errant of human nature in general, rather than guardians of particular conventions between men. The place of punishment can certainly be no other, than that where the crime was committed; for the necessity of punishing an individual for the general good subsists there, and there only'.[57]

In more recent years, the so-called principle of universality has also been upheld, whereby any State is empowered to bring to trial persons accused of international crimes regardless of the place of commission of the crime, or the nationality of the author or of the victim. This principle has been upheld in two different versions. According to the most widespread version, only the State where the accused is in custody can prosecute him or her (so-called *forum deprehensionis*, or jurisdiction of the place where the accused is apprehended).

This class of jurisdiction is accepted, at the level of customary international law, with regard to piracy (but see *infra*, **12.4.2**). At the level of treaty law it has been upheld with regard to *grave breaches* of the 1949 Geneva Conventions and the First Additional Protocol of 1977, *torture* (under Article 7 of the 1984 Torture Convention), as well as *terrorism* (see the various UN-sponsored treaties on this matter)[58] and *international drug trafficking*.[59] These treaties, however, do not confine themselves to granting the power to prosecute and try the accused. They also oblige States to do so, or alternatively to extradite the defendant to a State concerned (the principle of *aut prosequi et judicare, aut dedere*). This version of the principle of universality is also upheld by the national legislation of some States, such as Austria (Article 65.1.2 of the Penal Code), Germany (at least under the traditional construction of Articles 6.9 and 7.2 of the Penal Code; see however below) and Switzerland (see Articles 108 and 109 of the Military Penal Code, with regard to war crimes, and Article 6 bis of the Criminal Code, which has been held to be applicable to such crimes as torture).[60]

Under a different version of the universality principle, a State may prosecute persons accused of international crimes regardless of their nationality, the place of commission of the crime, the nationality of the victim, and even of whether or not the accused is in custody in the forum State.

This principle is upheld in such national legislations as that of Spain (in particular, with regard to genocide, war crimes, crimes against humanity, and terrorism; see Article 23 of the Law on Judicial Powers of 1985),[61] as well as Belgium (see the Laws of 1993 and 1999).[62] In addition, under the interpretation of the German Penal Code the German Supreme Court

(*Bundesgerichtshof*) propounded in a judgment of 21 February 2001, the same principle should also apply in Germany, at least whenever the obligation to prosecute is provided for in an international treaty binding upon Germany.[63] Perhaps one might also construe Article 7.5 of the Italian Criminal Code[64] to the effect that alleged authors of international crimes may be prosecuted even if they do not find themselves on Italian territory, provided that (i) the crimes are envisaged in international treaties ratified by Italy and (ii) under these treaties Italian courts may exercise jurisdiction.

This notion of the universality principle is legally admissible. The rationale behind it is twofold: (i) the crimes over which such jurisdiction may be exercised are of such gravity and magnitude that they warrant universal prosecution and repression (the Spanish Constitutional Court, in a judgment of 10 February 1997,[65] and the Spanish national court (*Audiencia nacional*) in an order of 4 November 1988[66] set out this view); (ii) the exercise of this jurisdiction does not amount to a breach of the principle of sovereign equality of States, nor does it lead to undue interference in the internal affairs of the State where the crime has been perpetrated (the *Audiencia nacional*, in two orders, of 4 and 5 November 1988 respectively,[67] as well as the German Federal High Court, in a judgment of 21 February 2001 in *Sokolović*,[68] took this view).

However, one should not be unmindful of the risk of abuse which reliance upon the broader conception of universality may involve. This in particular holds true for cases where the accused is a State official, who, because of the possible exercise by a foreign court of the universality principle, may end up being hindered in the exercise of his functions abroad, being de facto barred from travelling outside his state. This danger is however tempered by the existence of personal immunities accruing to senior State officials on official missions abroad, as well as to diplomatic and consular agents (see above, 5.2.3(b)-(e)). Nonetheless, it would be judicious for prosecutors, investigating judges, and courts to invoke this broad notion of universal jurisdiction with great caution, and only if they are fully satisfied that compelling evidence is available against the accused.

12.4.2 ARE STATES INTERNATIONALLY EMPOWERED OR EVEN OBLIGED TO PROSECUTE INTERNATIONAL CRIMES?

Although States tend to lay down in their legislation a limited range of legal grounds of criminal jurisdiction, one may well wonder whether they are nevertheless *legally* entitled under *customary* international law and in the absence of a legislative authorization, to exercise universality of jurisdiction (at least in the less broad of the two versions outlined above, 12.4.1) over war crimes, crimes against humanity, aggression, torture, and terrorism.

State practice provides only little assistance. So far most war crimes or crimes against humanity have been tried by national courts of States on whose territory the crime had been committed, under the territoriality and possibly the passive (or passive and active) nationality principles (think for example of the *Barbie, Touvier,* and *Papon* cases).[69] Or these crimes have been tried under special national legislation, such as that enacted in the UK, Canada, or Australia, relating to a specific set of crimes namely those committed by Nazis during the Second World War. Or else they have been tried under legislation enacted to implement such international treaties as the 1984 UN Convention on Torture. It would appear that the first case where a person accused of crimes against humanity has been tried in a State with which he had no links is *Eichmann* (although it could perhaps be argued that in fact the legal ground was that of 'passive nationality', conceived in a broad sense). It is however extremely significant that no State concerned protested against that trial: neither the two German States nor the countries on whose territory the acts of genocide planned or organized by Eichmann had been committed, nor the States of which the victims of genocide were nationals. Thus, States did not challenge the principle enunciated in 1962 by the Supreme Court of Israel whereby 'the peculiarly universal character of these crimes [against humanity] vests in every State the authority to try and punish anyone who participated in their commission'.[70] This proposition was taken up by a US court in *Yunis*[71] and *Demjanjuk*[72] and, in *Pinochet*, by Lords Browne-Wilkinson and Millet.[73] As we saw above, at **12.4.1**, recently at least some States have passed legislation upholding the universality principle, and their courts have begun to apply such principle.

The acceptance by States of the exercise of 'universal' jurisdiction by Israel, as well as the most recent practice of some States, are in line with the general principle enunciated in 1927 by the PCIJ in the *Lotus* case: States are free to exercise their criminal jurisdiction over acts performed outside their territory, whenever no specific international limitations (provided for either in treaties or in customary rules) restrict such freedom.[74] Indeed, one fails to discern any customary or treaty limitation on the power of States to try and punish crimes against humanity and other crimes perpetrated abroad by foreigners against other foreigners. However, one should not be unmindful of the fact that many national courts are not prepared to exercise universal jurisdiction if *express national legislation* to this effect is lacking.

For instance, according to the *US Restatement of the Law Third* (1986), 'Although international law is law of the United States, . . . a person cannot be tried in the federal courts for an international crime unless Congress adopts a statute to define and punish the offense . . . The act of Congress may, however, define the offense by reference to international law'.[75]

Similarly, in a judgment of 6 November 1995 in *Reporters sans frontières* v. *Mille Collines*, the Paris Court of Appeal held that it lacked jurisdiction over genocide, grave breaches of the four 1949 Geneva Conventions, crimes against humanity, and torture allegedly committed abroad by foreigners against foreigners. As far as 'genocide, war crimes and crimes against humanity' were concerned, the Court held that it lacked jurisdiction, because 'in the absence of provisions of domestic law international custom cannot have the effect of extending the extraterritorial jurisdiction of the French courts. In that respect, only the provisions of international treaties are applicable under the national legal system, provided they have been duly approved or ratified by France and, on account of their contents, the provisions of such treaties produce a direct effect'. As for grave breaches of the Geneva Conventions, the Court held that French courts lacked jurisdiction because no implementing legislation had been passed. Finally, with regard to torture, French courts did possess jurisdiction on account of the adoption by French authorities of implementing legislation of the 1984 UN Convention on Torture. However, in the case at issue the petitioners had not shown that they had suffered a direct damage from the alleged crimes.[76]

Furthermore, in two cases of 1999 (*Nulyarimma* v. *Thompson* and *Buzzacott* v. *Hill*) a

Federal Court of Australia dismissed claims of members of the aboriginal community that conduct engaged in by certain senior State officials was contributing to the destruction of the aboriginal people as an ethnic or racial group, thus amounting to genocide. The legal ground for the dismissal was that, although genocide was prohibited by an international peremptory norm as well as the 1948 Genocide Convention, and although a statute had been enacted approving ratification of that Convention, courts lacked jurisdiction over genocide because no legislation had been passed providing for the trial within Australia of persons accused of genocide.[77]

More difficult is the question whether international customary rules impose on States an *obligation* to prosecute and try the authors of alleged international crimes. Some commentators have given an affirmative answer to this query. Their arguments, however, do not prove compelling. Although there are a few international treaties providing for the so-called universal jurisdiction (with regard to grave breaches, the 1949 Geneva Conventions and the First 1977 Protocol; with regard to torture as a crime in time of peace there exists the 1984 Convention on Torture; various treaties on terrorism provide for universal jurisdiction), it seems difficult to prove the emergence of a customary rule imposing international obligations to prosecute and try or extradite. State practice supporting a contention to this effect is lacking.

In this respect, it seems significant that the Paris Court of Appeal, in its decision of 20 October 2000 in *Qaddafi*, cited the preamble of the Rome Statute of the ICC (whereby national courts of each State party to the Statute are duty bound to prosecute persons responsible for international crimes) as evidence of the obligation to prosecute alleged authors of international crimes, incumbent upon any contracting party as a result of 'the intent of the international community to prosecute the most serious facts, even though perpetrated by heads of State in the exercise of their functions, whenever they amount to international crimes, contrary to the demands of universal conscience'; however, in the case at issue, the Court had duly stressed that it had jurisdiction because the alleged crimes had been committed by foreigners abroad against *French* nationals.[78]

As for a possible emerging customary rule imposing an international obligation to prosecute and try alleged terrorists, or alternatively to hand them over to the States concerned, an admittedly not compelling piece of evidence is constituted by paragraph 5(b) of the GA Declaration of 1994 referred to above (see **12.2.6(a)**), that 'urges' States to, among other things, 'ensure the apprehension and prosecution or extradition of perpetrators of terrorist acts, in accordance with the relevant provisions of their national law'.

In addition, no general international principle may be relied upon to warrant the proposition that such an obligation has materialized in the international community. At most, one could argue that in those areas where treaties provide for such an obligation, a corresponding customary rule may have emerged or be in the process of crystallizing. Clearly, as soon as customary rules may be proved to have formed, they will reinforce for all the contracting parties the obligations to the same effect laid down in the aforementioned Conventions. They will impose on States not parties to any of those Conventions, or parties to only some of them, a significant obligation, with a correlative right for all other States to demand compliance with that obligation.

Nonetheless, it cannot be denied that at least with regard to the most odious international crimes such as, in particular, genocide and crimes against humanity, there exists a general obligation of international co-operation for their prevention and punishment. This general obligation, clearly referred to, with regard to genocide, by the ICJ in 1951 in *Genocide*[79] and restated in 1996 in *Application of the Convention on the Prevention and Punishment of the Crime of Genocide*,[80] may among other things entail for States the general duty to set up appropriate judicial mechanisms or procedures for the universal repression of those crimes.

12.4.2 TRENDS IN STATE PRACTICE

The penal repression of international crimes can be better assessed in its merits and shortcomings if considered in the light of the fundamental distinction drawn by Röling, with regard to war crimes, between 'individual' and 'system' criminality.[81] The former encompasses war crimes committed by combatants on their own initiative and for 'selfish' reasons (rape, looting, murder, and so on). The latter refers to war crimes perpetrated on a large scale, chiefly to advance the war effort, at the request of, or at least with the encouragement or toleration of, the government authorities (the killing of civilians to spread terror, the refusing of quarter, the use of prohibited weapons, the torture of captured enemies to obtain information, and so on). Normally 'individual criminality' is repressed by the culprit's national authorities (army commanders do not like this sort of misbehaviour, for it is bad for the morale of the troops and makes for a hostile enemy population). By contrast, 'system criminality' is normally repressed only by international tribunals or by the national jurisdiction of the adversary. There are, of course, exceptions, such as the *Calley* case, 'a typical example of system criminality',[82] urged upon the US authorities by American and foreign public opinion.

By and large, repression of 'individual criminality' is a more frequent occurrence than that of 'system criminality', for the simple reason that the latter involves an appraisal and condemnation of a whole system of government, of misbehaviour involving the highest authorities of a country.

It must be added that, strikingly, for about forty years the repressive system instituted by the 1949 Geneva Conventions with regard to grave breaches has not been put into practice. Only after the establishment of the ICTY and the ICTR have States commenced to resort to it.

Think, for instance, of the *Djajic*[83] and *Jorgic*[84] cases in Germany, of the *Sarik* case in Denmark,[85] of *Javor*[86] and *Munyeshayka*[87] in France and the *G.* case[88] in Switzerland.

In addition, as already pointed out, States have tended to confine themselves to the more traditional criteria and in practice to institute criminal proceedings primarily against alleged authors of crimes committed on their territory or against persons living on their territory and having acquired their nationality.

12.5 PROSECUTION AND PUNISHMENT BY INTERNATIONAL COURTS

12.5.1 REASONS FOR THE STRONG DEMAND FOR INTERNATIONAL CRIMINAL JUSTICE

(a) Past attempts

The demand for international criminal justice blew up, as it were, in the 1990s. However, it was not new. As early as 1919, after the First World War, the victors had agreed upon a few provisions of the peace treaty with Germany, signed at Versailles, where they provided for the punishment of the major parties responsible for war crimes and went so far as to lay down in Article 227 the responsibility of the German Emperor (Wilhelm II) for 'the supreme offence against international morality and the sanctity of treaties'.

The same provision envisaged the establishment of 'a special tribunal', composed of five judges (to be appointed by the USA, Britain, France, Italy, and Japan) and charged with trying the Emperor. The Allies were clearly motivated by their outrage at the atrocities perpetrated by the vanquished Powers, in particular Germany, and wished to set an example, although of course this was 'victors' justice'. However, the Netherlands, where the German Emperor had taken refuge, refused to extradite him, chiefly because the crimes of which he was accused were not contemplated in the Dutch Constitution. In addition, the aforementioned provisions of the Versailles Treaty were harshly criticized by some eminent publicists, among them the Italian leading jurist and politician, V. E. Orlando.[89]

As for the trials of German military personnel alleged to have committed war crimes, no international court was set up, nor were they tried by courts of the Allies, as was instead envisaged in Articles 228–30 of the Versailles Treaty. Eventually only 12 minor indictees out of the 895 Germans accused by the Allies (who comprised various generals and admirals including the Chief of Staff of the Army, General E. Ludendorff, General Paul von Hindenburg, later Chief of Staff of the Army, as well as the former Chancellor Bethmann-Hollweg) were brought to trial, but only before a German court, the Supreme Court sitting at Leipzig (and six of them were acquitted). Thus, the attempts at establishing some sort of international criminal justice ended up in failure (although some of the judgments delivered by the Leipzig Court against minor defendants set significant precedents, chiefly because of the high legal quality of those judgments).

The same attempts were repeated in similar historical circumstances, namely after the Second World War. Again this was 'victors' justice'. Two 'international' tribunals were set up, one to try the major German 'war criminals' (the Nuremberg IMT), the other to try the major Japanese leaders and politicians accused of very serious breaches of international law (the Tokyo Tribunal). The Allies instituted other tribunals in Germany: these were courts composed of judges from some of the allied countries (primarily US nationals) and sitting in judgment over minor alleged war criminals. Furthermore, German courts were authorized and indeed requested, under Law no. 10 passed by the Control Council established by the four major Powers (USA, Britain, France, and the Soviet Union) to try persons accused of war crimes, crimes against humanity, or crimes against peace.

The major drawbacks of the two 'international' Tribunals was that in practice they were composed of judges appointed by each of the four Powers; the prosecutors too were appointed by each of those Powers and acted under the instructions of each appointing State. Thus, the view must be shared that the two Tribunals were not international courts proper, but judicial bodies acting as organs common to the appointing States. The Nuremberg IMT admitted this legal reality when it stated that: 'The making of the Charter [of the IMT] was the exercise of the sovereign legislative power by the countries to which the German Reich unconditionally surrendered; and the undoubted right of these countries to legislate for the occupied territories has been recognised by the civilised world. . . . The Signatory Powers created this Tribunal, defined the law it was to administer, and made regulations for the proper conduct of the Trial. In doing so, they have done together what any one of them might have done singly; for it is not to be doubted that any nation has the right thus to set up special courts to administer law'.[90]

In spite of all their deficiencies, it was salutary that, by setting up these two 'international' Tribunals, for the first time States broke the monopoly of national jurisdiction over international crimes, a monopoly that until then had been the rule.

(b) The turning point in the early 1990s

A major breakthrough occurred in the early 1990s. Various factors led to a new ethos in the international community and a strong request for international criminal justice. Two, in particular, should be underscored.

First, the *end of the cold war* proved to be of crucial importance. It had significant effects. For one thing, the animosity that had dominated international relations for almost half a century dissipated. In its wake, a new spirit of relative optimism emerged, stimulated by the following factors: (a) a clear reduction in the distrust and mutual suspicion that had frustrated friendly relations and co-operation between the Western and the Eastern bloc; (b) the successor States to the USSR (the Russian Federation and the other members of the Confederation of Independent States) came to accept and respect some basic principles of international law; (c) as a result there emerged unprecedented agreement in the UN SC and increasing convergence in the views of the five permanent members, with the consequence that this institution became able to fulfil its functions more effectively.

Another effect of the end of the cold war was no less important. Despite the problems of that bleak period, during the cold war era the two power blocs had managed to guarantee a modicum of international order in that each of the Superpowers had acted as a sort of policeman and guarantor in its respective sphere of influence. The collapse of this model of international relations ushered in a wave of negative consequences. It entailed a fragmentation of the international community and intense disorder which, coupled with rising nationalism and fundamentalism, resulted in a spiralling of mostly internal armed conflicts, with much bloodshed and

cruelty. The ensuing implosion of previously multi-ethnic societies led to gross violations of international humanitarian law on a scale comparable to those committed
during the Second World War.

The other crucial factor was the *increasing importance of the human rights doctrine.*
Its emphasis on the need to respect human dignity and consequently to punish all
those who seriously attack such dignity begot the quest for, or at least gave a robust
impulse to, international criminal justice.

12.5.2 INTERNATIONAL TRIALS: MAIN MERITS

International tribunals enjoy a number of advantages over domestic courts, particularly those sitting in the territory of the State where atrocities have been committed.

First of all, it is a fact that national courts are not inclined to institute proceedings
for crimes that lack any territorial or national link with the State. Until 1994, when the
establishment of the ICTY gave a great impulse to the prosecution and punishment of
alleged war criminals, the criminal provisions of the 1949 Geneva Conventions had
never been applied. National courts are still State-oriented and loath to search for,
prosecute, and try foreigners who have committed crimes abroad against other foreigners. For them the short-term objectives of national concerns seem still to prevail.
This is also due in part to the failure of national parliaments to pass the necessary
legislation granting courts universal jurisdiction over international crimes.

Second, the crimes at issue being international, that is, serious breaches of international law, international courts are the most appropriate bodies to pronounce on
them. They are in a better position to know and apply international law.

Third, international judges may be in a better position to be fully impartial and
unbiased, or at any rate more even-handed than the national judges who have been
caught up in the milieu in which the crime under trial has been perpetrated. The
punishment of alleged authors of international crimes by international tribunals
normally meets with less resistance than national punishment, as it hurts national
feelings much less.

Fourth, international courts can investigate crimes with ramifications in many
countries more easily than national judges. Often the witnesses reside in different
countries, other evidence needs to be collected thanks to the co-operation of several
States, and in addition special expertise is needed to handle the often complex and
difficult legal issues raised in the various national legislations involved.

Fifth, trials by international courts may ensure some sort of uniformity in the
application of international law, whereas proceedings conducted before national
courts may lead to a great disparity both in the application of that law and the
penalties meted out to those found guilty.

Finally, the holding of international trials—enjoying greater visibility than national
criminal proceedings—signals the will of the international community to break with
the past, by punishing those who have deviated from acceptable standards of human
behaviour. In delivering punishment, the international community's purpose is not so

much retribution as stigmatization of the deviant behaviour, in the hope that this will
have a modicum of deterrent effect.

12.5.3 THE NEED FOR INTERNATIONAL CRIMINAL COURTS TO RELY UPON STATE CO-OPERATION

Some major features of international criminal courts stand out. Normally they do not
sit in the country where crimes falling under their jurisdiction have been perpetrated.
They are located in a distant country, or at any rate in a country not necessarily close
to the scene of the crimes. In short, they are not the *forum delicti commissi*.

As the Supreme Court of Israel stated in *Eichmann,* 'normally the great majority of the witnesses and the greater part of the evidence are concentrated in . . . the State [where the crimes
were committed] and [this] is therefore the most convenient place (*forum conveniens*) for the
conduct of the trial'.[91]

Another unique feature of these tribunals is that they exercise jurisdiction directly
over individuals living in a sovereign State and subject to the exclusive jurisdiction of
such State. In addition, in most cases when perpetrating the alleged crime these
individuals have acted *qua* State officials or at least at the instigation or with the
support or the endorsement or acquiescence of State authorities. In principle, international tribunals are therefore intended to cast aside the shield of sovereignty.
However—and this is another salient trait—in fact they cannot reach those individuals
without going through national authorities. These courts do have the power to issue
warrants for the seizure of evidence, and the searching of premises, and to issue
subpoenas or arrest warrants. However, they cannot enforce the acts resulting from
the exercise of those powers, for lack of enforcement agents working under their
authority and empowered freely to enter the territory of sovereign States and exercise
enforcement functions there, notably *vis-à-vis* individuals acting as State officials.
This is the major stumbling block of these courts and tribunals. They lack an
autonomous *police judiciaire* overriding national authorities. They are like giants
without arms and legs, who therefore need artificial limbs to walk and work.
These artificial limbs are the State authorities. If the co-operation of States is not
forthcoming, these tribunals are paralysed.

12.5.4 MAIN PROBLEMS BESETTING INTERNATIONAL CRIMINAL PROCEEDINGS

The crucial problem international criminal courts must face has already been mentioned: the need for States' co-operation. As long as States either refuse outright to
assist those courts in collecting evidence or arresting the indictees, or do not provide
sufficient assistance, international criminal justice can hardly fulfil its role. This of
course also applies to those cases, such as that of the ICTY, where assistance can be
provided by a multilateral force established under the aegis of the UN (reference is of

course made to the NATO-led forces operating in Bosnia and Herzegovina and, more recently, in Kosovo).

There also is a need for international criminal courts to assimilate the various judges, each with a different cultural and legal background. Another serious problem is the length of international criminal proceedings. This length results primarily from the adoption of the *adversarial* system, which requires that all the evidence be scrutinized orally through examination and cross-examination (whereas in the inquisitorial system the evidence is previously selected by the investigating judge). In addition, the protracted nature of proceedings is often accentuated by (i) the need to prove some ingredients of the crime (for instance, the existence of a widespread or systematic practice, in the case of crimes against humanity), by (ii) the need to look into the historical or social context of the crime, by (iii) the fact that often international crimes are complex offences perpetrated over large territories (frequently involving more than one State) and over a fairly long period of time, as well as by (iv) the huge difficulty in collecting evidence. It should also be noted that the adversarial system was conceived of and adopted in most common law countries as a fairly exceptional alternative to the principal policy choice, namely, avoidance of trial proceedings through plea bargaining. In fact, on account of this feature, the adversarial model works sufficiently well in most common law countries. However, in international criminal proceedings defendants tend not to plead guilty, among other things because of the serious stigma attaching to international crimes. They therefore prefer to stand trial, in spite of the length inherent in the examination and cross-examination of witnesses rendered, at the international level, more intractable by language problems. (While at the national level normally all proceedings are conducted in one language alone, before international courts at least two, and more often even three, languages are used, with the consequence that, among other things, all documents and exhibits need to be translated into various languages.) This factor, coupled with the frequent need of upholding a typical feature of the inquisitorial system, namely to keep the accused in custody, both in the pre-trial phase and during trial and appeal, makes for a state of affairs that in some cases might be seen as hardly consistent with the right to 'fair and expeditious trial' and the presumption of innocence accruing to any defendant.

Luckily international courts are aware of these and other practical problems, and are already putting in hand the necessary remedial measures.

12.6 MAJOR DIFFERENCES BETWEEN STATE RESPONSIBILITY AND INDIVIDUAL CRIMINAL LIABILITY

Finally, it is worth briefly outlining the elements differentiating these two kinds of responsibility as well as their points of contact.

International rules on 'ordinary State responsibility' substantially hinge on the notion of 'private justice'. Normally: (1) State responsibility only arises to the extent that individuals breaching international rules act on behalf of a State, that is, as *de jure* or de facto State officials; conduct of persons acting in a private capacity does not give rise to State responsibility whenever no involvement of a State can be proved. (2) The primary goal of this legal regime of responsibility is to bring about cessation of the breach or reparation of the damage, not punishment of the delinquent State; a reparative rather than punitive outlook is taken. (3) Only the State injured by the breach of an international rule may request cessation of the wrongful act or reparation. Only in exceptional cases of 'aggravated responsibility' (aggression, genocide, large-scale and massive breaches of human rights, etc.) are States not directly affected by these violations legally entitled to invoke the responsibility of the delinquent State. It is only in these cases that States do not act 'privately', but pursue a community interest on behalf of all members of the world community (or, in the case of multilateral treaties, of the group of parties to the treaty).

By contrast, individual criminal responsibility is based on the notions that: (1) Individuals behaving contrary to the most fundamental legal standards may be held criminally responsible regardless of whether they have acted in an official capacity, that is, both when they were State organs and when they acted as private individuals; their link with a State may be relevant (in the case of genocide, aggression, or crimes against humanity, when normally their action tends to be promoted, supported, acquiesced in, or condoned, by State authorities); legally, however, this link is not indispensable. (2) Prosecution and punishment are conducted in the interest of the world community; hence the power to institute proceedings belongs not only to those materially affected by the crime, but also to national courts, acting upon various grounds of jurisdiction (see **12.4.1**), or to international prosecutors, when international criminal courts are set up. (3) The primary goal of this class of responsibility is to punish the culprit.

Although these two categories of responsibility are clearly distinct, points of contact may however occur. In particular, in the case of genocide or aggression the two categories normally overlap or may be based on some common elements. For instance, when proceedings are instituted before an international court against a State held responsible for genocide, the court must establish whether those allegedly engaging in genocide acted with the intent to destroy members of a group; in other words, it must enquire into a mental element typical of criminal liability.

The two categories of responsibility do not replace but rather supplement each other, in various respects. First, some breaches of international rules perpetrated by State officials (such as war crimes) may give rise to both State responsibility and criminal liability: the former does not exclude the latter, and vice versa. Second, by and large, the regime of State responsibility is primarily intended to react to day-to-day, or ordinary, breaches of international law by State officials. The other legal regime is instead aimed at reacting to those breaches, by whoever perpetrated, that are so grave and inconsistent with internationally safeguarded values, as to demand the personal liability of their alleged perpetrators. Third, as we have seen above (**9.6.1**), in some respects the State obligation to prosecute and punish (or extradite) individuals charged with 'grave breaches' of the 1949 Geneva Conventions may be seen as a form of implementation of State responsibility for such breaches.

It is indisputable that individual criminal liability is more advanced than State responsibility. It is grounded on the notion of community interest and community right. To a large extent it partakes of the concept of justice as a public function, not as a private business. In addition, in many respects it is more effective in dissuading State officials from breaching international law (or at least those parts of international law that embody the most important values: peace, respect for human dignity, protection of groups from destruction, respect for a modicum of fair play, and in particular protection of civilians, in armed conflict). Even if it does not succeed in fulfilling a deterrent role, it can more effectively react to international breaches. Nevertheless, as long as international criminal justice is not rendered truly effective, by enabling criminal courts to have arrest warrants executed by national or international enforcement agencies, State responsibility will of necessity be needed, even in areas where the two kinds of responsibility may overlap. Indeed, if it proves impossible to arrest a head of State, a member of cabinet, or any other senior State official accused of international crimes, the only fall-back solution that remains it to activate State responsibility, either by bringing the case before an inter-State court such as the ICJ or, if such a court lacks jurisdiction, by resorting to counter-measures.

PART III

CONTEMPORARY ISSUES
IN INTERNATIONAL LAW

13

THE ROLE OF THE UNITED NATIONS

13.1 THE GRAND DESIGN OF THE POST-SECOND WORLD WAR PERIOD

As the US Secretary of State, Cordell Hull, recalled, '[f]rom the moment when Hitler's invasion of Poland revealed the bankruptcy of all existing methods to preserve peace, it became evident . . . that we must begin almost immediately to plan the creation of a new system'.[1]

The USA and the British did most of the planning. Two grand designs soon emerged, one advocated by the Americans, the other by the British. The former, strongly championed by Cordell Hull and President Roosevelt, hinged on a few main points: (1) resort to military force in international relations must be banned; (2) the traditional system of unilateral action, of military and political alliances, of spheres of influence and balance of power ought to be removed; all these mechanisms and practices must be replaced by a universal organization set up by peace-loving nations; (3) in this organization a major role was to be given to the most powerful allies fighting against the Axis Powers, namely the USA, the USSR, as well as Britain and France (which still had huge colonial empires), and China, which was to be associated with them. They were to be allotted the role of world policemen, responsible for enforcing peace; (4) economic and social co-operation was to be promoted so as to ensure economic progress and better working conditions with a view to forestalling future armed conflict resulting from dramatic economic inequalities; (5) colonial empires were to be dismantled, particularly if they belonged to 'weak nations', on three grounds: (a) for ideological reasons, that is, in order to realize the principle of self-determination of peoples throughout the world; (b) for political reasons, namely to avert future clashes and conflicts resulting from the existence in the world of over one billion 'brown people' resenting the domination of white minorities;[2] (c) for economic reasons: colonial empires distorted equality and free trade on the world market, one of the primary goals of the US neo-liberal approach; indeed, the colonialist Powers had access to cheap labour and cheap primary commodities in their colonies. However, the break-up of the colonial system must not be abrupt but gradual: an international trusteeship system was to gradually bring about the demise of that system (see also **18.1**).

The British scheme, relentlessly propounded by Churchill, accepted the idea of banning force and promoting economic and social co-operation, but also hinged on (1) the notion that world security could be safeguarded by the setting up of regional councils under a world council; (2) the maintenance of colonial empires or, alternatively, their gradual change into self-governing entities.

As the USA was by far the more powerful country, and had indeed become the most industrialized and militarily powerful State in the world, it easily gained the upper hand. However, it had to compromise with Britain over the question of colonialism, the more so because another future 'policeman', France, although temporarily 'defeated', very much clung to its colonial empire.

The Soviet Union played a relatively minor role in the establishment of the universal organization, the UN, and was primarily vocal on some political issues such as the veto power in the Security Council (SC), the proposed participation in the founding of the Organization of all 16 Soviet republics (eventually accepted by the Western allies only for Byelorussia and the Ukraine) and the upholding of the principle of self-determination.

The fundamental tenets of the future UN Charter were gradually agreed upon. This was done first in the Atlantic Charter, drafted by the USA and Britain in 1941, then by the three victorious Powers (the USA, Britain, and the Soviet Union) plus China, in a string of summits: at Moscow (October 1943), at Dumbarton Oaks (an estate in Washington DC, from 21 August to 7 October 1944), at Yalta (February 1945, without the participation of China). When the diplomatic conference designed to work out and approve the UN Charter was held (San Francisco, 25 April–26 June 1945), it was presented with a text elaborated by the Great Powers. To this text amendments, requiring a two-thirds majority, were technically permitted, although politically they were allowed only on relatively minor points. The 50 States gathered at San Francisco (most States of the world: the four convening Powers, the 42 States (including India, not yet independent) that had declared war either on Germany or on Japan, plus Argentina, Denmark, Byelorussia, and the Ukraine, the last two not yet recognized as independent States) could not but accept the key provisions of the Charter. Among these were: the provision on the establishment of a central organ consisting of a few countries, dominated by the five permanent members with veto power, and responsible for the maintenance of international peace and security; and the provision on domestic jurisdiction,[3] corresponding to the present Article 2.7, which was closely intertwined with the traditional principle on non-interference in the internal affairs of States (see below). However, small and medium-sized countries were able to contribute on some points, chiefly: (1) the laying down, in Article 51 (see **14.4.1**) of the right to individual and collective self-defence; (2) the expansion of the competence of the General Assembly (GA) (the collective body where every member State has one seat and one vote), which was empowered both to discuss any matter within the scope of the Charter and to make recommendations on questions concerning peace and security not being dealt with by the SC (see Articles 10 and 12); (3) the elevation of the Economic and Social Council, ECOSOC (the body charged with promoting co-operation on economic, social, cultural, educational, health, and related matters) to the rank of one of the principal organs of the new Organization; (4) the laying down of provisions on colonial matters (such as the Declaration regarding non-self-governing territories, contained in Article 73 and the provisions on the trusteeship system); (5)

the insertion of a provision establishing the prevalence of obligations imposed by the UN Charter over conflicting obligations, if any, deriving from other treaties (Article 103). A point of some contention was the principle of non-intervention, which was dear to the hearts of Latin American and other small countries (as was pointed out by a distinguished commentator: 'there was a widespread conviction among the middle and lesser States that some formal safeguard against intervention in their internal affairs was needed in an Organization in which the great Powers were to play a dominant role').[4] This principle was intended to be put into what became Article 2.4 (banning the use of force); the motion of Latin American and other countries had enough support to be inserted by a divided vote. However, in the end, the compromise (probably a perverse one) was to put it into Article 2.7 (safeguarding member States' 'domestic jurisdiction' from undue interference by the Organization).

It must be stressed that from the outset the new Organization was envisaged as a political body dominated by the Great Powers. Although they had taken upon themselves the task of safeguarding peace and security on behalf and in the interest of all nations of the world, they did not intend to make major concessions to small nations on matters they regarded as of crucial importance. In this connection, an exchange of views between Stalin, Churchill, and Roosevelt that occurred on 4 February 1945, at Yalta, is illuminating. While discussing the issue of voting procedures in the SC, Stalin noted that 'he would never agree to having any action of any of the Great Powers submitted to the judgment of the small powers'.[5] The other two leaders substantially agreed.[6]

Furthermore, the new Organization was to be a political entity pursuing political objectives, albeit within a legal framework. In its action it was not to be trammelled by legal technicalities, let alone by judicial restraints: efforts to make disputes on the interpretation of the Charter subject to the mandatory jurisdiction of its principal judicial organ, the ICJ, were rejected at San Francisco (they secured majority support but not the requisite two-thirds majority).[7]

13.2 GOALS AND STRUCTURE OF THE NEW ORGANIZATION

In the view of the founding fathers, the new Organization was to pursue a number of fundamental purposes: (1) to maintain peace and security (Article 1.1); (2) to bring about by peaceful means the adjustment or settlement of international disputes or situations which might lead to a breach of the peace (Article 1.1); (3) to develop friendly relations among nations based on respect for the principle of equal rights and self-determination of peoples (Article 1.2); in short, to promote, if not yet the gradual and internationally organized demise of colonial systems, at least the slow awakening of colonial countries to self-government; (4) to foster economic and social co-operation (Articles 1.3, 55); (5) to promote respect for human rights and fundamental freedoms for all persons (Articles 1.3, 55).

Other purposes of the Organization, clearly considered of minor importance by the founding fathers, were: (6) to promote disarmament and the regulation of armaments (Article 11.1); (7) to further respect for international law (Preamble) and encourage the progressive development of international law and its codification (Article 13.1.b).

Plainly, maintenance of peace and security was the crucial goal of the new entity. In 1939–45 the tension between force and law—persistent in the international community, as in any human grouping—had been magnified by the war. It had become clear that unless serious restraints were put on violence, the world would be heading for catastrophe. One should not believe, however, that the leaders were so naïve as to think that in 1945 one could radically break with the approach so forcefully set forth by Bismarck in the nineteenth century, when he reportedly said that 'the questions of our time will not be settled by resolutions and majority votes, but by blood and iron'.[8] Perhaps it was rather thought that, faced with two radically opposed methods for settling friction and disagreement, 'bullets' or 'words' (as Camus put it in 1947),[9] one ought bravely to endeavour opting as much as possible for the latter, while however being aware that the former would continue to be used.

Let us take a quick glance at the structure of the new Organization and how the various organs were to pursue the goals set by the founding fathers (and mothers).

The SC and the GA are the two principal organs. The GA, consisting of all member States, each having one vote, was granted a very broad competence: it was authorized to discuss and pronounce upon any matter within the province of the Organization (subject to some procedural restraints whenever a question relating to peace and security is being handled by the SC: see Article 12). Its decisions 'on important questions' (listed in Article 18.2) are made by a two-thirds majority of the members present and voting; others are taken instead by a majority of the members present and voting (Article 18.3). Its decisions (resolutions, recommendations, declarations) may not be legally binding *per se* (except for decisions concerning the 'internal life' of the Organization, such as those apportioning UN expenses among the member States (see Article 17.2), adopting rules of procedure (Article 21), establishing subsidiary organs (Article 22), electing members of the various other bodies, such as the SC, ECOSOC, etc., appointing the Secretary-General (Article 97), electing members of the ICJ pursuant to Article 8 of the Court Statute, etc.).

The SC consists of 15 members, some permanent (the so-called Big Five: China, France, the UK, Russia, and the USA), others elected every two years by the GA. Its competence is 'limited' to the maintenance of peace and security. Its decisions, except for those on procedural matters and on the election of members of the ICJ, may only be taken with an affirmative vote (or at least the abstention) of the five permanent members (the so-called veto power; see Article 27.3). They are taken by a vote of nine members (those on the election of judges of the ICJ may be taken by a vote of eight members: see Article 10 of the ICJ Statute, requiring the absolute majority of members of the SC). They may either be recommendatory in nature, or legally binding, pursuant to Article 25. The SC was to be assisted and advised by the Military Staff

Committee, consisting of the Chiefs of Staff of the permanent members; this body was to be responsible 'under the SC' for the strategic direction of any armed forces placed at the disposal of the SC. What is even more important, the military contingents that under Articles 43–5 member States were to put at the disposal of the SC for enforcement action in case of threats to the peace, breaches of the peace or aggression, were to act under SC control.

These two organs are at the top of the Organization. Their principal instrumentality was to be the *Secretariat*, headed by a *Secretary-General*, appointed by the GA upon the recommendation of the SC (Article 97). Three other main organs were to fulfil specialized functions: in the field of economic and social co-operation, the *Economic and Social Council* (ECOSOC), in some colonial matters, the *Trusteeship Council*, and in matters concerning international legal disputes, the *ICJ*.

ECOSOC consists of 54 member States elected by the GA for three years: its main task is to discuss, propose, recommend, promote studies, co-ordinate the action of specialized agencies (such as the International Labour Organization (ILO), UNESCO, the Food and Agriculture Organization (FAO), the World Health Organization (WHO), etc.), set up subsidiary bodies (such as the Commission on Human Rights, established in 1946 on the strength of Article 68), etc. in the fields within its competence.

Matters relating to some categories of non-independent countries (territories that were still under mandate, territories detached from 'enemy States as a result of the Second World War', other territories such as colonies voluntarily placed under trusteeship by the States responsible for their administration) were to be brought under the trusteeship system by virtue of special agreements. They were thus put under the control of the *Trusteeship Council*, consisting of members administering trust territories, permanent members of the SC that were not in such a position, and a number of members elected by the GA so as to ensure that membership was equally divided between States administering trust territories and those which did not (Article 86). The Charter puts the Trusteeship Council under the control of the GA or, when trusteeship agreements relate to 'strategic areas', of the SC (Article 83).

The *ICJ* is the principal judicial organ of the UN, authorized to settle legal disputes between States by binding judgments, or to issue Advisory Opinions at the request of the principal organs of the UN, that is the SC, the GA, or any other organ or specialized agency authorized by the GA. The ICJ consists of 15 judges elected by the GA and the SC. (Under Article 10.2 of the ICJ Statute, annexed to the UN Charter, when they elect judges for the ICJ, permanent members of the SC have no veto power; as pointed out above, it is therefore sufficient for a candidate to obtain eight out of 15 votes, whether or not the votes in his or her favour included those cast by the permanent members.)

13.3 PRINCIPAL ACHIEVEMENTS AND FAILURES
OF THE UN

13.3.1 GENERAL

From the outset agreement among the Great Powers who had drafted the Charter was considered the indispensable underpinning of the Organization (at Yalta, on 6 February 1945, Stalin had noted that 'the main thing was to prevent quarrels in future between the three Great Powers [USA, Britain, and the USSR] and the task, therefore, was to secure their unity for the future';[10] President Roosevelt fully shared this view).[11] However, as is well known, agreement did not last and the sudden worsening of the relations between the two leading States, the USA and the USSR, undermined the establishment of the collective security system. During the cold war (1946–89) the world split into two groups, each led by a Superpower. President Roosevelt's idea of the SC as 'a board of directors of the world' responsible for 'enforcing the peace against any potential miscreant'[12] fell asunder. Each of the two leading Powers took care of its own bloc to enforce order and stability there, and each respected the other's sphere of influence. Competition and conflict primarily erupted in relation to the Powers' grip on developing countries and control over strategic areas.

After the collapse of the Soviet Union and the end of the confrontation between the Eastern and Western coalitions, the world has been increasingly dominated by one Superpower, the USA. Nevertheless, the drastic change in the international scenario has not entailed the implementation of the security system envisaged in the Charter. The prevention of international and internal armed conflict or the prompt re-establishment of peace when these conflicts break out, disarmament, and a satisfactory regulation of international economic relations conducive to political stability in many countries, have remained the principal sore points.

Surprisingly, the UN has achieved much more in those areas that had been left somewhat in the background in 1945, than in those on which the founding fathers had focused their attention (maintenance of peace and security, settlement of disputes likely to endanger peace). The lukewarm attitude taken towards colonial countries was overturned and in the early 1960s colonialism had been practically swept away. In the area of human rights immense progress was made, with the adoption of exceedingly important Declarations and Conventions. The progressive development of international law was attained by the adoption of a number of Conventions codifying and developing international law.

13.3.2 MAINTENANCE OF PEACE AND SECURITY

The system inaugurated in 1945 was revolutionary indeed. It postulated that in future States ought to endeavour to settle their disputes peacefully and never use force (see Article 2.3 and 2.4 of the UN Charter), subject to the exception of self-defence; and that an international authority, the UN, would act as a world policing and enforce-ment agency. Thus, forcible self-help, traditionally a characteristic feature of the international community, was significantly restricted: it was left in the form of self-defence, provided for in Article 51 of the UN Charter, as well as, under Article 106 (a transitory provisions that has now become obsolescent), in the form of possible collective action by the five Great Powers to maintain peace, pending the coming into force of the agreements, referred to in Article 43, designed to make available to the SC armed forces, assistance, etc. And a centralized body (the SC) was vested with broad powers of forcible intervention (see Chapter VII of the Charter): any time it deter-mined under Article 39 that there was a threat to the peace, a breach of the peace, or an act of aggression, it could decide upon sanctions not involving the use of armed force, under Article 41, or take armed action against the aggressor or the State threatening the peace, under Article 42.

There were two momentous consequences. First, whereas previously the distinction between lawful and unlawful use of force either could not be made or was blurred, it had now become possible to say—at least in theory—whether a specific instance of use of force was lawful. Second, whereas previously (until the League of Nations), force could be used without any previous assessment by a third party, now an inter-national body, the SC, could decide to enforce peace after having determined the existence of a threat to the peace, a breach of the peace, or an act of aggression.

Self-defence was envisaged as an exception to this centralized collective security system. However, the UN Charter also set a number of limitations upon the right of self-defence enshrined in Article 51. This provision, subsequently turned into general international law, only allows the use of force in order to repel an 'armed attack', and subject to the procedural requirements that the SC must be immediately informed of the armed action in self-defence (Article 51 thus envisages self-defence as a sort of preliminary or provisional measure by which the victim of an armed attack may safeguard its rights for a limited period of time until such time as the centralized security mechanism begins to function).

The basic deficiencies of the collective security system outlined in the UN Charter were fourfold.

First, the idea of a collective monopoly of force by the five permanent members of the SC was, of course, based on their continuing agreement; in the case of dissent the so-called veto power (advocated by the USA and strongly endorsed at Dumbarton Oaks by the USSR) gave any of the five the right to cripple the functioning of the collective security system. (The veto power would have had a more sweeping scope and would have been essentially unqualified had the USSR prevailed in its opposition to Roosevelt's view—up to a point shared by Britain—that, when the SC was dealing with the *peaceful* settlement of disputes, but not with enforcement matters, a party to a dispute, including any of the Big Five, should not be entitled to cast a vote, because 'American concepts of fair play required that a party to a dispute not vote in judgment on itself'.)[13]

Second, the 'army' which should have been put at the disposal of the UN was not envisaged as an international army proper, exclusively dependent on the SC. Rather, it was to be composed of contingents placed at the disposal of the SC by the various member States through special agreements governing the number and type of forces and their degree of readiness. The SC would exercise its authority over national forces, which would act under the strategic and military direction of the 'Military Staff Committee' (see above, **13.2**). The Charter did not envisage that the State sending a contingent would continue to exercise command and control over it. However, the possibility of a 'dual allegiance' was not excluded altogether. Such a possible dual allegiance could not but result in a dangerous likelihood of the 'army' being paralysed by national States.

Third, force was only banned in 'international relations' (Article 2.4); it was consequently allowed in 'internal' affairs (for example, against rebels in the case of civil strife), and in the relations between colonial powers and dependent territories. As tensions within the various colonial empires had already become apparent and were to increase, the Charter left a huge host of potentially dangerous strains to be dealt with at the discretion of individual States, should political dissension and demands for change intensify to the point of armed conflict.

Fourth, to a large extent the UN Charter tended to uphold a concept more of 'negative peace', or absence of war, than 'positive' peace, or the introduction of justice for the purpose of preventing as far as possible political tensions from degenerating into armed conflicts. This is not to say that the UN closed its eyes to political reality and refrained from suggesting political solutions calculated to prevent armed conflicts. Indeed, co-operation in the economic, social, and political fields was promoted, obligations were imposed on colonial powers and a role for the UN was also envisaged to further co-operation as regards disarmament. However, this part of the UN Charter proved rudimentary and weak. Particularly unsatisfactory were the provisions concerning colonies and economic relations.

As a result of the cold war, the attempt at centralizing the use of force ended in failure and a 'UN army' was never established. The old institution of self-help acquired new importance, albeit with a number of qualifications. As a consequence the following developments have occurred.

(1) The two contending blocs set up separate organizations for 'collective self-defence' (NATO in 1949 and the Warsaw Pact in 1955). The world community returned to the traditional system of opposing political and military alliances.

(2) A trend emerged which was to become one of the distinguishing features of the present international community, namely, the tendency of States to make increasing use of the right of individual self-defence, to such an extent that a number of States now feel relatively confident to engage in war under the cloak of 'self-defence', without having to fear any decisive hindrance from the UN. At the same time States have endeavoured to broaden the concept of self-defence so as to include major forms of use of force short of war not covered by Article 51 of the Charter. Resort to unilateral use of force, under the cover of self-defence, or protection of nationals

abroad, or pre-emptive self-defence, occurred in a number of cases (for details see **Chapter 14**).

(3) The SC's inability to enforce peace led to two major developments: on the one side, enforcement by UN member States at the request, or upon authorization, of the SC; on the other, establishment of peace keeping as a mild replacement of or substitute for peace enforcement proper (see **Chapter 14**).

13.3.3 PROMOTION OF THE PEACEFUL SETTLEMENT OF DISPUTES LIKELY TO ENDANGER PEACE

The Charter enshrines the legal obligation of settling disputes by peaceful means (Articles 2.3, 33.1). However, the draftsmen were not interested in the peaceful settlement of *any* inter-State dispute. They were particularly concerned about disputes among States that could degenerate and imperil *peace*. They therefore laid down in Chapter VI of the Charter a set of provisions dealing with 'disputes the continuance of which is likely to endanger the maintenance of international peace and security'.

The purpose of intervention by the UN bodies is to prevent the breaking out of armed conflict. The machinery provided for in the UN Charter refers both to legal and to political disagreement, although, as we shall see, in the case of legal disputes a specific mode of settlement is suggested. The lack of distinction between the two classes of disputes is a sound development. All too often clashes between legal claims are politically motivated, or they have strong political implications, whereas political feuds frequently present legal overtones, or else one of the parties or even both of them employ legal arguments to buttress their political demands. If one of the major purposes of the world community is reconciliation of disputants so as to prevent their crossing swords, the better course of action is that, taken in 1945, of not making the selection of a certain mode of settlement conditional on the intrinsic character of the dispute.

The basic philosophy underlying the Charter is that every effort should be made to maintain peace and security. An obvious corollary is that whenever disagreements between States threaten to become explosive, and to endanger peace, the UN must step in and endeavour to defuse the situation. This, of course, implies that the Organization must always watch out for possible cracks in the fragile edifice of peace. The field of action of the Organization thus becomes very broad, for any disagreement evidently may escalate into a major conflict, except for the very minor and peripheral ones. Ross aptly stressed the great novelty of the Charter system in the following terms:

'The essence of the Charter, the point where it definitely breaks with the rules of traditional international law, is that it establishes the principle that every dispute (the continuance of which is likely to endanger the maintenance of international peace and security) is a public matter, so that whether the parties wish it or not, they must accept the fact that the dispute may be debated in the SC [or] the GA), if that organ considers such debate to be in the interests of peace. The parties are not obliged to seek the assistance of the Organization, but they are obliged to put up with its intervention.'[14]

With regard to disputes likely to endanger peace, the UN Charter provided that (i) each party to the dispute has the obligation to seek a solution 'by negotiation, enquiry, mediation, conciliation, arbitration, judicial settlement, resort to regional agencies or arrangements, or other peaceful means of their choice' (Article 33.1); (ii) any other State is authorized to bring any dispute or situation likely to endanger peace to the attention of the SC or the GA (Article 35; pursuant to paragraph 2, if the State is not a member of the UN, it must accept in advance the obligations of pacific settlement provided in the Charter; hence the SC's decision regarding the mode of peaceful settlement becomes binding on it); (iii) in the case of a dispute or situation which no State brings to the SC, this body is empowered to call upon the parties to settle their dispute by peaceful means (Article 33.2); (iv) the SC can investigate any dispute or situation in order to establish whether its continuance is likely to endanger peace (Article 34); (v) the SC can *recommend* 'appropriate procedures or methods of settlement' (Articles 36.1 and 37.2).

Clearly, the UN machinery for dispute settlement was rather weak, not only because the class of disputes or situations susceptible to be considered by the SC was relatively limited, but also because the powers of this body were confined to issuing recommendations (except for decisions to initiate investigations under Article 34).

Nonetheless, member States have brought to the attention of the SC disputes that clearly did not amount to a threat to the peace, and it has considered itself empowered to issue recommendations.

The SC has exercised its powers under Chapter VI on numerous occasions: in 1947, when it dealt with the dispute between Britain and Albania over the mines laid by Albania in the Corfu channel (a dispute that was then submitted to the ICJ), in 1948, when it handled the Kashmir dispute between India and Pakistan, in 1949, when it considered the dispute between Israel and Arab States. Later on it dealt with disputes over the Suez affair, the Congo, Namibia, Southern Rhodesia, up to, more recently, the crises in Nicaragua, Honduras, El Salvador, Guatemala, Cambodia, etc.

The fulfilment of this task has not led to any major achievements, on many grounds. The SC has not fully used the powers it derives from Chapter VI. Furthermore, it has sometimes felt that the public airing of the grievances of the parties to a dispute or those concerned in a situation was less appropriate for achieving a prompt settlement of the dispute or situation than private collective diplomacy. In addition, sometimes it has been felt that the SC sided with one of the parties concerned, rather than acting as a neutral promoter of the dispute settlement. On other occasions the contesting parties have felt that the SC was not prepared to push for a prompt and determinative settlement, nor was it willing, in the case of failure, to proceed to apply Chapter VII. This lack of political will has played into the hands of the contestants, or of one of them, with the resulting failure of the attempt at solving the case.

It should be noted that, under Article 14, the GA may recommend measures for achieving a 'peaceful adjustment of any situation . . . which it deems likely to impair the general welfare or friendly relations among nations'. This provision, couched in very broad terms, has given rise to an interesting practice.

In addition, the UN SG may play a role in dispute settlement. The Charter does not expressly give him this function, but many Secretaries-General have been asked, or have offered themselves, to act as mediators. The political and moral authority deriving from this high position within the UN structure has often proved useful at least to bring the parties to a common table by exercising good offices. In one case the SG was asked to act as arbitrator: in 1986 France and New Zealand jointly invited Péres de Cuéllar to arbitrate their dispute over the sinking of the *Rainbow Warrior*.

13.3.4 SELF-DETERMINATION OF PEOPLES

Despite the attempt of the USSR to set out in the Charter the goal of promoting independence for the colonial countries, in fact what was agreed upon in San Francisco was the gradual attainment of self-government by dependent peoples (and concomitantly, a moderate overhauling of colonial empires). The reference to self-determination contained in Articles 1.1 and 55 was conceived of in this limited manner. Article 73 (under Chapter X, entitled 'Declaration regarding non-self-governing territories') concerned the colonial territories that colonial Powers were not prepared to put under the trusteeship system, and with regard to which the relevant colonial Power simply had to report to the Secretary-General on minor matters (pursuant to Article 73e). Article 73 consistently envisaged that member States carrying responsibility for the administration of territories whose peoples had 'not yet attained a full measure of self-government' should engage in assisting them to develop self-government and build free political institutions. In contrast, the provisions on the international trusteeship system (to be established under UN authority for the administration and supervision of some limited categories of colonial territories: see above, **13.2**) contemplated self-government of colonial peoples, but also independence as might 'be appropriate to the particular circumstances of each territory and its peoples and the freely expressed wishes of the peoples concerned' (Article 76b). Complex machinery was set up, hinging on the Trusteeship Council, for national administration, under international supervision, of trust territories.

In short, the Charter kept alive the colonial system, although it divided colonial peoples into *two classes* (non-self-governing territories, and trust territories) and envisaged some measure of international scrutiny over the attainment, by the colonial Power, of the objectives of self-government (or, exceptionally, independence) that the colonial Power was now to pursue.

This is the area where the UN has been most successful. It is reported that, at San Francisco, it was generally believed that the UN could achieve general disarmament in a decade, whereas decolonization would take a century. Instead, only a few years after the adoption of the Charter the UN succeeded in beginning to dismantle colonial empires. It rapidly moved from a moderate, substantially neo-colonialist scheme primarily geared to self-government, to a courageous search for and promotion of independence. This bold development was facilitated by various factors: (1) the strong push given by the Soviet Union and eastern European socialist States to the fight against colonialism; (2) the increasingly lukewarm support of the USA to its colonial allies and the revival of the anti-colonialist attitude of that Great Power; (3) the growing insistence of colonial peoples on their 'right' to gain independence; this awareness was inculcated and spread by many debates in the Organization and the consequent UN resolutions and declarations, which hence were objectively instrumental in subverting the existing world order; it appears indisputable that those texts greatly incited national liberation movements to fight against colonialism, thereby contributing to the demise of the colonial system; (4) the growing economic and social costs, for European Powers, of maintaining their colonial systems, coupled with the decreasing importance and economic attractiveness, for them, of the primary goods they formerly exploited in colonial territories; (5) the rise to power in European colonial States of powerful social-democrat (Labour) parties adopting anti-colonialist stances.

Thus, in a matter of three decades (between 1947 and 1975), colonial empires were substantially brought down. The last colonies to acquire independence were the Portuguese colonies of Angola and Mozambique, in 1975, and Namibia, formerly a territory held by South Africa under a League of Nations mandate, in 1990. The status of Western Sahara and some small territories (the Virgin Islands, under the USA; New Caledonia, under French control; Tokelau, under New Zealand; plus some territories still under British control, such as the British Virgin Islands, Bermuda and the Falklands/Malvinas) remains one of the few unresolved problems. (It should however be noted that the population of some of these territories does not want independence, and neither the UN Charter nor the relevant GA resolutions require that they must choose independence.)

One of the merits of the UN was that it promoted the independence of colonial peoples (a) by peaceful means and, generally speaking, (b) by respecting the wishes and aspirations of the peoples concerned (through plebiscites and referendums).

However, the success of the UN in implementing self-determination was limited to colonial peoples (including Southern Rhodesia (now Zimbabwe) in 1980). Outside this category, it promoted (internal) self-determination in South Africa (in 1994) and the external self-determination of Eritrea (in 1996) and of East Timor (in 1999; in 1974 East Timor had been annexed by Indonesia, although the UN continued to consider that it was under Portuguese administration). Because of the basic attitude of most States towards territorial integrity and national sovereignty, the UN has been able or willing to foster internal self-determination in sovereign States only where it was to bring down governments practising an apartheid policy (see, however, *infra*, **13.3.6**).

13.3.5 ECONOMIC AND SOCIAL CO-OPERATION

In the area of economic and social co-operation the Charter simply stated, in Article 13.1(*b*), that the GA could initiate studies and make recommendations. However, a specialized body, the Economic and Social Council (ECOSOC) was made responsible for preparing studies, reports, and draft conventions, as well as recommendations (Article 62). Also Article 55 (at subparagraphs (*a*) and (*b*)) dealt with economic and social development, in particular with the creation of conditions necessary for social and economic progress. Here again, as in many other provisions of the UN Charter, a link was established with the maintenance of international peace and security. Conditions of stability and well-being were considered essential for the development and maintenance of peaceful relations among States. The link could also work the other way round: peace and security ensure a proper environment for economic and social development.[15]

However, no general principle was laid down in the Charter on the direction that economic and social co-operation should take in future. Policy decisions were left to the GA and ECOSOC or, more precisely, to the majority of States prevailing within them.

Over the years the GA and ECOSOC have undoubtedly promoted a great deal of co-operation among States in the social area, particularly with regard to human rights (see **Chapter 16**). However, in the field of economic co-operation the *huge hurdles to progress towards closing or at least narrowing the gap between developed and developing countries* have prevented any major breakthrough. The 1974 GA Declaration on the New International Economic Order and the Programme of Action relating thereto,[16] as well as the 1974 Charter on Economic Rights and Duties of States,[17] the 1986 Declaration on the Right to Development,[18] and the 1990 Declaration on International Economic Co-operation and the Revitalization of Economic Growth and Development of Developing Countries,[19] have proved a relative failure—among other things because the principles laid down there and supported by the overwhelming majority of developing countries, but opposed by some major industrialized States, were a far cry from real economic relations (see **Chapter 18**). A shift has occurred over the years: while in the 1970s industrialized countries were called upon to support developing countries in their efforts to further progress, recently the emphasis has been laid on the need for each country to be responsible for designing and implementing its own development policies.

Nevertheless, the UN has promoted economic co-operation in various fields, through some of its specialized agencies (FAO, WHO, the International Fund for Agricultural Development (IFAD)), or thorough such organs as the UN Conference on Trade and Development (UNCTAD) or the UN Development Programme (UNDP). UNDP has become very important as a means of co-ordinating various UN technical assistance activities. In 1970 the GA established a UNDP country-programme process, which was later strengthened and became the basic framework for co-ordinating assistance activities at the national level.[20] In addition, through one of its specialized agencies, the UN Industrial Development Organization (UNIDO),[21] it has promoted entrepreneurship and self-reliance, as well as cost-effective, ecology-sensitive industry in developing countries. Furthermore, it has promoted industrial co-operation and technology transfer. It also has served as a 'matchmaker' for North–South, South–South and East–West investment.

Within the general domain of economic and social co-operation, the UN activity that stands out for its importance and novelty is that concerning protection of the environment. As this topic will be discussed in **Chapter 17**, it may suffice here to recall that the UN has not only adopted three important Declarations (in 1972, 1982, and 1992), but also set up the United Nations Environment Programme (UNEP).[22] This body, together with the World Meteorological Organization (WMO), has been instrumental in highlighting the damage caused to the earth's ozone layer. In addition, UNEP has led major efforts to clean up pollution in the Mediterranean Sea as well as on beaches in a number of countries including Syria, Israel, Turkey, and Greece. Together with other specialized agencies such as the FAO the UN has also contributed to curbing global warming, preventing over-fishing, and limiting deforestation.

Finally, through the UN International Children's Fund (UNICEF), the UN has attempted to raise the general level of children's health and welfare in many developing countries. The UN has also provided an appropriate forum for negotiating the Convention on the Rights of the Child, the most widely ratified treaty ever, which entered into force in 1990.

In sum the UN, although it has greatly expanded, over the years, its range of action and tackled the most sensitive problems of our time, in the various social and economic fields with which it has dealt has been unable to go beyond *co-ordination and promotion*. This is only natural, since decision making in these matters still remains in the hands of *sovereign States*, and States are deeply divided by conflicting economic, political, and ideological interests. However, in the economic field the UN must be credited with promoting a shift from (a) government-to-government assistance to assistance by multilateral institutions and (b) from public investment to private investment as the engine of development (see however **Chapter 18**).

13.3.6 HUMAN RIGHTS

In the area of human rights as well the Charter was extremely cautious and tepid. In Article 55c it laid down that the Organization would 'promote' universal respect for human rights. In Article 13.1 it simply provided that the GA should 'initiate studies and make recommendations' for the purpose of 'assisting in the realization of human rights and fundamental freedoms for all without distinction as to race, sex, language, or religion'. Only 'studies and recommendations' were envisaged. However, ECOSOC could also prepare draft conventions and reports (Article 62).

In 1945 the international community still lacked an internationally agreed *list* of human rights to be respected by States and an internationally agreed *definition* of those rights. This is one of the reasons why it was still inconceivable that an international body could limit States' sovereignty by intruding in their internal affairs and making comments or recommendations on governments' internal structure or the relations between the State authorities and individuals. Therefore it was only natural for States to introduce Article 2.7 into the Charter. This clause, in providing for protection of States' 'domestic jurisdiction', objectively constituted a huge stumbling block to any incisive action by the UN in the field of human rights. It substantially barred the Organization from taking any step other than *general* recommendations (that is, recommendations addressed to all States), *general* studies or reports, and draft conventions. In other words, the Organization could not address matters relating to human rights in a specific country, for these were matters 'which are essentially within the domestic jurisdiction' of that State. Admittedly, in addition to envisaging tasks for the Organization, the Charter also laid down an obligation for States: through Article 56 all member States pledged themselves 'to take joint and separate action in co-operation with the Organization for the achievement of the purposes set forth in Article 55', including respect for human rights. This 'pledge' was however extremely vague.

In short, the Charter provisions concerning human rights only set forth a general programme of action. Detailed obligations and implementation mechanisms were not provided for. The Charter intended simply to proclaim human rights as a general goal both for States and for the Organization.

Over the years the UN has proved successful in promoting respect for human rights. In a matter of a few years the GA, by adopting in 1948 the Universal Declaration, was able to turn the few loose provisions of the Charter into a *decalogue of fundamental human rights and freedoms* (which, albeit without any legally binding force, possessed great moral authority). The next steps were the two Covenants of 1966 (see **16.4.2(b)**). They translated the provisions of the Declaration into binding legal rules. A string of treaties and Declarations followed (see **16.4.2(b)**). In addition to laying down obligations concerning respect for human rights, the Organization also set up a host of monitoring bodies.

One of the major achievements of the Organization was its remarkable contribution to putting an end to racist white supremacy in Southern Rhodesia (Zimbabwe) in 1980, and to bringing about the downfall of apartheid in South Africa in 1994.

The UN has also been instrumental in promoting the spread of democracy in the world. By providing electoral advice, assistance, and monitoring of electoral consultations, it has assisted (or, as in the case of Cambodia, enabled) people in a great many countries (including Namibia, El Salvador, Eritrea, Mozambique, Nicaragua, South Africa) to participate in free and fair elections.

The action of the UN in this area is impressive. Admittedly, many of the treaties concluded under the auspices of the Organization are still not universally binding. Furthermore, most monitoring mechanisms could be more effective and hard hitting. Nevertheless, for all its flaws, the whole array of instruments and mechanisms dealing with human rights at the universal level constitutes a great achievement. This becomes

apparent if one considers the action of the UN in this field against the general background of an international community consisting of sovereign States, each eager to
protect its own independence and autonomy against outside interference. The UN, by
strongly and unflinchingly promoting human rights, has introduced *a new ethos* in
the international community. It has gradually brought about a sort of Copernican
revolution: while previously the whole international system hinged on State sovereignty, at present individuals make up the linchpin of that community. To be sure,
States still play a crucial role in international dealings. However, now they are no
longer looked upon as perfect and self-centred entities. They are now viewed as
structures primarily geared to the furtherance of interests and concerns of individuals. Only a universal intergovernmental organization of the calibre of the UN
could have achieved this momentous result (for more details see **Chapter 16**).

13.3.7 DISARMAMENT

In the field of disarmament the Charter reached its lowest point. Article 11.1 simply
provided that the GA might 'consider general principles of co-operation . . . including
the principles governing disarmament and the regulation of armaments'. It added
that the GA could 'make recommendations with regard to such principles to the
Members or to the SC or to both'. Thus a matter indisputably of crucial importance
was relegated in the Charter to the back row. Probably the founding fathers felt that
the failure of all the provisions on this matter contained in the Covenant of the
League of Nations warranted a cautious approach and no great illusions. By and large
the framers of the Charter assumed that disarmament was a project to be negotiated
among a relatively few key States, but subject to principles agreed among the members
of the SC and the GA.

However, the GA took action to deal with the matter. Its first Commission (responsible for political and security matters) specialized in disarmament and from the
outset has discussed questions falling within this purview. In addition, in 1983 and
1988 the GA held a special session devoted to disarmament. It also set up the Committee on Disarmament, transformed in 1984 into the Conference on Disarmament.
Formally speaking the Conference is independent of the UN, although it uses UN staff
and annually reports to the GA, which can address recommendations to it. Furthermore, the GA established in 1984 (resolution 39/148H), as a subsidiary organ,
UNIDIR, a research institute on disarmament.

It is notable that a major disarmament treaty, namely the 1968 Treaty on the Non-
Proliferation of Nuclear Weapons, was negotiated following a GA resolution (1665-
XVI, of 5 December 1961) and within the UN Committee on Disarmament; it was
eventually adopted as resolution 2373-XXII of 12 June 1968. In addition, the Treaty is
subject to the verification procedures of an institution closely linked to the UN, the
International Atomic Energy Agency (IAEA). Furthermore, many treaties concluded
under the auspices of the UN include clauses on disarmament or denuclearization
(for instance: the 1959 Treaty on the Antarctic, Articles 1 and 5; the 1967 Treaty

on outer space, Article 4; the 1979 Treaty on the moon and other celestial bodies, Article 3).

Nevertheless, many other major treaties on disarmament have been negotiated and concluded *outside the UN*, or the Organization has played a relatively minor role in their negotiation. The reason is simple: the major nuclear Powers have felt that they had to reach agreement on crucial military matters on their own and outside a multilateral forum, where political and ideological pressure is likely to be put on them. Thus, the idea underlying the UN Charter, that States without serious armaments would have a voice through the GA, proved unworkable.

The treaties negotiated outside the UN include agreements on nuclear disarmament, agreements on arms control, and treaties on denuclearization.

Some have been directly negotiated by the two Great Powers: for instance, the Moscow Treaty of 5 August 1963 on nuclear testing in outer space, the treaty of 10 September 1996 on nuclear tests, the 1971 treaty banning the placing of nuclear weapons on the ocean floor, the 1972 treaty between the USSR and the USA on antiballistic missiles modified in 1974 (Salt I), followed by that of June 1979 (Salt II), the Washington treaty of 7 December 1987 on short-range missiles, the Start agreements I, of 31 July 1991 and II of 3 January 1993.

Other treaties have been negotiated within the Conference on Disarmament: for instance, the 1993 convention on chemical weapons, and the 1996 treaty for the complete ban on nuclear tests.

A number of treaties have been negotiated within regional frameworks: for instance, the 1967 treaty of Tlatelolco for the denuclearization of Latin America, the 1985 treaty of Rarotonga, denuclearizing the South Pacific, the 1995 treaty of Bangkok, for the denuclearization of South East Asia, and the 1996 treaty of Pelindaba, for the denuclearization of Africa.

Nonetheless, the UN, through the IAEA, has helped minimize the threat of nuclear war by inspecting nuclear reactors in at least 90 countries, to verify that nuclear materials were not diverted for military purposes.

13.3.8 CODIFICATION AND PROGRESSIVE DEVELOPMENT OF INTERNATIONAL LAW

Mention of international law was made in the Charter's preamble (where it was stated that one of the goals of the Organization was 'to establish conditions under which justice and respect for the obligations arising from treaties and other sources of international law can be maintained'). Article 1.1 provided that disputes should be 'settled peacefully in conformity with the principles of justice and international law'. Only Article 13.1(*a*) envisaged action on the matter: the GA was entrusted with making studies and recommendations for the purpose of 'encouraging the progressive development of international law and its codification'. Clearly, international law was not considered as one of the pillars for the construction of a new 'world order'. However, the need was felt to promote its updating and elaboration.

This is no doubt an area where the UN has gone beyond any expectation. It has fostered international law in a number of ways, some more traditional, others distinctly novel.

First, various UN bodies, in particular the GA, have succeeded in adopting draft conventions on major issues such as genocide, human rights, protection of women, rights of children, etc. These conventions, patiently worked out within UN bodies, chiefly the GA, have subsequently been ratified by a large number of States.

Second, the International Law Commission (ILC), a body consisting of experts in international law and diplomacy, has elaborated some important draft treaties codifying and progressively developing crucial areas of traditional international law (for example diplomatic immunities, consular immunities, the law of treaties, the law of the treaties between States and international organizations, State succession). These draft treaties, after receiving the approval of the GA, have been submitted to a Diplomatic Conference. The resulting legal texts have subsequently been ratified by a large number of States; in addition they have exercised considerable influence even outside the group of contracting parties.

Third, there are areas where the conflict between the political or economic interests of the various groups of States is staggering: for instance, regulation of international economic relations, protection of the environment, enunciation of the general principles that should govern international relations. In these areas, where it proved impossible to work out treaties, either directly by the GA or through the ILC, the GA has had recourse to creative legal thinking. It has promoted the elaboration of declarations or general resolutions. These texts, albeit devoid of any legally binding force, have the advantage of (1) laying down the major areas where most States may have reached some sort of understanding or agreement; (2) setting forth the major goals as well as the consequent policies that States ought to pursue in those areas; (3) establishing a sort of blueprint for international and national action; (4) laying the groundwork for the future development, at least on some of the issues envisaged; (5) gradually generating the possible crystallization of general binding rules or principles on some of the issues.

As examples of these declarations, one may recall the 1948 Universal Declaration on Human Rights (which had an important follow-up in the two 1966 Covenants and the numerous subsequent treaties), the 1960 Declaration on the granting of independence to colonial countries and peoples, the 1962 Declaration on permanent sovereignty over natural resources, the 1963 Declaration on principles governing activities in outer space, the 1970 Declaration on principles governing the seabed and ocean bed beyond national jurisdiction, the 1970 Declaration on Friendly Relations, the 1974 (ill-fated) Declaration on a New International Economic Order, the 1974 Declaration on the Definition of Aggression, as well as the various declarations on the environment (1972, 1982, and 1992; see *infra*, Chapter 17).

Fourth, various other UN bodies have greatly contributed to international law. Of course the principal merits in this area go to the ICJ, which through its judgments and advisory opinions has fleshed out many international rules or provided authoritative interpretations or elaborated on their contents and scope. However, also such political organs as the SC or the GA have provided in their resolutions, recommendations, or decisions a number of pronouncements on legal issues, that significantly clarify or develop some areas of international law.

Suffice it to mention a few examples: (1) in 1970, by laying down in the 1970 Declaration on Friendly Relations that colonial peoples may fight with all necessary means against colonial Powers forcibly depriving them of their freedom and independence, the GA contemplated a right to use force in international relations that was not envisaged in the UN Charter;[23] (2) in 1990 and 1991 the SC adopted resolutions 662 (1990) and 687 (1991) declaring among other things the annexation of Kuwait by Iraq to be null and void; (3) in 1991 the SC, by resolution 687 of 3 April 1991, adopted a decision regarding the delimitation of the frontier between Iraq and Kuwait, subsequently demarcated by the Secretary-General (S/22558); (4) again in 1991 the SC took the unprecedented step of establishing, by resolution 692 of 20 May 1991, the UN Compensation Commission charged with managing a fund for paying compensation for war damage caused by the unlawful Iraqi invasion and occupation of Kuwait; (5) the SC, by establishing in 1993 and 1994 the two International Criminal Tribunals (one for the former Yugoslavia, the other for Rwanda), imaginatively interpreted and applied Chapter VII, in particular Article 41 of the UN Charter (on measures not involving the use of force, that may be taken to counter a threat to the peace), as the ICTY stated in *Tadić* (*Interlocutory Appeal*).[24]

13.4 THE CURRENT ROLE OF THE UN

It is apparent from the above survey that since it came into existence the UN has often failed in three areas: (a) maintenance of peace and security, (b) disarmament, and (c) bridging the gap between industrialized and developing countries.

However, it would be disingenuous to apportion the blame to the UN itself. True, no one should gloss over the indisputable flaws of the Organization: bureaucratization; frequent mismanagement; overemphasis on discussing *ad infinitum* controversial matters, and passing hundreds of resolutions, as if verbal struggles and the consequent production of more written texts were by themselves to lead to changes in the political, diplomatic, and economic realm. However, for all its deficiencies and in spite of the lack of vision of some of its Secretaries-General, the primary failings of the UN must be traced back to the States behind it, chiefly the Great Powers. One should always bear in mind a few well-known, but true facts.

The Organization is based on a paradigm (the 'Kantian model', hinging on cooperation and the promotion of common, metanational values) that is profoundly dissimilar to that prevailing in the world community at large (the 'Grotian paradigm', typical of an anarchical society consisting of self-centred actors, each pursuing its short-term interests and scarcely concerned about community values). Indeed, although the two 'communities' almost coincide as far as their members are concerned, their structure and functioning is radically different (this is why it still seems questionable to speak of the UN Charter as the 'constitution' of the world community). As a result of the substantial chasm between the two models, the Organization must strive hard to rally all or most members States behind some general principles, in order to orient and channel their actions in a way conducive to the promotion of those common values and goals. In addition, the Organization, as such, lacks any real economic, political, or military power of its own. It must perforce rely on the support of member States, chiefly the Great Powers. However, only as long as the Great Powers consider that their general agendas can be reconciled with those of the Organization, are they prepared to lend it their support.

Furthermore, the structure of the Organization is in substance still that established in 1945 at San Francisco (except for some organs, such as the Trusteeship Council, which have lost their *raison d'être* in light of historical changes). The world, however, has changed radically. A more efficient apparatus would be needed, together with a SC representing not only the victors of the Second World War but the present constellation of economic and military power in the world. However, the two-thirds majority (including all the Permanent Members of the SC) required by Article 108 for amending the Charter makes it exceedingly difficult to introduce any major change.

Also, the position of the USA towards the Organization does not leave much room for improvement. The US policy, as set out in the 'Presidential directive no. 25' of 5 May 1994, makes it clear that the USA is prepared to participate in peace-keeping or peace-enforcement operations only to the extent that this participation is warranted by national US interest (and so long as the operations pursue clear objectives and are being sufficiently financed and of limited duration). According to the US State Department 'neither the US nor the international community have the mandate, nor the resources, nor the possibility of resolving every conflict of this kind'.[25] As rightly noted by Bertrand,[26] this statement is in fact a death sentence for collective security. In addition, the reform of the UN advocated by the USA is of limited scope: that State essentially insists on better management, on the enlargement of the SC to Germany and Japan (primarily to get these two States more involved in financing peace-keeping operations), and closer association of the UN with regional organizations or other organizations such as NATO, when it comes to peace enforcement.

Finally, no one could deny that in the world community there are a number of political problems that are objectively intractable on account of deep-rooted tensions and conflicting ethnic, political, and ideological claims. Conspicuous illustrations are Kashmir, Cyprus, the Middle East. There, not only UN diplomacy but also the diplomatic efforts undertaken by some Great Powers, chiefly the USA, have not led to any major breakthrough. It would be ungenerous to lay the blame at the door of the Organization for its failing to settle those situations and instead freezing them through its peace-keeping operations. Sometimes management of problems in a scarcely satisfactory manner and even delaying an appropriate solution may prove to be a better option than either outright neglect or handling of those issues by individual States or by groups of States substituting themselves for the UN.

It should be added, on the other hand, that over the years the UN has proved indispensable and indisputably successful in a great many areas.

Membership in the Organization has by now become a *test of legitimation* for any State. No new State can claim to be a legitimate and fully fledged member of the international community if it has not gained admission to the UN. The only conspicuous exception is Switzerland, whose motivations are unique and which in any case is gradually moving towards membership (and meanwhile enjoys the status of observer in the UN).

In addition, as everybody knows, the UN constitutes an *indispensable forum* where States may get together and engage in multilateral diplomacy, with a view to achieving political or legal agreement. The lack of such a world forum would render international dealings even more difficult.

Furthermore, what the UN has done in the fields of *decolonization, human rights, protection of the environment, development of international law,* and furthering *a set of new community values* (such as the principles of *jus cogens*) constitutes a great legacy. If the international community is so starkly different from that existing before the Second World War, this is primarily due to the UN.

Another major achievement of the UN has been to gradually get *non-State actors,* chiefly non-governmental organizations, but also some national liberation movements, involved in the international diplomatic process. In Article 71 the UN Charter only referred to non-governmental organizations ('The Economic and Social Council may make suitable arrangements for consultation with non-governmental organizations which are concerned with matters within its competence'). Since 1945 the UN has gradually integrated those organizations into its action and, by so doing, has greatly stimulated their birth and action. This is an exceedingly significant development: it shows that at the inter-State level an attempt has been made, with success, to integrate actors other than States into international dealings, to listen to their voices, to pay attention to their demands, to uphold their concerns as much as possible. Later on the same has occurred with regard to national liberation movements, which have been granted observer status in some UN bodies, and thus enabled to voice their claims (see **4.4**).

Finally, one should not underestimate the increasing tendency of the UN to link up with *regional organizations* (the OAS, the OAU, the Arab League, the EU, the Council of Europe, etc.) and even organizations that geographically speaking are not regional (for example, NATO and the OSCE), to promote and enhance their role in areas envisaged in Articles 52–4 of the UN Charter, that is in peaceful settlement of disputes and enforcement of peace and security. At present the UN is endeavouring to work in much closer partnership with those organizations. Indeed, in recent times some seminal ideas deeply rooted in Churchill's international vision of the 1940s and early 1950s, in particular the idea of the possible crucial role of regional organizations in the international community, are proving more and more fecund. It is highly probable that the international community will increasingly direct itself towards combined action of the universal Organization with regional bodies. Cross-fertilization, mutual assistance, and a wise *division of labour* may in the end prove instrumental in somewhat narrowing—to the extent that this is feasible—the present fissures of the world community.

14

COLLECTIVE SECURITY AND THE PROHIBITION OF FORCE

14.1 MAINTENANCE OF PEACE AND SECURITY BY CENTRAL ORGANS OR WITH THEIR AUTHORIZATION

Although the collective security system envisaged in the UN Charter (see **Chapter 13**) was never established, over the years the UN managed to achieve some significant results through collective measures that, albeit not expressly provided for in the Charter, have been increasingly accepted by the international community as legitimate enforcement or peacekeeping procedures.

14.1.1 RESORT TO FORCE BY STATES

On a few occasions *the SC authorized States to use force* against another State that had threatened peace or committed a breach of the peace or had engaged in aggression. This alternative road to the restoration of peace was taken in 1950. That year, taking advantage of the absence of the Soviet delegate (who did not attend SC meetings in protest over the failure of the UN to allow China to be represented in the UN by the People's Republic of China rather than nationalist China), the SC authorized member States, acting under US command, to assist South Korea to rebuff by force the aggression of North Korea and allowed them to use the UN flag in the course of military operations (resolutions 82, 83 and 84/1950). Similarly, in 1990 the SC authorized member States to use all necessary means—that is, to use force on large scale—to repel the Iraqi aggression against Kuwait (resolution 678/1990).

Being unable directly to take military measures, the SC also authorized member States to use force for several other different purposes. For instance, it adopted a host of authorizations to enforce economic measures previously decided upon.

Back in 1966 the SC called upon the UK to halt, 'by the use of force if necessary', ships carrying oil destined for Southern Rhodesia in flagrant breach of the embargo imposed by the SC against that country (resolution 221/1966; there ensued the incident of the Greek ship *Manuela*).[1]

Since then, particularly after the end of the cold war, the SC has often recommended States to undertake a limited use of force to secure compliance with economic sanctions previously adopted. Thus, for instance, by resolution 665 of 25 August 1990, the SC invited member States to inspect and verify the cargo and destination of every ship crossing the Gulf in order to ensure that they were not violating embargo measures imposed on Iraq. The SC also requested States to halt all inward and outward maritime shipping to ensure strict implementation of economic measures decided upon against the Federal Republic of Yugoslavia (resolutions 787/ 1992 and 820/1993), Somalia (resolution 794/1992), Haiti (resolutions 875/1993 and 917/1994), Liberia (resolution 1083/1997), and Sierra Leone (resolution 1132/1997). By the same token, the SC authorized NATO air strikes against Serb forces in Bosnia and Herzegovina.

Furthermore, *the SC gradually established a direct link between humanitarian crises and threats to the peace*, one of the three possible conditions that could trigger SC action under Chapter VII. It thus considerably enlarged the concept of threat to the peace laid down in Article 39 of the UN Charter, so as to include humanitarian crises within one State, which once were deemed to fall primarily within domestic jurisdiction. It subsequently authorized member States to use force to establish a secure environment for humanitarian relief operations.

Efforts were made to protect safe havens in Bosnia and Herzegovina on the basis of resolutions 836 and 844 (1993) authorizing member States, through the use of air power, to deter attacks against the safe areas. Operation *Restore Hope* in Somalia and Operation *Turquoise* in Rwanda were launched, respectively, on the basis of resolutions 794 and 929 (1992 and 1994). They consisted of large-scale military operations conducted by two 'coalitions of the willing'—led respectively by the USA and France—in order to achieve humanitarian objectives such as providing security and support for the distribution of relief supplies or ensuring the protection of displaced persons, refugees, and civilians at risk.

However, this practice of establishing a direct link between humanitarian crises and threats to the peace, that is, elevating those crises to threats to the peace, is not without its dangers. The SC is eager to retain discretionary power in this matter and tends to avoid explaining the nature of the link and the reasons for its action. As a result its practice lacks consistency and turns out to be selective. (For instance, African countries have assailed the fact that some humanitarian disasters in Africa, such as that in Sierra Leone, have not motivated the SC so strongly as some previous crises, such as that in Somalia.)

Through the enlargement of the notion of 'threat to the peace' the SC also authorized member States, acting nationally or through regional organizations or arrangements, to use force with a view to restoring democracy or public order. By resolution 940 (1994) the SC, after condemning the behaviour of the illegal de facto regime set up in Haiti, authorized member States to establish an international force and to use all necessary means to facilitate the departure of the military leaders and allow the return of the legitimately elected President, Jean-Bertrand Aristide.

More recently, following a request by Albania for SC action, the SC authorized member States to intervene there (resolution 1101/1997). The SC also authorized intervention in East Timor (resolution1264/1999) to prevent internal disorders from degenerating in combat situations.

The 'authorizations regime' reveals the gap between the original plan envisaged in Chapter VII and its implementation. The Council bears the overall political responsibility for authorized operations, but member States retain command and control over their armed forces with the sole obligation to report to the Council on a regular basis.

Notwithstanding its flaws, the 'authorizations system' has gradually become standing practice and it is widely recognized as consistent with Chapter VII of the Charter.[2]

14.1.2 MAINTENANCE OR RESTORATION OF PEACE BY REGIONAL OR OTHER ORGANIZATIONS

On a number of occasions the SC implicitly authorized regional or other organizations or arrangements to use force.[3] Thus, for instance, in the case of the former Yugoslavia, the SC authorized both maritime operations—to enforce the embargo—and air operations—to back up the peacekeeping force (UNPROFOR) protecting safe areas—obviously referring to a possible implementation through the Western European Union (WEU) and NATO. After the end of the war in 1995 it authorized (by resolution 1031/1995, followed by resolution 1088/1996) NATO to establish a multinational force in Bosnia-Herzegovina (IFOR, subsequently named SFOR) mandated to ensure—if necessary by the use of force—the implementation of the Dayton Agreement. Likewise, by resolution 1244 of 10 June 1999 adopted after the end of the war, the SC authorized NATO ('Member States and relevant international organizations'; NATO was mentioned in Annex 2) to deploy an international security presence in Kosovo to create and maintain an appropriate environment for the transitional administration of the region by the UN.

In 1999 the Kosovo crisis put this consolidated system at great risk. Given the massive gross violations of human rights perpetrated against the Kosovar population, NATO decided to attack the Federal Republic of Yugoslavia (Serbia and Montenegro), acting without any SC authorization. NATO's action is widely considered to amount to a gross breach of the UN Charter. (In addition, while conducting their military operations NATO armed forces breached on a few occasions important rules of international humanitarian law.) However, some commentators have contended that the SC, through resolution 1244/1999, endorsed NATO's action *ex post facto*, albeit taking a cautious approach.

At the present stage it is too early to determine whether there will emerge a customary rule legitimizing forcible intervention for humanitarian purposes without the need for a formal SC authorization.

14.1.3 MAINTENANCE OR RESTORATION OF PEACE UPON AUTHORIZATION OF THE GA

As early as 1950, in the face of Soviet opposition, the majority, dominated by the USA, contrived to *enhance the role of the GA* by the famous resolution 'Uniting for Peace' (377-V, adopted on 3 November 1950). The GA was empowered to recommend member States to adopt forcible measures against a State held responsible by the Organization for a breach of the ban on the threat or use of force. The resolution was adopted and the relevant new system was put into effect during the Korean War, 1950–1 (after the Soviet delegate came back to his seat within the SC and used his veto to paralyse that body). However, it did not provide a realistic alternative mainly because, following the wave of decolonizations in the 1960s, the majority within the GA was no longer favourable to the Western Powers who promoted the GA empowerment. Other solutions had to be put in place.

14.2 PEACEKEEPING OPERATIONS

As early as 1956 the temporary convergence between the two Superpowers led to the elaboration of a new and imaginative scheme: the use of '*peacekeeping' forces* (mostly known, on account of their headgear, as the UN Blue Helmets). The Suez crisis triggered the 'Uniting for Peace' mechanism (this time to circumvent British and French vetoes), but the mechanism was applied only in part. The GA entrusted the Secretary-General with the creation of UNEF (United Nations Emergency Force), a military force mandated to secure the cessation of hostilities and the withdrawal of British, French, and Israeli forces from the Egyptian territory, and—after the withdrawal—to serve as a buffer force between the Egyptian and Israeli armies.

UNEF provided the model for *traditional* peacekeeping operations, which show the following distinguishing traits. (1) They are composed of military personnel put at the disposal of the UN by member States and deployed in a troubled area with the *consent* of the territorial State. (2) They are generally under the exclusive authority of the SC (but can occasionally be under the authority of the GA, as happened with the creation of UNEF). The SC therefore bears responsibility for their overall political direction. In addition, their executive direction and command is entrusted to the UN Secretary-General, while command on the ground is given to the Chief of mission. (3) They have no power of military coercion, but can resort to arms only in self-defence (see, however, *infra*). (4) They are always requested to act in a neutral and impartial way. (5) They are financed through the regular budget of the Organization. The expenditures for peacekeeping forces relate to the maintenance of international peace and security; therefore they are obligatorily allotted by the GA under Article 17.2, as was confirmed by the ICJ in its Advisory Opinion on *Certain Expenses of the UN.*[4] Given the high costs of peacekeeping operations, the GA has occasionally established

Special Funds inviting voluntary contributions from member States to cover expenses.

Since 1956 the UN has established a large number of peacekeeping operations in different areas of the world. Classical peacekeeping operations, created on the basis of the UNEF model, have the main function of separating the contending parties, forestalling armed hostilities between them, and maintaining order in a given area. However, over the years they have come to perform a variety of tasks. Their number and complexity have greatly expanded since the end of the confrontation between Western and Eastern blocs: whereas 15 operations were set up before 1988, around forty operations have been established after that date.

Most of early and recent peacekeeping operations present the characteristics outlined above, but there have also been notable exceptions, especially related to the abandonment of the principle providing for the use of force only in self-defence. The United Nations Operation in Congo (ONUC) represents the first remarkable exception: the SC authorized ONUC to use force 'if necessary, in the last resort' to prevent 'the occurrence of civil war in the Congo' (resolution 161/1961) and later on to arrest and bring to detention foreign military and paramilitary personnel and mercenaries (Resolution 169/1961). More recently, the SC radically transformed the nature of the peacekeeping operation in Somalia (which thus was transformed from UNOSOM I into UNOSOM II), endowing it with enforcement powers under Chapter VII of the Charter (resolution 814/1993). Through resolution 836 adopted in June 1993, it also authorized UNPROFOR (the peacekeeping operation deployed in the territory of Bosnia and Herzegovina), 'acting in self-defence, to take the necessary measures, including the use of force, to reply to bombardments against the safe areas by any of the parties'. In all three cases UN forces were deployed where there was actually no peace to keep—that is, in situations of ongoing conflicts within States—and where a partial or total breakdown of governmental authorities had taken place. This trend of entrusting peacekeeping forces with enforcement functions has however been strongly criticized and did not develop to the point of creating a special category of UN peace-enforcement units, as the Secretary-General, Boutros Ghali, envisaged in his Agenda for Peace in 1992.[5]

In recent years the vast majority of UN forces have responded to intra-State conflicts or have intervened in internal disorder or immediate post-conflict situations. Several forces were established as a result of comprehensive peace agreements which, among other provisions, asked the UN to supervise the respecting and implementation of them (UNAVEM I, II, and III in Angola; ONUMOZ in Mozambique; UNAMIR in Rwanda; ONUSAL in El Salvador; UNTAC in Cambodia). Accordingly, the UN forces have included a large civilian component engaged in providing humanitarian assistance, furthering national reconciliation and promoting respect for human rights and fundamental freedoms, organizing and monitoring elections, and occasionally also assisting in rebuilding institutions and national capacities.

Very recently, two operations have been entrusted with the task of administering a region for a transitional period. The UN Mission in Kosovo (UNMIK) was created by resolution 1244/1999 to perform, *inter alia*, basic civilian administrative functions where and as long as required, organizing and overseeing the development of provisional institutions for democratic and autonomous self-government pending a political settlement, including the holding of elections; supporting, in co-ordination with international humanitarian organizations, humanitarian and disaster relief aid; maintaining civil law and order, including establishing local police forces and meanwhile, through the deployment of international police personnel to serve in Kosovo, protecting and promoting human rights and assuring the safe and unimpeded return of all refugees and displaced persons to their homes in Kosovo.

Similarly, the UN Transitional Authority in East Timor (resolution 1272/1999), established after the riots following the referendum granting the people independence from Indonesia, was assigned the following tasks: to provide security and maintain law and order throughout the territory of East Timor; to establish an effective administration; to assist in the development of civil and social services; to ensure the co-ordination and delivery of humanitarian assistance, rehabilitation, and development assistance; to support capacity-building for self-government; to assist in the establishment of conditions for sustainable development. The precedent for this kind of operation was set in 1962 when the GA established—upon the request of Indonesia and the Netherlands—a temporary executive authority (UNTEA) to administer the territory of West New Guinea pending its transfer to Indonesia (where it now forms the province of Irian Jaya).

Most complex situations have occasionally affected two other critical features of traditional peacekeeping operations: *consent of the territorial State* and *impartiality*. In some cases peacekeeping operations proceeded on the basis of a partial consent, in that they lacked the consent of one or more of the parties involved. As a consequence, impartiality as well was jeopardized. Nonetheless, the UN has always referred, and still does, to these features as the distinguishing traits of peacekeeping operations.

The 'peacekeeping' system—like the 'authorizations regime'—is at odds with that envisaged in Chapter VII of the UN Charter. Nevertheless, it has become one of the most important UN tools—often the only available one—and at present is universally recognized as consistent with the Charter.

On balance, peacekeeping operations have proved useful principally for the purpose of making the contending parties stop fighting, thereby avoiding more bloodshed. They have also turned out to be very helpful in assisting in the fulfilment of complex peace processes where the parties were willing to co-operate and build for the future. They are not actually designed to compel the parties to accept a solution imposed by the UN, but serve to help put into practice, on the spot, the solution agreed upon by the contending States. However, in the long run, peacekeeping operations may turn out to be counter-productive, for they freeze the situation without providing a real solution to the basic problems lying at the root of the conflict

This happened with UNFICYP in Cyprus and UNMOGIP in the Kashmir region. In contrast, it would seem that UNIFIL in Lebanon made the Israeli withdrawal from Lebanon in May–June 2000 possible and less dangerous; it also stabilized the situation in South Lebanon, where the Lebanese army, probably on advice from Damascus, still seems reluctant to deploy.

14.3 COLLECTIVE MEASURES NOT INVOLVING THE USE OF FORCE

'Sanctions' not involving the use of force are envisaged in the Charter (Article 41) and are not necessarily intended as a substitute for military action. It is however a fact that the relative failure of the UN collective system, and even of the imaginative substitutes subsequently set up, of necessity, led to *magnification* of the role and importance of these 'sanctions'. They too have been resorted to, both to respond to serious violations of international law amounting to a threat or a breach of peace, and to react to situations which, although not constituting a violation of international law, imperiled peace and security.

Often resort to these so-called sanctions is inversely proportionate to their coerciveness; in other words, the less coercive they are, the more frequently and effectively they are used. The reason is simple: States and international institutions cannot do without 'sanctions'. In the face of dissent in the SC and the consequent paralysis of collective enforcement machinery, the solution lies in relatively mild forms of pressure or exposure. They at least serve to express collective condemnation of misbehaviour by States. However, the effectiveness of these 'sanctions' depends first and foremost on the level of support they actually enjoy (they may not be implemented without active support by UN member States) and, second, on the quality of targeting (thus, arguably those against Libya succeeded because they were well targeted, consisting of a ban on flights and an embargo on arms).

14.3.1 ECONOMIC AND OTHER 'SANCTIONS'

In a few cases the SC has *decided* that member States should take certain *economic* or *commercial* measures against a delinquent State.

Cases in point are Southern Rhodesia (1966–79) and South Africa (1977–94), when the SC explicitly acted under Article 41 of the Charter, imposing an embargo on the import and export of certain goods, in the former case, and an embargo on the import of arms and other military *matériel*, in the latter. Subsequently the SC imposed economic sanctions or military embargoes against Iraq (by resolution 661 of 6 August 1990), Somalia (resolution 733 of 23 January 1992), Libya (by resolution 748 of 31 March 1992; the economic and other sanctions were repealed by resolution 1192 of 27 August 1998, after Libya handed over to the Dutch authorities the two Libyans accused of the terrorist attack on an American and French civil aircraft), the former Yugoslavia (by resolution 757 of 30 May 1992, followed by many resolutions against the FRY in 1993–9), Liberia (by resolution 788 of 19 November 1992), Haiti (by resolution 841 of 16 June 1993, followed by other resolutions in 1994), against a rebellious group in Angola, UNITA (by resolution 864 of 15 September 1993, followed by many other resolutions until 1998), against Sierra Leone (by resolution 1132 of 8 October 1997, followed by other resolutions in 1998), against the Taleban factions in Afghanistan (by resolution 1267 of 15 October 1999).

In other instances either the SC or the GA has *recommended* the adoption of measures such as the *breaking off of diplomatic relations*: for example, against South Africa (since 1962 on account of apartheid and later on also because of its illegal occupation of Namibia) and Portugal (between 1963 and 1975 because of its colonial policy).

Unfortunately, many of these decisions or recommendations have gone unheeded, owing to the lack of unanimous and substantial support by the whole international community (often the target State was aided by one or more Powers, which inevitably undermined UN condemnations).

14.3.2 NON-RECOGNITION OF ILLEGAL SITUATIONS

On several occasions, faced with unlawful behaviour of States it was not in a position to terminate, or against which it proved unable to recommend or enjoin effective sanctions, the UN has fallen back on non-recognition of the illegal situation.

This doctrine was first enunciated in early 1932. After the Japanese invasion of the Chinese province of Manchuria, H. L. Stimson, the US Secretary of State, declared that his Government 'cannot admit the legality of any situation de facto nor does it intend to recognize any treaty or agreement entered into between these Governments or agents thereof which may impair the treaty rights of the United States . . . and . . . it does not intend to recognize any situation, treaty or agreement which may be brought about by means contrary to the covenants and obligations of the Treaty of Paris of August 27, 1928'.[6]

The Special Assembly of the League of Nations adopted on 11 March 1932 a resolution along the same lines. In 1938 the Conference of American States passed at Lima a resolution on the non-recognition of acquisition of territory by force.

So far the SC and the GA have resorted to this class of sanctions with respect to a number of States: Israel, South Africa, Southern Rhodesia, Cyprus, and, in 1990, Iraq (by resolution 662 of 9 August 1990, the SC stated that the annexation of Kuwait by Iraq was null and void).

What is the import of UN pronouncements on non-recognition? Politically they rest on the idea that all actions contrary to certain basic values commonly accepted by the world community amount to deviations that should not be legitimized. Their aim is to isolate the delinquent State and compel it to change the situation that has been condemned. They constitute a last-resort measure in those cases where the UN has proved unable to bring about a return to legality by resorting to the sanctions provided for in the Charter: since the international organized community cannot nullify power, it must confine itself to emphatically withholding its endorsement.

Legally speaking these UN pronouncements entail a mutual undertaking on the part of the supporting States. States pledge themselves to avoid any international or internal act capable of turning the de facto situation into an internationally legal one. It follows that domestic courts of all those States must treat acts and transactions with the unlawful authority as null and void; on an international level, no act should be performed that might result in legalizing the situation in any way. The ensuing state of affairs is likely to be very complex: although many customary rules of international law have in fact been modified to take account of the universal principles which have recently emerged (see **Chapter 5**), those States which do not vote in favour of the UN resolutions cannot be forced to take the view that the effective situation is contrary to international law. Invoking the principle of effectiveness (see **1.7**) they can claim that they are entitled to consider that situation lawful and act accordingly. By contrast, the States who support the UN resolutions are authorized to regard the effective situation as unlawful, and to behave accordingly. Here, as in many other instances, one is confronted with a split in the attitude of the world community. Current international law makes allowance for this rift: although it does not render both tendencies legally warranted, it affords no means of making the majority view prevail.

14.3.3 CONDEMNATION BY THE SC

On a number of occasions *the SC has condemned serious violations of Article 2.4*, by defining them as acts of aggression. For instance, this happened in 1985, when the SC by resolution 573 condemned the Israeli attack on the PLO headquarters in Tunisia.

On other occasions the SC has simply condemned the use of force, without labelling it as aggression: see, for example, resolution 1177 of 26 June 1998, and resolution 1227 of 10 February 1999, by which the SC condemned the war between Ethiopia and Eritrea.

14.3.4 PUBLIC EXPOSURE, BY THE GA, OF GROSS VIOLATIONS

The failure of the UN to come to grips with the tremendous problems posed by forcible implementation of international law has impelled it to fall back on yet another 'sanction': public exposure of gross violations. This sanction normally consists in the adoption by the GA of resolutions condemning the unlawful conduct of States and in calls for the discontinuation of the deviant behaviour. So far the GA has passed resolutions of this class on several occasions, chiefly when member States have violated human rights or when they have disregarded basic principles of the Organization (as in the case of South Africa and Israel).

The fact that mere resort to exposure is seen as a sanction need not surprise us. Time and again States themselves have admitted the importance that public exposure can have as a means of exercising leverage on States. Thus, for instance, in 1975 the Greek representative said in the GA: 'Only intervention by various international and national organizations or protests of foreign Governments which truly respected the principles of freedom and democracy could exert an influence on dictators and guarantee some protection to political prisoners under totalitarian regimes.'[7] In the same vein, the UK delegate pointed out that 'if it was accepted that exposure was the most potent weapon available for combating torture, then the responsibility of the UN was very great indeed and there was cause to be grateful for the response to the GA's resolution [on torture, passed in 1975]'.[8]

Of course, one should not expect too much from this category of 'sanction', for more often than not the State concerned turns a deaf ear to international organizations. However, the beneficial effects of public condemnation can be appraised in the long term. It appears that States increasingly endeavour to avoid public strictures. In particular, they try to avoid being the target of repeated moral chastisements.

14.3.5 THE ESTABLISHMENT OF INTERNATIONAL CRIMINAL TRIBUNALS

On two occasions the SC, acting under Chapter VII, has *set up international criminal tribunals* designed to prosecute and punish the authors of atrocities perpetrated during armed conflict. It first established the International Criminal Tribunal for the Former Yugoslavia (ICTY, 1993) and one year later the International Criminal Tribunal for Rwanda (ICTR, 1994). They can be classified as measures not involving the use of force provided under Article 41 of the Charter, as was also affirmed by the ICTY Appeals Chamber in the *Tadić* (*Interlocutory Appeal*) case.

14.4 EXCEPTIONALLY PERMITTED RESORT TO FORCE BY STATES

14.4.1 SELF-DEFENCE

(a) General

Since aggression by another State constitutes a violation of the sovereign rights of the victim, in resorting to self-defence the latter engages in legal enforcement. This implies that self-defence must limit itself to rejecting the armed attack; it must not go beyond this purpose. As the ICJ stated in *Nicaragua*, self-defence only warrants 'measures which are proportional to the armed attack and necessary to respond to it'.[9] Consequently, (1) the victim of aggression must not occupy the aggressor State's territory, unless this is strictly required by the need to hold the aggressor in check and prevent him from continuing the aggression by other means. Furthermore, (2) self-defence must come to an end as soon as the SC steps in and takes over the task of putting an end to the aggression; however, this does not imply that self-defence must stop as soon as the SC has simply passed on the matter; it would rather seem that self-defence may continue until the SC has taken *effective* action rendering armed force by the victim State unnecessary and inappropriate, hence no longer legally warranted. If the SC fails to take action, (3) self-defence must cease as soon as its purpose, that is, to repel the armed attack, has been achieved. In other words, Article 51 and the corresponding norm of general international law do not authorize or condone any military action overstepping mere rejection of aggression. In particular, they prohibit prolonged military occupation and annexation of territory belonging to the aggressor.

As stated above, the failure of the UN collective system for enforcing peace resulted, among other things, in an expansion of resort to self-defence; in other words, it led to the invocation by States of Article 51 in cases which hardly amounted to self-defence or even in cases that were clearly not covered by the provision at issue.

Instances where Article 51 was invoked are: the USSR intervention in Hungary in 1956; the US intervention in the Dominican Republic in 1965; US participation in the Vietnam war in 1966; and intervention in Suez in 1967; the Israeli attack on Egypt in 1967; resort to force by the USA in the *Mayaguez* incident in 1975; the USSR intervention in Afghanistan in 1979; Israel's use of unilateral force in Uganda in 1976 (Entebbe airport), in Iraq in 1981 (Osiraq nuclear power station), and against Lebanon a number of times since 1978; the numerous attacks by South Africa on neighbouring States (Angola, Zambia) between 1976 and 1979 allegedly to stop terrorism from abroad; the military action of the UK against Argentina after the latter's invasion of the Falklands/Malvinas in 1982; the US intervention in Grenada in 1983, in Libya in 1986, and in Panama in 1989.

In practice States, particularly Great Powers, have tended to abuse this right. In addition to some cases mentioned below, under various headings, mention may be made of some instances where the USA has invoked Article 51 to warrant military actions that, in fact, had strong *punitive* connotations and also pursued a primarily *deterrent* purpose.

Thus, one may mention the US attack on Libya carried out on 14 April 1986. This attack, which caused the death of 37 persons, almost all civilians, was made in response to the bombing, in West Berlin, on 5 April, of a disco, allegedly carried out by Libyans. The USA justified their bombing as follows: 'Over a considerable period of time Libya has openly targeted American citizens and US installations. The most recent instance was in West Berlin on 5 April, where Libya was directly responsible for a bombing which resulted in the death of one US soldier and injury to a large number of American servicemen and other persons.'[10]

The USA also launched a number of missiles, on 26 June 1993, against Baghdad, allegedly in response to a planned terrorist attack on the former US President, Bush, which was due to have occurred two months earlier (on 14 April 1993), on a visit by Bush to Kuwait, an attack that was not carried out. In the UN SC the US delegate justified the American attack as follows:

'From all the evidence available to our intelligence community, we are . . . highly confident that the Iraqi Government, at its highest levels, directed its intelligence services to carry out an assassination attempt against President Bush . . . [T]his was a direct attack on the US, an attack that required a direct US response. Consequently President Clinton yesterday instructed the US Armed Forces to carry out a military operation against the headquarters of the Iraqi Intelligence Service in Baghdad. We responded directly, as we are entitled to do under Article 51 of the UN Charter, which provides for the exercise of self-defence in such cases. Our response has been proportionate and aimed at a target directly linked to the operation against President Bush. It was designed to damage the terrorist infrastructure of the Iraqi regime, reduce its ability to promote terrorism and deter acts of aggression against the US.'[11]

Similarly, on 20 August 1998, US submarines fired missiles against a military training camp in Afghanistan and a chemical plant in Sudan. This attack was in response to terrorist attacks organized by the group led by Osama bin Laden, including the shelling of the US embassies in Kenya and Tanzania. The justification for the US action was given by the US President on 21

August 1998 as follows: 'The US acted in exercise of our inherent right of self-defense consist-ent with Article 51 of the UN Charter. These strikes were a necessary and proportionate response to the imminent threat of further terrorist attacks against US personnel and facilities. These strikes were intended to prevent and deter additional attacks by a clearly identified terrorist threat. The targets were selected because they served to facilitate directly the efforts of terrorists specifically identified with attacks on US personnel and facilities and posed a continuing threat to US lives.'[12]

In other cases expansion of the notion of self-defence has occurred by the setting forth of a whole panoply of disparate legal grounds on which Article 51 was asserted to be applicable. As an illustration mention can be made of the US intervention in Panama, on 20 December 1989.

The US State Department maintained that the US intervention pursued the following purposes: '(1) to protect American lives (a US soldier in the US zone had been shot and killed by Panamanians), (2) to assist the lawful and democratically elected government in Panama in fulfilling its international obligations; (3) to seize and arrest General Noriega, an indicted drug trafficker; (4) to defend the integrity of US rights under the Panama Canal treaties'.[13] The formal justification of its military action, advanced by the USA, was as follows: 'The US has the inherent right of self-defence, as recognized in Article 51 of the UN Charter and Article 21 of the OAS Charter. This right of self-defence entitled the US to take necessary measures to defend US military personnel, US nationals and US installations. Further, the US has both the right and the duty under Article IV of the Panama Canal Treaty to use its armed forces to protect and defend the Canal and its availability to all nations. In addition, the legitimate democratically elected government of Panama was consulted and welcomes our actions.'[14]

(b) The question of ascertaining facts

A question that often arises in connection with individual (or collective) self-defence relates to the establishment of the facts amounting to the circumstances required for a State lawfully to resort to force in response to an armed attack. Often States tend to 'adjust' the facts to the needs for their justification of use of force in self-defence. As the ICJ judgment in *Nicaragua* forcefully showed,[15] the factual circumstances may prove at least as complex and important as legal issues. The problem is exacerbated by an important element: at the time of use of force States resorting to such use either monopolize control over the facts or possess a distinct advantage in establishing or 'organizing' facts. This is among other things rendered possible by the lack, or unavailability, of international mechanisms capable of timely and objective fact-finding. Under these circumstances, even the most implausible legal explanations may gain a semblance of credibility.

(c) Is anticipatory self-defence admissible?

A problem that has cropped up on several occasions and which in modern inter-national relations has become of *crucial importance* is whether Article 51 allows anticipatory self-defence, that is, a pre-emptive strike once a State is certain, or believes, that another State is about to attack it militarily.

Israel has resorted to anticipatory self-defence on various occasions: for example, in 1967 against Egypt, in 1975 against Palestinian camps in Lebanon, and in 1981 against Iraq (Israeli aircraft bombed Osiraq, an Iraqi nuclear reactor near Baghdad). Similarly, in 1980, in the UN SC, Iraq justified its armed attack on Iran by relying upon its right to pre-emptively strike at other countries preparing for war.

The rationale behind the doctrine of 'anticipatory' self-defence, stressed by all those who advocate it, is a strong meta-legal argument: in an era of missiles and nuclear weapons and of highly sophisticated methods of reconnaissance and intelligence, it would be naïve and self-defeating to contend that a State should await the attack by another country, in the full knowledge that it is certain to take place and likely to involve the use of very destructive weapons. As McDougall, one of the leading proponents of this view, wrote, to impose on States the attitude of 'sitting ducks' when confronted with an impending military attack 'could only make a mockery, both in its acceptability to States and in its potential application, of the Charter's main purpose of minimizing unauthorized coercion and violence across State lines'.[16] In 1981 the Israeli delegate echoed this doctrine in the SC.[17]

This non-legal rationale has been given a legal foundation by claiming that Article 51 did not suppress the pre-existing international rule on anticipatory self-defence, which was, therefore, left unaffected by the Charter.

The argument, developed by some eminent American and British jurists,[18] and advanced by Israel in the SC in 1981,[19] has been opposed by other distinguished publicists.[20] These publicists have substantially made two points. First, the alleged customary rule did not envisage a right of anticipatory self-defence proper, but a right of self-defence and self-preservation. Second, Article 51 wiped out all pre-existing law, and did not leave any room for self-defence except in the form it explicitly authorized.

However, in *Nicaragua* the ICJ authoritatively placed a different interpretation on Article 51, contrary to the second point just mentioned. It held that 'On one essential point, this treaty itself [that is, the UN Charter in Article 51] refers to pre-existing customary international law; this reference to customary law is contained in the actual text of Article 51, which mentions the "inherent right" (in the French text the "droit naturel") of individual or collective self-defence . . . The Court therefore finds that Article 51 of the Charter is only meaningful on the basis that there is a "natural" or "inherent" right of self-defence, and it is hard to see how this can be other than of a customary nature, even if its present content has been confirmed and influenced by the Charter . . . customary international law continues to exist alongside treaty law. Moreover the Charter, having itself recognized the existence of this right, does not go on to regulate directly all aspects of this content.'[21] Nevertheless, the Court did not specify the contents of the customary rules referred to in Article 51, in particular whether they included the old rule providing for a right to anticipatory self-defence. The Court noted that, as the parties to the dispute had not raised 'the issue of the lawfulness of a response to the imminent threat of armed attack', it did not intend to express any view on the matter.[22] Thus, this important decision of the Court cannot support any interpretation narrowing or broadening Article 51 with regard to the class of self-defence we are discussing.

A learned Israeli scholar, Y. Dinstein, propounded a middle-of-the-road view.[23] According to him one should distinguish between 'anticipatory self-defence', where an armed attack is merely foreseeable or even just conceivable, and 'interceptive self-defence', where an armed attack is 'imminent and practically unavoidable' because the other State 'has committed itself to an armed attack in an ostensibly irrevocable way'. In the latter case resort to self-defence would be legally warranted.[24] As illustrations of 'interceptive self-defence', the distinguished commentator suggested the hypothetical interception and sinking by the US Pacific Fleet of the Japanese carrier en route to the point from which it mounted the attack on Pearl Harbor in December 1941, as well as the Israeli initiation of the 'Six Days War' in 1967 'in response to an incipient armed attack by Egypt'.[25] Several objections can be raised against this view. First, it finds no basis in the text or context of Article 51. This provision speaks of 'armed attack' without making any distinction between different classes of such attack. Second, it is not supported by State practice, as we shall see in a moment. Third, it propounds a criterion that is no less loose and subjective than the one suggested by the proponents of the broadening of self-defence to 'anticipatory self-defence': how can one distinguish on the spot and in the heat of action between 'interceptive' and 'anticipatory' self-defence? Clearly, as the difference between these two categories boils down to different degrees of intensity, the perception of the would-be victim may vary. In short, the criterion at issue is not less conducive to arbitrary and dangerous decisions than the broadening of 'self-defence'.

If one undertakes a perusal of State practice in the light of Article 31 of the Vienna Convention on the Law of Treaties,[26] it becomes apparent that such practice does not evince agreement among States regarding the interpretation or the application of Article 51 with regard to anticipatory self-defence.

A number of States have advocated this class of self-defence. As early as 1946, in a Memorandum on the international control of atomic energy, the US State Department took a stand favourable to it, although primarily *de lege ferenda*,[27] as Jessup substantially noted.[28] However, in 1981, in the SC the USA took a firm position in favour of a broad notion of self-defence. The same view was propounded by Japan in 1968 and 1975, by Canada in 1981, as well as, as mentioned above, by Iraq in 1980 and Israel in 1975 and 1981. In addition, the UN did not condemn Israel in 1967 for its attack on Egypt nor Iraq for its attack in 1980 on Iran. Presumably this attitude was chiefly due to political considerations.

By contrast, when in 1975 Israel attacked Palestinian camps in Lebanon, in the SC not only developing and socialist countries but also all Western States including the USA, Japan, Sweden, France, Italy, and Britain condemned the Israeli action. The Lebanese delegate eloquently summarized the grounds on which the condemnation was based, as follows: 'Israel ... has stated that the aggression it undertook was not punitive but preventive in nature. This is a dangerous course to follow in international affairs. Are States to be allowed to determine on their own what should be termed preventive acts? If so, this will lead the world back to the law of the jungle, and far away from the international order based on the principles of the Charter of the United Nations.'[29]

Furthermore, in 1981, when the Israeli attack on the Iraqi nuclear reactor was discussed in the SC, the USA was the only State which (implicitly) indicated that it shared the Israeli concept of self-defence. In addition, although it voted for the SC resolution condemning Israel (resolution 487/1981), it pointed out after the vote that its attitude was only motivated by other considerations, namely Israel's failure to exhaust peaceful means for the resolution of the dispute.[30] All other members of the SC expressed their disagreement with the Israeli view, by unreservedly voting in favour of operative paragraph I of the resolution, whereby '[the SC] strongly condemns the military attack by Israel in clear violation of the Charter of the UN and the norms of international conduct'. Egypt[31] and Mexico[32] expressly refuted the doctrine of anticipatory self-defence. It is apparent from the statements of these States that they were deeply concerned that the interpretation they opposed might lead to abuse. In contrast, Britain, while condemning 'without equivocation' the Israeli attack as 'a grave breach of international law', noted that the attack was not an act of self-defence because 'it was not a response to an armed attack on Israel by Iraq. There was no instant or overwhelming necessity for self-defence. Nor [could] it be justified as a forcible measure of self-protection'.[33] It would thus seem that Britain upheld the doctrine of anticipatory self-defence in cases of 'instant and overwhelming necessity' and only denied that in the case under discussion these conditions were fulfilled.

Furthermore, in 1980, when the GA discussed Article 34 of the ILC Draft on State Responsibility, on self-defence, various States including Mexico, Romania, Iraq, Mongolia, Trinidad and Tobago, Poland, and Yugoslavia, stressed that Article 51 only warrants armed reaction to an aggression that is already under way.

This being so, it would seem that one should resort to the *object and scope of Article 51* and, more generally, Chapter VII of the UN Charter or even, to use the words of the ICJ in *Legality of the Use by a State of Nuclear Weapons in Armed Conflict*, 'the logic of the overall system contemplated by the Charter'.[34] The purpose of these provisions is to safeguard peace as much as possible, and for this purpose to establish a *collective* and *public* mechanism designed to prevent or put a stop to armed violence. The only exception is the '*private*' right of each State to protect itself against aggression pending the stepping in of collective bodies. Peace is regarded as the supreme value, and whatever may imperil or jeopardize such value should be removed or reined in as much as possible. If this is so, pre-emptive strikes should be banned, since they may easily lead to abuse, being based on subjective and arbitrary appraisals by individual States. It may thus be contended that, however *unrealistic* the ban imposed by Article 51 may prove to be in the present circumstances of warfare, States prefer to avoid *risks of abuse*. This should not be surprising. It is well known in any legal system that some classes of action are not susceptible to being properly defined and circumscribed in advance, involve a huge degree of discretion, and may have perilous consequences. In these instances legal legitimation of such actions might produce pernicious effects. Many legal systems make provision for cases where actions may prove illegal but in some respects justified on other grounds. Usually this is made, in criminal law, through the notion of 'mitigating circumstances'. Or else judicial or enforcement bodies in fact decide *not to legally* respond to breaches of law (this, in a way, has happened in the UN as well: the GA, which could be seen as the 'world jury', for better or worse, has sometimes harshly condemned recourse to force—for instance in the cases of Hungary, Grenada, Panama, Western Sahara—whereas on other occasions it has seemed to ignore or even approve such recourse: for instance in the cases of Goa, Tanzania and Uganda, the Central African Republic).

In the case of anticipatory self-defence, it is more judicious to consider such action as *legally prohibited*, while admittedly knowing that there may be cases where breaches of the prohibition may be justified on moral and political grounds and the community will eventually condone them or mete out lenient condemnation.

(d) Self-defence against armed infiltration and indirect aggression

While Article 51 clearly refers to an actual use of force taking place at a definite time (the crossing of frontiers by military troops, the bombing of territory by foreign aircraft, large-scale attack on foreign ships on the high seas, etc.) international practice shows that military aggression increasingly takes the form of gradual infiltration of armed forces and groups of voluntaries supported by a foreign government into the territory of another State. In these cases the 'invasion' of the territory of a State does not take place all of a sudden and on a large scale, but over a long period and piecemeal. This sort of aggression can also consist in organizing, assisting, fomenting, financing, inciting, or tolerating subversive or terrorist activities carried out against another State, either to overthrow its government or to interfere in civil strife (so-called indirect armed aggression). The problem arises of whether international law extends self-defence to include reaction to *invasion through infiltration of troops* and to *indirect armed aggression*.

The USA invoked the former category of aggression in the case of Vietnam: the American Government consistently held that individual self-defence by South Vietnam and collective self-defence by the USA were legitimized by the gradual infiltration of North Vietnamese troops and Vietcong into South Vietnam. The attitude of other States towards this view does not provide compelling evidence of the formation of a customary rule on the matter. However, the view agreed upon by States in the Definition of Aggression adopted in 1974 by the UN GA through resolution 3314-XXIX, seems to reflect customary law, as the ICJ authoritatively held in *Nicaragua*.[35] According to this view one may consider as armed attacks justifying self-defence those armed attacks made by armed bands, groups, irregulars, or mercenaries *sent by or on behalf of a State*, and of such a gravity as to amount to an armed attack conducted by regular forces. Anything short of these requirements may not warrant self-defence.

As for indirect armed aggression, various States (chiefly the USA, Israel and South Africa) have claimed that it warrants self-defence. In particular, Israel, on the occasion of its attacks against Palestinian camps in Lebanon (in 1970–83) and in Tunisia (in 1985), Southern Rhodesia (when it attacked Zambia in 1978–9), and South Africa, on the occasion of its attacks on SWAPO camps and troops in Angola and its raids into Lesotho, Zambia, and Swaziland (between 1976 and 1985) claimed that the violation of sovereign rights of the attacked State was justified by the fact that the latter tolerated or actively supported terrorist activities of guerrilla groups against the territory and assets of the attacking States.

However, the reaction of the international community has never been one of full and convinced acceptance of the legal justifications propounded by Israel, Southern Rhodesia, and South Africa. Indeed, the debates that took place on various occasions (in 1976, 1978, 1979, 1980, 1982, and 1984)[36] in the SC show that most States were opposed to the invocation of Article 51 and regarded the various instances of resort to force as illegal. In addition, the discussions on the principle of non-intervention which took place in the UN Special Committee on Friendly Relations in 1966–70 were revealing.

In 1964 the United Kingdom proposed to proclaim the right of any country to seek military assistance from third States, should it become the victim of unlawful intervention in the form of 'subversive activities leading to civil strife in which the dissident elements are receiving external support and encouragement'. In 1966 a group of Western countries (Australia, France, Canada, Italy, the UK, and the USA) took up and broadened that proposal, suggesting that the 'right of States in accordance with international law to take appropriate measures to defend themselves individually or collectively against intervention is a fundamental element of the inherent right of self-defence'. However, this proposal was strongly attacked in the Special Committee by a number of socialist and Third World countries, including Czechoslovakia, the United Arab Republic, Ghana, India, Lebanon, Algeria, and Mexico. They argued that the proposal was 'a dangerous departure from the UN Charter and from international law as generally accepted'; in particular, it ignored Article 51 and led to a dangerous broadening of the range of eventualities in which self-defence could be exercised under that provision of the Charter.

As a result of that criticism, the resolution's sponsors withdrew it and the final text of the Declaration on Friendly Relations simply refers to the 'relevant provisions of the Charter'. It should also be noted that the UN Special Committee for the Definition of Aggression eventually took the same stand, as is apparent, in particular, from the debates which took place within the Committee.

Furthermore, in *Nicaragua* the ICJ distinguished between various classes of threat or use of force. It pointed out that training or providing economic or military or logistical or other assistance to rebels fighting against the central authorities in another country may be regarded as a threat or use of force or as an intervention in the internal or external affairs of another State. However, it does not amount to armed attack (unless the provision of significant military support to an insurgency is major and demonstrable).[37] Hence, it does not entitle the target State to respond by self-defence against the assisting State.[38]

It thus seems difficult to contend that Article 51 authorizes self-defence against indirect armed aggression, or that a general rule has evolved authorizing States to invoke self-defence to repel such category of armed aggression. It would seem that State practice shows that entitlement to the right of self-defence against a State supporting an insurgency depends on (a) the level of such support, (b) the evidence of that support, and (c) the evaluation of that evidence by the ICJ or by another competent UN organ. It also depends, of course, on (d) the proportionality of the response and (e) the legality of the means used to respond.

(e) Collective self-defence

Article 51 grants any member State of the UN the right to use force in support of another State which has suffered an armed attack. This right, now incorporated in a general rule, has been interpreted to the effect that the intervening State must not be itself a victim of the armed attack by the aggressor (in which case it would act by way of 'individual' self-defence). Both the NATO treaty and the Treaty on the Warsaw Pact (now extinct) point in this direction. However, what is required is a prior bond (for example, a treaty) between the two States acting in self-defence or, if such a bond is lacking, an express request by the victim of the attack. In other words, a State cannot use force against a country which has attacked another State, without the request or the previous consent of the latter. In addition, it is for the victim State to establish that it has been militarily attacked. As was held by the ICJ in *Nicaragua*,

'[I]t is the State which is the victim of an armed attack which must form and declare the view that it has been so attacked. There is no rule of customary international law permitting another State to exercise the right of collective self-defence on the basis of its own assessment of the situation. Where collective self-defence is invoked, it is to be expected that the State for whose benefit this right is used will have declared itself to be the victim of an armed attack.'[39]

So far 'collective' self-defence (that is, intervention by one or more States in favour of the victim) has been invoked on a few occasions.

The USA relied on this defence in the case of Vietnam (in various official pronouncements, in particular the State Department Memorandum of 4 March 1966, the USA relied upon Article 51 for its military action in support of South Vietnam) and in Nicaragua, in 1981–4,[40] as did Britain in 1964 when it attacked Yemen to assist the Federation of Southern Arabia, and the Soviet Union in the case of Czechoslovakia (1968) and Afghanistan (1979). Collective self-defence was also referred to in the preamble of the resolution adopted by the SC after the Iraqi attack on Kuwait in 1990 and the request for assistance by the Kuwaiti government in exile (resolution 661 of 1990). However, as is well known, in that instance the SC authorized States to react to the Iraqi aggression against Kuwait.

The relative paucity of instances of 'collective' self-defence—in itself no doubt a felicitous feature of the present world community—is due to the tendency of States to hold aloof as much as possible from international armed conflicts or to side with one of the contending parties merely by sending arms and military equipment.

14.4.2 PROTECTION OF CITIZENS ABROAD

In various instances States have used force for the purpose of protecting their nationals whose lives were in danger in foreign territory.

In certain cases force has been used *without the consent* of the territorial State: Belgium intervened in the Congo in 1960; the USA in the Dominican Republic in 1965; the USA in Cambodian waters in 1975 (to rescue an American cargo boat and its crew captured by Cambodian armed forces); Israel in Uganda in 1976; the USA in Iran in 1980. In addition, as recalled above, the USA bombed Libya in 1986, Baghdad in 1993, and Afghanistan and Sudan in 1999 as a reaction to terrorist attacks on US nationals.[41]

In the first two cases the territorial State was not responsible for the threat to the life of foreign nationals, for such threat resulted from the collapse of the public order system. By contrast, in the third and fourth cases the local government was answerable, for it did not protect the lives of foreigners, but tolerated or even aided and abetted the activity of private individuals endangering foreign nationals.

In other cases military intervention was effected *with the consent* of the territorial State. Thus, the USA sent its troops to Lebanon in 1958 (although the principal grounds for American intervention, adduced both by the USA and Lebanon, were the request of the Lebanese Government and the applicability of Article 51 of the UN Charter, the US delegate to the SC also emphasized that US troops had been sent to Lebanon in order to protect American lives; he pointed out that US forces 'will afford security to the several thousand Americans who reside in that country'). Belgium did the same, with help from the USA in the Congo in 1964. The Federal Republic of Germany sent a commando unit to Mogadishu with the consent of Somalia in 1977. In 1978, French and Belgian troops intervened in the Shaba area at the request of Zaire. In 1983 the USA sent armed forces to Grenada. (They claimed that this was done at the request of the British Governor General, due to the collapse of local authorities;[42] independent reports disclosed that there was actually no imminent threat or danger to the lives of American citizens; the fact that US troops were stationed on the island after evacuating the American nationals confirmed that the ground for landing troops adduced by US authorities was indeed a mere pretext for unlawful forcible intervention. The UN GA did not uphold the legal grounds adduced by the USA and by resolution 38/7 of 1984 deplored the US intervention.) In 1989 the USA sent armed forces to Panama, among other things 'to protect American lives' after 'the legitimate democratically elected government of Panama [had been] consulted and [had] welcomed [the US] action'.[43]

In addition to the aforementioned cases one should mention the Larnaca incident of 1978. It is unique and anomalous and therefore cannot be put into the same category as the others just mentioned.

In February 1978 two terrorists killed the Egyptian Secretary-General of the Afro-Asian Peoples Solidarity Organization during a meeting of the Organization in Nicosia. After seizing hostages, among whom there were a few Egyptian nationals, the terrorists left Cyprus by aircraft but, being refused access by various countries, were obliged to return to Larnaca airport. While negotiations were under way between the Cypriot authorities and the terrorists, an Egyptian aircraft was allowed to land at Larnaca. When the Cypriot authorities realized that it carried a commando unit, they refused to authorize it to intervene. The Egyptians nevertheless opened fire against the terrorists, whereupon the Cyprus national guard in its turn fired against the Egyptians. As a result of the shoot-out several Egyptians and Cypriots were killed or wounded and the Cypriot authorities arrested the terrorists. A dispute between Egypt and Cyprus ensued. The former—while conceding that Cyprus had not authorized the use of force, claimed that it had not violated Cypriot sovereignty and had acted upon the principle of fighting terrorism. Cyprus, however, rejected Egyptian claims and firmly asserted that its sovereignty had been violated.

The case clearly does not fit into the class of incidents where States use force to protect their own nationals, first, because Egypt claimed its sole aim was to combat terrorists, and, second, because it contended that it had used force after being authorized by Cyprus to send a military aircraft to Larnaca.

One thing is striking: in most cases of use of force to protect nationals, the intervening State is a Western Power, and the State on whose territory the military action is carried out is a developing country. This situation is indicative of the present constellation of power in the world community. Of course, there is no denying that in nearly all the cases at issue there was either a real breakdown in the territorial system of public order, or an inability on the part of the local government to prevent the perpetration of unlawful acts against foreigners.

The second remarkable thing is that mostly Western States have expressed the view that armed intervention for the protection of nationals is internationally lawful, being authorized either by Article 51 of the UN Charter or by a customary rule unaffected by the Charter (the USA went so far as to adopt in 1948 regulations laying down the right of the USA to use force abroad to protect 'the lives and property' of American citizens 'against arbitrary violence': Article 0614, US Navy Regulations).[44]

By contrast, other countries have consistently opposed the legality of this class of resort to force. Except for the German intervention in Somalia (where the territorial State gave its consent), foreign intervention has often been attacked as contrary to international law. Thus, for instance, on the occasion of the armed action by the USA in Lebanon in 1958, Ethiopia stated in the GA:

'Ethiopia strongly opposes any introduction or maintenance of troops by one country within the territory of another country under the pretext of protection of national interest, protection of lives of citizens or any other excuse. This is a recognized means of exerting pressure by stronger Powers against smaller ones for extorting advantages. Therefore, it must never be permitted.'[45]

On the same occasion Poland argued that the protection of nationals abroad constituted an 'old pretext'.[46] And in 1978, on the occasion of the French and Belgian military operation in Zaire, the Soviet official news agency TASS stated that 'humanitarian intervention' was merely 'a fig leaf to cover up an undisguised interference in the internal affairs of Zaire'.[47]

On balance, it would seem that the objections of many States have not led to the obliteration of the general rule on the matter, evolved after the First World War (see **11.1.2**). However, this rule—which might be subsumed under the general notion of self-defence pursuant to Article 51 of the UN Charter—may only be resorted to *under very strict conditions*, dictated by the UN Charter system on the maintenance of peace and security. Its applicability in present-day conditions is justified by the weakness of the UN collective enforcement (clearly, had the UN SC armed forces at its disposal, to be dispatched immediately to places where human lives are in serious jeopardy, the rule would no longer be needed). The conditions to be fulfilled for the use of armed force to protect nationals abroad to be lawful, are as follows: (1) The threat or danger to the life of nationals—due either to terrorist attacks or to the collapse of the central authorities, or to the condoning by those authorities of terrorist or similar criminal activities—is serious. (2) No peaceful means of saving their lives are open either because they have already been exhausted or because it would be utterly unrealistic to resort to them. (3) Armed force is used for the exclusive purpose of saving or rescuing nationals. (4) The force employed is proportionate to the danger or threat. (5) As soon as nationals have been saved, force is discontinued. (6) The State that has used armed force abroad immediately reports to the SC; in particular, it explains in detail the grounds on which it has considered it indispensable to use force and the various steps taken to this effect.

It follows from this enumeration of conditions that the military interventions of Belgium in the Congo in 1960, of the USA in the Dominican Republic in 1965, of Israel in Uganda in 1976 were lawful. In contrast, the US intervention in Grenada in 1983 was unlawful (in particular, under the heading we are discussing—protection of citizens abroad). Similarly, the US bombing of Libya in 1986, of Baghdad in 1993, and of Afghanistan and Sudan in 1998 were contrary to the UN Charter.

14.4.3 ARMED INTERVENTION WITH THE CONSENT OF THE TERRITORIAL STATE

We should now ask ourselves whether the principle *volenti non fit injuria* (an illegal act is no longer such if the party whose rights have been infringed previously consented thereto), which is universally enshrined by State law, is also acknowledged as valid by the international community.

In traditional international law this principle was obviously in full force—each member being on a par with the others, there were no limits to the freedom of States and all rules could be derogated from. Thus each State was free to allow another to use force in any form on its own territory. Just as a State was able officially to sanction its own mutilation, dismemberment, or even its total extinction, so it could agree to allow another international subject to use force on its own territory.

Did the situation change once the use of force had been explicitly forbidden in the UN Charter and this ban had been enshrined as one of the pivots of the international community, with only a few very circumscribed exceptions? Since these exceptions did not include consent, can consent become an implicit exception? A close scrutiny of the Charter allows for only one conclusion: by explicit consent a State may authorize the use of force on its territory whenever, being the object of an 'armed attack', it resorts to individual self-defence and in addition authorizes a third State to assist it in 'collective self-defence'. What if the consenting State is not in fact the object of an 'armed attack'? For example, what if there is an insurrection within its territory, or if it is faced with serious disorders, and would like to appeal for help to another member of the international community?

A number of States tend to consider traditional law still fully valid and consequently hold that consent legitimizes the use of force because it precludes the violation of Article 2.4 of the Charter. In 1958, for instance, the British Foreign Secretary asserted:

'The structure of the Charter preserves the customary law by which aid may be given to a nation of the kind which I have described [in the face of civil strife fomented from abroad] . . . I do not believe that either the spirit or the letter of the Charter takes away the customary, traditional right'.[48]

Certain States all too readily claim their own military interventions to be lawful on account of consent (or request) by the State concerned. Thus, on more than one occasion, in cases of subversion in the territory of one State, other States have considered it quite legitimate to intervene, after a request to do so, either because the rebels were said to receive aid from third States, or because the consenting State was said to be the object of an 'armed attack', as laid down in Article 51.

Remember, for example, the Soviet intervention in Hungary in 1956 (when the USSR did not invoke Article 51), that of the USA in Lebanon, and of Britain in Jordan, both in 1958 (when both States invoked Article 51, as well as receiving consent), that of the USA in the Dominican Republic in 1965 (when the Americans also invoked the Charter of the OAS), in Grenada in 1983 (when the USA also referred to a regional treaty and to the 'right to protect nationals abroad'), not to mention Soviet intervention in Czechoslovakia in 1968 and in Afghanistan in 1979 (when the USSR both invoked Article 51 and allegedly received the consent of the territorial State in question).

To justify its armed intervention in Cyprus, in 1964 and 1974 Turkey invoked before the UN SC the 1960 Treaty of Guarantee between Cyprus, Greece, Turkey, and the UK, Article IV of which provided that in the event of a breach of the Treaty, and in so far as no common or concerted action proved possible, each of the three Guaranteeing Powers reserved 'the right to take action with the sole aim of re-establishing the state of affairs' created by the Treaty. Before the SC Greece and Cyprus rejected this interpretation, insisting that no 'military' action had been explicitly envisaged in the Treaty and in addition there had been no 'specific' consent by Cyprus to foreign military intervention.

The Panama Canal case should also be mentioned. Article V of the 1977 Panama Canal Treaty, laying down the principle of 'non-intervention in the internal affairs of the Republic of Panama', was unilaterally interpreted by the USA as consenting to the use of force by the USA in Panama. When the Treaty was submitted to the US Senate for the necessary authorization to ratification, Senator De Concini proposed a clause, accepted by the Senate as a 'condition' to ratification, whereby 'Notwithstanding the provisions of Article V or any other provision of the Treaty, if the Canal is closed, or its operations are interfered with, the United States of America and the Republic of Panama shall each independently have the right to take such steps as each deems necessary, in accordance with its constitutional processes, including the use of military force in the Republic of Panama, to reopen the Canal or restore the operations of the Canal, as the case may be'.[49] The Panamanian Government accepted the clause, without submitting it to a new plebiscite (the Treaty had already been approved by plebiscite). However, President Torrijos stated that Panamanians would not accept US intervention for defending or reopening the Canal, unless the USA was specifically invited.[50] In addition, Torrijos appended a declaration to the Panamanian instrument of ratification, stating among other things that Panama's 'political independence, territorial integrity and self-determination [were] guaranteed by the unshakable will of the Panamanian people'. The declaration went on to provide that 'Therefore, the Republic of Panama will reject, in unity and with decisiveness and firmness, any attempt by any country to intervene in its internal or external affairs'.[51] It would seem that the Panamanian response to the US 'condition' was intended to stultify its purpose of authorizing armed intervention. However, the State Department construed the Panamanian statement as not excluding or modifying 'the De Concini Condition or any other provision of the Treaties as ratified by the Senate'.[52] Whether or not this view was correct, it seems indisputable that, as some distinguished American commentators have rightly pointed out,[53] the US invasion and occupation of Panama in 1989 was not lawful, either on this ground (consent) or on one of the three other grounds put forward by the US Government, namely 'to safeguard lives of American citizens', to 'help restore democracy', and 'to bring General Manuel Noriega to justice': see above, **14.4.1(a)**.[54]

As a distinguished publicist rightly emphasized,[55] one should tread very warily, especially in the case of civil war, and never lose sight of certain general principles which emerged with a view to restricting the freedom of States.

According to this commentator, as a rule, it is necessary to ascertain that consent has not been vitiated by illegal pressure and has been issued by the legitimate authorities. Once these pre-liminary enquiries are completed, with specific reference to intervention in civil war or internal disorders one ought to distinguish between three main hypotheses. First, there is the case in which consent to the use of force was given by a State on whose territory an organized move-ment was not fighting the government 'with a general political object of replacing it; in this case the use of force was acceptable'. Second, one may envisage the case in which a substantial body of the population supported the insurrection 'and there is no question of foreign aid, moral or material, to the insurgents'; in such a case the use of force by a third State in support of the government can provoke objections 'on considerations of principle' because it could conflict with the principles of self-determination and non-interference, or for reasons of policy (the danger that these internal disturbances could escalate into an international conflict). The third case is that in which the rebels receive military aid from third States. In this case the use of force at the behest of the government is legitimate.

Clearly State practice makes extensive use of the consent exception, even though this practice hardly conforms to present-day international law. It would appear that many of the aforementioned cases of so-called armed intervention were unlawful, either because they were based on a misinterpretation of the relevant rules, or because the concrete situation adduced to justify intervention differed in reality from the one depicted by the intervening State. Often the rebels were not in fact receiving any 'external' aid, and certainly not in the form of massive 'military assistance'; or else, the individuals requesting or authorizing foreign intervention could not be regarded as the lawful authority of the 'inviting' State. Furthermore, whenever the intervening State (not to mention the 'consenting' State) justified the use of force by the need to repulse, in conformity with Article 51, an 'indirect armed aggression', the justification was based on a questionable interpretation of Article 51. Indeed, as we have already seen (**14.4.1(d)**), this provision does not allow the use of force against that particular form of 'aggression'.

The present legal regulation may be summarized as follows. First, consent must be freely given (that is, it cannot be wrested by any form of force, coercion, or duress: *coacta voluntas non est voluntas*); it must be real as opposed to merely 'apparent'. Second, it must be given by the lawful government, that is, by the authority empowered thereto by the constitution. Third, it may not be given as a blanket authorization for the future; it must be given ad hoc. Fourth, it may not validly legitimize the use of force against 'the territorial integrity or political independence' of the consenting or requesting State, contrary to Article 2.4 of the UN Charter. For instance, a State may not authorize another State to use force on its territory with a view to establishing control over the population of the consenting State, or to appropriating a portion of territory of that State. Fifth, consent cannot run counter to other principles of *jus cogens*. This would occur, for example, if force were authorized in order to deny or limit the right of peoples to self-determination, or if it turned out to be a case of interference in the domestic affairs of the State on whose territory force had been used, or if force involving atrocities were consented to for the purpose of putting down a rebellion or preventing secession.

14.4.4 ARMED REPRISALS AGAINST UNLAWFUL SMALL-SCALE USE OF FORCE

A few States (see below) and also some commentators have contended,[56] that a particular class of armed reprisals, that is, military action short of war in response to a single and small-scale armed action by another State, are legally authorized either by Article 51 or by a general rule on the matter. (As for serious violations of rules of international law other than Article 2.4 of the UN Charter, we have seen above, 11.3, that armed reprisals in response to them are prohibited by current international law, for only peaceful counter-measures are allowed, as even those would admit who are in favour of the legality of the class of reprisals we are now discussing.)

Before discussing this *particular* and *narrow* class of armed reprisals, it is fitting briefly to reconsider the legality of the *general category* of armed reprisals in modern international law.

States that carried out acts that can be regarded as military reprisals belong to the Western area: Britain, Israel, the USA, France, Portugal. For instance, in 1964, when the USA undertook bombing raids against North Vietnam in reply to the Gulf of Tonkin incident, the US Secretary of State, McNamara, spoke of 'retaliation'; the 1965 US air strikes against the same country following the North Vietnamese attacks at Pleiku were termed by the White House 'appropriate reprisal action'. In 1968 the Israeli Chief of Staff, General Bar Lev, defined as 'reprisals' both an Israeli attack against Egyptian installations and a raid against Beirut. Israel has had recourse to this class of armed reprisals in many instances since the early 1960s.

It would seem that also some cases where a State employed armed force under the cover of self-defence in fact fall under the category of armed reprisals: for instance, the US attack on Libya in 1986 (see above, 14.4.1(a)), as well as the US attack on Sudan and Afghanistan in 1998 (see 14.4.1(a)).

However, that no customary rule has evolved on this matter is evidenced by the fact that only some Western States have insisted on the legitimacy of armed reprisals when they themselves took such reprisals (strikingly, some of them, that is, France, Britain and the USA, went so far as to criticize resort to armed reprisal by *other* member States of the UN). That these reprisals are not authorized by Article 51, read in conjunction with Article 2.4, can be inferred from a literal and logical construction of those provisions and is corroborated by the subsequent practice of UN bodies, as indicative of the legal conviction of the States making up those bodies. In particular, mention may be made of various SC resolutions condemning reprisals 'as incompatible with the purposes and principles of the United Nations'[57] (this pronouncement is among other things intended to rule out the possibility of founding this category of reprisals on the last part of Article 2.4), as well as the statement in the 1970 GA Declaration on Friendly Relations (resolution 2625 XXV, adopted by consensus on 24 October 1970) whereby 'States have a duty to refrain from acts of reprisals involving the use of force' and, again, in 1981, in the GA Declaration on the Inadmissibility of Intervention and Interference in the Internal Affairs of States (resolution 36/103, adopted by consensus on 9 December 1981).

However, as has been rightly pointed out,[58] one should distinguish retaliatory armed force, which is normally a *delayed* response to the unlawful but small-scale use of force by another State, from an *immediate* armed reaction to a minor use of force. In the latter case, it is contended, the armed response is warranted, for otherwise the aggrieved State might turn out to be impotent in the face of a serious violation of international law by another State that causes an immediate and unavoidable threat to the life of the victims: in the end individuals belonging to law-abiding States would remain at the mercy of aggressive States. A distinguished commentator has crafted a useful expression for designating this class of cases: 'on-the-spot-reaction'.[59] He has suggested, as an example, the case of the patrol of a State that, moving along an international border, is hit by intense fire from military outposts of the neighbouring country; in this case, it is argued, the patrol can return fire. He also refers to the case of the destroyer of one particular State that on the high seas drops depth charges against the submarine of another State, 'and the submarine responds by firing torpedoes against the destroyer'. It would seem that in these cases the employment of military force by the target State is justified either because (a) the unlawful action involving force, undertaken by the other State, does not constitute an 'armed attack' pursuant to Article 51 of the UN Charter (the ICJ in *Nicaragua* stated that 'a mere frontier incident' does not amount to an armed attack),[60] or (b) there was no other means of avoiding an immediate peril to the life of persons belonging to the victim State: the ICJ in the *Corfu Channel* case admitted that a warship passing through an international waterway was entitled to 'retaliate quickly if fired upon' by the batteries of the coastal State.[61] Perhaps one could liken the condition in which the victim State finds itself in the circumstances at issue to 'distress' or to a 'state of necessity' legally warranting what would otherwise be illegal, namely armed reaction (see above 9.4.1(b)3).

In any event, the armed response is only authorized if it fulfils the conditions of *necessity* and *proportionality* generally required for the category of specific circumstances precluding wrongfulness of otherwise illegal acts,[62] as well as that of *immediacy*, inherent in the characteristic of this type of military response.[63]

14.4.5 IS RESORT TO FORCE TO STOP ATROCITIES
LEGALLY ADMISSIBLE?

It is apparent from the text and the context of the UN Charter that, although respect for human rights constitutes one of the main goals of the Organization, together with peace and self-determination, the Charter privileges peace to such an extent as to prohibit breaches of peace and security needed for ensuring observance of human rights. In other words, the Charter does not authorize individual States to use force against other States with a view to stopping atrocities. Such use may only be resorted to when the SC considers that this is exceptionally justified and acts accordingly, by authorizing the use of force. That this is the right interpretation of the Charter is borne out by the holding of the ICJ in *Nicaragua*.[64] State practice confirms the proposition.

India justified its armed intervention in East Pakistan in 1971 among other things as an act of self-defence against the Pakistani aggression and also on account of the inhuman conditions of the Bengali population in what later became Bangladesh. However in the SC the USA objected to the use of force, and in the GA opposition came from China, Albania, Jordan, Sweden, and other States.[65] When Vietnam intervened militarily in Cambodia in 1978, relying upon the notion of self-defence, in the ensuing debate in the UN SC many States clearly asserted that the UN Charter did not allow foreign intervention for the alleged purpose of safeguarding human rights.[66] When Tanzania attacked Uganda, in 1979, thus toppling the dictator Idi Amin, it to some extent relied on humanitarian grounds, citing the atrocities ordered or committed by the Ugandan dictator. However, although the attack was not discussed in the UN SC or in the GA, it would seem that eventually the international community did not endorse or condone the intervention, although it did not pronounce on its illegality.[67] When the French intervened in 1979 against Emperor Bokassa of the Central African Republic, after the atrocities had been condemned by the OAU Judicial Commission, there was no official pronouncement on that intervention. On the occasion of the 1999 NATO armed intervention in Kosovo, which had not been authorized by the SC, a number of States claimed that resort to force was legally warranted by the urgent need to put a stop to a 'humanitarian catastrophe' or, as other States put it, to the atrocities being perpetrated by the Serbs in Kosovo. (This stand was taken by such States as the USA, the UK, France, Canada, Belgium, the Netherlands, Italy, and others). However, many other States (including Russia, China, Cuba, Belarus, Ukraine, Namibia, India) strongly objected to that military action, arguing that it was blatantly contrary to the UN Charter, as it had not been authorized by the SC.[68]

It is apparent from a survey of State practice that an international customary rule, legally entitling individual States to take forcible measures to induce a State engaging in gross and large-scale violations of human rights to terminate such violations, has not crystallized. Indeed, *usus* is extremely limited and *opinio necessitatis*, though widespread, does not fulfil the requisite conditions of generality and non-opposition.

14.5 USE OF FORCE WHEN SELF-DETERMINATION IS DENIED

Although Article 2.4 only enjoins *States* to refrain from using force, arguably the corresponding customary rule addresses itself to any international legal subject, including national liberation movements. However, it would seem that gradually a customary rule has evolved providing for an exception to the broad scope of that customary rule banning force. This rule states that, if peoples subjected to colonial domination or foreign occupation, as well as racial groups not represented in government, are forcibly denied the right to self-determination, such peoples or racial groups are legally entitled to resort to armed force to realize their right to self-determination.

That the rule has evolved is evidenced by the acceptance by consensus of the 1970 Declaration on Friendly Relations as well as a string of subsequent GA resolutions (for example, resolutions 3314–XXIX of 14 December 1974 on the Definition of Aggression, Article 7; A/7185 Revision 1, paragraph 60; A/7402, paragraphs 6 and 61), as well as Article 1.4 of the 1977 First Additional Protocol to the 1949 Geneva Conventions.[69]

14.6 THE OLD AND THE NEW LAW CONTRASTED

It may prove useful to contrast the two basic patterns for enforcing law discussed in some detail in the previous paragraphs. The 'old' law rested on a few fundamental tenets: (1) the unfettered freedom of States to use force; (2) the consequent lack of a clear-cut distinction between enforcement proper (that is, resort to coercive action to compel observance of law) and use of force for realizing one's own interests; (3) the licence to use force without previously getting an international authority to establish whether a subjective right of the State resorting to force had in fact been violated; (4) the absence of any 'solidarity link' between the injured party and any third State, authorizing the latter to intervene to protect the rights of the former; international wrongs remained a 'private' occurrence between the delinquent State and the aggrieved party, except for those instances where there were already links based on treaties of alliance, in which case an ally might be affected by the wrongdoing and feel authorized to intervene; (5) the lack of any international agency capable of at least co-ordinating resort to force by individual States. In short, traditional law favoured major Powers: minor States derived no protection from general rules and consequently their own safeguard lay in the conclusion of treaties of alliance with one or more Great Powers.

In 1945 a consensus emerged to the effect that peace should henceforth constitute the overriding purpose of all members of the world community. Consequently, States agreed that the maintenance of peace should become a 'public' affair, that is to say, a matter of general concern, and that no country should be allowed to break or even jeopardize peaceful relations. The ensuing legal position is as follows: (1) The previously untrammelled right to use force has been suppressed; any use of force except in self-defence is totally banned. It should be noted, however, that the new international law has not abrogated the norms concerning the *modalities* of the use of force. In other words, if a State illegally engages in military action, it is bound to respect certain general principles and rules placing restraints on such action (see **Chapter 15**), the purpose being, of course, to ensure that any breaches of the general prohibitions referred to above do not degenerate into barbarism. (2) There is an international organization, the UN, which, in theory, is endowed with collective responsibility both for enforcing the law in extreme cases (that is, when breaches of international rules jeopardize peaceful relations) and more generally, for safeguarding peace, irrespective of any action taken by the aggrieved party, hence also in the event of its remaining passive in the face of aggression. Serious international breaches have become 'public' events, of concern for the whole international community. (3) Theoretically, the UN has a monopoly of force, in that it should intervene militarily in all the extreme cases just referred to. (4) Whenever international rules are disregarded without the breach falling within the category of 'armed attack', States are not authorized to react by force. Self-help, although still allowed, must be confined to *peaceful* reaction to international wrongs. (5) Even peaceful sanctions must be preceded by resort to other, peaceful, means of conflict resolution. Judicial adjudication, however, is not made compulsory. It may suffice that some peaceful settlement mechanism be used. Thus, even contemporary international law has not yet reached the stage typical of domestic legal systems, where ascertainment of legal situations must precede law enforcement. (6) A marked distinction between coercive or non-coercive measures of enforcement—which are lawful—and other instances of use or threat of military force—which are unlawful—has emerged. Thus, gradually, international law has come to uphold a distinction which is of fundamental importance and has for centuries been acted upon in municipal legal systems. As in the latter systems, in international law only the supreme collective body, the SC, is authorized to depart in exceptional circumstances from this distinction in the interest of the whole community. It can both *enforce the law* and *exercise 'police powers'*. What unfortunately strongly differentiates the world community from domestic legal systems is both the rudimentary character of the international enforcement machinery and also the fact that this distinction becomes somewhat blurred, in practice, owing to disagreement among States over the exact boundaries of the classes of lawful and unlawful use of force.

Can we say that this legal regime is a great innovation with respect to the previous one? In many respects it is indeed, but in the most important area, that of the condition of Great Powers, it has left the existing position almost unaffected. While in the past the lack of substantial restraints on the use of force simply confirmed that these Powers were the overlords in the world community, now the law goes so far as to consecrate their might, providing, as it does, that while they must not use force contrary to the Charter, transgression will not invite sanction under Chapter VII of the Charter owing to the veto power conferred on each of them. In spite of this huge shortcoming in the law, the Charter system was designed to afford legal and institutional protection to lesser or middle-sized countries, whenever they were not involved in a fight against one of the major Powers. To this extent the Charter made much headway towards the introduction of some kind of safeguarding of peace.

Finally, one should not pass over in silence a major factor which helps to forestall breaches of international law by States: the role of public opinion, especially in democratic countries. In this regard, it is fitting to quote the apposite and authoritative remarks of J. L. Brierly, on the enormous importance which international public opinion can and does have for the observance of the 'law of nations'. He noted in 1931 that international public opinion contains an apparent paradox:

'It is intrinsically a weaker force than opinion in the domestic sphere, yet it is in a sense more effective as a sanction of the law. For whereas an individual law-breaker may often hope to escape detection, a State knows that a breach of international law rarely fails to be notorious; and whereas again there are individuals so constituted that they are indifferent to the mere disapproval, unattended by pains and penalties, of others, every State is extraordinarily sensitive to the mere suspicion of illegal action.'[70]

15

LEGAL RESTRAINTS ON VIOLENCE IN ARMED CONFLICT

15.1 INTRODUCTION

It has become fashionable to quote the famous observation made in 1952 by Sir Hersch Lauterpacht that 'if international law is, in some ways, at the vanishing point of law, the law of war is, perhaps even more conspicuously, at the vanishing point of international law'.[1]

There is a lot of truth in this. More than any other corpus of legal rules, international law directly and transparently reflects power relations. It only partially restrains States' behaviour. War marks the passage from relatively harmonious relations to armed contention. War is the area in which power politics reach their peak and law relinquishes its control over international dealings. In the daily wrangle between force and law, the latter, of necessity, loses ground: international legal rules hold Armageddon only partially at bay. First, it refrains from imposing restraints on the most dangerous forms of armed violence. Second, all too often existing legal restraints are checkmated by sheer power. This state of affairs is only natural, given the mental disposition of most people and, what is even more important, the division of the world community into self-seeking nation-States, each of them claiming—as Suarez observed—to be a *communitas perfecta* (a perfect community).[2] Therefore, realistically one can simply require international law to *mitigate* at least some of the most frightful manifestations of the clash of arms. This is precisely what the rules on warfare endeavour to do.

15.2 CLASSES OF WAR

Since time immemorial wars have been armed conflicts involving in their cruelty and devastation the whole population of the contending parties, with civilians suffering no less than combatants. However, for a number of historical reasons between 1648 and 1789, wars tended to take the shape of contests between professionals, conducted as a sort of game and without any direct involvement of the civilian population. This was due to many factors: reaction to the sanguinary and drawn-out wars of the early seventeenth century; the development of costly armies consisting of highly trained professionals, whose death in war would be a great loss for States; the lack of national allegiance in military men and the consequent marked reluctance to fight unto the bitter end in defence of the State; the fact that the military profession was almost everywhere an apanage of the nobility, with the consequent feeling of belonging to the same social class common to the officers of all countries; the influence of aristocratic principles of chivalry.

However, the new ideals of the French Revolution and their implementation in this particular field (soldiers were no longer professionals; every citizen became a patriot and a member of a mass army) begot total wars. The devastating armed conflicts in which Napoleon engaged (1792–1815) soon provided an even more forceful negation of Rousseau's maxim that war was not a relationship between man and man but between State and State, where private persons were enemies only accidentally. The Prussian general, von Clausewitz, who had fought against Napoleon, eventually asserted in his treatise *On War* (1832) the need for wars to be life or death struggles involving the whole of the population of the contending States.

He was the first to perceive and lucidly expound the difference between the wars of the eighteenth century and the new total war. One should not believe that von Clausewitz's insistence on 'absolute war' (in his terminology),[3] and its ruthlessness, reflected a vicious longing for barbarity. In his view war in its new form had at least two merits. First, the decision to engage in armed conflict was no longer taken by a handful of leaders with no regard whatsoever for the population. Second, the savagery of modern war should prompt those in command to think twice before engaging in hostilities. The former proposition is in many respects questionable. Even in modern parliamentary democracies the leaders easily drum up support for any decision they may have made to initiate war for the pursuit of what they consider to be national interests. The waging of wars remains to a large extent in the hands of elites. The latter proposition is also open to criticism. Extreme cruelty in war has not stood in the way of the spread of armed conflict.

Most of the armed conflicts which spread after the Napoleonic period and are still raging today belong to the class described by von Clausewitz as total wars.

15.3 TRADITIONAL LAW IN A NUTSHELL

The bulk of traditional law was either restated and codified, or developed, at the Brussels Conference of 1874 and at the Hague Peace Conferences of 1899 and 1907. Interestingly, this law ultimately upheld the 'Rousseauesque', not the 'Clausewiztian' conception. Being based on the assumption that wars are clashes between States' armies, it distinguished between combatants and civilians and sought to shield the latter as much as possible from armed violence. The law under consideration essentially resulted from the tension and conflict of interest between: (1) Great Powers and lesser States; (2) naval Powers such as Britain and France, and other States

(Britain and France were very suspicious of any development in the law of naval warfare which might jeopardize their superiority. They therefore insisted on leaving belligerents as much freedom of action as possible at sea, whereas other States had of course contrary interests and were particularly eager to keep maritime commerce between belligerents and neutral States as unimpeded as possible); (3) countries interested in remaining aloof in cases of war on the one side, and States pursuing an expansionist policy, hence bent on war, on the other.

The rules worked out in 1874 and enacted by the 1899 and 1907 Conferences, as well as the customary law which had previously evolved, can be briefly summed up as follows. (These rules will be discussed in some detail later in the chapter.)

Only *inter-State armed conflicts* were regulated. No rule was adopted concerning civil wars. Fighting by insurgents remained under the sway of domestic criminal law (unless the State concerned granted the rebels the recognition of belligerency: see **4.1**).

The applicability of international conventions on warfare to armed conflicts was always uncertain and precarious. Indeed, all these conventions included the so-called *si omnes* clause, whereby they applied to an armed conflict on condition that all the belligerents were contracting parties. Consequently, it was sufficient for one belligerent not to be bound by a certain convention for the convention also to become inapplicable to the relationships between the other belligerents *inter se*: belligerents feared that, if another belligerent was not bound by a particular convention while they were, an imbalance would ensue to their disadvantage; they therefore preferred to opt for a solution favourable to them but detrimental to civilians (and ultimately to combatants as well): the convention would not apply to, hence restrain the freedom of, *any* belligerent. It follows that only customary law—hence the most general but also the loosest body of legal rules—was undisputedly applicable in any war.

Traditional law regarded as lawful combatants the members of regular armies, as well as militias or volunteer corps fulfilling a number of specific conditions (see **15.6.1(i)**). In addition it made allowance for the whole civilian population taking up arms on the approach of the enemy, provided certain conditions were met (see **15.6.1(i)**).

As for means of warfare, there existed few specific prohibitions of specific weapons, in addition to some general principles, very loosely set out. Various methods of combat were permitted as long as the parties could ensure that only belligerents could be targeted; in practice scant protection was granted to civilians. The principal means of ensuring compliance with law were left to each belligerent: it could resort to belligerent reprisals or to the prosecution and punishment of enemy combatants violating the laws of warfare.

In short, traditional international law tended to favour strong and middle-sized powers at least in three major areas: means of combat, methods of combat, and devices for inducing compliance with law.

Detailed rules on *neutrality*, that is, the relations between belligerents on the one side and third States on the other, were laid down. The interests of the former are clearly at variance with those of the latter: no belligerent wants third States to help its adversary by lending military or economic support; each belligerent is, therefore, interested in barring any dealings between third States and its enemy. By contrast, neutral States are keen to maintain unrestricted commercial dealings with the contending parties without, however, becoming embroiled in the armed conflict. The attitude of neutrality adopted in 1804–15 by the USA towards the countries engaged in the Napoleonic wars and, subsequently, the stand of Britain and other European countries in relation to the American Civil War (1861–5) greatly contributed to the development of a set of rules striking a fairly felicitous compromise between conflicting interests.

These were the main principles governing neutrality: (1) neutral States must refrain from giving any direct or indirect assistance to either belligerent; in particular they must prevent their territories from being used in the interest of one of the contesting parties (for example by enlisting troops); (2) belligerents must refrain from using the neutral territory for any warlike action and, should their troops take refuge in neutral territory, must acquiesce in their internment by the neutral State. However, (3) belligerents have the right to search and visit, and to seize, neutral vessels carrying contraband (that is, such goods as may assist the enemy in the conduct of war); in addition, they are entitled to blockade the enemy coast, thus preventing access to it by any vessel, including those of neutral States.

It should be noted that neither at The Hague, in 1899 and 1907, nor in other international forums was it possible to reach agreement on what categories of neutral goods constituted 'contraband', liable to seizure by belligerent warships. This in the end left belligerents free to designate as 'contraband' not only articles of undisputed military character, but also any other goods which, in their view, might serve the interests of the enemy. Thus a serious blow was struck to the interests of neutral States which considered their commercial dealings as vital.

15.4 NEW DEVELOPMENTS IN MODERN ARMED CONFLICT

In the period following the Hague codification, a series of events occurred which rendered it defective or inadequate in many respects.

In the first place, *new classes of combatants* emerged. During the Second World War partisans and resistance movements played a remarkable role in certain European countries occupied by Germany (Yugoslavia, France, The Netherlands, Poland, and the Soviet Union) as well as Italy in 1943 to 1945. They were not formally legitimized by existing law, because they operated in territories under military occupation, and also because they often lacked one or more of the requirements needed for lawful combatants (see 15.6.1(ii)). In particular, they normally did not carry arms openly, nor did they wear a distinctive sign recognizable at a distance. After the war a general feeling emerged among the Allies that resistance movements had acted for politically sound reasons; some provision should therefore be made in future for granting them legitimacy. When, subsequently, guerrilla warfare spread throughout the colonial countries, the majority of States felt that guerrillas, who normally do not fulfil the necessary legal conditions (see **15.6.1(ii)**), should be upgraded to the status of lawful combatants.

Second, war developed in two opposite directions: the '*wars of the rich*', that is, armed conflicts engaged in by highly developed countries using sophisticated weapons, and the '*wars of the poor*', struggles for national liberation waged by liberation movements in colonial or occupied territories and usually conducted by guerrillas. It should be noted that both classes of war (which often coexisted, as in the case of the Vietnam conflict between 1964 and 1974) have resulted in a staggering increase of civilian losses. In modern wars non-combatants are those who suffer most from armed violence.

Third, *new agencies of destruction* took pride of place: aircraft, first used in the war between Italy and Turkey (1911–12), then in the First World War (1914–18), proved of tremendous importance and effectiveness in the Spanish Civil War (1936–9) when German planes participated massively in the fighting. It subsequently became a major instrument of combat. Technological developments led to the creation of the atomic bomb and its use (on 6 and 9 August 1945, respectively at Hiroshima and Nagasaki), and subsequently to the manufacture and stockpiling of nuclear weapons. The arsenals of great and small Powers (the latter furnished by the former) have become bigger and bigger, with the addition of missiles, chemical weapons, and other arms.

Fourth, *civil wars* have become more and more widespread. Sometimes Great Powers fight each other by proxy, providing military assistance to the various factions struggling within the territory of sovereign States. In developing countries, historical and social conditions—chiefly tribal and political dissensions—generate clashes between opposing groups and facilitate the eruption of civil tumult.

Fifth, the laws of neutrality were ignored more and more frequently, and the whole institution of *neutrality gradually fell into decline*. This process began during the two World Wars, when the rules on neutrality turned out to put those States wishing to remain aloof in a situation no less hazardous than that of belligerents. Further factors were the establishment of the UN (which rested on the concept that, if the need arose, any member State should take armed action against an aggressor) and the proliferation of security pacts when it became apparent that the UN collective system was ineffective. A decisive blow to neutrality was struck by the creation of political groupings and alliances, each of them, sooner or later, siding with one of the belligerents during armed conflicts. This rendered the duties of impartiality, in particular the obligation not to assist either side militarily, obsolete. Furthermore, States increasingly considered that the impediments to commercial relations between neutrals and belligerents were economically disadvantageous and not warranted by the new circumstances.

15.5 THE NEW LAW: AN OVERVIEW

All these developments prompted States to revise and update the traditional rules on
warfare. (By contrast, they did not feel the need to make the laws of neutrality more
consonant with modern times.) The legislative process started in 1949, when four
Conventions on war victims (on the wounded and sick in the field; on the wounded,
sick, and shipwrecked at sea; on prisoners of war; on civilians) were adopted by a
Diplomatic Conference. To a vary large extent they gradually turned into customary
law. In 1977 another Diplomatic Conference adopted two Protocols, one on international, the other on internal armed conflicts. They extensively revised and updated
both the Hague Regulations of 1907 and the Geneva Conventions of 1949.
Subsequently a few treaties prohibiting some modern weapons have been agreed
upon.

The new law has not supplanted the old law; rather, it has generally elaborated and
supplemented it, or lent it greater clarity and precision.

Furthermore, the new law does not substantially depart from the 'Rousseauesque'
conception of armed conflicts, on which the traditional law rested. It does, of course,
endeavour to take account of the fact that modern wars increasingly tend to become
life-or-death, 'total' conflicts. Consequently, the new rules take into consideration the
growing involvement of both civilians and civilian installations (factories, etc.) in the
war effort. What matters, however, is that even the new body of rules has not abandoned the basic tenet that a distinction must always be made between combatants and
persons who do not take part (or no longer take part) in hostilities, and also between
military and civilian objectives.

Also, humanitarian law has become less geared to military necessity and increasingly impregnated with human rights values. The ICTY in *Tadić* (*Decision on Interlocutory Appeal*) rightly emphasized this new trend. When dealing with the distinction
between the law regulating international and that governing internal armed conflicts,
the Appeals Chamber pointed out that one of the most conspicuous developments of
modern humanitarian law was that it had been strongly influenced by human rights
doctrines:

'The impetuous development and propagation in the international community of human rights
doctrines . . . has brought about significant changes in international law, notably in the approach
to problems besetting the world community'. Thus, '[a] State-sovereignty-oriented approach
has been gradually supplanted by a human-being-oriented approach. Gradually the maxim of
Roman law *hominum causa omne jus constitutum est* (all law is created for the benefit of
human beings) has gained a firm foothold in the international community as well.'[4]

In addition, the '*si omnes* clause' (see **15.3**) has been gradually abandoned.
While the majority of the Hague Conventions has turned into customary law, recent
agreements such as the four 1949 Geneva Conventions, as well as the 1977 Protocols,
explicitly apply in the case of armed conflict to the States parties irrespective of

whether or not one of the belligerents is a contracting party. Today it has therefore become difficult or even impossible for belligerents to claim that they are free to disregard the existing law.

15.6 CURRENT REGULATION OF INTERNATIONAL ARMED CONFLICT

15.6.1 LAWFUL COMBATANTS

(i) Traditional law. It was in the interest of big Powers to exclude from the category of lawful combatants any person other than members of the regular army (as powerful States usually rely on standing armies of professionals and are likely to invade the territory of the adversary, they do not wish members of the enemy civilian population to be upgraded to the status of lawful combatants). In addition, in the case of military occupation, since powerful States normally find themselves in the position of the occupying power, it is to their advantage to place as many restrictions as possible on the rights of the population of the occupied territory. However, the opposition of a number of small and middle-sized States succeeded in the nineteenth century in extracting concessions for militias and volunteer corps as well as for the whole civilian population, and in excluding the possibility that the occupying power should acquire *ipso facto* sovereign rights over the territory it invaded.

The compromise solution reached by Great Powers with lesser States lay in granting the status of lawful combatant, in addition to regular armies, to militias and volunteer corps, provided the latter category fulfilled four conditions, namely: (1) that they be commanded by a person responsible for his subordinates; (2) that they wear a fixed distinctive sign recognizable at a distance; (3) that they carry arms openly; and (4) that they conduct their operations in accordance with the laws and customs of war. For another class of combatants (namely 'the inhabitants of a territory not under occupation who, on the approach of the enemy, spontaneously take up arms to resist the invading troops without having the time to organize themselves'; so-called *levée en masse*) two conditions only were required: that is, to carry arms openly and to respect the laws and customs of war.

In practice in the period between 1907 and 1939 wars were mainly fought by regular armies and on a few occasions only did other lawful combatants take part in hostilities on a large scale. In short, for a number of historical reasons, small countries did not in practice take advantage of the gains they had obtained on the normative level.

(ii) The new law

(1) *Partisans.* In 1949 the Third Geneva Convention added in Article 4.A.2 the category of 'organized resistance movements, belonging to a party to the conflict and operating in or outside their own territory, even if this territory is occupied', provided they fulfilled the same four conditions established in 1899 for other irregular combatants (a fifth condition was spelled out in 1949, stipulating that the combatants must be linked to a party to the conflict).

(2) *Guerrillas.* After 1949 the question of guerrilla fighters (that is, irregular combatants resorting to guerrilla warfare within the framework of inter-State wars or wars of national liberation) became increasingly important. In the 1974–7 Geneva Conference the debates were complex and protracted, but eventually led to the adoption of a compromise formula laid down in a particularly convoluted provision, Article 44. This stipulation leaves unaffected three of the requirements provided for in 1899 and 1949 for other categories of combatants (namely, being linked to a party to the conflict; being under a responsible command; and complying with the laws of war), while it reduces the two other criteria (carrying a distinctive sign recognizable at a distance, and carrying arms openly) to one: that combatants 'are obliged to distinguish themselves from the civilian population while they are engaged in an attack or in a military operation preparatory to an attack' (Article 44.3, first sentence). Thus the two traditional requirements are relaxed to the general condition of 'distinction from civilians' (presumably by insignia or any appropriate outward token, or by openly carrying weapons); in addition, combatants are only required to comply with this condition *during* an armed attack or immediately *prior* to it. Furthermore, if captured by the adversary, irregular combatants not fulfilling the condition do not forfeit their status of lawful combatants; consequently, they continue to be entitled to prisoner of war treatment, although they are liable to punishment for violating Article 44.3.

The requirements just mentioned were further relaxed with regard to such situations as wars of national liberation and military occupation. With respect to these situations the second sentence of Article 44.3 only requests that a combatant should carry his arms openly '(a) during each military engagement, and (b) during such time as he is visible to the adversary while he is engaged in a military deployment preceding the launching of an attack in which he is to participate'.

Thus guerrillas fighting in wars of national liberation or in occupied territory are favoured in two respects: first, the requirements exacted from them are less stringent than those necessary for irregular combatants fighting in 'normal' situations; second, they must fulfil these requirements under circumstances ('military engagement', etc.) which are narrower in scope than those for which guerrillas in 'normal' fighting must fulfil their conditions. However, in another important respect Article 44 is more exacting, or stricter, with guerrillas fighting in 'special' situations: if irregular combatants not satisfying the requirements of the second sentence of Article 44.3, are captured in the course of a war of national liberation or in occupied territory, they forfeit their status of lawful combatants and cannot therefore enjoy prisoner of war treatment.

The illustration given by Aldrich, a distinguished US lawyer who greatly contributed to the elaboration of Article 44, may be recalled. He mentioned the case of a guerrilla fighting in an occupied territory, who disguises himself as a civilian; if he is stopped and searched by occupying troops and suddenly draws his weapon and opens fire on the soldiers, on capture he will be deprived of prisoner of war status provided it can be proved that he was engaged in a military deployment preceding the launching of an attack. Only if he was not so engaged must he be treated as a prisoner of war.[5]

(3) *Mercenaries.* In 1960–70 the number of mercenaries became conspicuously large in Africa, where they were used both by the ruling elites (for internal security, intelligence, the training of special commandos, etc.) and by foreign powers as tools for organizing or strengthening movements to destabilize African regimes. Many an African State took a strong stand against the latter practice. Accordingly, both in the UN and at the Geneva Conference of 1974–7, African States claimed, with the support of other developing countries and the socialist group, that mercenaries should be treated as unlawful combatants (hence not entitled to the treatment of prisoners of war on capture). Western countries retorted that mercenaries fulfilling the various requirements of international law should be regarded as legitimate combatants, lest an ideological element be introduced into the laws of warfare, contrary to the basic humanitarian principle of equality of treatment.

The growing insistence on this issue by countries in the UN and the Organization of African Unity (OAU) found official recognition in the adoption of Article 47 at the Geneva Conference. The provision states in paragraph 1 that 'a mercenary shall not have the right to be a combatant or a prisoner of war' and then gives, in paragraph 2, the following definition of a mercenary:

'any person who (a) is specially recruited locally or abroad in order to fight in an armed conflict; (b) does, in fact, take a direct part in the hostilities; (c) is motivated to take part in the hostility essentially by the desire for private gain and, in fact, is promised, by or on behalf of a Party to the conflict, material compensation substantially in excess of that promised or paid to combatants of similar ranks and functions in the armed forces of that Party; (d) is neither a national of a Party to the conflict nor a resident of territory controlled by a Party to the conflict; (e) is not a member of the armed forces of a Party to the conflict; and (f) has not been sent by a State which is not a Party to the conflict on official duty as a member of its armed forces'.

15.6.2 CONDUCT OF HOSTILITIES: MEANS OF WARFARE

(i) *Traditional law.* Only those agencies of destruction which either were relatively ineffective or might imperil the life of their very users were proscribed. Thus explosive projectiles weighing under 400 grams were prohibited as belonging to the former category, whereas the other banned category covered such weapons as poison or

poisonous weapons, asphyxiating or deleterious gases, and automatic submarine contact mines. In contrast, really important and effective weapons were not banned,
however inhuman they might be.

This applies particularly to the use of aircraft for military purposes. In 1899 the Hague Conference adopted a Declaration prohibiting the discharge of explosives from balloons for a term of
five years. However, in 1907 there were already indications of the importance that balloons and
similar aerial devices might have for warlike purposes, and it was therefore agreed to 'prohibit,
for a period extending to the close of the Third Peace Conference [presumably five years, but the
Conference was never convened] the discharge of projectiles and explosives from balloons or by
other new methods of a similar nature'. The impact of the Declaration was weakened, first by
this proviso, and, second, by the fact that it was signed by a few countries only. It did not bear the
signatures of such major Powers as France, Germany, Italy, Japan, and Russia, with the consequence that, as the *British Manual on Land Warfare* of 1912 put it, the Declaration was
'practically without force'.

Apart from a few specific bans, the law of warfare included the general principle,
first stated in 1899 and reiterated in 1907, that 'it is expressly forbidden to employ
arms, projectiles, and material calculated to cause unnecessary suffering'. The principle, however, was very loose and lent itself to the most divergent interpretations. In
practice, it was taken to proscribe such minor arms as lances with a barbed head,
irregularly shaped bullets, projectiles filled with broken glass, and the like. Another
general principle which evolved in this period was that prohibiting indiscriminate
weapons (that is weapons which do not distinguish between combatants and civilians) or the indiscriminate use of weapons. But this was too vague to function as a
workable standard of behaviour (except in extreme cases).

(ii) New law. Also in recent times the *general principles*, to which reference has been
made above, have not played a significant role in recent international practice for they
are so loose as to be almost unworkable, save in extreme situations.

Specific bans on specific weapons have proved more useful. They list the arms on
which there is a general prohibition and describe the objective properties of the
weapons to be prohibited. In 1925 the Geneva Protocol prohibited the use of chemical
and bacteriological weapons. In 1972 the ban on bacteriological means of warfare was
restated and strengthened by a specific Convention designed to prohibit the manufacture and stockpiling of these agents of destruction. More recently, the use of three
categories of weapons was proscribed by a Convention adopted in 1980, to which
three Protocols were annexed (a fourth Protocol was adopted in 1995). The first
Protocol prohibits any weapon whose primary effect is to injure by fragments non-
detectable in the human body by X-rays. The second bans the use on land of mines,
booby traps, and other devices, if employed indiscriminately or when directed against
civilians (it was amended in 1996 with a view to strengthening restrictions on the use
of land mines). The third proscribes incendiary weapons, however not *per se* but if
such weapons are used to attack civilians or civilian objects, or military objectives
'located within a concentration of civilians'. The fourth Protocol prohibits blinding
laser weapons.

Strikingly, the First Protocol banning the use of 'any weapon the primary effect of which is to injure by fragments which in the human body escape detection by X-rays', concerns weapons that in fact do not exist. When the first move to ban such weapons was made, it was erroneously believed that US military forces had used them in Vietnam. Although it was later made clear that the weapons had actually not been used or even manufactured and that no State planned to include them in its arsenal, the ban was enacted, probably because major military Powers wished to show their readiness to make concessions and, in any case the issue was harmless (but the ban can serve the purpose of discouraging States from engaging in the manufacture of the weapon in question).

In 1976 a Convention was adopted within the UN on the prohibition of military and any other hostile use of environmental modification techniques. In 1997 States agreed upon the Ottawa Convention on the prohibition of the use, stockpiling, production, and transfer of antipersonnel mines and on their destruction.

The prohibition of specific weapons by specific bans or restrictions has two undoubted advantages. First, since the relevant international proscriptions refer to weapons by describing their objective features, a high degree of certainty is provided about the kind of weapons outlawed. By the same token, the prohibitions and restrictions are capable of providing normative guidance which is effective, even in the absence of an enforcement authority, as can be seen from the fact that, generally speaking, the various prohibitions of specific weapons have been respected even though there have been occasional violations.

This approach presents, however, two major drawbacks. First, as we saw above, so far international bans have concerned only those weapons which proved to be of minor military effectiveness or which, although militarily effective, might also present a risk to the belligerent using them. Accordingly, not only did bombing from aircraft fail to be prohibited, but—what is of course more important—no specific ban on the use of atomic and nuclear weapons has ever been enacted.

A second shortcoming is that even the bans on minor weapons can be easily bypassed by elaborating new and more sophisticated weapons which, while they are no less cruel, do not fall under the prohibition owing to new features.

(iii) Nuclear weapons. Let us now briefly consider a delicate and important issue, that of the legality of use of nuclear weapons.

In theory, nuclear weapons might be used in various different situations: (1) to launch an attack against another State, thus initiating a war proper (*aggressive first strike*); (2) to make a pre-emptive attack on another State, when the attacking State believes that the other State is about to launch a nuclear attack (*pre-emptive first strike*); (3) to respond in kind to a nuclear attack (or to an attack involving the extensive use of prohibited weapons of mass destruction) by another State (*second use in self-defence*); (4) to inflict devastating losses on the enemy in the course of a conventional war (*first use in a conventional war*); (5) to retaliate against the enemy's first use of nuclear weapons, or large-scale use of such prohibited weapons of mass destruction as chemical or bacteriological weapons, in the course of conventional war (*retaliatory use in a conventional war*). Nuclear Powers, which still support the so-called policy of deterrence, claim that they have the right to discourage military aggression by demonstrating that it will serve no purpose; they consequently claim to be entitled to resort to self-defence by using nuclear weapons (the enemy knows that, should it launch a first nuclear strike, its territory will be devastated by a nuclear response). Nuclear Powers thus justify the use of nuclear weapons listed under (2), (3) and (5) above.

What is the response of law? Since treaty prohibitions on or treaty authorizations of the use of nuclear weapons are lacking, and no specific customary rule has evolved on the matter, reliance must be placed on two sets of rules: those on resort to force (these are contained in the UN Charter and have by now turned into customary law), and the principles and customary rules of international humanitarian law.

Scant support can be drawn from State practice. An element of some weight is the protest lodged with the US Government on 10 August 1945, through Switzerland, by the Japanese Imperial Government, which stated that the atomic bomb dropped on Hiroshima (an instance of what I called above *first use in a conventional war*) was contrary to international law since it 'produced suffering not inferior to that caused by other weapons specifically prohibited by international law'. One may also mention the famous decision handed down in 1962 by the Tokyo District Court in *Shimoda et al*. In that decision the Court confined itself to passing judgment upon the lawfulness of the specific case of the bombings of Hiroshima and Nagasaki and did not claim to make a general pronouncement concerning atomic or nuclear weapons. The Court concluded that that bombing was unlawful for it was contrary both to the principle prohibiting indiscriminate attacks on undefended towns, and to the principle forbidding the use of weapons causing unnecessary suffering.[6]

Let us therefore discuss the various hypotheses suggested above, in the light of general legal principles.

As for an *aggressive first strike*, this—like any armed attack not in self-defence, by whatever weapon it may be carried out—would be clearly contrary to Article 2.4 of the UN Charter. The ICJ clearly recognized this in 1996 in its Advisory Opinion on *Legality of the Threat or Use of Nuclear Weapons*.[7]

In the case of a *pre-emptive first strike* by using nuclear weapons, it would seem that again this is contrary to Article 2.4, because Article 51 of the UN Charter does not authorize such strikes, whatever the arms involved (see **14.4.1(c)**). It should be noted that in its aforementioned Advisory Opinion the ICJ failed to address this important issue. Be that as it may, one should however not be blind to a hard and insurmountable fact: the nuclear Powers, in particular the five permanent members of the Security Council, all claim that they are entitled to use nuclear weapons to prevent a serious and imminent nuclear attack (and perhaps even a massive attack with weapons of mass destruction). Thus, the nuclear policy advocated by those Powers is in strident contrast with what seems to be the better interpretation of international law. This is a typical instance where, should the conflict between policy and law materialize, the latter would evidently cave in.

As for the *second use in self-defence* as defined above, it can be held to be lawful only if it meets various requirements. First, those of necessity and proportionality, as the ICJ stated in general terms in 1986 in *Nicaragua*[8] and repeated, with specific reference to the arms in issue, in *Legality of the Threat or Use of Nuclear Weapons*.[9] Second, the requirements deriving from two fundamental principles of international humanitarian law: that on protection of civilians, with the consequent obligation of always distinguishing between civilian and military objectives, and the principle whereby it is prohibited to cause unnecessary suffering to combatants. Third, the principles of neutrality, whereby belligerents must respect the inviolability of neutral powers. The ICJ admitted all of these requirements in its aforementioned Advisory Opinion.[10] However, it is doubtful whether nuclear weapons can be used in such a manner as to meet all these requirements (but some nuclear Powers claim that the so-called tactical nuclear weapons may be used in keeping with international law).

Surprisingly the Court also held that 'in view of the current state of international law, and of the elements of fact at its disposal, [it could not] conclude definitively whether the threat or use of nuclear weapons would be lawful or unlawful in an extreme circumstance of self-defence, in which the very survival of a State would be at stake'.[11] Two objections can be made against this ambiguous ruling. First, it does not clarify whether, in the instance of self-defence to which it alludes, the aforementioned requirements must be respected. In other words, did the Court intend to say that the law does not specify whether in the case of self-defence 'in which the very survival of the State would be at stake', that State could breach the principles of proportionality, the other two fundamental principles of humanitarian law and the principle of neutrality? Second, did the Court intend self-defence to encompass anticipatory or pre-emptive self-defence?

As for the *first use of nuclear weapons in a conventional war*, it would no doubt be contrary to the requirements just mentioned. It must therefore be held to be absolutely illegal.

In contrast, a *retaliatory use in a conventional war* would be lawful if it clearly met the requirements referred to above.

15.6.3 CONDUCT OF HOSTILITIES: METHODS OF COMBAT

(i) Traditional law. In traditional law on the conduct of hostilities one should distinguish between two sets of rules: those meeting the needs of all belligerents, regardless of the power they wielded; and those which instead were calculated to favour, directly or indirectly, the stronger States. The former includes such rules as those prohibiting treachery (Article 23(b) of the Hague Regulations); the killing or wounding of enemies who have 'laid down their arms or, no longer having any means of defence, have surrendered at discretion' (Article 23(c)); the declaration that no quarter will be given, in other words that even the defeated enemies willing to surrender will be killed (Article 23(d)); the improper use of flags of truce, of national flags, or of the military insignia and uniform of the enemy, the distinctive signs of the Geneva Conventions; and, lastly, pillage. Similarly, to this class belongs the rule allowing 'ruses

of war' and 'the employment of measures necessary for obtaining information about the enemy'. All these norms are clearly intended to introduce a minimum of fair play into the conduct of hostilities and actually serve the interests of all parties.

By contrast, when it comes to the rules prescribing how belligerents must behave in areas where civilians are located—areas that normally constitute the greatest part of the battlefield—it becomes apparent that the international regulations grant scant protection either to civilians or to the weaker belligerent. In short, belligerents must not attack, either from land or from sea, 'undefended towns, villages, dwellings, or buildings' '(Article 25 of the Hague Regulations). However, the concept of 'undefended town' was not defined, nor was a procedure envisaged for the reaching of an agreement between the contending parties about the 'undefended' status of a certain locality. As a consequence, an invading Power could refuse to consider a locality as 'undefended' even if it had been declared such by the adversary.

No less loose and defective were the rules governing the attack on 'defended' localities: Article 26 of the Hague Regulations merely provided that 'the officer in command of an attacking force must do all in his power to warn the authorities before commencing a bombardment, except in cases of assault', and Article 27 provided that 'all necessary steps must be taken to spare, as far as possible' churches, works of art, hospitals, and historic monuments.

(ii) The new law. Modern international regulation of methods of combat is very defective indeed. Following the spread of air warfare, which rendered the concept of 'undefended localities' still more uncertain, and in any event utterly obsolete, State practice has gradually brought about the emergence of three fundamental principles: (1) it is prohibited to attack civilian objects alone or to hit military and civilian objects indiscriminately; (2) when launching an attack, precautions must be taken to spare civilian objects; (3) in case an attack on military objectives cannot but cause incidental loss of civilian life or destruction of civilian objects, precautions must be taken so that such losses or destruction be not out of proportion to the military advantage. However, all three principles were so loose as to lend themselves to the most divergent interpretations. For one thing, for a long time the very concept of military objective was not clearly defined, and could therefore be extended at discretion. This circumstance, of necessity, weakened the principle about indiscriminate attacks. Second, 'precautions' cannot be defined in precise terms either. In this respect too, States retain great latitude. Consequently the second principle also turns out to be rather weak. Third, 'proportionality' is by definition very questionable, except in extreme cases (for example, if in order to destroy a tiny garrison controlling a bridge, the adversary annihilates a whole village surrounding the place where the garrison is located).

Although the three principles referred to above are vague and contain too many loopholes, they still provide a standard for at least the most glaring cases. One should not lose sight of the fact that were they lacking, no restraints on military power would exist and any war would soon turn into even worse carnage than the wars we have known so far.

The principles under consideration were clarified and given legal precision—to the extent, of course, that this was feasible in view of the open or covert opposition of major military Powers—in Protocol I of 1977.

A few illustrations of the trends emerging in the Conference may suffice. Article 52.2, for example, lays down a general definition of military objectives ('Those objects which by their nature, location, purpose or use make an effective contribution to military action and whose total or partial destruction, capture or neutralization, in the circumstances ruling at the time, offers a definite military advantage'). This definition is so sweeping that it can cover practically anything. More useful are the definitions of 'indiscriminate attacks' (Article 51.4 and 51.5), and 'precautionary measures' to be taken when launching an attack (Articles 57 and 58), or the various provisions on civilian objects (Articles 52–6), non-defended localities (Articles 59) and 'demilitarized zones' (Article 60).

Many of the relevant rules met, however, with the opposition of a number of strong military States (for instance, Britain, France, the USA). Some of them voiced great concern or took exception to the workability of the rules. Indeed, of the States just mentioned only Britain ratified the Protocol (however, with numerous and far-reaching reservations). It could therefore be contended that the most significant of those rules merely constitute contractual undertakings that will become binding on the ratifying States only. In other words, although they build upon, expand, and give precision to customary law, arguably they themselves have not yet become generally binding principles.

In 2000, in *Kupreškić et al*. Trial Chamber II of the ICTY stated that Articles 57 and 58, on precautionary measures against collateral civilian casualties, to be taken when attacking military objectives, 'are now part of customary international law, not only because they specify and flesh out general pre-existing norms, but also because they do not appear to be contested by any State, including those which have not ratified the Protocol'.[12] The Court went on to say that the loose nature of these rules, giving a wide margin of discretion to belligerents, could be somewhat restricted by resort to the Martens Clause (see above, **6.2.3**). It then indicated an interesting way of applying that clause to the particular problem at issue.[13]

One important advance made in 1977 should not, however, be passed over in silence. A rule was adopted prohibiting what was described as 'the use of methods or means of warfare which are intended or may be expected to cause such damage [i.e. widespread, long-term, and severe damage] to the natural environment and thereby to prejudice the health and survival of the population' (Article 55; see also Article 35.3). This provision was supported by practically all States. Its enactment had been preceded by various pronouncements by States during the Vietnam war to the effect that weapons damaging the environment were unlawful or should be banned. In addition, the rule is the outgrowth of greater concern in the world community for the environment, regardless of whether the threat occurs in time of peace or of war. One could therefore maintain that that provision already reflects a general consensus of States and thus is binding on all members of the world community. (However, in its 1996 Advisory Opinion on *The Legality of the Threat or Use of Nuclear Weapons*, the ICJ held that the 'powerful constraints' deriving from those provisions were only binding 'for all the States having subscribed to [the] provisions'.)[14]

15.6.4 PROTECTION OF WAR VICTIMS

In the past, more satisfactory than the rules on the conduct of hostilities were those protecting war victims, namely all the persons who do not take part in hostilities (civilians) or, having engaged in combat, are no longer in a position to do so (prisoners of war, the wounded, sick, or shipwrecked). In this area the Hague codification of 1899 and 1907, as well as some Geneva Conventions, made much headway.

At present the protection of war victims is the subject of extensive and detailed international legislation, to be found both in the four Geneva Conventions of 1949, and in Protocol I of 1977.

Lawful combatants who fall into the hands of the enemy, either because they surrender or because they are wounded, sick, or shipwrecked, are entitled to the status of *prisoner of war*: they may be interned in prisoner-of-war camps (that must located far from the combat zone). They must be held in good health and be treated humanely. They also have a set of rights (for example, against violence, intimidation, or insult); the Third Geneva Convention of 1949 spells them out in detail.

Under the Conventions civilians are satisfactorily protected to the extent that they are in the hands of the adversary either from the outset of the hostilities, or after the occupation of enemy territory. By contrast, those who happen to be in the theatre of military operations are only safeguarded by Protocol I.

What are the reasons for the difference between the section of the laws of warfare protecting the victims of war (with the exception just mentioned) and the other sections, such as that concerning means and methods of combat? Humanitarian considerations have counted more in this area than in others, where they have been outweighed by military demands. Plainly, it is in the interest of major military Powers to afford strong protection to war victims, while they are less concerned with prohibitions or restraints on the conduct of hostilities. On the other hand, small countries as well are interested in expanding the protection of war victims, if only for humanitarian reasons.

15.6.5 MEANS OF ENSURING COMPLIANCE WITH LAW

(i) Traditional law. One of the weakest points of traditional international law concerned the means for ensuring compliance with the laws of warfare. No third-party institution existed, nor was a third State or any independent commission ever entrusted with the task of scrutinizing the behaviour of belligerents. In the final analysis, each of them took upon itself the task of unilaterally determining whether the adversary abided by the law, and of enforcing it in cases of disregard.

Three devices were available and were in fact used to a great extent. (1) Belligerent reprisals (for example the maltreatment of prisoners of war, the unlawful bombardment of 'undefended' localities or of buildings immune from attack, etc.). Belligerent reprisals were a barbaric institution, ultimately leading to the killing of innocent combatants or civilians, punished for the misdeeds of their fellow countrymen. In addition, they lent themselves to abuses owing to the absence of any impartial verification of violations by the enemy. (2) Criminal punishment of enemy combatants or civilians guilty of 'war crimes', that is, serious violations of the laws of warfare. However, normally trials of war crimes were initiated after the war by the victor against nationals of the defeated country (whereas if proceedings were instituted during the hostilities, the adversary could easily retaliate by similarly prosecuting and punishing the enemies in his hands). (3) The payment of compensation for any violation perpetrated. Plainly, compensation was requested by the victor once the war was over, while the defeated had no means of doing likewise.

(ii) The new law

(1) *Reprisals.* As noted above, reprisals constitute the most rudimentary and widespread means of inducing the adversary to abide by the law. While traditional international law did not place any restraints with regard to the target of reprisals, the 1949 Geneva Conventions banned reprisals against 'protected persons' (prisoners of war, the wounded, sick, or shipwrecked, and civilians who found themselves in the hands of the enemy). These bans have by now turned into customary law. By contrast, reprisals against civilians were implicitly allowed in the theatre of military operations. This, of course, was a deplorable state of affairs, for reprisals are open to the worst abuses and, in addition, play ultimately into the hands of major military Powers (but States favourable to reprisals contend that, despite their shortcomings, they constitute the only effective sanction available to belligerents).

The 1974–7 Conference extended the ban to a series of civilian persons or civilian objects finding themselves on the battlefield (Articles 51.6; 53(c); 54.4; 55.2; 56.4 of Protocol I). However, the strong opposition of States such as France and Australia, and the misgivings entertained by a number of other States, may lead one to believe that those provisions remained treaty law, and consequently bind only those States which ratify or accede to the Protocol (without entering reservations).

A different view was taken in 2000, admittedly in an *obiter dictum*, by the ICTY in *Kupreškić et al.* Trial Chamber II put forward the proposition that 'the demands of humanity and the dictates of public conscience, as manifested in *opinio necessitatis*, have by now brought about the formation of a customary rule also binding upon those few States that at some stage did not intend to exclude the abstract legal possibility of resorting to the reprisals [against civilians not in the hand of the enemy belligerents, i.e. in the combat zone]'.[15] The Court among other things based its contention on the notion that 'while reprisals could have had a modicum of justification in the past, when they constituted practically the only means of compelling the enemy to abandon unlawful acts of warfare and to comply in future with international law, at present they can no longer be justified in this manner. A means of inducing compliance with international law is at present more widely available and, more importantly, is beginning to prove fairly efficacious: the prosecution and punishment of war crimes and crimes against humanity by national or international courts.'[16]

(2) *Penal repression of breaches.* As has already been stated above (**Chapter 12**) serious violations of international humanitarian law may be prosecuted and repressed both by national courts (that is, those of the national or territorial State, or of a third State, whenever the requisite conditions are met), and at the international level (by the ICTY, the ICTR, or the ICC and the Special Court for Sierra Leone, once they are established). This way of forestalling breaches of that body of law, and repressing them whenever they occur, is no doubt the most appropriate and fitting method of ensuring compliance with humanitarian law, for it is based on principles of fair trial and impartial finding of facts and law.

(3) *Protecting Powers.* The 1949 Geneva Conventions codified and improved on international practice concerning the designation of 'Protecting Powers' by belligerents for the purpose of safeguarding their interests as well as impelling the adversary to abide by international law.

In a nutshell, the Conventions provided that each of the belligerents could appoint a third State as 'Protecting Power'. But for the State to accomplish its tasks the consent of both belligerents was necessary. Thus the 1949 system hinged on a 'double-decker three-sided' relationship: the two belligerents and two third parties. Once a triangular agreement was reached, a third party could act as a 'Protecting Power' on behalf of each belligerent and scrutinize the implementation of the Conventions. (Nothing, of course, ruled out the possibility of a third State acting as Protecting Power for both belligerents). As the consent of all the States involved was necessary for the appointment and functioning of Protecting Powers it follows that if one of them withdrew consent the Protecting Power ceased to act. A significant advance of the 1949 Conventions lay in the provision of 'Substitutes for the Protecting Powers'. Of the three possibilities envisaged by the Conventions, the third stood out on account of its mandatory character: under Article 10/10/10/11, paragraph 3, the Detaining Power (that is, the State detaining the enemy wounded, shipwrecked, prisoners of war, or civilians) was duty bound to accept 'the offer of the services of a humanitarian organization, such as the International Committee of the Red Cross to assume the humanitarian functions performed by Protecting Powers under the present Convention'.

In practice the Protecting Powers system proved a (relative) failure. It was resorted to only in five cases: in 1956, in the Suez conflict (only, however, between Egypt on the one hand and France and the UK on the other); in the French-Tunisian conflict over Bizerte in 1961; in the short Goa affair in 1961, when India invaded the Portuguese colony; in the Indo-Pakistani war in 1971, although India soon withheld its consent; and in the 1982 Falklands-Malvinas conflict between Argentina and the UK (Switzerland acted on behalf of the UK whilst Brazil protected the interests of Argentina; however, neither State was formally designated as a Protecting Power). The various causes for its failure include belligerents' fear that they would recognize each other as a result of the appointment of Protecting Powers, the desire not to sever diplomatic relations, and the marked tendency not to enter into any agreement with the adversary.

One should also note both the propensity of States not to accept the offers of the

International Committee of the Red Cross (ICRC) to act as a substitute, as well as the reluctance of the ICRC to step in and take on the role of substitute.

The system instituted in Article 5 of the First Protocol of 1977 substantially takes up the 1949 system. It spells out that the consent of all the parties concerned is all important. Consent is made the linchpin of the system, and any automatic obligation, even that laid down in Article 10/ 10/10/11, paragraph 3 of the 1949 Conventions is done away with. Also (in paragraph 3) it sets up a procedure for facilitating the appointment of Protecting Powers: it eliminates some of the practical or political obstacles to the appointment of Powers, by specifying in paragraphs 5 and 6 that the designation and acceptance of Powers does not affect the legal status of the parties to the conflict or of any territory, and that diplomatic relations can be maintained by the belligerents despite the functioning of Powers.

15.7 CURRENT REGULATION OF INTERNAL ARMED CONFLICT

15.7.1 GENERAL FEATURES OF THE LEGAL REGULATION OF CIVIL STRIFE

The whole approach of international law to civil strife rests on an inherent clash of interests between the 'lawful' government on the one side (which is interested in regarding insurgents as mere bandits devoid of any international status) and rebels, on the other side (eager to be internationally legitimized). Third States may, and actually do, side with either party, according to their own political or ideological leanings, and this, of course, further complicates the question.

All rules governing the struggle between the lawful government and insurgents have one main feature in common: they do not grant rebels the status of lawful belligerents. In the eyes of both the government against which they fight and of third States, rebels remain criminals infringing upon domestic penal law. Consequently, if captured, they do not enjoy the status of prisoner of war but can be tried and punished for the mere fact of having taken up arms against the central authorities. Insurgents can be upgraded to the status of lawful combatants only if the incumbent Government decides to grant them the so-called recognition of belligerency. As pointed out earlier (see **4.1**), this recognition has only been accorded in the past and in extreme situations. The obsolescence of the recognition of belligerency derives mainly from the desire of the governments involved in civil commotion to wipe out rebellion as soon as possible, as well as from the interest of the third States in either remaining aloof or meddling de facto in the conflict without, however, going to the length of granting insurgents international legitimation. Thus rebels are normally in a greatly inferior position in relation to the central authorities against which they fight. If however the insurrectional government comes to possess international rights and duties, this achievement might perhaps entail for its armed forces the acquisition of the status of lawful combatants.

Another important feature of the corpus of rules concerning internal armed conflict is that most of them aim at protecting non-combatants only. Methods of combat are not regulated, except to the extent that they must aim at sparing civilians. In practice, there are almost no restraints on the armed engagements of government authorities and rebels *inter se*. States prefer to leave fighting substantially unrestricted on the clear assumption that, being militarily stronger than insurgents, they may quell rebellion more easily by remaining untrammelled by law. This concept is proving increasingly fallacious, for, at present, rebels are assisted in various ways, especially militarily, by third States, and armed violence is therefore carried out with intensity and cruelty on both sides.

15.7.2 CUSTOMARY LAW

As the ICTY Appeals Chamber stated in 1995 in *Tadić* (*Interlocutory Appeal*),[17] since the 1930s the traditional dichotomy between inter-State conflicts and civil strife, the former category governed by numerous international rules, the latter substantially left to the operation of national criminal law, has become blurred. As a consequence internal armed conflicts have increasingly been taken away from State sovereignty and regulated by international rules. The Court found four reasons for this development: the growing frequency of these conflicts; their becoming more and more cruel and protracted; the difficulty for third States to remain aloof; the impetuous propagation in the international community of the human rights doctrine.

The whole process started in the late 1930s. Owing to its ruinous effect and the magnitude of its armed hostilities, the Spanish Civil War (1936–9) acquired features comparable in several respects to an international war proper. This prompted the contending parties and several European States to affirm that certain general rules protecting civilians in inter-State wars were applicable to this conflict as well, and to all similar examples of civil strife. Thus, a very interesting phenomenon took shape, which has become a major trend of the present century: the increasing extension to civil wars of the principles applicable to international armed conflicts. The rules on which general consent emerged were: the ban on deliberate bombing of civilians; the prohibition on attacking non-military objectives; the rule concerning the precautions which must be taken when attacking military objects; the rule authorizing reprisals against enemy civilians and consequently submitting them to the general conditions exacted for reprisals.

The four rules in question apply to any internal armed conflict, provided it has the characteristics of the Spanish Civil War. That is to say, the insurgents must exhibit the following features: an organized administration effectively controlling a portion of the territory of the State; and organized armed forces capable of abiding by international law. Internal armed conflicts having a lesser degree of intensity, for example, instances of minor rebellions, or uprisings which do not take on the proportions of a civil war proper, are not covered by the rules.

The formation of general norms on civilians was substantially borne out by the unanimous adoption by the UN GA in 1968 of resolution no. 2444 (XXIII), and, again, in 1970, when resolution no. 2675 (XXV) was passed. Interestingly, on a par with these UN resolutions, recent practice has reaffirmed the applicability to civil wars of at least some general rules on civilians. The ICRC urged such applicability on several occasions (for instance, in 1964 during the conflict in the Congo and during the 1966–9 Nigerian civil war), on none of which did it encounter any significant opposition. That these rules on civilians gradually turned into customary law was also stated in 1995 by the ICTY Appeals Chamber in *Tadić* (*Interlocutory Appeal*).[18]

Unfortunately these fairly satisfactory conditions of law are not matched by its observance in practice. It is dispiriting to notice that the government and rebels of the same State—even though they pay lip-service to current legal standards, and in spite of the fact that, after all, the civilians suffering from the conflict are fellow nationals— rarely protect non-combatants as requested by law. This has been the case in recent occurrences such as the Nigerian conflict and the civil wars in Nicaragua, El Salvador, the former Yugoslavia, Colombia, and Chechnya. A possible explanation is that, first, civilians often take sides in domestic strife and actually contribute, at various levels, to the struggle, and, second, in many States the population is split into conflicting ethnic and cultural (or religious) groups, which consequently do not share the feeling of belonging to one and the same country.

Another body of customary rules has evolved out of a provision common to the four 1949 Geneva Conventions, namely Article 3. (In 1986 the ICJ stressed this point in *Nicaragua*; it held that the provisions of the common Article 3 'constitute a minimum yardstick' applicable to any armed conflict and 'reflect what the Court in 1949 [in the *Corfu Channel* case] called "elementary considerations of humanity"'.)[19] This Article has a much broader field of application than the aforementioned general rules on civilians, for it applies to any internal armed conflict, even to those which do not reach a high level of intensity. Article 3, which makes a point of leaving the legal status of insurgents unaffected, is meant to protect only the victims of hostilities, namely 'persons taking no active part' in them, to whom it grants a set of basic humanitarian safeguards.

First, non-combatants must not be attacked; in other words, they must not be identified as a military target and can never be the object of deliberate attacks. Furthermore, the contending parties must not resort to measures intended to intimidate or terrorize the civilian population. These prohibitions clearly follow from the provision banning the infliction of violence on the life and persons of non-combatants. In this connection, it is interesting to recall that in a document of 30 January 1970, the Legal Bureau of the Canadian Government stated *inter alia* that Article 3 outlaws 'acts of the type occurring at My Lai [in Vietnam]'.[20] This statement referred to the ban on physical violence against civilians, stemming from Article 3.

Second, pursuant to Article 3, the taking of hostages is prohibited. This practice, it must be emphasized, has frequently been resorted to during civil wars, including the Spanish conflict; the relevant provision is, therefore, of great value.

Third, all reprisals involving violence to the life and persons of non-combatants, or outrages upon their personal dignity, are forbidden.

Fourth, if members of the armed forces of the adversary, or civilians belonging to the opposing party and suspected of supporting it, are arrested and detained, or are put into internment camps, they must be treated humanely. In particular, no discriminatory treatment can be meted out to them, nor can they be submitted to torture, or to cruel, humiliating, or degrading measures. In the event of their being brought to trial, all judicial safeguards provided for in paragraph 1 of Article 3 must be observed.

Finally, the wounded and sick, including those belonging to the adversary, must be collected and cared for.

State practice developed after 1949 shows that Article 3 was invoked, reaffirmed, and relied upon on a number of occasions. Even when it was disregarded in practice, no State admitted violating it. This is no matter for surprise, for Article 3 essentially enshrines a handful of humanitarian principles proclaimed by States in other contexts, such as the various treaties on human rights.

The fact remains, however, that the instances of violation or disregard for the provisions of Article 3 greatly outnumber the instances of compliance. Nonetheless, all these instances of non-observance have not been such as to erode the rule. (Similarly, domestic criminal laws are not obliterated by their daily violation).

It should be added that some rules on the conduct of hostilities in international armed conflict have also gradually been extended to internal conflicts. The rationale for this development was spelled out by the ICTY in *Tadić* (*Interlocutory Appeal*):

'[E]lementary considerations of humanity and common sense make it preposterous that the use by States of weapons prohibited in armed conflicts between themselves be allowed when States try to put down rebellion by their own nationals on their own territory. What is inhumane, and consequently proscribed, in international wars, cannot but be inhumane and inadmissible in civil strife.'[21]

In the same case the Appeals Chamber concluded that one such customary rule was that prohibiting the use of chemical weapons.

The trend towards the gradual extension of general principles and rules governing inter-State conflicts to internal conflicts was strengthened and bolstered by the gradual jettisoning of the notion whereby war crimes can only be perpetrated in inter-State wars. In 1995 the ICTY, in the aforementioned decision in *Tadić* (*Interlocutory Appeal*), set forth the view that serious violations of customary or treaty rules governing internal conflicts may also amount, subject to certain conditions, to war crimes.[22] This view was confirmed by the Statute of the ICTR (Article 4), the case law of the two Tribunals, Article 8.2 of the 1998 Statute of the ICC, and the 1999 UN Secretary-General's 'Bulletin on Observance by United Nations Forces of International Humanitarian Law'.[23]

15.7.3 TREATY LAW

A number of treaties agreed upon after 1949 also regulate internal armed conflicts. However, unlike the common Article 3 of the four Geneva Conventions of 1949, they have not turned into customary law, or, in some instances, only some of their most fundamental provisions have ripened into general law, while the bulk of each treaty exclusively governs the conduct of the contracting parties. There exists a general treaty on this matter, the Second Additional Protocol of 1977, and some conventions regulating specific matters: the 1954 Hague Convention on Cultural Property (see Article 19), updated by the 1999 Second Hague Protocol on the same matter (see Article 22); the 1996 Amended Protocol II to the 1980 UN Convention on certain conventional weapons; this Protocol prohibits or restricts the use on land of mines, booby-traps and other devices (see Article 1.2); the 1997 Ottawa Convention on the Prohibition of the Use, Stockpiling, Production and Transfer of Anti-Personnel Mines (see Article 1). It would also seem that many States and the ICRC have taken the 1995 Protocol IV to the UN 1980 Convention, on blinding laser weapons, to apply to this category of conflict although it does not explicitly cover civil strife.

Unfortunately, the Second Geneva Protocol of 1977 was mutilated and stripped of some very significant provisions at the eleventh hour. What matters here is to emphasize that although nearly all its provisions were adopted by consensus, and although the Protocol itself was the subject of consensus approval, a number of Third World countries raised strong and unequivocal objections. This group included States such as Nigeria, Sri Lanka, India, Indonesia, Mexico, Ghana, Sudan, Zaire, Guatemala, the Philippines, Uganda—as well as Chile, which made a 'reservation' actually calculated to hamstring the Protocol, as far as its possible application to Chile was concerned. Some of these States went so far as to declare that the Protocol was 'superfluous' (Mexico), 'pointless' (India), 'quite unnecessary' (Uganda), and even to state that it 'did not involve any international agreement but simply a concession on the part of States which agreed to apply it to their own nationals' (Sudan). The number and content of the objections was such as to lead the Turkish delegation to state that the consensus was only apparent.[24]

The Protocol exhibits a general feature differentiating it from the rules generated by Article 3 and putting it on the same footing as the various rules on civilians which emerged as a result of the Spanish Civil War: it covers only large-scale armed conflicts, that is to say, civil strife presenting all the characteristics of intensity, duration, and magnitude of the Spanish and Nigerian civil wars. It does not apply to 'situations of internal disturbances and tensions, such as riots, isolated and sporadic acts of violence and other acts of a similar nature'. Thus, the progress made in 1977 turns out to be limited on a threefold score. First, one is struck by the paucity of the rules agreed upon. Second, these rules do not cover all classes of internal armed conflicts, but only those above a certain 'threshold'. Finally, third States tend not to demand compliance with the Protocol when it is being violated.

For instance El Salvador did not heed it in the least in the civil strife that raged between 1981 and 1992, and other contracting States made no attempt to press for its application (but some States, for instance Switzerland, clearly stated that the Protocol did apply).[25] In a few instances States clearly stated that armed violence going on in a foreign country was such that it qualified as an internal armed conflict (for instance, the German Government so stated in 1994 with regard to the clashes between Kurds and the authorities in Turkey).[26] In some cases national courts held that Protocol II applied to ongoing conflicts. Thus, in a judgment of 26 September

1994, the Court of Appeal of Santiago held in *Osvaldo Romo Mena* that the common Article 3 and Protocol II were applicable in September–November 1974 to the armed clashes in Chile.[27] In a judgment of 1995, the Constitutional Court of Colombia ruled that the Protocol did cover the internal armed conflict then in progress.[28] Similarly, in a decision of 31 July 1995 the Russian Constitutional Court ruled that the Protocol was applicable to the conflict in Chechnya.[29] However, it would seem that in spite of constant pressure from other States and international organizations, neither the Russian authorities nor the Chechen rebels are living up to the relevant legal standards.

All the same, the Protocol represents the maximum which States participating in the Geneva Conference, and particularly Third World countries, were prepared to concede. To attain a more satisfactory general regulation of civil wars it will be necessary to await the appearance of a more favourable attitude on the part of States.

15.8 THE ROLE OF LAW IN RESTRAINING ARMED VIOLENCE

Over the years mankind has witnessed steady progress in the sophistication, the devastating effects, and the cruelty of weapons and methods of combat. Illusions about a 'permanent peace' can no longer be entertained, and one watches with astonishment the succession of barbarous armed conflicts and the lack of any real advantage for mankind.

International legal control of warfare has kept pace with the developments in organized armed violence only to a limited extent. States and, in particular, major military Powers have not accepted sweeping restraints, with the consequence that this body of law is beset with deficiencies, loopholes, and ambiguity.

However, a realistic assessment of the present condition should not beget despair. Legal rules, however weak and defective, do restrict the behaviour of States and introduce a modicum of humanity into utterly inhuman conduct. The absence of normative standards would be even more regrettable: it would leave strong military Powers—or for that matter, any State, even the poor ones provided they were supported by one of the Great Powers—free of any restraint. Furthermore, it is precisely the nature of the laws of warfare referred to above (**15.1**) which makes it clear that here, more than in any other area, legal standards possess a significant metajuridical value: they serve as a moral and political yardstick by which public opinion, and non-governmental groups and associations can appraise if, and to what extent, States misbehave.

16

PROTECTION OF HUMAN RIGHTS

16.1 INTRODUCTION

Since 1945 the doctrine of human rights has been troubling and upsetting some, inflaming and thrilling others, whether individuals, groups, or non-governmental organizations, or members of cabinet, diplomats, or other State officials. At the State level, after the Second World War this doctrine has become, for some countries, one of the significant postulates of their foreign policy, of great use when blaming or denouncing other countries, or guiding their actions within international organizations. To other States this doctrine has become an incubus instead: it serves as a yardstick by which their behaviour is gauged and may be censured in international fora.

The arrival of human rights on the international scene is, indeed, a remarkable event because it is a subversive theory destined to foster tension and conflict among States. Essentially it is meant to tear aside the veil that in the past covered and protected sovereignty, giving each State the appearance of a fully armoured titanic structure, perceived by other States only 'as a whole', the inner mechanisms of which could not be tampered with. Today the human rights doctrine forces States to give account of how they treat their nationals, administer justice, run prisons, and so on. Potentially, therefore, it can subvert their domestic order and, consequently, the traditional configuration of the international community as well.

On the whole, one can say that within the international community this doctrine has acquired the value and significance which, within the context of domestic systems, was accorded to Locke's theory of a social contract, Montesquieu's concept of the separation of powers, and Rousseau's theory of the sovereignty of the people. Just as these political ideas eroded absolute and despotic monarchy, democratizing the foundations on which kingdoms rested, so the doctrine of human rights has lent, and still lends, in the world community, tremendous impetus to respect for the dignity of all human beings, and also to the democratization of States.

Why then did States support and even advocate this 'theory' at an international level, knowing full well that it diverged radically from the political philosophy of State sovereignty and the basic principle on which the 'Grotian model' rested? What political and ideological motives induced certain members of the international community to propound ideas likely to undermine and disrupt their own authority?

16.2 TRADITIONAL INTERNATIONAL LAW

Traditionally individuals were under the exclusive jurisdiction of the State of which they were nationals and where they lived. No other State could interfere with the authority of that State, which in a way had a sort of right of life and death over those individuals. Beyond national boundaries individuals could only be taken into consideration qua *citizens* of a foreign State. If they suffered damage abroad, their interests were safeguarded only to the extent to which their national State decided to exercise diplomatic protection (by approaching through diplomatic channels the State that had allegedly wronged one's nationals in their person or property, with a view to obtaining compensation for the damage caused and possibly punishment of the wrongdoers), or judicial protection (by bringing a claim on behalf of one's nationals before an international arbitral tribunal or court). Individuals were mere 'appendices' of the State to which they belonged, simple pawns in its hands, to be used, protected, or sacrificed according to what State interests dictated.

Gradually, however, a few exceptions, took shape. Treaties prohibiting the slave trade were concluded in the nineteenth century. Others banning both the slave trade and slavery as such were made in the twentieth century. Conventions were concluded after the First World War, under the auspices of the ILO, to protect the rights of workers. In the same period various treaties safeguarding religious, ethnic, and linguistic minorities were agreed upon. All these conventions and treaties, although founded to a great extent on humanitarian considerations, were also motivated by the self-interest of the contracting States.

The pressure to put a stop to the trade in black slaves came in part from those European countries which no longer had colonial interests in the Americas and were consequently keen to end the flow of cheap manpower to other countries. In the case of ILO Conventions, guaranteeing uniformity of treatment to workers in all the major areas of the world prevented certain countries from taking unfair advantage in the international market of low labour costs at home (see also **4.5.2(c)**). The treaties on minorities (with Czechoslovakia, Greece, Poland, Rumania, and Yugoslavia) as well as the peace treaties including clauses on minorities (those with Austria, Bulgaria, Turkey, and Hungary) were to some extent politically motivated: those European countries which had ethnic, linguistic, or religious affinities with groups living in other countries were eager for these groups to be respected and immune from undue hindrance and interference. What is even more important—as President Wilson pointed out at the Peace Conference on 31 May 1919, in an attempt to rebuff the opposition of States where minorities existed—the international protection of minorities aimed at safeguarding peace, besides attenuating the often harsh consequences of the territorial partitions effected in Europe by the Great Powers.[1]

Even so, it remains true that one of the motivations behind these three classes of treaties was the concept that certain groups or categories of individuals ought to be protected by international law for their own sake.

After the Second World War international protection of human beings as such increased at a staggering pace. Individuals were no longer to be taken care of, on the international level, *qua* members of a group, a minority, or another category. They began to be protected *qua* single human beings. Furthermore, the international standards on the matter were no longer motivated, even in part, by economic interests, although they were often dictated by political considerations.

Why did things change so drastically? The main reason was the shared conviction, among all the victorious powers, that the Nazi aggression and the atrocities perpetrated during the war had been the fruits of a vicious philosophy based on utter disregard for the dignity of human beings. One means of preventing a return to these horrors was the proclamation at all levels of certain basic standards of respect for human rights. This view was propounded with greatest force by the Western Powers (in particular the USA), for the simple reason that their whole political philosophy and indeed the fundamental legal texts of some of their national systems were based on a 'bill of rights'. Therefore, it came naturally to them to project their domestic concepts and creeds on to the international community.

The victors adopted a two-pronged strategy. They pursued, on the one hand, the development of international criminal law to meet the immediate need of bringing to justice and punishing German and Japanese war criminals who had committed inhuman acts. On the other hand, they set out to elaborate a set of general principles on human rights designed to serve as guidelines for the UN and its member States, the intent being that they would be gradually implemented and elaborated upon through traditional normative means, that is to say, treaties.

These two approaches, although distinct, supplement each other. Both stemmed from the desire to punish those guilty of atrocities and, by the same token, prevent the recurrence of similar acts in future by setting standards to be observed even in peacetime.

16.3 THE TURNING POINT: THE UN CHARTER

As pointed out above, the lead was taken in 1945 by Western countries and chiefly by the USA. President Roosevelt, in his message to Congress of 6 January 1941, had already listed the 'four freedoms', which he saw as important goals of future US foreign policy:

'In the future days, which we seek to make secure, we look forward to a world founded upon four essential human freedoms. The first is freedom of speech and expression—everywhere in the world. The second is freedom of every person to worship God in his own way—everywhere in the world. The third is freedom from want—which, translated into world terms, means economic understandings which will secure to every nation a healthy, peaceful life for its inhabitants—everywhere in the world. The fourth is freedom from fear—which translated into world terms, means a world wide reduction of armaments to such a point and in such a thorough fashion that no nation will be in a position to commit an act of aggression against any neighbour—anywhere in the world.'[2]

The lofty concepts enunciated by Roosevelt were taken up in the Atlantic Charter of 14 August 1941 and subsequently amplified by the US delegation to the Dumbarton Oaks Conference in 1944. In the 'US Tentative Proposals for a General International Organization' of 18 July 1944, it was suggested that the GA of the UN should be responsible for

'initiating studies and making recommendations for . . . the promotion of the observance of basic human rights in accordance with the principles or undertakings agreed upon by the States members of the International Organization'.[3]

It is apparent from this proposal that, once one moved from the proclamation of lofty principles at the political level to the adoption of treaty provisions, even the very State which had championed the inclusion of human rights among the matters under the jurisdiction of the UN eventually proceeded with the utmost caution. Indeed, it took pains to spell out that the Organization should have limited powers only. In particular, the standards on human rights by which member States should be guided were to be first accepted by them through the traditional process of treaty making. The American restraint was clearly motivated by domestic reasons: there were constitutional problems, which the acceptance of international obligations on human rights might raise, but also, and more importantly, in the USA in 1945 various racist laws were in force—and continued in force until the 1960s. These laws might easily expose the US Government to international censure and scrutiny if internationally binding obligations on human rights were enacted through the UN Charter.

At the Dumbarton Oaks Conference (August–October 1944), the initial opposition of the UK and the USSR led the USA to water down its proposals even further. In fact the provision on human rights produced by the four Powers (the USA, the USSR, the UK, and China), was quite weak. However, when the San Francisco Conference (April–June 1945) began, the four sponsoring Powers were confronted with a spate of bold amendments, mostly emanating from Latin American countries. This, as well as the conversion of the USSR to the cause of human rights (it put forward specific proposals on the matter, particularly on non-discrimination and self-determination of peoples), led the four Powers to consider it advisable to strengthen their proposals.

In the course of the San Francisco Conference three alignments emerged. On the one hand, there was a group of vocal Latin American countries (chiefly Brazil, Colombia, Chile, Cuba, the Dominican Republic, Ecuador, Mexico, Panama, and Uruguay) plus a few Western States (Australia, New Zealand, and Norway) joined by such nations as India. These countries put forward amendments substantially calculated to lay down an obligation to respect human rights. The second group of States included major Western Powers which, though favourable to the promotion of human rights, opposed the attempts to expand the sphere of action of the UN and to lay down definite obligations to respect human rights. The USA took a lead on this score, by strongly objecting to the broadening of Article 56 and also by insisting on the need to lay down a safeguarding clause protecting State sovereignty from undue interference from the Organization (the proviso that later became Article 2.7 on domestic jurisdiction). A third group, consisting of socialist countries (Byelorussia, Czechoslovakia, and Ukraine) led by the USSR, although substantially upholding the restrictive attitude of the second group just mentioned, distinguished itself by stressing the importance of the right of peoples to self-determination (a right which major Western countries, plus such colonial powers as Belgium, strongly opposed).

In addition, the USSR put forward proposals clearly showing that differences existed even in areas where there seemingly was agreement between East and West. Thus, for instance, when the four Great Powers met in San Francisco and discussed the proposal that the UN should promote 'respect for human rights', the USSR suggested that this should be followed by the words: 'in particular, the right to work, and the right to education'. The USA and the UK opposed this proposal, on the grounds that if it was specified which rights were to be protected, then others should be added—in particular the right to freedom of information and freedom of religion. Similarly, when at San Francisco the report of 'Technical Committee 3' (charged with discussing matters relating to economic and social co-operation) came to be discussed within Commission II of the Conference, the Soviet delegate drew attention to the part played by the USSR in improving on the Dumbarton Oaks proposals and specifically mentioned the principle of respect for human rights. He only spoke of economic, social, and cultural rights, however.[4]

The upshot of the lengthy discussions at San Francisco was that the first group of States did not obtain any substantial gains, while the other two groups reached a compromise which, to some extent, accommodated their mutual demands. The compromise consisted of the following provisions: (1) there was *no specific obligation* to take separate action for the promotion, let alone the protection, of human rights (see Article 56); (2) the right of self-determination of peoples was proclaimed (Articles 1 and 55), but only as a guiding principle for the Organization and in the *emasculated version of self-government*; (3) the powers of the GA in the field of human rights, already very weak (they boiled down to *making recommendations* and *conducting studies*), were further limited by the proviso of Article 2.7 (on domestic jurisdiction); (4) the Charter provisions on human rights were inspired by the conviction that respect for human rights should only be furthered as *a means of safeguarding peace*.

16.4 TRENDS IN THE EVOLUTION OF INTERNATIONAL ACTION ON HUMAN RIGHTS

Faced with this normative framework, member States of the UN were to decide how to make use of the loose formulas of the Charter. Broadly speaking, two possible courses of action were open to them. Either they could confine themselves to using the GA as a 'regular diplomatic conference' and accordingly draft conventions or stimulate States to pursue certain objectives by addressing general recommendations to them, in keeping with a liberal construction of Article 2.7. Arguably, to have achieved this would by no means have been a poor performance: the mere fact of detailing and spelling out in international instruments the human rights and fundamental freedoms, for the promotion of which States should strive, would have constituted a major accomplishment.

Alternatively, a less moderate course of action was available. By placing a strict interpretation on Article 2.7 the Organization could go beyond the mere elaboration of international standards, and call States to account, at least in cases of massive infringements of human rights. To this effect, the UN could turn the GA into the 'conscience of the world', by endowing it with the role of watchdog, to forestall or castigate egregious deviations from basic standards on human rights.

In the following pages we shall see that the UN (and regional organizations) gradually took the second path.

The majority in the UN and consequently the prevailing political philosophy underpinning UN action changed in the course of time. One can pinpoint four different phases. The first stage, which dated from the adoption of the UN Charter to the late 1950s, was characterized by Western dominance. At the regional level this approach led to the adoption, within the Council of Europe, of the 1950 European Convention on Human Rights, a landmark in the evolution of the international protection of human rights. The second stage, which started with the strengthening in the UN of the socialist group in 1955 and its taking the lead among the developing countries, had as its main feature the need for the West to come to terms with the other two groups, with the consequent striking of a number of important comprom-ises such as the two Covenants on human rights of 1966. The third stage, which started around 1974 and ended around 1990, was marked by the prevalence of devel-oping countries. It launched a new doctrine of human rights, which eventually gained the upper hand in many respects and aimed at supplanting or at least toning down, as much as possible, the views previously upheld by the GA. The present stage, which opened with the end of the cold war, has as its main feature the disappearance of three markedly differentiated groupings of States and the emergence of broad consensus on the need to consider respect for human rights a *sine qua non* for full international legitimation, that is, in order to participate in international intercourse.

It may prove helpful briefly to sketch out the philosophy and strategy of human rights championed in each stage by the prevailing majority of the time in the GA. A brief account of these philosophies will enable the reader better to understand the thrust of the legislative and monitoring output of the various international bodies.

16.4.1 THE FORMATIVE YEARS OF HUMAN RIGHTS DOCTRINES

(a) The Western doctrine

In the first years after the adoption of the Charter, the Western political philosophy easily prevailed. It can be summarized as follows: (1) Although it is not really possible to rank human rights in order of preference, civil and political rights appear to be of primary importance, especially certain rights such as freedom of thought and religion, which distinguish democracies from authoritarian States. (2) Self-determination constitutes only a general principle, not a full right of peoples. (3) International treaties laying down obligations in the field of human rights should be as clear and precise as possible; woolly terminology should be avoided, as should treaties which place too many restrictions on the freedom of individual States (lest a significant number of States failed to ratify the treaties). (4) It is not sufficient to approve international treaties to protect human rights; of equal importance is the establishment of international monitoring mechanisms to verify that the ratifying States are respecting these measures; without some kind of international supervision, treaties not only are of little practical use but may boil down to mere propaganda tools. (5) The promotion of human rights is an end to be pursued in its own right; it is not at any cost to be subordinated to the goal of attaining friendly relations between States.

(b) The socialist doctrine

Two important political events heralded the beginning of the second phase: the strengthening of the socialist group in 1955 owing to the admission of four eastern European countries to the UN and the fact that the highly confrontational spirit typical of the first years of the cold war began gradually to dwindle.

Briefly, the main points of the socialist 'doctrine' were as follows: (1) The UN Charter and later UN documents had led to the emergence of a universal principle by virtue of which all States must respect human rights without distinction of race, sex, language, or religion. To comply with this principle and with the international conventions which spelled it out, States must take the necessary legislative steps at a national level. Once this had been done, respect for human rights was *an internal question*: it was for the laws of each State to recognize human rights; responsibility for safeguarding these rights rested with the authorities of the State. (2) Nationals of a State must be content with bringing any alleged breach of human rights before State authorities; they must not be allowed to petition international agencies. (3) It was not for other countries or for the UN to interfere in this process; no intervention must be made in the internal affairs of States. (4) Care was to be taken to prevent the international protection of human rights from endangering peace or friendly international relations. (5) The role of the UN was limited to the elaboration of international instruments for ratification (or, in the case of recommendations, for consideration) by States, leaving individual countries to deal with the practical application at a national level. Socialist nations had a definite preference for treaties, perhaps because these are only binding on those countries which give their consent to them (by ratification or adherence). (6) The UN must concern itself with individual countries only in exceptional circumstances, that is, only when a State committed serious, repeated, and systematic violations of human rights, going against the universal principle mentioned above and endangering peace and friendly relations between States (a typical instance was *apartheid*). (7) In the interest of furthering human rights, it was of prime importance that improvements should be made in the international situation. International tension, the arms race, etc., were factors having a detrimental effect on human rights; consequently, one way of promoting respect for these rights was by fostering friendly and peaceful relations between States.

The preference of socialist countries was clearly for economic, social, and cultural rights; the right of self-determination; and the right of equality (with the consequent prohibition of discrimination, especially racial discrimination).

(c) The doctrine of developing countries

As pointed out above, the third stage was dominated by the Third World. In the early 1970s developing countries managed to elaborate their own philosophy and strategy of human rights. Thanks to their numerical superiority and vociferousness, they managed to propound their own aspirations without necessarily needing the support of socialist countries. However, in practice, this support was usually forthcoming, with the result that the West increasingly had to take a defensive stance. In spite of that, in important respects the majority in the UN did not go so far as to disregard basic Western demands.

The attitude of many developing countries towards civil and political rights was one of indifference, sometimes even hostility, for three main reasons.

First, fully to recognize the importance of this category of rights could undermine or weaken the authority of the government in such countries. Often developing nations were (and still are) torn by conflict between different groups and factions and in some cases even by tribal wars. Their principal aim, at least in the post-colonial period, must be to strengthen the authority of the State and not to favour centrifugal tendencies which could benefit from full recognition of the rights and freedoms of the individual.

The second reason is economic. Developing countries needed a strong central government if their economies were ever to get off the ground. With economic growth and the well-being of their populations as their aim, their tendency was rather to concentrate power in the hands of the government than to limit it by fostering the rights of the individual. The restriction of certain rights and liberties seemed to these countries to be justified by the need to give precedence to economic and social rights. To give a few examples: restrictions on freedom of movement and expatriation were regarded as justified by the need to stop the 'brain drain'; limitations on personal freedom and the right to start a family were considered to be justified by the need to slow down the birth rate; limitations on the rights and freedoms of trade unions (the right to strike, for example) were held to be warranted by the urgent need for economic development and industrialization, etc. In other words, not being in a position to protect all human rights, and often having to choose between civil and political rights on the one hand and economic and social rights on the other, these countries preferred to favour the latter. (The preference for economic and social rights also followed from the inherent character of these rights: as has been rightly stressed, they contribute to the 'build-up of State structures', whereas civil and political rights involve placing restraints on those structures.)

Third, the social structure typical of many African and Asian countries was (and often still is) that of a community with a leader exercising undisputed power. The Western European tradition is instead characterized by the tension and clash between freedom and overpowering authority. ('In all governments, there is a perpetual internecine struggle, open or secret, between Authority and Liberty; and neither of them can ever absolutely prevail in the contest', wrote Hume in 1742.)[5] This tension is alien to the culture of most developing countries. From a cultural point of view, the idea of a ruler with unlimited powers used to arouse neither criticism nor repulsion. ('The African concept of government is personal, not institutional. When the word "Government" is said the African thinks of the leader not, as the British, of a big building in which debates are held', Nyerere wrote in 1961.)[6] The leader expresses the needs of his people and stands up for their interests and they in turn submit to his will. In short, a curtailment of individual rights and freedoms to the benefit of the centralized authorities, which for a westerner brings to mind a whole tradition of rebellion against absolute authority, often appeared neither irrational nor to be condemned.

However, some developing countries had a motive of a different kind for opposing civil and political rights: the need to bolster autocratic regimes, which were (and still are) fairly common in the Third World. The arguments mentioned above were often used as an ideological justification for protecting despotic and authoritarian rulers from unwelcome interference from the UN.

The developing countries' doctrine of human rights was based on the following points: (1) In the present state of affairs at least, the realization of economic, cultural, and social rights is to be considered, if not an absolute priority, at any rate a major priority. (2) To this end, the international economic system must be altered, as it is to a large extent responsible for the undeveloped condition of the poorer nations and hence for the lack of recognition of fundamental rights in these countries. The establishment of a less unjust international order will be reflected inside these States. (3) When one of the developing countries is accused of violating civil and political rights, it makes no sense to criticize or condemn it; instead, the economic and social causes must be found and the domestic and international context for these violations understood. Violations can be brought to an end only by changing this context and eliminating the causes. It therefore appeared counterproductive—according to these States—for the UN to denounce or condemn certain States for alleged grave violations of human rights. The UN must try instead to bring about a change in international economic relations, thereby helping to remove the objective conditions which lead to violations. (4) There did exist exceptional cases of countries in which, for example, the government pursued a declared policy of racial discrimination (South Africa until the early 1990s; Rhodesia from 1965 to 1980) or denied the right of self-determination (Israel); the organized international community was to concentrate on these exceptional cases, which involved grave violations of all kinds of rights. (5) In fostering respect for human rights, resolutions of the UN GA should be preferred to treaties. This choice was dictated in part by the consideration that it was easier to make other States accept Third World views when they did not take the form of legally binding instruments. But developing countries also had a definite preference for resolutions because they are more flexible and adaptable than treaties, more suitable for general pronouncements laying down loose principles for action, than precise legislative instructions.

16.4.2 STANDARD SETTING

It is against the background of the various doctrines of human rights that the legislative and supervisory output of international bodies can be better appraised.

(a) The Universal Declaration (1948)

The first step was the attempt by the UN GA to draw up an international document on human rights acceptable to all members of the international community: to States as dissimilar ideologically and politically as the USA and the USSR; to nations with such different economic and political structures as the Western countries on the one hand and Ethiopia, Saudi Arabia, and Afghanistan on the other; to countries upholding differing religious philosophies, ranging from Christian (the nations of the West and Latin America), to Muslim (like Saudi Arabia, Afghanistan, Turkey, Pakistan, etc.), Hindu (like India), and Buddhist (like China).

It was therefore necessary to find the lowest common denominator, as regards the conception both of the relationship between State and individual, and of basic human rights. The attempt to forge a single, collective stand, a general 'philosophy' of human dignity, was successful, although agreement was only reached after lengthy discussions. The ensuing political document, the Universal Declaration of Human Rights of 10 December 1948, has two basic characteristics, one to do with its formal structure and the other with its content.

In formal terms, it is not legally binding, but possesses only moral and political force. In other words, it is simply a *recommendation* to States. About the content of the Declaration a little more needs to be said. On the whole, the view of human rights expressed in it is Western. More space and importance are allotted to civil and political rights than to economic, social, and cultural rights, and no mention at all is made of the rights of peoples. The position taken with regard to colonized peoples, who have been partially or completely denied their right to freedom, is purely formal. Nor does the Declaration say anything specific about economic inequalities between States (although today many commentators cite with increasing frequency Article 28 whereby 'Everyone is entitled to a social and international order in which the rights and freedoms set forth in the Declaration can be fully realized'). In addition, one could note that the Declaration did not consider the fact that some States, being underdeveloped, faced special problems when trying to guarantee certain basic rights, such as those to work, to education, to suitable housing, etc.

How did the West succeed in imposing its 'philosophy'? The socialist countries, though putting up a strong resistance to the fact that so little importance was being attributed to economic, social, and cultural rights, were in a minority. All they could do was abstain. Moreover, they had not yet fully worked out a clear strategy of their own. As for the Third World, it was at this stage to a large extent made up of Latin American countries with a Western outlook; the remaining countries simply did not have the strength or authority to stand up to the Western powers, which incidentally numbered among their delegates influential figures such as Eleanor Roosevelt and René Cassin.

In spite of its limitations, the Declaration was, however, of great importance in stimulating and directing the international promotion of human rights. It formulated *a unitary and universally valid concept of what values all States should cherish within their own domestic orders.* One particular category of States, the socialist countries, did not support it enthusiastically. Yet neither the latter nor developing nations regarded the Declaration as something from which they felt estranged—rather, they looked upon it as a document containing a valid core in need of completion. Consequently their subsequent efforts were directed not at eroding, let alone jettisoning, the Declaration, but rather at filling its gaps.

On the whole the Declaration remains a lodestar, which has guided the community of States as they gradually emerged from the dark age when the possession of armies, guns, and warships was the sole factor for judging the conduct of States, and there were no generally accepted principles for distinguishing good from evil in the world community.

(b) International treaties

Even before the Universal Declaration was adopted States had basically agreed on the need to translate its general principles into legally binding instruments.

A twofold strategy gradually unfolded. First, it was felt necessary to spell out the general standards of the Declaration in legally binding instruments of *general purport*, that is, covering the whole range of human rights. This was to be done both at the universal and at the regional level, where the relative political, ideological, and economic homogeneity of States rendered the task less difficult. Second, treaties were to be worked out in *specific* areas, notably those considered by the majority of States as being of greater significance and more in need of urgent international legislation (such as genocide, racial discrimination, etc.).

Thus at the universal level the Covenant on Civil and Political Rights (with an Optional Protocol) and that on Economic, Social, and Cultural Rights were adopted in 1966. At the regional level the European Convention on Human Rights was adopted in 1950, the Inter-American Convention on Human Rights in 1969, the African Charter on Human and Peoples' Rights in 1981; in 1994 the Council of the Arab League (with a membership of 22 States) passed the Arab Charter on Human Rights (although this is not yet in force).

The Covenants cover the whole range of fundamental rights. However, characteristically the right of property does not figure in either of them. Arguably, this was not due to the fact that the right was no longer considered a value worthy of international protection on a universal level, but rather to the inability of East and West to agree on the issue of compensation in case of expropriation. Be that as it may, this omission went along with the trend to erode and revise the international customary law which in the past had protected the private property of foreigners, requiring 'prompt, adequate, and effective' compensation in the case of expropriation or nationalization (see **18.9**).

In addition, for the first time in an international legal document we find the concept that formal or legal equality makes little sense if deep practical inequalities exist. This being the case, it appears right to give legal sanction to certain types of distinction when they come into being as a consequence of practical inequalities. Thus, Article 2.3 of the Covenant on Economic, Social, and Cultural Rights lays down that developing countries can establish to what extent they mean to allow foreigners the economic rights specified by the Covenant. In other words, they are authorized to discriminate between nationals and foreigners, so long as (a) this is justified by the country's economic circumstances and does not amount to discrimination against citizens of a particular State, and (b) the refusal to award the same status to foreigners and nationals does not lead to serious violations of other human rights. Other treaties that contain provisions envisaging 'affirmative action' for groups discriminated against include the 1965 Convention on racial discrimination (see, for example, Article 1.4) and the 1979 Convention on discrimination against women (see, for example, Article 4).

A host of specific treaties was hammered out, particularly at the universal level.

Suffice it to mention, among the most important, the Conventions on genocide (1948), on racial discrimination (1965), on discrimination against women (1979), on torture (1984), on the rights of the child (1989), and on migrant workers (1990).

16.4.3 THE TENDENCY TO OVERRULE THE OBJECTION OF DOMESTIC JURISDICTION

Over the years the UN tended to reject the objection of State sovereignty put forward by a number of States, and discussed various questions concerning human rights. In general, however, these questions concerned large-scale, flagrant violations of human rights, rather than isolated cases. The UN justified its 'intervention' on the grounds that these violations constituted a threat to peace and to friendly relations between States. The line taken was warranted in the same terms as those used while drafting the UN Charter: respect for human rights as a means of securing peace, thereby dispelling misgivings that the Organization would suffer from a paralysing fear of trespassing on State sovereignty. This 'intervention' could take various forms: public discussion in a UN body, adoption of a resolution on the matter, the making of appeals, requesting the State concerned to stop the violations forthwith, or even recommending to member States that peaceful sanctions should be taken against the delinquent State.

However, as a result of the growing network of international treaties and the establishment of the monitoring procedures to which we shall shortly refer, the conviction gradually took hold among UN members that 'intervention' in the affairs of individual States was fully justified, so long as *serious and large-scale violations* had been allegedly committed, regardless of whether they amounted to a threat to peace or to friendly relations between States.

To grasp the importance of this new trend and the sea change that has occurred, in the last few decades, in the relations between universal inter-State organizations and individuals living within member States and whose human rights are allegedly breached, one need only remember how the Council of the League of Nations reacted to the complaint of a German national of Jewish origin in 1933 (the *Bernheim* case), and, more generally, to large-scale and harsh discrimination against Jews in Germany.

In 1933 Franz Bernheim complained to the Council of the League of Nations about the breaches by Germany of the German-Polish Treaty of 1922, protecting minorities in Upper Silesia (at the time belonging to Germany); in particular, he insisted on the fact that the anti-Jewish laws promulgated in Germany in 1933, and by virtue of which he (like all Jewish employees) had been sacked by a German firm, were contrary to the Treaty.[7] The German delegate asked that the complaint be dismissed because Bernheim had no link with Upper Silesia.[8] The Polish delegate noted that admittedly from a formal point of view the Council could only deal with the fate of Jewish minorities in Upper Silesia. Nevertheless 'All members of the Council had . . . at least a moral right to make a pressing appeal to the German Government to ensure equal treatment for the Jews in Germany'.[9] He wrapped up his eloquent speech by stating that 'A minimum of rights must be guaranteed to every human being, whatever his race, religion, or mother tongue'.[10] A Committee of Jurists was appointed. It found Germany in the wrong but decided to take note of an assertion made previously by the German delegate: if some blame had to be assigned to Germany, confined obviously to Upper Silesia, it could only derive from 'errors due to misconstructions of internal [German] law by subordinate authorities; these errors would be corrected'.[11] On the strength of this affirmation the Council adopted a report inviting Germany to bring the violations to an end. It would seem that Germany made no follow-up to the Council's exhortation.

But the question of discrimination against Jews did not rest there. A few months later the question of whether in every modern civil State all citizens ought to enjoy equal treatment came up before a Committee of the League's Assembly. Germany insisted that this was an internal matter, while France took the contrary position, contending among other things that if a treaty protected minorities in one part only of a country, minorities were nonetheless to be protected in other parts of the territory of the country as well, for the treaty provisions must not be interpreted as excluding some categories of citizens from the benefits they granted (a clear reference to the *Bernheim* case).[12] The German delegate retorted that 'the Jewish problem in Germany [was] a special problem *sui generis* and [could] not possibly be treated . . . simply like an ordinary minority question'.[13] Although improved by the Greek delegate, N. Politis, the French proposal was rejected by Germany. Consequently, pursuant to Article 5 of the Covenant that required unanimity, the French-Greek proposal did not carry. Only three days after the rejection of that proposal, on 14 October 1933, Hitler announced Germany's withdrawal from the League, because other States were unprepared to grant 'true equality of rights' to it, and thereby put Germany in an 'undignified' position.

Respect for human dignity thus came up against its first stumbling block in Germany's firm stance that national sovereignty could not tolerate any international interference by an international body in internal affairs.

16.4.4 EXPANSION OF TERRITORIAL SCOPE OF HUMAN RIGHTS OBLIGATIONS

States, when they undertake obligations in the area of human rights, tend to consider that such obligations apply to individuals subject to their jurisdiction in their own territory. In other words, they construe these obligations as having a strictly territorial scope. This, for instance, was the interpretation they inclined to place on Article 2 of the UN Covenant on Civil and Political Rights, whereby 'Each state Party . . . undertakes to respect and to ensure to all individuals within its territory and subject to its jurisdiction the rights recognized in the present Covenant'.

However, international bodies responsible for scrutinizing compliance with human rights standards have increasingly interpreted those obligations as also having an *extraterritorial scope*. Thus, for instance, in 1995 the UN Human Rights Committee, in commenting on the report submitted by the USA, noted that it could not share the view of the US Government that the UN Covenant on Civil and Political Rights lacked extraterritorial reach under all circumstances. 'Such a view [it went on to point out] is contrary to the consistent interpretation of the Committee on this subject that, in special circumstances, persons may fall under the subject matter jurisdiction of a State party even when outside that State territory.'[14] More specifically, in *Delia Saldías de*

Lopez v. *Uruguay* the Committee had already ruled that Uruguay had violated the Covenant when its security forces had abducted and tortured in Argentina a Uruguayan citizen living there. It had noted that

'The reference in Article 1 of the Optional Protocol to "individuals subject to its jurisdiction" does not affect the above conclusion [that the Covenant also covered conduct of Uruguayans acting on foreign soil] because the reference in that Article is not to the place where the violations occurred, but rather to the relationship between the individuals and the State in relation to a violation of any of the rights set forth in the Covenant, wherever they occurred. Article 2.1 of the Covenant places an obligation upon a State party to respect and to ensure rights "to all individuals within its territory and subject to its jurisdiction", but it does not imply that the State party concerned cannot be held accountable for violations of rights under the Covenant which its agents commit upon the territory of another State, whether with the acqui-escence of the Government of that State or in opposition to it . . . In line with this, it would be unconscionable to so interpret the responsibility under Article 2 of the Covenant as to permit a State party to perpetrate violations of the Covenant on the territory of another State, which violations it could not perpetrate on its own territory'.[15]

In an important case (*Loizidou* v. *Turkey—Preliminary Objections*), the European Court of Human Rights carried this doctrine even further. The question had arisen of whether the denial by Turkish armed forces stationed in Northern Cyprus, of access by the applicant (a Cypriot) to her property in Northern Cyprus was imputable to Turkey and consequently fell under Turkey's jurisdiction pursuant to Article 1 of the European Convention on Human Rights. The Court gave an affirmative answer, rul-ing that what mattered was that Turkey had effective or overall control over the armed forces stationed in an area outside its national territory.[16] The Inter-American Com-mission of Human Rights spelled out this doctrine more forcefully in *Coard et al.* v. *US.* The question at issue was whether the USA could be found responsible for violating the 1948 American Declaration on the Rights and Duties of Man for allegedly holding incommunicado and mistreating 17 Grenadian nationals in Gre-nada in October 1983, when US and Caribbean armed forces invaded the island, deposing the 'revolutionary government'. In its report of 29 September 1999 the Commission replied in the affirmative, noting that

'Given that individual rights inhere simply by virtue of a person's humanity, each American State is obliged to uphold the protected rights of any person subject to its jurisdiction. While this most commonly refers to persons within a State's territory, it may, under given circumstances, refer to conduct with an extraterritorial locus where the person concerned is present in the territory of one State, but subject to the control of another State—usually through the acts of the latter's agents abroad. In principle, the inquiry turns not on the presumed victim's nationality or presence within a particular geographic area, but on whether, under the specific circumstances, the State observed the rights of a person subject to its authority and control'.[17]

This case law is consistent with the object and purpose of human rights obligations: they aim at protecting individuals against arbitrariness, abuse, and violence, regardless of the location where the State conduct occurs.

It follows from the above that States are to respect human rights obligations not only on their own territory but also abroad, when they exercise there some kind of authority or power, whether the individuals subject to this authority or power have the State's nationality or are foreigners. In addition, by exercise of authority one should mean not only the display of sovereign or other powers (law making, law enforcement, administrative powers, etc.), but also any exercise of power, however limited in time (for instance, the use of belligerent force in an armed conflict).

16.4.5 MONITORING OF COMPLIANCE

(a) Universal level

Clearly, in general the best means of ensuring respect for a right is to back it up with legal guarantees to be administered by a court of law. I have, however, already mentioned that in the international community the judicial settlement of disputes is often rendered all but impossible by the lukewarm attitude of many States. In the case of human rights, opposition to international adjudication is even stronger. The need to strike a compromise between State sovereignty and the requirement that States comply with international standards on human rights led to the establishment of a number of monitoring mechanisms—which, as pointed out above (**10.8.2**), are much weaker than international adjudication.

The principal mechanisms created in this period at the *universal* level were of two kinds: those established by international treaties and those set up by UN resolutions.

Among the former, one should mention—at the world level—the procedures created by the 1965 Convention on racial discrimination (monitored by the Committee on the Elimination of Racial Discrimination), by the Covenant on Civil and Political Rights of 1966, with its Optional Protocol (the monitoring body is the Human Rights Committee), that established in 1986 on the strength of the 1966 UN Covenant on Economic, Social, and Cultural Rights (this is monitored by the Committee on Economic, Social, and Cultural Rights), the one set up under the 1979 Convention on the elimination of discrimination against women (establishing a Committee with the same name), by the 1984 Convention on torture (on the strength of which the Committee against Torture was established), and the supervisory mechanism established by the 1989 Convention on the protection of the child.

Normally the Conventions just mentioned establish three supervisory procedures. (1) A procedure based on the examination of *periodic reports* submitted by States. (This is, of course, the weakest and it is no coincidence that it is the scrutiny that is applicable to all contracting States.) (2) The procedure of *inter-State complaints*, which a contracting State can set in motion against another party. (It can work only with regard to those States which, in addition to ratifying the Convention, have also accepted a special clause providing for the procedure. So far it has not yielded any major result, for obviously States refrain from engaging in reciprocal accusations.) (3) The procedure operating at the *request of individuals* or groups of individuals, who may file with the supervisory body a 'communication' setting out the violations allegedly perpetrated by a State. (Like the previous procedure, it is provided for in an 'optional clause', but it has proved effective, within the limitations inherent in any supervisory mechanism: see **10.8.2**.)

The monitoring mechanisms established by resolution are chiefly (a) those set up in 1967 by resolution 1235 (XLII) of the Economic and Social Council (ECOSOC); (b) others set up in 1970 by resolution 1503 (XLVIII) of the same body, and revised in 2000; as well as (c) the system of country or thematic special rapporteurs, gradually evolved in the 1990s by the Commission on Human Rights; and (d) the UN High Commissioner for Human Rights, established in 1993 by GA resolution 48/141.

The two procedures set up by ECOSOC are both complex and somewhat cumbersome. Both procedures depend upon several UN bodies such as the Sub-Commission for the Promotion and Protection of Human Rights (until 1999 called Sub-Commission for the Prevention of Dis-crimination and Protection of Minorities; it is composed of 26 experts nominated by govern-ments and elected by its 'parent' body, the Commission on Human Rights), the Commission on Human Rights (consisting of 53 member States), and ECOSOC (made up of 54 States), plus possibly a Commission of Investigation. They operate as a result, or at the behest, of 'communi-cations' (complaints) emanating from individuals or groups of individuals and deal with 'a consistent pattern of gross violations' only (that is, not with individual or sporadic infringements).

The procedure established in 1967 is *public*, for the discussion of the gross violations of human rights referred to in the 'communications' of individuals, is made in public sittings of the Commission on Human Rights, normally after receiving a report from the Sub-Commission. The Commission may eventually adopt resolutions deploring or condemning one or more particular States for their breaches of human rights.

In contrast, the procedure set up in 1970 and revised in 2000 is *confidential*: the 'communi-cations' from individuals and groups alleging human rights violations, which set in motion the whole process, are not made public (unless ECOSOC decides to release them, which happens very rarely). On the other hand, the identity of the countries under examination is announced by the Chairman of the Commission at the end of each yearly session. The final outcome of the procedure is made public if and when the Commission decides to submit a 'situation' to ECOSOC. Normally the Sub-Commission, after screening, through a Working Group, 'communi-cations' relating to gross and reliably attested violations of human rights, decides which situ-ations deserve thorough consideration. It then submits a report to the Working Group of the Commission dealing with these matters.

The *thematic procedure* deals both with gross violations and with individual infringements of groups of rights. The subjects for monitoring are often suggested by 'communications' from individuals and groups. The Commission, whenever it consider fit to undertake the examination of a particular theme ('a major phenomenon of human rights violations world-wide'), may appoint a Working Group, a special rapporteur or a representative, or an expert. Any of these may also undertake fact-finding missions in the countries concerned (with the countries' con-sent). In the event the Commission may pass recommendations to the States concerned as well as suggestions for remedying the breaches found.

The system of *country* or *thematic special rapporteurs* has gradually evolved to take account of special needs. Under this procedure the Commission on Human Rights entrusts either work-ing groups of experts, or individual experts (variously designated as special rapporteurs, repre-sentatives, experts), or even the UN Secretary-General or the UN High Commissioner for

Human Rights, with the task of examining, monitoring, and publicly reporting on the human rights situation in *a certain country* (e.g. Afghanistan, Cambodia, East Timor, the former Yugoslavia, Iraq, Burma/Myanmar, Occupied Arab Territories, Rwanda, Somalia, Sudan), or on *major human rights themes*, wherever the relevant problems might occur (for example, arbitrary detention; enforced or involuntary disappearances; extra-judicial, summary, or arbitrary executions; effects of foreign debt on the full enjoyment of economic, social, and cultural rights; the independence of judges and lawyers; internally displaced persons; mass exoduses; human rights of migrants; human rights and extreme poverty; religious intolerance; the right to restitution, compensation, and rehabilitation for victims of grave violations of human rights; torture; the adverse effects of illicit movement and dumping of toxic and dangerous products and wastes on the enjoyment of human rights; violence against women, its causes and consequences; actions against human rights defenders; housing; the right to food, etc.). The relevant rapporteurs may not only use information from any reliable source, but also make on-site country visits (provided the States concerned are agreeable).[18]

The primary function of the *High Commissioner* is to play 'an active role . . . in preventing the continuation of human rights violations throughout the world'. In substance, his or her role is to promote respect for human rights, in addition to providing advice, technical assistance, and cooperation. It would appear that so far, particularly after the initial period when the post was filled by a former diplomat, the High Commissioner has been significantly instrumental in drawing attention to gross violations, calling upon States to abide by international standards.

In order fairly to appraise the effectiveness of the aforementioned monitoring mechanisms, it must be appreciated that (a) they operate in an area where States, although they may have assumed international obligations, are not prepared to submit to international judicial scrutiny; and (b) this area covers matters that are politically extremely sensitive, and which may have international implications at the diplomatic, economic, or commercial level. Consequently, international bodies must tread gingerly, lest States withhold co-operation, thus leaving them unable to act, except for adopting condemnatory resolutions. Hence, the various international bodies concerned ought not to take an accusatory approach, that is, they should not engage in the attribution of responsibility to individual governments. Rather, they must opt for public exposure and pressure. (However, things are gradually changing in this respect; thus, for instance, the Working Group on arbitrary detention issues opinions which do in effect attribute 'responsibility' and various other rapporteurs increasingly tend to write their reports in a similar way.) More generally, they must take a 'conciliatory' rather than a 'confrontational' approach. Seen against this backdrop, the mechanisms under discussion may be considered to be reasonably effective in (a) focusing on countries or problems that deserve to be carefully scrutinized; (b) drawing the attention of States, international organizations, NGOs, and public opinion at large to some pivotal issues concerning human rights; (c) exerting pressure upon States with a view to inducing them gradually to improve their human rights record; (d) contributing to the creation of an international ethos requiring respect for at least some core human rights; (e) serving as a catalyst to the gradual elaboration of new international conventions or the adoption of general resolutions.

However, one should not ignore some major failings of these mechanisms: (1) They

tend to be so conditioned, in their unfolding, by political and diplomatic considerations, that often their final result is rather weak, being couched in terms that are too
general or too diplomatic. (2) The reports of the various working groups or individuals often fail to trickle down from the body of specialists or specialist organizations to public opinion at large. Consequently, a wealth of monitoring, information,
and expertise is eventually little used outside some restricted circles within the UN.

It should be added that recently the role of the High Commissioner for Human
Rights has proved to be more and more effective, as is shown, among other things, by
the action taken by the current Commissioner with regard to the armed conflict in
Chechnya and the follow-up made in various bodies to her visits to that area and her
talks with high-ranking officials in Moscow in 2000.

(b) Regional level

Regional supervisory mechanisms are more advanced. They are normally judicial
bodies, such as the European Court of Human Rights (ECHR), the Inter-American
Commission (IACHR) and the Inter-American Court of Human Rights
(IACourtHR). In contrast, the African Commission on Human Rights and the Rights
of Peoples (ACHR) is rather a monitoring body, still lacking judicial functions. An
African Court of Human Rights and Peoples' Rights is provided for in the Draft
Additional Protocol to the African Charter on Human and Peoples' Rights, of 1997.
This Protocol, however, has not yet entered into force.

Among the various judicial bodies just mentioned, the ECHR is by far the most
advanced. Under the 11th Protocol of 1994 (which considerably modified the previous system provided for under the 1950 European Convention on Human Rights),
since 1999 the Court has been a full-time judicial body consisting of 41 (now 43)
judges. Each of the 43 member States of the Council of Europe parties to the Convention may refer to the Court any alleged violation of the Convention and its Protocols
by another contracting State. In addition, any person subject to the jurisdiction of any
of the contracting States may address himself or herself to the Court claiming to be
the victim of a violation of the Convention or the Protocols. The petitioner fully
participates in the proceedings before the Court, on the same footing as the respondent State. However, judgments of the Court do not produce direct legal effects within
the national legal system of the State concerned. They are only binding at the
international level. Thus, if the Court finds that a State is in breach of one of the
obligations deriving from the relevant international instruments, that State is internationally bound to make reparation within its own legal system. It may happen that
the national legal system does not allow for this outcome, for example because the
breach has been brought into being by a national court through a final and irrevocable decision. In this case the Court shall afford just satisfaction to the injured person
(normally this is done through the payment, by the responsible State, of a certain
amount of money, as determined by the Court). If the State found responsible for a
breach of the Convention or the Protocols fails to comply with the judgment (as has
occurred in a few cases: see, for example, the *Loizidou* case against Turkey)[19] the only

'sanction' available is provided for in Article 8 of the Statute of the Council of Europe. Under this provision:

'Any Member of the Council of Europe which has seriously violated Article 3 [on respect for the rule of law and human rights] may be suspended from its rights of representation and requested by the Committee of Ministers to withdraw under Article 7. If such Member does not comply with this request, the Committee may decide that it has ceased to be a Member of the Council as from such date as the Committee may determine.'

Despite indisputable organizational problems, the huge backlog, and the slowness in bringing about changes in the legal systems of the various member States, no one can deny that the Court is playing a pivotal role in Europe. It is promoting and seeking to ensure full respect for human rights in countries as diverse as the UK and the Russian Federation, France and Slovakia, Germany and the former Yugoslav Republic of Macedonia. The Court is gradually effecting a harmonization, in the vast area of human rights, of the various legal systems. It is thus contributing to the creation of an extensive region in Europe where arbitrary or discriminatory action by governments is being strongly curtailed.

In *America*, the Commission and Court are playing an important role, although the *judicial means* at their disposal are not so advanced as those of the ECHR.

The IACHR, the headquarters of which are in Washington DC, is an autonomous organ of the Organization of American States (OAS) consisting of seven members elected by the GA of the OAS. It applies the 1969 American Convention on Human Rights, ratified by 25 Latin American and central American countries, plus Mexico (neither the USA nor Canada is a party to it). The Commission may receive individual petitions alleging human rights violations perpetrated by a member State of the OAS. (For those that are not parties to the Convention, the Commission applies the American Declaration of Rights and Duties of Man adopted in Bogotà in 1948.) If the petition is not regarded as inadmissible, the Commission may carry out investigations, including on-site visits, and hold hearings. It then offers to assist the parties in negotiating a friendly settlement, if they so desire. It may prepare a confidential report, containing possible recommendations to the respondent State. After a certain delay, and if the State has not taken any action on the report, the Commission may decide either to take the case to the Court, or to prepare a second report (giving among other things, a period of time to the State to resolve the case). After the elapse of that delay, the Commission may make its report public.

The Court is composed of seven judges (elected by the States parties to the American Convention on Human Rights) and has its seat in San José (Costa Rica). Only the Inter-American Commission and the States parties to the American Convention may bring cases before the Court. Proceedings may only be initiated against States that both are party to the Convention and also have recognized the Court's jurisdiction. The Court is also endowed with an advisory jurisdiction: it may issue an Advisory Opinion at the request of a member State or of an organ of the OAS. The Court may also issue, at the request of any member State of the OAS, an opinion on the compatibility of one of its national laws with Inter-American international instruments on human rights.

In spite of numerous difficulties of all kinds, the Commission and Court have done a remarkable job so far. They have issued important decisions as well as, in the case of the Court, Advisory Opinions. Given the survival of some authoritarian States on the American continent and the endemic problems of democracy in Latin America, the contribution of the two bodies to progress, the rule of law, and respect for human rights should not be underestimated.

16.4.6 HUMAN RIGHTS AND LITIGATION BEFORE MUNICIPAL COURTS

In some countries national courts take over, in a way, the functions of governments (which, all too often, seem unmoved by grave violations) and substitute themselves for international enforcement agencies that either do not exist or have proved extremely ineffectual.

Thus, since no international body had passed judgment on the lawfulness of the atomic bombing of Hiroshima and Nagasaki, and in addition the Japanese Government had eventually changed its mind on the matter, in 1963 a group of survivors sued the Japanese Government before the Tokyo District Court. They claimed compensation, arguing that by the peace treaty of 1952 that Government had unlawfully waived its rights and claims and those of its nationals towards the US Government, including the claims to compensation for the illegal atomic bombing. The Court pronounced that bombing illegal, although in the final analysis it held against the complainants (this is the famous *Shimoda* case).[20] In other cases domestic courts pass criminal judgment on individuals whom the territorial State failed to prosecute. The most important in this respect is the famous *Eichmann* case. In its judgment of 29 May 1962 the Supreme Court of Israel dismissed all the submissions of the appellant Eichmann who claimed that Israeli courts lacked jurisdiction over his alleged crimes because there was no territorial or personal link between those crimes and Israel. In its final remarks the Court held as follows:

'Not only do all the crimes attributed to the appellant bear an international character, but their harmful and murderous effects were so embracing and widespread as to shake the international community to its very foundations. The State of Israel therefore was entitled, pursuant to the principle of universal jurisdiction and in the capacity of a guardian of international law and an agent for its enforcement, to try the appellant. That being the case, no importance attaches to the fact that the State Israel did not exist when the offences were committed.'[21]

This judgment was in a way taken up by a US court in the *Yunis* case. Yunis, a resident and citizen of Lebanon accused of participating in the hijacking of a Jordanian airliner which resulted in the passengers (including several Americans) being held hostage, was brought to trial in the USA after being arrested by US authorities on the high seas. Yunis challenged the US courts' jurisdiction arguing that there was no nexus between the hijacking and the US territory (the aircraft never flew over US airspace and had no contact with US territory). In its judgment of 12 February 1988, the US District Court of the District of Columbia dismissed the defendant's motion and affirmed the jurisdiction of US courts. It held:

'Not only is the United States acting on behalf of the world community to punish alleged offenders of crimes that threatened the very foundations of world order, but the United States has its own interest in protecting its nationals.'[22]

The country where national courts have taken the most vigorous action against crimes committed abroad is the USA, where individuals and courts have taken down from the shelves and skilfully dusted off an old statute passed in 1789. This is the Alien Torts Claim Act, under which 'The [US] district courts shall have original jurisdiction of any civil action by an alien for a tort only, committed in violation of the law of nations or a treaty of the United States'. The US courts have applied this statute to gross violations of human rights perpetrated abroad by State officials (or individuals acting in a private capacity) against foreigners, thus obliging the culprits to pay compensation for those violations.

Since 1980 US courts have thus pronounced on torture in Paraguay (*Filartiga*),[23] political assassination ordered by Chilean authorities (*Letelier*),[24] torture and racial discrimination for economic gain in Argentina (*Siderman*),[25] torture, arbitrary arrest, and forced disappearance in Argentina (*Suarez-Mason*),[26] arbitrary killing in East Timor (*Todd* v. *Panjaitan*),[27] torture, summary execution, and forced disappearances in the Philippines (*Marcos*),[28] atrocities in Bosnia and Herzegovina (*Karadzic*),[29] torture and arbitrary detention in Haiti (*Avril*),[30] torture in Guatemala (*Gramajo*),[31] torture in Ethiopia (*Negewo*),[32] terrorist bombing in Lockerbie, Scotland (*Abdel Basset Ali Al-Megrahi and Lamen Khalifa Fhimah*).[33]

No one can deny the great significance of these US court decisions. In all these cases US courts filled the gap existing both at the international level (no international collective body took action, nor did other States intervene against the State to which the offending State officials belonged), and at the domestic level (no authority of the territorial State stepped in). Those courts therefore acted on behalf of the international community at large, to vindicate rights pertaining to human dignity. In so doing they proclaimed in judicial decisions some fundamental human values.

However, one should not be unmindful of the limits of this approach. First, these are *civil cases*, where the alleged perpetrator of serious crimes is only enjoined to pay compensation; no conviction is issued at the criminal level. In addition, normally the defendant is abroad when the decision is issued and can thus easily manage to avoid paying compensation. The decision thus ends up having an exclusively symbolic value. Second, as these are cases involving civil litigation only, the sued person may be, and normally is, absent (it is sufficient for him to be served a suit when in the USA). Thus, no in-depth examination of evidence takes place. Third, this judicial trend has occurred in one country only (courts of other countries such as Belgium and Spain are starting to act, but in the field of criminal law: see above, 12.4). There is the danger for courts of this country of setting themselves up as universal judges of atrocities committed abroad, a sort of humanitarian imperialism that may give rise to perplexities. By itself, this trend might not arouse misgivings, if it did not go hand in hand with the tendency of the US Executive to take upon itself the task of policing the world.

16.5 HUMAN RIGHTS AND CUSTOMARY INTERNATIONAL LAW

A significant feature of international legislation, case law, and monitoring activity of the relevant UN organs is that they have had a huge bearing on the traditional configuration of the international community. The human rights doctrine has substantially shaken up that configuration, bringing about significant changes in many areas of international law.

First of all, *certain important customary norms have gradually evolved*, chief and foremost among them the norm forbidding grave, repeated, and systematic violations of human rights (see **5.7**). Consistent practice and *opinio juris* or *opinio necessitatis* show that other rules now belong to the corpus of customary law: those banning slavery, genocide, and racial discrimination; the norm prohibiting forcible denial of the right of peoples to self-determination; as well as the rule banning torture. It should be noted that these rules not only bind all States belonging to the international community, whether they have ratified conventions on the subject or not; they also impose community obligations, as the ICJ stressed in the celebrated *dictum* in the *Barcelona Traction* case.[34] Moreover, they have also acquired the status of *jus cogens* (see **6.5.2**). Arguably, another customary rule is gradually crystallizing as a result of a host of UN GA resolutions, international treaties, as well as the increasing case law of the ICTY on rape and sexual assault; this is the rule banning gender discrimination.

In addition, since these customary rules impose community obligations (on this notion see above, **1.8.2**), there now exists a *legal entitlement* for any State or international organization competent in the area of human rights to request States where gross and large-scale violations of human rights are allegedly occurring to discontinue such violations. If they are not ended, States are authorized to take, in addition to diplomatic or economic steps amounting to retortion proper (see above, **11.5**), peaceful counter-measures (suspension or termination of treaties, withholding of economic assistance provided for in bilateral or multilateral treaties, etc.).

Individual counter-measures may be taken after the various means available within collective bodies have been exhausted, or have proved ineffective, or they may be taken with the authorization of an intergovernmental organization (see **11.4.1–2** and **14.3**). In contrast, it would seem that so far no customary rule has yet evolved to legitimize *forcible* counter-measures against massive and egregious infringements of human rights amounting to crimes against humanity (see **14.4.5**).

In practice, States tend to employ retortion more frequently than counter-measures proper. As instances one may recall the action taken since 1989 by the USA against Burma/Myanmar and referred to earlier (see **11.5**). Mention may also be made of the decision of the Italian Senate in 1999, upheld by the Italian Government,[35] to make economic assistance by Italy to Guatemala contingent upon Guatemala's implementation of the recommendations contained in the Final Report of 25 February 1999 of the Commission for Historical Clarification established through the Accord of Oslo of 23 June 1994 between the Government of Guatemala and the Guatemalan

National Revolutionary Unity.[36] It would appear that, in view of the Guatemalan failure to comply with the Report's recommendations, the Italian decision was carried through, although Guatemala considered that it amounted to unlawful interference in its domestic affairs.[37]

Furthermore, it may be argued that a general norm is currently in the process of coming into being which grants a *right to democratic governance* to all persons under the jurisdiction of a State.

This general norm first emerged as a result of the 'codification' of existing practice, in the principle of internal self-determination laid down in the 1970 UN Declaration on Friendly Relations; at that stage it was however confined to granting the right to equal access to government to racial groups denied such access. A number of subsequent factors gradually expanded that notion: the increasing ratification by States of the UN Covenants (which confer the right to internal self-determination to the whole people of each contracting State); the signing by 53 States (in Europe, and the USA and Canada) of the 1975 Helsinki Declaration (which explicitly grants the right of self-determination to all peoples) and its follow-up Declarations adopted by the Conference on Security and Co-operation in Europe (CSCE, as it then was) and explicitly laying down a right to democracy or to democratic institutions as a goal to be pursued by all States; the attitude taken in 1991–2 by the European Community on the occasion of the break-up of the Soviet Union and Yugoslavia and, in particular, the great emphasis laid by the Twelve EC States (as they then were) on respect for democracy and the rights of minorities; the spread of democratic governance to many Latin American countries, coupled with the formal upholding of the principles of democracy by both these States and other developing countries in other continents; the adoption of resolutions on democracy by the UN GA (for instance, resolutions 50/172, and 50/185, both of 1996), by the UN Human Rights Commission (for instance, resolutions 1999/57 of 28 April 1999, 2000/47 of 25 April 2000, 2000/167 of 4 October 2000), by the GA of the OAS (for instance, resolution 1080 (XXI-0/91) of 5 June 1991). Mention should also be made of mechanisms and institutions set up within the UN,[38] the OSCE,[39] or the OAS[40] on the monitoring of elections, to ensure a democratic process.

All these factors are clear indications of an important trend: States are increasingly accepting the idea that the right to democratic governance (also termed, in less stringent terms, internal self-determination) should have a broad purport and consequently apply to the people of each sovereign State. The fact that pronouncements of States to the contrary are isolated seems to bear out the contention that customary law is in the process of emerging.

What is meant by democracy? Opposition by many non-Western States to the Western model[41] leads one to believe that only some features of that model are now widely accepted: *representative* governance based on *regular, free, and fair elections*, and accountable to the electorate; *respect for human rights*; *rule of law*. It would seem that instead the notion of a multiparty political system is not yet agreeable to many States and therefore has not become part of the emerging international notion of democracy.

For the time being, the right to democracy has not yet taken root either as a human right belonging to all the individuals living in a State, or as a legal entitlement accruing to any State, to claim respect for democracy by other States. At present, the aforementioned notion of democracy is however used in international fora, on different scores. Thus, for instance, as we saw above (3.3) respect for democracy may constitute one of the criteria States adopt by for according or withholding recognition of new States. Similarly, that notion may be used in the UN in accrediting the representatives of the government of a State: as has happened in many instances (Haiti in 1992, Liberia in 1991–6, Afghanistan in 1996–8, Sierra Leone in 1997, Cambodia in 1997–8) the UN Credentials Committee has accredited, and entitled to participate in the UN GA as representatives of their respective States, the delegates of the government it considered democratic, even though that government was not yielding control over the population and the territory of the State.[42]

16.6 THE IMPACT OF HUMAN RIGHTS ON CUSTOMARY INTERNATIONAL LAW

The human rights doctrine has positively *influenced various fields of traditional international law*. It has helped to introduce a new paradigm in the international community, as the ICTY Appeals Chamber stated in 1995 in its seminal decision in *Tadić* (*Interlocutory Appeal*).[43]

Suffice it to mention here the impact on recognition of new States or governments (see **3.3**), international subjects (**3.1** and **4.2**), customary law (**6.2.3**), treaty making (**6.5**), reservations to treaties (**6.3.2(b)** and **6.5.5**), termination of treaties (**6.3.2(e)** and **6.5**), *jus cogens* (**6.5**), international monitoring of compliance with law (**10.8.2**), enforcement, including counter-measures (**11.3.1** and **11.4.2**), the administration of international criminal justice (**Chapter 12**), the laws of warfare or, to use a modern expression, the humanitarian law of armed conflict (**15.5**).

In all these areas the human rights doctrine has operated as a potent leaven, contributing to shift the world community from a reciprocity-based bundle of legal relations, geared to the 'private' pursuit of self-interest, and ultimately blind to collective needs, to a community hinging on a core of fundamental values, strengthened by the emergence of community obligations and community rights and the gradual shaping of public interests.

16.7 THE PRESENT ROLE OF HUMAN RIGHTS

The steady insistence on the need to respect human rights, by international law-making and monitoring bodies, and the impact these bodies have gradually had on States' behaviour, has produced a significant ripple effect. The whole international ethos has gradually, if almost imperceptibly, changed, so much so that some international supervisory bodies now consider warranted to depart from notions they themselves traditionally upheld. They currently consider it appropriate to place on those notions a much broader interpretation.

This trend has especially manifested itself in Europe and has in particular become apparent in the case law of the European Court of Human Rights. Indicative of this trend is the judgment delivered in 1999 by the European Court in *Selmouni* v. *France*. There, the Court, sitting as a Grand Chamber, unanimously held that the serious ill-treatment of persons detained in police custody, that it had regarded in previous cases (for example, in *Tomasi* v. *France*)[44] as manifestations of inhuman or degrading treatment contrary to Article 3 of the European Convention, were now to be termed torture, that is a much more serious breach of Article 3. The Court stated the following: '[H]aving regard to the fact that the [European Convention on Human Rights, of 1950] is a "living instrument which must be interpreted in the light of present-day conditions" . . . the Court considers that certain acts which were classified in the past as "inhuman and degrading treatment" as opposed to "torture" could be classified differently in future. *It takes the view that the increasingly high standard being required in the area of the protection of human rights and fundamental liberties correspondingly and inevitably requires greater firmness in assessing breaches of the fundamental values of democratic societies.*'[45]

Along these lines, the Court has modified, or even reversed, its jurisprudence in a number of other cases, all directed to enhance, more than in the past, the protection of human rights.[46]

In addition, the human rights doctrine has had the great merit of projecting domestic bills of rights on to the international stage, thereby pushing for the world-wide recognition of certain basic values hitherto only upheld within the national setting of a few countries. It also must be credited with prompting the UN to promote a deep sense of social justice and indignation against 'structural violence', in particular those historical situations (such as colonial or neo-colonial domination and apartheid, as well as poverty, malnutrition, and starvation in many poor countries) which have deprived whole groups or peoples of basic rights and freedoms. In other words, the UN has succeeded in moving from a static concept of human rights (conceived as a means of realizing international peace) to a dynamic doctrine which goes so far as to promote conflict and the disruption of the status quo for the sake of introducing social justice and respect for human dignity (this, as Röling correctly emphasized,[47] is what happened in the case of apartheid and former Rhodesia, where the UN willingly promoted rebellion against structural violence in the form of 'white rule').

It can be said that by now all, or nearly all, States agree on the following essential points. First, the dignity of human beings is a basic value that every State should try to protect, regardless of considerations of nationality, race, colour, gender, etc. Second, it is also necessary to aim at the achievement of fundamental rights of groups and peoples. Third, racial discrimination is universally considered one of the most repulsive and unbearable conditions. Fourth, even though some States may find it hard (either for economic reasons, or on organizational grounds) to achieve full respect for human rights, no State must engage in grave, repeated and large-scale violations of these rights. Fifth, when these large-scale violations are perpetrated, the international community is justified in 'intervening' by peaceful means.

Impressive headway has been made as far as norm setting is concerned, both at the universal and at the regional level. In contrast, from the vantage point of international scrutiny of observance of human rights, the balance sheet is less optimistic, at least at the universal level. Although a few important monitoring procedures have been instituted within the UN system or on the strength of some Conventions, so far they have not yielded conspicuous results. However, in assessing these procedures one ought to bear in mind that they are neither legally binding nor coercive (see **16.4.5(a)**). In consequence they can only be effective by exerting moral, psychological, and political pressure and by making use of public opinion (in the country concerned and in the whole international community). It follows that their effects can only be appreciated in the long run.

A general appraisal of the spread of the human rights doctrine and its incarnation in international rules and institutions should not, however, ignore one important fact: at the regional level, and especially in Europe, advanced judicial mechanisms have been set up that remedy in a substantially satisfactory manner violations of human rights perpetrated by member States.

Given the present structure and composition of the international community, what the UN and the relevant regional bodies have achieved so far constitutes the most that could be expected. Collective efforts must be made at all levels—not only by governments, but also, and above all, unofficially, by individuals, groups, associations, and other non-governmental bodies. To be sure, gross breaches of human rights will not cease overnight. What matters, however, is that one should not stop being indignant at such violations. As long as officials responsible for those breaches are called to account and other governments are prodded to react forcefully to oppression and injustice, there may be some hope of stemming inhumanity.

17

PROTECTION OF
THE ENVIRONMENT

17.1 TRADITIONAL LAW

Environment was defined in an international treaty of 1993 as including 'natural resources both abiotic and biotic, such as air, water, soil, fauna and flora and the interaction between the same factors; property which forms part of the cultural heritage; and the characteristic aspects of the landscape'.[1]

The question of the need to protect the environment exploded in the late 1960s. Since then it has increasingly become of crucial importance. At present States, international organizations, and individuals feel that it is imperative to take action to preserve the natural and human environment or at least avert its worsening. Before, the problem was not felt, for three main reasons. First, industrial developments had not spawned pollution and damage to the environment on a very large scale. Second, States still took a traditional approach to their international dealings: they looked upon them as relations between sovereign entities, each pursuing its self-interest, each eager to take care of its own economic, political, and ideological concerns, each reluctant to interfere with other States' management of their space and resources, and unmindful of general or community amenities. Third, public opinion was not yet sensitive to the potential dangers of industrial and military developments to a healthy environment.

Significant evidence of this traditional stand can be found in two cases brought before international courts before the late 1950s: the *Pacific Fur Seal* case (1893) and the *Trail Smelter* case (1938 and 1941). The former concerned a dispute between the USA and Britain over some issues relating to jurisdiction in the Behring Sea and—what is more relevant to our subject—the question whether the USA had a right of property and protection of fur seals outside its three-mile territorial waters. The latter case concerned relations between two industrial States, the USA and Canada. The USA accused Canada of damaging, through the industrial activities of a factory situated on its territory, the environment of the American State of Washington.

A brief mention of the *Pacific Fur Seal* case may be apposite. A group of States (the USA, Britain, France, Germany, Japan, Russia, Sweden, and Norway) interested in fur seal fisheries in the Behring Sea had failed to agree upon rules protecting fur seals from indiscriminate destruction and extermination resulting from over-exploitation. The USA and Britain therefore submitted to arbitration various issues relating to jurisdictional rights and the preservation of fur seals. In particular, one of the issues raised before the Arbitral Court was the question whether the USA had 'any right ... of protection or property in the fur seals frequenting the islands of the United States in Behring Sea when such seals are found outside the ordinary three-mile limit'.[2] On this issue the USA expressed an unusual and novel view. It based its claim on 'the established principles of the common and the civil law ... the practice of nations ... the laws of natural history, and ... the common interests of mankind'.[3] It asserted that it had a right of property over the fur seals outside its territorial sea; this right, however, did not make the USA 'absolute owners', for it was 'coupled with a trust for the benefit of mankind'; 'the human race [was] entitled to participate in the enjoyment'.[4] The USA also claimed to be the only State possessing the power of preserving fur seals. It stated the following: 'The United States, possessing, as they alone possess, the power of preserving and cherishing this valuable interest, are in a most just sense the trustee thereof for the benefit of mankind and should be permitted to discharge their trust without hindrance.'[5] In explaining the concepts of property and trust, it argued as follows: 'Every nation, so far as it possesses more than enough of the fruits of the earth to satisfy its own needs, is a *trustee* of the surplus for the benefit of those in other parts of the world who need them and are willing to give in exchange for them the products of their own labour, and this trust is *obligatory*.'[6] 'The coffee of Central America and Arabia is not the exclusive property of those two nations; the tea of China, the rubber of South America, are not the exclusive property of those nations where it is grown; they are, so far as not needed by the nations which enjoy the possession, the common property of mankind; and if nations which have the custody of them withdraw them, they are failing in their trust, and other nations have a right to interfere and secure their share.'[7] The British submissions were that the US claim was 'entirely without precedent'[8] and 'shorn of all support of international law and of justification from the usage of nations'.[9] It ran counter to the basic principles on the high seas and the right of all nations of the world to navigate and fish there. The Arbitral Court upheld the British view, holding that the USA had no 'right of protection or property in the fur-seals'.[10] It thus implicitly dismissed, among other things, the concept of 'trust for the benefit of mankind'. However, it also adopted regulations for the protection and preservation of fur seals. These regulations restricted fur seal fishing in many respects: under Article 1, the USA and Britain were to 'forbid their citizens and subjects ... to kill, capture or pursue at any time and in any manner whatever' fur seals 'within a zone of sixty miles around the Pribilov Islands, inclusive of the territorial waters'; Article 2 extended this prohibition to certain areas of the high seas for the period May–July; pursuant to Articles 3 and 4 only 'sailing vessels' with a 'special licence' were permitted to carry on fur seal fishing operations; under Article 6 the use of 'nets, fire arms and explosives' in such operations was however prohibited.[11]

In some respects the *Trail Smelter* case is probably more interesting. A Canadian smelter of zinc and lead ores, located in Trail, in British Columbia (Canada) was alleged to cause damage to trees, crops, and land in the American State of Washington due to emissions of sulphur dioxide fumes from the plant. These fumes, proceeding down the Columbia river valley and otherwise, entered the US territory. The Arbitral Court appointed by the USA and Canada was called upon to decide whether Canada was responsible for the damage and, if so, what indemnity it should pay to the USA.

The Court was asked to apply 'the law and practice followed in dealing with cognate questions in the United States of America as well as international law' (Article IV of the 1935 arbitration agreement). In its second decision (handed down on 11 March 1941), the Court stated that, generally speaking, every State has a duty at all times to protect other States against injurious acts by individuals within its jurisdiction;[12] more specifically, 'under the principles of international law, as well as the law of the United States, no State has the right to use or permit the use of its territory in such a manner as to cause injury by fumes in or to the territory of another or the properties or persons therein, when the case is of serious consequence and the injury is established by clear and convincing evidence'.[13] Consequently, the Court held Canada responsible for the conduct of the Trail Smelter and enjoined it to pay compensation to the USA. In addition, interestingly the Court also provided for future monitoring of the effects of the factory's activities on the environment, to prevent possible future damages to the US environment.

The issues raised in these cases were still looked at in the *perspective of State-to-State relations.* In *Pacific Fur Seal,* the Court rejected the US claim that by preserving the fur seals it would be acting as a trustee on behalf of mankind, and upheld instead the traditional view, advanced by Britain, that any good or asset on the high seas could be freely exploited by any State. In other words, it upheld the concept of the open sea as a *res communis omnium* (an asset that all may freely share), although admittedly, by issuing the regulations, it showed that it was concerned about over-fishing and eager to preserve the species. In the *Trail Smelter* case it was damage caused by one State to the environment of the other that triggered the legal claim. Legally the issue was not viewed as different from damage caused to private or public property, for instance by the inadvertent penetration of a foreign State's territory by armed forces. Nevertheless, there was an important novelty: for the first time an international tribunal propounded the principle that a State may not use, or allow its nationals to use, its own territory in such a manner as to cause injury to a neighbouring country.

Later, the idea gradually emerged that natural resources may be relevant not only to the individual States that can exploit them but also to all members of the international community and could be used in the interest of mankind. Thus, for instance, in the *Lac Lanoux* case (1957) the Arbitral Tribunal, while taking a traditional view of international law regulating relations between neighbouring States, alluded to the possibility of natural resources such as the water of a lake being exploited 'in the common interests of everybody'.

France had notified the Spanish Government that it intended to authorize the construction of a barrage utilizing the water of lake Lanoux. This lake lies in French territory at a very high altitude. Its waters flow through a tributary, the river Carol, an international waterway passing through France and Spain. The purpose of the barrage was to channel the lake's water through a hydroelectric power plant; the lake's water would have stopped flowing, so as to be used for the plant. To compensate for the cessation of the water flow, France would build a subterranean canal returning the same amount of water to the Carol river, at a point prior to its use by farmers in Spain. Spain objected that this scheme was contrary to treaty and customary law. The Court held that instead it did not infringe Spain's rights: France would neither pollute the waters to be returned to Spain, nor return less water than the quantity it intended to divert. The Court held that, 'assuming there was (*en admettant qu'il existe*) a principle which prohibits the upstream State from altering the waters of a river in such a fashion as seriously to prejudice the downstream State', in any event such principle did not apply in the case at issue because the French scheme did not alter the waters of the river Carol.[14] The Court went so far as to hold that there was no general international rule 'forbidding one State, acting to safeguard its legitimate interests, to put itself in a situation which would in fact permit it, in violation of its international pledges, seriously to injure a neighbouring State'.[15] However, the Court also stated the following: 'The growing ascendancy of man over the forces and secrets of nature has put into his hands instruments which he can use to violate his pledges just as much as for the common good of all (*pour le bien commun de tous*).[16]

17.2 NEW DEVELOPMENTS IN INDUSTRY AND TECHNOLOGY

In recent times a number of factors have increasingly brought about considerable damage, at an increasing pace, to the global environment: the growing importance of oil both for industrial production and for transport, the spread of nuclear plants, deforestation to make room for farmland or new housing, use of chlorofluorocarbons and other 'greenhouse' gases, use of outer space for scientific, industrial, or intelligence-gathering purposes, etc.

Damage is being caused both by industrialized States and, albeit to a lesser extent, by developing countries.

The former cause *air pollution* (by using transport vehicles, through industrial and domestic heating plants, waste incinerators, nuclear plants, etc.), *marine pollution* (by cleaning oil tanker hulls on the high seas; dumping wastes the disposal of which is expensive on land; through accidental running aground of tankers with the consequent discharge into the ocean of toxic products; through the discharge into the ocean—either directly, or through rivers flowing into the ocean—of land-based industrial pollution), *soil pollution* (mainly by dumping dangerous wastes in Third World countries), *water pollution* or *water shortage* (by contaminating groundwater through industrial wastes, sewage, etc., or depleting water resources), *global warming*, or the 'greenhouse effect' (caused by the emission of carbon dioxide and other gases used by industrial plants or for other purposes), as well as the *depletion of the ozone layer* as a result of the widespread use of chlorofluorocarbons (employed as refrigerants and in the manufacture of foam beverage containers, or for foam insulation).

Many *accidents* have brought to the fore the gravity of this condition. Suffice it to mention only a few: the sinking in 1967 of the *Torrey Canyon* (a ship registered under the flag of Liberia, which spilled over 117,000 tons of crude oil into the English Channel, causing extensive damage to the English and French coasts); the *Seveso* case (in 1976, in that town in Italy dioxine, a highly toxic substance released as a consequence of the explosion of a reactor in a chemical plant, polluted a vast area); the *Amoco Cadiz* accident (in 1978 a tanker registered in Liberia and owned by the US Standard Oil Company, ran aground off the coast of France, spilling a huge quantity of crude oil and fuel that created an oil slick 18 miles wide and eight miles long); the disintegration over Canadian territory, in 1978, of the Soviet satellite *Cosmos 954*, carrying a nuclear reactor filled with enriched uranium (as a result partly radioactive debris spread over vast parts of Canadian territory); the *Bophal* case (in 1984 an American owned chemical factory in Bophal, India, caused the death of about 2,500 persons); the *Chernobyl* accident (in 1986 an explosion occurred in one of the reactors in that Soviet nuclear plant; a radioactive cloud developed that drifted first towards Scandinavia and then southern Europe, crossing Germany, Austria, Switzerland, Yugoslavia, and Italy); the grounding in 1988 of the *Exxon Valdez* oil tanker (belonging to the multinational Exxon) and the consequent pollution of more than 1,000 miles of Alaskan shoreline, the killing of thousands of birds and marine mammals, and the disruption of fishing.

Developing countries too contribute to pollution. Rapid population growth, increasing industrialization, and massive urbanization have prompted many of these countries to proceed to deforestation so as to create cropland. In addition, because of widespread poverty many countries tend to use obsolete industrial plants as well as private cars having no devices against pollution. Furthermore, to make some earnings they often agree to the dumping on their territory of dangerous or toxic wastes produced by multinational corporations.

The measures, equipment, and general remedies to make good this catastrophic condition are exceedingly expensive. Consequently, big corporations and multi-nationals in developed countries are reluctant to adopt them, for fear that their production costs may dramatically soar and bring about a decrease in their competitiveness. Developing countries assert that, given their backwardness and poverty, they cannot afford to improve their conditions, unless they receive considerable financial assistance from industrialized States. As a result of these clashing interests, governments both in developed and developing countries proceed with great caution and constantly take account of the conflicting and immense economic interests at stake.

17.3 THE CURRENT REGULATION OF THE PROTECTION OF THE ENVIRONMENT

The practical problems briefly mentioned above, in particular the difficulty of impos-ing strict obligations on States or corporations, account for the unique features of the present international regulation of the environment. (1) In short, in this area only a *few general legal principles* have evolved (as we shall see below, at **17.3.1**, they are the principle imposing upon States the obligation not to allow their territory to be used in such a manner as to damage other States' environment; the principle enjoining co-operation for the protection of the environment; that requiring States immediately to notify other States of any possible risk to the environment; and the principle imposing the requirement to refrain from massive pollution of the atmosphere or the seas). (2)

Possibly, one or two *customary rules* also have crystallized on matters relating to the law of the sea (see **17.3.1**). (3) General problems have been regulated through so-called *soft law*, that is, by means of a string of non-binding resolutions and declarations. (4) *Very numerous treaties* have been concluded on specific matters; many of these treaties are however '*framework agreements*' in that they only provide a general framework for further negotiation of agreements. (5) Normally no specific or ad hoc judicial procedure has been established to deal with cases of non-compliance with existing rules; instead, *supervisory and preventive mechanisms* have been set up. (6) A number of *international institutions* have been established with the general task of endeavouring to stave off further degradation of the environment.

In the following paragraphs I shall consider each of these unique features. It will become clear that in this area States have shown considerable imagination and engaged in innovative legal engineering. They have crafted principles, rules, and monitoring mechanisms designed to strike a balance between *two conflicting requirements*: the dramatic urgency to put a stop to the deterioration of the environment besides forestalling new damages, on the one hand; the necessity realistically to take into account the huge economic and social costs involved in this process both for developed States and even more for developing countries, on the other.

It will also be clear that, because of the need to weigh up and reconcile as much as possible these two conflicting requirements, at the legal level progress has been less conspicuous than one would have expected or desired. True, the environment is no longer conceived of in a State-sovereignty-oriented perspective, as an asset that may belong to each State and in whose protection only the State concerned may be legally and practically interested. The environment has come to be regarded as a *common amenity*, as an asset in the safeguarding of which all should be interested, regardless of where the environment is or may be harmed. Nevertheless, the normal consequence of this approach has not been drawn on the legal plane: no *specific obligation to protect the environment* has arisen in general international law with the characteristics of a community obligation, that is, an obligation towards all the other members of the international community, attended by a *corresponding legal entitlement* accruing to all the other members of the world community, to demand fulfilment of the obligation. However, most of the general principles we will consider below do impose community obligations. In particular, in cases of breach of the general principle prohibiting massive pollution of the atmosphere or of the seas any State, whether or not damaged, may invoke the 'aggravated responsibility' of the polluting State (see above, **9.5**). In addition, the role of calling upon or requesting individual States, on behalf of the international community, to protect the environment is in practice played by the numerous international bodies established under the various conventions and treaties agreed upon in this area. Those international institutions act to safeguard *community values and concerns*. Their action is of crucial importance; they are indispensable in the present configuration of the world community. One might consider that this is simply a fall-back solution, and that it would have been far better to grant to every State the right to demand of any other State compliance with international legal standards on the environment. However, it is more realistic to entrust international bodies with the task of promoting compliance with those standards. Given the motivations and the economic interests behind the international regulation of the environment, international bodies can better act than individual States on behalf of groups or of the whole international community.

Another interesting trend in international environmental law should be emphasized. As already pointed out above (2.6), the law of the environment has increasingly been influenced by, and been seen in the perspective of, the law of development and human rights law. In some respects it has in its turn influenced international humanitarian law (in that this body of law increasingly aims at protecting the environment in time of armed conflict). This a healthy and meritorious trend, for it testifies to the increasing need for various bodies of law to become integrated; what is even more important, it emphasizes the need to look upon the environment from the angle of human rights and development promotion, by taking into account in particular the demands of developing countries.

17.3.1 GENERAL PRINCIPLES

State practice and case law show that only few general principles have evolved. The first and more general one is that *enjoining every State not to allow its territory to be used in such a way as to damage the environment of other States or of areas beyond the limits of national jurisdiction.* This principle was first set out by the Arbitral Court in the *Trail Smelter* case. It is substantially based on an even more general obligation, enunciated in 1949 by the ICJ in the *Corfu Channel* case (every State is under the obligation 'not to allow knowingly its territory to be used for acts contrary to the rights of other States').[17] It was subsequently proclaimed, among other things, in Principle 21 of the 1972 Stockholm UN Declaration on the Human Environment (see *infra*). It was also restated in two decisions, of 1979 and 1983, of the Rotterdam Tribunal in the case, *Handelskwekerij G.-J. Bier B.V. Stichting Reinwater v. Mines de Potasse d'Alsace S.A.*[18] In its generally accepted purport, this principle is not State sovereignty oriented. In other words, it is intended to protect not only the environment of each other State, as an asset belonging to it, but also the environment as a *common amenity.* This is among other things borne out by the dictum of the ICJ in *Legality of the Threat or Use of Nuclear Weapons,* whereby:

'The environment is not an abstraction but represents the living space, the quality of life and the very health of human beings, including generations unborn. The existence of the general obligation of States to ensure that activities within their jurisdiction and control respect the environment of other States or of areas beyond national control is now part of the corpus of international law relating to the environment'.[19]

The Court came back to this principle in the *Case Concerning the Gabcíkovo-Nagymaros Project,* where it stressed the importance it attached to 'respect for the environment', 'not only for States but also for the whole of mankind'.[20]

Another general principle, attested to by the general and increasing concern of States about the environment and borne out by the great number of treaties concluded in this area, is that *imposing upon States the obligation to co-operate for the protection of the environment.* This principle had already been alluded to in the decision in *Trail Smelter,* and was restated in Principle 24 of the 1972 Stockholm Declaration. It is of course much looser than the previous one but already reflects a new approach to environmental issues, based on the assumption that the environment is a matter of *general* concern. It follows from this principle that every State must co-operate for the protection of this precious asset, regardless of whether or not its own environment has been or may be harmed. Of course, given its looseness, this principle can only be applied jointly with the customary rule on good faith: every State must in good faith endeavour to co-operate with other States with a view to protecting the environment. A blunt refusal to co-operate, unaccompanied by a statement of the reasons for such attitude, would amount to a breach of the principle.

A less vague principle is that requiring every State immediately to *notify other States of the possible risk that their environment may be damaged or affected* by an accident that has occurred on its territory or in an area under its jurisdiction. This principle evolved as a reaction to the failure of the Soviet Union urgently to inform other States of the Chernobyl nuclear accident in 1986. The Vienna Convention on early notification of nuclear accidents, adopted at record speed that same year, greatly contributed to the crystallization of this principle, which was later restated in Principle 18 of the 1992 Rio Declaration.

Another general principle is that referred to above (**17.3**), enjoining States *to refrain from causing massive pollution of the atmosphere or the seas.*

A general principle, which however has a less broad import for it only applies to relations between riparian States of an international river, was propounded in 1983 by the Rotterdam Tribunal in the case of *G.-J. Bier* v. *Mines de Potasse* mentioned above (although the court classified the principle as a 'general principle of law recognized by civilized nations'). A Dutch grower had claimed that the huge quantity of salt dumped into the Rhine by potassium mines in Alsace as a by-product of potassium production damaged his crops. The Court held that in the last decade a general principle had evolved whereby

'the upstream users of an international river are no longer entitled to the unrestricted use of (the waters) of such a river, and are bound, when taking decisions concerning its use, to take reasonable account of the interests of other users in downstream areas'.[21]

So much for general principles. As for *specific customary rules,* it would seem that none has evolved for the specific purpose of protecting the environment. This view was put forward by the Rotterdam Tribunal in 1979 in the aforementioned case and seems to be borne out by practice. However, some commentators have contended that at least in the law of the sea, a few customary rules crystallized as a result of the discussions and the long process of elaboration of the 1982 Law of the Sea Convention, and were eventually codified in that Convention.

Reference is specifically made to the general obligation to 'protect and preserve the environment' laid down in Article 192. Reference is also made to the right of coastal States to conserve and manage living and non-living natural resources and to preserve the marine environment (codified in Article 56(a) of the Convention), as well as to the right of coastal States to take measures in the territorial sea to conserve marine biological resources, to preserve the marine environment, and to prevent, reduce, and control marine pollution (codified in Article 21).

Some commentators also contend that another area of emerging general norms is that concerning the conservation of marine living resources (see, for example, the 1982 Convention on the Conservation of Antarctic Marine Living Resources (CCAMLR), the 1995 UN Agreement on Straddling Fish Stocks and Highly Migratory Fish Stocks, etc.).

It should be noted that recently, in two *European Communities Hormones* cases brought before WTO Panels, the European Communities contended that the 'precautionary principle' (whereby one should take all necessary precautions to avoid damage to the environment; see *infra*) had become a customary rule of international law or, at least, a general principle of law.[22] However, the other parties to the disputes disagreed. Thus, the USA suggested that it was indeed more an 'approach' than a principle,[23] while Canada submitted that it was 'an emerging principle of law' which might in the future crystallize into a general principle of law recognized by civilized nations.[24] Neither the Panels,[25] nor the Appellate Body[26] took any stand on the matter.

In sum, if it is argued that customary rules have evolved or are emerging, it must also be noted that this occurs sector by sector, for instance, in the field of the law of the sea. Probably general rules—more specific than the aforementioned general principles—and encompassing the whole field of the environment will take shape in the near future, as a result of the gradual expansion of this sector-oriented evolution.

17.3.2 GENERAL GUIDELINES LAID DOWN IN 'SOFT LAW' DOCUMENTS

International guidelines for protecting the environment have been laid down in a host of legally non-binding international instruments adopted by UN Conferences or bodies. The principal ones are: the 1972 Stockholm Declaration, passed by the 1972 UN Conference on the Human Environment, the 1982 World Charter for Nature, proclaimed by consensus by the UN General Assembly, the 1992 Rio Declaration on the Environment and Development, adopted by a UN Conference. These instruments, together with other non-binding instruments such as codes of conduct, belong to the category of so-called soft law (see **7.6.2**). They lay down standards of action that States, international organizations, corporations, and individuals should pursue. Although they are not legally binding (except when they codify or crystallize general principles or rules), they evince the consensus of the international community on the path to be taken to tackle environmental issues. They are much less than binding legal rules but much more than simple desiderata of individual States or organizations. What is even more important, they point to the *general approach to the environment* that States, intergovernmental organizations, national or multinational corporations, and individuals should adopt, each at its or his own level.

These guidelines can be summed up as follows.

First, the environment is an asset belonging to mankind, to be safeguarded for the benefit of everybody including future generations (Principle 2 of the 1972 Stockholm Declaration;[27] see also the preamble of the 1982 World Charter for Nature).[28]

Second, nature is a general asset that must be protected, along the lines set out in the various provisions of the 1982 World Charter for Nature, and further developed, in some respects, in the 1992 Rio Declaration.[29]

Third, States, international organizations, and individuals share responsibility for the protection of the environment and should therefore co-operate to this effect (Principles 4, 24, and 25 of the Stockholm Declaration).

Fourth, States have common but differentiated responsibilities, depending on whether they are industrialized or developing countries (Principle 7 of the 1992 Rio Declaration). To safeguard the environment adequately, developing countries need financial and technological assistance, stability of prices, and adequate earnings for primary commodities and raw material, as well as the free flow of up-to-date scientific information and transfer of experience in environmental technologies. In addition, standards and criteria that may be valid for the most advanced countries may prove inappropriate, or of unwarranted social cost, for developing countries (Principles 9, 10, 20, and 23 of the Stockholm Declaration, further elaborated upon in the 1992 Rio Declaration).

Fifth, in promoting development, States should always be guided by the notion of 'sustainable development', propounded in many treaties and declarations. This notion intends to cover 'development that meets the needs of the present without compromising the ability of future generations to meet their own needs' (this is the definition offered in the Report made in 1987 to the UN GA by the World Commission on Environment and Development (WCED) chaired by the Norwegian Prime Minister, G. H. Brundland).

Sixth, States should endeavour to prevent damage to the environment by taking precautionary measures (Principle 15 of the Rio Declaration).[30]

Seventh, the polluter should 'in principle' bear the cost of pollution, 'with due regard to the public interests and without distorting international trade and investment' (Principle 16 of the Rio Declaration).

17.3.3 TREATIES

A very large number of treaties have been concluded in this area. Some are bilateral, most are multilateral, some are of universal scope, many are regional in character. Normally they cover very specific aspects of the environment (for instance, marine pollution by dumping of wastes, pollution from ships, protection of the Mediterranean Sea against pollution, trans-boundary movement of hazardous wastes, oil pollution, long-range trans-boundary air pollution, protection of the ozone layer, civil liability for damage resulting from activities dangerous to the environment). The choice of this particular law-making process is only natural: in an area where enormous economic interests are at stake States prefer to proceed with utmost prudence and are prepared to be legally bound only by those rules which they themselves have contributed to hammering out and have then duly accepted. In contrast, they are not willing to be bound by general rules emerging in the international community as a product of the majority of States. In short, in this delicate area States prefer to adopt a *consensual* attitude. However, as has been rightly noted, States are increasingly abandoning the approach taken in the early years and based on the working out of *sectoral* treaties, covering specific issues (the so-called first generation treaties on the environment). They now tend to adopt a *universalist and global* approach. As instances of the so-called second-generation treaties one can cite the 1992 Framework Convention on Climate Change[31] together with the 1997 Kyoto Additional Protocol,[32] as well as the 1992 Convention on Biological Diversity.[33] However, this new approach has not completely replaced the traditional or sectoral one.

In addition, the extreme caution of States has prompted them to craft a special category of treaties: *framework conventions*. These are treaties that enshrine some basic principles, or lay down general guidelines, or set out international and national policies. At the same time they provide for the elaboration and adoption of future treaties (or, in some cases, special protocols adopted together with the framework convention) laying down specific obligations. As instances of this category one may mention the 1976 Convention for the protection of the Mediterranean Sea against pollution (followed by various additional protocols), the 1979 Convention on long-range trans-boundary air pollution, the 1985 Convention for the protection of the ozone layer, the 1992 Framework Convention on climate change. The advantage of this approach is that step by step States can come to a gradual agreement on specific legal obligations, after having established some general binding guidelines.

17.3.4 MECHANISMS FOR PROMOTING OR ENSURING COMPLIANCE

(a) General

States have rightly felt that there was little point in trying to ensure compliance with international rules on protection of the environment by resorting to traditional judicial mechanisms and, in cases of persistent non-compliance, to rules on State responsibility. Questions of the environment cannot be settled by black-and-white decisions, that is by simply deciding whether a State has abided by an international rule or has violated it. First, most of the time international rules governing this matter are not always so clear-cut and specific as one might expect. Second, once the breach of a rule has occurred it may be too late for judicial or quasi-judicial bodies to step in, for the damage to the environment may be of such magnitude that the payment of compensation proves inadequate to the loss or destruction of precious natural assets. Third, the delinquent State may be unable to pay compensation, because of its dire financial conditions, its underdevelopment, or other reasons. Fourth, the damage may have been caused by private persons, without any State responsibility (for instance, on account of lack of due diligence) being involved. Fifth, it may happen that the damage has been caused not to one or more specific States but to the whole international community, and for diplomatic, political, or other reasons no State is prepared to institute judicial or other proceedings against the law-breaking State. In short, it has been rightly considered that this is an area where what is needed is *prevention*, carried out by *collective bodies* acting on behalf of the international community or at least a group of States. It has been felt that the primary task of these bodies should be to *monitor* the conduct of States and, in case of non-compliance, *assist* the deviant State in remedying the damage. Sanctions should be envisaged only as a last resort and in case of repeated non-compliance.

The above remarks are not intended to imply that legal disputes may not arise between two or more States and that they may not be settled by recourse to arbitral or judicial proceedings. Indeed, most treaties on the environment, even those that provide for monitoring mechanisms, do not rule out such recourse; they even explicitly provide for it. This, for instance, holds true for the 1985 Convention on the Protection of the Ozone Layer (Article 11) and the 1992 Convention on Climate Change (Article 14). The fact however remains that in reality States tend to shun judicial proceedings and rely primarily on supervisory procedures.

(b) Monitoring mechanisms

As stated earlier (**10.8.2**), monitoring bodies see to it that States conform with the applicable international standards on protection of the environment. They therefore act on behalf either of the collectivity of States behind a particular treaty, or of the whole of humanity (in the case of bodies established within universal organizations such as the UN). Monitoring mechanisms have the task of both verifying whether States are complying with international standards and promoting respect for such standards. Clearly, the role these mechanisms play is well attuned to the realities of the present international community.

A survey of the numerous treaties on the environment shows that the most widespread supervisory systems may be grouped into four main classes: (a) States' self-reporting procedures; (b) inspection; (c) so-called non-compliance procedures; (d) preventive global monitoring.

Many treaties on the environment provide for the obligation of States to prepare *periodic reports* on their implementation. These reports are normally transmitted to the Secretariat established by the treaty, or to the Secretariat of the organization in charge of the particular treaty (this for instance, is provided for in Article VIII of the 1973 Convention on International Trade in Endangered Species of Wild Fauna and Flaura (CITES)).[34] In other cases the reports are submitted, through the Secretariat, to the Conference of the States parties (this, for instance, is provided for in Article 12 of the 1992 Framework Convention on Climate Change; a similar provision can be found in Article 26 of the 1992 Convention on Biological Diversity). In most cases

State reports are examined by the Secretariat, which submits to the Conference of States parties draft recommendations, to be discussed and, if possible, adopted by the Conference.

Of course monitoring through *on-site inspection* is far more incisive. Inspections are made either by a joint organization or body or by individual contracting States.

This supervisory method is envisaged, for instance, in the 1959 Antarctic Treaty,[35] under which each State party may carry out inspections and report to the 'Consultative Parties', which then discuss the reports in their meetings (the 1991 Protocol on Environmental Protection strengthens this monitoring).[36] The 1973 International Convention for the Prevention of Pollution by Ships (MARPOL)[37] entrusts with monitoring tasks both the flag State and the State where boats dock. The 1992 Niue Treaty on Co-operation in Fisheries Surveillance and Law Enforcement in the South Pacific Region provides for inspection on the sea (carried out on the strength of the Pacific Patrol Boat Programme, by boats of the contracting States) and by the air (carried out by aircraft of Australia and New Zealand).[38] Other treaties confer the power of inspection on collective bodies. For example, the Schedule adopted in 1971 to the 1949 Convention for the Regulation of Whaling established a scheme of international observers, appointed by the International Whaling Commission, but nominated and paid by governments. The 1973 Convention on International Trade in Endangered Species of Wild Fauna and Flaura (CITES) provides that the Secretariat, after receiving States' reports, may authorize an inquiry, the result of which is submitted to the Conference of States parties, which in turn may make recommendations to the relevant State (Article 13). A more effective supervisory system is that provided for in the 1972 UNESCO Convention Concerning the Protection of the World Cultural and Natural Heritage,[39] under which an intergovernmental Committee ensures 'systematic' monitoring of the state of conservation of world heritage sites, as well as 'reactive' monitoring when these sites are threatened by natural disasters or human activities.

A third and more advanced supervisory system, the so-called *non-compliance procedure*, was first established in 1990 with regard to the 1987 Montreal Protocol on Substances that Deplete the Ozone Layer. It has subsequently been taken up in other treaties (notably in the 1992 Framework Convention on Climate Change, the 1994 Protocol on the Reduction of Sulphur, additional to the 1979 Convention on Long-Range Trans-boundary Air Pollution,[40] and the 1994 UN Convention to Combat Desertification).[41] This monitoring system is much stronger than the other ones and shares some features with the judicial settlements of disputes. In particular, (a) the proceedings may have a contentious character (the State complained of may appear before the monitoring body to put forward its arguments and submissions) and (b) the outcome of the procedure may be the adoption of a binding decision (imposing what in practice amounts to a sanction).

Normally this procedure unfolds as follows (the one established in 1990 and subsequently improved upon will be taken as a model). The Secretariat, if after examining States' periodic reports, considers that a State is not complying with the treaty, may make a report to the Meeting of States Parties as well as the Implementation Committee (a permanent body consisting of representatives of ten contracting States, and normally meeting twice a year). Similarly, the Secretariat may forward to the Committee the objections and misgivings (called

'reservations') expressed by a State party and supported by 'corroborating information', concerning another contracting State's implementation of its obligations. In addition, a State party
may report to the Committee, through the Secretariat, that, 'despite having made its best, bona
fide efforts, it is unable to comply fully with its obligations'. The Committee discusses the
Secretariat's report, or the complaining State's 'reservations', or the submissions of the States
about its own inability to fulfil the Protocol's obligations. It may invite to its discussion the
State complained of or self-reporting. It then makes a report to the meeting of States parties.
This gathering shall 'decide upon and call for steps to bring about full compliance with the
Protocol'. The measures that the meeting may adopt, listed in Annex V, include: (a) 'appropriate
assistance, including assistance for the collection and reporting of data, technical assistance,
technology transfer and financial assistance, information transfer and training'; (b) the issuing
of cautions; (c) 'suspension, in accordance with the applicable rules of international law concerning the suspension of the operation of a treaty, of specific rights and privileges under the
Protocol, whether or not subject to time limits, including those concerned with industrial
rationalization, production, consumption, trade, transfer of technology, financial mechanism and
institutional arrangements'.

A fourth system is different from those so far discussed in that it is not primarily
designed to verify whether States infringe international rules for the protection of the
environment. Rather, it aims at *collecting data and information* on the environment so
as better to prevent possible damage to the environment. The most important system
belonging to this category is the Global Environment Monitoring System (GEMS)
established within the framework of the Earth-Watch Programme designed by UNEP
(see *infra*). It is directed 'to assemble and assess information on the human and
natural environment in order to anticipate environmental degradation and alert the
international community to ways in which human activities may be interfering with
the functioning of the biosphere and with human well-being'.

17.4 INSTITUTIONAL BODIES IN CHARGE OF
PROTECTION OF THE ENVIRONMENT

As soon it emerged that the protection of the environment was bound to become one
of the crucial issues of the whole international community, international bodies were
set up and entrusted with broad powers of promoting protection of natural resources
and the human environment.

Among the institutions with a universal scope, mention should be made of the
United Nations Environment Program (UNEP), a subsidiary body of the UN established in 1972 by GA resolution 2997.

UNEP consists of: (a) a Governing Council of 58 members elected by the GA meeting annually
and reporting, though ECOSOC, to the GA; and (b) a Secretariat, with its headquarters in
Nairobi. UNEP promotes international environmental co-operation, co-ordinates programmes
and projects on the environment, and stimulates action by States and international organizations in this area.

In 1992 the UN GA established by resolution 47/191 the UN Commission on Sustainable Development (CSD), consisting of 53 States elected by ECOSOC and a Secretariat based in New York. The Commission is called upon, among other things, to 'enhance international co-operation and rationalise the intergovernmental decision-making capacity for the integration of environment and development issues'. It is guided by the Rio Declaration and must pursue the objective of achieving 'sustainable development'. Other international institutions dealing with the environment have been set up within the framework of such intergovernmental agencies as FAO, UNESCO, IMO, etc.

In addition, there exist many bodies operating at the regional level, such as those active within the European Union, the OECD, the OSCE, the OAS, and the South Pacific region.

Furthermore, numerous treaties on the environment establish international Secretariats, which co-ordinate or monitor and promote actions in the area covered by each treaty. There also exist such institutions as 'Man and the Biosphere', the World Heritage Commission, etc.

17.5 STATE RESPONSIBILITY AND CIVIL LIABILITY FOR ENVIRONMENTAL HARM

17.5.1 STATE RESPONSIBILITY

Under general rules on 'ordinary' State responsibility (see **9.4**) States incur international responsibility when they perform unlawful activities thereby bringing about damage to another State. The question arises however of whether the injuring State bears responsibility on account of fault (that is, if it failed to exercise due diligence) or instead regardless of any negligence, that is simply because of its risk-creating conduct. A further problem is whether States are responsible for activities *that are not prohibited by international law*, and nevertheless cause harm or damage to other States.

These difficult questions are sometimes settled by treaty regulations. For instance, the 1972 Convention on International Liability for Damage Caused by Space Objects[42] provides for various forms of responsibility: absolute liability (Article II)[43] and liability based on fault (Article III). In addition, it contemplates causes of exoneration from absolute liability (Article VI).[44] However, when no treaty provisions are applicable, the aforementioned legal issues remain largely unsettled. Indeed, it would seem that no clear-cut general rules have yet crystallized in this area, mainly because States are still reluctant to accept a legal regulation that might have serious economic consequences. However, whatever solution is preferred in the *general* field of the law of State responsibility for the two issues just mentioned, in the *particular* field of protection of the environment a solution favourable to the environment seems to commend itself. Arguably, States are increasingly feeling the need to safeguard the environment as a crucial constituent part of the common heritage of mankind, so much so that it has been enshrined in innumerable international instruments, some of them legally binding. The whole spirit and the very thrust of modern law of the environment should lead to opting for solutions capable of enhancing the safeguarding of the environment. It could therefore be maintained that, at least in the field of the environment, fault or negligence is not required for State responsibility to arise (that is, a State may be held accountable, hence liable to pay compensation, for serious damage to the environment even if it acted with due diligence). By the same token, it could be asserted that a State may also be held responsible for lawful activities, whenever they result in serious harm to the environment. As indicative of the emergence of a rule in this sense one may mention the *Trail Smelter* case (see above, **17.1**), and the accidents the *Fukuryu Maru* and *Cosmos*, although in neither case has the relevant State admitted its responsibility.

In 1954 a US nuclear test off the Marshall Islands in the South Pacific caused injury to many members of the crew of the Japanese fishing boat *Fukuryu Maru*, which was exposed to nuclear fallout. It should be noted that before the conduct of the tests, the Japanese ambassador to the USA had requested assurances from the United States that compensation would be paid in the event of damage or economic loss to Japanese fishermen resulting from the nuclear test.[45] After the tests the US Government agreed to pay $US 2m. without however formally admitting responsibility.[46] The same occurred as a result of the disintegration over Canadian territory of the Soviet satellite *Cosmos 954*, in 1978. The Canadian authorities, after searching and finding the partly radioactive debris scattered on Canadian territory, requested compensation for the cost incurred in locating and recovering the debris. In 1981 the Soviet Union agreed to pay compensation ($Can. 3m.), without adverting to any responsibility it might have incurred.[47]

Some commentators have rightly noted that claims that a State bears international responsibility may have to face a host of other legal problems as well as serious practical hurdles: (1) It may be difficult to prove the existence of a causal link between the culpable activity and the harm, particularly in the case of air pollution or when it is asserted that the damage has arisen as a result of activities performed years before; furthermore, harmful effects may arise as a result of many concomitant factors (for instance, smog, combined with fog and pollutants produced by industry, domestic heating, and gas emissions from motor vehicles, may cause respiratory ailments if there is no wind, whereas they may be swept away by strong wind). (2) It may prove difficult to identify the author of environmental harm, particularly in the case of long-range pollution. (3) In most cases harmful effects are caused by individuals or multinational corporations. It is still unclear whether States, in addition to being responsible for (a) the conduct causing environmental damage, of persons who are State officials or who act on behalf of the State, as well as (b) lack of due diligence in the case of damage caused by private activities of persons or entities not acting on their behalf, may also be held accountable for acts of private persons not involving any conduct or omissions of *de jure* or de facto State officials. However, the State's general duty to avoid as much as possible, or at any rate to be cognizant of, the commission of international wrongful acts on its territory, to some extent alluded to by the ICJ in the *Corfu Channel* case,[48] might provide some basis for States' international liability. (4) The assessment of damages proves to be extremely difficult and complicated in view of the numerous factors that should be taken into account (this seems to be borne out by the decision delivered in 1984 in the *Amoco Cadiz* case by the US District Court for the Northern District of Illinois, which envisaged numerous categories of damage such as clean-up operations by public employees, the cost of using public buildings for those operations, coastline and harbour restoration, ecological harm, etc.).[49]

As noted above, practice shows that in many instances States are inclined to pay compensation for their own risky activities without however admitting any international responsibility.

17.5.2 CIVIL LIABILITY

The liability of individuals, of national or multinational corporations, or of States, *under domestic law*, is regulated by municipal law and, in many instances, by a number of international treaties dealing with specific matters (damage caused by nuclear installations, oil pollution, exploration or exploitation of seabed mineral resources, pollution of the marine environment, damage caused by waste, the transport of dangerous goods, etc.). Among general treaties on the matter, mention should be made of the 1993 Council of Europe Convention on Civil Liability for Damage Resulting from Activities Dangerous to the Environment.[50] Other Conventions regulate civil responsibility arising in specific matters.[51]

Generally speaking, liability is incurred by the owner of the ship causing the damage, the operator of nuclear installations, or of installations for the exploitation of seabed mineral resources, or (in the case of damage caused by the transport of dangerous goods) by the registered owner or person controlling the road vehicle or inland navigation vessel or operator of a railway line. Normally a strict liability approach is taken, that is, subject to a few exceptions, the author of the damage is liable regardless of intent or negligence. As a rule jurisdiction over claims for compensation belongs to the courts of the party in whose territory the incident occurred.

The 1968 EEC Convention on Jurisdiction and Enforcement of Judgements in Civil and Commercial Matters[52] provides in Article 3 that a defendant can be sued in tort before the courts of the place where the harmful event occurred, without however specifying whether by this place is intended the place where the wrongful conduct occurs (place of the polluter, etc.), or the place where the harm is suffered (place of the victim). In a judgment handed down on 30 November 1976 in *G.-J. Bier* v. *Mines de Potasse* the European Court of Justice ruled that the draftsmen of the Convention had in mind the interests of the injured party and consequently the choice of the forum must be left to the plaintiff.[53]

Of course, the rendering of a judgment by a national court may not suffice. It may prove necessary to seek and obtain recognition and enforcement of that judgment in the country where the victim resides or the assets of the party complained of are located, so as to obtain proper compensation.

A number of treaties provide for the execution of judgments delivered by foreign courts. For instance, Article XI of the 1962 Brussels Convention on the Liability of Operators of Nuclear Ships[54] stipulates that a final judgment entered by a court having jurisdiction (that is, a court of the licensing State or of the Contracting State in whose territory nuclear damage has been sustained) is recognized in the territory of any other Contracting State. Similarly Article XII, paragraphs 1 and 2 of the 1963 IAEA Vienna Convention on Civil Liability for Nuclear Damage[55] stipulates that final judgments that are recognized are enforceable in the territory of any State party. Article 31 of the 1968 EEC Convention on Jurisdiction and Enforcement of Judgments in Civil and Commercial Matters[56] provides that decisions rendered in one of the contracting States may be executed in another Contracting State on request by any interested party. Article IX.3 of the 1969 Civil Liability Convention for Oil Pollution Damage[57] provides that judgments rendered in one of the contracting States are recognizable and enforceable in the courts of all the other parties.

17.6 LIBERALIZATION OF TRADE VERSUS PROTECTION OF THE ENVIRONMENT

So far we have seen that protection of the environment has become one of the most urgent needs of the present international community. In the following chapter we will see that in the last few years liberalization of world trade has become another top priority of this community, and a special organization is now ensuring the attainment of this goal: the WTO. We should now ask ourselves whether these two basic demands of the world community are in conflict and, if so, whether an attempt is being made to reconcile them.[58]

In some respects measures concerning trade have been used as a tool for ensuring a more effective protection of the environment. Thus, for instance, some treaties such as the 1987 Montreal Protocol on Substances that Deplete the Ozone Layer[59] envisage the taking of trade sanctions against those States that do not comply with the minimum standards on the environment laid down in the relevant treaties.[60]

Generally speaking, however, liberalization of trade and protection of the environment are on a 'collision course'. Indeed, the first goal is directed to abolishing any form of State protectionism so as to ensure the free flow of international trade. By contrast, the other goal may require strong State intervention: for instance, it may prove necessary for State authorities to stop the importation of goods injurious to health or noxious to the environment; or it may appear necessary to intervene in the area of goods processing or manufacturing by limiting those forms that prove excessively harmful to the environment.

The need to reconcile free trade with environmental protection has become more and more compelling in recent years. The Articles of Agreement of the GATT (the entity that was incorporated into the WTO in 1994: see *infra*, **18.7.3**) did not explicitly provide for any exemption concerning the environment from the rules on free trade. Article XX, paragraph (b) admitted exemptions 'necessary to protect human, animal

or plant life or health' and paragraph (g) exempted measures 'relating to the conservation of exhaustible natural resources if such measures are made effective in conjunction with restrictions on domestic production or consumption'. However sweeping,
these clauses were not broad enough to cover non-living finite resources (such as oil,
coal, and gas) or such broad notions as ecosystem protection or biological diversity.

The States negotiating the Uruguay Round were aware of the problems. In 1994
they set up a Committee on Trade and Development charged with (a) identifying 'the
relationship between trade measures and environmental measures in order to
promote sustainable development'; and (b) making recommendations on 'whether
any modifications of the provisions of the multilateral trading system are required'.
However, it would seem that so far the Committee has not achieved much.

Nevertheless, some progress was made both at the level of conclusion of
agreements, and at that of settlement of disputes.

In 1994 the Agreement on Technical Barriers to Trade (TBT) was concluded. Its
Article 2.2 provides that 'technical regulations shall not be more trade-restrictive than
necessary to fulfil a legitimate purpose . . . *inter alia* . . . protection of human health or
safety; animal plant life or health; or the environment'.[61]

The dispute-settling mechanisms envisaged in the WTO, namely, the panels
charged with deciding upon disputes between parties to the WTO (see above, **10.8.1**)
have increasingly dealt with environmental issues and over time have opened up to
demands relating to protection of the environment.

Thus, WTO panels pronounced upon cases relating to trade measures adopted by States to
conserve animal species beyond their territory (*Tuna-Dolphin* case—Mexico v. USA; and
Shrimps-Turtles case—India, Pakistan, and Thailand v. USA). In the former case the Panel
admitted the right to adopt unilateral trade measures designed to protect the global environment as long as such measures are consistent with international standards as well as
international rules on the exercise of jurisdiction.[62] In the latter case the Appellate Body held
that requiring from exporting countries compliance with, or the adoption of, certain policies
prescribed by the importing country for the sake of protecting the environment (in the case at
issue: requiring the adoption of fishing technology capable of avoiding the incidental killing of
sea turtles) was not *per se* contrary to Article XX.[63] The Appellate Body also took a stand
favourable to environmental requirements in *Standards for Reformulated and Conventional
Gasoline* (Venezuela v. USA). Venezuela had assailed as discriminatory US measures imposing,
on environmental grounds, stricter criteria than those demanded of domestic fuel, on foreign
import of fuel; in its view clean air was not an 'exhaustible natural resource', hence it did not
fall under the permissive clauses of Article XX. The Appellate Body held instead that clean air is
a natural resource that can be depleted by pollutants.[64]

18

LEGAL ATTEMPTS AT NARROWING THE GAP BETWEEN NORTH AND SOUTH

18.1 THE COLONIAL RELATIONSHIP

It is impossible to understand the current problems of developing countries without being aware of the general historical background. It may therefore prove useful to get a broad, though necessarily over-simplified view of the patterns along which powerful European countries benefited economically from the natural resources of colonial territories, or such other countries as those in Latin America, which, though independent in the early nineteenth century, were long under de facto domination of industrialized States.

Colonial expansion was decisively stimulated by the advent in the eighteenth century of industrial development in Europe, chiefly in Britain, which witnessed rapid industrial growth in the period 1780–1840. As Britain had few natural resources of its own (among these coal and iron), but was capable of manufacturing goods in relatively high volumes and efficiently, it found it useful to import primary commodities (cocoa, tea, coffee, sugar, wheat, tobacco, bananas, rubber, tin, bauxite, copper, iron ore, mercury, petroleum, tungsten, nickel, manganese ore, etc.). Thus it proved of immense value to the Western economy to invest in colonial territories or in such backward countries as those of Latin America, for the purpose of extracting the raw materials available there.

The impact of advanced economic activity on the archaic structure of underdeveloped territories resulted in the creation of a 'dual' or 'hybrid' economy.[1] Two different patterns of economic activity came to exist side by side, namely: (a) a dynamic and modern sector, export oriented and based on the capitalistic model, and (b) the general sector of the economy, essentially based on pre-capitalistic structures and geared to subsistence agriculture. The former sector, geared to producing and exporting *raw materials*, was controlled by foreign enterprises but availed itself of cheap local labour. Colonial penetration, based on the recruitment of local manpower, had a favourable impact on the standard of living of the population in the region where foreign enterprises were set up. It stimulated a certain amount of economic activity. It also had other useful side-effects in such areas as health, sanitation, or infrastructures (harbours, lines of communication, telegraphs, transport, etc.). In spite of these beneficial effects, no structural modification in the overall economic system of developing countries was brought about. In the main, Western economic dominance produced the highly adverse effect of not promoting a global and self-sustaining development process involving all economic sectors. The economic structure of backward nations remained 'dual'. Indeed, with the passage of time this character became even more conspicuous, even though later on in certain developing countries more complex structures evolved.

The condition of developing countries worsened after the First World War. The USA became the leading economic force in the world. Owing both to its consistent protectionist policy and its vast natural resources, its requirement of imported primary commodities was relatively low (see also **13.1** and **18.4**). This attitude resulted in the steady decline of the exports from developing nations which, in its turn, further accentuated the economic imbalance between North and South.

18.2 MAIN FEATURES OF DEVELOPING COUNTRIES' ECONOMIC STRUCTURE

It is of course difficult to set down the principal economic characteristics of emergent countries in a concise manner, if only because these nations differ widely. They include huge and populous countries such as China, India, Nigeria, Indonesia, and Brazil and tiny nations such as Grenada, Swaziland, or Nauru. They range from such States as Bangladesh, Chad, or the Central African Republic, with a backward and rudimentary economy, to such countries as Mexico, Venezuela, Nigeria, India, Pakistan, Indonesia, Singapore, South Korea, where considerable progress towards industrialization has been made and one or more sectors of the economy have advanced along lines similar to those prevailing in Western States (Mexico and South Korea joined, in 1994 and 1996 respectively, the Organization for Economic Cooperation and Development, OECD, an organization that brings together industrialized States sharing the principles of a market economy, a pluralist democracy, and respect for human rights).

Nevertheless, a few generalizations are possible, with the usual caveat that they tend to over-simplify reality.

The principal characteristics of an underdeveloped economy may be summed up as follows: (1) The dominant economic activity is agriculture. (2) Often a 'dual' or hybrid' economy exists, as described above; sometimes the economy even consists of three sectors: the traditional area where subsistence (agricultural) economy predominates; the sector geared to foreign trade (production and export of raw materials; this is what is currently termed a *monoculture economy*); and a sector of light industry producing articles of general consumption such as textiles and processed foodstuffs, earmarked for the domestic market. (3) Both agriculture and manufacturing are often conducted on a family basis, that is, primarily in family-size, cottage-type units, rather than in industrial productive units. (4) The agricultural and industrial equipment is primitive, or at any rate not very sophisticated; as a consequence, labour productivity is relatively low and the output comparatively poor. (5) So-called concealed unemployment prevails, that is, a situation whereby if the number of workers employed is reduced, there is no fall in production, even without changing the capital stock and the production techniques. (6) There is a low level of capital stock. The accumulation of capital necessary for the acquisition of better industrial equipment and more generally for productive investment, in particular with a view to terminating the *monoculture economy* and thus undertaking *differentiated economic activities*, often does not come about. There are two principal reasons for this failure. First, the low labour productivity does not give rise to that excess of production over consumption which allows private saving. In other words, agricultural and industrial output primarily serve to ensure the subsistence of workers. Second, that part of the national product not earmarked for labour force subsistence often goes to a small wealthy elite, normally made up of landowners, a few industrial entrepreneurs, and political leaders. This causes what economists call 'the vicious circle of poverty'[2]: the labour output is too small to permit the accumulation of capital necessary to improve and modernize the agricultural and industrial equipment, so as to increase labour and investment productivity. (7) What economists call 'conglomerative factors' worsen the economy of these countries. The industrialization of an area presupposes a number of infrastructures (lines of communication, electric power, supplies of piped water, training of local manpower, public administration, etc.). In turn, these infrastructures make further investment profitable. Lack of, or scant, industrialization and ancillary facilities in developing countries make it more advantageous for capital-exporting countries to invest in industrialized areas of the world. Indeed, even cheap manpower in developing nations does not outweigh the profitability of investment in areas where a whole range of infrastructures already exists. In addition, conglomerative factors also operate with regard to the demands of industrial workers. If a factory is set up in a backward area, the workers' earnings cannot be spent only on purchasing the factory's output; a market must be created, which itself can further stimulate economic activity. The optimum solution would lie in setting up, instead of one big factory, a number of small industrial units capable of producing a wide range of products to be sold to the workers. However, below a minimum size modern factories are not profitable. Consequently the installation of a new factory in a developing country may be attended by the lack of an adequate domestic market, so that all the beneficial effects of industrialization fail to materialize. (8) A further complicating factor for the economy of these countries is the steady increase in population.

18.3 THE MOST FUNDAMENTAL ECONOMIC NEEDS OF DEVELOPING COUNTRIES

Given their economic structure and conditions, developing nations clearly need international economic relations that depart markedly from the liberal, free-market approach taken and advocated by industrialized States, chiefly the USA. This approach, it is well known, is grounded on the principle of free trade and free competition, in particular the abolition of trade tariffs and other devices that distort the world market. Instead, it is important for developing countries to enjoy 'discriminatory treatment', that is treatment taking account of their problems, hence different and more advantageous than that existing between developed countries. More specifically, these countries need: (a) stabilization of the price of primary commodities, so as to avoid price fluctuations and decline, to the detriment of the producers; (b) trade preferences and concessions, in particular trade barriers on their imports and preferential treatment for their exports, notably the most-favoured-nation treatment (on this notion see *infra*, **18.7.3**), without, however, any concession to developed countries in return; (c) foreign investment, in particular to promote economic activities in areas other than production and export of local raw materials; (d) economic assistance, in particular the rescheduling or even the cancellation of foreign debt; (e) transfer of modern technology; (f) training of skilled workers.

In addition to these problems, others are created by some of the developing countries themselves. Often the State structure is authoritarian. Only in a few countries does one find that truly democratic processes have been put in place. It is not unusual for political leaders to be inclined to act more in the interest of the ethnic group or the elite to which they belong than in the interest of the whole population, and in particular that of the innumerable people who suffer from poverty, malnutrition, and lack of education and health care. Frequently corruption is rife, both among civil servants and at a higher level, that of politicians. In many countries internecine conflicts between ethnic, tribal, or religious groups are rampant and frequently result in armed clashes and much bloodshed. On top of that, some States tend to choose inadequate economic policies (for instance, lack of encouragement of the private sector).

Plainly, whenever developing countries are beset by these problems, foreign assistance may only prove fruitful if accompanied by better or more democratic governance at home.

18.4 INTERNATIONAL ECONOMIC INSTITUTIONS ESTABLISHED TOWARDS THE END OF THE SECOND WORLD WAR

To appraise the demands of developing countries for an international economic order more responsive to their needs, it may prove useful first compendiously to describe the philosophy and motivations behind the establishment of international economic institutions towards the end of the Second World War.

The Second World War left Europe in a shambles: the economies of both Western European countries and the Soviet Union had been disrupted by the fighting or converted to the war effort. Japan too was on its knees. The USA was the only big Power whose territory had been spared by invasion or bombardment and whose economy had been boosted by the war. After the war it became by far the most powerful State militarily; it was in its interest to increase its economic power by allowing its capital to be invested abroad, thus expanding its economy on a world scale. The US economic expansion on European territory and in the Far East was salutary, at least in the short run, to the countries disrupted by war. They could not but benefit from the flow of American capital into their markets. Hence they keenly welcomed the restructuring of international economic relations propounded by the USA. To implement the new scheme it was, however, necessary to dismantle all the barriers that over the years had been erected in the world community by States increasingly bent on protectionism (this of course includes colonialist countries, which drew much benefit from the exploitation of primary commodities produced in colonial territories). Thus the USA launched a *free trade and free market philosophy*. In addition, it succeeded in having three important international institutions (the World Bank, the IMF, and the GATT) established for the purpose of creating the necessary international mechanisms for realizing that philosophy on a multilateral, stable, and continuing basis.

The World Bank was given the task of mobilizing and collecting money from private sources on the international capital market, with a view to lending it to those States most in need of foreign investment.

The IMF was designed to ensure international monetary stability. It aimed to ensure that single States did not alter international trade conditions by monetary contrivances (such as unilateral devaluations of their currencies) designed to protect the national economy at the expense of foreign countries. In addition, it was designed to help finance temporary balance-of-payment deficits of member States, caused by fluctuations in the price of products on the international market, or by domestic problems. Such financing was clearly to serve as a device for preventing States from finding themselves constrained to resort to protectionism.

The GATT was intended to abolish traditional tariff restrictions on free trade which greatly hampered free competition on the world market.

These institutions, to a large extent imbued with a free market and free competition philosophy, were harshly criticized by developing countries, particularly as soon as such countries acquired independence. As pointed out above, with regard to North–South relations, emergent nations advocated two principles conflicting with that philosophy: 'preferential treatment' and 'positive discrimination'. Slowly, under the strong pressure of developing countries, all three international institutions attuned their policy, at least in part, to the North–South question, albeit in a manner which developing countries still consider inadequate.

18.5 THE PRINCIPAL DEMANDS AND THE LEGAL STRATEGY OF DEVELOPING COUNTRIES

Initially (between 1946 and the late 1950s) disadvantaged countries insisted on their need to obtain financial and technical assistance from industrialized nations, so as rapidly to get off the ground. Then they gradually realized that this sort of assistance was totally inadequate to cope with the far-reaching problems besetting them. The prices of the primary commodities they produced (sugar, coffee, tea, cocoa, rubber, and so on; see above, **18.1**) were steadily declining on the world market, while at the same time there was a steady increase in the price of manufactured or semi-manufactured goods, that is, goods which poor countries had to import both to meet their growth requirements and also to create the infrastructure necessary for promoting foreign investment. In consequence, a decline in the exports of developing countries and an increase in their imports took place; as a result, their balance of payments deficit worsened at staggering speed. From the early 1960s to the early 1970s they therefore increasingly insisted on 'trade, not aid', that is, trade conditions more favourable to them.

In the early 1970s the accession of a great number of formerly dependent African and Asian countries to political independence rendered developing countries more pugnacious and vocal. In addition, following the 1973 Arab–Israeli war, the Arab oil-producing countries decided upon a boycott of industrialized countries. The worried reaction of the West emboldened the Arab States, which set up an association of oil exporting countries (OPEC). All these factors led developing countries to (a) reconsider the whole international economic system and (b) put forward audacious and far-reaching demands concerning the reshaping of international economic relations, so as to adopt measures that, instead of being palliatives, could come to grips with the substance of international structural relations.

To attain their political objectives, at the *legal level* these countries could not count on the formation of *customary rules* upholding their demands. Normally the growth of custom is a slow process, and those countries were eager to effect very swiftly the changes for which they were fighting. Furthermore, custom requires a large convergence of States on the substance of new standards; in the matter at issue there was however strong opposition from the industrialized countries which, considering that some of their fundamental interests were at stake, were not prepared to tie their hands by accepting new international rules. In their legal strategy, developing countries had therefore to fall back on two possible norm-setting processes: the adoption of *general declarations by the GA*, and the working out of international agreements. The first process has of course the major disadvantage of not creating binding legal standards. It can create only the so-called soft law, which is no real law at all, but only guidelines and norms. Soft law thus may lead to the formation of customary rules, if the other States are willing gradually to accept as binding those standards and norms, or it may be the start of the gradual making of international agreements, or it may set up new international institutions that serve as catalysts or promoters of gradual change. The other norm-setting process (*treaty making*) obviously requires that States reach agreement, and that a fairly large number of States be prepared to become party to such agreements.

As we shall see, developing countries followed both paths. They pushed for the adoption of general declarations by the GA, with a view both to setting out general guidelines and to promoting the establishment of new institutions geared to development. They also insisted on the making of agreements in at least some areas.

Thus in 1974 they got the UN GA to adopt a Declaration on the *New International Economic Order* (NIEO), with a Programme of Action, and a Charter of Economic Rights and Duties of States. In 1982 they managed to have adopted by the Diplomatic Conference on the Law of the Sea a Convention incorporating the concept of the '*common heritage of mankind*'. In 1986 they pushed through the GA a Declaration on the *right to development.* Over time, these attempts have ended up in relative failure, both because they were too ambitious, and on account of the strong opposition of industrialized countries.

The NIEO was intended to be a *global challenge* to existing international economic relations. Its *main tenets* were the following: (1) Developing countries must be entitled to regulate and control the activities of multinational corporations operating within their territory. (2) They must be free to nationalize or expropriate foreign property on conditions favourable to them. (3) They must be free to set up associations of primary commodities producers similar to OPEC; all other States must recognize this right and refrain from taking economic, military, or political measures calculated to restrict it. (4) International trade should be based on the need to ensure stable, equitable, and remunerative prices for raw materials, generalized non-reciprocal and non-discriminatory tariff preferences, as well as transfer of technology to developing countries; and should provide economic and technical assistance without any strings attached. By and large the principles laid down in the GA texts on the NIEO amounted to a set of standards of achievement primarily possessed of political and rhetorical value only. With the passage of time it became increasingly clear that they could not be translated into reality unless some conditions, including a favourable attitude on the part of industrialized countries, were met. Nevertheless, although the NIEO never really got off the ground as a normative scheme, some of its mechanisms proved viable (for instance, the Restrictive Business Practice Code, or RBP Code, adopted in 1980 by the UN GA as a non-legal, non-binding code of conduct, or the Common Fund for Commodities, which came into force in 1989 to assist commodity-producing emergent countries).

As pointed out above (**3.5.4**), the concept of a *common heritage of mankind* was launched as early as 1967 by the Maltese Ambassador Arvid Pardo in the UN GA.[3] It aimed to establish an international legal regime of the seabed and the ocean floor solely for peaceful purposes, and for the benefit of mankind as a whole. The concept of a 'common heritage of mankind' as a general standard for the exploitation of new natural resources incorporated five main elements: (a) the exclusion of a right of appropriation; (b) the duty to exploit the resources in the interest of mankind in such a way as to benefit all, including developing countries; (c) the duty to explore and exploit for peaceful purposes only; (d) the duty to pay due regard to scientific research; (e) the duty duly to protect the environment. As we have seen above, the concept was first upheld in the 1979 Treaty on the Moon and other Celestial Bodies. However, eventually in the treaty the crucial point of the common heritage concept, that is, the question of how to share the benefits deriving from the exploitation of resources in outer space, was left unresolved. In contrast, Pardo's ideas were to some extent taken up in the 1982 Convention on the Law of the Sea. However, industrialized countries firmly opposed the new concepts, with the result that for a long time they refrained from ratifying the Convention. A breakthrough occurred in 1994, when States reached agreement on a text designed to revise part XI of the Convention (on the main aspects of the 1994 Agreement, see above, **3.5.4**). In short, the substance of the notion of a common heritage of mankind was largely diluted, although not altogether jettisoned.

Let us now move on to the third principle advocated by developing countries and which has so far remained a dead letter. It is the principle whereby all human beings have *a right to development*. This principle, first suggested by Senegal in the UN GA as early as 1966, was later enshrined in various GA resolutions, culminating in the Declaration of 1986. It states the following: (1) The right to development is an inalienable right whereby 'every human being and all peoples are entitled to participate in, and contribute to, and enjoy economic, social, cultural and political development' (Article 1 of the Declaration). (2) 'The human person is the central subject of development and should be the active participant and beneficiary of the right to development' (Article 2.1). (3) States have 'the right and the duty to formulate appropriate national development policies' (Article 2.3) and the 'duty to take steps, individually and collectively, to formulate international development policies with a view to facilitating the full realization of the right to development' (Article 4.1). Plainly, these provisions, and others included in the Declaration, set out loosely worded political goals, rather than legal guidelines. In addition they did not specify to what extent the right at issue should be conceived of as a right of individuals towards their States, or of peoples, and whether the holder of the corresponding obligations should be States *vis-à-vis* individuals or States towards one another. On the whole, this and other similar texts were misguided. Clearly, their motivation was twofold.

Proclaiming the 'right to development' meant reformulating the whole problem of development in terms of a 'fundamental right'. This served to bring the demand for a restructuring of the world economic order into focus and indeed to dramatize such demand: clearly, if you speak of a 'right' it follows that there must exist a duty falling upon somebody. Second, the new concept served to bring the whole momentum of the human rights doctrine—with its panoply of ideas, patterns, and machinery—to bear on all the problems of international economic relations. Nevertheless, developing countries won a pyrrhic victory, for the verbal proclamation and the verbal insistence on the new 'right' did not lead to any major tangible result. Perhaps the chief merit of the whole action for this new 'right' was the bringing to the fore of two important underlying ideas: development does not merely amount to economic growth, but also involves a human dimension; furthermore, it directly concerns not only governments but the whole population; consequently its realization should not be to the sole advantage of ruling elites.

18.6 THE ACTION OF THE WORLD COMMUNITY: GENERAL

It was essentially after the adoption of the UN Charter and the gradual accession of many developing countries to independence, that the international community awoke to the plight of these countries. Four main factors account for this breakthrough: (1) The gradual dismantling of colonial empires unveiled the real conditions of colonial territories and made it clear that political independence was not sufficient. (2) The increasing impact of socialist ideologies on international relations convinced statesmen that they could no longer turn a blind eye to cruel social realities. (3) Some young leaders of developing countries, fully aware of the real conditions of their nations, started vociferously to demand assistance as a way of compensation for the past exploitation by colonial States. (4) The UN offered emergent States a crucial forum where they could put forward their demands and try to reach some sort of compromise with the industrialized States.

The international community has adopted a *three-pronged strategy* in response: (a) a partial modification of international economic and financial institutions (the World Bank, the International Monetary Fund, the GATT and the WTO), so as to make them more responsive to the needs of developing countries; (b) the promotion of multilateral co-operation geared to the development of those countries; (c) the establishment of mechanisms designed to guarantee foreign investments in developing countries.

18.7 MODIFICATION OF INTERNATIONAL ECONOMIC INSTITUTIONS

Developing countries have repeatedly endeavoured to prompt the financial and economic institutions established in the aftermath of the Second World War at the behest of the USA to adjust their policies so as to take account of their special conditions.

18.7.1 THE INTERNATIONAL BANK FOR RECONSTRUCTION AND DEVELOPMENT (THE WORLD BANK)

The World Bank, created in 1944 at the Bretton Woods Conference, is an intergovernmental organization (it later became a UN Specialized Agency). It is corporate in form, all its capital stock being owned by its member States; the amount of their shares is established on the basis of the quotas set for participating in the IMF.

The World Bank also draws its lending resources from money it borrows from private sources through the sale of Bank obligations to investors in capital markets, stock transactions, the earning of interest on its lending, and the commissions and charges arising from the granting of loans.

The central organ is the Board of Governors, consisting of a Governor and an alternate appointed by each member State. Its decisions are taken by a 'weighted voting' system. Each member is allotted the same basic number of votes, namely, 250; additional votes are allocated in proportion to a country's quota. It follows that the voices of the wealthiest countries are stronger than those of the others. Many of the Bank's powers vested in the Board of Governors are delegated to the Executive Board, at present consisting of 22 Directors. The Bank's President (by tradition, a US national) is elected by the Directors.

The statutory goals of the Bank include 'the encouragement of the development of productive facilities and resources in less developed countries'. Since its earliest years the Bank has pursued this goal. Its other statutory goals, namely, 'the restoration of economies destroyed or disrupted by war' and 'the re-conversion of productive facilities to peacetime needs', were primarily attained through activities carried out directly by the USA (by means of the Marshall Plan). The Bank's principal activity is lending money to member States, to 'political subdivisions thereof', or to business enterprises in the territory of members. If the borrower is not a government, the loan must be guaranteed by the government in whose territory the project financed by the loan is located. Loans, made only for technically and economically valid projects, are long term and incur current interest rates.

To meet the needs of poor countries the Bank changed its lending techniques, with regard to the countries concerned. Thus, it made loan terms longer, and differentiated between the interest rates charged to industrialized States and those to developing nations (the rate for loans granted to the former is higher by 0.50 per cent). In addition it decided to grant at least part of such loans in local currency. Furthermore,

more recently, the Bank has made loans that are primarily designed to protect the environment in developing countries. Thus, in 1990, in agreement with the UNDP and UNEP (the UN Environment Programme), the Global Environment Facility was established. It is financed though contributions from over 60 countries; the Bank is in charge of administering these contributions.

In addition, in 1956 the Bank amended its Articles of Agreement, so as to set up the IFC (see *infra*, **18.8.2**) and, in 1960, the IDA (see *infra*, **18.8.2**).

Furthermore, to promote private investments in developing countries and the settlement of disputes arising out of these investments, the Bank established the ICSID and the MIGA (see *infra*, **18.9.2**).

18.7.2 THE INTERNATIONAL MONETARY FUND (IMF)

The IMF was established, together with the World Bank, in 1944, for the main purpose of safeguarding the stability of foreign exchange. Through the Agreement establishing the IMF, the previously unrestricted sovereignty of States in monetary matters was seriously limited. The Agreement provided for a fixed parity between all currencies and gold (the USA had undertaken to fix the convertibility of US dollars into gold at a fixed rate of 35 dollars per ounce. In this way a fixed parity between US dollars, gold, and the various currencies was established; plainly, this arrangement was designed to ensure relative stability in foreign exchange). However, in 1978 the system envisaged in 1944 and based on the *gold exchange standard* was discarded. Gold was dethroned as the common denominator of the par value regime in international monetary transactions and States were allowed to refer to its market rate in their mutual relations. Since 1978 member States of the IMF have been free to choose their exchange rate system (free floating, joint floating, pegging the national currency to that of another State, etc.).

In 1944 States also undertook to refrain from introducing restrictions on payments or transfers for current international transactions as defined by the Articles of Agreement instituting the IMF, multiple currency practices, or discriminatory arrangements, unless authorized by the Articles of Agreement or by the IMF.

As a sort of countervailing measure to the limitations on their sovereignty in monetary matters, member States had a (mainly conditional) right to draw the currency of another member from the Fund whenever they needed it to correct temporary disequilibria in their balance of payments. The purpose of this right accruing to member States was to allow them to overcome their balance of payment difficulties without being compelled to resort to all those protectionist measures the IMF had been set up to prevent.

At present the IMF's financial resources are made up of the quotas subscribed by each member. Quotas consist in part of Special Drawing Rights (SDRs) and other reserve currencies, and in part of States' national currencies (SDRs form a reserve asset that the IMF can allocate to members; States entitled to benefit from the SDRs can be allocated currency to meet balance of payment outflows). Management of the resources is entrusted to two departments: the General

Department (responsible for conducting all the major operations and holding the Fund's assets) and the SDR Department (responsible for all transactions and operations).

The central organ of the IMF is the Board of Governors, consisting of a Governor and an alternate appointed by each member State. Most of the IMF's powers are vested in the Board of Governors, which can delegate them to the Executive Board. The Executive Board consists of a variable number of Executive Directors (at present they are 24), partly designated by the most important members, partly elected every two years by the remaining members, by a complex voting procedure. Both the Board of Governors and the Executive Board follow the 'weighted voting' system (already described above, with reference to the World Bank: see **18.7.1**). Consequently in the IMF also the voice of the wealthiest countries is stronger than that of the others. However, the practice of deciding by consensus (see above, **2.5.6**) has increasingly spread.

The Managing Director is another central organ of the IMF. He is selected by the Executive Board (he cannot be either a Governor or a Director). He is the head of the operating staff. Unlike Governors and Directors, he and his staff owe their duty exclusively to the Fund.

As a result of the demise of the Gold Exchange System, the Fund turned from a monetary institution into a lending institution (although to some extent lending was always basic to the fund: J. M. Keynes is reported to have said, 'You have to understand that the Bank is a Fund, and the Fund is a Bank', that is, the Fund gives overdrafts as loans).

The gradual opening of the Fund to *developing countries* took place both through the growing participation of these countries in the IMF decision-making process, and through the growing influence of developing countries on the drafting of provisions regulating the IMF and the use of its resources. Furthermore, to meet the specific needs of developing countries the Fund set up mechanisms designed to increase the lending of financial resources to those countries. This has come about through the increase in the maximum limit on authorized drawing, and through the establishment of special resources designed to take into account the wide range of causes of disequilibria in the balance of payments. Such mechanisms include the Compensatory Financing Facility, established in 1963 and expanded in subsequent years. It is designed to provide additional resources to States exporting primary products and which encounter problems due to temporary shortfalls in receipts for exports. Another such mechanism is the Extended Facility, established in 1974, which in turn grants assistance, for longer periods of time and in larger amounts than normal, to States which suffer serious deficits in their balance of payments owing to structural maladjustments in production, trade, or prices.

18.7.3 THE GENERAL AGREEMENT ON TARIFFS AND TRADE (GATT) AND THE WORLD TRADE ORGANIZATION (WTO)

(i) The GATT. The combination of international currency stability and the institutionalized mobilization of private capital to promote the free flow of investment to countries short of money did not suffice for the realization of the grand design

launched by the USA in the post-war period—a design which constituted a bold projection on to the world community of a pattern of economic order typical of capitalist countries. The free enterprise, free market, and free competition postulates would have become empty words if protectionism in trade had survived. Hence, after the establishment of the IMF and the World Bank, the need soon arose to complete the foundations of the new economic order by abolishing trade barriers.

In 1947 a new scheme was set up in the shape of the General Agreement on Tariffs and Trade (GATT). The Agreement, unlike the Articles instituting the Bank and the IMF, did not create an international organization; however, over the years an organizational structure did evolve, operating between the 'sessions' of the contracting parties, held twice a year in Geneva. Unlike the Bank and the IMF, the GATT is based on the equal voting power of each party or, in other words, not on the weighted-voting system.

The core of the GATT is the set of obligations that it imposes on the contracting States, a very complex and technical network of stipulations.

The first obligation imposes the requirement that each member grant all other parties *most-favoured-nation treatment* in the field of imports or exports, that is, to treat other GATT members in the same manner as the country to which it grants the most favourable conditions. Why was this clause deemed necessary for the purpose of achieving free trade? Clearly, if a great number of States loyally apply this clause, it follows that discriminations between them tend gradually to fall down and a regime of equality in their trade relationship is established.

If, say, France must grant all other members the most-favoured-nation treatment, this means that in relations between France and all GATT members the same dues will apply as those in force between France and the country it treats best. Thus there will be complete equality between all countries concerned. Similarly, if Japan is to grant the same treatment to all GATT members as to its most-favoured nation, this implies that between Japan and all other members there will be complete equality. It may, however, happen that France gives better treatment to a third country than the treatment accorded by Japan to the nation it favours most. In this case, a difference of treatment between France and Japan, *inter se*, will ensue, for the former will extend to the latter (and to all countries members of the GATT) a better treatment than the treatment granted by Japan to France (and to all the other members of the GATT). Thus, the operation of the clause does not necessarily beget *complete* equality among all members of the GATT. In practice, however, this imbalance is somewhat tempered by the fact that, on the whole, the granting of commercial treatment is based on reciprocity. Therefore, at least when members of the GATT accord each other special advantages, these advantages extend to all other members. If, say, Sweden and Algeria enter into an agreement providing, on a mutual basis, for special facilities as regards imports and exports of certain commodities, each of them must extend the same treatment to all other members of the GATT. (This, however, does not imply that between two other GATT members, say Mexico and Italy, the imports or exports of the same commodities are subject to the same regime. In other words, even in this case equality is not absolute.)

Another obligation prescribes that imported goods be treated *no worse than domestic goods under internal taxation or regulation measures* (Article III). Thus, while the most-favoured-nation clause is designed to provide non-discriminatory treatment for imports from different foreign countries, this obligation puts foreign goods on the same footing as those produced domestically. The obligation, it is plain, strikes at the very heart of the protectionist tendency of most States. These two obligations are closely related to, and supported by, the general obligation gradually to reduce customs duties by way of *bilateral or multilateral negotiations ('rounds')* (Article XXVIII, *bis*). The first rounds dealt mainly with tariff reductions and were conducted bilaterally, whereas later negotiations, conducted on a multilateral approach, included other areas (anti-dumping and non-tariff measures).

While these are the principal obligations laid down in the Agreement, they are attended by further obligations calculated to strengthen the principle of non-discrimination and equality of treatment in other specific areas, where States tend to depart from free trade postulates. Thus the Agreement prohibits: quantitative restrictions on both imports and exports (such restrictions are often introduced to protect national products from foreign competition); dumping (that is, the practices by which 'products of one country are introduced into the commerce of another country at less than the normal value of the products'), if 'it causes or threatens material injury to an established industry in the territory of a contracting party or materially retards the establishment of a domestic industry'. In addition, the Agreement restricts the freedom of States to grant subsidies, particularly export subsidies.

When imposing all these obligations, the framers of the Agreement were, of course, aware that special situations existed of which they ought to take account. This is why they provided for a set of exceptions, some of which were laid down in the original Agreement, whereas others were added in later years when the practical operation of the GATT rendered them necessary. The exceptions can be grouped under three different headings. The first group of exceptions is aimed at *general situations*. Thus Article XXV stipulates that the contracting parties, acting jointly, may by a specific vote waive an obligation laid down in the Agreement. Article XIX provides for the use of temporary restraints on imports if the latter are causing serious injuries to domestic industry. Furthermore, Articles XII to XIV permit the use of quotas on imports in case of balance of payments crises. Finally, Articles XX and XXI provide for exceptions for the purpose of implementing national health and safety regulations as well as those pertaining to national security. A second group of exceptions aims at allowing the maintenance of *preferences* between members of special regional groupings (Article XXIV). These exceptions in particular concern such groupings as custom unions (for example the EC) and free trade areas (for example, EFTA). A third group of exceptions, as will be seen, relates to *developing countries*.

(ii) The GATT and the problems of developing countries. As stated above, the GATT's goal of progressively bringing about the elimination of trade barriers could prove detrimental to the economy of developing countries, because the backwardness of their industrial development and the consequent higher costs of production cannot but render their products less competitive than those from highly industrialized countries. Third World countries therefore needed some protection for their economy, in the form of *trade barriers on their imports* and *preferential treatment for their exports*.

The most-favoured-nation clause referred to above did not meet the demands of emergent countries. It was designed to put on the same footing States having similar economic structures, whereas it was ill-suited for developing countries. In addition, until the 1986–94 Uruguay Round, the clause did not cover areas crucial to backward countries, namely agriculture, textiles, and clothing, areas in which industrialized States permitted levies, quotas, and subsidies so as to protect themselves from the products of developing countries.

The need for a preferential treatment of developing countries was first acknowledged through the revision, brought about at the Review Session of 1954–5, of Article XVIII. The amendment essentially recognized the structural nature of developing countries' balance of payments problems and attenuated the requirement of prior approval in regard to measures deviating from the GATT's obligations for the promotion of a particular industry.

The changes introduced in 1965 were more significant. A Protocol amending the General Agreement was adopted and a special section, Part IV, called 'Trade and Development', was added to the Agreement. Part IV of the Agreement codifies in the multilateral trading system the concept of *non-reciprocity* in trade negotiations between developed and developing countries. Thus, developing countries have been allowed: (i) with a view to promoting the establishment of particular industries, to modify or withdraw tariff concessions previously made for manufactured products of industrialized countries; (ii) to impose quantitative restrictions on the importation of foreign goods in order to safeguard their financial position and ensure an adequate level of monetary reserves. Industrialized countries, in their turn, undertook, first, to accord high priority to the reduction or elimination of barriers to products of particular export interest for developing countries; second, to refrain from introducing, or increasing the incidence of, customs duties or non-tariff import barriers on those products; and, third, to refrain from imposing new fiscal measures which could hamper significantly the growth of consumption of primary products from developing countries.

Part IV of the GATT was further elaborated in 1979, in the decision known as the *Enabling Clause*. This Clause consolidated both the concept of 'differential and more favourable treatment' for developing countries and the principle of non-reciprocity in trade negotiations. Under the Clause members of the GATT parties to a trade agreement were authorized 'to accord differential and more favourable treatment to developing countries, without according such treatment to other contracting parties'. However, this Clause has the drawback that it does not legally oblige industrialized States to grant the treatment it provides for to developing countries. It merely authorizes them to grant that treatment.

(iii) The WTO. The Uruguay Round's Final Act of 1994 strengthened the GATT's institutional machinery through the establishment of the World Trade Organization (WTO). This organization is a single *institutional framework* encompassing the GATT plus all the agreements and legal instruments negotiated in the Uruguay Round (the GATT, now called the GATT 1994, and other agreements relating to trade in goods; the General Agreement on Trade in Services (GATS); the Agreements on Trade-

Related Property (TRIPs) and on Trade-Related Investment Measures (TRIMs); the Understanding on Dispute Settlement (DSU); and so on).

The WTO is not a successor organization to the GATT. However, contracting parties to GATT 1947 that accept all the undertakings deriving from the Uruguay Round automatically become original members of the WTO. Other States may accede to the Organization, on condition that they accept the undertakings deriving from the Uruguay Round (some exceptions are however envisaged, concerning the so-called 'pluri-lateral agreements'). At present, the WTO has more than 130 members (about 100 are developing countries), accounting for over 90 per cent of world trade. Over 30 other States are negotiating membership.

In practice the structure of the WTO has formalized that with which the GATT had progressively endowed itself. It consists of a Ministerial Conference (meeting at least every two years); a General Council (composed of the representatives of the member States; it meets in the intervals between each session of the Conference and also meets as the Trade Policy Review Body or the Dispute Settlement Body); the Goods Council, Services Council and Intellectual Property Council, reporting to the General Council; a Director General heading the staff and appointed by the Ministerial Conference. The first and second Ministerial Conference (Singapore, 1996; Geneva, 1998) beefed up the WTO structure by establishing working groups relating to specific sectors within the general field of action of the Organization.

As in the GATT, decisions are normally taken by consensus; majority voting is envisaged, but so far it has not been resorted to.

The reduction of the imbalance detrimental to emergent countries was one of the reasons for the establishment of the WTO. The WTO incorporated all the major provisions of the GATT relating to developing countries, including the 'Enabling Clause'. The Clause is the legal basis of (a) the *Generalized System of Preferences*, whereby developed countries offer non-reciprocal preferential treatment (such as zero or low duties on imports) to products originating in developing countries; it is for preference-giving countries unilaterally to determine which countries and which products are included in their schemes; (b) the *Global System of Trade Preferences*, whereby developing countries that are members of the Group of 77 (see **2.5.5**) exchange trade concession among themselves (UNCTAD providing technical assistance to beneficiaries); and (c) *regional arrangements among developing countries*.

In addition, the GATS allows developing countries some preferential treatment. It also should be noted that, following a decision of June 1999, the WTO General Council may grant waivers allowing developing countries to provide preferential tariff treatment to products of least-developed countries. Waivers may also be granted to developed countries. (Recent examples include the EC-France trading agreements with Morocco, the Canadian tariff treatment for Commonwealth Caribbean countries, the US-Andean Trade Preference Act.)

Nevertheless, one should not pass over in silence the reservations expressed by some commentators with regard to the failure of the new trading system fully to take into account developing countries' needs. Thus, it has been noted that generally speaking the new disciplines and normative standards proclaimed within the WTO mean that developing countries no longer have available to them economic options (trade barriers, export or import subsidies, etc.) that industrialized States resorted to in the early twentieth century to promote their own development and industrialization.[4] In addition, some specific standards prove of little benefit or even disadvantageous to emergent countries. Thus, for instance, the Agreement on Subsidies and Countervailing Measures prohibit subsidies normally used by developing countries, whereas they exempt from the prohibition *agricultural subsidies* used by developed States. Furthermore, arguably the Agreements on Trade-Related Intellectual Property (TRIPs) tend to favour technology producers and owners more than technology users and importers.[5]

18.8 MULTILATERAL CO-OPERATION FOR DEVELOPMENT

The notion of development co-operation commonly covers all the activities undertaken by the more industrialized States to promote the economic progress of the more disadvantaged countries. When States carry out these activities within the framework of an international organization, development co-operation takes on the nature of *multilateral* co-operation, in contrast to the co-operation that every State, in pursuing its foreign policy goals, may undertake at the *bilateral* level.

In addition to these two modalities of co-operation, recently forms of so-called *multi-bilateral* co-operation have taken shape. They are mixed in nature: they are performed by an international organization, but subject to the priorities and conditions established by the industrialized State willing to finance the specific co-operation activities. This class of co-operation has the advantage of reconciling the interests of all the parties concerned. The granting States, as in bilateral co-operation, are in charge of the policy decisions, management, and financing; international organizations, as in the case of multilateral co-operation, are entrusted with implementation; the beneficiary States, in their turn, may count on a relatively steady flow of assistance, which however is filtered through by the international organization.

At the universal level, the UN and its Specialized Agencies constitute the necessary reference point for development co-operation of a *technical* nature. Through the transfer of know-how, carried out in the form of donations, technical co-operation primarily aims at furthering the most efficacious use, by the beneficiary States, of their own economic resources.

In contrast, development co-operation of a *financial* nature is organized, at the universal level, by the organizations falling within the ambit of the World Bank, notably the International Development Agency (IDA). This class of co-operation aims at mobilizing capital so as to increase the financial resources of poor countries. Unlike technical co-operation, it is not carried out in the form of donations, but through the making of loans to backward countries on conditions more advantageous to them than those prevailing on the world market.

The concept of *North–South co-operation* has been accompanied by the gradual emergence of the concept of the need for development co-operation between countries belonging to the same class of less industrialized States: so-called *South–South co-operation*. The final Act of the Bandung Conference of 1955 (attended by 29 Afro-Asian countries) for the first time officially recognized this form of co-operation. Significant developments followed in the first seven conferences of non-aligned countries as well as, within the UN framework, in UNCTAD. South–South co-operation pursues the goal of establishing an economic circuit alternative to the existing one; to this end, it emphasizes the importance of the collective autonomy of developing countries. The ensuing economic relations established by the countries under discussion, and defined as Technical Co-operation between Developing Countries (TCDC) have had many ups and downs. Nevertheless, in the 1980s and 1990s trade exchanges between developing countries increased.

Recently a growing tendency has emerged towards 'bilateralization' of multilateral co-operation. By the same token, a tendency is also shaping up to 'privatize' certain aspects of multilateral co-operation by increasingly having resort to non-governmental organizations (NGOs) as well as other non-governmental entities from industrialized countries. Commentators from developing countries have argued that this growing bilateralization and privatization may gradually weaken or undermine the viability of some of the existing multilateral institutions and mechanisms, or even lead to their gradual obsolescence.

18.8.1 TECHNICAL CO-OPERATION

(i) The first steps. In an initial stage, namely between 1946 and the early 1960s, both the lack of clear vision and an operational scheme, on the part of most developing countries, and the resistance of developed countries, resulted in the establishment, within the UN, of forms of technical co-operation totally inadequate for coping with the far-reaching problems of developing countries.

The UN at first dealt with the issue by establishing the Technical Assistance Programme (TAP), which is still in operation (GA resolution 200(III) of 4 December 1948). This Programme, financed through the system provided for in Article 17.2 of the UN Charter (that is, through compulsory apportionment by the GA), mainly envisaged the sending of missions of experts and technicians to developing countries, the granting of scholarships, and the establishment of training and research centres. Later the GA established the Expanded Programme of Technical Assistance (EPTA) (resolution 304-IV). This Programme was financed by a Special Fund, contributed voluntarily by member States. The assistance provided mainly consisted of furnishing expert advice, the individual training of local personnel, the provision and dissemination of technical information, and the supply of equipment for demonstration purposes.

(ii) The establishment of UNDP. As stated above, a turning point occurred in the second half of the 1960s. In the late 1950s and early 1960s the prices of the primary commodities produced by developing countries were steadily declining on the world market while the prices of manufactured or semi-manufactured goods developing

countries had to import were steadily increasing. It thus became imperative to reconsider the whole international economic system.

It is within this new context that the GA, by resolution 2029-XX of 22 November 1965, established the UN Programme for Development (UNDP). This Programme, which replaced both EPTA and the Special Fund, was set up in order to co-ordinate and streamline the assistance previously granted by various UN specialized agencies. It is at present the UN's largest source of development assistance and the main body responsible for co-ordinating assistance.

UNDP's resources consist of voluntary contributions, which States announce in a special conference ('pledging conference') annually convened by the UN SG. There also exist the so-called contributions for the financing of activities provided for in the programmes; they are paid by the countries benefiting from the activities carried out by the UNDP on their territory.

UNDP is a subsidiary organ of ECOSOC. It is headed by an Administrator, responsible to an Executive Board consisting of 36 States representing all major regions and both donors and 'programme countries'. The Board reports, through ECOSOC, to the GA. It sets policy guidelines and discusses and approves the volume of assistance allocated to each country, as well as all country programmes. With a view to realizing a decentralization of the Programme, side by side with this central structure there exists a local structure, consisting of Country Offices, resident representatives, the resident co-ordinator, and regional bureaux.

After the major legislation passed in 1994–5 by the Executive Board, the UNDP's overriding goals are now (a) eradication of poverty through 'sustainable human development'; and (b) building capacity for good governance (through democratization and political empowerment of the poor by participating in and strengthening civil society organizations, by strengthening judicial, electoral, and parliamentary systems, by focusing on human rights and the rule of law, etc.).

(iii) UNCTAD. Within the UN, technical assistance to developing countries has also been provided through UNCTAD, whose principal purposes are 'to maximize the trade, investments and developing opportunities of developing countries'. UNCTAD is currently implementing over 300 projects of technical assistance in more than 100 countries.

UNCTAD was established in 1964 by the UN GA, after a Conference held under the auspices of the UN had adopted a set of resolutions laying down the principles on which the institution was to work in future. Legally speaking UNCTAD is a subsidiary body of the GA. However, it has an autonomous and conspicuously complex structure, consisting of: (a) a Conference, composed of all the member States and meeting every four years; (b) a permanent executive body, the Trade and Development Board, open to all members, currently 144 States. It meets twice a year (for 'regular sessions') and up to three times a year for 'executive sessions' dealing with urgent policy issues as well as management and institutional matters; and (c) a Secretariat, headed by a Secretary-General, who is appointed by the UN Secretary-General and needs to be confirmed by the GA.

UNCTAD has an operational budget (covering the organizational expenditures) drawn from the UN regular budget, and a budget covering its technical co-operation activities, that is instead financed from extra-budgetary resources provided by donors (the major industrialized

States including France, Germany, Italy, Japan, the Netherlands, Sweden, Switzerland, the UK, the USA), beneficiary countries (developing countries are increasingly financing UNCTAD's technical co-operation activities in their own territory), as well as organizations (UNDP, the World Bank, the Inter-American Development Bank, the EU Commission, etc.).

As we saw above (**18.5**), it is within UNCTAD that *a new philosophy and an attendant new strategy of development* were worked out and approved, at the instigation of developing nations.

They basically hinged on (a) the need to pursue an international division of labour; (b) the elimination by developed countries of existing trade barriers hampering the access of primary products from developing countries; (c) the stabilization of the price of primary commodities; (d) non-reciprocity in commercial agreements, which means that preferential treatment must be granted to developing countries whereas the latter are not required to reciprocate.

(iv) UNIDO. Another important institution was established in 1966: the UN Industrial Development Organization (UNIDO). It was set up by a GA resolution (2152-XXI). It has the status of a Specialized Agency. UNIDO neither provides nor lends money to developing countries. It carries out studies and surveys geared to the problems of industrialization of poor countries. It also serves as a global forum for the exchange of information, analysis, and advice on industrial policies and institutions, between industrially developed and developing countries, business associations, and individual companies. Furthermore, it serves as a provider of services to governments, institutions, and enterprises in recipient (that is, developing) countries.

These services range from simple advice and counsel to providing engineers to implement global agreements on reducing greenhouse gases and industrial pollution, or transferring appropriate technology from one country to another, or helping solve sensitive problems of waste management. Normally, in agreement with the client country, UNIDO makes available its own experts or may draw upon specialists from other agencies or from States or private corporations. Similarly, UNIDO may find investors for projects and industries, or providers of equipment, technology, or techniques.

UNIDO is composed of 168 States, mostly developing countries, plus a number of industrialized States (the USA and Canada are conspicuously absent). It is made up of a General Conference, which meets every two years and, among other things, elects representatives to the 53 seats on the Industrial Development Board and to the 27 seats on the Programme and Budget Committee, besides appointing the Director-General.

UNIDO's financial resources come from a '*regular budget*'. This budget, covering expenditures to be met from assessed contributions, provides for administration, research, and other regular expenses of the Organization. In contrast, and acceding to a request made at the outset by industrialized countries, technical co-operation is funded, through the '*operational budget*', from other sources (voluntary contributions from donor countries and institutions, allocations by the UNDP, etc.).

(v) The WTO. The World Trade Organization (WTO), on which see *supra*, **18.7.3(iii)**, takes part in technical co-operation by (a) assisting recipient countries in understanding and implementing agreed international rules on trade, (b) achieving their full

participation in the multilateral trading system, and (c) directing technical assistance towards human resource development and institutional capacity building.

The WTO tries to attain these goals by carrying out an array of activities, some in the country or the region concerned, others at the WTO headquarters in Geneva: seminars (for instance, on anti-dumping, customs valuation, subsidies, and countervailing measures, or on broader topics such as the functioning of the WTO and multilateral trade negotiations), workshops, technical missions (designed to assist countries in drafting and preparing legislation and regulations, etc.), briefing sessions for Geneva-based delegations or visiting officials, technical co-operation in electronic form.

Funding for technical co-operation comes from three sources: (a) the WTO's regular budget; (b) voluntary contributions from WTO members (a number of WTO members have decided, as an interim solution, to finance the activities at issue through the establishment of a Global Trust Fund (GTF) for WTO Technical Co-operation; one of its aims is to minimize the administrative costs and procedures following from a multiplicity of trust funds on a national basis); (c) cost sharing, either by the host country or by other countries.

Technical co-operation activities are overseen by a Committee on Trade and Development (CTD).

18.8.2 FINANCIAL CO-OPERATION

At the universal level, financial co-operation with developing countries is effected through a group of institutions headed by the World Bank, and most notably the International Development Association (IDA).

The IDA was established in 1960 on the initiative of the USA. It is an affiliate of the World Bank, and avails itself of its structure. Its financial resources consist of capital subscribed by the member States and by supplementary contributions from several members.

The IDA supplements the World Bank's functions and pursues the primary task of financing the development of poor countries by granting development loans on terms more liberal than those granted by the Bank. The financial resources of the IDA consist of capital subscribed by the member States and by supplementary contributions from several members. It operates by making loans for a term of 50 years, with a ten-year initial grace period, no interest charge, and a service charge of three-quarters of one per cent per annum. The areas where it has concentrated are, first, electric power supply; communications and transportation; and second, agriculture and education.

Besides the length of the term of loans and the lack of any interest charge, another feature of IDA's operations was designed to uphold some developing countries' requests: greater participation of such countries in the decision-making process. However, the fact remains that the majority is firmly kept in the hands of industrialized States.

Two more bodies are linked to the World Bank: ICSID and MIGA (see below, **18.9.2**). In 1965 the International Finance Corporation (IFC) was set up for the purpose of promoting private foreign investment in developing countries. This institution is an affiliate of the Bank and its structure is that of the Bank. It aims primarily at participating in private loans and other investments and, when private capital is not available, supplementing private investment from its own resources.

18.9 THE PROMOTION OF FOREIGN INVESTMENT IN DEVELOPING COUNTRIES

18.9.1 TRADITIONAL LAW AND CHALLENGES TO IT

To understand the impact of developing countries' demands on the legal regulation of foreign investment, it is necessary first to take a quick look at the law that existed before they took action to change it.

Traditional international rules governing foreign investment required that any time a country to which foreign capital had been exported or where companies had been established expropriated or nationalized them, it was duty bound to pay *compensation*. These rules were contested by the Soviet Union following the Soviet nationalizations in 1918 and 1925 and by Mexico in the wake of the nationalizations involved in the Mexican Agrarian Reform of 1927 and the nationalization of foreign oil property in 1938. Eventually the Soviet Union, after refusing to pay any compensation at all, had to bow to the economic and political pressure of other States and grudgingly complied with the prevailing international standards. As for Mexico, it admitted that 'adequate compensation' was to be paid (unless the expropriation of foreign property was discriminatory, in which case no compensation was due), but insisted that the time and manner of payment must be determined by its own laws. The USA reacted indignantly and the Secretary of State, Cordell Hull, in a famous note of 22 August 1938, formulated the US doctrine of compensation, as follows: 'No government is entitled to expropriate private property, for whatever purpose, without provision for *prompt, adequate and effective payment* therefor'.[6] Mexico eventually yielded to the economic superiority of the USA and this celebrated formula was subsequently considered by Western countries to encapsulate the basic requirements for lawful expropriations.

The problem exploded again after the Second World War, when developing countries increasingly became politically independent and tried to get off the ground economically as well. They felt impelled to expropriate foreign property because their natural resources were to a large extent in foreign hands. One of the ways of achieving rapid economic advance lay in appropriating foreign assets without this constituting an excessive financial burden for the expropriating State.

In addition to those carried out by eastern Europe socialist countries in 1946–8, expropriations were made by Iran in 1951, Egypt in 1956, Cuba in 1959, Sri Lanka in 1963, Indonesia in 1965, Tanzania in 1966, Bolivia in 1969, Algeria in 1971, Somalia in 1970–2, Chile in 1972, Libya in 1978.

Developing States increasingly challenged the 'prompt, adequate and effective' formula and contended that (a) only 'adequate' or 'appropriate' compensation was due, and in addition (b) the modalities of its determination were to be left to the nationalizing State. Their demands were upheld first in the GA Declaration on

Permanent Sovereignty over Natural Resources (resolution 1803-XVII, adopted by consensus in 1962) and then in Article 2.2(c) of the Charter of Economic Rights and Duties of States (GA resolution 3281-XXIX, adopted by majority vote in 1974). However, most Western States voted against that provision or abstained, making clear that in their view it run counter to existing law. The ensuing status of customary international law is thus left unclear, industrialized States clinging to the Hull formula and developing countries insisting on the new legal views upheld by the majority of UN bodies.

18.9.2 NEW DEVICES ADOPTED TO BREAK THE LEGAL DEADLOCK

Faced with this unsatisfactory legal regulation, States have eventually sought to avoid harsh conflicts by resorting to *devices and compromises* which, to some extent, accommodate the demands of both categories of States involved, namely, capital-exporting and capital-importing States. After all, it is in the interest of both categories not to stretch things too far. In cases of total disagreement, if the country of the investors does not want to use extra-legal pressure, its nationals end up seeing their interests sacrificed. Similarly, nationalizing or expropriating countries do not gain much from a refusal to negotiate, for the other country concerned can retaliate by discontinuing its assistance, if any, or by discouraging private investment in other ways.

The famous Hickenlooper Amendment of 1963 to the US Foreign Assistance Act of 1961, named after the US Senator, was precisely designed to suspend assistance to any government dispossessing US nationals of their property without due compensation, until such time as this government had taken 'the appropriate steps'.

Three main devices have been adopted to avoid or forestall clashes: (1) hammering out *lump sum agreements*; (2) resort to the International Centre for Settlement of International Disputes (ICSID) for *compulsory conciliation or arbitration* in cases of dispute; (3) reliance on *insurance protection* by the investors.

Lump sum agreements are international treaties by which the expropriating State allocates a single sum of money, which is determined on the basis of various criteria, and normally goes halfway to meeting the conflicting requests of the two States concerned. In some cases (as in the nationalization of the Suez Canal Company by Egypt in 1956, where a settlement was reached in 1958) an agreement is concluded whereby a sum not entirely meeting the claims of the dispossessed foreigners is paid in instalments over a period of several years. In other instances the dispossessing State grants compensation in kind: this, for instance, happened in the Bolivian nationalizations of 1969, when Bolivia compensated foreign countries through the sale of gas to them.

Resort to the ICSID was rendered possible by the elaboration, in 1965, by the Bank, of the Convention on the Settlement of Disputes between States and Nationals of other States. The ICSID was established as a permanent institution discharging conciliatory or arbitral functions to settle disputes between private investors and States that are beneficiaries of foreign investment. The parties to an investment dispute that have ratified the Convention are given the option to resort to conciliation or arbitration and the ICSID provides the appropriate machinery.

A similarly widespread practice is that of turning to investment guaranteeing mechanisms designed to provide insurance protection for private investment abroad. The insurance can be granted at the national or at the international level.

As for the former, suffice it to mention the US Agency, the Overseas Private Investment Corporation (OPIC). It was established in 1969 as a self-supporting corporation totally owned by the US Government. It provides insurance to American enterprises investing abroad against three classes of non-commercial risk: (a) inconvertibility of foreign currency into US dollars; (b) expropriation of investment by the host Government; (c) war, revolution, or insurrection.

At the international level, the Multilateral Investment Guarantee Agency (MIGA) has acquired increasing importance. It was set up in 1985 for the purpose of promoting investment flows to developing countries: its main task is to guarantee investments against non-commercial risks in host countries. Four categories of risk are mentioned in the Convention instituting MIGA: (a) transfer risk, which occurs when the host country decides upon restrictions on currency conversion and transfer; (b) expropriation, the result of which is to deprive the investor of his ownership or control; (c) breach of contract; (d) war or 'civil disturbance' in the host country.

18.9.3 TOWARDS A REVIVAL OF THE HULL FORMULA?

It would seem that recently State practice has tended to uphold traditional standards on compensation. This, at least, is what transpires from a string of bilateral agreements made since the early 1980s and providing for compensation under criteria very close to the old 'prompt, adequate and effective' formula. Similarly, this formula has been taken up in the non-binding Guidelines adopted by the Bank in 1992. Nevertheless, these trends are not so widespread as to lead one to believe that that Hull clause has now turned into customary law. In this respect it seems significant that in 1994 the Iran-US Claims Tribunal, in *Shahin Shaine Ebrahimi et al.* did not take a position favourable to it.[7] In a well-argued and elaborate decision, the Tribunal held that the Hull standard does not represent 'the prevailing standard of compensation'. Rather, in its view customary international law favours an 'appropriate compensation' standard.[8] The Tribunal also specified the purport of this standard:

'The gradual emergence of this [customary international] rule [on "appropriate compensation"] aims at ensuring that the amount of compensation is determined in a flexible manner, that is, taking into account the specific circumstances of each case. The prevalence of the "appropriate" compensation standard does not imply, however, that the compensation *quantum* should be always "less than full" or always "partial".[9] [Various awards on this matter] reflect a consistent concern not to determine the amount of compensation rigidly, i.e. without taking into account the specific circumstances of each concrete case'.[10]

18.10 A TENTATIVE STOCK-TAKING

One of the major results of the developing countries' action for development can be seen in the fact that this issue has become one of the central questions of the world community. The idea that industrialized States should assist poor countries has solidly taken root, with the attendant feeling of social solidarity. In addition, a whole array of guidelines, goals, and institutions has been set up for the purpose of putting solidarity into practice.

Recently major industrialized countries have increasingly turned their attention to the needs of developing countries, particularly in Africa. Thus, since the 1988 Toronto Summit the G7 Group (now G8) has pledged to cancel, or at least significantly reduce, the foreign debt of the poorest countries. At the same time the existing international institutions (chiefly UNDP, UNCTAD, UNIDO, as well as the WTO) are constructively helping to reduce the gap between North and South.

They are also insisting on the need for a *linkage* between development and other matters. In particular, they are increasingly emphasizing the need for disadvantaged countries to promote development by simultaneously ensuring and also enhancing *respect for human rights* and *protection of the environment*. In some cases assistance and co-operation have been made *conditional* on respect for international standards on human rights and the environment (this trend may be seen, for instance, in the action of the European Communities). This is a healthy development. In particular, so far 'conditionality' has not been used as a devious instrument for seeking the imposition of Western political, economic, or cultural patterns of behaviour. Rather, most of the time it has been employed as a means of promoting *community values* increasingly shared by the whole world community.

Past experience has shown that the legal tools available to States for assisting backward countries may be successfully used. The adoption of GA resolutions may prove useful as long as they set out realistic and clearly defined blueprints for action. Institutions established by the UN and other intergovernmental organizations are an indispensable channel of assistance and a crucial factor of transformation and change. International agreements can help create conditions conducive to healthy progress in poor countries. As usual, *law* provides helpful instruments, institutions and conceptual equipment. What is often missing is the *political will* of powerful States—too often bent on the pursuit of short-term interests, and frequently excessively self-centred—to use those tools. However, other factors also stand in the way of a more rapid progress: in particular, huge economic difficulties. In addition, one should not be unmindful of the excessive political rhetoric of some developing countries, as well as the propensity for mismanagement and corruption, or authoritarian governance, that can still be discerned in some of these countries.

NOTES

Chapter 1

1. It is worth recalling Hobbes's penetrating remark on this phenomenon (which of course is also to be found within the domestic setting of States, whenever individuals act as State organs). After pointing out that the Romans applied the term *persona*, or mask, 'like the one tragic and comic actors wore in theatre', to all the individuals speaking on behalf of others, he went on to say, 'Indeed, in the theatre it was understood that it was not the actor who spoke, but somebody else, Agamemnon for example, in that the actor put on the fictitious face of Agamemnon and consequently was Agamemnon throughout the play; this transmutation was later accepted even without the false face (*sine facie ficta*): it was sufficient for the actor to declare which "*persona*" he would impersonate. Fictions of this kind are no less necessary to the State than in theatre, on account of the negotiations and transactions of the absent (*propter absentium commercia et contractus*). As regards the civil use of the concept of "person", it can be defined as follows: a person is the one to whom either his own words and deeds or those of somebody else are attributed (*persona est, cui verba et actiones hominum attribuuntur vel suae vel alienae*). Consequently, just as one and the same actor can impersonate different "persons" on different occasions, so any man can represent more human beings.' (T. Hobbes, "Elementorum Philosophiae Sectio Secunda: De Homine" (1658), in T. Hobbes, *Opera philosophica quae latine scripsit omnia* (London: W. Molesworth, 1966, ii, at 130).

2. For the relevant diplomatic notes see RDI, 3 (1924), at 339 et seq. and the documents published in Ministero degli Affari Esteri, *I documenti diplomatici italiani*, VII Series; 1922–35, vol. 2 (Rome: Istituto Poligrafico dello Stato, 1955), LIV–503. E. Anchieri, 'L'affare di Corfù alla luce dei documenti diplomatici italiani', *Il Politico*, 20 (1955), 374–95. For a careful examination of the debates in the League of Nations see K. Strupp, 'L'incident de Janina entre la Grèce et l'Italie', RGDIP, 301 (1924), 1–30255–84; A. Philippe, *Le role de la Société des Nations dans l'affaire de Corfou* (Lille: Editions Camille Robbe, 1924). See also J. Barros, *The Corfu Incident of 1923, Mussolini and the League of Nations* (Princeton, N.J.: Princeton University Press, 1963).

3. H. Kelsen, *Principles*, at 10.

4. S. Hoffmann, 'International Law and the Control of Force', in K. Deutsch and S. Hoffmann, eds., *The Relevance of International Law* (Garden City, N.Y.: Anchor Books, 1971), at 36.

5. H. Triepel, 'Les rapports entre le droit interne et le droit international', HR (1923), at 106.

6. BILC, 3, at 705.

7. Ibid., at 704.

8. PCIJ, Series A, no. 23, at 27.

9. See *Annuaire de l'Institut de droit international*, 63(II) (1990), 338–40. The resolution was proposed by the distinguished Italian international lawyer, G. Sperduti.

10. The significance of Article 1 was first emphasized by L. Condorelli and L. Boisson de Chazournes, 'Quelques remarques à propos de l'obligation des Etats de "respecter et faire respecter" le droit international humanitaire "en toutes circonstances"' in *Etudes et essais en l'honneur de J. Pictet* (Geneva: M. Nijhoff Publishers, 1984), 17–35. The ICJ held that Article 1 had turned into customary international law in *Nicaragua* (ICJ Reports (1986), at 114, para. 220).

11. ICJ, Order of 13 September 1993, in ICJ Reports (1993), at 444–5, para. 115.

12. On the various instances of current international protection of 'community interests' see the important considerations by B. Simma, 'From Bilateralism to Community Interest in International Law', HR, 250 (1994–VI), esp. at 256 et seq.

13. See M. Wight, 'Western Values in International Relations', in H. Butterfield and M. Wight, eds., *Diplomatic Investigations* (London: Allen and Unwin, 1967); M. Wight, G. Wight, and B. Porter, eds., *International Theory—The Three Traditions* (Leicester and London: Leicester University Press, 1991), in particular at 137 ff.

Wight distinguishes between the Machiavellian, Grotian, and Kantian traditions.

14. H. Bull, *The Anarchical Society: A Study of Order in World Politics* (London and Basingstoke: Macmillan, 1977), at 24–7; id., 'The Importance of Grotius in the Study of International Relations', in H. Bull, B. Kingsbury, and A. Roberts, eds., *Hugo Grotius and International Relations* (Oxford: Oxford University Press, 1990), esp. at 71–93.

Bull distinguishes between the Hobbesian or realist tradition, the Kantian or universalist tradition, and the Grotian or internationalist tradition.

R. Falk has taken up these notions and discussed them in many articles (see, in particular, 'A New Paradigm for International Legal Studies: Prospects and Proposals', in R. Falk, F. Kratochwil, and S. H. Mendlovitz, eds., *International Law: A Comparative Perspective* (Boulder, Col., and London: Westview, 1985), 651–702. See also R. Jackson, *The Global Governance—Human Conduct in a World of States* (Oxford: Oxford University Press, 2000), 378–85.

Chapter 2

1. J. R. Strayer, *On the Medieval Origins of the Modern State* (Princeton, N.J.: Princeton University Press, 1979), at 9–10.

2. G. Jellinek, 'Die Entwicklung des Ministeriums in der Konstitutionellen Monarchie' (1883), in *Ausgewählte Schriften und Reden* (Berlin: O. Häring, 1911), ii, at 98.

3. See text in Parry, i, at 198–269 and 319–56.

4. Under this scheme, peace was to be enforced. Pursuant to Article 123 of the Treaty of Münster, the victim of a threat to peace or any serious violation was not to resort to war, but should 'exhort the offender not to come to any hostility, submitting the cause to a friendly composition or to the ordinary proceedings of justice'. Article 124 envisaged a cooling-off period, lasting as long as three years; if at its expiry no settlement has been reached, the injured State was entitled to wage war, and all the other contracting parties were to assist it by using force. In addition, States were duty-bound to refrain from giving military assistance to the offender, nor could they allow its troops to pass through or stay in their territories (Article 3). Thus, the collective security system envisaged in 1648 hinged on the following notions: (i) a sweeping ban on the use of force; (ii) a prohibition on individual self-defence, except after the expiry of a long period; (iii) the duty of all States other than the victim of a wrong to act in collective self-defence. This scheme, which strongly resembles the one that was set up in 1919 under the League of Nations system, was never put into effect. Though weak and rudimentary by modern standards, it was too far ahead of its time and in harsh conflict with the interests and predispositions of States. Members of the international community followed a different pattern of behaviour, based on both the untrammelled right of individual States to resort to war whenever they considered it appropriate and the lack of any obligation to give military assistance to the victims of attacks by other States.

5. C. H. Alexandrowicz, 'The Afro-Asian World and the Law of Nations (Historical Aspects)', HR, 123 (1968-I), at 125.

6. H. Otsuka, 'Japan's Early Encounter with the Concept of the Law of Nations', JYIL, 13 (1969), at 56.

7. Alexandrowicz, (cit above, note 5), at 151.

8. See text in Parry, vol. 165, 483.

9. See text in Moore, *Digest*, vi, at 368–72.

10. H. Staudacher, *Die Friedensblockade* (Leipzig: von Duncker und Humblot, 1909), at 29–31.

11. It was first used in 1780 by Bentham in his *Introduction to the Principles of Morals and Legislation*. Since then it increasingly replaced the previous terms 'law of nations' and 'droit des gens'. As the Italian philologist P. Peruzzi showed ('A European Word-Formation Pattern', *Archivio filologico italiano* 41 (1976), 76–85), other factors besides the strictly linguistic motivated this change, or were instrumental in making it widespread: the emotional appeal and the growing importance of the concept of 'nation', the spread of 'international industrial exhibitions', and the setting up in 1864, in London, of the 'International Working Men's Association', commonly known as the 'First International' or simply, 'The International'.

12. On the Eurocentrism dominating this stage of development of the world community, see in particular Y. Onuma, 'When Was the Law of International Society Born?—An Inquiry of the History of International Law from an Intercivilisation Perspective', *Journal of the History of International Law* 2 (2000) 1–66, in particular at 27 et seq.

13. E. M. Spiers, 'The Use of Dum Dum Bullets in Colonial Warfare', *The Journal of Imperial and Commonwealth History*, 4 (1975), at 6–7.

14. H. Grotius *On the Law of War and Peace*, tr. F. W. Kelsey (Oxford: Clarendon Press, 1925), at 653 (Book III, Ch. IV).

15. See AJIL, Supplement I (1907), at 1–6.

16. See Hay's Note in USFR (1903), at 5.

17. R. Albrecht-Carrié, *The Meaning of the First World War* (Englewood Cliffs, N.J.: Prentice Hall, 1965), at vi.

18. R. Lansing, *War Memoirs* (Indianapolis: The Bobbs-Merrill Co., 1935, repr. Westport, Conn.: Greenwood Press, 1970), at 341.

19. See above, note 4.

20. N. Politis, *Les Nouvelles Tendances du droit international* (Paris: Librairie Hachette, 1927), at 91–2.

21. 'La civilization mécanique vient de parvenir à son dernier degré de sauvagerie', *Combat*, 8

August 1945, reprinted in A. Camus, *Essais* (Paris: Gallimard, 1984), at 291.

22. D. K. Fieldhouse, *Colonialism 1870–1945* (London: Wiedenfeld and Nicolson, 1981), at 15.

23. B. O. Nwabueze, *Constitutionalism in the Emergent States* (London: C. Hurst and Co., 1973), at 24.

Chapter 3

1. M. Wight, G. Wight, and B. Porter, eds., *International Theory—The Three Traditions* (London: Leicester University Press, 1991), at 139.

2. RIAA, 1, at 389.

3. See e.g. R. Müllerson, *International Law, Rights and Politics* (London and New York: Routledge, 1994), at 130; R. Rich, 'Recognition of States: the Collapse of Yugoslavia and the Soviet Union', EJIL, 4 (1993), at 36–65.

4. See text in EJIL, 4 (1993), at 76–7.

5. Ibid., at 74–7.

6. Ibid., at 74–6.

7. Ibid., at 77–80 and 80–4.

8. Ibid., at 90.

9. RIAA, 1, at 379.

10. In 1997 the UN Human Rights Committee stated in its General Comment No. 26 that 'once the people are accorded the protection of the rights under the Covenant, such protection devolves with territory and continues to belong to them, notwithstanding change in government of the State party, including dismemberment in more than one State or State succession or any subsequent action of the State party designed to divest them of the rights guaranteed by the Covenant'. Human Rights Committee, General Comment 26 (61), UN Doc. A/53/40, Annex VII, 8 December 1997, para. 4. See also http://www1.umn.edu/humanrts/gencomm/hrcom26.htm. On this matter see M.T. Kamminga, 'State Succession in Respect of Human Rights Treaties', EJIL, 7 (1996), at 469 ff.; B. Simma, 'From Bilateralism to Community Interest in International Law', HR, 250 (1994-VI), at 354–8.

11. ILR, 96, at 732.

12. RIAA, 2, at 838.

13. ICJ Reports (1959), at 240 and 255.

14. Res. 16 of the 1964 Meeting of Heads of State and Government of the OAU (see M. Shaw, *Title to Territory in Africa: International Legal Issues* (Oxford: Oxford University Press, 1986), at 185–7.

15. ICJ Reports (1986), at 565, para. 20. See also *Land, Island and Maritime Frontier Dispute*, ICJ Reports (1992), at 386–8, paras 40–3.

16. See text in EJIL, 3 (1992), at 183–4.

17. ICJ Reports (1969), at 22, para. 19.

18. ICJ Reports (1969), at 53.

19. ICJ Reports (1982), at 18 ff.

20. ICJ Reports (1984), at 246 ff.

21. ICJ Reports (1985), at 13 ff.

22. ICJ Reports (1993), at 37 ff.

23. It is reported in A. Pardo, *The Common Heritage: Selected Papers on Oceans and World Order 1967–74* (Malta: Malta University Press, 1975), at 31, 64, 85.

Chapter 4

1. See E. W. Hall, *A Treatise on International Law*, 8th edn. (Oxford: Clarendon Press, 1924), 44–5.

2. Ibid., at 41–2.

3. YILC, 2 (1972), at 139, para. 181.

4. ICJ Reports 1996, at 75, para. 19.

5. Ibid., at 78, para. 25.

6. For a careful description of traditional international organizations active in economic fields, see W. Kaufmann, 'Les unions internationales de nature économique', HR, II (1924), 181–290.

7. See D. Anzilotti, 'Gli organi comuni nelle società di Stati', RDI, 8 (1914), at 156–64, repr. in his *Scritti di diritto internazionale pubblico* (Padua: Cedam, 1956), i, at 605–14.

8. Text in RDI, 23 (1931), at 386–9. See ibid., at 389–91, a note by M. Scerni.

9. ICJ Reports (1949), at 179.

10. Ibid.

11. Ibid.

12. RDI, 69 (1986), at 146–52, in particular at 150–1.

13. ICJ Reports (1949), at 178.

14. See UN Yearbook (1948), at 400.

15. RDI, 69 (1986), at 884–89, in particular at 886–7 (English translation, partially followed here, in IYIL, 7 (1986–7), at 295–8).

16. RDI, 69 (1986), at 887.

17. Award of 31 July 1989, in RIAA, 20, at 138–9, paras 49–52.

18. PCIJ, Ser. B, no. 15, at 17–18.

19. J. Westlake, *Chapters on the Principles of International Law* (Cambridge: Cambridge University Press, 1894), at 2; Kelsen, *Principles*, at 124–6.

20. D. Anzilotti, 'L'azione individuale contraria al diritto internazionale', *Rivista di diritto internazionale e legislazione comparata*, 5 (1902), at 8–43, repr. in

his *Scritti di diritto internazionale pubblico* (Padua: Cedam, 1956), i, at 211 ff.

21. *Trial of the Major War Criminals before the International Military Tribunal, Nuremberg 14 November 1945–1 October 1946* (Nuremberg: 1947), i, at 233.

Chapter 5

1. On these principles see R. Ago, *Lezioni di diritto internazionale* (Milan: Giuffré, 1943), at 65 et seq.

2. See UNCIO, vi, at 332.

3. V. E. Orlando, 'Francesco Crispi' (1923), in *Scritti varii di diritto pubblico e scienza politica* (Milan: Giuffré, 1940), at 400.

4. R. Lansing, *The Peace Negotiations—A Personal Narrative* (Boston and New York: Houghton Mifflin Company, 1921), at 102–3.

5. See AJIL, 29 (1935), 502–7 and 30 (1936), at 123–4.

6. Whiteman, v, 208–14; UN Yearbook (1960), at 196–8.

7. For references see N. Ronzitti, 'La cattura di un individuo all'estero: in margine al caso Argoud', RDI, 48 (1965), 74–9.

8. Decision of 2 October 1921, in AILC, 17, 5–11, at 8–9.

9. Judgment of 15 June 1992, 504 U.S. 655 (1992), also to be found at http://caselaw.lp.findlaw.com/scripts.

10. This was a follow-up to the *Caroline* case (see **11.1.2**). Alexander McLeod was one of the British officers who in 1837 went into US territory to help fight against Canadian rebels assisted by US nationals. McLeod helped to capture the US ship *Caroline* used by the rebels, and killed an American citizen. When in 1840 he went to the US State of New York on business, he was arrested and indicted for the killing of the US national as well as arson. The British Ambassador to the USA protested, arguing that McLeod had acted in an official capacity. He stated that the destruction of the *Caroline* was 'a public act of persons in her Majesty's service, obeying the order of their superior authorities'; it could therefore 'only be the subject of discussion between the two national Governments' and could 'not justly be made the ground of legal proceedings in the United States against the persons concerned' (Moore, Digest, ii, at 24). The US Secretary of State Webster admitted in a note to the US Attorney-General that McLeod was not to be held responsible: 'That an individual, forming part of a public force, and acting under the authority of his Government, is not to be

held answerable as a private trespasser or malefactor, is a principle of public law sanctioned by the usages of all civilized nations, and which the Government of the United States has no inclination to dispute . . . an individual may claim immunity from the consequences of acts done by him, by showing that he acted under national authority . . . individuals connected in it [a State transaction] cannot be arrested and tried before the ordinary tribunals, as for the violation of municipal law' (ibid., at 25–6). Nevertheless, McLeod was not released but had to stand trial, on the ground that some legal technicalities of the laws of the State of New York did not allow his release (and indeed in 1842 the US Congress passed a law providing for the removal of cases involving international relations from State courts to Federal courts). He was later acquitted (see also R. Y. Jennings, 'The *Caroline* and *McLeod* Cases', AJIL 32 (1938), 92–9).

11. As the UN Secretary-General stated in his ruling of 6 July 1986, the French Government, after admitting that the two French nationals who had blown up the *Rainbow Warrior* were French officers and had acted under military orders, sought their 'immediate return' while at the same time stating that France was ready to give an apology and pay compensation to New Zealand for the damage suffered (RIAA, 20, at 224). However, New Zealand insisted that 'the sinking of the *Rainbow Warrior* involved not only a breach of international law, but also the commission of a serious crime in New Zealand for which the two officers received a lengthy sentence from a New Zealand court' (ibid.). According to New Zealand, 'their release to freedom would undermine the integrity of the New Zealand system'. New Zealand only admitted that it was prepared to have the prisoners serve their sentences outside New Zealand (ibid.).

12. E. de Vattel, *Le droit des gens, ou principes de la loi naturelle* (Paris: J.-P. Aillaud, 1830), i, at 47 ('Préliminaires', para. 18).

13. The Chamber held that 'customary international law protects the internal organization of each sovereign State: it leaves it to each sovereign State to determine its internal structure and in particular to designate the individuals acting as State agents or organs. Each sovereign State has the right to issue instructions to its organs, both those operating at the internal level and those operating in the field of international relations, and also to provide for sanctions or to the remedies in case on noncompliance with those instructions. The corollary of this exclusive power is that each State is entitled to claim that acts or transactions performed by one of its organs in its official capacity be attributed to the

State, so that the individual organ may not be held accountable for those acts or transactions.' (Judgment of 29 October 1997, para. 41). '[Official actions of State organs] cannot be the subject of sanctions or penalties [taken by foreign States] for conduct that is not private but undertaken on behalf of a State. In other words, State officials cannot suffer the consequences of wrongful acts which are not attributable to them personally but to the State on whose behalf they act: they enjoy so-called "functional immunity"' (ibid., para. 38). 'The few exceptions relate to one particular consequence of the [customary] rule. These exceptions arise from the norms of international criminal law prohibiting war crimes, crimes against humanity and genocide' (ibid., para. 41).

14. ILR, 100, at 372.

15. 168 U.S. 250 (1897). See AILC, 7, 193 ff., at 195.

16. ILM, 21 (1982), at 107.

17. [1983] AC 244 at 261–2 *per* Lord Wilberforce.

18. [1984] AC 580 at 598–9, *per* Lord Diplock.

19. See http://www.un.org/law/ilc/texts/fimmfra.htm.

20. Decision of 19 March 1992, no. 3468, in RDI, 75 (1992), 403–7.

21. Decision of 15 July 1992, no. 329, in RDI, 75 (1992), 395–402. For the English translation see ILR, 101, 394 et seq.

22. See, for instance, the decision of 6 June 1956 in *Royaume de Grèce* v. *Banque Julius Bär and Co.*, in *Recueil des Arrêts* 1956, 75–93 in particular grounds 7–10; decision of 30 April 1986 in *Königreich Spanien* v. *Firma X et al.*, ibid., 1986, 148–55, in German (legal grounds 3–5); decision of 19 January 1987 in *S.* v. *République socialiste de Roumanie et al.*, ibid., 1987, 172–77 (legal ground 3).

23. The Court noted that 'Claims against a general current bank account of the embassy of a foreign State which exists in the State of the forum and the purpose of which is to cover the embassy's costs and expenses are not subject to forced execution by the State of the forum' (ILR, 65, at 164).

24. [1984] 2 All ER 6; ILR, 74, 180 et seq.

25. See text in *Schweizerische Zeitschrift für internationales und europäisches Recht*, 2 (1992), 570–2.

26. See the decision of 10 February 1960 in *République Arabe Unie* v. *dame X*, in *Recueil des arrêts*, 1960, 23–33 (see in particular the fifth legal ground).

27. Decision of 18 July 1979, no. 48, in IYIL, 4 (1978–9), at 147.

28. This proposition was enunciated, among others, by British courts. See, for instance, *Dickinson* v. *Del Solar* [1930] 1 KB 376, reprinted in BILC, vi, at 142–4. In its decision of 31 July 1929 the King's Bench Division held that 'Diplomatic privilege does not impart immunity from legal liability, but only exemption from local jurisdiction. The privilege is the privilege of the Sovereign by whom the diplomatic agent is accredited' (at 144).

29. See, for instance, *Kirloy* v. *Windsor*, decided in 1978 by the US District Court, Northern District of Ohio, Eastern Division, in Digest of US Practice, 1978, at 641–3 (where one also finds the position of the US State Department); the decisions of the King's Bench Division of 21 January 1952 and the Court of Appeal of 20 May 1952 in *Sayce* v. *Ameer Ruler Sadiq Mohsammad Abbasi Bahawalpur State*, in BILC, 7, at 657 and 662.

See also the decision of the Italian Court of Cassation of 11 March 1921 in *Nobili* v. *Emperor Charles I of Austria*, in *Giurisprudenza italiana*, 1921, I, Part I, at 371–4 (reprinted in A. Santa Maria, ed., *La Giurisprudenza di diritto internazionale;* I, 1921–5 (Naples: Editore Jovene, 1997), at 45–7. English summary in Annual Digest, 1919–22, at 136.

30. See the order issued on 18 February 1987 by the Rome Tribunal in *Bigi*, in RIDIPP, 24 (1988), at 360.

31. For instance, see the opinion issued on 12 May 1961 by the Swiss Foreign Department, in ASDI, 21 (1964), at 171; the decision by the London Court of Appeal of 24 March 1964, in *Zoerrsch* v. *Waldock and another*, ILM 3 (1964), at 525 and BILC, 8, at 837.

32. Decision of 9 April 1925, text (in French) in JDI, 53 (1926), at 65.

33. See *Ministère Public* v. *P.*, Court of Brussels, decision of 5 June 1965, in *Journal des Tribunaux* (Brussels), 1966, at 30–1.

34. See the decision of the Supreme Court of Japan in *The Empire* v. *Chang and others*, in Annual Digest, 1919–22, at 288.

35. See the Rome Tribunal's order of 16 February 1966 in *Imp. A.B.*, in *Archivio penale*, 1966, II, at 212.

36. See decision of 8 May 1971, by the Court of Appeal of Venice, in *P.M.* v. *Zappi Mentore*, in *Rivista penale*, 1971, II, at 1255–60.

37. See the order of 18 February 1987 by the Rome Tribunal in *Bigi* (cit. above, note 29).

38. See Hackworth, iv, at 458.

39. See for instance the decision of the Police Court of the District of Columbia in *District of Columbia* v. *Vinard L. Paris*, AJIL, 33 (1939), at 787–91; the decision of the Court of Appeal of

Ontario in *Re Regina and Palacios* (in CYIL, 23 (1985), at 412–13).

See also *Shaw* v. *Shaw*, decision by the British High Court of 9 February 1979, in ILR, 78, 483–90.

For other cases as well as State practice see J. Salmon, *Manuel de droit diplomatique* (Brussels: Bruylant, 1994), 404–8.

40. See UNCIO, vi, at 355.

41. See UNCIO, vi, at 559, as well as 334 (see also 720–1).

42. ICJ Reports (1986), at 104, para. 195.

43. ICJ Reports (1986), at 145, para. 290. In *North Sea Continental Shelf* the Court had already referred to the principle, with special emphasis on its applicability to negotiations (ICJ Reports (1969), at 47–8, paras 86–7).

44. PCIJ, Advisory Opinion of 23 July 1923, Series B, no. 5, at 27 (the Court held that 'It is well established in international law that no State can, without its consent, be compelled to submit its disputes with other States either to mediation or to arbitration, or to any other kind of pacific settlement. Such consent can be given once and for all in the form of an obligation freely undertaken, but it can, on the contrary, also be given in a special case apart from any existing obligation').

45. R. Lansing, *The Peace Negotiations—A Personal Narrative* (Boston and New York: Houghton Mifflin Co., 1921), 93–105, in particular at 96–7.

46. See ibid., at 97 (quoting from a note he wrote on 20 December 1918, in Paris).

47. See judgment of 20 August 1998, http://www.lexum.unmontreal.ca/csc-scc/en/pub/1998/vol2/html/1998scr2–0217.html, para. 126.

48. ICJ Reports (1975), at 33 (paras 58–9). The Court reaffirmed the importance of self-determination, 'one of the essential principles of contemporary international law', in *Case Concerning East Timor*, Reports 1995, at 102 (para. 29).

49. E. Roosevelt, 'The Universal Validity of Man's Right to Self-Determination', US Dept. of State Bulletin, 27 (8 December 1952), at 919.

50. ICJ Reports (1986), at 100–1, para. 190.

51. AJIL, 74 (1980), at 418–20, in particular at 419.

52. Various delegates stated that the rules of international law protecting fundamental rights belong to *jus cogens*. See in particular the statements by the representative of Finland (United Nations Conference on the Law of Treaties, First Session (Vienna, 26 March–24 May 1968), *Official Records*, at 295, para. 13), Kenya (ibid., 296, para. 31), Sierra Leone (ibid., 300, para. 9), Uruguay (ibid., 303, para. 48: the delegate of that country considered that 'the systematic

violation of human rights' was prohibited by *jus cogens*), Cyprus (ibid., 306, para. 69), France (ibid., 309, para. 32: the French delegate stated that 'The substance of *jus cogens* was what represented the undeniable expression of the universal conscience, the common denominator of what men of all nationalities regarded as sacrosanct, namely, respect for and protection of the rights of the human person'), and Canada (ibid., 323, para. 22), as well as the Federal Republic of Germany (United Nations Conference on the Law of Treaties, Second Session (Vienna, 9 April–22 May 1969), *Official Records*, at 96, para. 26).

53. ICJ Reports (1966), at 298.

54. Text in EJIL 3 (1992), at 182–3.

55. Text in EJIL 3 (1992), 184.

56. See ICJ Reports (1975), at 29 ff., paras 48–53.

57. RDI, 69 (1986), at 886.

58. EJIL, 3 (1992), at 182–3.

59. Ibid., at 183–4.

60. S. Hoffmann, *Duties Beyond Borders—On the Limits and Possibilities of Ethical International Politics* (Syracuse, N.Y.: Syracuse University Press, 1981), at 124.

61. See http://www.lexum.unmontreal.ca/csc-scc/en/pub/1998/vol.2/html/1998scr2–0217.html, para. 130.

Chapter 6

1. See Anzilotti, *Corso*, i, at 71–6.

2. See *Keyn* (*The Franconia*) (1876) and the *West Rand Central Gold Mining Co. Ltd.* (1905) cases. In 1876, in *Keyn* (*The Franconia*), a British court held that 'To be binding, [international] law must have received the assent of the nations who are to be bound by it. This assent may be express, as by treaty or the acknowledged concurrence of governments, or may be implied from established usage' (*per* Cockburn, C.J., in BILC, 2, at 780).

In 1905 another British court took the same stand in *West Rand Central Gold Mining Co. Ltd.* It held that international law 'rests upon a consensus of civilised States . . . It included rules or practices "so universally approved or assented to as to be fairly termed . . . law"' (BILC, 2, at 289). 'It is quite true that whatever has received the common consent of civilised nations must have received the assent of our country, and that to which we have assented along with other nations in general may properly be called international law' (ibid., at 291).

3. In the *Lotus* case, the PCIJ stated as follows: 'The rules of law binding upon States . . . emanate

from their own free will as expressed in conventions or by usages generally accepted as expressing principles of law and established in order to regulate the relations between these co-existing independent communities or with a view to the achievement of common aims' (PCIJ, Series A, no. 10, at 18).

4. The US counsel had invoked principles of justice and morality. The British counsel dismissed this claim, noting that 'International law, properly so called, is only so much of the principles of morality and justice as the nations have agreed shall be part of those rules of conduct which shall govern their relations one with another. In other words, international law, as there exists no external superior power to impose it, rests upon the principle of consent. In the words of Grotius, *Placuitne gentibus?* Is there the consent of nations?' (Moore, *History and Digest*, i, at 871). When the President of the Tribunal asked the counsel for Great Britain whether it only referred to written agreement, he replied: 'When I say "to which they have agreed" of course I mean not merely or necessarily by a formal or express or written agreement, but by any mode in which agreement may be manifested, by which the Tribunal may arrive at the conclusion that they have so agreed' (ibid., at 872). It should be noted that the USA did not challenge the British views on this matter. The Tribunal did not pronounce on the issue, although generally speaking it upheld the British claims.

5. In *The Antelope*, the US Supreme Court had to deal in 1825 with the question of whether the arrest by American authorities of a Spanish vessel engaged in the slave trade was lawful. It held the arrest unlawful, for, although the slave trade was at the time normally prohibited, previously it had been legal and States favourable to that trade were entitled not to abide by the new rule. The Court held that 'No principle of general law is more universally acknowledged, than the perfect equality of nations. Russia and Geneva have equal rights. It results from this equality, that no one can rightfully impose a rule on another. Each legislates for itself, but its legislation can operate on itself alone. A right, then, which is vested in all by the consent of all, can be devested [sic] only by consent; and this trade [of slaves] in which all have participated, must remain lawful to those who cannot be induced to relinquish it. As no nation can prescribe a rule for others, none can make a law of nations; and this traffic remains lawful to those whose governments have not forbidden it' (AILC, 1, at 35–56, in particular at 45).

6. In 1903, in *Fishbach and Friedricy* the umpire of the German-Venezuelan Mixed Claims Commission held that 'Any nation has the power and the right to dissent from a rule or principle of international law,

even though it is accepted by all the other nations' (RIAA, 10, at 397).

7. The three principles are: *lex posterior derogat priori* (a later law repeals an earlier law), *lex posterior generalis non derogat priori speciali* (a later law, general in character, does not derogate from an earlier law which is special in character), and *lex specialis derogat generali* (a special law prevails over a general law).

8. The sources of international law were enumerated in Article 38 of the Statute of the PCIJ (corresponding to the present Article 38 of the Statute of the ICJ) as follows:

'1. The Court, whose function is to decide in accordance with international law such disputes as are submitted to it, shall apply:

a) international conventions, whether general or particular, establishing rules expressly recognized by the contesting States;

b) international custom, as evidence of a general practice accepted as law;

c) the general principles of law recognized by civilized nations;

d) subject to the provisions of Article 59 ['The decision of the Court has no binding effect except between the parties and in respect of that particular case'], judicial decisions and the teachings of the most highly qualified publicists of the various nations, as subsidiary means for the determination of the rules of law.

2. This provision shall not prejudice the power of the Court to decide a case ex aequo et bono, if the parties agree thereto.'

One should not be misled by this provision into believing that treaties override customary rules. In fact the sources of international law are listed in Article 38 in the order in which they should be used by the Court. Treaties being special *ratione personae* and possibly even *ratione materiae vis-à-vis* customary rules, the Court should look into them before resorting to customary rules, if any.

9. Kelsen, *Principles*, at 307–8.

10. M. Giuliano, *La comunità internazionale e il diritto* (Padua: Cedam, 1950), at 161 ff.; R. Ago, *Scienza giuridica e diritto internazionale* (Milan: Giuffré, 1950), at 78–108; G. Barile, 'La rilevazione e l'integrazione del diritto internazionale non scritto e la libertà d'apprezzamento del giudice', *Comunicazioni e studi*, 5 (1953), at 150 ff.

It should be noted that as early as 1928 D. Anzilotti had written that customary rules are 'spontaneous, almost unconscious manifestations of certain needs of social life' (*Corso*, at 73; *Cours*, at 74).

11. For the *North Sea Continental Shelf* case, see ICJ Reports (1969), para. 74.

12. In *Nicaragua*, in establishing the content of customary rules on the 'non-use of force and non-intervention', the Court stated the following:

'It is not to be expected that in the practice of States the application of the rules in question should have been perfect, in the sense that States should have refrained, with complete consistency, from the use of force or from intervention in each other's internal affairs. The Court does not consider that, for a rule to be established as customary, the corresponding practice must be in absolutely rigorous conformity with the rule. In order to deduce the existence of customary rules, the Court deems it sufficient that the conduct of States should, in general, be consistent with such rules, and that instances of State conduct inconsistent with a given rule should generally have been treated as breaches of that rule, not as indications of the recognition of a new rule. If a State acts in a way prima facie inconsistent with a recognized rule, but defends its conduct by appealing to exceptions or justifications contained within the rule itself, then whether or not the State's conduct is in fact justifiable on that basis, the significance of that attitude is to confirm rather than to weaken the rule' (ICJ Reports (1986), at 98, para. 186).

13. See ICJ Reports (1969), at 43, para. 74.

14. For the words of the *North Sea Continental Shelf* case, see ICJ Reports (1969), 44, para. 77.

15. See B. Cheng, 'United Nations Resolutions on Outer Space: "Instant" International Customary Law?', IJIL, 5 (1965), 23–43.

16. Text in RDI, 19 (1940), at 93–5.

17. Text, in French, in *Zeitschrift für internationales Recht*, 32 (1924), at 474, in footnote.

18. See text quoted in note 16 above, at 94.

19. Ibid.

20. The Convention had been adopted by the Sixth Pan-American Conference. See text in M.O. Hudson, *International Legislation* (Washington, D.C.: Carnegie Endowment, 1931–50), iv, 2401 et seq., and AJIL, 22 (1928), Suppl., 138 et seq.

21. For a very recent case where a court has played down the role of *usus*, on account of the entry into play of the Martens Clause, see the judgment of the ICTY, Trial Chamber II, in *Kupreskić et al.*, 14 January 2000, para. 527 (on the question of reprisals against civilians).

22. See A. Cassese, 'The Martens Clause: Half a Loaf or Simply Pie in the Sky?', EJIL, 11 (2000), 193–202.

23. Ibid., 209–10.

24. For a perusal of this case law see ibid., at 202–8.

25. See ibid.

26. For a perceptive and in-depth analysis of the various scholarly and judicial views concerning the doctrine of the 'persistent objector' see M. Mendelson, 'The Formation of Customary International Law', HR, 272 (1998), at 227–44.

27. See The American Law Institute, *Restatement of the Law Third, The Foreign Relations Law of the United States* (St. Paul, Minn.: American Law Institute Publishers, 1987), I, at 18, 26 (§102d) and 32 (note 2). The passage quoted is at 32.

28. See the *Fisheries* case (ICJ Reports (1951), at 131) and previously the *Asylum* case (ICJ Reports (1950), at 277–8). In addition to being *obiter dicta*, neither case appears to provide a watertight pronouncement about the existence of a customary rule or principle on the matter.

For references to the pleadings of the UK and Norway in *Fisheries*, see M. Mendelson, 'The Formation of Customary International Law', cit. at note 26, 235, note 216.

29. See Judge Tanaka's Dissenting Opinion in the *South West Africa* case (ICJ Reports (1966), at 291).

30. Judgment of 25 May 1926, PCIJ, Series A, no. 7, at 29.

31. ICJ Reports (1978), at 39, para. 96.

32. Ibid.

33. Ibid., at 41–4, paras 100–6.

34. Ibid., at 44, para. 107.

35. ICJ Reports (1994), at 121, para. 25.

36. ICJ Reports (1951), at 15–30.

37. See ECHR, *Belilos* case, Series A, no. 132 (1988), para. 60; *Weber* case, Series A, no. 177 (1990), paras 38–40; *Loizidou* case (preliminary objections), Series A, no. 310 (1995), paras 90–8.

38. Human Rights Committee, General Comment 24/52 on Issues relating to Reservations to the UN Covenant on Civil and Political Rights, adopted on 2 November 1994, para. 17, in ILM, 34 (1995), at 845. The Committee has offered the following rationale for the conclusion just referred to:

'[Human rights] treaties, and the [UN] Covenant [on Civil and Political Rights] specifically, are not a web of inter-State exchanges of mutual obligations. They concern the endowment of individuals with rights. The principle of inter-State reciprocity has no place ... And because the operation of the classic rules on reservations is so inadequate for the Covenant, States have often not seen any legal interest in or need to object to reservations. The absence of protest by States cannot imply that a reservation is either compatible or incompatible with the object and purpose of the Covenant. Objections have been occasional, made by some but not by others, and on grounds not always specified . . . In short, the pattern is so unclear that it is not safe to assume that a non-objecting State thinks that a particular reservation is acceptable. In the view of the Committee, because of the special characteristics of the Covenant as a human rights treaty, it is open to question what effect objections have between States inter se . . . It necessarily falls to the Committee to determine whether a specific reservation is compatible with the object and purpose of the Covenant' (ibid., paras 17 and 20).

It should be noted that the USA, the UK, and France strongly objected to the Committee's views on the severability of reservations contrary to the object and purpose of human rights treaties: see HRLJ, 16 (1995), at 422 ff.

See also YILC (1997), II, Part Two, at 48–9, 53–6, paras 75–87, 124–56.

39. See *Rawle Kennedy v. Trinidad and Tobago*, decision of 31 December 1999, Communication no. 845/1999 (CCPR/C/67/D/84571999), paras 6.4–6.7.

40. Anzilotti, *Corso*, at 102, 104, 107. Anzilotti had already made this statement in the first edition of his *Corso*, I (*Parte generale*) (Roma: Athenaeum, 1912), at 203.

41. 17 US (4 Wheaton), 316 at 407–37, 4 L. Ed. 579 (1819).

42. US Supreme Court, 252 U.S. 416, in AILC, 10, 373–8, at 376–7.

43. PCIJ, Advisory Opinions of 23 July 1926 on *Competence of the ILO Concerning Personal Work of the Employer*, Series B, no. 13, at 18, and of 8 December 1927 on *Jurisdiction of the European Commission of the Danube*, Series B, no. 14, at 64.

44. See the Advisory Opinions in *Reparation* (ICJ Reports (1949), at 180, 182), in *Effects of Awards of Compensation made by the U.N. Administrative Tribunal* (ICJ Reports (1954), at 56–7), in the *Expenses* case (ICJ Reports (1962), 167–8) and in *Namibia* (ICJ Reports (1971), at 47–9, 52). See also the Court's Advisory Opinion in *Legality of the Use by a State of Nuclear Weapons in Armed Conflict* (ICJ Reports (1996), at 78–81, paras 25–6).

45. Frédéric II, 'Histoire de mon temps, Avant-propos', in *Œuvres posthumes de Frédéric II, roi de Prusse* (Berlin: Voss et Fils, 1789), i, at 11, 14.

46. Bismarck wrote the following: 'Observance of treaties between Big States is relative indeed, as soon as it is put to test "in the struggle for existence". No big nation will be prompted to sacrifice its existence on the altar of fidelity to a treaty, if obliged to choose between the two. The [maxim] *ultra posse nemo tenetur* [no one is bound beyond what he can do]

cannot be invalidated by any treaty clause' (Otto Fürst von Bismarck-Schönhauser, *Gedanken und Erinnerungen* (Stuttgart and Berlin: Cotta, 1922), ii, at 287.

47. Reportedly President De Gaulle, upon signing an important treaty with Germany, stated that international agreements 'are like roses and young girls; they last while they last' (see *The Economist* (London), 18 March 1972, at 6).

48. Human Rights Committee, General Comment 26(61), adopted by the Committee at its 1631st meeting, http://www1.umn.edu/humanrts/gencomm/hrcom26.htm, para. 2.

49. Ibid., para. 3.

50. See in particular the splendid comments by E. Jimenez de Aréchaga, 'International Law in the Past Third of a Century', HR, 159 (1978-I), at 14–26.

51. ICJ Reports (1971), at 47.

52. ICJ Reports (1972), at 67.

53. ICJ Reports (1973), at 18.

54. ICJ Reports (1997), paras 46–7; see also paras 101–4, where the Court discussed Article 61 of the Vienna Convention.

55. Ibid., para. 123.

56. ICJ Reports (1969), at 39.

57. ICJ Reports (1973), at 14.

58. ICJ Reports (1969), at 41.

59. ICJ Reports (1974), at 23–6.

60. See United Nations Conference on the Law of Treaties, First Session (Vienna, 26 March–24 May 1968), *Official Records*, Summary Records of the Plenary Meetings and of the Meetings of the Committee of the Whole, at 300, para. 9.

61. Ibid., at 312–13, paras 55–63.

62. Ibid., at 322, para. 6.

63. Ibid., at 327, paras 68–70.

64. Ibid., at 309–10, paras 26–34. The French delegate admitted, however, that respect for human rights constituted 'the substance of *jus cogens*' (ibid., para. 32). See also United Nations Conference on the Law of Treaties, Second Session (Vienna, 9 April–22 May 1969), *Official Records*, Summary Records of the Plenary Meetings of the Committee of the Whole, at 93–5, paras 7–18.

65. *Official Records* of the First Session, cit. at note 60, at 323–4, paras 25–31, and, more clearly, *Official Records* of the Second Session, cit. at note 64, at 103, paras 30–1.

66. *Official Records* of the First Session cit. at note 60, at 295, paras 18–19.

67. Ibid., at 305–6, paras 66–71.

68. Ibid., at 310, paras 35–8.

69. Ibid., at 311, paras 41–3.

70. Ibid., at 315, paras 1–5.

71. Ibid., at 323, paras 21–4.

72. E. Jimenez de Aréchaga, 'International Law in the Past Third of a Century', HR, 159 (1978-I), at 64.

73. R. Ago, 'Droit des traités à la lumière de la Convention de Vienne', HR, 134 (1971-III), at 297.

74. United Nations Conference on the Law of Treaties, 1968, *Official Records* of the First Session, cit. at note 60, at 472, para. 12.

75. He said: 'In supporting the principle [of *jus cogens*], care must be taken not to exaggerate its scope, either in a positive direction, by making of it a mystique that would breathe fresh life into international life, or in a negative direction, by seeing in it an element of the destruction of treaties and of anarchy . . . It was in the nature of things that, in practice, that type of treaties [sc. contrary to *jus cogens*], a flagrant challenge to the international conscience, would be infrequent and that instances of treaties that would be null and void as the result of the application of that rule [on *jus cogens*] would be rare.' *Official Records* of the First Session, (cit. above note 60), at 303, para. 48.

76. It is widely recognized in the international community that gross or systematic racial discrimination runs contrary to the most fundamental norms of international law. It should be noted that Article 4(1) of the UN Covenant on Civil and Political Rights provides in terms that 'in time of public emergency which threatens the life of the nation' no derogation is admissible from the principle of non-discrimination. The US *Restatement of the Law Third, Restatement of the Law—The Foreign Relations Law of the United States* (St. Paul, Minn.: American Law Institute Publishers, 1987), vol. 2, at 167, states that the international norms prohibiting 'systematic racial discrimination' are peremptory in character. That racial discrimination is prohibited by *jus cogens* was also maintained by many States at the Vienna Diplomatic Conference on the Law of Treaties (see above, **5.8**).

77. See in particular the decision of the ICTY in *Furundžija* (judgment of 10 December 1998), at paras 153–57, as well as the judgment of the House of Lords of 24 March 1999 in *Pinochet* (Lord Browne-Wilkinson, in ILM 38 (1999), at 589, Lord Hope of Craighead, ibid., at 626, and Lord Millet, ibid, at 649–50).

78. ICJ Reports (1996), at 257, para. 79.

79. See ICTY Trial Chamber II, in *Kupreskić et al.*, Judgment of 14 January 2000, para. 520.

80. Decision no. 53 of 13 October 1993, in *Az Alkotmànybirosg Hatà rosatai*, 1994, 2832–9, at 2836 (unofficial English translation by an expert translator on file with the author).

81. See the order of 6 November 1998 in *Pinochet* by a Belgian *Juge d'instruction*, in *Revue de droit pénal et de criminologie* 79 (1999), at 286. As for Switzerland, see the official message of the Swiss Government (*Conseil fédéral*) to Parliament: *Message relatif au Statut de la Cour pénale internationale, à la loi fédérale sur la coopération avec la Cour pénale internationale ainsi qu'à une révision du droit pénal*, of 15 November 2000, at 470, para. 5.2.

82. See references in Chapter 5, at note 51.

83. In *Kuwait v. Aminoil* it had been claimed by one of the parties that permanent sovereignty over natural resources had become 'an imperative rule of *jus cogens* prohibiting States from affording, by contract or by treaty, guarantees of any kind against the exercise of the public authority in regard to all matters relating to natural riches'. In its decision of 24 March 1982 the Arbitral Tribunal bluntly rejected this submission. It stated the following: 'This contention lacks all foundation. Even if [General] Assembly Resolution 1803 (XVII) [on permanent sovereignty over natural resources] adopted in 1962, is to be regarded, by reason of the circumstance of its adoption, as reflecting the then state of international law, such is not the case with subsequent resolutions which have not had the same degree of authority. Even if some of their provisions can be regarded as codifying rules that reflect international practice, it would not be possible from this to deduce the existence of a rule of international law prohibiting a State from undertaking not to proceed to a nationalization during a limited period of time. It may indeed well be eminently useful that "host" States should, if they so desire, be able to pledge themselves not to nationalize given foreign undertakings within a limited period; and no rule of public international law prevents them from doing so' (ILR, 66, at 587–8, para. 90(2)).

In *Determination of the Maritime Boundary between Guinea-Bissau and Senegal* Guinea-Bissau had argued that the rule enshrining the right of peoples to self-determination had the character of *jus cogens*; similarly, some of the corollaries of the rule, including the principle of permanent sovereignty over natural resources, had the character of a peremptory norm. According to Guinea-Bissau the Agreement of 1960 between France (former colonial Power of Senegal) and Portugal (former colonial Power of Guinea-Bissau) fixing the maritime boundaries between the two countries was contrary to those rules of *jus cogens* in two respects: (i) it constituted an alienation of territory, and as such was contrary to the principle of permanent sovereignty over natural resources; (ii) 'the process of liberation' was already under way at the time of the signature of the Agreement, thereby rendering the Agreement incompatible with the right of peoples to self-determination; indeed, according to Guinea-Bissau, as from the initiation of the process of national liberation, the colonial State was no longer entitled to exercise its *jus tractatus*, that is the right to conclude agreements on behalf of the colonial people. In its decision of 31 July 1989 the Arbitral Tribunal dismissed both contentions. It held that the principle of permanent sovereignty over natural resources did not apply to the case at issue because before 1960 'the maritime boundaries between the two countries had not been determined, and consequently neither of the two States could assert that a particular portion of the maritime area was "its own"'. Furthermore, the Tribunal held that Guinea-Bissau had not proved the existence of a peremptory norm restricting the power of a colonial Power to conclude agreements with respect to the colonial territory; in addition, in the case under dispute the alleged restriction of the colonial Power's *jus tractatus* was not admissible because in 1960 the war of national liberation had not yet begun and recognition by the United Nations of the national liberation movement in Guinea-Bissau had only come in 1973. Consequently, at the relevant time Portugal had the legal capacity to make treaties for Guinea-Bissau (ILR, 83, at 24–30).

84. See judgment of 10 December 1998, paras 154–7.

85. See English text in EJIL 4 (1993), at 90 and French original in RGDIP 92 (1993), at 594.

86. Judge Padilla Nervo stated in his Separate Opinion that 'customary rules belonging to the category of *jus cogens* cannot be subjected to unilateral reservations' (ICJ Reports (1969), at 97); Judge Tanaka argued in his Dissenting Opinion that a reservation would be null and void if it were 'contrary to an essential principle of the continental shelf institution which must be recognized as *jus cogens*' (ibid., at 182), and Judge ad hoc Sørensen stated in his Dissenting Opinion that the acceptance of a reservation had the effect of establishing a special contractual relationship between the parties concerned and '[p]rovided the customary rule does not belong to the category of *jus cogens*, a special contractual relationship of this nature is not invalid as such' (ibid., at 248).

87. General Comment 24(52), adopted on 2 November 1994, in UN Doc CCPR/C/21/Rev.1/Add. 6 (1994), para. 8 (see also http://hei.unige.ch/humanrts/gencomm/hrcom24. htm).

The Committee went on to say: 'Accordingly, a State may not reserve the right to engage in slavery, to torture, to subject persons to cruel, inhuman or degrading treatment or punishment, to arbitrarily deprive persons of their lives, to arbitrarily arrest or detain persons, to deny freedom of thought, conscience and religion, to presume a person guilty unless he proves his innocence, to execute pregnant women or children, to permit the advocacy of national, racial or religious hatred, to deny to persons of marriageable age the right to marry, or to deny to minorities the right to enjoy their own culture, profess their own religion, or use their own language. And while reservations to particular clauses of Article 14 may be acceptable, a general reservation to the right to a fair trial would not be'.

88. See the resolution adopted on 1 September 1983 on 'New Problems of Extradition'. In section IV it is stated that 'In cases where there is a well-founded fear of the violation of the fundamental rights of an accused in the territory of the requesting State, extradition may be refused, whosoever the individual whose extradition is requested and whatever the nature of the offence of which he is accused'. See Institute of International Law, *Yearbook*, vol. 60, Part II, Session of Cambridge (Paris: A. Pedone, 1983), at 306.

89. Decision of the US Court of Appeals, District of Columbia Circuit, 1 July 1994, in ILR 103, at 618.

90. Ibid., at 612–19. The decision of the District Court is ibid., at 598–603, that of the Court of Appeals is ibid., at 604–12.

91. See Judgment cit., at paras 154–7.

92. See the orders (*autos)* of the Spanish National Criminal Court (*Audiencia Nacional*) in *Adolfo Francisco*, of 4 November 1998, legal ground no. 8. The accused had been charged with genocide, terrorism and torture. The Court held that the Argentinian laws of amnesty could be regarded as contrary to *jus cogens* and in contravention of international treaties concluded by Argentina (text in *El Derecho Jurisprudencia*).

See also the order of 5 November 1998 issued by the same Court in *Augusto Pinochet*, on the same matter, concerning a Chilean law on amnesty, legal ground no. 8 (the accused had been charged with genocide, torture and terrorism). See text in *El Derecho Jurisprudencia*.

93. Ibid., para 155.

94. In its 'Message relatif à la Convention pour la prévention et la répression du crime de génocide, et révision correspondante du droit pénal' sent to Parliament on 31 March 1999, the Swiss Government (*Conseil Fédéral*) stated the following : 'Dans la mesure où l'interdiction du génocide est une règle impérative du droit des gens (*jus cogens*), les Etats ne peuvent pas convenir de l'écarter. Il est ainsi probable qu'un traité de paix consacrant une amnistie pour des actes de génocide ne devrait pas être considéré comme valable en droit. Il en résulte que sous l'angle du droit international, une législation nationale qui autoriserait ou même ordonnerait un génocide contre un groupe déterminé ne pourrait en aucun cas servir de légitimation à ses auteurs et à leurs complices' (at 4916).

95. Judgment, cit., para. 156.

96. See order of 6 November 1998 by a Belgian *Juge d'instruction* in *Pinochet*, in *Revue de droit pénal et de criminologie*, 79 (1999), at 288.

97. ILR 103, at 618.

98. See judgment of 24 March 1999, opinion of Lord Millet, in ILM 38 (1999), 649–50; cf. the opinion of Lord Browne-Wilkinson, ibid., 589–91.

99. See for instance the statements by the Agent and one of the Counsel (Professor Brownlie) for the Federal Republic of Yugoslavia (Serbia and Montenegro) before the ICJ in *Legality of Use of Force*, Hearing of 10 May 1999 (morning), at 13 and 25 (the prohibition of the use of force belongs to *jus cogens*).

100. For instance, in its order of 15 December 1979 in *United States Diplomatic and Consular Staff in Tehran, Provisional Measures*, the Court stated that 'while no State is under any obligation to maintain diplomatic or consular relations with another, yet it cannot fail to recognize the imperative obligations inherent therein, now codified in the Vienna Conventions of 1961 and 1963, to which both Iran and the United States are parties' (ICJ Reports (1979), at 20, para. 41. In the Advisory Opinion of 8 July 1996 on *Legality of the Threat or Use of Nuclear Weapons*, the Court stated that the fundamental rules of humanitarian law applicable in armed conflict 'are to be observed by all States whether or not they have ratified the conventions that contain them because they constitute intransgressible principles of international customary law' (ICJ Reports (1996), at 257, para. 79). However, President Bedjaoui, in his Declaration, said that those rules 'form part of *jus cogens*' (ibid., at 273, para. 21).

In 1986, in *Nicaragua* the Court mentioned that both Nicaragua and the USA, respectively in their Memorial and Counter-Memorial, had asserted that the prohibition of the use of force had come to be recognized as *jus cogens*. After mentioning these concordant views, the Court refrained however from setting forth its own view on the matter (ICJ Reports (1986), at 100–1, paras 190–1).

101. See HR, 159 (1978-I) (cit. above, at note 72), at 65.

102. See Judgment of 3 November 1982, in *Arrêts du Tribunal Fédéral Suisse, Recueil Officiel*, vol. 108, I, at 408–13, para. 8a.

103. Ibid., at 410–12.

104. See Judgment of 12 December 1975, in *Arrêts du Tribunal Fédéral Suisse, Recueil Officiel*, vol. 101, I, at 541, para. 7b (in German).

105. See *Arrêts du Tribunal Fédéral Suisse, Recueil Officiel*, vol. 111, I, at 412, para. 8a.

106. See *Sener* (22 March 1983), in *Arrêts du Tribunal Fédéral Suisse, Recueil Officiel*, vol. 109, I, at 72, para. 6aa (in German); *Bufano et al.* (21 May 1986), ibid., vol. 112, I, at 222, para. 7 and 224, para. 7; *P. v. Office Fédéral de la police* (21 May 1986), ibid., vol. 117, I, 340, para. 2 (on good faith); *X v. Office Fédéral de la police* (3 November 1995), ibid., vol. 121, II, at 299, para. 3 and 301, para. 5; *X v. Office Fédéral de la police* (11 September 1996), ibid., vol. 122, II, at 379–80, para. 2d.

Chapter 7

1. *Corso*, at 297.

2. Report of the Panel, paras 7.114–7.124.

3. Ibid., paras 7.125–7.126.

4. ICJ Reports (1969), at 25, paras 27–8.

5. ICJ Reports (1974), 267–71.

6. ICJ Reports (1986), at 132, para. 261.

7. Case decided by a Chamber of the ICJ: see ICJ Reports (1986), at 573–4, paras 39–40.

8. During the Spanish-American war in 1898 US naval forces entered Manila Bay (the Philippines were under Spanish sovereignty) and cut the Manila–Hong Kong submarine telegraph cables that had been laid by a British corporation. Great Britain presented a claim for compensation on behalf of that company. The Tribunal disallowed the claim. It held the following:

'[E]ven assuming that there was in 1898 no treaty and no specific rule of international law formulated as the expression of a universally recognised rule governing the case of the cutting of cables by belligerents, it cannot be said that there is no principle of international law applicable. International law, as well as domestic law, may not contain, and generally does not contain, express rules decisive of particular cases; but the function of jurisprudence is to resolve the conflict of opposing rights and interests by applying, in default of any specific provision of law, the corollaries of general principles, and so to find—exactly as in the mathematical sciences—the solution of the problem. This is the method of jurisprudence; it is the method by which the law has been gradually evolved in every country resulting in the definition and settlement of legal relations as well as between States as between private individuals' (RIAA, 6, at 114–15).

9. Advisory Opinion of 18 July 1996, ICJ Reports (1996), at 266, para. 105(2)(E). In their declarations or dissenting opinions some judges construed the passage quoted in the text as a *non liquet*: see Bedjaoui, ibid., at 271, paras 14–15; Vereshchetin, ibid., at 279–81; Schwebel, ibid., at 322–3; Higgins, ibid., at 584, para. 7 and 590, paras 29–30.

10. ICJ, *The Corfu Channel* case (Merits), ICJ Reports (1949), at 22.

11. ICJ Reports (1986), at 114, para. 219.

12. Ibid., (1986), at 566, para. 23.

13. ICTY, Trial Chamber II, Judgment of 10 December 1998, para. 183.

14. See text in ILM, 36 (1997), 399 et seq.

15. The Arbitral Tribunal stated the following: 'Referring to the Tribunal's duty to act according to "relevant legal and equitable principles," some may argue that the foregoing rulings are improperly based on purely "political" considerations and lack any adequate basis in law or equity. For reasons previously explained, we disagree. One of the unique qualities of the present arbitration is that it inherently encompasses political considerations, requiring as it does that the Tribunal allocate political responsibilities between the Entities in a manner that will advance the goals of Dayton. Moreover, although the Tribunal has a duty to make a final decision as soon as "that can be done consistent with relevant legal and equitable principles" (Award Para. 102), it should not act until matters have become sufficiently stabilized to allow it to put in place a solution that is likely to endure over the long term (see Award Para. 101). We therefore think there is both legal and equitable justification for ordering a relatively short delay to collect additional facts relating both to probable future compliance with Dayton and the future relationship between the two Entities' (para. 20).

16. See text in ILM (1999), at 536 ct seq.

17. See *Neptune* case (*United States* v. *Great Britain*), decision of 25 June 1797 (Opinion of Commissioner Pinkney), in Lapradelle and Politis, i, at 156–7 (it should be noted that the Commissioner did not mention national legislation but only some famous publicists). See however the Opinion of Commissioner Trumbull, ibid., at 177–8.

18. PCA, Award of 11 November 1912 on *Russian Indemnities* case, in RIAA, 11, at 443 (original French; for the English text see AJIL, 7 (1913), at 178 ff.).

19. PCA, *Pious Funds of the Californias*, award of 14 October 1902, in RIAA, 9, at 12.

20. See *Fabiani* case, award of 30 December 1896, in La Fontaine, *Pasicrisie*, at 356.

21. See the award delivered on 29 March 1900 by the Arbitral Tribunal of Delagoa (*Portugal* v. *US and Great Britain*), in La Fontaine, *Pasicrisie*, at 402 as well as the award rendered on 29 November 1902 by Judge Asser in the *Cape Horn Pigeon et al.* case, in Lapradelle and Politis, ii, at 285.

22. For the debates in the Committee cited in the text see League of Nations, Permanent Court of International Justice, Advisory Committee of Jurists, *Procès-verbaux of the Proceedings of the Committee, June 16th–July 24th 1920* (The Hague: van Langenhuysen Brothers, 1920), at 286–339.

23. See the speech of Baron Descamps in *Procès-Verbaux*, cit. at note 22, at 322–5. See also the proposal he put forward at the 13th Meeting, ibid., at 306.

24. Ibid., at 323–4 (text of the speech made by Descamps to introduce his proposal).

25. Ibid., at 318.

26. Ibid., at 310–11.

27. See the statements of Root, ibid., at 293–4 and 308–10, of Ricci-Busatti, ibid., at 315–25, and of Lord Phillimore, ibid., at 315–27.

28. Ibid., at 287.

29. Ibid., at 294.

30. See the text submitted by Root, ibid., at 344; at the 15th Meeting Mr Root pointed out that he had prepared the text 'in collaboration with Lord Phillimore' (ibid., at 331).

31. PCIJ, *Mosul Boundary* case, Series B, no. 12 (1925), at 32.

32. PCIJ, *Chorzow Factory*, Merits, Series A, no. 17 (1928), at 29.

33. PCIJ, *Chorzow Factory* case, Series A, no. 17, at 31 ('one party cannot avail himself of the fact that the other has not fulfilled some obligation, or has not had recourse to some means of redress, if the former party has, by some illegal act, prevented the latter from fulfilling the obligation in question, or from having recourse to the tribunal which would have been open to him').

34. See Anzilotti's Dissenting Opinion in the *Prise d'eau à la Meuse*, Series A/B, no. 70, at 50.

35. PCIJ, *Brazilian Loans*, Series A, no. 20–1, at 114.

36. The Lebanese Judge Ammoun, in his Dissenting Opinion in *North Sea Continental Shelf*, harshly and rightly criticized the outmoded and discriminatory reference to 'civilised nations'. See ICJ Reports (1969), at 133–4.

37. See ICJ, *Nuclear Tests* case, ICJ Reports (1974), at 268, para. 46 ('One of the basic principles governing the creation and performance of legal obligations, whatever their source, is the principle of good faith').

38. See Judgment no. 963, ILO Administrative Tribunal, 1989, at 6 ('Toute autorité est liée par la règle qu'elle a elle-même édictée aussi longtemps qu'elle ne l'a ni modifiée, ni abrogée. Il s'agit là d'un principe général du droit en vertu duquel les règlements ne disposent que pour l'avenir. Le principe s'impose à toutes les autorités, car il constitue le fondement de tous les rapports juridiques').

See also ICJ, *Nicaragua*, ICJ Reports (1986), at 114, paras 218–220; *Case Concerning the Frontier Dispute*, ICJ Reports (1986), at 566, para. 23.

In its judgment in *Furundžija* the ICTY, faced with the legal issue of deciding whether forced oral penetration constituted rape as a crime against humanity or a war crime, after establishing that there was no uniformity in the national legislation of States, had recourse to a general principle. It held that the 'general principle of respect for human dignity is the basic underpinning and indeed the very raison d'être of international humanitarian law and human rights law; indeed, in modern times it has become of such paramount importance as to permeate the whole body of international law. This principle is intended to shield human beings from outrages upon their personal dignity, whether such outrages are carried out by unlawfully attacking the body or by humiliating and debasing the honour, the self-respect or the mental well-being of a person'. The Tribunal drew the conclusion that it was 'consonant with this principle that such an extremely serious sexual outrage as forced oral penetration should be classified as rape'. ICTY, Trial Chamber II, Judgment of 10 December 1998, para. 183.

39. See ILO, Administrative Tribunal, Judgments, 66th Session, 7. ICTY, Trial Chamber II, Judgment of 14 January 2000 in the *Kupreskić et al.* case, para. 623.

40. ICJ, Advisory Opinion on *South West Africa*, ICJ Reports (1971), at 31; *Aegean Sea* case, ICJ Reports (1978), at 33.

41. ICTY, Appeals Chamber, *Tadić* case (judgment of 2 October 1995), para. 42.

42. ICJ, *Judgments of the ILO Administrative Tribunal*, ICJ Reports (1956), at 85. In its Advisory Opinion on *Application for Review of Judgment no. 158*, ICJ Reports (1973), at 181, the Court stated that: 'General principles of law and the judicial character of the Court do require that, even in advisory proceedings, the interested parties should necessarily have an opportunity, and on the basis of equality, to submit all the elements relevant to the questions which have been referred to the review tribunals. But that condition is fulfilled by the submission of written statements.'

43. Sentencing Judgment of 29 November 1996, para. 31.

44. Judgment, cit. above, note 13, paras 174–81.

45. Judgment, cit. above, note 39, para. 637 ff., in particular 680 ff.

46. Judgment of 30 March 2000, para. 796.

47. *New Jersey* v. *Delaware*, 291 US 361, at 383.

48. See Moore, *History and Digest*, i, 543–682; see also B. Seidel, 'The Alabama', in *Encyclopedia*, i, at 97–9.

49. RIAA, 2, at 829 ff., in particular 838–40.

50. Judgment of 31 July 1928, in RIAA, 2, at 1013 ff., in particular 1025–8.

51. ICJ Reports (1970), at 32, para. 33.

52. ICJ Reports (1966), at 38–47.

53. ICJ reports (1969), 32–43.

54. ICJ Reports (1974), 267–71.

55. ICJ Reports (1986), 38–66, 94–106, 106–12, 113–15.

56. ICTY Appeals Chamber, Judgment of 5 October 1995, paras 94–137.

57. ICTY, Trial Chamber II, Judgment of 14 January 2000, paras 637–748.

58. P. Cahier, 'Le rôle du juge dans l'élaboration du droit international', in J. Makarczyk, ed., *Essays in Honour of K. Skubiszewski* (The Hague, London, Boston: Kluwer, 1996), at 358 ff. A different view is taken by G. Abi-Saab, 'De la Jurisprudence—Quelques réflexions sur son rôle dans le développement du droit international', in M. Perez Gonzalez, ed., *Hacia un nuevo orden internacional y europeo: Estudios en homenaje al Profesor Don Manuel Diez de Velasco* (Madrid: Tecnos, 1993), at 20 ff.

59. ICJ Reports (1949), at 182.

60. ICJ Reports (1951), at 24.

61. ICJ Reports (1955), at 22–54.

62. ICJ Reports (1969), at 46–48.

Chapter 8

1. For citations of Moser's works and the writings of subsequent scholars, see H. Triepel, *Völkerrecht und Landesrecht* (Leipzig: Hirschfeld, 1899), at 114, notes 1–6.

2. C. Bergbohm, *Staatsvertäge und Gesetze als Quellen des Völkerrechts* (Dorpat: C. Mattiesen, 1877), in particular at 59–91, 102–10; A. Zorn, *Grundzüge des Völkerrechts*, 2nd edn. (Leipzig: J. J. Weber, 1903), at 5–9; M. Wenzel, *Juristische Grundprobleme—Zugleich eine Untersuchung zum Begriff des Staates und Problem des Völkerrechts* (Berlin: F. Dümmlers, 1920), at 351–9, 385–421 (for a penetrating criticism of Wenzel's contribution, see A. Verdross, *Die Einheit des rechtlichen Weltbildes auf Grundlage der Völkerrechtsverfassung* (Tübingen: Mohr, 1923), at 55–62).

3. H. Triepel, *Völkerrecht und Landesrecht*, cit. above, note 1, in particular at 156 ff.; D. Anzilotti, 'Teoria generale della responsabilità dello Stato nel diritto internazionale' (1902), in *Scritti di diritto internazionale pubblico*, I (Padua: Cedam, 1956); id., 'L'azione individuale contraria al diritto internazionale' (1902), ibid., at 211–41; id., 'Il diritto internazionale nei giudizi interni' (1905), ibid., at 314 ff.; id., *Corso* (1928), at 49–63.

4. Anzilotti, *Corso*, at 52.

5. W. Kaufmann, *Die Rechtskraft des Internationales Rechtes und das Verhältnis der Staatsgesetzgebungen und der Staastorgane zu demselben* (Stuttgart: F. Enke, 1899), in particular at 1–86. Kaufman had already outlined his general views in his book on *Die mitteleuropäischen Eisenbahnen und das internationale öffentliche Recht. Internationale Studien und Beiträge* (Leipzig: Duncker and Humblot, 1893), at 112–13, 121–4, 129–31. See also id., 'Die modernen nichtstaatlichen internationalen Verbände und Kongresse und das internationale Recht', *Zeitschrift für Völkerrecht und Bundesstaatsrecht*, 2 (1908), at 419–40, in particular at 438 ff.

6. W. Kaufmann, *Die Rechtskraft*, cit. above, note 5, at iii–iv.

7. Ibid., at 77–9 as well as 62–4.

8. Ibid., at 60–5.

9. Ibid., at 77–85.

10. Anzilotti criticized Kaufmann's views: 'Il diritto internazionale nei giudizi interni' (1905) (cit. above, note 3), at 292; as did P. Heilborn, *Grundbegriffe des Völkerrechts* (Berlin, Stuttgart, and Leipzig: Verlag von W. Kohlhammer, 1912), at 92–5, and M. Wenzel, *Juristische Grundprobleme* (cit. above, note 2), at 352–4.

On Kaufmann's views see F. Münch, 'Wilhelm Kaufmann und der ursprüngliche Monismus', *Die Friedenswarte*, 53 (1955–6), at 117 ff., in particular 120–2.

11. H. Kelsen, *Das Problem der Souveränität und die Theorie des Völkerrechts-Beitrag zu einer reinen Rechtslehre* (Tübingen: J. C. Mohr (P. Siebeck), 1920), at 120 ff.; id., *Allgemeine Staatslehre* (Berlin: J. Springer, 1925), at 119 ff.; id., *Les Rapports de système entre le droit interne et le droit international public*, HR, 1926 (IV), at 227–331, in particular at 289 ff.; id., *Principles*, at 190–6.

12. Ibid., at 194–5.

13. Ibid., at 354.

14. Ibid., at 446–7.

15. In *Polish Nationals in Danzig* the Court stated that: 'It should . . . be observed that . . . according to generally accepted principles . . . a State cannot adduce as against another State its own constitution with a view to evading obligations incumbent upon it under international law or treaties in force' (PCIJ, Series A/B, no. 44 (1931), at 24). See also the *Free Zones* case (PCIJ, Series A/B, no. 46, at 167).

16. See e.g. the *Georges Pinson* case brought before the France-Mexico Claims Commission (decision of 18 October 1928, in RIAA, 5, at 393–4), as well as the decision of the President of the ICTY in *Blaškić* (decision of 3 April 1996, para. 7).

17. See PCIJ, Series B, no. 10, at 20. See also Brownlie, *Principles of International Law*, 5th edn. (Oxford: Clarendon Press, 1998), at 35 and authors cited in n. 22 (this distinguished author adds that 'However, in general a failure to bring about such conformity is not in itself a direct breach of international law, and a breach arises only when the state concerned fails to observe its obligations on a specific occasion'). M. B. Akehurst and P. Malanczuk, *Akehurst's Modern Introduction to International Law* (London: Routledge, 1997), at 64.

18. See Articles 49(1), 50(1), 129(1), and 146(1) of the 1949 Geneva Conventions.

19. See Article 5 of the 1948 Convention on Genocide, Article 2(1)(d) of the 1965 Convention on Racial Discrimination, Article 2(2) of the 1966 Covenant on Civil and Political Rights, Articles 4 and 5 of the 1984 Convention on Torture.

20. In his decision of 3 April 1966 in *Blaškić*, the President of the ICTY held that Article 29 of the ICTY Statute, on the obligation of States to cooperate with the Tribunal, had such a nature and effect, and consequently Croatia, by not enacting implementing legislation, was in breach of international law (see paras 8–11).

21. See Article 88 of the Rome Statute, which pro-

vides as follows: 'States parties shall ensure that there are procedures available under their national law for all the forms of cooperation which are specified under this Part [Part 9, on International Co-operation and Judicial Assistance]'.

22. The Tribunal stated that: '[G]iven the importance that the international community attaches to the protection of individuals from torture, the prohibition against torture is particularly stringent and sweeping. States are obliged not only to prohibit and punish torture, but also to forestall its occurrence: it is insufficient merely to intervene after the infliction of torture, when the physical or moral integrity of human beings has already been irremediably harmed. Consequently States are bound to put in place all those measures that may pre-empt the perpetration of torture. . . . It follows that international rules prohibit not only torture but also (i) the failure to adopt the national measures necessary for implementing the prohibition and (ii) the maintenance in force or passage of laws which are contrary to the prohibition. . . . [I]n the case of torture, the requirement that States expeditiously institute national implementing measures is an integral part of the international obligation to prohibit this practice' (ICTY, Trial Chamber II, *Prosecutor* v. *Furundžija*, Judgment of 10 December 1998, paras 148–9; see also para. 150).

23. This system is differently termed by some courts or commentators. Thus, Lord Denning in a famous case (*Trendtex Trading Corporation* v. *Central Bank of Nigeria*), distinguished between *incorporation* and *transformation* as follows: 'One school of thought holds to the doctrine of incorporation. It says that the rules of international law are incorporated into English law automatically and considered to be part of English law unless they are in conflict with an Act of Parliament. The other school of thought holds to the doctrine of transformation. It says that the rules of international law are not to be considered as part of English law except in so far as they have been already adopted and made part of our law by the decisions of the judges, or by Act of Parliament, or long established custom. The difference is vital when you are faced with a change in the rules of international law. Under the doctrine of incorporation, when the rules of international law change, our English law changes with them. But, under the doctrine of transformation the English law does not change. It is bound by precedent. It is bound down to those rules of international law which have been accepted and adopted in the past. It cannot develop as international law develops.' [1977] 1 QB 529 at 553–4.

24. See for instance Cass. 16 June 1947, in *Pasicri-*

sie belge (1947), I, at 268; Cass. 27 November 1950, ibid. (1951), I, at 182.

25. Decision of 26 May 1966, in *Journal des Tribunaux* (1966), at 463.

26. Decision of 18 December 1979, in *Pasicrisie belge* (1980), I, at 480.

27. Article 10(1) of the 1947 Italian Constitution provides that 'The Italian legal order shall conform with the generally recognised rules of international law'.

Article 25 of the 1949 German Constitution provides that 'The general rules of public international law shall be an integral part of federal law. They shall take precedence over the laws and shall directly create rights and duties for the inhabitants of the federal territory'.

Article 98(2) of the 1947 Constitution of Japan provides that 'The treaties concluded by Japan and established laws of nations shall be faithfully observed'. On this provision, in as much as it deals with treaties, see the decision of the Japanese Supreme Court of 16 December 1959 in *Shigeru Sakata et al.*, in JAIL, 4 (1960), at 103 ff.

Article 28(1) of the 1975 Greek Constitution states that 'The generally recognized rules of international law as well as international conventions as of the time they are sanctioned by law and become operative according to the conditions therein shall be an integral part of domestic Greek law and shall prevail over any contrary provision of law. The enforcement of international law and international conventions to aliens always depends on the condition of reciprocity'.

As for Uzbekistan, see the Preamble and Article 17 of the Constitution ('Recognizing priority of the generally accepted norms of international law'). However, with a striking inconsistency Article 15 provides for the 'absolute supremacy' of the laws of the Republic of Uzbekistan.

See also Article 6 of the Constitution of Turkmenistan and Article 8 of the Constitution of Belarus.

28. Section 232 of the South African Constitution provides that 'Customary international law is law of the Republic unless it is inconsistent with the Constitution or an act of Parliament'.

29. See AILC, ii, at 427. See also 420–2.

30. For *Fujii* see ILR, 19 (1952), at 312. It is also available at http://login.findlaw.com/sinpts/callaw destca/col2d/38/718.html.

31. For the *Lockheed* case see Order of 6 February 1979, in *Giurisprudenza costituzionale*, Supp. 24 (1979), at 94–5.

32. Judgment of 14 April 1981, in NYIL (1982), at 367, no. 150.

33. See RGDIP (1995), at 1015.

34. See the decision of the Italian Court of Cassation of 8 May 1989 (*Polo Castro* case), RDI, 73 (1990), at 1042–4.

35. Decision of 30 October 1998, in *Rev. fr. droit admn.* (1998), 1081–90. See also JDI (1999), at 675 ff.

36. Decision no. 450 of 2 June 2000, in http:/www.courdecassation.fr/agenda/arrets/99–60274.htm.

37. Decision of 22 January 1999, no. 98–408 DC, at http://www.conseil-constitutionnel.fr.

38. 'La République peut reconnaître la juridiction de la Cour pénale internationale dans les conditions prévues par le traité signé le 18 Juillet 1998' (Constitutional law of 8 July 1999, No. 99–568, at http://www.legifrance.gouv.fr, or in *Journal Officiel, Lois et Décrets*, 9 July 1999, No. 157, at 10175.)

39. See Article 28(1) of the 1975 Greek Constitution, cited at note 27.

40. Article 96(1) of the Spanish Constitution provides as follows: 'Validly concluded international treaties once officially published in Spain, shall constitute part of the internal legal order. Their provisions may only be abrogated, modified or suspended in the manner provided for in the treaties themselves or in accordance with general norms of international law.'

41. Article 91(3) of the 1983 Constitution of the Netherlands provides that 'Any provisions of a treaty that conflict with the Constitution or which lead to conflicts with it may be approved by the Chambers of the States General only if at least two-thirds of the votes cast are in favour'. Article 94 states that 'Statutory regulations in force within the Kingdom shall not be applicable if such application is in conflict with provisions of treaties that are binding on all persons or of resolutions by international institutions'. This provision has been construed as entailing that treaty provisions, if self-executing, take precedence over both laws and the Constitution (E. A. Alkema, 'Foreign Relations in the 1983 Dutch Constitution', NILR, 31 (1984), at 320).

42. On constitutional courts and international law see, for instance, W. Czaplinsky, 'International Law and Polish Municipal Law: Recent Jurisprudence of the Polish Supreme Judicial Organs', in ZaöRV, 53 (1993–II), at 871–81; G. M. Danilenko, 'The New Russian Constitution and International Law', AJIL, 88 (1994), at 460–4; V. S. Vereshchetin, 'New Constitutions and the Old Problem of the Relationship between International Law and National Law', EJIL, 7 (1996), at 34–7; J. Henderson, 'Reference to International Law in Decided Cases of the First Russian Constitutional Court, in R. Müllerson, M. Fitzmaurice, and M. Andenas, eds., *Constitutional Reform and International Law in Central and Eastern Europe* (The Hague and Boston: Kluwer Law International, 1998), at 59 ff.; G. M. Danilenko, 'Implementation of International Law in CIS States: Theory and Practice', EJIL, 10 (1999), at 56–63.

43. Judgment of 16 July 1954, no. 2539, in *Foro italiano*, 1 (1955), at 41.

44. See text in AILC, 2nd Series, vol. 12, at 386. The Court went on to say: 'This court acknowledges the validity of the government's position that Congress has the power to enact statutes abrogating prior treaties or international obligations entered into by the United States . . . However, unless this power is clearly and unequivocally exercised, this court is under a duty to interpret statutes in a manner consonant with existing treaty obligations. This is a rule of statutory construction sustained by an unbroken line of authority for over a century and a half' (ibid., at 387).

45. It would seem that this also applies to the holding of the Constitutional Court of Hungary, whereby 'The Constitution and domestic regulations are to be interpreted in such a way, that generally accepted rules of international law shall be effective' (judgment of 13 October 1993, in *East European Constitutional Review* 2–3 (1993–4), at 10).

For a list of US cases see those cited in the aforementioned decision in *US* v. *Palestine Liberation Organization* (cit. above, note 44), at 386–7.

In 1996 in the *AZAPO* case the South African Constitutional Court stated among other things that ' . . . the lawmakers of the Constitution should not lightly be presumed to authorize any law which might constitute a breach of the obligations of the State in terms of international law' (1996 (4) SA 671 (CC), at 688, para. 28).

46. For the Italian authors see: C. Fabozzi, *L'attuazione dei trattati internazionali mediante ordine di esecuzione* (Milan: Giuffré, 1961), at 163–5; R. Quadri, *Diritto internazionale pubblico*, 5th edn. (Naples: Liguori, 1968), at 78–9; B. Conforti, *Diritto internazionale*, 5th edn. (Naples: Editoriale Scientifica, 1997), at 316.

The Russian publicist is E. T. Usenko, 'Theoretical Problems in the Relation of International Law to Municipal Law', *Soviet Yearbook of International Law*, 1977, at 87.

47. See the Belgian Judgment of 27 May 1971. See text translated into English in *Common Market Law Reports* (1972), at 330 ff. Original French in *Pasicrisie belge* (1971), at 886 ff.

48. See the decision of 19 January 1993, no. 10. The Court held that the provisions implementing a number of international treaties ratified by Italy, and concerning a fundamental right of the accused (the right to be informed promptly and in detail in a language which he understands of the nature and cause of the criminal charge against him) were in force in Italy, not having been repealed by subsequent Italian legislation, because they were 'rules deriving from a source based on an atypical [lawmaking] competence, as such not susceptible of being repealed or amended by means of ordinary legislation' (in RDI, 76 (1993), at 261).

49. Decision of 24 July 2000, rec. 408/1999, in *El Derecho, Jurisprudencia* (2000/25122), at 3–4, legal grounds 6 through 9.

50. Article 92 of the 1978 Spanish Constitution provides as follows: 'By means of an organic law (*ley organica*), authorization may be granted for the conclusion of treaties which attribute to an international organization or institution the exercise of competences derived from the Constitution. It is the responsibility of the *Cortes Generales* [the Spanish Parliament] or the Government, depending on the cases, to guarantee compliance with these treaties and the resolutions emanating from the international or supranational organizations which have been entitled by this cession.'

In an opinion (*dictamen*) of 9 September 1993, no. 984/93, the Council of State (*Consejo de Estado*) held that 'by virtue of Article 96.1 of the Constitution [for the text of this provision, see above, note 40], resolutions of those international organizations of which Spain is a member can be assimilated to treaties made by Spain; as a consequence these resolutions are automatically incorporated into our internal legal system as soon as they have been perfected at the international level and are published in Spain's Official Journal (*Boletín Oficial del Estado*). However, publication in the Official Journal of the relevant Organization may suffice whenever this is provided for in the treaty establishing the Organization' (in Consejo de Estado, *Recopilación de Doctrina Legal 1993* (Madrid: Boletín Oficial del Estado, 1994), at 1–5).

In the Spanish practice, binding resolutions of the Security Council (for example those on Iraq and the former Yugoslavia) have been published in the Official Journal, thus becoming automatically binding within the Spanish legal system.

51. By a decision of 8 November 1963 the Court of Cassation (Criminal Section) assimilated Chapter V of Annex 9 adopted by the Governing Body of ICAO to the treaty establishing the Organization, with the obvious consequence that it was considered sufficient for those annexes or regulations to be published in the *Journal Officiel* for them to be binding within the French legal system (in *Bulletin Crim.*, 1963, n. 315, at 667–71).

By a decision of 30 December 1977 the Constitutional Council (*Conseil constitutionnel*) held that the binding force in France of EC regulations was the direct consequence of international commitments previously taken by France (in *Recueil des décisions du Conseil constitutionnel* (1977), at 44 and 46).

52. The first category of EC directives covers cases where, the interpretation of national legislation being uncertain, such legislation must be construed in keeping with Community directives. The second category embraces directives that specify or clarify an obligation already laid down in the EC treaties, or opts between two possible interpretations of a treaty's provisions. The third category encompasses directives which impose on States obligations not necessarily involving the passing of ad hoc implementing legislation. In this case the directive may be relied upon before national courts, by individuals against a member State, as far as its general legal effects are concerned. See B. Conforti, *Diritto internazionale*, cit. above, note 46, at 325–9.

53. See Article 96(1) of the 1978 Constitution of Spain, cited at note 40.

Article 92 of the Dutch Constitution (enacted in 1953, revised in 1956, and updated in 1983) provides: 'Legislative, executive and judicial powers may be conferred on international institutions by or pursuant to a treaty, subject, where necessary, to the provisions of Article 91 paragraph 3 [which provides that treaties conflicting with the Constitution should be approved by Parliament by a two-thirds majority].' Article 93 provides as follows: 'Provisions of treaties and of resolutions by international institutions, which may be binding on all persons by virtue of their contents, shall become binding after they have been published.' Article 94 stipulates that 'Statutory regulations in force within the Kingdom shall not be applicable if such application is in conflict with provisions of treaties that are binding on all persons or of resolutions by international institutions'.

Article 28(2) of the Greek Constitution provides that 'with a view to meeting important national interests and promoting co-operation with other States, it is possible to confer, by treaty or international agreement, competences provided for in the Constitution on bodies of international organizations'.

54. Article 94 provides as follows:

1. The giving of the consent of the State to obligate itself

to something by means of treaties or agreements shall require prior authorization of the *Cortes Generales* in the following cases:

  (a) Treaties of a political nature.

  (b) Treaties or agreements of a military nature.

  (c) Treaties or agreements which affect the territorial integrity of the State or the fundamental rights and duties established in Title I.

  (d) Treaties or agreements which imply important obligations for the public treasury.

  (e) Treaties or agreements which involve modification or repeal of some law or require legislative measures for their execution.

2. The Congress and the Senate shall be immediately informed of the conclusion of the treaties or agreements.

55. See for instance opinion (*dictamen*) no. 650/95 of 30 March 1995, in Consejo de Estado, *Recopilación de Doctrina Legal 1995* (Madrid: Boletín Oficial del Estado, 1996), at 10–11; opinion no. 288/95 of 16 March 1995, ibid., at 13–16; opinion no. 3.777/96 of 14 November 1996, *Recopilación etc. 1996*, at 11.

56. See for instance opinion no. 2.479/94 of 19 January 1995, *Recopilación etc. 1995*, ibid., at 12–13; opinion no. 209/95 of 23 February 1995, ibid., at 32–4; opinion no. 2.484/95 of 14 December 1995, ibid., at 38–9; opinion no. 318/97, in *Recopilación etc. 1997*, at 15–16.

57. See for example opinion no. 3.393/98 of 10 September 1998, in *Recopilación etc. 1998*, at 18–20.

58. See for instance opinion no. 3.306/97 of 10 July 1997, in *Recopilación etc. 1997*, at 1–2; opinion no. 449/97 of 6 February 1997, ibid., at 7–9; opinion no. 1.301/97 of 10 April 1997, ibid., at 10–11; opinion no. 6.351/97 of 5 February 1998 in *Recopilación etc. 1998*, at 27–9.

59. See for instance opinion no. 336/97 of 6 February 1997, in *Recopilación etc. 1997*, at 3; opinion no. 201/98 of 5 February 1998, in *Recopilación etc. 1998*, at 11–14.

60. See for instance opinion no. 961/95 of 15 June 1995, in *Recopilación etc. 1995*, at 35–36; opinion no. 1.371/98 of 23 April 1998, in *Recopilación etc. 1998*, at 5–6; opinion no. 3.690/98 of 1 October 1998, ibid., at 6–8; opinion no. 477/98 of 26 February 1998, ibid., at 14–16.

61. See for instance opinion no. 3.421/96 of 24 October 1996, in *Recopilación etc. 1996*, at 1–4; opinion no. 1.365/96 of 11 April 1996, ibid., at 6–8 (about an exchange of diplomatic notes for the provisional application of a treaty with Portugal); opinion no. 5.572/97 of 20 November 1997, in *Recopilación etc. 1997*, at 13–15.

In contrast, in its opinion no. 4.532/98 of 17 December 1998 the Council of State stated that the making of a specific agreement providing for the provisional application of a Convention of 1995 among member States of the European Union required parliamentary authorization: see *Recopilación etc. 1998*, at 8–11.

Chapter 9

1. Thus, in some cases, e.g. *Caire* (RIAA, v, 529–31) decided in 1929, the France-Mexico Claims Commission upheld the 'doctrine of the objective responsibility of the State'. In the *Union Bridge Company* case a UK-US Arbitral Tribunal held in 1924 that the UK was responsible for the appropriation, during the Boer War (1899–1902) of US neutral property in South Africa, even if the British officer who had appropriated that property had mistakenly believed that it was not neutral. The Tribunal held that the international liability of the UK was 'not affected either by the fact that he [the British officer] did so under a mistake as to the character and ownership of the material or that it was a time of pressure and confusion caused by war, or by the fact, which, on the evidence, must be admitted, that there was no intention on the part of the British authorities to appropriate the material in question' (RIAA, vi, at 141). Also in other cases international courts held that a State was responsible even if its officials had committed *bona fide* errors in judgement. See e.g. the *Wanderer* case (RIAA, vi, 68–77), the *McLean* case (ibid., 82–5) as well as *Kling* (RIAA, iv, 578–81).

By contrast, in other cases, such as *Lighthouses*, decided in 1956 by the PCA (RIAA, xii, at 217–18; ILR 23, at 659), the State was not held responsible among other things because the event ('the disastrous effects' of a fire that had destroyed the temporary premises and the stores of a French firm evicted by the Greek authorities) was not 'foreseeable'. And in their dissenting opinions in the *Corfu Channel* case Judges Krylov (ICJ Reports (1949), at 71–2) and Ecer (ibid., at 127–8) explicitly upheld the doctrine of fault.

2. ICJ, Advisory Opinion of 29 April 1999, in Reports 1999, at 87, para. 62.

3. RIAA, 9, at 468.

4. RIAA, 5, at 534–8, in particular 536.

5. RIAA, 4, at 274 (the USA was held responsible for the action of the authorities of the State of Texas against a Mexican national).

6. RIAA, 5, at 530. See also Ann. Dig., 5 (1929–30), no. 91.

7. RIAA, 4, at 116.

8. Ibid., at 173–90, in particular 174–5, 177.

9. Still unreported. Although the issue of whether Qaddafi was de facto or *de jure* Head of State had been discussed in the pleadings before the court, in its decision the Court of Appeals did not go into it. It took it for granted that he was the Head of State of Libya.

10. See Press release of the French Ministry of Foreign Affairs, 20 October 2000 (www.doc.diplomatie.fr). See also *International Herald Tribune*, 21 October 2000, at 2.

On 13 March 2001 the Court of Cassation overturned the ruling by the Court of Appeals, without however contesting that Qaddafi was in effect the Head of State of Libya. See on this decision S. Zappalà, 'Do Heads of State in office enjoy immunity from jurisdiction for international crimes? The Qadhafi case before the French *Cour de Cassation*', in EJIL, 12 (2001), forthcoming.

11. ICJ Reports (1986), at 45 ff., paras 75–86, 93–115.

12 See the still unreported judgment of 21 February 2001, in *X.*, 3 StR 372/00, at 10–11 of the typescript.

13. See Judgment of 15 July 1999, paras 98–145.

14. ICJ Reports (1980), at 30, para. 58.

15. Ibid., at 30–4, paras 59–68.

16. Ibid., at 36, para. 74.

17. See ILC, Fiftieth Session (1998), A/CN.4/490/Add.5, paras 283–4.

18. D. Anzilotti, *Teoria generale della responsabilità dello Stato nel diritto internazionale* (Florence: Lumache, 1902), reprinted in *Scritti di diritto internazionale pubblico* (Padua: Cedam, 1956), ii, at 89, and *Corso*, at 425.

19. See R. Ago's Third Report on State Responsibility, YILC (1971), II, First Part, paras 73–4.

20. See YILC (1973), II, at 183, para. 12.

21. See *Yuille, Shotridge and Co.* (UK and Portugal, judgment of 21 October 1861, in La Pradelle and Politis, ii, at 109); *Alabama* (USA and UK, judgment of 14 September 1872, ibid., at 880–8, 893, 889); PCIJ, *Wimbledon* case (Series A, no. 1, at 32); *Responsabilité de l'Allemagne* (RIAA, ii, at 1068–77). See also *Eagle Star* (RIAA, v, at 141–2).

22. Gill, a British national working at a power plant in Mexico, was forced to flee in night attire with his family when revolutionary forces attacked the power plant. During the attack a considerable amount of personal property was taken or destroyed by the revolutionary forces. The UK-Mexico Claims Commission held that Mexico was responsible for its failure to suppress or punish the attack. However, the Commission stated that 'there may be a number of cases, in which absence of action is not due to negligence or omission but to the impossibility of taking immediate and decisive measures, in which every Government may temporarily find themselves, when confronted with a situation of a very sudden nature . . . authorities cannot be blamed for omission or negligence, when the action taken by them has not resulted in the *entire* suppression of the insurrections, risings, riots or acts of brigandage, or has not led to the punishment of *all* the individuals responsible. In those cases no responsibility will be admitted' (RIAA, v, at 159).

23. PCIJ, *Serbian Loans* case, Series A, nos 20–1, at 39–40.

24. RIAA, xx, at 252–3, paras 76–7.

25. See YILC (1979), II, First Part, at 60, para. 131.

26. La Pradelle and Politis, i, at 704–5.

27. See YILC (1979), II, First Part, at 60, para. 130.

28. See RIAA, xx, 253–5, paras 78–9.

29. Ibid., 256–9, paras 83–8.

30. See the Opinion of Judge Pinkney in Moore, *International Adjudications*, iv, at 398–400. See also a summary of the case in YILC (1980), II, First Part, at 34, para. 48.

31. YILC (1980), II, at 28.

32. See text in ILM 9 (1970), at 25.

33. ICJ Reports (1997), paras 51–2, 56–7. See also paras 58–9.

34. *Spanish Zone of Morocco*, RIAA, ii, at 722–7.

35. *Martini* case, RIAA, ii, at 1002.

36. *The Palmarejo and Mexican Gold Fields Ltd* (UK-Mexican Claims Commission), RIAA, v, at 301–2; *Compagnie générale des asphalts de France*, RIAA, ix, at 389–98. The Umpire stated the following: 'The umpire is not disregardful of the claim of the honourable Commissioner for Venezuela that, since the duties were not, in fact, again paid, the claimant company has suffered no loss, and hence, in equity, has no rightful demand for their repayment; but it is the opinion of the umpire that an unjustifiable act is not made just because, perchance, there were not evil results which might well have followed. The claimant Government has a right to insist that its sovereignty over its own soil shall be respected and that its subject shall be restored to his original right before consequent results shall be discussed. The umpire having found that the requirement of import duties before clearance was an unlawful exaction and a wrongful assumption of Venezuelan sovereignty on British soil, it is just and right, and therefore justice and equity [sic] that these duties be restored to the claimant company' (at 398).

37. See http://www.fas.org/irp/news/1998/02/980227_mossadf.htm.

38. See text of the letter of the US ambassador in *International Herald Tribune*, 12 April 2001, at 8 ('We are very sorry the entering of China's airspace and the landing did not have verbal clearance'). The Chinese government had insisted that the Chinese authority had heard no distress calls or requests for permission to enter Chinese airspace and so the landing was illegal (see *International Herald Tribune*, 14–15 April 2001, at 1 and 41).

39. RIAA, xi, at 457–61 and 471–7.

40. See ICJ Reports (1949), at 35, and ILR, 82, at 577, respectively.

41. RIAA, xxviii, at 443, para. 81. See also at 444–6 (paras 84–98).

42. Article 19 paragraphs 2 and 3 of the previous Draft provided that:

'2. An internationally wrongful act which results from the breach by a State of an international obligation so essential for the protection of fundamental interests of the international community that its breach is recognized as a crime by that community as a whole constitutes an international crime.

3. Subject to paragraph 2, and on the basis of the rules of international law in force, an international crime may result, *inter alia*, from:

(a) a serious breach of an international obligation of essential importance for the maintenance of international peace and security, such as that prohibiting aggression;

(b) a serious breach of an international obligation of essential importance for safeguarding the right of self-determination of peoples, such as that prohibiting the establishment or maintenance by force of colonial domination;

(c) a serious breach on a widespread scale of an international obligation of essential importance for safeguarding the human being, such as those prohibiting slavery, genocide and apartheid;

(d) a serious breach of an international obligation of essential importance for the safeguarding and preservation of the human environment, such as those prohibiting massive pollution of the atmosphere or the seas'.

43. For the notion of 'integral obligations' see G. Fitzmaurice, in *Second Report on the Law of Treaties*, in YILC (1957), II, at 54, para. 126 (speaking of treaties on disarmament and control of armaments, the distinguished international lawyer pointed out that 'unless the contrary is expressly provided by the treaty, the obligation of each party . . . is necessarily dependent on a corresponding performance of the same thing by all the other parties, since it is of the essence of such a treaty that the undertaking of each party is given in return for a similar undertaking by the others. Particular breaches by individual parties would therefore justify corresponding particular non-observances by the others: and a general, or really fundamental breach by one party, amounting to a repudiation, would ensure for all practical purposes an end to the treaty').

See also J. Crawford, *Third Report on State Responsibility*, A/CN.4/507, 10 March 2000, paras 91 and 106, as well as the *Statement* to the ILC by the Chairman of the 2000 ILC Drafting Committee, G. Gaja, ILC Draft (2000), at 31–2.

For the denomination 'interdependent' obligations see B. Simma, 'The Work of the International law Commission at its 52nd Session (2000)', forthcoming (Fitzmaurice had already propounded the notion of 'interdependence of obligations', *Second Report*, at 54, n. 73).

44. Most, if not all, treaties on disarmament or arms control include a clause providing for withdrawal. As an example of these clauses Article X(1) of the 1968 Treaty on the Non-Proliferation of Nuclear Weapons can be mentioned: 'Each party shall in exercising its national sovereignty have the right to withdraw from the Treaty if it decides that extraordinary events, related to the subject matter of this Treaty, have jeopardized the supreme interests of its country. It shall give notice of such withdrawal to all other Parties to the Treaty and to the UN Security Council three months in advance. Such notice shall include a statement of the extraordinary events it regards as having jeopardized its supreme interests.' It is submitted that this clause, when inserted in treaties providing for a collective monitoring and sanctioning mechanism in case of breach by one of the contracting parties, should be strictly construed and only made applicable to cases where the non-compliance with the treaty, established by the collective monitoring body, is very serious, and the responsible State does not discontinue it in spite of the findings and possible sanctions of the collective body. This proposition applies to such treaties as the 1967 Tlatelolco Treaty Banning Nuclear Weapons in Latin America, the 1984 Convention on the Prohibition of the Development, Production and Stockpiling of Bacteriological (Biological) and Toxin Weapons and on Their Destruction, and the 1993 Convention on the Development, Production, Stockpiling and Use of Chemical Weapons and on Their Destruction.

45. For the contrary view, see *Third Report on State Responsibility*, cit. above, note 43, at para. 106, n. 195.

46. See *Bulletin of the European Communities*, 1980, no. 4, 20–6, at 25.

47. Statement of the Belgian delegate in the SC:

UN doc. S/PV.2472, 6 September 1983, at 11. See also the statement of Sweden (ibid., 2471, at 41).

48. For Canada, see ILM (1983), at 1199–1200; for the USA see *Dept. of State Bulletin*, October 1983, at 1 et seq. For Japan see ILM (1983), at 1201–3.

49. See in particular J.I. Charney, 'Third State Remedies in International Law', *Michigan Journal of International Law*, 10 (1989), 57–101; J. A. Frowein, 'Reactions by Not Directly Affected States to Breaches of Public International Law', HR, 248 (1994-IV), 416–22.

50. Judgment of 10 December 1998, para. 142.

51. Judgment of 14 January 2000, paras 517–18.

52. ICJ Reports (1986), at 114, para. 220.

53. UN Doc. A/SPC/35/SR.27, para. 8.

54. Judgment of 29 October 1997, para. 26.

55. Ibid., para. 36.

56. See M. Veuthey, 'Pour une politique humanitaire', *Mélanges Pictet* (Geneva and The Hague: M. Nijhoff Publishers, 1984), at 1002.

57. See *European Communities Bulletin*, 1984, no. 2, at 95, no. 3, at 80.

58. See Jordan National Report on State Practice, 1998 (submitted to the ICRC in 1999), ch. 6.2.

59. Written reply to a parliamentary question, in *Bundestag*, doc. 13/718, 13th Legislative Period, 9 March 1995 (http://dip.bundestag.de/btd/13/007/1300718.asc, at 3, para. 6).

60. See, for example, SC res. 681 (1990), paras 5 and 6; GA resolutions 32 /91, of 13 December 1977, para. A(4), and 39/95 of 14 December 1984, paras B(4) and C(9). See also the Secretary-General's report of 21 January 1988, UN Doc S/19443, para. 27.

61. Council of Europe, Committee of Ministers, declaration of 18 February 1993, para. 4 (http://cm.coe.int/ta/decl/71993/93decl.htm).

Chapter 10

1. See the report of the Commission of Inquiry in J. B. Scott, *The Hague Court Reports*, First Series (New York, 1916), at 404–13 and AJIL, 2 (1907), at 929. See also A. Mandelstam, 'La commission internationale d'enquête sur l'incident de la Mer du Nord', RGDIP (1905), at 161–90, 350–415.

2. See J. B. Scott, above, note 1, vol. 7, at 413, 614.

3. See ibid., Second Series (New York, 1932), at 135 as well as AJIL, 16 (1922), at 485–92.

4. Martens' statement is quoted in League of Nations, Permanent Court of International Justice, *Advisory Committee of Jurists* (1922), at 22 and 695.

5. Conférence de La Haye, *Actes et Documents* (The Hague, 1907), ii, at 235. See also *Advisory Committee of Jurists* (cit. above, note 4), at 695.

6. See the final Report of the Committee of Jurists, in *Advisory Committee of Jurists* (cit. above, note 4), at 695.

7. See ibid., at 696.

8. PCIJ, Series A, no. 5, at 27–8.

9. ICJ Reports (1951), at 78.

10. A notable exception is recourse to this method by the USA and Chile in 1992–3, in the *Letelier and Moffit* case: these two persons had been assassinated in Washington DC in 1976, allegedly by a Chilean intelligence officer acting under instructions of the central Chilean authorities. Chile denied responsibility but was prepared to make an *ex gratia* payment equivalent to the amount it would have paid had its responsibility been established. The Inquiry Commission was thus simply called upon to determine the quantum of the *ex gratia* payment. See ILM, 30 (1992), at 422; ILM, 31 (1993), at 1.

11. See J. Collier and V. Lowe, *The Settlement of Disputes in International Law* (Oxford: Oxford University Press, 1999), at 26–7.

12. See RGDIP (1985), 854–9.

13. See http://www.un.org/News/Press/docs/1999/19990610.SC6686.html.

14. PCIJ, Series A, no. 5, at 27–8.

15. ICJ Reports (1951), at 78.

16. See http://www.worldbank.org/icsid/bluefintuna/main.htm.

Chapter 11

1. On the *Amelia Island* case see Moore, *Digest*, ii, 406–8; *Right to Protect Citizens in Foreign Countries*, at 51–2.

2. See Moore, *Digest*, ii, 402–5; *Right to Protect Citizens in Foreign Countries*, at 52–3.

3. On the *Caroline* case see Moore, *Digest*, ii, at 409–14; Lord McNair, *International Law Opinions* (Cambridge: Cambridge University Press, 1956), ii, at 221–30; R. Jennings, 'The *Caroline* and *McLeod* cases', AJIL, 23 (1938), at 82–99.

4. M. Offutt, *The Protection of Citizens Abroad by the Armed Forces of the United States* (Baltimore: Johns Hopkins University Press, 1928), at 12 ff.

5. For the text of the arbitral award see RIAA, ii, at 1013–33. The part on reprisals is at 1026–9.

6. See text in H. Wehberg, *Institut de Droit International—Tableau général des résolutions (1873–1956)* (Basle: Editions juridiques et sociologiques S.A., 1957), 167–70.

7. RIAA, ii, at 417.

8. RIAA, xxviii, at 443, para. 81.

9. ICJ Reports (1986), paras 176 and 195.

10. ICJ Reports (1996), paras 37–50, in particular 42 and 46.

11. For this practice see D. Bowett, 'Reprisals Involving Recourse to Armed Force', AJIL, 66 (1972), at 7, n. 23.

12. See the practice carefully reported and perceptively commented upon by R. Barsotti, 'Armed Reprisals', in A. Cassese, ed., *The Current Legal Regulation of the Use of Force* (Dordrecht, Boston, and Lancaster: Martinus Nijhoff Publishers, 1986) at 79–110.

13. See ICJ Reports (1980), at 38–42 (paras 80–9).

14. See C. Dominicé, 'Représailles et droit diplomatique', in *Festschrift für Hans Huber* (Bern: Stämpfli, 1981), 541–52; E. Zoller, *Peacetime Unilateral Remedies: An Analysis of Countermeasures* (Dobbs Ferry, New York: Transnational Publishers, 1984), 84–9; L.-A. Sicilianos, *Les réactions décentralisées à l'illicite—Des contre-mesures à la légitime défense* (Paris: Librairie générale de droit et jurisprudence, 1990), 344–51; C. Focarelli, *Le contromisure nel diritto internazionale* (Milan: Giuffré, 1994), at 97–110.

15. On this point see in particular C. Focarelli, *Le contromisure*, cit. above, note 14, at 516–22, and the apt remarks on the significance of the ICJ dictum in *US Diplomatic and Consular Staff in Tehran* by B. Conforti, *International Law and the Role of Domestic Legal Systems* (Dordrecht, Boston, and London: M. Nijhoff, 1993), at 184, n. 53.

16. See RIAA, ii, at 1026–8.

17. RIAA, xviii, at 443, para. 83.

18. ICJ Reports (1997), at para. 85.

19. See Tokyo Higher Court, decision of 1953 [no more details about the date are provided] in *Anglo-Iranian Oil Co. v. Idemitsu Kosan Kabushiki Kaisha* (*Nissho Maru* case), in ILR, 20 (1953), at 312–16; Hamburg Court, decision of 22 January 1973, *Chilean Copper Nationalization* case, in ILM, 12 (1973), at 274. The Court felt that the claimants *as individuals* were not entitled to claim damages on the plane of international law, nor were they able, as a result of the *doctrine of sovereign immunity*, to pursue a claim on the plane of municipal law, in the USA.

20. See text in Friedman, ii, at 1699–1700.

21. Court of Cassation, decision of 8 December 1954 in *Bulletin des arrêts de la Cour de Cassation, Chambres Civiles* (1954), at 298.

22. Hague District Court, 20 February 1962, ILR, 33 (1962), at 30.

23. Aden Supreme Court, 9 January 1953, *Rose Mary* case, ILR, 20 (1953), at 317.

24. Venice Court, decision of 11 March 1953, *Miriella* case, ILR, 22 (1955), at 23.

25. 376 US 398 (1964), ILM, 3 (1964), at 394.

26. 748 F. 2nd 790 (2nd Cir. 1984).

27. See ILM, 30 (1992), at 422; ILM, 31 (1993), at 1.

28. See, in particular, B. Conforti, *The Law and Practice of the United Nations* (The Hague, London, and Boston: Kluwer Law International, 2000), at 185–94.

29. Ibid., at 214–17.

30. General Comment, para. 3.

31. Ibid., para. 5.

32. Ibid., para. 16.

33. Ibid., para. 10.

34. See also, for the relevant references, L.F. Damrosch, 'Enforcing International Law Through Non-Forcible Measures', HR, 269 (1977), 91–9.

Chapter 12

1. Under Article 101 of the 1982 Convention on the Law of the Sea, which can be deemed to reflect and codify customary international law, piracy consists of any of the following acts:

'(a) any illegal acts of violence, detention or any act of depredation, committed for private ends by the crew or passengers of a private ship or private aircraft and directed: (i) on the high seas, against another ship or aircraft, or against persons or property on board such ship or aircraft; (ii) against a ship, aircraft, persons or property in a place outside the jurisdiction of any State;

(b) any act of voluntary participation in the operation of a ship or of an aircraft with knowledge of facts making it a pirate ship or aircraft;

(c) any act of inciting or of intentionally facilitating an act described in subparagraph (a) or (b).'

2. See US Department of the Army, *The Law of Land Warfare*, July 1956, para. 499 ('The term "war crime" is the technical expression for a violation of the law of war by any person or person, military or civilian. Every violation of the law of war is a war crime').

3. For the British Manual see The War Office, *The Law of War on Land* (being Part III of the Manual of

Military Law) (London, 1958), para. 624 (this definition is very similar to that contained in the US Military Manual).

4. See ICTY, *Tadić* case, Judgment of 2 October 1995, para. 94. The Tribunal went on to give an example of a non-serious violation: 'the fact of a combatant simply appropriating a loaf of bread in an occupied village' would not amount to such a breach, 'although it may be regarded as falling foul of the basic principle laid down in Article 46(1) of the [1907] Hague Regulations [on Land Warfare] (and the corresponding rule of customary international law) whereby "private property must be respected" by any army occupying an enemy territory'.

5. Judgment of 3 March 2000, at para. 176.

6. See ICTY, *Tadić*, Judgment of 2 October 1995, paras 95–137. The ICTY Appeals Chamber stated the following:

'A State-sovereignty-oriented approach has been gradually supplanted by a human-being-oriented approach. Gradually the maxim of Roman law *hominum causa omne jus constitutum est* (all law is created for the benefit of human beings) has gained a firm foothold in the international community as well. It follows that in the area of armed conflict the distinction between interstate wars and civil wars is losing its value as far as human beings are concerned. Why protect civilians from belligerent violence, or ban rape, torture or the wanton destruction of hospitals, churches, museums or private property, as well as proscribe weapons causing unnecessary suffering when two sovereign States are engaged in war, and yet refrain from enacting the same bans or providing the same protection when armed violence has erupted "only" within the territory of a sovereign State? If international law, while of course duly safeguarding the legitimate interests of states, must gradually turn to the protection of human beings, it is only natural that the aforementioned dichotomy [belligerency–insurgency] should gradually lose its weight' (ibid., para. 97).

7. See ICTY, Judgment of 2 October 1995, para. 83. Judge G. Abi-Saab held in his Separate Opinion (ibid., at 4–6) that the customary rule referred to above, in the text, had already crystallised.

8. For instance, citizens of the Allies (such as French Jews under the Vichy regime (1940–4)); nationals of States not formally under German occupation and, therefore, not protected by the international rules safeguarding the civilian population of occupied territories: this applied to Austria, annexed by Germany in 1938, and Czechoslovakia (following the Munich Treaty in 1938, the Sudeten territory was annexed by Germany, and the rest of the country became the so-called Protectorate of Bohemia and Moravia, in 1939). The Germans also harassed and murdered stateless Jews and gypsies.

9. See the statements made on 2 February 1945, at the Malta Conference, by the British Foreign Secretary, Anthony Eden (in FRUS, *The Conferences at Malta and at Yalta, 1945*, at 507) and on 9 February 1945 at Yalta, by Prime Minister Churchill (ibid., at 849). See also the Memorandum of 4 September 1944 on 'Major War Criminals', by the Lord Chancellor, Sir John Simon, reproduced in B. F. Smith, *The American Road to Nuremberg—The Documentary Record, 1944–1945* (Stanford, Ca.: Hoover Institution Press and Stanford University, 1982), at 31–3 and notes at 227. Another member of the Cabinet, Clement Attlee, had proposed including industrialists and military leaders, plus von Papen and Seyss Inquart, in the shoot-on-sight list (see Smith, cit., at 227).

Later Churchill changed his mind (see his top secret telegram to Roosevelt of 22 October 1944, in FRUS, cit. at 400).

10. The Soviet position is reported by the British Foreign Secretary, Eden, in FRUS (cit. above, note 9), at 507 ('Mr. Eden said that when this [question] was discussed in October [1943, at the Moscow meeting of Foreign Ministers] Marshal Stalin had disagreed with our view favouring some summary executions and had said that some form of judicial procedure was necessary').

11. E. Schwelb, 'Crimes against Humanity', BYIL, 23 (1946), at 193–5, 206–7. The words cited in the text are at 207.

12. Sir Hartley Shawcross, in *Speeches of the Chief Prosecutors at the Close of the Case Against the Individual Defendants* (London: H.M. Stationery Office, Cmd. 6964, 1946), at 63.

13. See the Motion adopted by all Defence Counsel on 19 November 1945, in *Trial of the Major War Criminals Before the International Military Tribunal, Nuremberg 14 November 1945–1 October 1946* (Nuremberg, 1947), Nuremberg I, at 168–9.

14. Ibid.

15. Ibid.

16. Ibid., at 219.

17. See B. V. A. Röling and C. F. Ruter, eds., *The Tokyo Judgment*, vol. 2 (Amsterdam: Apa University Press, 1977), at 1048 ff.

18. The Peace Treaties with Italy, Romania, Hungary, Bulgaria, and Finland included terms providing for the punishment of these crimes.

19. See text in *Bull. crim.* (1993), no. 143, at 351–5. See also RGDIP (1994), at 471–4, with a comment by D. Alland (at 474–82).

20. In the *Enigster* case, the District Court of Tel Aviv rightly stated that 'a person who was himself persecuted and confined in the same camps as his

victims can, from the legal point of view, be guilty of a crime against humanity if he performs inhumane acts against his fellow prisoners. In contrast to a war criminal, the perpetrator of a crime against humanity does not have to be a man who identified himself with the persecuting regime or its evil intention' (in ILR, 18 (1951), at 542).

21. The *T. and K.* case was brought before the German Supreme Court in the British Occupied Zone (the accused had been charged with burning down a synagogue in 1938): see *Entscheidungen des Obersten Gerichtshofes für die Britische Zone* (Berlin and Hamburg: Walter de Gruyter and Co., 1950), i, at 198–202.

See also the *Finta* case, decisions by the Ontario Court of Appeal (Decision of 29 April 1992, 92 D.L.R. (4th), 1–153) and the Supreme Court of Canada (Decision of 24 March 1994; in (1994) 1 R.C.S., 701–877). The accused, a Hungarian national by birth who had in 1956 become a Canadian citizen by naturalization, had been charged with war crimes and crimes against humanity pursuant to Section 7 (#.71) of the Canadian Criminal Code as a result of his conduct in Hungary during the Second World War). In his capacity as captain of the Royal Hungarian Gendarmerie, which acted under the direct command of the German SS, he had allegedly been in charge of the 'de-jewification' of the Hungarian town of Szeged during the spring of 1944, more specifically the expropriation, concentration, and eventual deportation, primarily to Auschwitz and Birkenau, of 8,617 Hungarian Jews.

22. Also in relation to the frame of mind of the agent mention may be made of a number of cases brought before the German Supreme Court in the British Occupied Zone. Most of these cases concern denunciations by Germans to the police or military authorities of Jews or political opponents, with the consequence that the denounced persons were arrested and imprisoned or severely ill-treated; some such cases concern the burning of synagogues in 1938.

In the *Sch.* case, a person had in 1943 denounced his landlord to the Gestapo for his statements against Hitler; as a result the man had been arrested and sentenced to death. The Court held that for the conduct in question to amount to a crime against humanity, 'the awareness and the intent' of the agent to deliver the victim to 'despotic powers' was sufficient. In other words, the Court stressed the link between the single action of the accused and the entire system of abuse and violence inherent within the Nazi regime.

It is notable that the German Supreme Court held that the existence of a link or nexus between an offence against humanity and a general policy or a systematic practice of abuses did not necessarily imply that the author of the crime against humanity intended by his action to further or promote the violent and brutal practice of the regime within which the crime had been committed. Nor was it required that the agent should approve the final result of his action. In other words, the Court simply required an *objective link* between that act and the policy or practice as well as the awareness of such policy or practice; not necessarily the intention to commit the crime for the purpose of pursuing that policy or practice, or a state of mind which approved the outcome of the crime (decision of 26 October 1948, in *Entscheidungen* (cit. above, note 21), i, 122–6, at 124).

Both the *Barbie* case (decisions of 20 December 1985, in ILR, 78, at 137–41 and of 3 June 1988, in ILR 200, at 331–7) and the *Touvier* case (decisions of the Paris Court of Appeal of 13 April 1992 and the Court of Cassation, of 27 November 1992, in ILR, 100, at 337–64) both brought before the French Court of Cassation, confirm this approach.

On denunciations, it is fitting to mention a Decision of 16 November 1948 *(J. and R.* case) in which the German Supreme Court of the British Zone sought to satisfy itself if, in a case of denunciation of two persons to the police and their subsequent arrest and death in prison, the author of the denunciation possessed the requisite mental element. In this connection the Court noted that what was required for a crime against humanity was that the perpetrator intended to wrong and injure the victim in connection with the Nazi system of violence and tyranny. In other words, the perpetrator must know that, given the characteristics of the Nazi regime, the consequences of his action would be such as to negate the humanity of the victims. The Court went on to point out that the perpetrator could be held responsible, even if he had not thought of the grave consequences of his action, for 'he was obliged to consider them'. The perpetrator could only then be held unaccountable when he could not have predicted the inhuman consequences of his action because of the particular features of the specific case (see *Entscheidungen* (cit. above, note 21), i, at 167–71).

See, for instance, *E. et A.* case, Decision of 17 August 1948, ibid., at 61–2; *Sch.* case, Decision of 26 October 1948, ibid., at 125–6; *Z.* case, Decision of 15 February 1949, ibid., at 291; *Ehel, M.* case, Decision of 24 May 1949, ibid., ii, at 68–9.

That the perpetrator need not have a racist or inhuman frame of mind can be seen, for instance, in a case concerning the denunciation of a Jew by a member of the German SS, where the German Supreme Court in the British Occupied Zone held that for the *mens rea* in a crime against humanity to exist, it is not necessary that the agent acted 'out of inhumane convictions'. See *K.* case, Decision of 27 July 1948, ibid., i, at 50.

23. See *Law Reports of Trials of War Criminals*, vii, at 25; Friedman, ii, at 1520.

24. See *Law Reports of Trials of War Criminals*, xiii, at 17.

25. See ILR, 36: District Court, Judgment of 12 December 1961, at 5; Supreme Court, Judgment of 29 May 1962, at 277.

26. The *Jorgić* judgment of 26 September 1997, in BGH/STR 3 215/98. The Court found the defendant guilty of genocide and sentenced him to life imprisonment. The most significant part of the judgment is that relating to *mens rea*. The Court held that the intent to destroy a group 'means destroying the group as a social unit in its specificity, uniqueness and feeling of belonging: the biological-physical destruction of the group is not required' (Section III, para. 1). Also the Court's findings about the factual and psychological elements from which one can infer the existence of 'intent' are extremely interesting.

27. Judgment of 30 April 1999, in *Neue Zeitschrift für Strafrecht*, 8 (1999), at 396–404 (with a note by K. Ambos, ibid., at 404–6).

28. Both decisions are still unreported. For *Sokolović* see BGH 3 StR 372/00, and for *Kusljić* see BGH 3 StR 244/00.

29. Judgment of 2 September 1998, at 204–8.

30. Judgment of 21 May 1999, at 41–9.

31. Judgment of 14 December 1999, paras 78–83.

32. ICJ, Advisory Opinion on *Reservations to the Convention on the Prevention and Punishment of Genocide*, in ICJ Reports (1951), at 23.

33. For the Syrian proposal see UN doc. A/C6/234.

34. Judgment of 22 February 2001, paras 488–97.

35. Judgment of 2 September 1998, para. 593.

36. Judgment of 10 December 1998, para. 162.

37. House of Lords, judgments of 25 November 1998, 15 January 1999, and 24 March 1999 (see text of this third judgment in ILM 38 (1999), 581–663).

38. Judgment of 10 December 1998, para. 146.

39. *Aksoy v. Turkey*, judgment of 18 December 1996, para. 62.

40. *Selmouni v. France*, judgment of 28 July 1999, paras 96–105.

41. 630 F 2d 876 (2d Cir. 1990).

42. Judgment of 10 December 1998, at para. 146.

43. Judgment of 16 November 1998, at paras 455–74.

44. Judgment cit. above, note 35, para. 257.

45. Judgment cit. above, note 33, paras 483–97.

46. *Trials of the Major War Criminals*, cit. above, note 13, vol. I, at 186.

47. Article 16 of the Draft Code provides that: 'An individual, who, as leader or organizer, actively participates in or orders the planning, preparation, initiation or waging of aggression committed by a state, shall be responsible for a crime of aggression' (UN doc. A/51/332).

48. The SC has defined as 'acts of aggression' some actions or raids by South Africa and Israel. See, for example, resolution 573 of 4 October 1985 (on Israeli attacks on PLO targets), and resolution 577 of 6 December 1985 (on South Africa's attacks on Angola).

49. In *Nicaragua*, in addressing the issue of aggression defined in Article 3(g) of the Definition as the fact that a State 'sends or is substantially involved in sending into another State armed bands with the task of engaging in armed acts against the latter State of such gravity that they would normally be seen as aggression', the Court held that 'This description . . . may be taken to reflect customary international law. The Court sees no reason to deny that, in customary law, the prohibition of armed attacks may apply to the sending by a State of armed bands to the territory of another State, if such an operation, because of its scale and effects, would have been classified as an armed attack rather than as a mere frontier incident had it been carried out by regular armed forces' (ICJ Reports (1986), para. 195).

50. Convention to Prevent and Punish the Acts of Terrorism Taking the Form of Crimes Against Persons and Related Extortion that are of International Significance, of 2 February 1971, in D. J. Musch, ed., *Terrorism—Documents of International and Local Control*, 14 (Dobbs Ferry, New York: Oceana Publications Inc., 1997), at 523–8. The Convention was signed by 22 Latin or Central American countries, plus the USA and Sri Lanka.

51. Still unpublished, at 2–4 of the typescript.

52. Still unpublished, at 2–3 of the typescript.

53. See S. Zappalà, 'Do Heads of State in Office Enjoy Immunity from Jurisdiction for International Crimes? The Qadhafi Case before the French Cour de Cassation', EJIL, 12 (2001), forthcoming.

54. See text of the Belgian order in *Revue de droit pénal et de criminologie*, 79 (1999), at 278 et seq. of the Belgian order. As for the House of Lords' decision of 24 March 1999 on *Pinochet*, see ILM 38

(1999), 593–95 Lord Browne-Wilkinson), 621–27 (Lord Hope of Craighead), 651–2 (Lord Miller).

55. See ICJ, Arrest Warrant of 11 April 2000 (*Democratic Republic of the Congo* v. *Belgium*), verbatim records of the public sitting held on 21 November 2000, CR 2000/33, at http://www.icj.org, and the public sitting of 23 November 2000, CR 2000/35, ibid.

56. See ILR, 36, at 302–3.

57. C. Beccaria, *An Essay on Crimes and Punishments*, translated from the Italian, 4th edn. (London: F. Newberry, 1775), repr. (Brooklyn Village: Branden Press Inc., 1983), at 64. For the original text see C. Beccaria, *Dei delitti e delle pene*, a cura di F. Venturi (Turin: G. Einaudi, 1965), at 71–2.

58. See for instance Article 7 of the Hague Convention for the suppression of unlawful seizure of aircraft of 1970; Article 7 of the Montreal Convention on the suppression of unlawful acts against the safety of civil aviation (sabotage), of 1971; Article 8 of the 1979 Convention against the taking of hostages; Article 7 of the 1988 Convention for the suppression of unlawful acts against the safety of maritime navigation.

59. See for instance Article 36 of the New York Convention of 1961, Article 22 of the Vienna Convention of 1971, and Articles 4 and 6(9) of the New York Convention of 1988.

60. Article 65.1.2 of the Austrian Penal Code provides that Austrian criminal law may apply in respect of offences committed abroad, so long as the acts are also punishable in the place where they were performed, and provided that the offender, if a foreigner, is in Austria and may not be extradited to another State.

In Germany Article 6.9 of the Penal Code provides that German criminal law shall apply to offences committed by non-nationals abroad if such offences are made punishable by an international treaty binding upon Germany. Article 7(2)2 of the same Penal Code allows for prosecution of foreigners apprehended in Germany for crimes perpetrated abroad, if they are not extradited (either because a request for extradition was never made, or was refused, or because extradition is not feasible).

Articles 108 and 109 of the Swiss Military Penal Code provide for universal jurisdiction over violations of international humanitarian law and the laws and customs of war. Article 6 bis of the Swiss Criminal Code makes the Code applicable to crimes committed abroad (i) whenever Switzerland is obliged to pursue such crimes under an international treaty, and provided that (ii) the act is also punishable in the State where it was committed, and

(iii) the perpetrator is in Switzerland and is not extradited.

61. Article 23 of the 1985 Law on Judicial Power provides that Spanish courts have jurisdiction over crimes committed outside Spain when such crimes constitute genocide, terrorism, or other crimes which Spain is obliged to prosecute under international treaties.

62. Under a law of 16 June 1993 Belgian courts have jurisdiction over grave breaches of the 1949 Geneva Conventions and 1977 Protocols, no matter where such offences are committed, by whom or against whom they are committed, and whether or not the offender is on Belgian territory. A law of 3 February 1999 added genocide and crimes against humanity to the international crimes over which Belgian courts possess universal jurisdiction.

63. The Court noted that in its decision of 29 November 1999 the Court of Appeal (*Oberlandsgericht Düsseldorf*), following the traditional German case law, had held that a factual link was required by law (*legitimierender Anknüpfungspunkt*) for a German court to exercise jurisdiction over crimes committed abroad by foreigners (in the case at issue the offender was a Bosnian Serb accused of complicity in genocide perpetrated in Bosnia). The Court of Appeal had found this link in the fact that the accused had lived and worked in Germany from 1969 to 1989 and had thereafter regularly returned to Germany to collect his pension and also seek work. After recalling these findings by the Court of Appeal, the Supreme Court added: 'The Court however inclines, in any case under Article 6 para. 9 of the German Criminal Code, not to hold as necessary these additional factual links that would warrant the exercise of jurisdiction . . . Indeed, when, by virtue of an obligation laid down in an international treaty, Germany prosecutes and punishes under German law an offence committed by a foreigner abroad, it is difficult to speak of an infringement of the principle of non-intervention' (Judgment of 21 February 2001, 3 StR 372/00, still unreported, at 19–20 of the typescript).

64. Under this provision Italian nationals or foreigners who commit abroad any crime 'for which either special legislative provisions or international treaties establish that the Italian criminal law shall apply, may be punished under Italian law'.

65. See Judgment of 10 February 1997, no. 21/1997, *El Derecho, Jurisprudencia*, at 6, legal ground 3A. The Court held that the Spanish legislator had intended 'to attribute universal scope to the Spanish jurisdiction over those specific crimes [mentioned in Article 23 of the 1985 Law on Judicial Power], on

account both of the gravity of these crimes and the need for international protection.'

66. Order (*auto*) of 4 November 1988, in *don Adolfo Francisco (Scilingo)*, in *El Derecho, Jurisprudencia*, at 3, legal ground 2. The Court held that it was contrary to the spirit of the Genocide Convention to interpret Article 6 of this Convention (which provides that the accused may be tried either by a territorially competent court or by an international court) to the effect that such provision would limit the jurisdiction of States. This interpretation would run counter to the fact that genocide is 'regarded as a crime of extreme gravity in the whole world and affects directly the international community, indeed all humanity, as is intended by the same Convention'.

67. See order of 4 November 1998 in *don Adolfo Francisco (Scilingo)*, in *El Derecho, Jurisprudencia*, at 8, legal ground 10; order of 5 November 1998, in *don Augusto (Pinochet)*, ibid., at 8, legal ground 9.

The *Audiencia Nacional* rightly held in the two orders (*autos*) that Article 2.1 of the UN Charter, proclaiming the principle of sovereign equality of all member States, does not bar States from exercising universal criminal jurisdiction. As the Court put it: 'When the Spanish judicial authorities apply Article 23.4 [of the aforementioned Law], they neither invade, nor interfere with, the sovereignty of the State where the crime was perpetrated. They simply exercise the Spanish sovereignty with regard to international crimes. Spain derives its jurisdiction over those crimes from the principle of universal prosecution of certain crimes, a notion of international law upheld in the Spanish internal legislation'.

68. See the judgment mentioned in note 62.

69. For the *Barbie* case, see ILR, 100, at 331. See ibid., for the *Touvier* case, at 337, and for *Papon* (Assises Bordeaux, 2 April 1998).

70. See Judgment of 29 May 1962, in ILR, 36, at 287. See also at 298–304. The Court concluded as follows: 'Not only do all the crimes attributed to the appellant bear an international character, but their harmful and murderous effects were so embracing and widespread as to shake the international community to its very foundations. The State of Israel therefore was entitled, pursuant to the principle of universality of jurisdiction and in the capacity of a guardian of international law and an agent for its enforcement, to try the appellant' (ibid., at 304).

71. District Court of Columbia, judgment of 12 February 1988, 681 F. Supp. 896 (DDC), at 903.

72. *Demjanjuk* v. *Petrowsky et al.*, decision of 31 October 1985 in 776 F. 2d 571 (6th Cir. 1985), *cert. Denied* 475 US 1016 (1986).

73. *Regina* v. *Bow Street Magistrate, ex parte Pinochet* (no. 3) (1999) 2 WLR 827, at 911–12. He stated that 'crimes prohibited by international law attract universal jurisdiction under customary international law if two criteria are satisfied. First, they must be contrary to a peremptory norm of international law so as to infringe *jus cogens*. Secondly, they must be so serious and on such a scale that they can justly be regarded as an attack on the international legal order' (at 649).

74. The PCIJ held that 'Far from laying down a general prohibition to the effect that States may not extend the application of their laws and the jurisdiction of their courts to persons, property and acts outside their territory, it [international law] leaves them in this respect a wide measure of discretion which is only limited in certain cases by prohibitive rules; as regards other cases, every State remains free to adopt the principles which it regards as best and most suitable' (PCIJ, Judgment of 7 September 1927, Series A, no. 10, at 19).

75. The American Law Institute, Restatement of the Law Third, *Restatement of the Law—The Foreign Relations Law of the United States*, I (St. Paul, Minn.: American Law Institute Publishers, 1987), at 255–6 (para. 404, n. 1).

76. Text in *Situation*, 27 (1995–6), at 48–51. English (partial) translation in M. Sassoli and A. A. Bouvier, eds., *How Does Law Protect in War?* (Geneva: ICRC, 1999), at 1342–3.

77. See text in ILM, 39 (2000), 20–68. One of the three judges, Merkel, disagreed, contending that a legislative act creating genocide as an offence and granting jurisdiction to courts was not necessary for the court to exercise jurisdiction over genocide (however, he also concluded for the dismissal of the claims, on other legal grounds).

78. See decision of 20 October 2000, at 4–5.

79. ICJ Reports (1951), at 23.

80. ICJ Reports (1996), II, at 616, para. 31.

81. B. V. A. Röling, 'The Significance of the Laws of War', in A. Cassese, ed., *Current Problems of International Law* (Milan: Giuffré, 1975), at 137–9.

82. Ibid., at 139. For the text of the *Calley* case, see Friedman, ii, at 1703 et seq. (Judge Advocate's statement) and *International Lawyer*, 8 (1974), at 523 et seq. (decision of the Court of Military Appeals).

83. *Bayerisches Oberstes Landesgericht*, decision of 23 May 1996, 3 StR 20/96.

84. See above, note 26.

85. High Court, decision of 25 November 1994, case S-3396/94.

86. Cour de Cassation, 26 March 1996, in *Bulletin Criminel* (1996), 379–82.

87. Cour de Cassation, decision of 6 January 1998, *Bulletin Criminel* (1998), 3–8 (see also *Juris-Classeur Pénal, La semaine juridique*, 41, (7 October 1998), at 1758–9, with a comment by J.-F. Roulot at 1759–61.

88. Tribunal militaire de division I, decision of 18 April 1997, in http.//www.cicr.org/ihl-nat.

89. V. E. O. Orlando, 'Il processo del Kaiser' (1937), in *Scritti varii di diritto pubblico e scienza politica* (Milan: Giuffré, 1940), at 97 ff.

90. See *Trial of the Major War Criminals*, cit. above, note 13, I, at 218.

91. See ILR, 36, at 302.

Chapter 13

1. C. Hull, *Memoirs* (New York: Macmillan, 1948), ii, at 1625.

2. The expression 'brown people' was used by President Roosevelt, according to a memo by C. Taussig: see W. R. Louis, *Imperialism at Bay: The United States and the Decolonization of the British Empire, 1941–1945* (New York: Oxford University Press, 1978), at 486.

3. On the various proposals relating to domestic jurisdiction see in particular R. B. Russel, *A History of the United Nations Charter—The Role of the United States 1940–1945* (Washington D.C.: The Brookings Institution, 1958), 463–4, 785, 900–10.

4. L. Preuss, 'Article 2, Paragraph 7 of the Charter of the United Nations and Matters of Domestic Jurisdiction', HR, 74 (1949-I), at 573.

5. See FRUS, *The Conferences at Malta and Yalta—1945*, at 589. On the same occasion A. Y. Vyshinsky ('First Deputy People's Commissar for Foreign Affairs', in other words, Deputy Foreign Minister, of the Soviet Union) 'said to Mr Bohlen [Assistant to the US Secretary of State and interpreter of President Roosevelt at the Yalta Conference] that they would never agree to the right of the small powers to judge the acts of the Great Powers, and in reply to an observation by Mr. Bohlen concerning the opinion of the American people he replied that the American people should learn to obey their leaders', ibid., at 590.

6. See ibid., 589–91. Churchill quoted the saying 'The eagle should permit the small birds to sing and care not wherefor they sang' (at 590), while Bohlen, in reply to an inquiry by Churchill about

the US position on the voting procedure in the SC, mentioned 'the story of the Southern planter who had given a bottle of whiskey to a Negro as a present. The next day he asked the Negro how he had liked the whiskey, to which the Negro replied that it was perfect. The planter asked what he meant, and the Negro said if it had been any better it would not have been given to him, and if it had been any worse he could not have drunk it' (590–1).

7. See UNCIO, 13, at 633–4, 645–6.

8. See A. J. P. Taylor, *Rumors of War* (London: Hamish Hamilton, 1952), at 44.

9. A. Camus, *Essais* (Paris: Gallimard, 1984), at 352.

10. See FRUS, *The Conferences at Malta and Yalta—1945*, at 666.

11. Ibid., at 667.

12. H. Kissinger, *Diplomacy* (New York: Simon and Schuster, 1995), at 395.

13. In the opinion of the USA, permanent members of the SC were to place themselves, at least with regard to judicial or quasi-judicial procedures, on an equal footing with other States. For the US position, see FRUS, *The Conferences at Malta and Yalta—1945*, at 46–7; see also 56–62, 66–8, 660–2, 682–4, 995–6. See also E. R. Stettinius, jr, *Roosevelt and the Russians—The Yalta Conference* (Garden City, New York: Doubleday and Co., 1949), 135–50.

For the British position, see FRUS, cit., at 46, 663–7. As to the Soviet position, see ibid., at 46, 63–4, 68–71.

See also R. B. Russel (cit. at note 3), at 445–50, 458–9, 497–506.

14. A. Ross, *The United Nations: Peace and Progress* (New York: The Bedminster Press, 1966), at 190.

15. See GA res. S-18/3, adopted on 1 May 1990, during the Special Session on International Economic Co-operation.

16. GA res. 3201 (S-VI), adopted on 1 May 1974; GA res. 3202 (S-VI), adopted on the same day.

17. GA res. 3281 (XXIX), adopted on 13 December 1974.

18. GA res. 41/128, adopted on 4 December 1986.

19. See GA res. 45/199 of 21 December 1990.

20. See GA res. 2688 (XXV), adopted on 11 December 1970; GA res. 32/197, Annex, adopted on 20 December 1977.

21. GA res. 2152 (XXI), adopted on 17 November 1966.

22. GA res. 2997 (XXVII), adopted on 15 December 1972.

23. See A. Pellet, 'La formation du droit international dans le cadre des Nations Unies', EJIL, 6 (1995), at 417.

24. ICTY, Appeals Chamber, Judgment of 2 October 1995, paras 32–7.

25. Cited by M. Bertrand, 'The UN as an Organization. A Critique of its Functioning', EJIL, 6 (1995), 352.

26. Ibid.

Chapter 14

1. This Greek ship was stopped and searched by a British man-of-war without opposition from the Greek authorities. Another Greek ship, the *Joanna-V*, had been searched on the high seas off the coast of Bernia, Mozambique, prior to the S.C. resolution, triggering strong protests from the Greek government. On these two incidents see, for the relevant references, V. Gowlland-Debbas, *Collective Responses to Illegal Acts in International Law* (Dordrecht, Boston, and London: Nijhoff, 1990), at 400–19 as well B. Conforti, *The Law and Practice of the United Nations*, 2nd Edn. (The Hague-London-Boston: Kluwer, 2000) at 280.

2. See D. Sarooshi, *The United Nations and the Development of Collective Security: the Delegation by the UN Security Council of its Chapter VII Powers* (Oxford: Clarendon Press, 1999); N. Blokker, 'Is the Authorization authorized? Powers and practice of the UN Security Council to authorize the use of force by "coalitions of the able and willing"', EJIL, 11 (2000), 541–68.

3. For the relevant cases see H. Freudenschuss, 'Between Unilateralism and Collective Security: Authorization of the Use of Force by the Security Council', EJIL, 5 (1994), at 492 et seq.; G. Gaja, *Use of Force Made or Authorized by the United Nations*, in C. Tomuschat, ed., *The United Nations at Age Fifty. A Legal Perspective* (The Hague, Boston: Kluwer Law International, 1995), at 39 et seq.

4. ICJ Reports (1962), at 151.

5. See R. Higgins, 'Peace and Security. Achievement and Failures', EJIL, 6 (1995), at 459. See also M. Frulli, 'Le operazioni di peacekeeping delle Nazioni Unite e l'uso della forza', RDI, 84 (2001), forthcoming.

6. AJIL, 26 (1932), at 342.

7. See GAOR, XXXth Session, 3rd Committee, 2160th Meeting, para. 14.

8. Ibid., 2167th Meeting, para. 1.

9. ICJ Reports (1986), para. 176.

10. AJIL, 80 (1986), at 633.

11. UN Doc. S/PV.3245, at 6.

12. AJIL, 83 (1989), at 162.

13. AJIL, 84 (1990), at 547.

14. AJIL, 84 (1990), at 548.

15. ICJ Reports (1986), at 20–92.

16. M. McDougall, 'The Soviet-Cuban Quarantine and Self-Defense', AJIL, 57 (1963), at 597, 601.

17. He declared that the scope of the concept of self-defence had 'broadened with the advance of man's ability to wreak havoc on his enemies. Consequently the concept took on new and far wider application with the advent of the nuclear era. Anyone who thinks otherwise has simply not faced up to the horrific realities of the world we live in today, and that is particularly true for small States whose vulnerability is vast and whose capacity to survive a nuclear strike is very limited'. See UN Doc. S/PV.2288, at 40; ILM, 19 (1981), at 989.

18. C. H. M. Waldock, 'The Regulation of the Use of Force by Individual States in International Law', HR, 82 (1952), at 498; J. Stone, *Aggression and World Order* (London: Stevens, 1958), at 44; D. W. Bowett, *Self-Defence in International Law* (Manchester: Manchester University Press, 1958), at 187–92; M. S. McDougall and F. P. Feliciano, eds., *Law and Minimum World Public Order* (New Haven, Conn.: New Haven Press, 1961), at 232–41; M. A. Kaplan, and N. Katzenbach, *The Political Foundations of International Law* (New York: Wiley, 1961), at 210 ff.; S. Schwebel, 'Aggression, Intervention and Self-Defence in Modern International Law', HR, 136 (1972-II), at 479 ff.; see also S. Schwebel, Dissenting Opinion, ICJ, *Nicaragua*, ICJ Reports (1986), at 347; O. Schachter, *International Law in Theory and Practice* (Dordrecht, Boston, and London: Nijhoff, 1991), at 151–2; R. Higgins, *Problems and Process— International Law and How to Use It* (Oxford: Clarendon Press, 1994), 242–3.

19. With reference to the attack on Osiraq, the Israeli delegate stated the following: 'In destroying Osiraq, Israel performed an elementary act of self-preservation, both morally and legally. In so doing, Israel was exercising its inherent right of self-defence as understood in general international law and as preserved in Article 51 of the UN Charter. A threat of nuclear obliteration was being developed against Israel by Iraq, one of Israel's most implacable enemies. Israel tried to have that threat halted by diplomatic means. Our efforts bore no fruits. Ultimately we were left with no choice. We were obliged to remove that mortal danger. We did it cleanly and effectively.' See UN Doc. SPV.2280, 2 June 1981, in ILM (1981), at 970.

20. H. Kelsen, *The Law of the United Nations*,

(London: Stevens, 1950), at 797–8; H. Wehberg, 'L'interdiction du recours à la force. Le principe et les problèmes qui se posent', HR, 78 (1951-I), at 81; P. C. Jessup, *A Modern Law of Nations—An Introduction* (New York: Macmillan, 1952), 165–7; I. Brownlie, *International Law and the Use of Force by States* (Oxford: Oxford University Press, 1963), at 264 ff.; K. Skubiszewski, 'Use of Force by States. Collective Security. Law of War and Peace', in M. Sørensen, ed., *Manual of Public International Law* (London: Macmillan, 1968), at 767; P. L. Lamberti Zanardi, *La legittima difesa nel diritto internazionale* (Milan: Giuffré, 1972), at 191 ff.; B. V. A. Röling, 'On the Prohibition of the Use of Force', in A. R. Blackshied, ed., *Legal Change—Essays in Honour of J. Stone* (New York: Butterworths, 1983), at 276 ff.

21. ICJ Reports (1986), at 94, para. 176.

22. Ibid., at 103, para. 194.

23. Y. Dinstein, *War, Aggression and Self-Defence*, 2nd edn. (Cambridge: Cambridge University Press, 1994), at 188–91.

24. Ibid., at 190.

25. Ibid., at 191 and 192–3. With reference to the first hypothetical case, Dinstein notes that, if the US sinking of the Japanese carrier had taken place 'and the Americans would have succeeded in aborting an onslaught which at one fell swoop managed to change the balance of military power in the Pacific, it would have been preposterous to look upon the United States as answerable for inflicting an armed attack upon Japan' (at 189). With regard to the Israeli initiation of the war in 1967 Dinstein points out the following: 'True, no single Egyptian step, evaluated alone, may have qualified as an armed attack. But when all the measures taken by Egypt (especially the peremptory ejection of the United Nations Emergency Force from the Gaza Strip and the Sinai Peninsula; the closure of the Straits of Tiran; the unprecedented build-up of Egyptian forces along Israel's borders; and constant sabre-rattling statements about the impending fighting) were assessed in the aggregate, it seemed to be crystal-clear that Egypt was bent on an armed attack, and the sole question was not whether war would materialize but when' (at 191).

26. Pursuant to Article 31(3), in the interpretation of a treaty,

'There shall be taken into account, together with the context:

(a) any subsequent agreement between the parties regarding the interpretation of the treaty or the application of its provisions;

(b) any subsequent practice in the application of the treaty which establishes the agreement of the parties regarding its interpretation;

(c) any relevant rules of international law applicable in the relations between the parties'.

27. It noted the following: 'It is . . . clear that an "armed attack" is now something entirely different from what it was prior to the discovery of atomic weapons. It would therefore seem to be both important and appropriate under present conditions that the treaty [the proposed agreement on control of atomic warfare] define "armed attack" in a manner appropriate to atomic weapons and include in the definitions not simply the actual dropping of an atomic bomb, but also certain steps in themselves preliminary to such action.' See Dept. State Bull., 2702 (1946), at 164.

28. Jessup rightly noted that the US clarification was suggested because it was not clear from Article 51 whether anticipatory self-defence was authorized. See P. C. Jessup, *A Modern Law of Nations* (cit. above, note 20), at 167.

29. SCOR, Thirtieth Year, 1859th Meeting, 4 December 1975, at 11, para. 99.

30. ILM, 19 (1981), at 985 and 996.

31. ILM, 19 (1981), at 980.

32. Mexico said the following: 'It is inadmissible to invoke the right to self-defence when no armed attack has taken place. The concept of preventive war, which for many years served as justification for the abuses of powerful States, since it left it to their discretion to define what constituted a threat to them, was definitively abolished by the Charter of the UN'. Ibid., at 991–2.

33. ILM, 19 (1981), at 977.

34. ICJ Reports (1996), at 80, para. 26.

35. ICJ Reports (1986), at 103–4, para. 195.

36. See references in A. Cassese in J.-P. Cot and A. Pellet, eds., *La Charte des Nations Unies—Commentaire article par article*, 2nd edn. (Paris: Economica, 1991) at 781–2.

37. ICJ Reports (1986), at para. 195.

38. ICJ Reports (1986), at 103–4, 218–19, paras 195, 228, 230.

39. ICJ Reports (1986), at 103–4, para. 195.

40. The ICJ in *Nicaragua* rejected the US justification of collective self-defence: see ICJ Reports (1986), at 103–6, paras 194–201, and 146, para. 292(2).

41. For the more recent practice see N. Ronzitti, *Rescuing Nationals Abroad through Military Coercion and Intervention on Grounds of Humanity* (Dordrecht, Boston, and Lancaster: M. Nijhoff, 1985), at

26 ff. For the older practice see *Right to Protect Citizens in Foreign Countries*, at 51 ff.

42. See AJIL, 78 (1984), at 200, 662.

43. See AJIL, 84 (1990), at 545, 547.

44. In 1993 the UK Foreign Minister stated in the House of Commons that 'Force may be used in self-defence against threats to one's nationals if: (a) there is good evidence that the target attacked would otherwise continue to be used by the other State in support of terrorist attacks against one's nationals; (b) there is, effectively, no other way to forestall imminent further attacks on one's nationals; (c) the force employed is proportionate to the threat'. See BYIL, 64 (1993), at 732.

45. See GAOR, 3rd Emergency Special Session, 742nd Plenary Meeting, 20 August 1958, para. 75.

46. Ibid., 740th Plenary Meeting, 19 August 1958, para. 84.

47. See *Keesing's Contemporary Archives* (1978), at 29128.

48. Quoted by I. Brownlie (cit. above, note 20), at 326.

49. See the text of the Treaties of 1977 on Panama and the various US reservations and conditions and understandings at http://lcweb2.locgov/frd/cs/panama/pa-appnb.html.

50. See W. J. Jorden, *Panama Odyssey* (Austin, Texas: University of Texas Press, 1984), at 585.

51. The provisions cited in the text constitute paragraph 3 of the Panamian declaration. For the full text see *US Senate Debate on the Panama Canal Treaties: A Compendium of Major Statements, Record Votes and Relevant Events*, prepared for the Committee on Foreign Relations, US Senate, 95th Congress, 2nd Session, February 1979 (Washington, D.C.: Government Printing Office, 1979), at 557.

52. See AJIL, 78 (1984), at 204–7.

53. See V. P. Nanda, 'The Validity of United States Intervention in Panama Under International Law', AJIL, 84 (1990), at 500–1; L. Henkin, 'The Invasion of Panama Under International Law', CJTL, 29 (1991), at 302–3, 309–10. A contrary view was put forward by A. D. Sofaer, 'The Legality of the United States Action in Panama', CJTL, 29 (1991), at 287–8. See also D. Wippman, 'Treaty-Based Intervention: Who Can Say No?', *University of Chicago Law Review*, 62 (1995), at 680–4.

54. Statement by the US President G. Bush, made on 3 January 1990, Office of the Press Secretary, the White House.

55. See I. Brownlie (cit. above, note 20), at 317–27.

56. D. Bowett, cit. above, note 18, at 270–1; id., 'Reprisals Involving Recourse to Armed Force', AJIL,

66 (1972), at 3; K. Skubiszewski, cit. above, note 19, at 754; Y. Dinstein, *War, Aggression and Self-Defence* (cit. above, note 23), at 215–26.

57. See, for instance, SC resolution 111 of 19 January 1956; SC resolution 171 of 9 April 1962; SC resolution 188 (1964), para. 1; SC resolution 270 (1969).

58. See for example I. Brownlie (cit. above, note 20), at 305. See also Dinstein (cit. above, note 23), at 214–15.

59. Ibid., at 214.

60. ICJ Reports (1986), at 103, para. 195.

61. ICJ Reports (1949), at 31.

62. In *Nicaragua* the ICJ mentioned that the parties agreed 'in holding that whether the response to the [armed] attack is lawful depends on observance of the criteria of the necessity and the proportionality of the measures taken in self-defence' (IJC Reports (1986), at 103, para. 194), and seemed implicitly to uphold this view.

63. Cf. Dinstein (cit. above, note 23), at 215.

64. ICJ Reports (1986), at 134–5, para. 268.

65. For the appropriate references see Ronzitti (cit. above, note 41), at 95–7; S. D. Murphy, *Humanitarian Intervention* (Philadelphia: University of Pennsylvania, 1996), at 99–100.

66. For references see Ronzitti (cit. above, note 41), at 98–101, Murphy (cit. above, note 65), at 103–4.

67. For references see Ronzitti (cit. above, note 41), at 102–6; Murphy (cit. above, note 65), at 105–7.

68. For the indication of the position of various States, I refer the reader to my article, 'A Follow-Up: Forcible Humanitarian Countermeasures and *Opinio Necessitatis*', EJIL, 10 (1999), at 791–8.

69. For references see A. Cassese, *Self-Determination of Peoples—A Legal Reappraisal* (Cambridge: Cambridge University Press, 1995), at 150–8, 197–8.

70. J. L. Brierly, 'Sanctions' (1931), in *The Basis of Obligation in International Law* (Oxford: Oxford University Press, 1958), at 203.

Chapter 15

1. H. Lauterpacht, 'The problem of the revision of the law of war', BYIL, 29 (1952), at 382.

2. On Suares's concept of the State as a *communitas perfecta* see J. Brierly, *The Basis of Obligation in International Law and Other Papers* (Oxford: Oxford University Press, 1958), at 361 ff., 367 ff.

3. C. von Clausewitz, *On War*, ed. with an introduction by A. Rapaport (Harmondsworth: Penguin, 1971), at 384.

4. Decision of 2 October 1995, para. 97.

5. G. Aldrich, 'New life for the laws of war', AJIL, 75 (1981), at 773–4.

6. See text in Friedman, ii, at 1688 ff.

7. ICJ Reports (1996), at 266, para. 105C.

8. ICJ Reports (1986), at 94, para. 176.

9. ICJ Reports (1996), note 7, at 245, para. 41.

10. Ibid., paras 42, 78–87, 88–9.

11. Ibid., paras 96–7, and 105E.

12. Judgment of 14 January 2000, para. 524.

13. Ibid., para. 526.

14. ICJ Reports (1996), at 242, para. 31.

15. Judgment of 14 January 2000, para. 533.

16. Ibid., para. 530.

17. Judgment (cit. above, note 4), para. 97 ff.

18. Ibid., para. 100 ff.

19. ICJ Reports (1986), at 114, para. 218.

20. See CYIL, 9 (1971), at 301.

21. Judgment (cit. above, note 4), para. 119.

22. Ibid., paras 128–34.

23. UN Doc. ST/SGB/1999/13, of 6 August 1999.

24. For the various statements on Protocol II, see Diplomatic Conference on Humanitarian Law of Armed Conflict (1974–77), *Official Records*, vii, at 199, 203, 251, 201, 250.

25. See the memorandum of the Swiss Foreign Department in ASDI (1987), 185–7.

26. See the Reply of the German Government to a written question of a member of the Bundestag, in *Bundestag*, doc. 12/8458, 7 September 1994.

27. See text (in English) in M. Sassoli and A. A. Bouvier, eds., *How does Law Protect in War?* (Geneva: ICRC, 1999), at 895–900.

28. Ibid., 1357–70.

29. For the text of the judgment (in English), see *Human Rights Journal*, 17 (1996), at 133–8. See the perceptive comment by P. Gaeta, 'The Armed conflict in Chechnya before the Russian Constitutional Court', EJIL, 7 (1996), 563–70.

Chapter 16

1. See FRUS, *The Paris Peace Conference 1919*, iii (Washington, D.C.: Government Printing Office, 1943), 406–8.

2. See US Congress, *Hearings Documents*, 77th Congress, 1st Session.

3. See the text of the 'Tentative Proposals' as an appendix to R.B. Russel, *A History of the United Nations Charter—The Role of the United States 1940–1945* (Washington, D.C.: The Brookings Institution, 1958), 995–1006, at 997.

4. For the relevant statements on human rights made at San Francisco see in particular UNCIO, vol. 3, 296 ff.; vol. 8, at 56, 80–1, 85, 90–1. In particular, for the Soviet statement referred to in the text, see vol. 8, 56–7.

5. D. Hume, 'Essays, Literary, Moral and Political', in *Essays and Treatises on Several Subjects* (Edinburgh, 1804), i, at 27 ff.

6. J. Nyerere, 'The African and Democracy', in J. Duffy and R. A. Manners, eds., *Africa Speaks* (Princeton: Princeton University Press, 1961), at 33.

7. See League of Nations, *Official Journal*, Year XIV, July 1933, at 833–935 and October 1933, *Special Supplement* no. 114, at 1–3 and 22.

8. League of Nations, *Official Journal*, Year XIV, July 1933, at 839.

9. Ibid., at 841.

10. Ibid., at 841.

11. Ibid., at 842.

12. League of Nations, *Official Journal*, 1933, *Special Supplement* no. 120 (Minutes of the Sixth Committee—Political questions), at 28.

13. Ibid., at 42.

14. UN Doc. CCPR/C/79/Add 50 (1995), para. 19.

15. Decision of 29 July 1981 (communication no. 52/1979), in Human Rights Committee, *Selected Decisions (Second to Sixteenth sessions)* (New York: UN, 1985), at 91, paras 12.2–12.3.

16. Series A., no. 310, 23 February 1995, para. 62; *Merits*, 18 December 1996, para. 57.

17. Case no. 10.951, Report no. 109/99, 29 September 1999, para. 37.

18. For an up-to-date and thorough examination of these procedures see B. Rudolf, *Die thematischen Berichterstatter und Arbeitsgruppen der UN-Menschensrechtskommission* (Berlin and Heidelberg: Springer, 2000). See, in particular, the survey of the Working Group on arbitrary arrest and its major contribution to the development of a 'case law' on the matter (at 199–334) as well as the final appraisal of the effectiveness of these mechanisms (at 543–61).

19. *Loizidou* case—*Preliminary Objections*, Series A, no. 310 (1995).

20. Text of the judgment (in English) in Friedman, ii, at 1688 ff. See Chapter 11, note 20.

21. ILR, 36, at 304.

22. See 681 F. Supp. 896 (DDC 1988), at 903.

23. 630 F. 876 (2d Cir. 1980).

24. 748 F. 2d 790 (2d Cir. 1984).

25. 965 F. 2d 699 (9th Cir. 1992).

26. 672 F. Supp. 1531 (N.D. Cal. 1987).

27. Decision of 26 October 1994, 92–12255 D. Mass.

28. 25 F. 3d 1467 (9th Cir. 1994).

29. 70 F. 3d 232 (2d Cir. 1995).

30. 812 F. Supp. 207 (S.D. Fla 1993).

31. 886 F. Supp. 162 (D. Mass. 1995).

32. Court Appeal 11th Cir. no. 93–9133 (10 January 1996).

33. Court Appeal 2d Cir. no. 95–7930 (16 November 1996).

34. ICJ Reports (1970), para. 33.

35. See *Senato della Repubblica*, XIII Legislatura, 634th Seduta pubblica, *Resoconto sommario e steno-grafico*, 17 June 1999, in http://notes3.senato.it/ ODG-PU . . . /1dad.

36. See *Guatemala—Memory of Silence, Report of the Commission for Historical Clarification—Conclusions and Recommendations* (n. p., 1999).

37. See C. Tomuschat, 'Vergangenheitsbewälti-gung durch Aufklärung: Die Arbeit der Wahrheit-skommission in Guatemala', in U. Fastenrath, ed., *Internationaler Schutz der Menschenrechte* (Dresden and Munich: Dresden University Press, 2000), at 173, n. 53.

38. See for instance the Report of the UN Secretary-General on 'Enhancing the effectiveness of the principle of periodic and effective elections' (A/ 52/474, 1997) on the various UN missions for elect-oral assistance; the other Report of the same organ on 'Support by the United Nations system of the efforts of Governments to promote and consolidate new or restored democracies' (A/52/513, 1997).

39. For instance, the Office for Democratic Institutions and Human Rights (ODIHR) deploys election observation missions to OSCE participating States to assess the implementation of OSCE com-mitments relating to elections.

40. For example, the Unit for the Promotion of Democracy (UPD) is a body within the General Secretariat of the OAS responsible for activities in support of democratic consolidation in the member States.

41. See, for instance, the statements made in 1999 by various States in the UN Human Rights Commis-sion: India (*Summary Records*, 57th Meeting, E/ CN.4/1999/SR 57, para. 7), Pakistan (ibid., para. 11), Cuba (ibid., para. 21), Russia (ibid., para. 29), Indo-nesia (ibid., para. 40), and China (ibid., paras 41–2); see http://www.unhchr.ch/huridocda/. See also the statements made by some States in the same organ, in 2000: Pakistan (*Summary Records* 62nd meeting,

E/CN.4/2000/SR.62, paras 11 and 43–5), Cuba (ibid., paras 40–2 and 56), Sudan (ibid., para. 47), China (ibid., paras 52–3), Swaziland (ibid., para. 54).

42. For the necessary references, see also M. Grif-fin, 'Accrediting Democracies: Does the Credentials Committee of the United Nations Promote Dem-ocracy Through its Accreditation Process, and Should It?', *New York University J. of Int. Law and Pol.*, 32 (2000), 725–85, in particular 745 ff.

43. Judgment of 2 October 1995, para. 97 (the text of the *dictum* is reproduced in 15.5).

44. Judgment of 27 August 1992, in HRLJ (1992), 453 ff., paras 115–16.

45. Judgment of 29 July 1999, appl. no. 25803/94, para. 101 (emphasis added).

46. See for instance *Borgers v. Belgium* (judgment of 30 October 1991, Series A, no. 214-A), where it would seem that the Court reversed its previous judgment in *Delcourt v. Belgium* (judgment of 17 January 1970, Series A, no. 11). See also *Labita v. Italy* (judgment of 6 April 2000), when the Court expanded the scope of Article 3 by holding that 'the lack of a thorough and effective investigation into the credible allegation made by the applicant that he had been ill-treated by wardens when detained' in a specific Italian prison, amounted to a violation of Article 3 (paras 130–6).

47. B. V. A. Röling, 'Peace-Research and Peace-Keeping' in A. Cassese, ed., *United Nations Peace-Keeping: Legal Essays* (Alphen: Sijthoff and Noord-hoff, 1978), at 250–2.

Chapter 17

1. Council of Europe Convention on Civil Liabil-ity for Damage Resulting from Activities Dangerous to the Environment, done at Lugano, 21 June 1993, Article 2.10 (text of the Convention in ILM, 32 (1993), at 1228–46).

2. Moore, *History and Digest*, i, at 801. It should be noted that as early as 1887 the US Secretary of State, Bayard, had sent a note to France, Germany, Britain, Japan, Russia, Sweden, and Norway, urging inter-national co-operation, and stating among other things that 'It is well known that the unregulated and indiscriminate killing of seals in many parts of the world has driven them from place to place, and, by breaking up their habitual resorts, has greatly reduced their number' (ibid., at 776). The note went on to stress 'the common interest of all nations in preventing the indiscriminate destruction and con-sequent extermination of an animal which contrib-utes so importantly to the commercial wealth and general use of mankind' (ibid.).

3. Ibid., at 811. See also at 827–9.

4. Ibid., at 834 and 835.

5. Ibid., at 814.

6. Ibid., at 834.

7. Ibid., at 853.

8. Ibid., at 819.

9. Ibid., at 845. See, at 870–1 and 875–7, the sharp and rather sarcastic British comments on the US views on the right to 'property and protection'.

10. Ibid., at 939 (original text of the award in French) and 849 (English translation).

11. See ibid., at 949–51. See, at 922–9, a report on the negotiations on the regulations.

12. RIAA, iii, at 1963.

13. Ibid., at 1965.

14. RIAA, xii, at 308. For the English translation see ILR, 24, at 101 ff., at 129.

15. Ibid., at 305. For the English translation see ILR, 24, at 126.

16. Ibid. For the English translation see ILR, 24, at 126. See also D. Rauschning, 'Lac Lanoux Arbitration', in *Encyclopedia*, 3, at 111–13.

17. ICJ, *The Corfu Channel Case (Merits)*, ICJ Reports (1949), at 22.

18. For the judgment of 8 January 1979 delivered by the Rotterdam Court, see NYIL, 11 (1980), at 326–33. For the judgment of 16 December 1983, see NYIL, 15 (1984), at 471–84.

19. ICJ Reports (1996), at 241–2, para. 29.

20. ICJ Reports (1997), at 41, para. 53.

21. Case cit. above, at note 18. See NYIL, 15 (1984), at 479.

22. See WTO Appellate Body Report of 16 January 1998, AB-1997–4, para. 121.

23. See ibid., para. 122.

24. See ibid.

25. US Panel Report, paras 8.157–8; Canada Panel Report, paras 8.160–1.

26. Appellate Body (cit. above, note 22), para. 123.

27. 'The natural resources of the earth including the air, water, land, flora and fauna and especially representative samples of natural ecosystems must be safeguarded for the benefit of present and future generations through careful planning or management, as appropriate.'

28. GA resolution 37/7 (1982), UN Doc. A/37/51(1982).

29. ILM, 31 (1992), at 874 ff.

30. It provides that 'In order to protect the environment, the precautionary approach shall be widely applied by States according to their capabilities. Where there are threats of serious or irreversible damage, lack of full scientific certainty shall not be used as a reason for postponing cost effective measures to prevent environmental degradation'.

31. ILM, 31 (1992), at 849 ff.

32. ILM, 37 (1998), at 22–43.

33. ILM, 31 (1992), at 818 ff.

34. ILM, 12 (1973), at 1085 ff.

35. 402 UNTS, 71; see also AJIL, 54 (1960), at 477 ff.

36. See ILM, 30 (1991), at 1455 ff.

37. ILM, 12 (1973), at 1319 ff.

38. See ILM, 32 (1993), at 136 ff.

39. ILM, 11 (1972), at 1358 ff.

40. ILM, 33 (1994), at 1540–55.

41. Ibid., at 1328.

42. 961 UNTS, at 187 ff.

43. Article II stipulates that 'A launching State shall be absolutely liable to pay compensation for damage caused by its space object on the surface of the earth or to aircraft in flight'.

44. Under Article VI.1 the launching State can be exonerated from absolute liability if it establishes 'that the damage has resulted either wholly or partially from gross negligence or from an act or omission done with intent to cause damage on the part of the claimant State or of natural or juridical persons it represents'. Paragraph 2 provides that 'No exoneration whatever shall be granted in cases where the damage has resulted from activities conducted by a launching State which are not in conformity with international law including, in particular, the Charter of the United Nations and the Treaty on Principles Governing the Activities of States in the Exploration and Use of Outer Space, including the Moon and Other Celestial Bodies'.

45. See the Japanese note of 25 January 1956 in Whiteman, 4, at 575.

46. See Settlement of Japanese Claims for Personal and Property Damages Resulting from Nuclear Tests in the Marshall Islands, in *Treaties and Other International Acts Series (United States)*, at 3160.

47. See ILM, 18 (1979), at 899.

48. The Court held that 'as State practice shows . . . a State on whose territory or in whose waters an act contrary to international law has occurred, may be called upon to give an explanation . . . A State cannot evade such a request by limiting itself to a reply that it is ignorant of the circumstances of the act and of its authors. The State may, up to a certain point, be bound to supply particulars of the use made by it of

the means of information and inquiry at its disposal' (ICJ Reports (1949), at 18). However, the Court went on to say that the mere fact of a State's control over a territory does not entail that the State knew or ought to have known of the commission of unlawful acts. 'This fact [the Court concluded] by itself and apart from other circumstances, neither involves *prima facie* responsibility nor shifts the burden of proof' (ibid.).

49. See decision of 1979 in AILC, 4 (1979–86), at 399 ff.; see in particular the subsequent decision of 1992 *In the matter of Oil Spill by the Amoco Cadiz off the Coast of France on March 16, 1978*, 954 F. 2d 1279 (7th Cir. 1992), at 1299–1302.

On the various problems referred to in the text, see in particular A. Kiss and D. Shelton, *International Environmental Law* (New York and London: Transnational Publishers Inc. and Graham and Trotman Ltd, 1991), at 350 ff.

50. ILM, 32 (1993), at 1228 ff.

51. See, e.g., the 1960 Convention on Third Party Liability in the Field of Nuclear Energy and the Additional Protocol of 1964 (in UNTS, 956, no. 13706) and the 1962 Convention on the Liability of Operators of Nuclear Ships (in IAEA, International Conventions on Civil Liability for Nuclear Damage, Legal Series no. 4 (Vienna, 1966), at 36 ff.).

52. ILM, 8 (1969), at 229 ff.

53. Judgment of 30 November 1976, no. 21/76, CMLR, 1977, at 284.

54. For references see note 51.

55. ILM, 2 (1963), at 727 ff.

56. ILM, 8 (1969), at 229 ff.

57. ILM, 9 (1970), at 45 ff.

58. See in particular F. Francioni, 'La tutela d'ambiente e la disciplina del commercio internazionale', in *Diritto e Organizzazione del Commercio Internazionale dopo la creazione dell'Organizzazione Internazionale del Commercio* (Naples: Editoriale Scientifica, 1998), at 147 ff.; id., 'Environment, Human Rights and the Limits of Free Trade', as well as D. French, 'The Changing Nature of "Environmental Protection": Recent Developments Regarding Trade and the Environment in the European Union and the World Trade Organization', NILR, 47 (2000), at 1 ff.

My exposition draws upon these writings.

59. ILM, 26 (1987), at 1541 ff.

60. For various instances of international environmental agreements mandating the use of trade restrictions with a view to eliciting compliance, see R. Wolfrum, 'Means of Ensuring Compliance with and Enforcement of International Environmental Law', HR, 272 (1998), 59 et seq.

61. Text at http://www.wto.org/english/docs_e/legal_e/17-tbt.wpf.

62. See ILM, 33 (1994), at 839 ff.

63. See ILM, 38 (1999), at 118 ff.

64. See ILM, 35 (1996), at 274 ff.

Chapter 18

1. For this notion see C. Furtado, *Development and Underdevelopment* (Berkeley: University of California Press, 1964), at 127–40, in particular 129.

2. For this, and other economic notions used in this chapter, see C. Napoleoni, *Economic Thought of the Twentieth Century*, trans. and ed. by A. Cigno (London: Martin Robertson and Co., 1972), at 145 ff.

3. See A. Pardo, *The Common Heritage: Selected Papers on Oceans and World Order 1967–74* (Malta: Malta University Press, 1975), at 31, 64, 85.

4. See A. A. Yusuf, 'Developing Countries and the Multilateral Trade Rules: The Continuing Quest for "an Equitable Playing Field"', in L. Boisson de Chazournes and V. Gowlland-Debbas. eds., *The International Legal System in Quest of Equity and Universality, Liber Amicorum G. Abi-Saab* (The Hague-London-Boston: Kluwer, 2001), at 389–409.

5. Ibid.

6. Text in AJIL, 32 (1938), Suppl., at 192 (emphasis added).

7. Final Award of 12 October 1994, unpublished, typewritten text (95 pp.). The Award was rendered by Chamber Three, presided over by Judge G. Arangio-Ruiz. See also the Separate Opinion of Judge Allison, paras 4–37 (on the standard in question).

8. Ibid., para. 88.

9. Ibid.

10. Ibid., para. 93.

INDEX